CLASSICS IN EDUCATION

CLASSICS IN EDUCATION

Edited by

WADE BASKIN

PHILOSOPHICAL LIBRARY
New York

CONTENTS

v

FOREWORD

The anthologist is forced at the outset to decide which works are to be included and the order in which they are to be presented. Because of its very nature and scope, CLASSICS IN EDUCATION invites censure from anyone who has given serious attention to the history of the general theory and practice of education. The decisions made in each instance reflect the personal bias and the limitations of the anthologist. Here, for instance, readers may detect a preference for writers who have stressed those values upon which our culture is founded, who have initiated new trends or made significant advances in the art and science of teaching, or who have appealed to every age because their works are suffused with deep insights and intuitions, with lofty aspirations and ideals, and have the power to stimulate creative thought. The names of men like Plato and Aristotle, Montaigne and Rousseau, Froebel and Pestalozzi, Dewey and Kilpatrick, Russell and Whitehead immediately come to mind and obviously deserve a place on anyone's list, but I have laid a broad basis for criticism by choosing one text rather than another—and by excluding a host of worthy candidates from my final list. Considerations of space always restrict the freedom of the anthologist, and the same is true of the form, accessibility and availability of texts. Finally, I have invited criticism by including a disproportionate number of recent American documents and of materials relating to developments in China and Russia. Only time will permit evaluation of the judgments expressed in connection with their inclusion.

The complexity of the material covered here is such that only two arrangements—the chronological and the alphabetical— seemed practical. Besides convenience, the alphabetical arrangement has the advantage of putting on an equal footing what is remote in time and what is immediate, with the result that it avoids implying that value judgments may or should be predicated on chronology.

To all those whose efforts, accomplishments, and sacrifices have made possible the completion of this undertaking, I owe a debt of gratitude. In preparing the introductory material for the selections that follow, I have drawn freely from the works of Morris Bishop, Sidney D. Braun, Lawrence A. Cremin, T. D. Jarman, H. I. Marrou, and Hermann Weimer, as well as from the works of other writers mentioned elsewhere. Though acknowledgements appear at the beginning of each entry, I wish here to express my appreciation for permission to use copyrighted materials to Jerome S. Bruner, James B. Conant, Mrs. Marian Kilpatrick, and B. F. Skinner; to the editors of *Educational Leadership, Journal of the Proceedings and Addresses of the National Education Association,* McGraw-Hill Company, Inc., *School and Society,* and *Teachers College Record;* and to Gene Franks, who prepared a translation of Vives' essay especially for this collection. In locating and assembling materials, I have had the generous help of Professor Franks, Mary Castleberry, Rose Carter, Lahoma Clark, Mamie Harris, Clyde Jackson, Raymond Piller, Sam Pool, Mildred Trammell, and Mildred Williams. The task of reading proofs was shared by Sybil Barkley, Jo ann Freeman, Margaret Johnson, Brenda Lane, and Betty Robertson. Finally, for acquiescing to the curtailment of many activities and diversions, including a summer vacation — and for providing many pleasant interruptions during the long sessions given over to the preparation of the anthology — I owe a debt of gratitude and an apology to Pat, Wade, Danny, and Michael.

W. B.

Southeastern State College

x

CLASSICS IN EDUCATION

ARISTOTLE

ARISTOTLE (c. 384-322 B.C.) Ranked by common consent as the world's leading philosopher, Aristotle possessed one of the few truly encyclopedic minds ever produced. His plan for the education of youth, modified and enlarged to constitute the Trivium and the Quadrivium of the Middle Ages, dominated the intellectual life of the Western world for more than a thousand years.

He was born at Stagira in 384 or 383 B.C. and died at Chalcis in 322 B.C. Son of the personal physician to King Amyntas II, he was orphaned at an early age and brought up by a relative, Proxenus, in Atarnea. At the age of eighteen he went to Athens, where he joined Plato's Academy. During the next twenty years he studied Platonic, Socratic, and pre-Socratic philosophy as well as many related disciplines. Besides writing a number of dialogues in defense of Platonic philosophy, he probably taught at the Academy for several years. Following the appointment of Speusippus as Plato's successor, he went with his friend Xenocrates to Assus, a city in Asia Minor, where he joined a circle formed by Hermias, the ruler of the city. He married the daughter of Hermias, who was a political ally of King Philip of Macedonia, and shortly thereafter accepted the task of educating the young prince who became known to posterity as Alexander the Great. When Alexander succeeded his father in 336 B.C., Aristotle returned to his home in Stagira. Realizing that he was now opposed in his thinking to much that was being taught at the Academy, he founded a new school in the northeast part of Athens. Alexander died suddenly in 323 B.C. and anti-Macedonian sentiment soon made Athens a dangerous place of residence for Aristotle, who observed that he left the city in order to prevent the Athenians from committing a second sin against philosophy. He died at Chalcis on the island of Euboea in 322 B.C.

It was as founder of the Lyceum at Athens that Aristotle made his most important contribution to education. He taught art, physics, natural science, politics, logic and philosophy, and he planned far-reaching projects which, when carried out by himself and his students, culminated in the systematization of the whole field of knowledge. A careful and practical thinker, he invented the science of logic (though he does not mention it as a definite part of philosophy); he conceived it as a method of inquiry or investigation and in this way provided later thinkers with a

1

"tool" (*organon*) for examining inductively the confused objects of sense, discovering relations, and deducing further truths. His scholarship embraced the whole range of human knowledge, and his practice of strolling down the shady paths of the Lyceum gave to his school of philosophy the name Peripatetic.

In a number of his works Aristotle dealt at length with the subject of education. Many views that have profoundly influenced the intellectual history of the West are expressed in *Rhetoric, Poetics,* and *Nicomachean Ethics,* but it was in *Politics* that he set out to develop the concepts that "in men, reason and mind are the end toward which nature strives" and that "every man ought to aim at what is possible, what is becoming." Though his discussion is incomplete, the curriculum which he proposes here, together with his concept of man as a political animal whose happiness can be achieved only through pursuit of the common good, can leave little doubt about the importance which he attached to the education of youth. Avoidance of extremes, practicability, appropriateness — these considerations determined the elaboration of the system, which changed drastically under the influence of Philo of Alexandria, Sextus Empiricus, St. Augustine, and others, but which regained its original form under Martianus Capella and dominated education for the next millennium.

THE GOLDEN MEAN*

There are three things which make men good and virtuous: these are nature, habit, and reason. In the first place, everyone must be born a man and not some other animal; in the second place, he must have a certain character, both of body and soul. But some qualities there is no use having at birth, for they are altered by habit, and some gifts of nature may be turned by habit to good or bad. . . . We have already determined what natures are likely to be most easily molded by the hands of the legislator. All else is the work of education. We learn some things by habit and some by instruction.

*   *   *

*From the seventh and eighth books in Aristotle's *Politics,* in Bohn's Classical Library.

2

Equality consists in the same treatment of similar persons, and no government can stand which is not founded upon justice. Nature herself has given the principle of choice when she made a difference between young and old (though they are really the same in kind), of whom she fitted the one to govern and the others to be governed. No one takes offense at being governed when he is young, nor does he think himself better than his governors, especially if he will enjoy the same privilege when he reaches the required age. We conclude that from one point of view governors are identical, and from another different. And therefore their education must be the same and also different.

* * *

Now the soul of man is divided into two parts, one of which has reason in itself, and the other, not having reason in itself, is able to obey reason. And we call a man good because he has the virtues of these two parts. In which of them the end is more likely to be found is no matter of doubt to those who adopt our division, for in the world both of nature and of art the inferior always exists for the sake of the better or superior, and the better or superior is that which has reason. The reason too, in our ordinary way of speaking, is divided into two parts, for there is a practical and a speculative reason, and there must be a corresponding division of actions; the actions of the naturally better principle are to be preferred by those who have it in their power to attain to both or to all, for that is always to every one the most eligible which is the highest attainable by him. The whole of life is further divided into two parts, business and leisure, war and peace, and all actions into those which are necessary and useful, and those which are honorable. And the preference given to one or the other class of actions must necessarily be like the preference given to one or other part of the soul and its actions over the other; there must be war for the sake of peace, business for the sake of leisure, things useful and necessary for the sake of things honorable. All these points the statesman should keep in view when he frames his laws; he should consider the parts of the soul and their functions, and above all the better and the

3

end; he should also remember the diversities of human lives and actions. For men must engage in business and go to war, but leisure and peace are better; they must do what is necessary and useful, but what is honorable is better. In such principles children and persons of every age which requires education should be trained.

* * *

We have already determined that nature and habit and reason are required, and what should be the character of the citizens has also been defined by us. But we have still to consider whether the training of early life is to be that of reason or habit, for these two must accord, and when in accord they will then form the best of harmonies. Reason may make mistakes and fail in attaining the highest ideal of life, and there may be a like evil influence of habit. Thus much is clear in the first place, that, as in all other things, birth implies some antecedent principle, and that the end of anything has a beginning in some former end. Now, in men reason and mind are the end towards which nature strives, so that the birth and moral discipline of the citizens ought to be ordered with a view to them. In the second place, as the soul and body are two, we see also that there are two parts of the soul, the rational and the irrational, and two corresponding states — reason and appetite. And as the body is prior in order of generation to the soul, so the irrational is prior to the rational. The proof is that anger and will and desire are implanted in children from their very birth, but reason and understanding are developed as they grow older. Wherefore, the care of the body ought to precede that of the soul, and the training of the appetitive part should follow: none the less our care of it must be for the sake of the reason, and our care of the body for the sake of the soul.

* * *

After the children have been born, the manner of rearing them may be supposed to have a great effect on their bodily strength.

4

It would appear from the example of animals, and of those nations who desire to create the military habit, that the food which has most milk in it is best suited to human beings; but the less wine the better, if they would escape diseases. Also all the motions to which children can be subjected at their early age are very useful. But in order to preserve their tender limbs from distortion, some nations have had recourse to mechanical appliances which straighten their bodies. To accustom children to the cold from their earliest years is also an excellent practice, which greatly conduces to health, and hardens them for military service. Hence many barbarians have a custom of plunging their children at birth into a cold stream; others, like the Celts, clothe them in a light wrapper only. For human nature should be early habituated to endure all which by habit it can be made to endure; but the process must be gradual. And children, from their natural warmth, may be easily trained to bear cold. Such care should attend them in the first stage of life.

The next period lasts to the age of five; during this no demand should be made upon the child for study or labor, lest its growth be impeded; and there should be sufficient motion to prevent the limbs from being inactive. This can be secured, among other ways, by amusement, but the amusement should not be vulgar or tiring or riotous. The Directors of Education, as they are termed, should be careful what tales or stories the children hear, for the sports of children are designed to prepare the way for the business of later life, and should be for the most part imitations of the occupations which they will hereafter pursue in earnest. Those are wrong who (like Plato) in the Laws attempt to check the loud crying and screaming of children, for these contribute towards their growth, and, in a manner, exercise their bodies. Straining the voice has an effect similar to that produced by the retention of the breath in violent exertions. Besides other duties, the Directors of Education should have an eye to their bringing up, and should take care that they are left as little as possible with slaves. For until they are seven years old they must live at home; and therefore, even at this early age, all that is mean and low should be banished from their sight and hearing.

*   *   *

No one will doubt that the legislator should direct his attention above all to the education of youth, or that the neglect of education does harm to states. The citizen should be molded to suit the form of government under which he lives. For each government has a peculiar character which originally formed and which continues to preserve it. The character of democracy creates democracy, and the character of oligarchy creates oligarchy; and always the better the character, the better the government.

Now for the exercise of any faculty or art a previous training and habituation are required; clearly therefore for the practice of virtue. And since the whole city has one end, it is manifest that education should be one and the same for all, and that it should be public, and not private—not as at present, when everyone looks after his own children separately, and gives them separate instruction of the sort which he thinks best; the training in things which are of common interest should be the same for all. Neither must we suppose that any one of the citizens belongs to himself, for they all belong to the state, and are each of them a part of the state, and the care of each part is inseparable from the care of the whole. In this particular the Lacedaemonians are to be praised, for they take the greatest pains about their children and make education the business of the state.

That education should be regulated by law and should be an affair of state is not to be denied, but what should be the character of this public education, and how young persons should be educated, are questions which remain to be considered. For mankind are by no means agreed about the things to be taught, whether we look to virtue or the best life.

Neither is it clear whether education is more concerned with intellectual or with moral virtue. The existing practice is perplexing; no one knows on what principle we should proceed—should the useful in life, or should virtue, or should the higher knowledge, be the aim of our training; all three opinions have been entertained. Again, about the means there is no agreement; for different persons, starting with different ideas about the nature of virtue, naturally disagree about the practice of it.

There can be no doubt that children should be taught those useful things which are really necessary, but not all things; for occupations are divided into liberal and illiberal; and to young children should be imparted only such kinds of knowledge as will be useful to them without vulgarizing them. And any occupation, art, or science, which makes the body or soul or mind of the freeman less fit for the practice or exercise of virtue, is vulgar; wherefore we call those arts vulgar which tend to deform the body, and likewise all paid employments, for they absorb and degrade the mind.

There are also some liberal arts quite proper for a freeman to acquire, but only a certain degree, and if he attend to them too closely, in order to attain perfection in them, the same evil effects will follow. The object also which a man sets before him makes a great difference; if he does or learns anything for his own sake or for the sake of his friends, or with a view to excellence, the action will not appear illiberal; but if done for the sake of others, the very same action will be thought menial and servile. The received subjects of instruction, as I have already remarked, are partly of a liberal and partly of an illiberal character.

The customary branches of education are four in number: (1) reading and writing, (2) exercises, (3) music, to which is sometimes added (4) drawing. Of these, reading and writing and drawing are regarded as useful for the purposes of life in a variety of ways, and gymnastic exercises are thought to infuse courage. Concerning music a doubt may be raised. In our own days most men cultivate it for the sake of pleasure, but originally it was included in education because nature herself, as has often been said, requires that we should be able not only to work well but to use leisure well, for I must state once again that the first principle of all action is leisure. Both are necessary, but leisure is better than occupation and is its end. The question that ought to be asked, therefore, is this: what ought we to do when at leisure? Clearly we ought not to be amusing ourselves, for amusement then would be the end of life. . . . Leisure of itself gives pleasure and happiness and enjoyment of life, and these are experienced not by the busy man but by the man who has

7

leisure. For he who is occupied has in view some unattained end, but happiness is an end inasmuch as all men deem it to be accompanied by pleasure and not by pain. Such pleasure is regarded differently by different persons, however, and varies according to the habit of individuals. The pleasure of the best man is the best and springs from the noblest sources.

It is clear, then, that some branches of learning and education must be studied merely with a view to leisure spent in intellectual activity. These are to be valued for their own sake, whereas those kinds of knowledge which are useful in business are to be deemed necessary and exist for the sake of other things. That explains why our fathers accepted music as a part of education, not because of its necessity or its utility, since it is not necessary or useful in the same manner as reading and writing, which are useful in money-making, in running a household, in acquiring knowledge, and in politics . . . There remains, then, the use of music for intellectual enjoyment in leisure, and this is evidently the reason for its introduction.

*   *   *

It is evident, then, that there is a sort of education in which parents should train their sons, not as being useful or necessary, but because it is liberal or noble. Whether this is of one kind only or of more than one, and if so, what they are and how they are to be imparted, must still be determined. This much we are now in a position to say, that the ancients witness to us, for their opinion may be inferred from the fact that music is one of the received and traditional branches of education. Furthermore, it is clear that children should be instructed in some useful things —for example, in reading and writing—not only for their usefulness but also because many other sorts of knowledge are acquired through them. With a like view they may be taught drawing, not to prevent their making mistakes in their own purchases, or in order that they may not be imposed upon in the buying or selling of articles, but rather because it makes them judges of the beauty of the human form. To be seeking always after the useful does not become free and exalted souls. Now it is clear that in educa-

8

tion habit must go before reason, and the body before the mind; and therefore boys should be handed over to the trainer, who creates in them the proper habit of body, and to the wrestling-master, who teaches them their exercises.

* * *

Of these states which in our own day seem to take the greatest care of children, some aim at producing in them an athletic habit, but they only injure their forms and stunt their growth. Although the Lacedaemonians have not fallen into this mistake, yet they brutalize their children by laborious exercises which they think will make them courageous. But in truth, as we have often repeated, education should not be exclusively directed to this or to any other single end. And even if we suppose the Lacedaemonians to be right in their end, they do not attain it. For among barbarians and among animals courage is found associated, not with the greatest ferocity, but with a gentle and lionlike temper. There are many races who are ready enough to kill and eat men, such as the Achaeans and Heniochi, who both live about the Black Sea; and there are other inland tribes, as bad or worse, who all live by plunder, but have no courage. It is notorious that the Lacedaemonians, while they were themselves assiduous in their laborious drill, were superior to others, but now they are beaten both in war and gymnastic exercises. For their ancient superiority did not depend on their mode of training their youth, but only on the circumstance that they trained them at a time when others did not. Hence we may infer that what is noble, not what is brutal, should have the first place; no wolf or other wild animal will face a really noble danger; such dangers are for the brave man. And parents who devote their children to gymnastics while they neglect their necessary education, in reality vulgarize them; for they make them useful to the state in one quality only, and even in this the argument proves them to be inferior to others. We should judge the Lacedaemonians not from what they have been but from what they are; for now they have rivals who compete with their education; formerly they had none.

It is an admitted principle that gymnastic exercises should be employed in education and that for children they should be of a lighter kind, avoiding severe regimen or painful toil, lest the growth of the body be impaired. The evil of excessive training in early years is strikingly proved by the example of the Olympic victors; for not more than two or three of them have gained a prize both as boys and as men; their early training and severe gymnastic exercises exhausted their constitutions. When boyhood is over, three years should be spent in other studies; the period of life which follows may then be devoted to hard exercise and strict regimen. Men ought not to labor at the same time with their minds and with their bodies; for the two kinds of labor are opposed to one another, the labor of the body impedes the mind, and the labor of the mind the body.

*　　*　　*

We accept the division of melodies proposed by certain philosophers into ethical melodies, melodies of action, and passionate or inspiring melodies, each having, as they say, a mode or harmony corresponding to it. But we maintain further that music should be studied, not for the sake of one, but of many benefits, that is to say, with a view to education, purification . . . intellectual enjoyment, relaxation and recreation after exertion. It is clear, therefore, that all the harmonies must be employed by us, but not all of them in the same manner. In education ethical melodies are to be preferred, but we may listen to the melodies of action and passion when they are performed by others. For feelings such as pity and fear, or, again, enthusiasm, exist very strongly in some souls, and have more or less influence over all. Some persons fall into a religious frenzy, whom we see disenthralled by the use of mystic melodies, which bring healing and purification to the soul. Those who are influenced by pity or fear and every emotional nature have a like experience, others in their degree are stirred by something which specially affects them, and all are in a manner purified and their souls lightened and delighted. The melodies of purification likewise give an innocent pleasure to mankind. Such are the harmonies and the melodies in which those who perform music at the theater should be invited to compete. But since the spectators are of two kinds—the one free and educated, the other a vulgar crowd composed of mechanics, laborers, and the like—there ought to be contests and exhibitions instituted for the relaxation of the second class also. And the melodies will correspond to their minds; for as their minds are perverted from the natural state, so there are exaggerated and corrupted harmonies which are in like manner a perversion. A man receives pleasure from what is natural to him, and therefore professional musicians may be allowed to practice this lower sort of music before an audience of a lower type. But, for the purposes of education, as I have already said, those modes and melodies should be employed which are ethical, such as the Dorian; though we may include any others which are approved by philosophers who have had a musical education. The Socrates of the Republic is wrong in retaining only the Phrygian mode along with the Dorian, and the more so because he rejects the flute; for the Phrygian is to the modes what the flute is to musical instruments—both of them are exciting and emotional. Poetry proves this, for Bacchic frenzy and all similar emotions are most suitably expressed by the flute, and are better set to the Phrygian then to any other harmony. The dithyramb, for example, is acknowledged to be Phrygian, a fact of which the connoisseurs of music offer many proofs, saying, among other things, that Philoxenus, having attempted to compose his Tales as a dithyramb in the Dorian mode, found it impossible, and fell back into the more appropriate Phrygian. All men agree that the Dorian music is the gravest and manliest. And whereas we say that the extremes should be avoided and the mean followed, and whereas the Dorian is a mean between the other harmonies (the Phrygian and the Lydian), it is evident that our youth should be taught the Dorian music.

Two principles have to be kept in view, what is possible, what is becoming: at these every man ought to aim. But even these are relative to age; the old, who have lost their powers, cannot very well sing the severe melodies, and nature herself seems to suggest that their songs should be of the more relaxed kind. Wherefore the musicians likewise blame Socrates, and with justice, for

11

rejecting the relaxed harmonies in education under the idea that they are intoxicating, not in the ordinary sense of intoxication (for wine rather tends to excite men), but because they have no strength in them. And so with a view to a time of life when men begin to grow old, they ought to practice the gentler harmonies and melodies as well as the others. And if there be any harmony, such as the Lydian above all others appears to be, which is suited to children of tender age, and possesses the elements both of order and of education, clearly we ought to use it, for education should be based upon three principles—the mean, the possible, the becoming.

ROGER ASCHAM

ROGER ASCHAM (1515-1568). The bookish learning of the grammar school and the university had little appeal to the politician, the courtier, the man of action. The Middle Ages had separated the education of the clerk and the knight but the Renaissance had revived the Greek ideal of a balanced education involving both mind and body. The new inclination "to joyne learning with cumlie exercises" was duly noted by Roger Ascham, author of *The Scholemaster*, one of the earliest works in English on the theory and practice of teaching.

Born in Kirby Wiske, Yorkshire, England, in 1515, he was brought up in the family of Sir Anthony Wingfield, who sent him to Cambridge, where he distinguished himself in mathematics, music, and the classical languages. His lectures at St. John's, where he received his M. A. in 1537, were so popular that students from the other colleges at Oxford came to hear him. In 1548 he became tutor to Princess Elizabeth, and two years later he accepted an appointment as secretary to Sir Richard Morison, ambassador to Emperor Charles V. Later he served as Latin secretary to Mary Tudor and as private tutor to Queen Elizabeth I. Between 1563 and 1568, the year of his death, he worked on his two-volume masterpiece. In the first book he urges the teacher to use gentleness rather than force in inducing the child to study; in the second he outlines his famous method of teaching Latin prose composition, the heart of English classical education, by means of double translation. Though he was constantly aware of what today would be called the "psychology of learning," his main concern was with the education of the whole man. Like Sir Thomas Elyot, he stressed training in manners and morals, and he expressed chagrin over the acceptance of the "italianate" behavior of the youth of his time.

THE IDEAL COURTIER AND THE
ITALIANATE ENGLISHMAN*

To ride comely, to run fair at the tilt or ring, to play at all weapons, to shoot fair in bow or surely in gun, to vault lustily, to run, to leap, to wrestle, to swim, to dance comely, to sing and play of instruments cunningly, to hawk, to hunt, to play at tennis and all pastimes generally which be joined with labour, used in open place and on the daylight, containing either some fit exercise for war or some pleasant pastime for peace, be not only comely and decent, but also very necessary, for a courtly gentleman to use.

* * *

To join learning with comely exercises Conto Baldassare Castiglione in his book, *Cortegiano*, doth timely teach: which book, advisedly read and diligently followed but one year at home in England, would do a young gentleman more good, I wiss, than three years travel abroad spent in Italy. . . . And besides good precepts in books, in all kinds of tongues, this court also never lacked many fair examples for young gentlemen to follow. And, surely, one example is more valuable, both to good and ill, than twenty precepts written in books. . . . Present examples of this present time, I list not to touch, yet there is one example for all the gentlemen of this court to follow, that may well satisfy them, or nothing will serve them, nor no example move them to goodness and learning.

It is your shame (I speak to you all, you young gentlemen of England), that one maid should go beyond you all, in excellency of learning and knowledge of divers tongues. Point forth

---

*From *The Scholemaster*, first published in 1570 and reprinted by E. Arber in 1870.

14

six of the best given gentlemen of this court, and all they together shew not so much good will, spend not so much time, bestow not so many hours, daily, orderly and constantly, for the increase of learning and knowledge, as doth the Queen's Majesty herself. Yea I believe that, beside her perfect readiness in Latin, Italian, French and Spanish, she readeth here now at Windsor more Greek every day than some prebendary of this church doth read Latin in a whole week. And that which is most praiseworthy of all, within the walls of her privy chamber she hath obtained that excellence of learning, to understand, speak and write, both wittily with head and fair with hand, as scarce one or two rare wits in both the universities have in many years reached unto. Amongst all the benefits that God hath blessed me withal, next the knowledge of Christ's true religion, I count this the greatest, that it pleased God to call me to be one poor minister in setting forward these excellent gifts of learning in this most excellent Prince. Whose only example if the rest of our nobility would follow, then might England be, for learning and wisdom in nobility, a spectacle to all the world beside.

*   *   *

Take heed therefore, ye great ones in the court, yea, though ye be the greatest of all, take heed what ye do, take heed how ye live. For as you great ones used to do, so all mean men love to do. You be indeed makers or marrers of all men's manners within the realm. For though God hath placed you to be chief in making of laws, to bear greatest authority, to command all others, yet God doth order that all your laws, all your authority, all your commandments, do not half so much with mean men, as doth your example and manner of living. And for example even in the greatest matter, if you yourselves do serve God gladly and orderly for conscience sake, not coldly and sometime for manner sake, you carry all the court with you, and the whole realm beside, earnestly and orderly to do the same. If you do otherwise, you be the only authors of all misorders in religion, not only to the court, but to all England beside. Infinite shall be made cold

15

in religion by your example that never were hurt by reading of books.

And in meaner matters, if three or four great ones in court will needs outrage in apparel, in huge hose, in monstrous hats, in garish colours, let the Prince proclaim, make laws, order, punish, command every gate in London daily to be watched, let all good men beside do everywhere what they can, surely the misorder of apparel in mean men abroad shall never be amended, except the greatest in court will order and mend themselves first.

* * *

Sir Richard Sackville, that worthy gentleman of worthy memory, as I said in the beginning, in the queen's privy chamber at Windsor, after he had talked with me for the right choice of a good wit in a child for learning, and of the true difference betwixt quick and hard wits, of alluring young children by gentleness to love learning, and of the special care that was to be had to keep young men from licentious living, he was most earnest with me, to have me say my mind also, what I thought concerning the fancy that many young gentlemen of England have to travel abroad, and namely to lead a long life in Italy. His request, both for his authority and good will toward me, was a sufficient commandment unto me to satisfy his pleasure with uttering plainly my opinion in that matter. "Sir," quoth I, "I take going thither and living there for a young gentleman that doth not go under the keep and guard of such a man, as both by wisdom can, and authority dare rule him, to be marvellous dangerous." And why I said so then, I will declare at large now: which I said then privately and write now openly, not because I do contemn either the knowledge of strange and diverse tongues, and namely the Italian tongue, which next to the Greek and Latin tongue I like and love above all other; or else because I do despite the learning that is gotten, or the experience that is gathered in strange countries; or for any private malice that I bear to Italy, which country, and in it namely Rome I have always specially honoured. Because, time was, when Italy and Rome have been, to the great good of us that now live, the best breeders and bringers up of the worthiest men, not only for wise speaking, but also for well doing in all civil affairs, that ever was in the world. But now, that time is gone, and though the place remain, yet the old and present manners do differ as far as black and white, as virtue and vice. Virtue once made that country mistress over all the world. Vice now maketh that country slave to them that before were glad to serve it. All men seeth it: they themselves confess it, namely such as be best and wisest amongst them. For sin, by lust and vanity, hath and doth breed up everywhere common contempt of God's word, private contention in many families, open factions in every city: and so, making themselves bond to vanity and vice at home, they are content to bear the yoke of serving strangers abroad. Italy now is not that Italy, that it was wont to be: and therefore now not so fit a place, as some do count it, for young men to fetch either wisdom or honesty from thence.

*   *   *

But I am afraid that over many of our travellers into Italy do not eschew the way to Circe's court, but go, and ride, and run, and fly thither. They make great haste to come to her: they make great suit to serve her: yea, I could point out some with my finger, that never had gone out of England, but only to serve Circes in Italy. Vanity and vice, and any licence to ill living in England was counted stale and rude unto them. And so, being mules and horses before they went, returned very swine and asses home again, yet everywhere very foxes with subtle and busy heads, and, where they may, very wolves with cruel malicious hearts. A marvellous monster, which for filthiness of living, for dullness to learning himself, for wiliness in dealing with others, for malice in hurting without cause, should carry at once in one body the belly of a swine, the head of an ass, the brain of a fox, the womb of a wolf. If you think we judge amiss, and write too sore against you, hear what the Italian saith of the Englishman, what the master reporteth of the scholar: who uttereth plainly, what is taught by him, and what learned by you, saying, *Englese italianato, è un diavolo incarnato*, that is to say, you remain men in shape and fashion, but become devils in life and condition. This is not the opinion of one for some private spite, but the judgment of all in a common proverb, which riseth of that learning and those manners which you gather in Italy: a good schoolhouse of wholesome doctrine and worthy masters of commendable scholars, where the master had rather defame himself for his teaching, than not shame his scholar for his learning. A good nature of the master and fair conditions of the scholars. And now choose you, you Italian Englishmen, whether you will be angry with us for calling you monsters, or with the Italians for calling you devils, or else with your own selves, that take so much pains and go so far to make your selves both. If some yet do not well understand what is an Englishman Italianated, I will plainly tell him. He, that by living and travelling in Italy, bringeth home into England out of Italy the religion, the learning, the policy, the experience, the manners of Italy. That is to say, for religion papistry or worse: for learning less commonly than they carried out with them: for policy a factious heart, a discoursing head, a mind to meddle in all men's matters: for experience plenty of new mischiefs never known in England before: for manners variety of vanities, and change of filthy living. These be the enchantments of Circes, brought out of Italy to mar men's manners in England; much by example of ill life, but more by precepts of fond books, of late translated out of Italian into English, sold in every shop in London, commended by honest titles the sooner to corrupt honest manners, dedicated over boldly to virtuous and honourable personages, the easier to beguile simple and innocent wits. It is pity that those which have authority and charge to allow and disallow books to be printed, be no more circumspect herein than they are. Ten sermons at Paul's Cross do not so much good for moving men to true doctrine, as one of those books do harm with enticing men to ill living. Yea, I say farther, those books tend not so much to corrupt honest living, as they do to subvert true religion. More papists be made, by your merry books of Italy, than by your earnest books of Louvain. And because our great physicians do wink at the matter, and make no count of this sore, I, though not admitted one of their fellowship, yet having been many years a prentice to God's true religion, and trust to continue a poor journey-man therein all days of my life, for the duty I owe and love I bear both to true doctrine and honest living, though I have no authority to amend the sore myself, yet I will declare my good will to discover the sore to others.

ST. AUGUSTINE

ST. AUGUSTINE (354-430). The foremost of the Latin Church Fathers absorbed the civic and pagan culture represented by Roman liberal education and was, until the time of his conversion in 386, a teacher of rhetoric and grammar. Primarily influenced by Greek speculative philosophy, he tried to interpret his new faith in terms of his first learnings. Living in the period of the disintegration of the Roman Empire, he contributed significantly to the strengthening of the position of the Christian church and to the history of philosophy, literature, and Christian education.

The story of his youth is told with moving simplicity in his great spiritual autobiography, the *Confessions*. Born at Tagaste in Roman North Africa on November 13, 354, Aurelius Augustinus was educated for a career as a teacher. At the age of seventeen he went to Carthage where he excelled in rhetoric and became acquainted with the dissipations of a large city. He completed his studies, taught grammar at Tagaste for two years, and established his own school of rhetoric at Carthage. The reading of Cicero's Hortensius fired him with the desire to find a philosophy that would give meaning and purpose to his existence, but he failed to achieve his goal through study of Scripture, Manichaeanism, or teachings of the Academic school. The end of his moral confusion came in 386 through a sudden conversion of will. Through the great writings of his maturity and his dedication to the task of rescuing human souls, he left his mark on the entire tradition of Western civilization. He died at Hippo on August 28, 430, while the Vandals were laying siege to his episcopal town.

St. Augustine favored a rhetorical training for the clergy, but he insisted that the content of the training in grammar and rhetoric should be that of Scripture and Christian writings rather than that of the classics. Under his influence education assumed a new character: the method was traditional (the understanding of written texts through the application of "certain rules"), but the object — the understanding of Scripture, the basis of the Christian faith — was new and was attainable only through diligent study.

The selection that follows is from the *Confessions* (written when St. Augustine was about forty-five), long regarded as a manual of self-analysis.

*CONFESSIONS**

I came to boyhood, or rather it came to me, displacing infancy. Nor did that depart,—(for whither went it?)—and yet it was no more. For I was no longer a speechless infant, but a speaking boy. This I remember; and have since observed how I learned to speak. It was not that my elders taught me words (as, soon after, other learning) in any set method; but I, longing by cries and broken accents and various motions of my limbs to express my thoughts, that so I might have my will, and yet unable to express all I willed, or to whom I willed, did myself, by the understanding which Thou, my God, gavest me, practise the sounds in my memory. When they named any thing, and as they spoke turned towards it, I saw and remembered that they called what they would point out, by the name they uttered. And that they meant this thing and no other, was plain from the motion of their body, the natural language, as it were, of all nations, expressed by the countenance, glances of the eye, gestures of the limbs, and tones of the voice, indicating the affections of the mind, as it pursues, possesses, rejects, or shuns. And thus by constantly hearing words, as they occurred in various sentences, I realized gradually for what they stood; and having broken in my mouth to these signs, I thereby gave utterance to my will. Thus I exchanged with those about me these current signs of our wills, and so launched deeper into the stormy intercourse of human life, yet depending on parental authority and the beck of elders.

O God my God, what miseries and mockeries did I now experience, when obedience to my teachers was proposed to me, as proper in a boy, in order that in this world I might prosper, and

*Translated by Edward B. Pusey.

excel in tongue-science, which should serve to the praise of men, and to deceitful riches. Next I was put to school to get learning, in which I (poor wretch) knew not what use there was; and yet, if idle in learning, I was beaten. For this was judged right by our forefathers; and many, passing the same course before us, framed for us weary paths, through which we were fain to pass; multiplying toil and grief upon the sons of Adam. But, Lord, we found that men called upon Thee, and we learnt from them to think of Thee (according to our powers) as of some great One, who, though hidden from our senses, couldst hear and help us. For so I began, as a boy, to pray to Thee, my aid and refuge; and broke the fetters of my tongue to call on Thee, praying Thee, though small, yet with no small earnestness, that I might not be beaten at school. And when Thou heardest me not, (*not thereby giving me over to folly*) my elders, yea, my very parents, who yet wished me no ill, mocked my stripes, my then great and grievous ill.

Is there, Lord, any of soul so great, and cleaving to Thee with so intense affection, (for a sort of stupidity will in a way do it); but is there any one, who, from cleaving devoutly to Thee, is endued with so great a spirit, that he can think as lightly of the racks and hooks and other torments, (against which, throughout all lands, men call on Thee with extreme dread,) mocking at those by whom they are feared most bitterly, as our parents mocked the torments which we suffered in boyhood from our masters? For we feared not our torments less; nor prayed we less to Thee to escape them. And yet we sinned, in writing or reading or studying less than was exacted of us. For we wanted not, O Lord, memory or capacity, whereof Thy will gave enough for our age; but our sole delight was play; and for this we were punished by those who yet themselves were doing the like. But elder folks' idleness is called "business"; that of boys, being really the same, is punished by those elders; and none commiserates either boys or men. . . .

In boyhood itself, however, (so much less dreaded for me than youth,) I loved not study, and hated to be forced to it. Yet I was forced; and this was well done towards me, but I did not well; for, unless forced, I had not learnt. But no one doeth well against his will, even though what he doth, be well. Yet neither did they well who forced me, but what was well came to me from Thee, my God. For they were regardless how I should employ what they forced me to learn, except to satiate the insatiate desires of a wealthy beggary, and a shameful glory. But Thou, *by whom the very hairs of our head are numbered,* didst use for my good the error of all who urged me to learn; and my own, who would not learn, Thou didst use for my punishment—a fit penalty for one, so small a boy and so great a sinner. So by those who did not well, Thou didst well for me; and by my own sin Thou didst justly punish me. For Thou hast commanded, and so it is, that every inordinate affection should be its own punishment.

But why did I so much hate the Greek which I studied as a boy? I do not yet fully know. For the Latin I loved; not what my first masters, but what the so-called grammarians taught me. For those first lessons, reading, writing, and arithmetic, I thought as great a burden and penalty as any Greek. And yet whence was this too, but from the sin and vanity of this life, because *I was flesh, and a breath that passeth away and cometh not again?* For those first lessons were better certainly, because more certain; by them I obtained, and still retain, the power of reading what I find written, and myself writing what I will; whereas in the others, I was forced to learn the wanderings of one Aeneas, forgetful of my own, and to weep for dead Dido, because she killed herself for love; the while, with dry eyes, I endured my miserable self dying among these things, far from Thee, O God my life.

For what more miserable than a miserable being who commiserates not himself; weeping the death of Dido for love to Aeneas, but weeping not his own death for want of love to Thee, O God. Thou light of my heart, Thou bread of my inmost soul, Thou Power who givest vigour to my mind, who quickenest my thoughts, I loved Thee not. I committed fornication against Thee, and all around me thus fornicating there echoed "Well done! well done!" *for the friendship of this world is fornication against Thee;* and "Well done! well done!" echoes on till one is ashamed not to be thus a man. And all this I wept not, I who wept for Dido slain, and "seeking by the sword a stroke and wound extreme," myself seeking the while a worse extreme, the extremest and lowest of Thy creatures, having forsaken Thee, earth passing into the earth. And if forbid to read all this, I was grieved that I might not read what grieved me. Madness like this is thought a higher and a richer learning, than that by which I learned to read and write.

But now, my God, cry Thou aloud in my soul; and let Thy truth tell me, "Not so, not so. Far better was that first study." For, lo, I would readily forget the wanderings of Aeneas and all the rest, rather than how to read and write. But over the entrance of the Grammar School is a curtain drawn! true; yet is this not so much an emblem of anything recondite, as a cloak of error. Let not those, whom I no longer fear, cry out against me, while I confess to Thee, my God, whatever my soul will, and acquiesce in the condemnation of my evil ways, that I may love Thy good ways. Let not either buyers or sellers of grammar-learning cry out against me. For if I question them whether it be true, that Aeneas came on a time to Carthage, as the Poet tells, the less learned will reply that they know not, the more learned that he never did. But should I ask with what letters the name "Aeneas" is written, every one who has learnt this will answer me aright, as to the signs which men have conventionally settled. If, again, I should ask, which might be forgotten with least detriment to the concerns of life, reading and writing or these poetic fictions? who does not foresee, what all must answer who have not wholly forgotten themselves? I sinned, then, when as a boy I preferred those empty to those more profitable studies, or rather loved the one and hated the other. "One and one, two;" "two and two, four;" this was to me a hateful sing-song: the wooden horse lined with armed men, and the burning of Troy, and "Creusa's shade and sad similitude," were the choice spectacle of my vanity. . . .

Stage-plays also carried me away, full of images of my miseries, and of fuel to my fire. Why is it, that man desires to be made sad, beholding doleful and tragical things, which yet himself would by no means suffer? yet he desires as a spectator to feel sorrow at them, and this very sorrow is his pleasure. What is this but a miserable madness? for a man is the more affected with these actions, the less free he is from such affections. Howsoever, when he suffers in his own person, it is usually called misery: when he compassionates others, then it is mercy. But what sort of compassion is this for feigned and scenical passions? for the auditor is not called on to relieve, but only to grieve: and he applauds the actor of these fictions the more, the more he grieves. And if the calamities of those persons (whether of old times, or mere fiction) be so acted, that the spectator is not moved to tears, he goes away disgusted and criticising; but if he be moved to passion, he stays intent, and weeps for joy. . . .

And now I was chief in the rhetoric school, whereat I joyed proudly, and I swelled with arrogancy, thought (Lord, Thou knowest) for quieter and altogether removed from the subvertings of those "Subverters" (for this ill-omened and devilish name, was the very badge of gallantry) among whom I lived, with a shameless shame that I was not even as they. With them I lived, and was sometimes delighted with their friendship, whose doings I ever did abhor, i.e. their "subvertings," wherewith they wantonly persecuted the modesty of strangers, which they disturbed by a gratuitous jeering, feeding thereon their malicious mirth. Nothing can be liker the very actions of devils than these. What then could they be more truly called than "subverters?" themselves subverted and altogether perverted first, the deceiving spirits secretly deriding and seducing them, wherein themselves delight to jeer at, and deceive others.

Among such as these, in that unsettled age of mine, learned I books of eloquence, wherein I desired to be eminent, out of a damnable and vain glorious end, a joy in human vanity. In the ordinary course of study, I fell upon a certain book of Cicero, whose speech almost all admire, not so his heart. This book of his contains an exhortation to philosophy, and is called *"Hortensius."* But this book altered my affections, and turned my prayers to Thyself, O Lord; and made me have other purposes and desires. Every vain hope at once became worthless to me; and I longed with an incredibly burning desire for an immortality of wisdom, and began now to arise, that I might return to Thee. For not to sharpen my tongue, (which thing I seemed to be purchasing with my mother's allowances, in that my nineteenth year, my father being dead two years before,) not to sharpen my tongue did I employ that book; nor did it infuse into me its style, but its matter. . . .

I resolved then to bend my mind to the holy Scriptures, that I might see what they were. But behold, I see a thing not understood by the proud, nor laid open to children, lowly in access, in its recesses lofty, and veiled with mysteries; and I was not such as could enter into it, or stoop my neck to follow its steps. For not as I now speak, did I feel when I turned to those Scriptures; but they seemed to me unworthy to be compared to the stateliness of Cicero, for my swelling pride shrunk from their lowliness, nor could my sharp wit pierce the interior thereof. Yet were they such as would grow up in a little one. But I disdained to be a little one; and, swollen with pride, took myself to be a great one. . . .

So was I speaking, and weeping in the most bitter contrition of my heart, when, lo! I heard from a neighbouring house a voice, as of boy or girl, I know not chanting, and oft repeating, "Take up and read; Take up and read." Instantly, my countenance altered, I began to think most intently, whether children were wont in any kind of play to sing such words: nor could I remember ever to have heard the like. So checking the torrent of my tears, I arose; interpreting it to be no other than a command from God, to open the book, and read the first chapter I should find. For I had heard of Antony, that coming in during the reading of the Gospel, he received the admonition, as if what was being read, was spoken to him; *Go, sell all that thou hast, and give to the poor, and thou shalt have treasure in heaven, and come and follow me.* And by such oracle he was forthwith converted unto Thee. Eagerly then I returned to the place where Alypius was sitting, for there had I laid the volume of the Apostle when I arose thence. I seized, opened and in silence read that section, on which my eyes first fell: *Not in rioting and drunkenness, not in chambering and wantonness, not in strife and envying: but put ye on the Lord Jesus Christ, and make not provision for the flesh,* in concupiscence. No further would I read; nor needed I: for instantly at the end of this sentence, by a light as it were of serenity infused into my heart, all the darkness of doubt vanished away.

Then putting my finger between, or some other mark, I shut the volume, and with a calmed countenance made it known to Alypius. And what was wrought in him, which I knew not, he thus shewed me. He asked to see what I had read: I shewed him; and he looked even further than I had read, and I knew not what followed. This followed, *him that is weak in the faith, receive;* which he applied to himself, and disclosed to me. And by this admonition was he strengthened; and by a good resolution and purpose, and most corresponding to his character, wherein he did always very far differ from me, for the better, without any turbulent delay he joined me. Thence we go in to my mother; we tell her; she rejoiceth: we relate in order how it took place; she leaps for joy, and triumpheth, and blesseth Thee, *Who art able to do above that which we ask or think;* for she perceived that Thou hadst given her more for me, than she was wont to beg by her pitiful and most sorrowful groanings. For Thou convertedst me unto Thyself, so that I sought neither wife, nor any hope of this world, standing in that rule of faith, where Thou hadst shewed me unto her in a vision, so many years before. And Thou didst *convert her mourning into joy,* much more plentiful than she had desired, and in a much more precious and purer way than she erst required, by having grandchildren of my body.

FRANCIS BACON

FRANCIS BACON (1561-1626). The youngest of eight children born to Sir Nicholas Bacon, lord keeper of the great seal under Queen Elizabeth, and of Lady Ann, sister-in-law of Lord Burghley, Elizabeth's trusted adviser, was destined for public service. He had the outstanding intellect of Elizabethan England, and his genius soon brought him to the attention of the queen, who named him "the young lord keeper." Pope called him "the wisest, brightest, meanest of mankind," but a more objective critic would attribute to him the very qualities to which we owe the achievements of modern science.

Bacon grew up in York House in London and spent his early years in the glittering precincts of the court. At the age of twelve he entered Trinity College, Cambridge, where he studied until 1575. Soon after joining the company of Gray's Inn, he interrupted his studies of the law in order to accompany the English ambassador to Paris. The death of his father in 1579 forced him to forsake diplomacy and return to the law. He became an utter barrister in 1582 and took his seat in the House of Commons in 1584. Knighted in 1603, he was made solicitor-general in 1607, attorney-general in 1613, privy councilor in 1616, lord keeper of the great seal in 1617, lord chancellor in 1618. In the same year he was created Baron Verulam, and three years later Viscount St. Alban. Bacon was deeply impressed by the political philosophy of Machiavelli and had long advocated a pragmatic morality in his writings. It is regrettable that his completely materialistic philosophy brought about his disgrace. In 1621 he confessed to the charge of having taken bribes and was deprived of his offices and sentenced to a fine and to imprisonment. Though the fine was converted into a trust fund for his own use and his imprisonment was limited to a few days, he was permanently excluded from Parliament and was politically a broken man. He summed up his fate in these words: "I was the justest judge that was in England these fifty years, but it was the justest sentence in Parliament that was in these two hundred years." In the last five years that remained to him, he devoted his time to legal and scientific studies. His death on April 9, 1626, came as a consequence of a chill contracted during the course of an experiment involving the use of snow as a preservative of meat.

Bacon is popularly remembered for his informal and engaging *Essays,* but these were for him merely a means of relaxation. He wrote more than thirty philosophical works in Latin, the most valuable being the *Novum Organum* (1620), in which he described the true method of science and divorced the new science from superstition, theology, and antiquated philosophical concepts. His eloquence and his ability to fashion into a connected system the new mode of thinking made him the guiding spirit of modern philosophy. The *Advancement of Learning,* the only philosophical work published by him in English, gave a review of the state of knowledge in his time and outlined a system of classifying the various branches of knowledge. His eloquent plea for the unprejudiced observation of facts, despite the fact that he promised far more than he achieved, made him the most revered prophet of the scientific outlook.

OF STUDIES*

Studies serve for delight, for ornament, and for ability. Their chief use for delight is in privateness and retiring; for ornament, is in discourse; and for ability, is in the judgment and disposition of business. For expert men can execute, and perhaps judge of particulars, one by one; but the general counsels, and the plots and marshaling of affairs come best from those that are learned. To spend too much time in studies is sloth; to use them too much for ornament is affectation; to make judgment wholly by their rules is the humor of a scholar. They perfect nature, and are perfected by experience; for natural abilities are like natural plants, that need pruning by study; and studies themselves do give forth directions too much at large, except they be bounded in by experience. Crafty men contemn studies; simple men admire them; and wise men use them: for they teach not their own use; but that is a wisdom without them and above them, won by observation. Read not to contradict and confute; nor to believe and take for granted; nor to find talk and discourse; but to weigh and consider. Some books are to be tasted, others to be swallowed, and some few to be chewed and digested: that

*From *The Works of Francis Bacon,* edited by James Spedding and others (London, 1857).

is, some books are to be read only in parts; others to be read, but not curiously; and some few to be read wholly, and with diligence and attention. Some books also may be read by deputy, and extracts made of them by others; but that would be only in the less important arguments, and the meaner sort of books; else distilled books are like common distilled waters, flashy things. Reading maketh a full man; conference a ready man; and writing an exact man. And therefore, if a man write little, he had need have a great memory; if he confer little, he had need have a present wit; and if he read little, he had need have much cunning, to seem to know that he doth not. Histories make men wise; poets witty; the mathematics subtle; natural philosophy deep; moral grave; logic and rhetoric able to contend. *Abeunt studia in mores.* Nay, there is no stone or impediment in the wit, but may be wrought out by fit studies, like as diseases of the body may have appropriate exercises. Bowling is good for the stone and reins; shooting for the lungs and breast; gentle walking for the stomach; riding for the head; and the like. So if a man's wit be wandering, let him study the mathematics; for in demonstrations, if his wit be called away never so little, he must begin again: if his wit be not apt to distinguish or find differences, let him study the schoolmen; for they are *cymini sectores*: if he be not apt to beat over matters, and to call one thing to prove and illustrate another, let him study the lawyers' cases: so every defect of the mind may have a special receipt.

OF CUSTOM AND EDUCATION*

Men's thoughts are much according to their inclination; their discourse and speeches according to their learning and infused opinions; but their deeds are after as they have been accustomed. And therefore, as Machiavel well noteth (though in an evil-favored instance), there is no trusting to the force of nature nor to the bravery of words, except it be corroborate by custom. His

*Ibid.

30

instance is, that for the achieving of a desperate conspiracy, a man should not rest upon the fierceness of any man's nature, or his resolute undertakings; but take such as one as hath had his hands formerly in blood. But Machiavel knew not of a Friar Clement, nor a Ravillac, nor a Jaureguy, nor a Baltazar Gerard; yet his rule holdeth still that nature, nor the engagement of words, are not so forcible as custom. Only superstition is now so well advanced, that men of the first blood are as firm as butchers by occupation; and votary resolution is made equipollent to custom even in matter of blood. In other things the predominancy of customs is everywhere visible; insomuch as a man would wonder to hear men profess, protest, engage, give great words, and then do just as they have done before; as if they were dead images, and engines moved only by the wheels of custom. We see also the reign or tyranny of custom, what it is. The Indians (I mean the sect of their wise men) lay themselves quietly upon a stack of wood, and so sacrifice themselves by fire. Nay the wives strive to be burned with the corpses of their husbands. The lads of Sparta, of ancient time, were wont to be scourged upon the altar of Diana, without so much as queching, I remember, in the beginning of Queen Elizabeth's time of England, an Irish rebel condemned, put up a petition to the deputy that he might be hanged in a withe, and not in an halter; because it had been so used with former rebels. There be monks in Russia, for penance, that will sit a whole night in a vessel of water, till they be engaged with hard ice. Many examples may be put of the force of custom, both upon mind and body. Therefore, since custom is the principal magistrate of man's life, let men by all means endeavor to obtain good customs. Certainly custom is most perfect when it beginneth in young years: this we call education; which is, in effect, but an early custom. So we see, in languages the tongue is more pliant to all expressions and sounds, the joints are more supple to all feats of activity and motions, in youth than afterwards. For it is true that late learners cannot so well take the ply; except it be in some minds that have not suffered themselves to fix, but have kept themselves open and prepared to receive continual amendment, which is exceeding rare. But if the force of custom simple and separate be great, the force of custom copulate and conjoined and collegiate is far greater. For there example teacheth, company comforteth, emulation quickeneth, glory raiseth: so as in such places the force of custom is in this exaltation. Certainly the great multiplication of virtues upon human nature resteth upon societies well ordained and disciplined. For commonwealths and good governments do nourish virtue grown, but do not much mend the seeds. But the misery is, that the most effectual means are now applied to the ends least to be desired.

THE NEW METHOD*

1. Man, as the minister and interpreter of nature, does and understands as much as his observations on the order of nature, either with regard to things or the mind, permit him, and neither knows nor is capable of more.

2. The unassisted hand, and the understanding left to itself, possess but little power. Effects are produced by the means of instruments and helps, which the understanding requires no less than the hand. And as instruments either promote or regulate the motion of the hand, so those that are applied to the mind prompt or protect the understanding.

3. Knowledge and human power are synonymous, since the ignorance of the cause frustrates the effects. For nature is only subdued by submission, and that which in contemplative philosophy corresponds with the cause, in practical science becomes the *rule.*

4. Man, whilst operating, can only apply or withdraw natural bodies; nature, internally, performs the rest.

5. Those who become practically versed in nature, are the

*From *Novum Organum,* (London, 1620). Aphorisms 1-38 are from *The Works,* edited by Basil Montague, (Philadelphia, 1842). Aphorisms 39-49 are from *The Works,* edited by Spedding.

mechanic, the mathematician, the physician, the alchymist, and the magician; but all (as matters now stand) with faint efforts and meagre success.

6. It would be madness, and inconsistency, to suppose that things which have never yet been performed, can be performed without employing some hitherto untried means.

7. The creations of the mind and hand appear very numerous, if we judge by books and manufactures: but all that variety consist of an excessive refinement, and of deduction from a few well known matters; not of a number of axioms.

8. Even the effects already discovered are due to chance and experiment, rather than to the sciences. For our present sciences are nothing more than peculiar arrangements of matters already discovered, and not methods for discovery, or plans for new operations.

9. The sole cause and room of almost every defect in the sciences is this; that whilst we falsely admire and extol the powers of the human mind, we do not search for its real helps.

10. The subtilty of nature is far beyond that of sense or of the understanding: so that the specious meditations, speculations, and theories of mankind, are but a kind of insanity, only there is no one to stand by and observe it.

11. As the present sciences are useless for the discovery of effects, so the present system of logic is useless for the discovery of the sciences.

12. The present system of logic rather assists in confirming and rendering inveterate the errors founded on vulgar notions, than in searching after truth; and is therefore more hurtful than useful.

13. The syllogism is not applied to the principles of the sciences, and is of no avail in intermediate axioms, as being very unequal to the subtilty of nature. It forces assent, therefore, and not things.

14. The syllogism consists of propositions, propositions of words, words are the signs of notions. If, therefore, the notions (which form the basis of the whole) be confused and carelessly

abstracted from things, there is no solidity in the superstructure. Our only hope, then, is in genuine induction.

15. We have no sound notions either in logic or physics; substance, quality, action, passion, and existence are not clear notions; much less, weight, levity, density, tenuity, moisture, dryness, generation, corruption, attraction, repulsion, element, matter, form, and the like. They are all fantastical and ill defined.

16. The notions of less abstract natures, as man, dog, dove; and the immediate perceptions of sense, as heat, cold, white, black, do not deceive us materially, yet even these are sometimes confused by the mutability of matter and the intermixture of things. All the rest, which men have hitherto employed, are errors; and improperly abstracted and deduced from things.

17. There is the same degree of licentiousness and error in forming axioms, as in abstracting notions: and that in the first principles, which depend on common induction. Still more is this the case in axioms and inferior propositions derived from syllogisms.

18. The present discoveries in science are such as lie immediately beneath the surface of common notions. It is necessary, however, to penetrate the more secret and remote parts of nature, in order to abstract both notions and axioms from things, by a more certain and guarded method.

19. There are and can exist but two ways of investigating and discovering truth. The one hurries on rapidly from the senses and particulars to the most general axioms; and from them as principles and their supposed indisputable truth derives and discovers the intermediate axioms. This is the way now in use. The other constructs its axioms from the senses and particulars, by ascending continually and gradually, till it finally arrives at the most general axioms, which is the true but unattempted way.

20. The understanding when left to itself proceeds by the same way as that which it would have adopted under the guidance of logic, namely, the first. For the mind is fond of starting off to generalities, that it may avoid labour, and after dwelling a little on a subject is fatigued by experiment. But these evils are augmented by logic, for the sake of the ostentation of dispute.

21. The understanding when left to itself in a man of a steady, patient, and reflecting disposition, (especially when unimpeded by received doctrines,) makes some attempt in the right way, but with little effect; since the understanding, undirected and unassisted, is unequal to and unfit for the task of vanquishing the obscurity of things.

22. Each of these two ways begins from the senses and particulars, and ends in the greatest generalities. But they are immeasurably different; for the one merely touches cursorily the limits of experiment, and particulars, whilst the other runs duly and regularly through them; the one from the very outset lays down some abstract and useless generalities, the other gradually rises to those principles which are really the most common in nature.

23. There is no small difference between the *idols* of the human mind, and the *ideas* of the divine mind; that is to say, between certain idle dogmas, and the real stamp and impression of created objects, as they are found in nature.

24. Axioms determined upon in argument can never assist in the discovery of new effects: for the subtilty of nature is vastly superior to that of argument. But axioms properly and regularly abstracted from particulars, easily point out and define new particulars, and therefore impart activity to the sciences.

25. The axioms now in use are derived from a scanty handful, as it were, of experience, and a few particular of frequent occurrence, whence they are of much the same dimensions or extent as their origin. And if any neglected or unknown instance occurs, the axiom is saved by some frivolous distinction, when it would be more consistent with truth to amend it.

26. We are wont, for the sake of distinction, to call that human reasoning which we apply to nature, the anticipation of nature, (as being rash and premature;) and that which is properly deduced from things, the interpretation of nature.

27. Anticipations are sufficiently powerful in producing unanimity, for if men were all to become even uniformly mad, they might agree tolerably well with each other.

28. Anticipations again will be assented to much more readily than interpretations; because, being deduced from a few instances,

and these principally of familiar occurrence, they immediately hit the understanding, and satisfy the imagination; whilst, on the contrary, interpretations, being deduced from various subjects, and these widely dispersed, cannot suddenly strike the understanding; so that, in common estimation, they must appear difficult and discordant, and almost like the mysteries of faith.

29. In sciences found on opinions and dogmas, it is right to make use of anticipations and logic, if you wish to force assent rather than things.

30. If all the capacities of all ages should unite and combine and transmit their labours, no great progress will be made in learning by anticipations; because the radical errors, and those which occur in the first process of the mind, are not cured by the excellence of subsequent means and remedies.

31. It is in vain to expect any great progress in the sciences by the superinducing or engrafting new matters upon old. An instauration must be made from the very foundations, if we do not wish to revolve forever in a circle, making only some slight and contemptible progress.

32. The ancient authors, and all others, are left in undisputed possession of their honours. For we enter into no comparison of capacity or talent, but of method; and assume the part of a guide, rather than of a critic.

33. To speak plainly, no correct judgment can be formed, either of our methods, or its discoveries, by those anticipations which are now in common use; for it is not to be required of us to submit ourselves to the judgment of the very method we ourselves arraign.

34. Nor is it an easy matter to deliver and explain our sentiments: for those things which are in themselves new can yet be only understood from some analogy to what is old.

35. Alexander Borgia said of the expedition of the French into Italy, that they came with chalk in their hands to mark up their lodgings, and not with weapons to force their passage. Even so do we wish our philosophy to make its way quietly into those minds that are fit for it, and of good capacity. For we have no

need of contention where we differ in first principles, and our very notions, and even in our forms of demonstration.

36. We have but one simple method of delivering our sentiments: namely, we must bring men to particulars, and their regular series and order, and they must for a while renounce their notions and begin to form an acquaintance with things.

37. Our method and that of the skeptics agree in some respects at first setting out: but differ most widely and are completely opposed to each other in their conclusion. For they roundly assert that nothing can be known; we, that but a small part of nature can be known by the present method. Their next step, however, is to destroy the authority of the senses and understanding, whilst we invent and supply them with assistance.

38. The idols and false notions which have already preoccupied the human understanding, and are deeply rooted in it, not only to beset men's minds, that they become difficult of access, but even when access is obtained, will again meet and trouble us in the instauration of the sciences, unless mankind, when forewarned, guard themselves with all possible care against them.

39. There are four classes of Idols which beset men's minds. To these for distinction's sake I have assigned names, — calling the first class *Idols of the Tribe;* the second, *Idols of the Cave;* the third, *Idols of the Market-place;* the fourth, *Idols of the Theatre.* . . .

41. The Idols of the Tribe have their foundation in human nature itself, and in the tribe or race of men. For it is a false assertion that the sense of man is the measure of things. On the contrary, all perceptions as well of the sense as of the mind are according to the measure of the universe. And the human understanding is like a false mirror, which, receiving rays irregularly, distorts and discolours the nature of things by mingling its own nature with it.

42. The Idols of the Cave are the idols of the individual man. For every one (besides the errors common to human nature in general) has a cave or den of his own, which refracts and discolours the light of nature; owing either to his own proper

37

and peculiar nature; or to his education and conversation with others; or to the reading of books, and the authority of those whom he esteems and admires; or to the differences of impressions, accordingly as they take place in a mind preoccupied and predisposed or in a mind indifferent and settled; or the like. So that the spirit of man (according as it is meted out to different individuals) is in fact a thing variable and full of perturbation, and governed as it were by chance. Whence it was well observed by Heraclitus that men look for sciences in their own lesser worlds, and not in the greater or common world.

43.   There are also Idols formed by the intercourse and association of men with each other, which I call Idols of the Marketplace, on account of the commerce and consort of men there. For it is by discourse that men associate; and words are imposed according to the apprehension of the vulgar. And therefore the ill and unfit choice of words wonderfully obstructs the understanding. Nor do the definitions or explanations wherewith in some things learned men are wont to guard and defend themselves, by any means set the matter right. But words plainly force and overrule the understanding, and throw all into confusion, and lead men away into numberless empty controversies and idle fancies.

44.   Lastly, there are Idols which have immigrated into men's minds from the various dogmas of philosophies, and also from wrong laws of demonstration. These I call Idols of the Theatre; because in my judgment all the received systems are but so many stage-plays, representing worlds of their own creation after an unreal and scenic fashion. Nor is it only of the systems now in vogue, or only of the ancient sects and philosophies, that I speak; for many more plays of the same kind may yet be composed and in like artificial manner set forth; seeing that errors the most widely different have nevertheless causes for the most part alike. Neither again do I mean this only of entire systems, but also of many principles and axioms in science, which by tradition, credulity, and negligence have come to be received. But of these several kinds of Idols I must speak more largely and exactly, that the understanding may be duly cautioned.

45. The human understanding is of its own nature prone to suppose the existence of more order and regularity in the world than it finds. And though there be many things in nature which are singular and unmatched, yet it devises for them parallels and conjugates and relatives which do not exist. Hence the fiction that all celestial bodies move in perfect circles; spirals and dragons being (except in name) utterly rejected. Hence too the element of Fire with its orb is brought in, to make up the square with the other three which the sense perceives. Hence also the ratio of density of the so-called elements is arbitrarily fixed at ten to one. And so on of other dreams. And these fancies affect not dogmas only, but simple notions also.

46. The human understanding when it has once adopted an opinion (either as being the received opinion or as being agreeable to itself) draws all things else to support and agree with it. And though there be a greater number and weight of instances to be found on the other side, yet these it either neglects and despises, or else by some distinction sets aside and rejects; in order that by this great and pernicious predetermination the authority of its former conclusions may remain inviolate. And therefore it was a good answer that was made by one who when they showed him hanging in a temple a picture of those who had paid their vows as having escaped shipwreck, and would have him say whether he did not now acknowledge the power of the gods,— "Aye," asked he again, "but where are they painted that were drowned after their vows?" And such is the way of all superstition, whether in astrology, dreams, omens, divine judgments, or the like; wherein men, having a delight in such vanities, mark the events where they are fulfilled, but where they fail, though this happen much oftener, neglect and pass them by. But with far more subtlety does this mischief insinuate itself into philosophy and the sciences; in which the first conclusion colours and brings into conformity with itself all that come after, though far sounder and better. Besides, independently of that delight and vanity which I have described, it is the peculiar and perpetual error of the human intellect to be more moved and excited by affirmatives than by negatives; whereas it ought properly to hold itself

indifferently disposed towards both alike. Indeed in the establishment of any true axiom, the negative instance is the more forcible of the two.

47. The human understanding is moved by those things most which strike and enter the mind simultaneously and suddenly, and so fill the imagination; and then it feigns and supposes all other things to be somehow, though it cannot see how, similar to those few things by which it is surrounded. But for that going to and fro to remote and heterogeneous instances, by which axioms are tried as in the fire, the intellect is altogether slow and unfit, unless it be forced thereto by severe laws and overruling authority.

48. The human understanding is unquiet; it cannot stop or rest, and still presses onward, but in vain. Therefore it is that we cannot conceive of any end or limit to the world; but always as of necessity it occurs to us that there is something beyond. Neither again can it be conceived how eternity has flowed down to the present day; for that distinction which is commonly received of infinity in time past and in time to come can by no means hold; for it would thence follow that one infinity is greater than another, and that infinity is wasting away and tending to become finite. The like subtlety arises touching the infinite divisibility for lines, from the same inability of thought to stop. But this inability interferes more mischievously in the discovery of causes: for although the most general principles in nature ought to be held merely positive, as they are discovered, and cannot with truth be referred to a cause; nevertheless the human understanding being unable to rest still seeks something prior in the order of nature. And then it is that in struggling towards that which is further off it falls back upon that which is more nigh at hand; namely, on final causes: which have relation clearly to the nature of man rather than to the nature of the universe; and from this source have strangely defiled philosophy. But he is no less an unskilled and shallow philosopher who seeks causes of that which is most general, than he who in things subordinate and subaltern omits to do so.

49. The human understanding is no dry light, but receives an infusion from the will and affections; whence proceed sciences

which may be called "sciences as one would." For what a man had rather were true he more readily believes. Therefore he rejects difficult things from impatience of research; sober things, because they narrow hope; the deeper things of nature, from superstition; the light of experience, from arrogance and pride, lest his mind should seem to be occupied with things mean and transitory; things not commonly believed, out of deference to the opinion of the vulgar.

PLAN FOR THE ADVANCEMENT OF LEARNING*

We divide the whole of the work into six parts: the first whereof gives the substance, or general description of the knowledge which mankind at present possess; choosing to dwell a little upon things already received, that we may the easier perfect the old, and lead on to new; being equally inclined to cultivate the discoveries of antiquity, as to strike out fresh paths of science. In classing the sciences, we comprehend not only the things already invented and known, but also those omitted and wanted; for the intellectual globe, as well as the terrestrial, has both its frosts and deserts. It is therefore no wonder if we sometimes depart from the common divisions. For an addition, while it alters the whole, must necessarily alter the parts and their sections; whereas the received divisions are only fitted to the received sum of the sciences, as it now stands. With regard to the things we shall note as defective; it will be our method to give more than the bare titles, or short heads of what we desire to have done; with particular care, where the dignity or difficulty of the subject requires it, either to lay down the rules for effecting the work, or make an attempt of our own, by way of example, or pattern, of the whole. For it concerns our own character, no less than the advantage of others, to know that a mere capricious idea has not presented the subject to our mind, and that all we desire and aim at is a wish.

*From *Advancement of Learning*, edited by Joseph Devey, New York, 1901.

41

For our designs are within the power of all to compass, and we ourselves have certain and evident demonstrations of their utility. We come not hither, as augurs, to measure out regions in our mind by divination, but like generals, to invade them for conquest. And this is the first part of the work.

When we have gone through the ancient arts, we shall prepare the human understanding for pressing on beyond them. The second object of the work embraces the doctrine of a more perfect use of reason, and the true helps of the intellectual faculties, so as to raise and enlarge the powers of the mind; and, as far as the condition of humanity allows, to fit it to conquer the difficulties and obscurities of nature. The thing we mean, is a kind of logic, by us called The Art of interpreting Nature; as differing widely from the common logic, which, however, pretends to assist and direct the understanding, and in that they agree: but the difference between them consists in three things, viz., the end, the order of demonstrating, and the grounds of inquiry.

The end of our new logic is to find, not arguments, but arts; not what agrees with principles, but principles themselves: not probable reasons, but plans and designs of works—a different intention producing a different effect. In one the adversary is conquered by dispute, and in the other nature by works. The nature and order of the demonstrations agree with this object. For in common logic, almost our whole labor is spent upon the syllogism. Logicians hitherto appear scarcely to have noticed induction, passing it over with some slight comment. But we reject the syllogistic method as being too confused, and allowing nature to escape out of our hands. For though nobody can doubt that those things which agree with the middle term agree with each other, nevertheless, there is this source of error, that a syllogism consists of propositions, propositions of words, and words are but the tokens and signs of things. Now, if the first notions, which are, as it were, the soul of words, and the basis of every philosophical fabric, are hastily abstracted from things, and vague and not clearly defined and limited, the whole structure falls to the ground. We therefore reject the syllogism, and that not only as regards first principles, to which logicians do not apply them, but also with respect to intermediate propositions, which the syllogism contrives to manage in such a way as to render barren in effect, unfit for practice, and clearly unsuited to the active branch of the sciences. Nevertheless, we would leave to the syllogism, and such celebrated and applauded demonstrations, their jurisdiction over popular and speculative acts; while, in everything relating to the nature of things, we make use of induction for both our major and minor propositions; for we consider induction as that form of demonstration which closes in upon nature and presses on, and, as it were, mixes itself with action. Whence the common order of demonstrating is absolutely inverted; for instead of flying immediately from the senses, and particulars, to generals, as to certain fixed poles, about which disputes always turn, and deriving others from these by intermediates, in a short, indeed, but precipitate manner, fit for controversy, but unfit to close with nature; we continually raise up propositions by degrees, and in the last place, come to the most general axioms, which are not notional, but well defined, and what nature allows of, as entering into the very essence of things.

But the more difficult part of our task consists in the form of induction, and the judgment to be made by it; for that form of the logicians which proceeds by simple enumeration, is a childish thing, concludes unsafely, lies open to contradictory instances, and regards only common matters, yet determines nothing: while the sciences require such a form of induction, as can separate, adjust, and verify experience, and come to a necessary determination by proper exclusions and rejections.

Nor is this all; for we likewise lay the foundations of the sciences stronger and closer, and begin our inquiries deeper than men have hitherto done, bringing those things to the test which the common logic has taken upon trust. The logicians borrow the principles of the sciences from the sciences themselves, venerate the first notions of the mind, and acquiesce in the immediate informations of the senses, when rightly disposed; but we judge, that a real logic should enter every province of the sciences with a greater authority than their own principles can give; and that such supposed principles should be examined, till they become absolutely clear and certain. As for first notions of the mind, we suspect all those that the understanding, left to itself, procures; nor ever allow them till approved and authorized by a second judgment. And with respect to the informations of the senses, we have many ways of examining them; for the senses are fallacious, though they discover their own errors; but these lie near, while the means of discovery are remote.

The senses are faulty in two respects, as they either fail or deceive us. For there are many things that escape the senses, though ever so rightly disposed; as by the subtilty of the whole body, or the minuteness of its parts; the distance of place; the slowness or velocity of motion; the commonness of the object, etc. Neither do the senses, when they lay hold of a thing, retain it strongly; for evidence, and the informations of sense, are in proportion to a man, and not in proportion to the universe. And it is a grand error to assert that sense is the measure of things.

To remedy this, we have from all quarters brought together, and fitted helps for the senses; and that rather by experiments than by instruments; apt experiments being much more subtile than the senses themselves, though assisted with the most finished instruments. . . .

Our natural history is not designed so much to please by its variety, or benefit by gainful experiments, as to afford light to the discovery of causes, and hold out the breasts to philosophy; for though we principally regard works, and the active parts of the Sciences, yet we wait for the time of harvest, and would not reap the blade for the ear. We are well aware that axioms, rightly framed, will draw after them whole sheaves of works: but for that untimely and childish desire of seeing fruits of new works before the season, we absolutely condemn and reject it, as the golden apple that hinders the progress.

With regard to its collection; we propose to show nature not only in a free state, as in the history of meteors, minerals, plants, and animals; but more particularly as she is bound, and tortured, pressed, formed, and turned out of her course by art and human industry. Hence we would set down all opposite experiments of the mechanic and liberal arts, with many others not yet formed into arts; for the nature of things is better discovered by the torturings of art, than when they are left to themselves. Nor is it only a history of bodies that we would give; but also of their cardinal virtues, or fundamental qualities; as density, rarity, heat, cold, etc., which should be comprised in particular histories.

The kind of experiments to be procured for our history are much more subtile and simple than the common; abundance of them must be recovered from darkness, and are such as no one would have inquired after, that was not led by constant and certain tract to the discovery of causes; as being in themselves of no great use, and consequently not sought for their own sake, but with regard to works: like the letters of the alphabet with regard to discourse.

In the choice of our narratives and experiments we hope to have shown more care than the other writers of natural history; as receiving nothing but upon ocular demonstration, or the strictest scrutiny of examination; and not heightening what is delivered to increase its miraculousness, but thoroughly purging it of superstition and fable. Besides this, we reject, with a particular mark, all those boasted and received falsehoods, which by a strange neglect have prevailed for so many ages, that they may no longer molest the sciences. For as the idle tales of nurses do really corrupt the minds of children, we cannot too carefully guard the infancy of philosophy from all vanity and superstition. And when any new or more curious experiment is offered, though it may seem to us certain and well founded; yet we expressly add the manner wherein it was made; that, after it shall be understood how things appear to us, men may beware of any error adhering to them, and search after more infallible proofs. We, likewise, all along interpose our directions, scruples and cautions; and religiously guard against phantoms and illusions.

Lastly, having well observed how far experiments and history distract the mind; and how difficult it is, especially for tender or prejudiced persons, to converse with nature from the beginning, we shall continually subjoin our observations, as so many first glances of natural history at philosophy; and this to give mankind some earnest, that they shall not be kept perpetually floating upon the waves of history; and that when they come to the work of the understanding, and the explanation of nature, they may find all things in greater readiness. This will conclude the third part.

After the understanding has been thus aided and fortified, we shall be prepared to enter upon philosophy itself. But in so difficult a task, there are certain things to be observed, as well for instruction as for present use. The first is to propose examples of inquiry and investigation, according to our own method, in certain subjects of the noblest kind, but greatly differing from each other, that a specimen may be had of every sort. By these examples we mean not illustrations of rules and precepts, but perfect models, which will exemplify the second part of this work, and represent, as it were, to the eye, the whole progress of the mind, and the continued structure and order of invention, in the most chosen subjects, after the same manner as globes and machines facilitate the more abstruse and subtile demonstrations in mathematics. We assign the fourth part of our work to these examples, which are nothing else than a particular application of the second part of our undertaking.

The fifth part is only temporary, or of use but till the rest are finished; whence we look upon it as interest till the principal be paid; for we do not propose to travel hoodwinked, so as to take no notice of what may occur of use in the way. This part, therefore, will consist of such things as we have invented, experienced, or added, by the same common use of the understanding that others employ. For as we have greater hopes from our constant conversation with nature than from our force of genius, the discoveries we shall thus make may serve as inns on the road, for the mind to repose in, during its progress to greater certainties. But this, without being at all disposed to abide by anything that is not discovered, or proved, by the true form of induction. Nor need any one be shocked at this suspension of the judgment, in a doctrine which does not assert that nothing is knowable; but only that things cannot be known except in a certain order and method: while it allows particular degrees of certainty, for the sake of commodiousness and use, until the mind shall enter on the explanation of causes. Nor were those schools of philosophers, who held positive truth to be unattainable, inferior to others who dogmatized at will. They did not, however, like us, prepare helps for the guidance of the senses and understanding, as we have done, but at once abolished all belief and authority, which is a totally different and almost opposite matter.

The sixth and last part of our work, to which all the rest are subservient, is to lay down that philosophy which shall flow from the just, pure and strict inquiry hitherto proposed. But to perfect this, is beyond both our abilities and our hopes, yet we shall lay the foundations of it, and recommend the superstructure to posterity. We design no contemptible beginning to the work; and anticipate that the fortune of mankind will lead it to such a termination as is not possible for the present race of men to conceive. The point in view is not only the contemplative happiness, but the whole fortunes, and affairs, and powers, and works of men. For man being the minister and interpreter of nature, acts and understands so far as he has observed of the order, the works and mind of nature, and can proceed no further; for no power is able to loose or break the chain of causes, nor is nature to be conquered but by submission; whence those twin intentions, human knowledge and human power, are really coincident; and the greatest hindrance to works is the ignorance of causes.

The capital precept for the whole undertaking is this, that the eye of the mind be never taken off from things themselves, but receive their images truly as they are. And God forbid that ever we should offer the dreams of fancy for a model of the world; but rather in his kindness vouchsafe to us the means of writing a revelation and true vision of the traces and molds of the Creator in his creatures.

WILLIAM BAGLEY

WILLIAM BAGLEY (1874-1946). The dignity and importance of teaching as a profession was uppermost in the mind of William Chandler Bagley throughout his long and active period of service to education in America. Chief critic of progressive education and leading exponent of a modified form of traditionalism, he helped to organize the group known as the Essentialists, who would direct more attention to systematic work, to the fundamentals or essentials established by tradition, to rather formal teaching procedures.

Born in Detroit, Michigan, on March 15, 1874, he graduated from Michigan Agricultural College in 1895, took the M. S. Degree at the University of Wisconsin in 1898, and received his doctorate from Cornell University in 1900. He taught in public schools and in normal schools from 1895 to 1897 and from 1901 to 1908.

Always proud of his profession, he preferred to be listed in *Who's Who* as "teacher" rather than as "educator" or "professor," and he censured schools systems for allowing unfair discrepancies to exist between the salaries of administrators and those paid to teachers.

In 1908 he accepted a position as professor of education at the University of Illinois, where he remained until he accepted a similar position at Teachers College. During his long tenure at Teachers College (1917-1940) thousands of students came directly under his influence and could never forget the dignity and importance which he attached to the work of the classroom teacher. He died on July 1, 1946.

Dr. Bagley delivered a lecture to foreign students on December 18, 1928, under the auspices of the International Institute of Teachers College. Obviously pleased by the advances that had already been made in improving the qualifications of American teachers and establishing the prestige of the teaching profession, he expressed his confidence that "our profession will prove neither recreant nor inadequate to its great trust and its great opportunity." The following article is based on his lecture.

THE PROFESSION OF TEACHING IN THE
UNITED STATES*

The development of American education has been beset from the outset by handicaps and obstacles, many of which undoubtedly confront our fellow-workers in other countries, but some of which are indigenous, so to speak, to our own soil, growing out of our own peculiar traditions and *mores*: our deep-seated and thoroughly dynamic ideals of local self-government; the diverse standards of our conglomerate population; the sharply contrasting needs and interests of our urban and rural people; our fondness for quantity-production and our delight in numerical magnitudes; our distrust of the expert; our zeal in making laws and our zest in breaking them; and a host of other factors and forces, many of which work in quite opposite directions, but all of which have cooperated to make extremely difficult the development of an educational system which would be constructively effective on a nation-wide basis.

And yet these unique factors in our problem, even though they have constituted serious handicaps to educational effort, have also been, perhaps for that very reason, a stimulating challenge, the continued response to which has resulted in progress of a most substantial sort, with promises for the future that should give hope and inspiration to those in other countries who are facing problems similar in difficulty although in many instances quite different in kind.

The advancement in the status of the teacher's calling, while the most recent of the large developments in American education, is in some respects the most significant and promises for the future the most far-reaching results. It is also, I believe, a development quite unprecedented in the history of education and, so far as I know, it is unparalleled in other countries.

*From *School and Society*, XXIX (January 26, 1929), pp. 101-110. Reprinted by permission of the editor of *School and Society*.

In reviewing the handicaps that have beset this development, it goes without saying that many of them are not at all peculiar to our country. Something akin to contempt for the work of teaching, especially in the lower schools, has found expression, I suppose, in all ages and in all climes. It was the Englishman, Bernard Shaw, who coined the famous epigram, "Those who can, do; those who can not, teach." The immortal Boswell, in a ponderous effort to explain why Samuel Johnson was so complete and pitiable a failure as a teacher of youth, ventured the following sage reflection:

"The art of communicating instruction, of whatever kind, is much to be valued; and I have ever thought that those who devote themselves to this employment, and do their duty with diligence and success, are entitled to very high respect from the community, as Johnson himself often maintained. Yet I am of the opinion that the greatest abilities are not only not required in this office, but render a man less fit for it."

While this patronizing attitude of thinly veiled contempt for the work of teaching is no new thing and not at all confined to our own country, I believe that it has constituted a far more serious handicap to the development of our profession here than it has elsewhere.

In the first place, until recently, the teaching-personnel of our public schools has been transient and unstable. Twenty years ago, the average period of service of the public-school teacher was not more than four years, which meant that tens of thousands of teachers remained only one, two or three years in the service. The occupation was distinctly recognized in most communities as temporary, and those who from force of circumstances were compelled to make it a life work were naturally regarded with something akin to pity. For the able and ambitious, teaching was openly taken up as a stepping-stone to what both the teacher and the public thought of as worthier callings. One of the early university professors of education, in whose classes I sat thirty years ago, laughingly referred to public-school teachers as a group made up chiefly of immature women and feeble men.

Along with this condition, of course, went the parallel fact that the teachers as a whole were pitifully unprepared for their work. Twenty years ago, more than a majority of the public-school teachers had had no education beyond the high school, and more than ten thousand were limited in their education to what the elementary school provided.

Although every state maintained professional schools for teachers not one in four of those employed in the public schools was a product of such an institution. As short a time ago as 1916, Judd and Parker asserted in an official bulletin of the Bureau of Education that the United States gave less attention to the training of teachers than did any other civilized nation. With brief tenure and lack of training quite naturally went meager compensation, and in a country where occupations won public regard in direct proportion to the material rewards that they provided, this condition was in itself a sufficient stigma to the teacher's calling.

Closely related to the handicaps which transiency, instability, low training standards and meager preparation placed in the way of professional development was the unequal competition with other occupations for talented recruits. This was most serious, of course, in connection with the problem of drawing able men into the profession. Not only did the vast development of business and industry multiply the opportunities for building huge individual fortunes, but the spectacular achievements of our captains of industry, finance and organization caught the public imagination, bringing to successful efforts in those fields a measure of renown and popular adulation beside which even the material rewards were of quite subordinate value.

There are one or two incidents in my own life that may give a concrete setting to the conditions to which I have referred. Some forty years ago I was a schoolboy in the city of Detroit. As cities went, even in those days, Detroit was an unpretentious, rather conservative urban center, surpassed in wealth, population and promise by nearly a score of American cities. One day in the early nineties, while walking along one of the streets of the city, I saw a little group gathered around a queer-looking conveyance drawn up alongside the curb. I joined the crowd, and found that

51

the object of their interest was what we then called a horseless carriage. A young man was rather frantically engaged in overhauling the machinery, every now and again making a desperate effort to get the clumsy contraption to show some signs of life. As long as I watched, his efforts were rewarded only by a wheezy cough from the crude engine, echoed, of course, by the jeers of the crowd. That jeering crowd little dreamed that the scene which they were witnessing for the first time would be reenacted within the next thirty years on ten thousand city streets and country roads by hundreds of thousands of exasperated drivers of self-propelled vehicles; still less did they dream that the evolution of that clumsy, horseless carriage would cause their city to out-distance all but three of its competitors in population and wealth and make it the world center for the most highly organized branch of modern industry; least of all did they dream that the young man who was struggling so desperately to conjure a vital spark in that new-fangled internal-combustion engine was in all likelihood the man who, within three decades, would be recognized and acclaimed as the type and symbol of American genius at its own unique best.

It is not at all to be wondered at that the marvelous expansion of American industry, with its overwhelming rewards of wealth and fame for successful effort, should have cast a shadow over fields of endeavor less spectacular, less appealing to the concrete imagination of the public, less obviously creative of new values. It is small wonder that, with competition of this sort, the latter fields were unable to attract so large a share of superior talent as has been the case in many other countries. The relative paucity of our national contributions to pure science, to literature, music and the other fine arts, and to statesmanship of the first order may be explained at least in part by this factor. Obviously an occupation so modestly rewarded as teaching and one that offers so few opportunities for renown would have, under these conditions, a relatively low place in public esteem.

The effect of all this upon the morale of the teaching group may be readily inferred. Those who remained for any length of time in the profession acquired, in many cases, an inferiority

52

complex of large dimensions. They openly regretted that they had not taken up another occupation. Just as openly, they advised young people against teaching as a career and commiserated one another over their hard lot. About eight years ago in visiting the college in Michigan where I spent my undergraduate days, I called on one of the two or three of my former instructors who still survived. He asked me what I had been doing over the years and where I was located. I told him that I had been teaching and was still engaged in that occupation. Then he asked me where I had come from when I entered college. He shook his head sadly when I told him, and then, with a sincere sigh of pity, he said, "And just think what you might have become if you had only gone back to Detroit and entered the automobile business." I left his office and my old college with a deep sense of my failure to reflect any worthy credit on my *alma mater*.

I could multiply concrete examples of this sort from my own experience and that of my friends, but enough has been said to indicate one of the most serious obstacles that the development of a real profession of teaching has confronted in our country. With what I have said regarding the instability, inadequate training and transiency of the great rank and file of teachers, this may give us a sufficient background against which to project the advances that our profession has made.

To-day, many of the conditions to which I have referred are radically different from what they were fifteen, ten, even five years ago. The period of service of the average teacher has been extended from four or five years to at least eight or nine years. The level of training has advanced to a much higher plane—where fifteen years ago the median public-school teacher had no more than a high-school education at most, to-day it is probable that 60 per cent of these teachers have had two years or more in advance of high-school graduation. In several states the proportion is nearly 100 per cent. The number of college graduates in the public-school service has also shown a remarkable increase. The enrolment in our normal schools and teachers' colleges has doubled in the past five years, and the output of these professional schools is now so large that, for the first time in our history, there is an actual surplus of trained teachers in most of the cities and in some of the states.

This condition has led to significant advances in the standards of our professional schools. Many of the former two-year normal schools have advanced the requirements for elementary-school teachers three years and some are now on a full four-year basis. Paralleling these advances there has been a really remarkable development within the profession, some of the outstanding trends of which I shall mention a little later. In public esteem, too, the teacher's calling has made significant advances.

Like most profound changes, these developments have been brought about in part by conscious and deliberate purposing, and in part by the fortunate operation of forces and factors that are largely beyond either individual or social control. Let us consider first these latter, impersonal factors.

Primarily, of course, one must recognize the unprecedented material prosperity of our country. This has made possible both a wider extension of educational opportunity and a keener demand for better schools and better teachers. As a result, the level of teachers' salaries has advanced significantly, and is still advancing in spite of a tendency toward the stabilization of wage and salary levels in other occupations. Teaching can now compete with other callings on terms much more nearly equal than have prevailed heretofore.

This, however, does not tell the whole story, for the contrasts with the spectacular rewards of business and industry still persist. Yet for some reason the influence of this contrast is less noticeable to-day than it was only a few years ago. This may be due to a recognition on the part of the public that these huge material rewards in the very nature of things can go to only a very few of the most capable or the most fortunate, while the rank and file must necessarily fare much more modestly.

Back of all this, however, is another set of facts, the full significance of which we are probably not yet in a position to grasp. The leaven of the Industrial Revolution, which has been responsible for so many fundamental social changes, is still working, and working in a more thoroughgoing fashion in our country

54

than anywhere else. The report of the American Federation of Labor, recently published, reveals the astounding fact that, in spite of the vast development of American industry in the present decade, the number of persons actually engaged in manufacturing has decreased by approximately a million since 1920. In other words, the improvement of automatic machinery has not only kept pace with the expansion of industry; it has sent a million workers to seek other means of earning a living. In this country, too, much more than in other countries, the influence of the Industrial Revolution has profoundly affected agriculture. Power-driven machinery has apparently replaced no fewer than 800,000 farm workers since 1920.

As a mere layman in economics, it would be presumptuous in me to attempt an interpretation of these facts. I can not escape the conclusion, however, that they are related in a very direct way to the opportunities that our profession has recently enjoyed to augment its numbers, advance its standards and stabilize its service. If I am right in my inferences, these developments in invention and industrial organization are actually driving men and women out of industry and farming into the white-collar occupations. Not only have the traditional professions grown in numbers—there are 250,000 more professional workers now than in 1920, according to the Federation's report—but a veritable multitude of other white-collar occupations are advancing toward a professional status in the sense that specific and often prolonged courses of education are willingly undertaken by those seeking either employment or advancement. Banks, department stores, the great hotel syndicates, insurance companies and public service corporations are developing elaborate schools for the training of their personnel. In at least one of the big insurance companies the vice-president in charge of education is one of the highest paid and most highly respected of the executives. With this emphasis upon specialized training, there has naturally been a corresponding emphasis upon an extended and thoroughgoing general education which shall serve as a background for the specialized courses; hence another reason why the high-school enrolment has trebled in fifteen years and why the college enrolment has doubled in ten years.

May I say parenthetically that it is of the utmost significance to education that this recent turn of the Industrial Revolution has not only reduced the proportion of workers needed in industry and farming, but has also increased the numbers needed in the white-collar occupations? The development of type-setting machinery, for example, made it possible for one operator to do the work of four compositors, and thus reduced the demand for the old-time printer, but the economy and efficiency of the new process greatly multiplied the demand for writers, editors, illustrators and advertising specialists. In fact, every department of automatic machines for mass-production has opened new fields of useful employment almost all of which have meant a stepping-up of the intellectual level of the work involved. Within the past decade this change has been going on with unprecedented acceleration; hence the heavy demands now made upon the schools and colleges are something more than a mere reflex of our economic prosperity; in a very real sense, they are the expression of a tremendously enlarged need on the part of millions of people for a type of instruction and discipline that will mean for them a genuine intellectual advance. Hence the recent controversy in our field regarding the possibilities of raising through education the mass-levels of effective intelligence is concerned with something more than a merely academic question. Upon the issue that this controversy involves hangs the future of our industrialized civilization.

I have suggested that the recent development of our profession has been conditioned in part by impersonal forces, largely economic in character, which have operated to expand the field of our service, to increase the demands made upon us and to give us more and better recruits. The net result has been an almost complete transformation of the conditions under which we have been working. May I impress particularly the fact that, so far as its outward manifestations are concerned, this transformation has come very suddenly—almost overnight, so to speak? Many of our fellow-workers are still rubbing their eyes and wondering whether it is not all a dream. Others are still, in a manner of speaking, fast asleep—working on programs which reflect needs that seemed genuine enough a few years ago, but which can now be seen as based upon quite erroneous assumptions regarding the trends of contemporary civilization; programs, for example, that would keep the farm boys on the farms to compete with gasoline engines and combined harvesters; and programs for premature vocational training based on the theory that the white-collar occupations are overcrowded when they are apparently the only occupations that have not been seriously overcrowded in the past few years and are to-day the occupations in which there are evidences of the greatest expansion.

It need hardly be said that the situation which confronts us is fairly unique to our own country. Other nations undoubtedly need heavier emphasis upon agricultural and trade education and less emphasis upon intellectual education. Be that as it may, it is clear enough that some of our own students of education have made some rather bad guesses during the past two decades and that some of them are still repeating their stereotyped pleas even though the need for their particular variety of reform no longer exists. On the other hand, it is equally true that the progress of our profession has been influenced in a very powerful positive fashion by the students of education. While they have undoubtedly made mistakes in some of their efforts to define social problems and to construct programs that would work toward the solution of these problems, they have played an important part in laying the foundations upon which a real and great profession of teaching is even now arising.

For upward of thirty years, a steadily increasing number of men and women have been devoting their lives to the serious study of the educational problem. The pioneers of this group were a few scattering school executives who conceived of their duties as comprehending something beyond the machinery of organization and the routine of administration, and who set a splendid example of constructive leadership and truly creative effort. One of these men was William Torrey Harris, who infused into the city school system of St. Louis a vigorous new life and who later served with distinction as the federal commissioner of education. Another was Francis W. Parker, who, as head of the schools of Quincy, Massachusetts, was the founder in America of what we now call the progressive school of educational theory; another was William H. Maxwell, the first superintendent of the schools of Greater New York. A fourth was Calvin Kendall, for many years superintendent of schools in Indianapolis and during the latter part of his life commissioner of education for the State of New Jersey.

Among the early colleagues and companions of these executives were the first professors of education in the colleges and universities. The real development of these departments of education may be dated from about 1890. Two years before, Clark University had been founded under the leadership of Stanley Hall, and during the following decade Clark was a nursery of educational ideals and enthusiasms. Then came the development of Teachers College under James E. Russell, and at the University of Chicago the pioneer work of John Dewey. From Clark and Columbia and Chicago men and women in increasing numbers went out to other colleges and universities either to establish or to remodel on a true university basis the departments of education. State universities, like those of Wisconsin, Iowa, Minnesota, California and Illinois, became in their turn centers of instruction, research and inspiration directed toward the problems of teaching and learning, of administration and supervision in the public schools. Private and endowed institutions like Peabody, Stanford, Yale and Harvard assumed their share of the great task.

The influence of this development of the university study of education upon the profession of teaching has been profound. In the first place, it has provided for the professional education of teachers a substantial body of knowledge. The recency of this development is exemplified by the fact that many of the men who have done the pioneer work are still in their prime. . . .

A second influence of the university study of education has been a new access of self-respect on the part of the teaching personnel. The inferiority complex, to which I referred as one of the handicaps to our professional development, is gradually but certainly giving place to a sense of professional pride and dignity, tempered as it should be and as I hope it always will be, by a keen sense of the complexities of our problem and of the serious responsibilities which one must assume who would do even the humblest work in the field of teaching.

A third influence is one of the most significant of all. The university study of education has played a most important part in integrating the teaching profession. As Dean Russell told you a few weeks ago, something akin to the old-world caste distinction between the education of the masses and the education of the classes has persisted even in our unit system which otherwise so closely articulates the elementary and secondary schools. With us, the distinction has been one primarily of training and material rewards. The elementary-school teacher has represented a narrower and briefer training than the high-school teacher and even now receives in most of our school systems a distinctly lower salary. It has been a popular belief, shared by many members of the profession itself, that the work of teaching increases in difficulty, dignity and importance as one goes up the age scale. The university study of education has probably done more than anything else to reveal the fallacy of this popular belief, and to correct the injustice that has been done to the younger children in our schools by a deliberate policy which uses the lower grades as the testing ground for the immature and inexperienced teachers, the permanent abode of the weak and the indolent, and the final resting-place of the old and decrepit. To-day there is a growing conviction that no phase or field of teaching can lay valid claim to being more difficult or more important than any other phase. Discriminations and distinctions as to salaries are breaking down, as, for example, in the gradual extension of the single-salary schedule which does away with all distinctions except those that are based upon training, experience and meritorious service.

This general movement has been a powerful force in integrating our profession vertically, so to speak. Other forces have been operating to integrate the profession horizontally or geographically. Chief among these are our educational organizations. Foreign students sometimes wonder why, with our lack of any centralized educational authority in the nation as a whole, with the lack

59

even of highly centralized state systems, our schools all over the country are in fundamental ways very much alike, dominated by the same aims and ideals, following fairly similar programs of study, governed by essentially uniform standards. The answer is simple. While our school systems are essentially local, the teaching profession is essentially national. For seventy years the educational leaders of the nation have met annually to discuss their common problems, but it has been only within the past twenty years that the state and national organizations have really represented the profession as a whole. Today these organizations are made up of, and controlled very largely by, the rank and file of elementary and secondary teachers. The National Education Association has grown in active membership from 10,000 to 200,000 in a single decade. Its policies are now determined by a representative assembly made up largely of delegates elected by the state associations. Many of the latter, in turn, are controlled by similar representative assemblies elected by district and local associations. The total enrolment in all of these organizations aggregates nearly three quarters of a million, which means that three out of every four members of our profession can have a vote and a voice in determining where our profession will go and how it will get there — in formulating our collective ideals and devising the means of realizing them through collective action. To this end the national association employs a headquarters staff with a personnel of more than one hundred men and women, including expert research workers, editors, legislative agents, publicity agents and specialists in the major educational fields. Several of the state organizations have similar staffs, and practically all of them employ full-time secretaries and publish official journals. May I emphasize the fact that this development has taken place almost entirely within a single decade?

One of the striking characteristics of this and other phases of our professional development has been the clear-cut tendency toward a thoroughgoing democracy. Not only are the distinctions between the elementary-school service and the high-school service being obliterated, but the equally unfortunate distinctions between the classroom teacher and the executive and supervisory officials are being minimized. In our professional organizations, as in our classes in education, all the workers in our field can meet on a common footing.

This tendency, which has been abetted by many of the administrators themselves, merits an especial emphasis in a discussion of the profession of teaching in the United States. It is distinctly a conscious effort to counteract in education some of the admitted evils that elaborate organization has brought about in business and industry. In the latter fields, the magnification of the executive and supervisory officers in contrast with those who do the first-hand work has perhaps been inevitable. Quite naturally, as our school systems expanded, a similar hierarchy of administrative authority was established, and the distinctions involved in this administrative hierarchy became in effect professional distinctions. To be transferred from the first-hand work of teaching boys and girls to an executive or administrative post was generally, and still is in many places, looked upon as a professional promotion. Under these conditions a large city school system became quite analogous to a great factory with its board of directors, its superintendent, managers, foremen, bosses and "hands." In school work, the classroom teachers were the "hands."

Now whatever may be the advantages or the dangers of such a hierarchy in business and industry, it works veritable mischief when applied to education. A simple contrast will, I think, make this clear.

If I buy an automobile I am not particularly concerned, except from a humanitarian point of view, with the workmen who have actually put it together. I can be reasonably certain that a few highly competent engineers designed the car, that a few others devised elaborate machinery for making and testing the various parts, and that a competent hierarchy of executives, superintendents, managers, foremen and bosses formed a responsible overhead for supervising its construction. The factory hands who operated the automatic machinery, screwed up the nuts, clinched the cotter-pins and sprayed on the paint and varnish: these may have been morons or they may have been near-geniuses; they may have had no interest whatsoever in their work beyond their paychecks or they may have been true craftsmen with a fine pride in good workmanship; they may have been human automata going through their motions with as little real understanding of what it all meant as the machines that they operated, or they may have been men of keen insight, seeing their work in clear relation to the completed product. To me, merely as a purchaser of an automobile, it would make little difference. I can trust the machinery of production and testing under the supervision of the overhead. In fact, I can be fairly certain that if any one of the factory-hands were a near-genius and tremendously interested in his work for its own sake and able to see his work clearly in its relation to the completed product, he would very quickly be taken from the ranks and promoted to the overhead.

So much if I should buy an automobile.

When I send my children to school, however, my attitude toward the person who does the actual, first-hand work of their education is almost completely reversed. It is true that I would wish plans and specifications of that education to be well drawn by highly competent students of the problem; I would like the textbooks to be authoritative and well-written; I would like the tests to be objective and accurate; I would like an organization that would guarantee a healthful school environment. But above all I would want for my children a real teacher. No virtues of the "overhead" could compensate for a teacher who had no interest in his work, who saw nothing beyond his pay-check, who found no joy and left no pride in doing his work as well as it could be done irrespective of the material rewards that it brought, who had no vision of what it meant and no understanding of what his efforts contributed to the completed product.

One of the prominent objectives of our profession at the present time is to give to those who do the actual first-hand work of teaching an adequate recognition. Within the past ten years there has been a distinct tendency toward the participation of classroom teachers in the construction of educational policies and programs. In some school systems, councils elected by the teachers have a recognized function in the government of the schools. Probably the most characteristic expression of this tendency, however, is found in the work that is now going on all over the country in the revision and construction of curricula by groups of classroom teachers.

While practices such as these tend to dignify the actual first-hand work of teaching, they have, I think, an even deeper significance. They represent a quite new type of control for public education — and a type of control which has vast possibilities for the future. It goes without saying that some of the results will be disappointing. There must necessarily be groping and stumbling and blundering; but in the end the progress that is made is likely to be both substantial and enduring.

And this I take it is the fundamental justification of democracy as a mode of social control. Autocratic leadership gets results more quickly; and, under extremely competent leadership, the results may mean genuine progress. But dependence upon autocratic leadership suffers under two handicaps. In the first place, a really competent leader may not appear for years or even generations; in the second place, progress which is made possible only by a dictatorship is not likely to be sustained when the strong hand loses its grip. Given a reasonably high level of trained intelligence, the democratic group will be able to carry on even if competent leadership does not appear; and although its progress may be slow, it is much more likely to be certain and sustained.

I have attempted to present in general outline the development of the profession of teaching in the United States. I have called attention to some of the typical handicaps that this development has encountered; to the economic forces which have transformed in a striking fashion some of these handicaps; to the contributions that the students of education have made to our professional development; and to some of the factors that have worked toward professional solidarity and integration. I have probably set forth certain of the characteristics of our profession as though they were full-fledged achievements rather than ideals and aspirations many of which are still far from realization. My aim has been, however, to portray substantial trends, in the future fruition of which some of our dreams may come true. Certain it is that the present situation is full of promise. Whether this great army of

63

teachers, now numbering in all branches of education upward of a million men and women, can think together and work together toward the fulfilment of this promise is another question. There are, of course, social forces and economic factors that will constitute handicaps in the future as similar forces and factors have been handicaps in the past. But personally I am optimistic; the transformation that I have myself witnessed in thirty years is so thoroughgoing that I can not but believe that another generation will carry us much further on the road to better things. It is literally true that through our profession every significant unit in our vast population can be touched and quickened. It is within our power as an organized and responsible group to make the American school the greatest single constructive force in American life. I have every faith that our profession will prove neither recreant nor inadequate to its great trust and its great opportunity.

ST. BASIL

ST. BASIL (c. 330-379). Born in Caesarea around 330, St. Basil, known as Basil the Great, studied at Byzantium and Athens, then observed the life of the hermits in Syria and Egypt before retiring to the desert of Pontus to found the monastic order known as Basilians. Son of a teacher of rhetoric and himself a teacher in Caesarea, he was actively engaged in the education of youth until his death around 379.

Because of his conservatism and his penchant for organization, he has been called a Roman among the Greeks. Ordained a priest about 365, the Cappadocian Father refused to admit that Rome had claim to primacy in the Christian Church, but he promoted the union of the two great branches of Christianity. In his role as founder of monastic institutions he substituted for the ascetic life of the hermit a communal existence centered around charitable services and hard work.

St. Basil held ancient writers in high esteem and regarded the study of their works as a preparation for the study of Scripture and Christian writings. He was among the first Greek Fathers to assert that pagan literature had an important place in the education of Christians. His classic solution to the problem of adapting the writings of the pagans to the needs of youth, sometimes called the theory of the honeybee, is put forward in his *Address to Young Men,* a part of which is presented here: Christians must not condemn pagan literature in principle but must, like the bee, select only what is acceptable from the Christian point of view. Werner Jaeger credited St. Basil with writing "the charter of all Christian higher education for centuries to come."

*THE RIGHT USE OF GREEK LITERATURE**

Do not be surprised if to you, who go to school every day, and who, through their writings, associate with the learned men of old, I say that out of my own experience I have evolved something more useful. Now this my counsel, that you should not un-

*From St. Basil's *Address to Young Men on the Right Use of Greek Literature,* translated by Frederick Morgan Padelford (New York: Henry Holt and Company, 1902).

qualifiedly give over your minds to these men, as a ship is surrendered to the rudder, to follow whither they list, but that, while receiving whatever of value they have to offer, you yet recognize what it is wise to ignore. Accordingly, from this point on I shall take up and discuss the pagan writings, and how we are to discriminate among them.

II. We Christians, young men, hold that this human life is not a supremely precious thing, nor do we recognize anything as unconditionally a blessing which benefits us in this life only. Neither pride of ancestry, nor bodily strength, nor beauty, nor greatness, nor the esteem of all men, nor kingly authority, nor indeed, whatever of human affairs may be called great, do we consider worthy of desire, or the possessors of them as objects of envy; but we place our hopes upon the things which are beyond, and in preparation for the life eternal do we all things that we do. . . .

III. If, then, there is any affinity between the two literatures, a knowledge of them should be useful to us in our search for truth; if not, the comparison by emphasizing the contrast, will be of no small service in strengthening our regard for the better one. With what now may we compare these two kinds of education to obtain a simile? Just as it is the chief mission of the tree to bear its fruit in its season, though at the same time it puts forth for ornament the leaves which quiver on its boughs, even so the real fruit of the soul is truth, yet it is not without advantage for it to embrace the pagan wisdom, as also leaves offer shelter to the fruit, and an appearance not untimely.

IV. Perhaps it is sufficiently demonstrated that such heathen learning is not unprofitable for the soul; I shall then discuss next the extent to which one may pursue it. To begin with the poets, since their writings are of all degrees of excellence, you should not study all of their poems without omitting a single word. When they recount the words and deeds of good men, you should both love and imitate them, earnestly emulating such conduct. But when they portray base conduct, you must flee from them and stop up your ears, as Odysseus is said to have fled past the song of the sirens, for familiarity with evil writings paves the way for

66

evil deeds. Therefore the soul must be guarded with great care, lest through our love for letters it receive some contamination unaware, as men drink in poison with honey. We shall not praise the poets when they scoff and rail, when they represent fornicators and winebibbers, when they define blissfulness by groaning tables and wanton songs. Least of all shall we listen to them when they tell us of their gods, and especially when they represent them as being many, and not at one among themselves. For, among these gods, at one time brother is at variance with brother, or the father with his children; at another, the children engage in truceless war against their parents. The adulteries of the gods and their amours, and especially those of the one whom they call Zeus, chief of all and most high, things of which one cannot speak, even in connection with brutes, without blushing, we shall leave to the stage.

I have the same words for the historians, and especially when they make up stories for the amusement of their hearers. And certainly we shall not follow the example of the rhetoricians in the art of lying. For neither in the courts of justice nor in other business affairs will falsehood be of any help to us Christians, who, having chosen the straight and true path of life, are forbidden by the gospel to go to law. But on the other hand we shall receive gladly those passages in which they praise virtue or condemn vice. For just as bees know how to extract honey from flowers, which to men are agreeable only for their fragrance and color, even so here also those who look for something more than pleasure and enjoyment in such writers may derive profit for their souls. Now, then, altogether after the manner of bees must we use these writings, for the bees do not visit all the flowers without discrimination, nor indeed do they seek to carry away entire those upon which they light, but rather, having taken so much as is adapted to their needs, they let the rest go. So we, if wise, shall take from heathen books whatever befits us and is allied to the truth, and shall pass over the rest. And just as in culling roses we avoid the thorns, from such writings as these we will gather everything useful, and guard against the noxious. So, from the very beginning, we must examine each of their teachings, to harmonize it with our ultimate purpose, according to the Doric proverb, "testing each stone by the measuring-line."

V. Since we must needs attain to the life to come through virtue, our attention is to be chiefly fastened upon those many passages from the poets, from the historians, and especially from the philosophers, in which virtue itself is praised. For it is of no small advantage that virtue become a habit with a youth, for the lessons of youth make a deep impression, because the soul is then plastic, and therefore they are likely to be indelible. . . .

VI. Almost all who have written upon the subject of wisdom have more or less, in proportion to their several abilities, extolled virtue in their writings. Such men must one obey, and must try to realize their words in his life. For he, who by his works exemplifies the wisdom which with others is a matter of theory alone, 'breathes; all others flutter about like shadows.' I think it is as if a painter should represent some marvel of manly beauty, and the subject should actually be such a man as the artist pictures on the canvas. To praise virtue in public with brilliant words and with long drawn out speeches, while in private preferring pleasures to temperance, and self-interest to justice, finds an analogy on the stage, for the players frequently appear as kings and rulers, though they are neither, nor perhaps even genuinely free men. . . . But every man is divided against himself who does not make his life conform to his words, but who says with Euripides, 'The mouth indeed hath sworn, but the heart knows no oath.' Such a man will seek the appearance of virtue rather than the reality. But to seem to be good when one is not so, is, if we are to respect the opinion of Plato at all, the very height of injustice.

VII. But let us bring our discussion back again to the examples of noble deeds. A certain man once kept striking Socrates, the son of Sophroniscus, in the face, yet he did not resent it, but allowed full play to the ruffian's anger, so that his face was swollen and bruised from the blows. Then when he stopped striking him, Socrates did nothing more than write on his forehead, as an artisan on a statue, who did it, and thus took out his revenge. Since these examples almost coincide with our teachings, I hold that such men are worthy of emulation. . . .

68

VIII. I have called to mind the wreaths and the fighters. These men endure hardships beyond number, they use every means to increase their strength, they sweat ceaselessly at their training, they accept many blows from the master, they adopt the mode of life which he prescribes, though it is most unpleasant, and, in a word, they so rule all their conduct that their whole life before the contest is preparatory to it. Then they strip themselves for the arena, and endure all and risk all, to receive the crown of olive, or of parsley, or some other branch, and to be announced by the herald as victor.

Will it then be possible for us, to whom are held out rewards so wondrous in number and in splendor that tongue can not recount them, while we are fast asleep and leading care-free lives, to make these our own by half-hearted efforts? . . . For after we have actually endured many hardships, we shall scarcely gain those blessings to which, as said above, nothing in human experience is comparable. Therefore we must not be lightminded, nor exchange our immortal hopes for momentary idleness, lest reproaches come upon us, and judgment befall us, not forsooth here among men, although judgment here is no easy thing for the man of sense to bear, but at the bar of justice, be that under the earth, or wherever else it may happen to be. While he who unintentionally violates his obligations perchance receives some pardon from God, he who designedly chooses a life of wickedness doubtless has a far greater punishment to endure. . . .

IX. In a word, he who would not bury himself in the mire of sensuality must deem the whole body of little worth, or must, as Plato puts it, pay only so much heed to the body as is an aid to wisdom. [Rep. iii. 403-412] or as Paul admonishes somewhere in a similar passage: 'Let no one make provision for the flesh, to fulfill the lusts thereof.' [Rom. xiii. 14.] Wherein is there any difference between those who take pains that the body shall be perfect, but ignore the soul, for the use of which it is designed, and those who are scrupulous about their tools, but neglectful of their trade? On the contrary, one ought to discipline the flesh and hold it under, as a fierce animal is controlled, and to quiet, by the lash of reason, the unrest which it engenders in the soul, and

69

not, by giving full rein to pleasure, to disregard the mind, as a charioteer is run away with by unmanageable and frenzied horses. So let us bear in mind the remark of Pythagoras, who, upon learning that one of his followers was growing very fleshy from gymnastics and hearty eating, said to him, 'Will you not stop making your imprisonment harder for yourself?' Then it is said that since Plato foresaw the dangerous influence of the body, he chose an unhealthy part of Athens for his Academy, in order to remove excessive bodily comfort, as one prunes the rank shoots of the vines. Indeed I have even heard physicians say that over-healthiness is dangerous. Since, then, this exaggerated care of the body is harmful to the body itself, and a hindrance to the soul, it is sheer madness to be a slave to the body, and serve it. . . .

X. To be sure, we shall become more intimately acquainted with these precepts in the sacred writings, but it is incumbent upon us, for the present, to trace, as it were, the silhouette of virtue in the pagan authors. For those who carefully gather the useful from each book are wont, like mighty rivers, to gain accessions on every hand. For the precept of the poet which bids us add little must be taken as applying not so much to the accumulation of riches, as of the various branches of learning. In line with this Bias said to his son, who, as he was about to set out for Egypt, was inquiring what course he could pursue to give his father the greatest satisfaction: "Store up means for the journey of old age." By *means* he meant virtue, but he placed too great restrictions upon it, since he limited its usefulness to the earthly life. For if any one mentions the old age of Tithonus or of Arganthonius, or of that Methuselah who is said to have lacked but thirty years of being a millenarian, or even if he reckons the entire period since the creation, I will laugh as at the fancies of a child, since I look forward to that long, undying age, of the extent of which there is no limit for the mind of man to grasp, any more than there is of the life immortal. For the journey of this life eternal I would advise you to husband resources, leaving no stone unturned, as the proverb has it whence you might derive any aid. From this task we shall not shrink because it is hard and laborious, but, remembering the precept that every man ought to choose the better life, and expecting that association will render it pleasant, we shall busy ourselves with those things that are best. For it is shameful to squander the present, and later to call back the past in anguish, when no more time is given.

In the above treatise I have explained to you some of the things which I deem the most to be desired; of others I shall continue to counsel you so long as life is allowed me. Now as the sick are of three classes, according to the degrees of their sickness, may you not seem to belong to the third, or incurable, class, nor show a spiritual malady like that of their bodies! For those who are slightly indisposed visit physicians in person, and those who are seized by violent sickness call physicians, but those who are suffering from a hopelessly incurable melancholy do not even admit the physicians if they come. May this now be your plight, as would seem to be the case were you to shun these right counsels!

JEROME S. BRUNER

JEROME S. BRUNER (1915-   ). The most influential and widely read book of the present decade, so far as professional educators are concerned, may well be the report by its director of a conference of scientists and teachers arranged by the National Academy of Sciences to consider the improvement of the teaching of science in the public schools. One reviewer (Paul Goodman in the *New York Herald Tribune*) called it a classic, "comparable for its philosophical centrality and humane concreteness to some of the essays of Dewey." The author of *The Process of Education,* published in 1960 by the Harvard University Press, is Jerome Seymour Bruner, professor of psychology and director of Harvard's Center for Cognitive Studies.

The eminent psychologist and public opinion expert was born in New York City on October 1, 1915. He received his bachelor's degree from Duke in 1937 and his doctorate in psychology from Harvard in 1941. After serving as associate director of the Office of Public Opinion Research (1943-1944), he accepted an appointment to Harvard, where he has taught since 1945. He is active in a number of learned societies and has investigated the cognitive processes, especially perception, memory, thinking and attitude formation, and experimental and social psychology. He is co-author of *Opinions and Personality* and has written, (in addition to *The Process of Education*), *On Knowing, Essays for the Left Hand, A Study of Thinking,* and several important articles.

In the following essay, adapted from an address given in 1963, Bruner tries to formulate a theory of instruction. Aware that we are living through a revolution in education, he challenges old dogmas and warns that our very survival may depend on its successful outcome.

NEEDED: *A THEORY OF INSTRUCTION**

Over the past several years it has become increasingly clear to me, as to any thinking person today, that both psychology and the field of curriculum design itself suffer jointly from the lack of a theory of instruction. Such a theory of instruction would indeed be interesting just for its own sake, for purely theoretical reasons. There cannot be, for example, a theory of development which leaves somehow to chance the question of the way in which societies pace and structure the experiences with which children come in contact; and to talk about the nature of development without talking about the way in which society does and can structure the sequence, is to be as intellectually foolish as it is to be morally irresponsible. So even if one were seeking only a better theory about the nature of man, one would indeed want a theory of instruction as one of the instruments by which one understood man and how he was shaped by his fellow man.

Yet we also realize that a theory of instruction is about as practical a thing as one could possibly have to guide one in the process of passing on the knowledge, the skills, the point of view and the heart of a culture. Let us, then, see whether we can set forth some possible theorems that might go into a theory of instruction.

Elements of a Theory

What do we mean by a theory of instruction? I found myself beginning this exercise by putting down theorems that tried to separate what we might mean by a theory of instruction from

*From *Educational Leadership* (May, 1963), pp. 523-532. Copyright © 1963 by the Association for Supervision and Curriculum Development. Reprinted by permission of Dr. Bruner and the editor of *Educational Leadership*.

other kinds of theories that have been current. The first thought that occurred to me is that in its very nature a theory of instruction is *prescriptive* and not *descriptive*. Such a theory has the aim of producing particular ends and producing them in ways that we speak of as optimal. It is not a description of what has happened when learning has taken place — it is something which is normative, which gives you something to shoot at and which, in the end, must state something about what you do when you put instruction together in the form of courses. Now, this is not a very surprising thing, yet I am struck by the fact that many persons in the field of education have assumed that we could depend on other kinds of theories than the theory of instruction to guide us in this kind of enterprise. For example, I find that the dependence upon learning theory among educators is as touching as it is shocking. The fact of the matter is that the learning theory is not a theory of instruction; it is a theory that describes what takes place while learning is going on and after learning has taken place.

There is no clear-cut way in which one can derive wisdom, or indeed implication, from learning theory that will guide him in the constructing of a curriculum. When I say a theory of instruction is prescriptive, I mean it is *before the fact*. It is before learning has taken place and not while and after learning has taken place. Let me give you an example of the kind of difficulty you get into when you assume that you can use the slender reed of learning theory to lean on. Take, for example, the case of programed instruction.

There is in the current doctrine (I will call it) of programed instruction the idea that somehow you should take small steps, that each increment should be a small step. Now, this idea is derived willy-nilly from a theory of learning which states that learning is incremental and goes in small steps. Nowhere in the evidence upon which such a theory is based — and it is only partial evidence — nowhere is there anything that says that simply because learning takes place in small steps the *environment* should be arranged in small steps. And so we set up a curriculum that also has small steps. In doing so we fail to take sight of the fact that indeed organisms from vertebrate on up through the highest primate, man, operate by taking large packets of information and breaking these down into their own bite size and that unless they have the opportunity to do that, learning may become stereotyped. At least it is a worthy hypothesis about instruction.

A theory of instruction must concern itself with the relationship between how things are presented and how they are learned. Though I myself have worked hard and long in the vineyard of learning theory, I can do no better than to start by warning the reader away from it. Learning theory is not a theory of instruction. It describes what happened. A theory of instruction is a guide to what to do in order to achieve certain objectives. Unfortunately, we shall have to start pretty nearly at the beginning, for there is very little literature to guide us in this subtle enterprise.

What shall a theory of instruction be about? I would propose that there are four aspects of such a theory. First, a theory of instruction should concern itself with the factors that predispose a child to learn effectively; and there are many such factors that predispose. These are factors which, on the whole, precede the child's entry into our scholastic care. These factors relate to his earliest childhood and indeed one might say that we should provide some theorems for a theory of toys, and for a theory of family, and for a theory of stimulation, because the thing that comes to mind here is the question of what kind of stimulation ought a child to have before he is faced with this formidable thing we call a schoolroom and a teacher. What sorts of identification might he best form? How shall we bring his linguistic level up to a point where he is able to handle things symbolically? I shall not treat further these predispositions because what I want to do after this introduction of the different aspects of the theory is to go back and have a look at each one of these in detail, so let me pass on now to a second aspect of a theory of instruction.

It should concern itself with the optimal structuring of knowledge. By this, I mean that for any body of knowledge there is a minimal set of propositions, or statements, or images from which one can best generate the rest of what exists within that field. For example, from the conservation theorems plus a little more, a great deal of physics can be reconstructed. This is the "guts" of physics.

Now, I think when we speak of the optimal structuring of knowledge, we probably have three things in mind about this set of underlying propositions. They should have the power of simplifying the diversity of information within the field, somehow rendering the particular redundant, making it clear that this case is just a sub-case of something else, that one fact is not the same as every other fact. I speak of this power of simplification as the economy of a structure. Secondly, such a structure would enable you to generate new propositions to go beyond the information given. This I would speak of as the productiveness of a structure. And finally, there is another aspect of the structure of knowledge which has to do with the extent to which it increases the manipulability of knowledge. It is classically the case, for example, that when you put something into words it now becomes possible for you to take that thing which before you only intuited in some rough way and to subject it to the combinings and re-combinings that are made possible by the transformative powers of language. And this I want to speak of as the power of a structure. In thinking of structure, then, we shall want to consider economy, productiveness, and power. All of these things are relative to a learner. It does not do to say simply that because physics has great economy, great productiveness, and great power as practiced by a Feinman or a Purcell, that therefore you have children ape those distinguished scientists. You take the child where you find him and give him the structure that is economical, productive and powerful for him and that allows him to grow.

A third aspect of a theory of instruction deals with the optimal sequence that is required for learning. In what order do we present things? If you are presenting the Napoleonic period, where do you start? If you would give a sense of the sixteenth century, do you begin with the fact that mercantile prices and prosperity were going up at a booming rate, whereas the rents that were got by the landlords were not going up because there were long-term leases? You might. If you want to produce drama, you would.

76

But, we will return to that because there is a question of how to give the learner a place from which to take off, something upon which to build. What order to do it? What exercises do you give him to strengthen the sinews of his own thinking? What type of representation do you use? How much particular? How much generality?

Finally, a fourth aspect of a theory of instruction should concern itself with the nature and pacing of rewards and punishments and successes and failures.

To sum up then, a theory of instruction should be constructed around four problems: predispositions, structures, sequences, and consequences.

Predisposition

What can we say about the factors that predispose a student to be a learner? Let us begin with the following simple proposition: that in order to learn or to solve problems, it is necessary that alternatives be explored and that you cannot have effective learning or problem solving without the learner's having the courage and the skill to explore alternative ways of dealing with a problem.

It seems that if you take this as the first proposition concerning predisposition, there are three things that immediately can be said. First, that if this is the case, learning in the presence of a teacher, or a tutor, or an instructor should somehow minimize the risks and the severity of the consequence that follows upon exploration of alternatives. It should be less risky for a child to explore alternatives in the presence of a teacher, than without one present. It is obvious that, at the level of coping with nature in the raw, the child searching for food on his own would stand more risk of eating toadstools and poisoning himself, and thereby bringing exploration to a close.

Yet there are other less obvious things that have to do with the closing down of the exploration of alternatives. A teacher or parent can instill the fear of being a fool. That can surely paralyze the will to explore alternatives, for the moment an unreasonable

77

alternative is made to seem like a foolish one, the inner freedom to explore is limited by the requirements of face saving. The encouragement of exploration of alternatives requires some practical minimization of the severity of consequences following exploration.

It seems to me, further, that one of the ways in which a sense of alternatives to be explored can be opened, is to increase the informativeness of error. To increase the informativeness of error essentially involves making clear to the child what produced a failure. One of the major functions of a teacher is to lead the child to a sense of why he failed. I do not mean why he failed in terms of a characterological analysis; I mean in terms of the nature of what it is that he is doing. If you can somehow make the child aware that his attempted answer is not so much a wrong answer, as an answer to another problem, and then get him back on the track, it becomes possible for the child to reduce the confusion that is produced by picking a wrong alternative. One of the things that, I believe, keeps us from exploring alternatives is precisely the confusion of making the wrong choice.

Still another goad to the exploration of alternatives is through the encouragement of "subversiveness." I mean that you must subvert all of the earlier established constraints against the exploration of alternatives. This kind of subversiveness has to do with a healthy skepticism toward holy cows, prefabricated doctrines, and stuffed shirtliness. Let there be no question or doubt that is "not nice to express." The moment you as teachers lose your role as subversives in this respect, you are doing the child an injustice and yourself an injustice as a teacher. I want to rescue the word "subversion" from the wrong senses to which it has been put in recent years.

When we think about predispositions to learn, we have to bear in mind that the very relationship that we have with our pupils is a privileged relationship involving authority and direction; that is to say, the exchange is uneven. We know; they do not. Since that is the case, it becomes very necessary for us not to use this implicit authoritative relationship as a means of using our own office as a way of establishing truth and falsity. It is so

78

easy in the mind of the impressionable child to equate truth with Miss Smith!

The nature of learning in a school situation requires at least a dyadic relation; at least two people are involved, and usually many more than two. This obvious point requires that there be some set of minimal social skills that a child brings with him to a learning situation. We do not know much about the nature of these social skills that are required for an exchange of information. The act of exchanging information mutually, or even of accepting information and working on it until you make it your own, is not well understood. In addition to minimum social skills, there are elementary intellectual skills that are necessary for a first encounter with school learning. We "know" this, but we do little either to investigate these elementary skills or to devise ways of strengthening them. I am thinking principally of linguistic skills. Where a child has been socially underprivileged in his early years, it may be necessary for example to look squarely at the situation and say: This child, before he can go on in these subjects, simply needs more linguistic training or all of our words will be just mere wind going by his ears. I do not mean vocabulary, but, rather, development of the full transformative power of language which our linguists are only now beginning to understand.

It is necessary for the beginning child to have certain kinds of manipulative and almost intuitive geometric skills. We have started studies of children on the borders of the Sahara in the interior of Senegal. We are struck at the difference in the behavior of American children and children in the African bush who do not have toys with mechanical or geometrical constraint to play with. We take it for granted that our children can deal with geometrical forms, put them together and take them apart, yet the fact of the matter is that it should not be taken for granted. The experience of manipulating materials gives our children a stock of images and geometric transformations that permit them to work geometrically and mechanically in a way that our African subjects cannot. These elementary forms of intellectual skills are essential. Is there more that we can do that we are not doing?

My last point before passing on to the topic of structure in

79

learning has to do with attitudes toward the use of mind. These are predisposing factors of an enormously important kind. For example, we know that these vary to some extent, speaking sociologically, by class, by ethnic group, by culture. There is no question, for example, that in terms of social class, very frequently you will find in the lowest social class an attitude toward life that is governed by the concept of luck. This means that there is really nothing you can do by your own efforts, that things happen to a considerable extent by luck. The business of applying the mind, the idea that man has a chance if he will use his mind, is an attitude which is not frequently present and which has to be created. This is an extremely *difficult* thing to do and I hope no one asks me how do you do it, because I do not know. Yet it is quite clear that we must use the most intelligent opportunism we can muster, to do anything we can to get the idea started that by the use of mind one can increase effectiveness or any other desired state. We also know that different ethnic groups have different attitudes toward the use of mind, and again, I do not think we take full advantage of this. The Muslim-African culture, for example, has an attitude toward the use of mind that it should be used principally for grasping the word that has been passed on. This is not the kind of use of mind that makes for what might be called a very active, vigorous mind.

Structure of Knowledge

Now let us turn to the question of the structure of knowledge, its economy, productiveness, and power as related to the capacities of a learner. The first point relates to theorem in the theory of computation proposed by Turing. Turing proposed that any problem that can be solved can be solved by simpler means. That is the theorem. Out of this theorem has come the technology of computing machines. What it says — and it says this only for so-called well-defined problems with unique solutions — is that however complicated the problem, we can break it down into a set of simpler elementary operations and finally end up with operations as simple as: make a mark, move a mark, take the mark out, put the mark back, etc. These elementary operations are then combined into sub-routines that are more complex and then these are combined, etc. The machine succeeds in being practically interesting because it can run off so many of these operations in so short a time. Turing's theorem has a certain relevance to the structure of knowledge; it, in a sense, is another way of stating what by now I am afraid has become an old saw: that any subject can be taught to anybody at any age in some form that is honest. There is always some way in which complicated problems can be reduced to simpler form, simple and step-by-step enough for a child to grasp.

Now, to move ahead one step, I believe it can be said that knowledge about anything can, generally speaking, be represented in three ways, three parallel systems of processing information. One of these is what I call the enactive representation of knowledge. How do you tie a running bowline? You will reply that you can't quite say it or draw it, but that you will show me by tieing one. Try to tell somebody how to ride a bicycle, or ski. It is knowing by doing. It is the way in which the young child on a seesaw "knows" Newton's Law of Moments. He knows that in order to balance two children on the other side he has to get farther out on his side, and this is the Law of Moments, but known enactively. Only with time do children free themselves from this tendency to equate things with the actions directed toward them. We never free ourselves from it completely. Let me, now speak of ikonic representation. If somebody says to me, for example, "What's a square?" I might say, "Well, a square is a set of sets such that the number of elements in each set is equal to the number of sets." This is a good definition of a square, formalistically. Yet the fact of the matter is that there is another way of representing a square, by an image. It isn't a square, it's an image of a square, and it's a useful image — we can start with it. Many of the things we use in representing knowledge have this ikonic property. I use the word "ikonic" because I do not really mean a kind of imitation of nature. Let us not run down the importance of these useful images. They have limits, these representing pictures.

Finally, a third way in which knowledge can get represented is symbolically. By this I mean in words or in those more powerful versions of words, powerful in one way in any case, mathematical symbols. I think you can turn around the Chinese proverb to the effect that one picture is worth a thousand words. For certain purposes one word is worth a thousand pictures. For example, draw a picture of "implosion"; and yet the idea of implosion as such was one of the basic notions that led to the idea of thermonuclear fusion. Implosion is the concept that results from the application of a contrast transformation on the more familiar concept of explosion. The word was so important that it was classified as top secret during the war. It is this capacity to put things into a symbol system with rules for manipulating, for decomposing and recomposing and transforming and turning symbols on their heads that makes it possible to explore things not present, not picturable, and indeed not in existence.

Now the three modes of representation do not disappear as we grow older; quite to the contrary, they remain with us forever. When we speak of the application of Turing's theorem to the question of structuring of knowledge, it is in reference to the representation forms we have been discussing. Early in life and also early in our mastery of a subject we may have to represent things in terms of what we do with them — in much the same way as a child "knows about" balance beams by knowing what to do on a seesaw. We may then emerge with an image of it, however non-rigorous the image may be. Then and only then can language and symbol systems be applied with some degree of likelihood that their reference will be understood. I do not think I can say anything more important than that. You create a structure, not by starting off with the highest brow symbolic version, but by giving it in the muscles, then in imagery and then giving it in language, with its tools for manipulation. The basic task is to orchestrate the three kinds of representations so that we can lead the child from doing, to imaging what he has done, and finally to symbolization.

Usually in a college catalog when a course is listed it will say something about a "prerequisite." Let me urge that any topic also has internal prerequisites in addition to the things that you are supposed to have mastered beforehand. The internal prerequisites may indeed be just precisely the easier modes of representation that get one to a less rigorous, more imageful or enactive grasp of a subject before it gets converted either into ordinary or mathematical language. The way you get ahead with learning is to translate an idea into those non-rigorous forms that can be understood. Then one can, with their aid, become more precise and powerful. In mathematics such techniques are called "heuristics." Their use often constitutes a prerequisite to grasping a subject in its full depth. This is most of what is meant when we speak of "spiral curriculum."

Optimal Sequence

With respect to the sequence in which material is presented, different sequences are obviously needed to achieve different objectives. The idea of one right sequence is a myth. You have to be quite clear about what kind of learning you are trying to produce before you can specify what is a good sequence for presenting it. There are sequences that can be described for the production of parrots. We use them all the time. But there is also a sequence that is particularly interesting in that it seems to increase the likelihood that knowledge will be converted into a structure that is economical, productive and powerful — and therefore transferable. It is worth pausing over.

I would like to suggest that if you wanted to do this, the first thing that you might do is to try leading the child to grasp a structure by induction from particular instances. You would give him lots of particular instances and let him recognize their underlying regularity. If you want the child to transfer his learning to new situations you had better give him some practice in transfer while he is learning.

The second thing you might try is the use of contrast in your sequence. The fish will be the last to discover water. Economy of representation often makes it necessary for the child to see the contrasting case. Often concepts are structured in terms of contrast and can only be fully understood in terms of them. To grasp the meaning of community in arithmetic — that $3 \cdot 4 = 4 \cdot 3$ — often may require that we recognize the non-commutative case of ordinary language — that for quantifiers, for example, "very much" is not equal to "much very" or as a little girl once put it "black shoe" isn't "shoe black."

Third, if one wants a sequence that is going to produce powerful learning, avoid premature symbolization. Do not give them that word to parrot before they know what it is about either by manipulation or in images. Ask yourselves how much you understand about simultaneous equations.

Fourth, you might try to give the child practice at both leaping and plodding. Let him go by small steps. Then let him take great leaps, huge guesses, without guessing he is deprived of his rights as a mind. We cannot get all of the evidence. It is often by guessing that we become aware of what we know.

Another question related to sequence has to do with what I would call "revisiting." Rarely is everything learned about anything in one encounter. Yet we seem to be so impelled to cover, to get through the Elizabethan Period, and on through such-and-such period that we forget the obvious point — that the pot is rarely licked clean at one swipe. Perhaps we would do well to take music listening as a model. It is not simply a matter of mastering this subject, or even of converting it into more powerful form. Rather, revisit means an opportunity of connecting what we have learned now with what else we know. Why is such an obvious point so often ignored?

Reward and Punishment

Now the question of pacing reward and punishment for success and failure. First distinguish two states. One is success and failure; the other one is reward and punishment. By success and failure, I mean the end state that is inherent in a task. The problem is solved or not solved or close to solved. By reward and punishment, I mean something quite different. It relates to the consequences that follow upon success and failure — prizes, scoldings, gold stars, etc.

It is often the case that emphasis upon reward and punishment, under the control of an outside agent such as a teacher or parent, diverts attention away from success and failure. In effect, this may take the learning initiative away from the child and give it to the person dispensing the rewards and punishments. This will be the more likely if the learner is not able to determine the basis of success and failure. One of the great problems in teaching, which usually starts with the teacher being very supportive, is to give the rewarding function back to the learner and the task. Perhaps we can do this by rewarding good errors so that the child becomes aware of the process of problem solving as worthy as well as the fruits of successful outcome. In any case, I wish to mention these matters to suggest that old dogmas about the role of "reinforcement" can be looked at afresh. The independent problem solver is one who rewards and punishes himself by judging the adequacy of his efforts. Equip him with the tools for thinking and let him be his own man.

Some Conclusions

I should warn you, in conclusion, to beware of the likes of us. We do not have a tested theory of instruction to offer you. What is quite plain is that one is needed and I would propose that we work together in its forging.

I warn you for a good reason. Educators are a curiously doctrinal or ideological kind of people. You are given to slogans and fight and bleed in their behalf. You have looked to psychology for help and have often been misled into accepting mere hypotheses as the proven word. It is partly because it is so hard to test the adequacy of ideas in an educational setting.

Now we are living through a great revolution in education. Our survival may depend on its successful outcome — our survival as the human race. I know no group in our society more devoted to the common weal than our educators. In this era of new curricula, new teaching arrangements, new automated devices, your best rudder is a healthy sense of experimentation backed by a skepticism toward educational slogans.

If we are to move toward a serviceable and sturdy theory of instruction — and I think we are — then your greatest contribution will be a willingness to give new ideas a try and full candor in expressing your reactions to how things worked. The prospect is strenuous, but gains to be won are enormous. I wish you well.

NICHOLAS MURRAY BUTLER

NICHOLAS MURRAY BUTLER (1862-1947). An American educator, publicist, and Nobel laureate, Nicholas Murray Butler was born at Elizabeth, New Jersey, on April 2, 1862. One of the most outstanding men of his generation, he graduated from Columbia College in 1882 and received his doctorate two years later. After studying in Berlin and Paris, he returned to Columbia as an assistant in philosophy in 1885 and during the next five years moved rapidly up the educational hierarchy, becoming in turn tutor, adjunct professor, the first dean of the faculty of philosophy, and professor of philosophy and education. He organized Teachers College and served as its first president (1886-1891). He founded the *Educational Review* in 1889, served as president of the National Education Association in 1895, and became president of Columbia University in 1901, at which time he began to play an increasingly important role in international relations.

During the forty-four years of his presidency he demonstrated great talent as an administrator, transforming a provincial college into one of the world's largest and most progressive universities. Aside from his direction of the University, his time was largely spent on a life-long crusade for world peace. His activities made him an intimate of many notables of his time, earned him many honorary degrees and invitations to address various European parliaments, and led to his sharing the Nobel peace prize with Jane Addams in 1931.

WHAT KNOWLEDGE IS OF MOST WORTH?*

Mankind is divided into warring camps, and while electricity and steam have bound the nations of the earth together, questions of knowledge and of belief have split up every nation into sects. In all this tumult it is difficult to catch the sound of the dominant note. Each suggested interpretation seems to lead us

*From *The Meaning of Education, and Other Essays and Addresses* (New York, The Macmillan Company, 1898).

further into the tangled maze, where we cannot see the wood for the trees. Standards of truth are more definite than ever before; but standards of worth are strangely confused, and at times even their existence is denied.

Amid all this confusion, however, a light has been growing steadily brighter for those who have eyes to see. In our own century two great masters of thought have come forward, offering, like Ariadne of old, to place in our hands the guiding thread that shall lead us through the labyrinth — the German Hegel and the Englishman Herbert Spencer. And as the nineteenth century closes, amid the din of other and lesser voices, we seem to hear the deeper tones of these two interpreters swelling forth as representative of the best and most earnest endeavors, from two totally different points of view, of human seekers after light. Each has taken the whole of knowledge for his province, each has spread out before us a connected view of man and his environment, and each would ". . . Assert Eternal Providence and justify the ways of God to men." These great teachers typify the catholicity and the scientific method that are so characteristic of the best expressions of our modern civilization. Whatever of insight we have gained into history, into philosophy, into art, and into nature, they have incorporated in their systematic thinking and have endeavored to illumine with the light of their controlling principles. Hegel, schooled in the teachings of Kant and of Fichte, and coming early to an appreciation of the seed-thought of Plato and Aristotle, Bruno and Spinoza, has taught us in unmistakable language that independent, self-active being is the father of all things. Spencer, feeling the thrill of that unity which makes the cosmos one (and receiving from Lamarck and Von Baer the hint that led him to see that the life of the individual furnishes the clew to the understanding of the life of the aggregate, whether natural or social), has formulated into a single and understandable law of progress the terms of that development, or evolution, which has been more or less dimly before the mind of man since thought began. The German with his principle of self-activity, and the Englishman with his law of evolution, offer us a foothold for our knowledge and our faith, and assure us that it will safely support them. From the one we learn the eternal reasonableness of all that is or can be, while the other teaches us the character of the process by which the visible universe, that every day presents new wonders to our gaze, has been builded out of the primeval star-dust. At their hands the two sublime and awe-inspiring verities of Kant — the starry heavens above and the moral law within — find their places in the life of the spirit, and together testify to its eternity and its beauty.

Despite the fact that our age is one of unexampled scientific and industrial progress, yet nothing in all our modern scientific activity is more striking than the undisputed primacy of thought — thought not in antagonism to sense, but interpretative of the data of sense. Idealism, shorn of its crudities and its extravagances, and based on reason rather than on Berkeley's analysis of sense-perception, is conquering the world. What Plato saw, Descartes, Leibniz, Kant, and Hegel have demonstrated. . . .

What, then, does this primacy of thought signify, and what is its bearing upon our educational ideals? Obviously the possession of a conclusion such as this, wrested from nature by the hand of science and from history by that of philosophy, must serve in many ways to guide us in estimating the importance of human institutions and of educational instruments. We cannot accept either of these, without question, from the hands of a tradition to which our modern philosophy and our modern science were wholly unknown; nor can we blindly follow those believers in a crude psychology who would present us with so many mental faculties to be trained, each by its appropriate formal exercise, as if they were sticks of wood to be shaped and reduced to symmetry and order. Mental life, as Wundt so forcibly says, "does not consist in the connection of unalterable objects and varying conditions: in all its phases it is process; an active, not a passive, existence; development, not stagnation." Herein is mental life true to nature. Like nature, it is not fixed, but ever changing, and this unceasing change, necessary to both growth and development, gives to life both its reality and its pathos. It also gives to education its unending character, and to mankind the clew to education's wisest processes.

The question that I am asking — what knowledge is of most worth? — is a very old one, and the answers to it which have been handed down through the centuries are many and various. It is a question which each age must put to itself, and answer from the standpoint of its deepest and widest knowledge. The wisest philosophers have always seen, more or less clearly, the far-reaching character of the question and the great importance of the answer. Socrates and Plato, Augustine and Aquinas, were under no illusions as to it; but often in later years the deeper questions relating to the relative worth of subjects of study have been either entirely lost sight of or very superficially dealt with. Bacon clothes in attractive axiomatic form some very crude judgments as to the relative worth of studies. Rousseau outlines an educational program that ruined his reputation for sobriety of judgment. Herbert Spencer turns aside for a moment from his life-work to apotheosize science in education, although science is, by his own definition, only partially unified knowledge. . . . In similar fashion, others holding a brief for some particular phase or department of knowledge, have come forward crying Eureka! and proclaiming that the value of all studies must be measured in terms of their newly discovered standard. The very latest cry is that studies and intellectual exercises are valuable in proportion as they stimulate enlarged brain-areas, thus making the appreciation of Shakespeare, of Beethoven, and of Leonardo da Vinci solely a function of the circulation of the blood.

But to sciolists of this type philosophy and science can now make common answer. If it be true that spirit and reason rule the universe, then the highest and most enduring knowledge is of the things of the spirit. That subtle sense of the beautiful and the sublime which accompanies spiritual insight, and is part of it — this is the highest achievement of which humanity is capable. It is typified, in various forms, in the verse of Dante and the prose of Thomas à Kempis, in the Sistine Madonna of Raphael, and in Mozart's Requiem. To develop this sense in education is the task of art and literature, to interpret it is the work of philosophy, and to nourish it the function of religion. Because it most fully represents the higher nature of man, it is man's highest possession, and those studies that directly appeal to it and instruct it are beyond compare the most valuable. This has been eloquently and beautifully illustrated by Brother Azarias. "Take a Raphael or a Murillo," he says. "We gaze upon the painted canvas till its beauty has entered our soul. The splendor of the beauty lights up within us depth unrevealed, and far down in our inner consciousness we discover something that responds to the beauty on which we have been gazing. It is as though a former friend revealed himself to us. There is here a recognition. The more careful has been our sense-culture, the more delicately have our feelings been attuned to respond to a thing of beauty and find in it a joy forever, all the sooner and the more intensely do we experience this recognition. And therewith comes a vague yearning, a longing as for something. What does it all mean? The recognition is of the ideal." Toward the full recognition and appreciation of this insight into the great works of the spirit, whether recorded in literature, in art, or in institutional life, higher education should bend all its energies. The study of philosophy itself, or the truly philosophic study of any department of knowledge — however remote its beginnings may seem to be — will accomplish this end. The ways of approach to this goal are as many as there are human interests, for they are all bound together in the bonds of a common origin and a common purpose. The attainment of it is true culture, as Matthew Arnold has defined it: "the acquainting ourselves with the best that has been known and said in the world, and thus with the history of the human spirit." . . .

But education, as Mr. Froude has reminded us, has two aspects. "On one side it is the cultivation of man's reason, the development of his spiritual nature. It elevates him above the pressure of material interest. It makes him superior to the pleasures and pains of a world which is but his temporary home, in filling his mind with higher subjects than the occupations of life would themselves provide him with." It is this aspect of education that I have been considering, for it is from this aspect that we derive our inspiration and our ideals. "But," continues Mr. Froude, "a life of speculation to the multitude would be a life of idleness and uselessness. They have to maintain themselves in industrious independence in a world in which it has been said there are but three possible modes of existence — begging, stealing, and working; and education means also the equipping a man with means to earn his own living." It is this latter and very practical aspect of education that causes us to feel at times the full force of the question of worth in education. Immediate utility makes demands upon the school which it is unable wholly to neglect. If the school is to be the training-ground for citizenship, its products must be usefully and soundly equipped as well as well disciplined and well informed. An educated proletariat — to use the forcible paradox of Bismarck — is a continual source of disturbance and danger to any nation. Acting upon this conviction, the great modern democracies — and the time seems to have come when a democracy may be defined as a government, of any form, in which public opinion habitually rules — are everywhere having a care that in education provision be made for the practical, or immediately useful. This is as it should be, but it exposes the school to a new series of dangers against which it must guard.

Utility is a term that may be given either a very broad or a very narrow meaning. There are utilities higher and utilities lower, and under no circumstances will the true teacher ever permit the former to be sacrificed to the latter. This would be done if, in its zeal for fitting the child for self-support, the school were to neglect to lay the foundation for that higher intellectual and spiritual life which constitutes humanity's full stature. This foundation is made ready only if proper emphasis be laid, from the kindergarten to the college, on those studies whose subject-matter is the direct product of intelligence and will, and which can, therefore, make direct appeal to man's higher nature. The sciences and their application are capable of use, even from the standpoint of this higher order of utilities, because of the reason they exhibit and reveal. Man's rational freedom is the goal, and the sciences are the lower steps on the ladder that reaches to it.

BALDASSARE CASTIGLIONE

BALDASSARE CASTIGLIONE (1478-1529). The Italian count, Baldassare Castiglione, provided the ideal portrait of the scholar-gentleman in *Il Cortegiano* (*The Courtier*), which Dr. Johnson called "the best book that was ever written upon good breeding."

Born near Mantua in 1478, Castiglione completed his education at the University of Milan and took an active part in the campaigns and diplomacy of the Italian wars. In 1504 his services were sought by the Duke of Urbino, and in this way he gained access to the most renowned courts of Italy. According to his own account, it was soon after the death of his protector in 1508 that Castiglione set to work on the treatise that was to bring him universal acclaim. His self-appointed task was to reunite the Greek ideals of action and learning.

His treatise in dialogue form yields an unforgettable portrait of the ideal courtier — the man of action, the man engaged in the service of a prince, adept on the field and in the council chamber, the man completely at ease in the society of ladies and gentlemen. It became a classic of its kind; written in Italian rather than Latin, it was widely translated into other languages (the first English translation was made by Sir Thomas Hoby in 1861) and seemed to typify the spirit of the Renaissance in its liveliest and most human form. The following extract from *The Courtier* is a slightly revised version of Leonard E. Opdycke's translation.

On February 7, 1529, Castiglione died in Toledo, Spain. His greatest tribute was probably that paid him by Charles V, to whom he had been sent as papal nuncio five years earlier: "I tell you that here has died one of the finest gentlemen of the world."

THE PERFECT GENTLEMAN*

"I am of the opinion that the principal and true profession of the Courtier ought to be that of arms; which I would have him follow actively above all else, and be known among others as

*From *The Book of the Courtier*, translated by Leonard E. Opdycke (New York: Charles Scribner's Sons, 1901).

bold and strong, and loyal to whomsoever he serves. And he will win a reputation for these good qualities by exercising them at all times and in all places, since one may never fail in this without severest censure. And just as among women, their fair fame once sullied never recovers its first luster, so that reputation of a gentleman who bears arms, if once it be in the least tarnished with cowardice or other disgrace, remains forever infamous before the world and full of ignominy. Therefore the more our Courtier excels in this art, the more he will be worthy of praise; and yet I do not deem essential in him that perfect knowledge of things and those other qualities that befit a commander; since this would be too wide a sea let us be content, as we have said, with perfect loyalty and unconquered courage, and that he be always seen to possess them. For the courageous are often recognized even more in small things than in great; and frequently in perils of importance and where there are many spectators, some men are to be found, who, although their hearts be dead within them, yet, moved by shame or by the presence of others, press forward almost with their eyes shut, and do their duty God knows how. While on occasions of little moment, when they think they can avoid putting themselves in danger without being detected, they are glad to keep safe. But those who, even when they do not expect to be observed or seen or recognized by anyone, show their ardour and neglect nothing, however paltry, that may be laid to their charge — they have that strength of mind which we seek in our Courtier. . . .

"Therefore let the man we are seeking, be very bold, stern, and always among the first, where the enemy are to be seen; and in every other place, gentle, modest, reserved, above all things avoiding ostentation and that impudent self-praise by which men ever excite hatred and disgust in all who hear them."

Then my lord Gaspar replied:

"As for me, I have known few men excellent in anything whatever, who do not praise themselves; and it seems to me that this may well be permitted them; for when anyone who feels himself needs have daring to do them, and confidence in himself, and must not be abject or mean in spirit, yet very modest in speech, showing less confidence in himself than he has lest his self-confidence lead to rashness."

The Count now paused a little, and messer Bernardo Bibbiena said, laughing:

"I remember what you said earlier, that this Courtier of ours must be endowed by nature with beauty of countenance and person, and with a grace that shall make him so agreeable. Grace and beauty of countenance I think I certainly possess, and this is the reason why so many ladies are ardently in love with me, as you know; but I am rather doubtful as to the beauty of my person, especially as regards these legs of mine, which seem to me decidedly less well proportioned than I should wish: as to my bust and other members, however, I am quite content. Pray, now, describe a little more in particular the sort of body that the Courtier is to have, so that I may dismiss this doubt and set my mind at rest."

After some laughter at this, the Count continued:

"Of a certainty that grace of countenance can be truly said to be yours, nor need I cite further example than this to show what manner of thing it is, for we unquestionably perceive your aspect to be most agreeable and pleasing to everyone, albeit the lineaments of it are not very delicate. Still it is of a manly cast and at the same time full of grace; and this characteristic is to be found in many different types of countenance. And of such sort I would have our Courtier's aspect; not so soft and effeminate as is sought by many, who not only curl their hair and pluck their brows, but gloss their faces with all those arts employed by the most wanton and unchaste women in the world; and in their walk, posture and every act, they seem so limp and languid that their limbs are like to fall apart; and they pronounce their words so mournfully that they appear about to expire upon the spot: and the more they find themselves with men of rank, the more they affect such tricks. Since nature has not made them women, as they seem to wish to appear and be, they should be treated not as good women but as public harlots, and driven not merely from the courts of great lords but from the society of honest men.

"Then coming to the bodily frame, I say it is enough if this be neither extremely short nor tall, for both of these conditions excite a certain contemptuous surprise, and men of either sort are gazed upon in much the same way that we gaze on monsters. Yet if we must offend in one of the two extremes, it is preferable to fall a little short of the just measure of height than to exceed it, for besides often being dull of intellect, men thus huge of body are also unfit for every exercise of agility, which thing I should much wish in the Courtier. And so I would have him well built and shapely of limb, and would have him show strength and lightness and suppleness, and know all bodily exercises that befit a man of war: whereof I think the first should be to handle every sort of weapon well on foot and on horse, to understand the advantages of each, and especially to be familiar with those weapons that are ordinarily used among gentlemen; for besides the use of them in war, where such subtlety in contrivance is perhaps not needful, there frequently arise differences between one gentleman and another, which afterwards result in duels often fought with such weapons as happen at the moment to be within reach: thus knowledge of this kind is a very safe thing. Nor am I one of those who say that skill is forgotten in the hour of need; for he whose skill forsakes him at such a time, indeed gives token that he has already lost heart and head through fear.

"Moreover I deem it very important to know how to wrestle, for it is a great help in the use of all kinds of weapons on foot. Then, both for his own sake and for that of his friends, he must understand the quarrels and differences that may arise, and must be quick to seize an advantage, always showing courage and prudence in all things. Nor should he be too ready to fight except when honour demands it, for besides the great danger that the uncertainty of fate entails, he who rushes into such affairs recklessly and without urgent cause, merits the severest censure even though he be successful. But when he finds himself so far engaged that he cannot withdraw without reproach, he ought to be most deliberate, both in the preliminaries to the duel and in the duel itself, and always show readiness and daring. Nor must he act like some, who fritter the affair away in disputes and controversies, and who, having the choice of weapons, select those that neither cut nor pierce, and arm themselves as if they were expecting a cannonade; and thinking it enough not to be defeated, stand ever on the defensive and retreat, — showing therein their utter cowardice. And thus they make themselves a laughing-stock for boys, like those two men of Ancona who fought at Perugia not long since, and made everyone laugh who saw them." . . .

"If I remember rightly, Sir Count, I think you have repeated several times this evening that the Courtier must accompany his actions, gestures, habits, in short his every movement, with grace; and this you seem to regard as an universal seasoning, without which all other properties and good qualities are of little worth. And indeed I think that in this everyone would allow himself to be persuaded easily, since from the very force of the word, it may be said that he who has grace finds grace. But since you said that this is oftentimes the gift of nature and of heaven and, even when not thus perfect, can with care and pains be made much greater — those men who are born so fortunate and so rich in this treasure as are some we see, seem to me in this to have little need of other master; because that benign favour of heaven almost in despite of themselves leads them higher than they will, and makes them not only pleasing but admirable to all the world. Therefore I do not discuss this, it not being in our power to acquire it of ourselves. But they who have received from nature only so much, that they are capable of becoming graceful by pains, industry and care — I long to know by what art, by what training, by what method, they can acquire this grace, as well in bodily exercises (in which you esteem it to be so necessary) as also in everything else that they may do or say. Therefore, since by much praise of this quality you have aroused in all of us, I think, an ardent thirst to pursue it, you are further bound, by the charge that my lady Emilia laid upon you, to satisfy that thirst by teaching us how to attain it."

"I am not bound," said the Count, "to teach you how to become graceful, or anything else; but only to show you what manner of man a perfect Courtier ought to be. Nor would I in any case undertake the task of teaching you this perfection; especially having said a little while ago that the Courtier must know how to wrestle, vault, and do many other things, which I am sure you all know quite as well as if I, who have never learned them, were to teach you. For just as a good soldier knows how to tell the smith what fashion, shape and quality his armour ought to have, but cannot show how it is to be made or forged or tempered; so I perhaps may be able to tell you what manner of man a perfect Courtier ought to be, but cannot teach you what you must do to become one.

"Yet to comply with your request as far as is within my power — although it is almost a proverb that grace is not to be learned — I say that whoever would acquire grace in bodily exercises (assuming first that he be by nature not incapable), ought to begin early and learn the rudiments from the best masters. And how important this seemed to King Philip of Macedon, may be seen from the fact that he chose Aristotle, the famous philosopher and perhaps the greatest that has ever been in the world, to teach his son Alexander the first elements of letters. And of the men whom we know at the present day, consider how well and how gracefully my lord Galeazzo Sanseverino, Grand Equerry of France, performs all bodily exercises; and this because in addition to the natural aptitude of person that he possesses, he has taken the utmost pains to study with good masters, and always to have about him men who excel and to select from each the best of what they know; for just as in wrestling, vaulting and in the use of many sorts of weapons, he has taken for his guide our friend messer Pietro Monte, who (as you know) is the true and only master of every form of trained strength and ability, — so in riding, jousting and all else, he has ever had before his eyes the most proficient men that were known in those matters.

"Therefore he who wishes to be a good pupil, besides performing his tasks well, must put forth every effort to resemble his master, and, if it were possible, to transform himself into his master. And when he feels that he has made some progress, it will be very profitable to observe different men of the same calling, and governing himself with that good judgment which must ever be his guide, to go about selecting now this thing from one and that thing from another. And as the bee in the green meadows is ever wont to rob the flowers among the grass, so our Courtier must steal this grace from all who seem to possess it, taking from each that part which shall most be worthy praise; and not act like a friend of ours whom you all know, who thought he greatly resembled King Ferdinand the Younger of Aragon, and made it his care to imitate the latter in nothing but a certain trick of continually raising the head and twisting one side of the mouth, which the king had contracted from some infirmity. And there are many such, who think they gain a point if only they be like a great man in some thing; and frequently they devote themselves to that which is his only fault.

"But having before now often considered whence this grace springs, laying aside those men who have it by nature, I find one universal rule concerning it, which seems to me worth more in this matter than any other in all things human that are done or said: and that is to avoid affectation to the uttermost and as it were a very sharp and dangerous rock; and, to use possibly a new word, to practice in everything a certain nonchalance that shall conceal design and show that what is done and said is done without effort and almost without thought. From this I believe grace is in large measure derived, because everyone knows the difficulty of those things that are rare and well done, and therefore facility in them excites the highest admiration; while on the other hand, to strive and as the saying is to drag by the hair, is extremely ungraceful, and makes us esteem everything slightly, however great it be.

"Accordingly we may affirm that to be true art which does not appear to be art; nor to anything must we give greater care than to conceal art, for if it is discovered, it quite destroys our credit and brings us into small esteem. And I remember having once read that there were several very excellent orators of antiquity, who among their other devices strove to make everyone believe that they had no knowledge of letters; and hiding their knowledge they pretended that their orations were composed very simply and as if springing rather from nature and truth than from study and art; the which, if it had been detected, would have made men wary of being duped by it.

"Thus you see how the exhibition of art and study so intense destroys the grace in everything. Which of you is there who does not laugh when our friend messer Pierpaolo dances in his peculiar way, with those capers of his — legs stiff to the toe and head motionless, as if he were a stick, and with such intentness that he actually seems to be counting the steps? What eye so blind as not to see in this the ungracefulness of affectation — and in many men and women who are here present, the grace of that nonchalant ease (for in the case of bodily movements many call it thus), showing by word or laugh or gesture that they have no care and are thinking more of everything else than of that, to make the onlooker think they can hardly go amiss?"

JOHN AMOS COMENIUS

JOHN AMOS COMENIUS (1592-1670). "The pioneer of modern educational science" was born in Moravia on March 28, 1592, and died in Amsterdam on November 15, 1670. The name of the devoted Moravian churchman who initiated the age of educational reform was really Jan Komensky, and the source of his ideas may be traced to a strange blend of theological mysticism (his belief in prophecies, dreams, and revelations is revealed in the prophetic work *Lux in Tenebris*) and modern science.

Comenius studied at Herborn in Nassau and at Heidelberg, became rector of a school at Pierov, and later served as pastor of a church at Fulnek. He fled to Lissa, in Poland, after the battle of Prague in 1620. Ten years later he published *Pansophiae prodromus,* in which he tried to systematize all human knowledge and make it accessible to everyone. In 1638 he went to Sweden, where he reorganized the state school system. His plan to accomplish the same mission in England was unsuccessful because the Puritan Revolution was inimical to educational reform.

As a youth Comenius displayed an eagerness for knowledge, but recognized that the schools of his time suffered from many defects in method and discipline. As head of the Moravian gymnasium at Lissa, he was able to devote his attention to the theory and practice of education. He studied the works of Bacon and Ratich but found in them "defects and gaps." By "reducing everything to the immovable law of nature" he finally produced the *Great Didactic,* "which shows the art of readily and solidly teaching all men all things."

In 1650 Comenius established a model school at Patak in Hungary. It was here that he published his famous *Janua linguarum reserata,* an outline of a method for teaching languages not very different from the "new key" or audio-lingual method now in favor. His *Orbis pictus,* the most famous of all his writings, was designated to lay a solid foundation for knowledge by utilizing accurate sense perceptions: "The foundation of all knowledge consists in representing clearly to the senses sensible objects so that they can be easily apprehended." His illustrated textbook, which contained "the pictures and names of all the principal things in the world and of all the principal occupations of men," was the first of its kind.

The following selections are representative of the writings in which he tried to establish a science of education. Though his psychology was somewhat primitive, his recognition of the need for sound organization of the school system, for compulsory free education, and for techniques and programs of instruction adapted to the capacity and interest of the learner mark him as amazingly modern.

THE SCIENCE OF EDUCATION*

In all the operations of nature development is from within.

For example: in the case of a bird it is not the claws, or the feathers, or the skin that are first formed, but the inner parts; the outer parts are formed later, at the proper season.

Imitation. In the same way the gardener does not insert his graft into the outer bark nor into the outside layer of wood, but making an incision right into the pith, places the graft as far in as it will go.

In this way he makes the joint so firm that the sap cannot escape, but is forced right into the shoot, and uses all its strength in vivifying it.

So, too, a tree, that is nourished by the rain of heaven and the moisture of the earth, assimilates its nutriment, not through its outer bark, but through the pores of its inmost parts. On this account the gardener waters, not the branches, but the roots. Animals also convey their food, not to their outer limbs, but to the stomach, which assimilates it and nourishes the whole body. If, therefore, the educator of the young give special attention to the roots of knowledge, the understanding, these will soon impart their vitality to the stem, that is, to the memory, and finally blossoms and fruits, that is to say, a facile use of language and practical capacity will be produced.

Deviation. It is on this point that those teachers fall into error who, instead of thoroughly explaining the subjects of study to the boys under their charge, give them endless dictations, and make them learn their lessons off by heart. Even those who wish to explain the subject-matter do not know how to do so, that is to say, do not know how to tend the roots or how to engraft the graft of knowledge. Thus they fatigue their pupils, and resemble

---

*From *The Great Didactic of John Amos Comenius,* edited by M. W. Keatinge (London: Adam and Charles Black, 1896).

a man who uses a club or a mallet, instead of a knife, when he wishes to make an incision in a plant.

Rectification. It therefore follows

(i) That the scholar should be taught first to understand things, and then to remember them, and that no stress should be laid on the use of speech or pen, till after a training on the first two points.

(ii) That the teacher should know all the methods by which the understanding many be sharpened, and should put them into practice skilfully.

Nature, in its formative processes, begins with the universal and ends with the particular.

Deviation. From this it follows that it is a mistake to teach the several branches of science in detail before a general outline of the whole realm of knowledge has been placed before the student, and that no one should be instructed in such a way as to become proficient in any one branch of knowledge without thoroughly understanding its relation to all the rest.

Rectification. The remedy for this want of system is as follows: at the very commencement of their studies, boys should receive instruction in the first principles of general culture, that is to say, the subjects learned should be arranged in such a manner that the studies that come later introduce nothing new, but only expand the elements of knowledge that the boy has already mastered. Just as a tree, even if it live for a hundred years, puts forth no new branches, but only suffers those that already exist to develope and to spread.

(i) Each language, science, or art must be first taught in its most simple elements, that the student may obtain a general idea of it. (ii) His knowledge may next be developed further by placing rules and examples before him. (iii) Then he may be allowed to learn the subject systematically with the exceptions and irregularities; and (iv), last of all, may be given a commentary, though only where it is absolutely necessary. For he who has thoroughly mastered a subject from the beginning will have little need of a commentary, but will soon be in the position to write one himself.

Nature begins by a careful selection of materials.

Deviation. It follows from this: (1) That it is best to devote the mind to the pursuit of wisdom while it is still fresh, and before it has acquired the habit of dissipating its strength over a variety of occupations; and that the later the education begins, the harder it will be for it to obtain a hold, because the mind is already occupied by other things. (2) That the result must be bad if a boy be instructed by several teachers at once, since it is scarcely possible for them all to use the same method, and, if they do not, the boy's mind is drawn first in one direction and then in another, and its development is thus hindered. (3) That it shows great lack of judgment if moral instruction be not made the first point when the education of children or of older boys is commenced; since, when they have been taught to control their feelings, they will be the more fit to receive other instruction.

Rectification. Therefore

(i) Education should be commenced early.

(ii) The pupil should not have more than one teacher in each subject.

(iii) Before anything else is done, the morals should be rendered harmonious by the master's influence.

Nature prepares its material so that it actually strives to attain the form.

Thus the chicken in the egg, when sufficiently formed, seeks to develope itself still further, moves, and bursts the shell or breaks through it with its break. After escaping from its prison, it takes pleasure in the warmth and nutriment provided by its mother, opens its beak expectantly and swallows its food greedily. It rejoices to find itself under the open sky, exercises its wings, and, later on, uses them with enjoyment; in a word, it displays a keen desire to fulfil all its natural functions, though throughout the whole process of development it advances step by step.

Imitation. The gardener also must bring it about that the plant, properly provided with moisture and with warmth, take pleasure in its vigorous growth.

Deviation. Therefore, those who drive boys to their studies, do them great harm. For what result can they expect? If a man have no appetite, but yet takes food when urged to do so, the result can only be sickness and vomiting, or at least indigestion and indisposition. On the other hand, if a man be hungry, he is eager to take food, digests it readily, and easily converts it into flesh and blood. Thus Isocrates says: "He who is anxious to learn will also be learned." And Quintilian says: "The acquisition of knowledge depends on the will to learn, and this cannot be forced."

Rectification. Therefore

(i)   The desire to know and to learn should be excited in boys in every possible manner.

(ii)   The method of instruction should lighten the drudgery of learning, that there may be nothing to hinder the scholars or deter them from making progress with their studies.

The desire to learn is kindled in boys by parents, by masters, by the method of teaching, and by the authority of the state.

By parents, if they praise learning and the learned in the presence of their children, or if they encourage them to be industrious by promising them nice books and clothes, or some other pretty thing; if they commend the teachers (especially him to whom they entrust their sons) as much for their friendly feeling towards the pupils as for their skill in teaching (for love and admiration are the feelings most calculated to stimulate a desire for imitation); finally, if, from time to time, they send the child to him with a small present. In this way they will easily bring it about that the children like their lessons and their teachers, and have confidence in them.

By the teachers, if they are gentle and persuasive, and do not alienate their pupils from them by roughness, but attract them by fatherly sentiments and words; if they commend the studies that they take in hand on account of their excellence, pleasantness, and ease; if they praise the industrious ones from time to time (to the little ones they may give apples, nuts, sugar, etc.); if they call the children to them, privately or in the class, and show them pictures of the things that they must learn, or explain to them optical or geometrical instruments, astronomical globes, and such-like things that are calculated to excite their admiration; or again,

105

if they occasionally give the children some messages to carry to their parents. In a word, if they treat their pupils kindly they will easily win their affections, and will bring it about that they prefer going to school to remaining at home.

Nature developes everything from beginnings which, though insignificant in appearance, possess great potential strength.

Terrible deviation. In direct opposition to this principle a terrible mistake is generally made in schools. Most teachers are at pains to place in the earth plants instead of seeds, and trees instead of shoots, since, instead of starting with the fundamental principles, they place before their pupils a chaos of diverse conclusions or the complete texts of authors. And yet it is certain that instruction rests on a very small number of principles, just as the earth is composed of four elements (though in diverse forms); and that from these principles (in accordance with the evident limits of their powers of differentiation) an unlimited number of results can be deduced, just as, in the case of a tree, hundreds of branches, and thousands of leaves, blossoms, and fruits are produced from the original shoot.

Rectification. In the meantime we may draw three conclusions:
(i) Every art must be contained in the shortest and most practical rules.
(ii) Each rule must be expressed in the shortest and clearest words.
(iii) Each rule must be accompanied by many examples, in order that the use of the rule may be quite clear when fresh cases arise.

Nature does not hurry, but advances slowly.

Deviation. For the young, therefore, it is torture
(i) If they are compelled to receive six, seven, or eight hours' class instruction daily, and private lessons in addition.
(ii) If they are overburdened with dictations, with exercises, and with the lessons that they have to commit to memory, until nausea and, in some cases, insanity is produced.

If we take a jar with a narrow mouth (for to this we may compare a boy's intellect) and attempt to pour a quantity of water into it violently, instead of allowing it to trickle in drop by drop, what will be the result? Without doubt the greater part of the liquid will flow over the side, and ultimately the jar will contain less than if the operation had taken place gradually. Quite as foolish is the action of those who try to teach their pupils, not as much as they can assimilate, but as much as they themselves wish; for the faculties need to be supported and not to be over-burdened, and the teacher, like the physician, is the servant and not the master of nature.

Rectification. The ease and the pleasantness of study will therefore be increased:

(i)   If the class instruction be curtailed as much as possible, namely to four hours, and if the same length of time be left for private study.

(ii)   If the pupils be forced to memorise as little as possible, that is to say, only the most important things; of the rest they need only grasp the general meaning.

(iii)   If everything be arranged to suit the capacity of the pupil, which increases naturally with study and age.

Nature compels nothing to advance that is not driven forward by its own mature strength.

Deviation. Now the faculties of the young are forced:

(i)   If boys are compelled to learn things for which their age and capacity are not yet suited.

(ii)   If they are made to learn by heart or do things that have not first been thoroughly explained and demonstrated to them.

Rectification. From what has been said, it follows

(i)   That nothing should be taught to the young, unless it is not only permitted but actually demanded by their age and mental strength.

(ii)   That nothing should be learned by heart that has not been thoroughly grasped by the understanding. Nor should any feat of memory be demanded unless it is absolutely certain that the boy's strength is equal to it.

(iii)   That nothing should be set boys to do until its nature

107

has been thoroughly explained to them, and rules and procedures have been given.

Nature assists its operations in every possible manner.

Deviation. It is therefore cruelty on the part of a teacher if he set his pupils work to do without first explaining it to them thoroughly, or showing them how it should be done, and if he do not assist them in their first attempts; or if he allow them to toil hard, and then loses his temper if they do not succeed in their endeavours.

What is this but to torture the young? it is just as if a nurse were to force a child to walk, while it is still afraid to stand on its legs, and beat it when it failed to do so. Nature's teaching is very different, and shows that we ought to have patience with the weak as long as their strength is insufficient.

Rectification. From this it follows:

(i)   That no blows should be given for lack of readiness to learn (for, if the pupil do not learn readily, this is the fault of no one but the teacher, who either does not know how to make his pupil receptive of knowledge or does not take the trouble to do so).

(ii)   That the subjects that have to be learned by the pupils should be so thoroughly explained to them, that they can understand them as well as they understand their five fingers.

(iii)   That, as far as is possible, instruction should be given through the senses, that it may be retained in the memory with less effort.

For example, the sense of hearing should always be conjoined with that of sight, and the tongue should be trained in combination with the hand. The subjects that are taught should not merely be taught orally, and thus appeal to the ear alone, but should be pictorially illustrated, and thus develope the imagination by the help of the eye. Again, the pupils should learn to speak with their mouths and at the same time to express what they say with their hands, that no study may be proceeded with before what has already been learned is thoroughly impressed on the eyes, the ears, the understanding, and the memory. With this object, it is desirable to represent pictorially, on the walls of the class-room, everything that is treated of in the class, by putting up either precepts and rules or pictures and diagrams illustrative of the subjects taught. If this be done, it is incredible how much it assists a teacher to impress his instruction on the pupils' minds. It is also useful if the scholars learn to write down in their note-books or among their collections of idioms everything that they hear or read, since in this way the imagination is assisted and it is easier to remember them later on.

Nothing is produced by nature of which the practical application is not soon evident.

For example, when a bird is formed it is soon evident that the wings are intended for flying and the legs for running. In the same way every part of a tree has its use, down to the skin and the bloom that surround the fruit.

Therefore

Imitation. The task of the pupil will be made easier, if the master, when he teaches him anything, show him at the same time its practical application in every-day life. This rule must be carefully observed in teaching languages, dialectic, arithmetic, geometry, physics, etc. If it be neglected, the things that you are explaining will seem to be monsters from the new world, and the attitude of the pupil, who is indifferent whether they exist or no, will be one of belief rather than of knowledge. When things are brought under his notice and their use is explained to him, they should be put into his hands that he may assure himself of his knowledge and may derive enjoyment from its application.

Therefore

Those things only should be taught whose application can be easily demonstrated. . . .

Nature produces nothing that is useless. . . .

[Imitation] in schools. In schools therefore

(i)   Nothing should be studied, unless it be of undoubted use in this world and in the world to come, — its use in the world to come being the more important (Jerome reminds us that knowledge, that is to be of service to us in heaven, must be acquired on earth).

(ii) If it be necessary to teach the young much that is of value solely in this world (and this cannot be avoided), care must be taken that while a real advantage is gained for our present life, our heavenly welfare be not hindered thereby.

Why then pursue worthless studies? What object is there in learning subjects that are of no use to those who know them and the lack of which is not felt by those who do not know them? subjects, too, which are certain to be forgotten as time passes on and the business of life becomes more engrossing? This short life of ours has more than enough to occupy it, even if we do not waste it on worthless studies. Schools must therefore be organised in such a way that the scholars learn nothing but what is of value.

ACTIVITY AND EXPRESSION*

1. Boys ever delight in being occupied in something, for their youthful blood does not allow them to be at rest. Now as this is very useful, it ought not to be restrained, but provision made that they may always have something to do. Let them be like ants, continually occupied in doing something, carrying, drawing, construction, and transposing, provided always that whatever they do be done prudently. They ought to be assisted, by showing them the forms of all things, even of playthings; for they cannot yet be occupied in real works, and we should play with them. We read that Themistocles, supreme ruler of the Athenians, was once seen riding with his son on a long reed as a horse, by a young unmarried citizen; and observing that he wondered how so great a man could act so childishly, he begged of him not to relate the incident to any one until he himself had a son, — thus indicating that when he became a father, he would be better able to understand the affection of parents for

*From *School of Infancy,* edited by Will S. Monroe (Boston, 1893).

their children, and that he would cease to be surprised at the conduct which now seemed to him childish.

2. Inasmuch as children try to imitate what they see others do, they should be permitted to have all things, excepting such as might cause injury to themselves, such as knives, hatchets, and glass. When this is not convenient, in place of real instruments they should have toys procured for their use; namely, iron knives, wooden swords, plows, little carriages, sledges, mills, buildings, etc. With these they may amuse themselves, thus exercising their bodies to health, their minds to vigor, and their bodily members to agility. They are delighted to construct little houses, and to erect walls of clay, chips, wood, or stone, thus displaying an architectural genius. In a word, whatever children delight to play with, provided that it be not hurtful, they ought rather to be gratified than restrained from it; for inactivity is more injurious to both mind and body than anything in which they can be occupied.

3. Now advancing according to their years, in the first year they will have sufficient mechanical knowledge for children, if they learn why they open their mouths for food, hold up their heads, take anything in their hands, sit, stand, etc.; all these things will depend rather on nature than nurture.

4. In the second and third years their mechanical knowledge may be extended; for now they begin to learn what it is to run, to jump, to agitate themselves in various ways, to play, to kindle and extinguish, to pour out water, to carry things from place to place, to put down, to lift up, to lay prostrate, to cause to stand, to turn, to roll together, to unroll, to bend, to make straight, to break, to split, etc.; all these things ought to be allowed, nay, when opportunity serves, they ought to be shown them.

5. The fourth, fifth, and sixth years will and ought to be full of labors and architectural efforts; for too much sitting still or slowly walking about on the part of a child is not a good sign; to be always running or doing something is a sure sign of a sound body and vigorous intellect; therefore, whatever attracts their attention, that ought not to be denied, but rather be given

them; that which is done should be properly done, and with a view to future usefulness.

6. Children in this maternal school ought also, in their fourth and fifth year, to be exercised in drawing and writing, according as their inclination may be noticed or excited, supplying them with chalk (poorer persons may use a piece of charcoal), with which they may at their will make dots, lines, hooks, or round O's, of which the method may be easily shown, either as an exercise or amusement. In this way they will accustom the hand to the use of the chalk, and to form letters, and they will understand what a dot is, and what a little line, which will afterwards greatly abridge the labors of the teacher.

7. In this stage dialectics (reasoning), beyond the natural, or such as is obtained in practice, cannot be introduced; but in whatever manner those persons conduct themselves, who associate with children, whether rationally or irrationally, such will the children be.

8. The elements of arithmetic can scarcely be propounded to children in the third year; but soon they can count up to five or ten, or at least pronounce the numbers correctly; they may not at first understand what those numbers really are, but they will of themselves observe the use to which this enumeration is applied. In the fourth, fifth, and sixth years it will be sufficient if they count up to twenty in succession, and be able clearly to distinguish that seven is more than five, and fifteen more than thirteen; what is an even and what an odd number, which they may easily learn from the play which we call odds and evens. To proceed farther than this in arithmetic would be unprofitable, nay, hurtful; for nothing is so difficult to fix in our minds as numbers.

9. About the second year the principles of geometry may be perceived, when we say of anything it is large or small; they will afterwards know easily what is short or long, wide or narrow. In the fourth year they may learn the different forms; for example, what is a circle, what are lines, what a square. At length they may learn the names of the common measures, such as a finger's breadth, a span, a foot, a pint, a quart, a gallon. What-

ever comes spontaneously to their own knowledge, they themselves should be shown how to measure, to weigh, thus comparing the one with another standard of measurement.

10. Music is especially natural to us; for as soon as we see the light we immediately sing the song of paradise, thus recalling to our memory our fall, A, a! E, e! I maintain that complaint and wailing are our first music, from which it is impossible to restrain infants; and if it were possible, it would be inexpedient, since it contributes to their health; for as long as other exercises and amusements are wanting, by this very means their chests and other internal parts relieve themselves of their superfluities. External music begins to delight children at two years of age; such as singing, rattling, and striking of musical instruments. They should therefore be indulged in this, so that their ears and minds may be soothed by concord and harmony.

11. In the third year the sacred music of daily use may be introduced; namely, that received as a custom to sing before and after dinner, and when prayers are begun or ended. On such occasions they ought to be present, and to be accustomed to attend and conduct themselves composedly. It will also be expedient to take them to public worship, where the whole assembly unites in singing the praises of God. In the fourth year it is possible for some children to sing of themselves; the slower ones, however, ought not to be forced, but permitted to have a whistle, a drum, or pipes, so that by whistling, drumming, and piping they may accustom their ears to the perceptions of various sounds, or even to imitate them. In the fifth year it will be time to open their mouths in hymns and praises to God, and to use their voices for the glory of their Creator.

12. These things parents, in singing or playing with children, may easily instil into their minds; the memory is now more enlarged and apt than previously, and will, with greater ease and pleasure, imbibe a larger number of things in consequence of the rhythm and melody. The more verses they commit to memory, the better will they be pleased with themselves, and the glory of God be largely promoted. Blessed is the home where voices resound with music.

THE COMMUNIST PARTY
OF THE U.S.S.R.

The *First Programme* of the Communist Party, adopted in 1903, called on the working class to fight for the overthrow of the Czarist government and the establishment of the dictatorship of the proletariat; the *Second Programme,* adopted in 1919, called for the building of a socialist society; the *Third Programme,* adopted on October 31, 1961, calls for the building of a Communist society. The role of education in the attainment of the prime objective of the Party is Section V of the *Programme*: "In the struggle for the victory of communism, ideological work becomes an increasingly powerful factor. . . . The Party considers that the paramount task in the ideological field in the present period is to educate all working people in a spirit of ideological integrity and devotion to communism. . . . Special importance is attached by the Party to the moulding of the rising generation." That educational competition between the United States and the U.S.S.R. will be intensified in the coming years is obvious. Soviet plans involve enormous expansion in the controlled use of mass media, conventional programs of instruction, and experimental techniques and devices, such as audio-visual aids and programmed learning. Senator William Fulbright judiciously observed recently (December 10, 1963) that the Russians "are spending almost twice as much of their gross national product on education as this country is. I predict that history will show that it is in this area that the real struggle will be determined."

"The Tasks of the Party in the Spheres of Ideology, Education, Instruction, Science, and Culture," presented here in full, deserves serious — and critical — attention.

114

THE TASKS OF THE PARTY IN THE SPHERES OF IDEOLOGY, EDUCATION, INSTRUCTION, SCIENCE, AND CULTURE*

Soviet society has made great progress in the socialist education of the masses, in the moulding of active builders of socialism. But even after the socialist system has triumphed there persist in the minds and behavior of people survivals of capitalism, which hamper the progress of society.

In the struggle for the victory of communism, ideological work becomes an increasingly powerful factor. The higher the social consciousness of the members of society, the more fully and broadly their creative activities come into play in the building of the material and technical basis of communism, in the development of communist forms of labour and new relations between people, and, consequently, the more rapid and successfully the building of communism proceeds.

The Party considers that the paramount task in the ideological field in the present period is to educate all working people in a spirit of ideological integrity and devotion to communism, and cultivate in them a communist attitude to labour and the social economy; to eliminate completely the survivals of bourgeois views and morals; to ensure the all-round, harmonious development of the individual; to create a truly rich spiritual culture. Special importance is attached by the Party to the moulding of the rising generation.

The moulding of the new man is effected through his own active participation in communist construction and the development of communist principles in the economic and social spheres, under the influence of the educational work carried out by the Party, the state, and various social organizations, work in which

*Section V on *The Programme of The Communist Party of the Soviet Union* (Moscow: Foreign Languages Publishing House, 1961).

the press, radio, cinema, and television play an important part. As communist forms of social organisation are created, communist ideas will become more firmly rooted in life and work and in human relations, and people will develop the ability to enjoy the benefits of communism in a rational way. Joint planned labour by the members of society, their daily participation in the management of state and public affairs, and the development of communist relations of comradely co-operation and mutual support, recast the minds of people in a spirit of collectivism, industry, and humanism.

Increased communist consciousness of the people furthers the ideological and political unity of the workers, collective farmers, and intellectuals and promotes their gradual fusion in the single collective of the working people of communist society.

The Party sets the following tasks:

1. *In the Field of Development of Communist Consciousness*

(a) *The Shaping of a Scientific World Outlook.* Under socialism and at a time when a communist society is being built, when spontaneous economic development has given way to the conscious organisation of production and social life as a whole, and when theory is daily translated into practice, it is of prime importance that a scientific world outlook be shaped in all working people of Soviet society on the basis of Marxism-Leninism, an integral and harmonious system of philosophical, economic and socio-political views. The Party calls for the education of the population as a whole in the spirit of scientific communism and strives to ensure that all working people fully understand the course and perspectives of world development, that they take a correct view of international and domestic events and consciously build their life on communist lines. Communist ideas and communist deeds should blend organically in the behaviour of every person and in the activities of all collectives and organisations.

The theoretical elaboration and timely practical solution of new problems raised by life are essential to the successful advance of society to communism. Theory must continue to illumine the road

116

of practice, and help detect and eliminate obstacles and difficulties hindering successful communist construction. The Party regards it as one of its most important duties to further elaborate Marxist-Leninist theory by studying and generalising new phenomena in the life of Soviet society and the experience of the world revolutionary working-class and liberation movements, and creatively to combine the theory and the practice of communist construction.

(b) *Labour Education.* The Party sees the development of a communist attitude to labour in all members of society as its chief educational task. Labour for the benefit of society is the sacred duty of all. Any labour for society, whether physical or mental, is honourable and commands respect. Exemplary labour and management in the social economy should serve to educate all working people.

Everything required for life and human progress is created by labour. Hence every able-bodied man must take part in creating the means which are indispensable for his life and work and for the welfare of society. Anyone who received any benefits from society without doing his share of work, would be a parasite living at the expense of others.

It is impossible for a man in communist society not to work, for neither his social consciousness, nor public opinion would permit it. Work according to one's ability will become a habit, a prime necessity of life, for every member of society.

(c) *The Affirmation of Communist Morality.* In the course of transition to communism, the moral principles of society become increasingly important; the sphere of action of the moral factor expands and the importance of the administrative control of human relations diminishes accordingly. The Party will encourage all forms of conscious civic self-discipline leading to the assertion and promotion of the basic rules of the communist way of life.

The Communists reject the class morality of the exploiters; in contrast to the perverse, selfish views and morals of the old world, they promote communist morality, which is the noblest and most just morality, for it expresses the interests and ideals of the whole of working mankind. Communism makes the ele-

117

mentary standards of morality and justice, which were distorted or shamelessly flouted under the rule of the exploiters, inviolable rules for relations both between individuals and between peoples. Communist morality encompasses the fundamental norms of human morality which the masses of the people evolved in the course of millenniums as they fought against vice and social oppression. The revolutionary morality of the working class is of particular importance to the moral advancement of society. As socialist and communist construction progresses, communist morality is enriched with new principles, a new content.

The Party holds that *the moral code of the builder of communism* should comprise the following principles:

devotion to the communist cause; love of the socialist motherland and of the other socialist countries;

conscientious labour for the good of society — he who does not work, neither shall he eat;

concern on the part of everyone for the preservation and growth of public wealth;

a high sense of public duty; intolerance of actions harmful to the public interest;

collectivism and comradely mutual assistance: one for all and all for one;

humane relations and mutual respect between individuals — man is to man a friend, comrade and brother;

honesty and truthfulness, moral purity, modesty, and unpretentiousness in social and private life;

mutual respect in the family, and concern for the upbringing of children;

an uncompromising attitude to injustice, parasitism, dishonesty, careerism and money-grubbing;

friendship and brotherhood among all peoples of the U.S.S.R.; intolerance of national and racial hatred;

an uncompromising attitude to the enemies of communism, peace and the freedom of nations;

fraternal solidarity with the working people of all countries, and with all peoples.

(d) *The Promotion of Proletarian Internationalism and Socialist*

118

Patriotism. The Party will untiringly educate Soviet people in the spirit of proletarian internationalism and will vigorously promote the international solidarity of the working people. In fostering the Soviet people's love of their country, the Party maintains that with the emergence of the world socialist system the patriotism of the members of socialist society is expressed in devotion and loyalty to their own country and to the entire community of socialist countries. Socialist patriotism and socialist internationalism necessarily imply proletarian solidarity with the working class and all working people of all countries. The Party will continue perseveringly to combat the reactionary ideology of bourgeois nationalism, racism, and cosmopolitanism.

(e) *All-Round and Harmonious Development of the Individual.* In the period of transition to communism, there are greater opportunities of *educating a new man, who will harmoniously combine spiritual wealth, moral purity and a perfect physique.*

All-round development of the individual has been made possible by historic social gains — freedom from exploitation, unemployment and poverty, from discrimination on account of sex, origin, nationality or race. Every member of society is provided with equal opportunities for education and creative labour. Relations of dependence and inequality between people in public affairs and in family life disappear. The personal dignity of each citizen is protected by society. Each is guaranteed an equal and free choice of occupation and profession with due regard to the interests of society. As less and less time is spent on material production, the individual is afforded ever greater opportunities to develop his abilities, gifts, and talents in the fields of production, science, engineering, literature, and the arts. People will increasingly devote their leisure to public pursuits, cultural intercourse, intellectual and physical development, scientific, technical and artistic endeavour. Physical training and sports will become part and parcel of the everyday life of people.

(f) *Elimination of the Survivals of Capitalism in the Minds and Behavior of People.* The Party considers it an integral part of its communist education work to combat manifestations of bour-

119

geois ideology and morality, and the remnants of private-owner psychology, superstitions, and prejudices.

The general public, public opinion, and extensive criticism and self-criticism must play a big role in combating survivals of the past and manifestations of individualism and selfishness. Comradely censure of anti-social behaviour will gradually become the principal means of doing away with manifestations of bourgeois views, customs and habits. The power of example in public affairs and in private life, in the performance of one's public duty, acquires tremendous educational significance.

The Party uses ideological media to educate people in the spirit of a scientific materialist world conception, to overcome religious prejudices without insulting the sentiments of believers. It is necessary to conduct regularly broad atheistic propaganda on a scientific basis, to explain patiently the untenability of religious beliefs, which were engendered in the past when people were overawed by the elemental forces and social oppression and did not know the real causes of natural and social phenomena. This can be done by making use of the achievements of modern science, which is steadily solving the mysteries of the universe and extending man's power over nature, leaving no room for religious inventions about supernatural forces.

(g) *The Exposure of Bourgeois Ideology.* The peaceful coexistence of states with different social systems does not imply any ease of the ideological struggle. The Communist Party will go on *exposing the anti-popular, reactionary nature of capitalism* and all attempts to paint bright pictures of the capitalist system.

The Party will *steadfastly propagate the great advantages of socialism and communism over the declining capitalist system.*

The Party advances the scientific ideology of communism in contrast to reactionary bourgeois ideology. Communist ideology, which expresses the fundamental interests of the working class and all working people, teaches them to struggle, to live and work, for the happiness of all. It is the most humane ideology. Its ideals are to establish truly human relations between individuals and peoples, to deliver mankind from the threat of wars of extermination, and bring about universal peace and a free, happy life for all men on earth.

2. *In the Field of Public Education*

The transition to communism implies training that will make people communist-minded and highly-cultured, people fitted for both physical and mental labour, for active work in various social, governmental, scientific, and cultural spheres.

The system of public education is so organised as to ensure that the instruction and education of the rising generation are closely bound up with life and productive labour, and that the adult population can combine work in the sphere of production with further training and education in keeping with their vocations and the requirements of society. Public education along these lines will make for the moulding of harmoniously developed members of communist society and for the solution of a cardinal social problem, namely, the elimination of substantial distinctions between mental and physical labour.

The main tasks in the field of instruction and education are:

(a) *Introduction of Universal Compulsory Secondary Education.* In the next decade compulsory secondary general and poly-technical eleven-year education is to be introduced for all children of school age, and eight-year education for young people engaged in the national economy who have not had the appropriate schooling; in the subsequent decade every one will have the opportunity to receive a complete secondary education. Universal secondary education is guaranteed by the development of general and polytechnical education, professional training combined with socially useful labour of school children to the extent of their physical capacity, and a considerable expansion of the network of all types of general schools, including evening schools, which provide a secondary education in off-work hours.

Secondary education must furnish a solid knowledge of the fundamentals of the basic sciences, an understanding of the principles of the communist world outlook, and a labour and polytechnical training in accordance with the rising levels of science and

121

engineering, with due regard to the needs of society and to the abilities and inclinations of the students, as well as the moral, aesthetic and physical education of a healthy rising generation.

In view of the rapid progress of science and engineering, the system of industrial, professional and vocational training should be improved continuously, so that the skills of those engaged in production may develop together with their better general education in the social and natural sciences and with the acquisition of specialised knowledge in engineering, agronomy, medicine, and other fields.

(b) *The Public Upbringing of Children of Pre-School and School Age.* The communist system of public education is based on the public upbringing of children. The educational influence which the family exerts on children must be brought into ever greater harmony with their public upbringing.

The growing number of pre-school institutions and boarding-schools of different types will fully meet the requirements of all working people who wish to give their children of pre-school and school age a public upbringing. The importance of the school, which is to cultivate love of labour and knowledge in children and to raise the younger generation in the spirit of communist consciousness and morality, will increase. An honourable and responsible role in this respect falls to teachers, and to the Komsomol and Young Pioneer organisations.

(c) *Creation of Conditions for High-Standard Instruction and Education of the Rising Generation.* The Party plans to carry out an extensive programme for the construction of schools and cultural-education establishments to meet fully the needs of education and instruction. All schools will be housed in good buildings and will go over to a one-shift time-table. They will all have study work-shops and chemical, physical and other laboratories; rural schools will also have their own farming plots; large factories will have production training shops for school children. Modern facilities — cinema, radio, and television — will be widely used in schools.

For physical training and aesthetic education, all schools and extra-scholastic establishments will have gymnasiums, sports grounds and facilities for the creative endeavour of children in music, painting, sculpture, etc. The network of sports schools, sports grounds, tourist camps, skiing centres, aquatic stations, swimming-pools, and other sports facilities will be expanded in town and country-side.

(d) *Higher and Secondary Special Education.* In step with scientific and technical progress, higher and secondary special education, which must train highly-skilled specialists with a broad theoretical and political background, will be expanded.

Shorter working hours and a considerable improvement in the standard of living of the entire population will provide everyone with an opportunity to receive a higher or secondary special education if he so desires. The number of higher and secondary specialised schools, evening and correspondence schools in particular, as well as higher schools at factories, agricultural institutes (on large state farms), studios, conservatoires, etc., must be increased in all areas of the country with the support of factories and trade unions and other social organisations. The plan is to considerably increase every year the number of students at higher and secondary specialised schools; special education will be afforded to tens of millions of people.

3. *In the Field of Science*

Under the socialist system of economy, scientific and technical progress enables man to employ the riches and forces of nature most effectively in the interests of the people, to discover new forms of energy and to create new materials, to develop means of weather control, and to master outer space. Application of science in production becomes a decisive factor of rapid growth of the productive forces of society. Scientific progress and the introduction of scientific achievements into the economy will remain an object of special concern to the Party.

Most important are the following tasks:

(a) *Development of Theoretical Investigations.* The further perspectives of scientific and technical progress depend in the present period primarily on the achievements of *the key branches*

123

of natural science. A high level of development in *mathematics, physics, chemistry, and biology* is a necessary condition for the technical, medical, agricultural, and other sciences.

Theoretical research will be promoted to the utmost, primarily in such decisive fields of technical progress as electrification of the whole country, comprehensive mechanisation and automation of production, transport and communications, the application of chemistry to the leading branches of the national economy, industrial uses of atomic energy. This applies to:

studying the power and fuel balance of the country, finding the best ways and means of utilising the natural sources of power, working out the scientific fundamentals of a single power grid, discovering new power sources and developing methods of direct conversion of thermal, nuclear, solar, and chemical energy into electric power, and solving problems related to control of thermonuclear reactions;

working out the theory and principles of designing new machines, automatic and telemechanical systems, intensively developing radioelectronics, elaborating the theoretical foundations of computing, control and information machines, and technically improving them;

investigating chemical processes, working out new, more efficient technologies and creating inexpensive high-quality artificial and synthetic materials for all branches of the national economy: mechanical engineering, building, the manufacture of household goods and mineral fertilisers, and creating new preparations for use in medicine and agriculture;

improving existing methods and devising new, more effective methods of prospecting minerals and making comprehensive use of natural wealth.

Big advances are to be made in the development of all the biological sciences in order successfully to solve medical problems and achieve further progress in agriculture. The main tasks to be solved by these sciences in the interests of mankind are: ascertainment of the essence of the phenomena of life, the biological laws governing the development of the organic world, study of the physics and chemistry of living matter, elaboration

124

of various methods of controlling vital processes, in particular, metabolism, heredity and directed changes in organisms. It is essential to develop more broadly and deeply the Michurin line in biology, which is based on the proposition that conditions of life are primary in the development of the organic world. Medicine must concentrate on discovering means of preventing and conquering cancer, virulent, cardio-vascular, and other dangerous diseases. It is important to study and extensively use microorganisms in the economy and the health services, among other things for the production of foods and feedstuffs, vitamins, antibiotics and enzymes, and for the development of new agricultural techniques.

Artificial earth satellites and spaceships have, by enabling man to penetrate into outer space, provided great opportunities of discovering new natural phenomena and laws and of investigating the planets and the sun.

In the age of rapid scientific progress, the elaboration of the philosophical problems of modern natural science on the basis of dialectical materialism, the only scientific method of cognition, becomes still more urgent.

There must be intensive development of research work in the *social sciences,* which constitute the scientific basis for the guidance of the development of society. Most important in this field is the study and theoretical generalisation of the experience gained in communist construction; investigation of the key objective laws governing the economic, political and cultural progress of socialism and its development into communism, and elaboration of the problems of communist education.

The task of economic science is to generalise new phenomena in the economic life of society, and to work out the national economic problems whose solution promotes successful communist construction. Economists must concentrate on finding the most effective ways of utilising material and labour resources in the economy, the best methods of planning and organising industrial and agricultural production, and elaborating the principles of a rational distribution of the productive forces and of the technical and economic problems of communist construction.

125

The investigation of the problems of world history and contemporary world development must disclose the law-governed process of mankind's advance towards communism, the change in the balance of forces in favour of socialism, the aggravation of the general crisis of capitalism, the breakup of the colonial system of imperialism and its consequences, and the upsurge of the national-liberation movement of peoples.

It is important to study the historical experience of the Communist Party and the Soviet people, tried and proved successful in practice, the objective laws of development of the world socialist system and the world Communist and working-class movement.

It is essential, in the future as well, to firmly defend and develop dialectical and historical materialism as the science of the most general laws of development of nature, society and human thinking.

The social sciences must continue to struggle with determination against bourgeois ideology, against Right-Socialist theory and practice, and against revisionism and dogmatism; they must uphold the purity of the principles of Marxism-Leninism.

(b) *Ties Between Science and Production.* Close ties with the creative labour of the people and practical communist construction are an earnest of a fruitful development of science.

In conformity with the requirements of economic and cultural development, it is essential to extend and improve the network of research institutions, including those attached to the central bodies directing economic development and those attached to the economic councils, and the network of research laboratories and institutes at the major industrial plants and in farming areas; to develop research at higher educational establishments; to improve the geographical distribution of research institutions and higher educational establishments, and to ensure the further development of science in all the Union republics and major economic areas.

The research institutions must plan and co-ordinate their work in the most important fields of research in accordance with the plans of economic and cultural development. The role of the collective opinion of scientists in directing scientific work will increase. Free comradely discussions promoting the creative solu-

126

tion of pressing problems are an essential condition for scientific development.

The Party will adopt measures to extend and improve the material facilities of science and to enlist the most capable creative forces in scientific pursuits.

It is a point of honour for Soviet scientists to consolidate the advanced positions which Soviet science has won in major branches of knowledge and to take *a leading place in world science* in all the key fields.

4. *In the Field of Cultural Development, Literature and Art*

Cultural development during the full-scale construction of communist society will constitute the closing stage of a great cultural revolution. At this stage all the necessary ideological and cultural conditions will be created for the victory of communism.

The growth of the productive forces, progress in engineering and in the organisation of production, increased social activity of the working people, development of the democratic principles of self-government, and a communist reorganisation of everyday life depend in very large measure on the cultural advancement of the population.

Absorbing and developing all the best that has been created by world culture, communist culture will be a new, higher stage in the cultural progress of mankind. It will embody the versatility and richness of the spiritual life of society, and the lofty ideals and humanism of the new world. It will be culture of a classless society, a culture of the entire people, of all mankind.

(a) *All-Round Advancement of the Cultural Life of Society.* In the period of transition to communism, creative effort in all fields of culture becomes particularly fruitful and accessible to all members of society. Soviet literature, music, painting, cinema and theatre, television and all the other arts, will attain higher standards in their ideological make-up and artistry. People's theatres, mass amateur art, technical invention and other forms of creative endeavour by the people will become widespread. The advancement of artistic and creative activities among the masses will

127

ensure the appearance of new gifted writers, artists, musicians and actors. The development and enrichment of the arts are based on a combination of mass amateur endeavour and professional art.

The Party will work unremittingly to ensure that literature, art, and culture flourish, that every individual is given full scope to apply his abilities, that the people are educated aesthetically and develop a fine artistic taste and cultural habits. The artistic element will ennoble labour still more, make living conditions more attractive, and lift man up spiritually.

To provide the material basis for cultural development on a grand scale:

book publishing and the press will be vigorously developed, and the printing and paper industries will be expanded accordingly;

there will be more libraries, lecture halls and reading-rooms, theatres, houses of culture, clubs, and cinemas;

the country-wide radio diffusion network will be completed; television stations covering all industrial and agricultural areas will be built;

people's universities, people's theatrical companies, and other amateur cultural organisations will be widely developed;

a large network of scientific and technical laboratories and of art and cinema studios will be provided for the use of all who have the inclination and ability.

The Party considers it necessary to distribute cultural institutions evenly throughout the country in order gradually to bring the cultural standard of the countryside level with that of the town and achieve rapid cultural progress in all the newly-developed areas.

(b) *Enhancement of the Educational Role of Literature and Art.* Soviet literature and art, imbued with optimism and dynamic communist ideas, are great factors in ideological education and cultivate in Soviet people the qualities of builders of a new world. They must be a source of joy and inspiration to millions of people, express their will, their sentiments and ideas, enrich them ideologically and educate them morally.

The highroad of literature and art lies through the strengthening of their bond with the life of the people, through faithful

128

and highly artistic depiction of the richness and versatility of socialist reality, inspired and vivid portrayal of all that is new and genuinely communist, and exposure of all that hinders the progress of society.

In the art of socialist realism, which is based on the principles of partisanship and kinship with the people, bold pioneering in the artistic depiction of life goes hand in hand with the cultivation and development of the progressive traditions of world culture. Writers, artists, musicians, theatrical workers, and film makers have every opportunity of displaying creative initiative and skill, using manifold forms, styles, and genres.

The Communist Party shows solicitude for the proper development of literature and art and their ideological and artistic standards, helps social organisations and literary and art associations in their activities.

(c) *The Expansion of International Cultural Relations.* The Party considers it necessary to expand the Soviet Union's cultural relations with the countries of the socialist system and with all other countries for the purpose of pooling scientific and cultural achievements and of bringing about mutual understanding and friendship among the peoples.

JAMES B. CONANT

JAMES B. CONANT (1893-   ). Internationally renowned as a scientist, scholar, statesman, author and educator, Dr. James Bryant Conant is perhaps best known to teachers and to parents for his comprehensive and authoritative report on *The American High School Today* and the recommendations contained in his report for improving public secondary education.

Born at Dorchester, Massachusetts, on March 26, 1893, he graduated from Harvard in 1913 and earned his doctorate there in 1916. He was appointed there in 1916. He was appointed instructor in chemistry in 1916 and professor of organic chemistry in 1927. In 1933 he became president of Harvard University. He later served as chairman of the National Defense Research Committee, a capacity in which he co-ordinated the original effort to develop the atomic bomb project, as a senior adviser to the National Science Foundation and to the Atomic Energy Commission, as United States High Commissioner for Germany, and as Ambassador to Germany.

Dr. Conant's life-long interest in education is reflected both in his scholarly publications and in his popular writings. He has written two textbooks in chemistry and demonstrated great success in writing about science for nonscientists, as in *On Understanding Science* (1947). Bringing the objectivity of his scientific training to the investigation of problems and issues of vital importance on the American educational scene, he has produced, in addition to the widely publicized report previously mentioned, the following significant works: *Education and Liberty* (1953), *The Education of American Teachers* (1963), and *Shaping Educational Policy* (1964).

Dr. Conant traveled from state to state gathering material for his report on *The American High School Today*. After considering the unique nature of our educational system and discovering some alarming deficiencies he formulated twenty-one specific recommendations for improving the curriculum and organization of the secondary school. His highly rational judgments reflect careful thought and deserve the nationwide attention they are still receiving. As one reviewer of the report noted, "Dr. Conant's attitude is that of a peaceful reformer, but that attitude, supported by a battery of well-aimed facts, gives this book great power to improve American education."

RECOMMENDATIONS FOR IMPROVING PUBLIC SECONDARY EDUCATION*

Before presenting a number of specific recommendations addressed to school board members and school administrators, a few words of explanation may be in order. My recommendations are based on what I have observed. Almost without exception, I can point to one or more schools in which the recommended type of organization or practice can be found, not as an experiment but as something tried and tested over a period of years. Taken together, they outline the important characteristics of a satisfactory high school which is widely comprehensive, and the recommendations must be judged as a whole, for some taken separately would be almost impossible to put into effect.

Because I have been interested in determining the characteristics of a satisfactory comprehensive high school, this section of the report may appear too conservative for the taste of many readers. Yet it follows from the premises of my study that my recommendations would include only what I had found to be well-established features of at least one school. I have seen a number of interesting new departures, such as the use of television, which in my opinion have not yet developed to a point where they can be regarded as firmly established features of a comprehensive school. I hardly need emphasize the importance of experimentation and the desirability of innovation in all phases of education. It would be most unfortunate if the conservative recommendations in this section, necessarily presented in rather dogmatic form, should lead anyone to believe I was in favor of

*From *The American High School Today* (New York: Signet Books, 1964). Copyright © 1949 by James Bryant Conant and originally published by McGraw-Hill Company, Inc. Reprinted by permission of Dr. Conant, the publishers, and Educational Testing Service of Princeton, New Jersey.

freezing the development of the curriculum or the organization of a high school.

As a matter of fact, I can easily draw up a long list of urgent problems which can be solved only by schools trying out new ideas and then evaluating the new departures as carefully as possible. To mention only a few items, new areas of vocational work in electronics for boys appear to need exploration, and successful adventures in this field should be brought to the attention of all concerned with vocational education. I found widespread dissatisfaction with the course in world history. Furthermore, I found few teachers or administrators who were willing to endorse a four-year sequence in social studies because of their doubts as to the value of what would be taught the fourth year. Therefore, experimentation, evaluation, and discussion of the findings of social science teachers would seem to me to be high on the list of priorities in curriculum development. There is ferment in many areas of instruction: a new approach to physics is being rapidly developed; there are several new approaches to a four-year sequence of mathematics; foreign language teachers in some school systems are starting instruction in lower grades. If I had been engaged in passing judgment on the details of the content of courses, I think I should not have been able to assess any of these new developments. Time must tell which of them are successful. But one must rejoice at the evidence on all sides of a new spirit of examination of the high school curriculum. Undoubtedly new ideas about the organization of the school day and the allocation of time among various subjects should be tried out and tested as should the possibility of moving algebra as well as languages into the lower grades. Ten or even five years from now, at least some of my recommendations may need serious revision because of what has been demonstrated as successful practice. In short, there is no inconsistency between adapting the best from what has been well tried and tested and having an open mind about the outcome of experiment now planned or underway.

Some of the recommendations which follow would involve an increase in the budget and therefore require school board action;

they would have to be explained to the community to receive support. These recommendations are of particular importance to the school boards and to the citizens to whom each school board is responsible. Other recommendations concern the details of school organization and curriculum; in the first instance, these recommendations belong in the province of the school administrators. I assume that if a school is functioning satisfactorily the relationship between the school board, the superintendent, and the principal will be such that changes introduced by the principal and superintendent will be fully explained to the school board which, in turn, can explain them to the public.

I should like at this point to restate my judgment, based upon months of traveling and visits to schools in eighteen states as well as upon discussions with many, many school administrators, that three things are necessary to have a good high school, provided that it is of sufficient size: *first,* a school board composed of devoted, intelligent, understanding citizens who realize fully the *distinction between policy-making and administration; second,* a first-rate superintendent; and *third,* a good principal. I assume that the school board will leave the development of the curriculum to the administrative officers and the teaching staff but will be kept informed of all developments. Furthermore, the members will reserve the right to ask the superintendent, and through the superintendent the principal, searching questions about the details of the curriculum. They will not only reserve this right but exercise it from time to time.

One final word of warning addressed to school board members. Some of the recommendations listed below can be put into effect at the beginning of the school year without upsetting in any way the morale of the teaching staff. Other recommendations, however, can be effective only if a majority of the teachers are convinced of their wisdom. If an administrative officer feels that these recommendations should be introduced, his first task would be to examine the problems involved with committees of teachers and then persuade the teachers that the recommendations should be given a thorough trial. I have in mind particularly the controversial subject of ability grouping, any recommendations in

133

regard to marking or grading, and the requirements for admission to advanced courses.

Recommendation 1: The Counseling System

In a satisfactory school system the counseling should start in the elementary school, and there should be good articulation between the counseling in the junior and senior high schools if the pattern is 6-3-3 or between the counseling in the elementary school and the high school if the system is organized on an 8-4 basis. There should be one full-time counselor (or guidance officer) for every two hundred fifty to three hundred pupils in the high school. The counselors should have had experience as teachers but should be devoting virtually full time to the counseling work; they should be familiar with the use of tests and measurements of the aptitudes and achievements of pupils. The function of the counselor is not to supplant the parents but to supplement parental advice to a youngster. To this end, the counselor should be in close touch with the parent as well as the pupil. Through consultation, an attempt should be made each year to work out an elective program for the student which corresponds to the student's interest and ability as determined by tests of scholastic aptitude, the recorded achievement as measured by grades in courses, and by teachers' estimates. The counselors should be sympathetic to the elective programs which develop marketable skills; they should also understand the program for the slow readers and be ready to cooperate with the teachers of this group of students.

In guiding the more able students, the counselor should be on the lookout for the bright boy or girl whose high ability has been demonstrated by the results of aptitude tests given from time to time but whose achievement, as measured by grades in courses, has been low. The problem of motivating such pupils is a difficult one. I should like to emphasize at this point the importance of recognizing fully the role of adequate motivation in determining the eventual success of any student.

The framework in which the counselor operates depends upon

134

school policy. For example, the policy of the school in regard to the vocational programs should be such as to insure that these programs are *not* used as dumping grounds for those of low academic ability. Furthermore, it should be school policy that the counselor arrange a meaningful sequence of courses in the elective programs of all the pupils. In a comprehensive high school of the type I am considering, a meaningful sequence for a majority of the students would be a series of courses leading to the development of marketable skills (see Recommendation 7). In Recommendation 9 I set forth what I believe should be the minimum program of the academically talented. In most of the schools I have visited, there was relatively little pressure on the part of parents to have less-than-average students take difficult subjects. More often the counselors' main task was to persuade parents that their bright offspring should elect such subjects as eleventh- and twelfth-grade mathematics, physics, and foreign languages. On the other hand, I am familiar with a number of schools where the situation is just reversed.

My views about counseling and guidance are based not only on my observations in the fifty-five schools I visited, but also on a special report prepared for me by Dr. R. C. Lloyd, Special Assistant to the Superintendent of the Baltimore, Maryland, Public Schools. He visited a variety of schools and talked with many guidance officers in the course of his investigations.

Recommendation 2: *Individualized Programs*

It should be the policy of the school that every student has an individualized program; there would be no classification of students according to clearly defined and labeled programs or tracks such as "college-preparatory," "vocational," "commercial." In advising the student as to his elective program, the counselor will be guided by the minimum program recommended as a matter of school policy for the academically talented or by recommended sequences leading to the development of skills marketable on graduation. It will turn out that many students of similar ability and vocational interests will have almost identical programs, but

135

a student who has elected an academic sequence may shift to a vocational sequence and vice versa. Furthermore, with individualized programs, the students themselves do not feel that they are labeled according to the program they have chosen in the ninth or tenth grade. If flexibility is combined with a declaration of policy in regard to the programs for the academically talented and if a good guidance service is available, the academic inventory should show results as satisfactory as the results in a school which has a clear-cut academic or college-preparatory track.

A feeling of prestige is apt to be attached to those who are enrolled in an academic program if the school is rigidly divided into groups with different programs; and there will be pressure from ambitious parents to have their children, irrespective of ability, enrolled in the college preparatory track. Such pressures are difficult to resist and may lead many students to attempt advanced mathematics, physics, and foreign language courses which they cannot handle.

Recommendation 3: Required Programs for All

(a) *General Education.* The requirements for graduation for all students should be as follows:

Four years of English, three or four years of social studies — including two years of history (one of which should be American history) and a senior course in American problems or American government — one year of mathematics in the ninth grade (algebra or general mathematics), and at least one year of science in the ninth or tenth grade, which might well be biology or general physical science. By a year, I mean that a course is given five periods a week throughout the academic year or an equivalent amount of time. This academic program of general education involves nine or ten courses with homework to be taken in four years and occupies more than half the time of most students, whatever their elective programs.

(b) *The Elective Program.* The other requirement for graduation should be successful completion of at least seven more courses, not including physical education. *All students should be*

136

urged to include art and music in their elective programs. All students should be advised to have as the central core of their elective program significant sequences of courses, either those leading to the development of a marketable skill or those of an academic nature.

(c) *Standards for Pass and Failure.* This recommendation is directed to the principal of the high school and involves the kind of policy with which a school board should not be directly concerned. In order to assist the counselors in their work of guiding the students into programs which the students can handle effectively, the teachers of the advanced academic *elective* courses — foreign languages, mathematics, and science — should be urged to maintain high standards. They should be told not to hesitate to fail a student who does not meet the minimum level of performance they judge necessary for a mastery of the subject in question. In other words, the work in the academic elective courses should be judged on a standard of performance so high that students who do not have the ability to handle the subjects are discouraged from electing these courses and prevented from continuing in the sequence. On the other hand, for the *required* courses another standard should be applied. Since these courses are required of all, irrespective of ability, a student may be given a passing grade if he has worked to full capacity whether or not a certain level of achievement has been reached. A series of examinations in English composition (Recommendation 6) should insure the development of a minimum skill in composition; an eleventh grade test in arithmetic followed by a remedial twelfth-grade course is likewise to be recommended.

Recommendation 4: Ability Grouping

In the required subjects and those elected by students with a wide range of ability, the students should be grouped according to ability, subject by subject. For example, in English, American history, ninth-grade algebra, biology, and physical science, there should be at least three types of classes — one for the more able in the subject, another for the large group whose ability is about average, and another for the very slow readers who should be handled by special teachers. The middle group might be divided into two or three sections according to the students' abilities in the subject in question. This type of grouping is not to be confused with across-the-board grouping according to which a given student is placed in a particular section in *all* courses. Under the scheme here recommended, for example, a student may be in the top section in English but the middle section in history or ninth-grade algebra.

Ability grouping is a highly controversial subject among administrators and teachers. I have met competent teachers who argued vigorously for heterogeneous grouping in all classes — that is to say, they argued that students of widely different academic abilities and reading skills should be in the same class. Other teachers were equally certain that justice cannot be done to either the bright student or the slow reader if both receive instruction in the same class. Some of those who feel that heterogeneous grouping is a mistake advocate across-the-board grouping or tracking. Others advocate grouping the students according to their ability in the subject in question.

In those subjects elected by a relatively small fraction of the student body, such as advanced mathematics and twelfth-grade physics, something approaching ability grouping comes about as a consequence of the elective nature of these subjects. As a rule, few if any of the boys and girls in the bottom half of the class in terms of academic ability are bold enough to elect these courses. In some schools, the majority of the students in these courses come at least from the top 15 to 25 per cent. In a few schools the biology course was divided according to ability into two groups, and the teachers thought it would be much better if three groupings were available. To some degree, ability grouping in science courses may be a consequence of the proper labeling of different courses in the same subject. For example, a course labeled "biology" is more likely to be taken by the able and ambitious students than one labeled "life science," which will be taken by the less bright students.

Recommendation 5: *A Supplement to a High School Diploma*

The awarding of a diploma is evidence only that a student has (1) completed the required work in general education to the best of his ability, and (2) has finished satisfactorily a certain sequence of elective courses. In addition to the diploma, each student should be given a durable record of the courses studied in four years and the grades obtained. The existence of such a record should be well publicized so that employers ask for it rather than merely relying on a diploma when questioning an applicant for a job about his education. The record might be a card that could be carried in a wallet.

Recommendation 6: *English Composition*

The time devoted to English composition during the four years should occupy about half the total time devoted to the study of English. Each student should be required to write an average of one theme a week. Themes should be corrected by the teacher. In order that teachers of English have adequate time for handling these themes, no English teacher should be responsible for more than one hundred pupils.

To test the ability of each student in English composition, a schoolwide composition test should be given in every grade; in the ninth and eleventh grades, these composition tests should be graded not only by the teacher but by a committee of the entire school. Those students who do not obtain a grade on the eleventh-grade composition test commensurate with their ability as measured by an aptitude test should be required to take a special course in English composition in the twelfth grade.

In all the schools visited, at least three years of the study of English were required; in many schools, four. On the basis of conversations with teachers, I became convinced that half of this time should be devoted to English composition and that students, particularly those with academic ability, should be given ample opportunity through practice to develop their skill in English composition. English teachers were strongly of the opinion that, for

139

the best instruction, themes should be corrected by the regular teacher, who, in turn, should discuss them with the students. Obviously, adequate instruction in English composition requires that teachers not be overloaded. In one school I visited, the use of composition tests as recommended above has been found a highly satisfactory device for improving the work in composition.

Recommendation 7: Diversified Programs for the Development of Marketable Skills

Programs should be available for girls interested in developing skills in typing, stenography, the use of clerical machines, home economics, or a specialized branch of home economics which through further work in college might lead to the profession of dietitian. Distributive education should be available if the retail shops in the community can be persuaded to provide suitable openings. If the community is rural, vocational agriculture should be included. For boys, depending on the community, trade and industrial programs should be available. Half a day is required in the eleventh and twelfth grades for this vocational work. In each specialized trade, there should be an advisory committee composed of representatives of management and labor. Federal money is available for these programs.

The school administration should constantly assess the employment situation in those trades included in the vocational programs. When opportunities for employment in a given trade no longer exist within the community, the training program in that field should be dropped. The administration should be ready to introduce new vocational programs as opportunities open in the community or area. In some communities, advanced programs of a technical nature should be developed; these programs often involve more mathematics than is usually required for the building trades or auto mechanics programs.

As stated in Recommendation 3 (a), the students enrolled in programs which develop marketable skills should also be enrolled in English, social studies, and other courses required for graduation. Furthermore, efforts should be made to prevent isolation from the other students. Homerooms may be effective means to this end (see Recommendation 20).

The reader of this report who is not familiar with educational terminology must keep in mind that the word *vocational* has a special connotation when used by high school people. A vocational program is usually one supported by federal money flowing through the state agency in charge of vocational education and matched by state funds. The conditions under which this money can be spent are generally defined by the Smith-Hughes and George-Barden Acts and specifically defined by the state supervising agency. As indicated earlier in this report, states vary greatly in the rules which they have adopted for the expenditure of these federal funds. The federally supported vocational programs must involve fifteen hours a week in the shops in the eleventh and twelfth grades and also require one period of related subjects such as mechanical drawing and mathematics. Examples of vocational subjects included are building trades, auto mechanics, the training of tool and die mechanics, printing, electrical work, metal trades including welding, and agriculture. In some schools essentially the same amount of time is devoted to the vocational work, although no federal funds are involved.

Excellent examples of vocational programs were found in a number of schools. To give one example, those boys enrolled in a building trades course built a house which was sold before the completion of their work. The money was put into a revolving fund for the building of a house by the succeeding class. I was assured in several communities that those who did well in the building trades program could find employment at once as carpenters. In other schools where no building trades program was in existence, the reason was the absence of employment opportunities for carpenters. I mention this particular situation as illustrating how necessary it is to tie vocational programs to employment opportunities in each community.

The training of tool and die mechanics requires expensive and elaborate machine shops. I was surprised how frequently I encountered such shops. I was impressed by the obvious interest

141

of the students in shopwork. Programs for mechanics flourished in cities where the local trades were ready to employ those who had developed the skills requisite for a skilled workman fashioning tools and handling metals. I was told in several communities that the boys who had successfully completed such a program could at once obtain positions in local factories and gain a full year in an apprentice program. In some communities where there was a local junior college, high school graduates specializing in machine shop programs could study courses at the junior college level and, with the mastery of more applied mathematics, take the first step in becoming tool designers.

The line between the industrial arts program and the vocational shop program for boys is not an easy one to draw. One may say that the industrial arts program provides a survey of the different skilled trades involving the use of tools and the working of materials as diverse as leather, wood, and metal. In the schools in which there are strong vocational shop programs for boys, the industrial arts courses can be considered as preparatory or exploratory courses.

I observed that the presence of strong vocational work under the Smith-Hughes Act in a comprehensive high school provides somewhat the same stimulus to those in the industrial arts program as does the offering of a college-level course in the twelfth grade to all who have elected an academic program. The fact that able boys are in a position to anticipate by at least a year the regular work of apprenticeship in the skilled trades means that the others who are doing shopwork see high standards of excellence before them. It seemed to me that the whole atmosphere in the industrial arts shops was more professional in those schools which had strong vocational programs than it was in the schools which did not.

Where local opportunities permit, students in some of the vocational programs may obtain experience by working on jobs outside the school. This work experience program has been expanded in recent years. Its success, I was told, depends on the close relationship between the supervisor of the schoolwork and the employer. The work on the job must be related to the work in the school. I found a few cases in which there was some dissatisfaction with this arrangement on the part of the school authorities because of the time the students were away from school. But more often the principal as well as the students regretted that there were not more opportunities available for providing students with work experience.

Distributive education in some localities has been developed to a high degree. In this program work experience is provided for both boys and girls in retail shops in the community. The program is usually elected more heavily by girls than by boys. Instruction in the school is related to the work on the job. Success depends on the number of openings in local stores and the attitude of the employer. I found only one school in which the principal had decided against this program and refused to introduce it.

Recommendation 8: Special Consideration for the Very Slow Readers

Those in the ninth grade of the school who read at a level of the sixth grade or below should be given special consideration. These pupils should be instructed in English and the required social studies by special teachers who are interested in working with such students and who are sympathetic to their problems. Remedial reading should be part of the work, and special types of textbooks should be provided. The elective programs of these pupils should be directed toward simple vocational work, and they should be kept out of the regular vocational programs for boys, the distributive education program, and the regular commercial program for girls. These students should not be confused with mentally retarded students. The education of the mentally retarded is a special problem which in some states is also handled in the regular high school through special instruction and the use of special state funds.

In every school visited, a certain fraction of the entering class was composed of boys and girls whose reading ability was several grades below that of their classmates. For example, there might

143

be as many as 10 or 15 per cent of the students reading at the fourth-, fifth-, or sixth-grade level. These slow readers have great difficulty with the required courses in English and social studies. Common practice was to include a few of these slow readers in each of the regular classes in English and social studies and to trust the skill of the teacher to develop these students' capacities through individual attention. Many teachers frankly admitted this task was an almost hopeless undertaking. If one book is used for the entire class, the slow readers are hardly able to read the book. In about half the schools I visited, some special provisions were made for this group of students. In only a few schools, however, were the provisions commensurate with the difficulties of the task. Nevertheless, there seems to be an increasing interest in this challenging educational problem.

The improvement of reading ability is, of course, the paramount problem, and work with remedial reading must be provided. However, in the opinion of teachers involved, it is very difficult, even with the best of instruction, to raise the reading level of these students more than two grades. Only a few are able to reach the degree of efficiency that enables them to enter regular classes in English and social studies later in their high school course. Whether or not greater attention to reading difficulties in the lower grades would have improved this situation in the schools I visited, I am not prepared to say. But those who are well informed about the teaching of reading emphasize that the development of reading skill must be a continuous process throughout the school years.

The whole problem of the instruction in the first eight grades and the relation of the inadequacies in this area to the problems of the high school is a subject on which I have no basis to report.

Recommendation 9: The Programs of the Academically Talented

A policy in regard to the elective programs of academically talented boys and girls should be adopted by the school to serve as a guide to the counselors. In the type of school I am discussing the following program should be strongly recommended as a minimum:

Four years of mathematics, four years of one foreign language, three years of science, in addition to the required four years of English and three years of social studies; a total of eighteen courses with homework to be taken in four years. This program will require at least fifteen hours of homework each week.

Many academically talented pupils may wish to study a second foreign language or an additional course in social studies. Since such students are capable of handling twenty or more courses with homework, these additional academic courses may be added to the recommended minimum program. If the school is organized on a seven- or eight-period day (Recommendation 12), at least one additional course without homework (for example, art or music) may also be scheduled each year.

If as school policy a minimum academic program including both mathematics and a foreign language is recommended to the academically talented pupils and their parents, the counselors will have the problem of identifying as early as possible the members of the group. It may well be that, in the next lower 10 or 20 per cent of the boys and girls in terms of scholastic aptitude on a national basis, there are a number who ought to be guided into similar but less rigorous programs.

In some schools sequential courses in music theory and composition are offered which involve a considerable amount of homework. These are not the usual courses in music, however, which I encountered in my visits. Students with special aptitude for music might well be advised to elect such a sequence as an *addition* to the minimum program instead of a second foreign language. I do know, however, experienced public school administrators who would argue for the *substitution* of this sequence or a second language for twelfth-grade mathematics and twelfth-grade science in the case of girls. In this connection, I should like to point out that the above recommendation is in no way the equivalent of establishing a rigid academic track or labeled program. Since the recommendation is intended only as a guide to counselors, its adoption in no way prevents the counselor from advising exceptional programs in exceptional cases.

The essence of the recommendation is that students who have the ability to handle effectively both mathematics and a foreign language (by definition, the "academically talented") should be urged to study both subjects in grades nine through twelve.

On a national basis, the group we are referring to as the "academically talented" constitutes about 15 per cent of the high school population. The percentage may be smaller or larger in particular schools, depending on the chance distribution of academic talent in a given year. National norms for aptitude tests will provide a rough guide as to what fraction of a given class in a school has academic ability corresponding approximately to that of the upper 15 per cent on a national basis. In giving advice to an individual student, the counselor should be guided by aptitude and achievement tests and by the success of the pupil each year as measured by his grades in the academic courses. In advising parents as to what courses are too difficult for their children, the counselor should likewise be guided by test data and by grades in courses. The recommended program is intended only for those students who have ability in *both* mathematics and foreign languages. If the counselor becomes convinced that a student is having difficulty with one or the other subject, he should then decide the student in question is not academically talented. For students of considerable academic ability in one field only, special programs should be devised. *If the scholastic aptitude test scores and lower grade records indicate that a student is in the upper 15 per cent on a national basis, the presumption should be that the recommended minimum academic program can be carried.*

In some schools, the main problem stems from the tendency of some academically talented pupils either to elect an easy program or to enroll in a vocational sequence to prepare for an immediate job. In other schools, the reverse situation is found: the main problem the counselor faces is persuading the overambitious parent of a child with little academic ability that eleventh- and twelfth-grade mathematics, physics, and foreign languages are too difficult.

The question might be raised as to why a school board should adopt the policy I have recommended. What are the arguments in favor of an academically talented student's electing a wide program of at least eighteen courses with homework? To my mind the most compelling argument is that the student in question has potentialities shared with only a relatively few contemporaries, probably not more than 15 per cent of his age group. If these potentialities are not developed as far as possible during the school years, they may never be fully developed. From the point of view of the individual, failure to develop talent in school may be the equivalent of locking many doors. For example, without mathematics and science in high school, it would be difficult later to enter an engineering school, to take a premedical course in college, and impossible to begin a scientific career in a university. If something approaching mastery of a foreign language is not attained before graduation from high school, it may never be attained.

The loss to the individual from not electing a suitable program in high school is clear. So too is the loss to the nation. From the 15 per cent of the youth who are academically talented will come the future professional men and women. These people ought to have as wide and solid an education as possible. It is in the national interest to have them develop their capacities to the full and start this development as early as possible. My recommended program differs from many I have seen in that it is not a specialized program in either mathematics and science or in foreign languages. If a student completes this wide program in high school, his range of choice of college majors is far greater than if he had specialized earlier.

Concerning the Preparation for College. Some might argue for my recommendation by saying that the program outlined is the proper college-preparatory program. But those who argue this way lay themselves open to serious counterarguments. I have carefully avoided the use of the phrase "college-preparatory." To my mind, the academically talented youth ought to elect a full program of stiff courses in high school and ought to go to college. But the reasons for the first imperative are only distantly related to those that support the second. The fact of the matter is that today in

147

the United States it is impossible to relate the details of a high school course of study to the subsequent work of a student in a college or university, unless the collegiate work is defined in very specific terms. Requirements for admission to an undergraduate engineering college can be clearly stated in terms of the knowledge of mathematics and science demanded in the freshman professional courses. But it would be out of the question for all colleges and universities to require a similar high school preparation in mathematics and science. There is such a wide variety of possible courses of study open to undergraduates in our colleges and universities that the concept of specific preparation for college work is almost without meaning. Even in institutions with a highly selective admission policy, it is possible for a very bright boy to complete with honors his college course although he enters with little knowledge of science, mathematics, or a foreign language. If he majors in history or English literature, for example, the only high school courses which can be regarded as direct preparation for college are those in English and social studies. To be sure, such a young man will be forever handicapped by the fact that his potentialities were not fully developed in the high school years, but so far as his work in college is concerned, it could be maintained he had been "prepared."

Uniform standards for admission to college are impossible in the United States for a number of reasons. Even the degree of uniformity existing among the colleges that used the College Entrance Examination system of fifty years ago cannot be re-established. High school people naturally resist any attempt on the part of college admission officers to prescribe the content of courses or even the pattern of courses. And it must be remembered that from some communities many boys and girls of only average academic ability are propelled by social pressures toward a four-year college. For better or worse, in many sections of the country this type of student must be given at least an opportunity to try college work. In some states practically the only requirement for admission to the state-supported institutions of higher learning is the possession of a high school diploma. Private colleges exist that have no higher requirements for admission and in which

148

those with little preparation and only a modicum of ability can obtain a bachelor's degree. In a word, the idea is completely illusory that the high school curriculum might be stiffened by agreement as to entrance requirements on the part of colleges and universities.

The Misinterpretation of the Results of Tests. The mounting numbers of potential college candidates have led to the requirements by an increasing number of collegiate institutions that candidates for admission take certain of the tests administered by the College Entrance Examination Board. These tests are quite different from the subject-matter examinations of even twenty-five years ago. Two types of objective test are used: one is aimed at measuring the student's aptitudes for scholastic work; the other, his achievement in certain subjects. Since there is considerable misunderstanding among citizens about the tests that are now given on a national scale, a few words on this subject may not be out of order. In the first place, one type of test (the SCAT, for example), is designed to measure aptitude. The distribution of the scores on such a test clearly does not indicate the quality of the teaching in a particular school. If one school has a mean score for the graduating class far higher than another, this differential does *not* mean that the first school is a better school than the other. If one thinks of these aptitude tests as measuring the brightness or dullness of the pupils, and the achievement tests as measuring how much pupils have learned, he is on fairly safe ground.

Scholarships are being awarded nationally on the basis of uniform tests. Since only the very top students in terms of aptitude can obtain high scores on these tests, a comparison of the success or failure of these pupils from different schools is in no way a valid comparison of the total education provided by the schools. To a large degree, it is a fortunate accident if a school has enrolled in its graduating class a few students with the very high aptitude necessary to do well in these tests. The school can indeed be proud if a student wins one of these awards, and the community should pay at least as much tribute to academic as to athletic talent. Obviously the school has directed the highly gifted student into a profitable course of study. No evidence is available from the outcomes of these national scholarship tests, however, as to what sort of program the majority of the academically talented elected, nor as to how successful, in general, are the teachers of the academic subjects.

Recommendation 10: Highly Gifted Pupils

For the highly gifted pupils some type of special arrangement should be made. These pupils of high ability, who constitute on a national basis about 3 per cent of the student population, may well be too few in number in some schools to warrant giving them instruction in a special class. In this case, a special guidance officer should be assigned to the group as a tutor and should keep in close touch with these students throughout their four years of senior high schoolwork. The tutor should see to it that these students are challenged not only by course work but by the development of their special interests as well. The identification of the highly gifted might well start in the seventh or eighth grade or earlier.

If enough students are available to provide a special class, these students should take in the twelfth grade one or more courses which are part of the Advanced Placement Program. This program has been developed in recent years by schools and colleges working cooperatively under the aegis of the College Entrance Examination Board. Under the program a student in the twelfth grade may take such courses as college mathematics, college English, or college history and, after passing suitable examinations, may be given college credit for the courses and also sophomore standing in these subjects. This program should be adopted not only because of the benefits which accrue to the students involved, but because it may well have a good influence on students of somewhat less ability by raising the tone of the whole academic program. Information about this program may be obtained by writing to the Director of the Advanced Placement Program, College Entrance Examination Board, 475 Riverside Drive, New York, New York 10027.

Recommendation 11: The Academic Inventory

In order to provide meaningful statistics about the education of the academically talented, a school board through the superintendent should ask the principal each year to provide an academic inventory. As explained earlier, the academic inventory summarizes the programs of the academically talented students in the senior class without giving their names. In a school in which the range of intellectual ability corresponds to the national norm, 15 per cent of the students would be included in this inventory. In other schools the percentage may vary. The academic inventory should include information as to what per cent of the academically talented boys and girls went on to a two-year college, a four-year college, or a university. This academic inventory of the graduating class might well be published each year.

It should be pointed out that, while the academic inventory is at first sight a measure of the effectiveness of the counseling service, such is often not the case. In the first place, the policy of the school, as determined by the school board, superintendent, and principal, may slight foreign languages or may even allow English and social studies to be neglected if the boys or girls (usually the boys) are keen on taking the maximum amount of mathematics and science. Furthermore, the elective programs of the pupils always represent the resultant of the counselors' advice and the pupils' and parents' interests and desires. I might note here that the program I recommended earlier for the academically talented is an elective program. If it were required, there would be no need for an academic inventory.

Recommendation 12: Organization of the School Day

The school day should be so organized that there are at least six periods in addition to the required physical education and driver education which in many states occupy at least a period each day. A seven- or eight-period day may be organized with periods as short as forty-five minutes. Under such an organiza-

151

tion, laboratory periods as well as industrial arts courses should involve double periods.

The flexibility provided by such an arrangement is to be contrasted with the rigidity of that of the six-period day. With a six-period day, one period of which is taken up by physical education, the academically talented student cannot elect the wide academic program recommended above and at the same time elect art, music, and practical courses. The importance of this recommendation can hardly be overemphasized in connection with the education of academically talented students.

Whether the school is organized into a six-, seven-, or eight-period day I found to be a matter of great importance as well as of controversy among school administrators. A number of administrators with whom I talked felt that a six-period day places the elective programs in a strait jacket. Therefore, these administrators have preferred a seven- or eight-period day with periods sometimes running as short as forty minutes. On the other hand, I met administrators who felt strongly that periods of nearly a full hour are essential and who urged that the school day be lengthened to make a seven-period day possible. In some places the school day is far too short.

Recommendation 13: Prerequisites for Advanced Academic Courses

Standards in advanced courses should be such that those who enroll in each successive course of a sequence have demonstrated the ability required to handle that course. To this end, admission to eleventh-grade mathematics should depend upon the student's receiving at least a C in tenth-grade mathematics, and for admission to twelfth-grade mathematics at least a C should be required in the eleventh-grade course. Similarly, if the physics course is given in the twelfth-grade, it should be open only to those students who have studied three years of mathematics and obtained a grade of at least C in each course. Also, in the foreign language sequence, a grade of C should be required for entry into the second-year course.

152

Recommendation 14: Students Should Not be Given a Rank in Class According to Their Grades in All Subjects

In many schools, it is customary to designate a rank in class on graduation as determined by the marks received; the position of valedictorian is usually held by the student whose rank is number one. The ranking is calculated by averaging the grades in all subjects taken during the four years. I have found that in many schools the desire to rank high has led bright students to elect easy courses in order to obtain high grades. This fact emerges clearly from an examination of many programs sent to us by schools as part of their academic inventories. The use by some colleges and universities of rank in class as the basis of their admission policies has increased this tendency of bright boys and girls to avoid stiff programs. Following the practice in at least one school visited, I strongly recommend that the graduating class not be ranked on the basis of grades obtained in ALL subjects and that a valedictorian not be named on this basis. Admission officers in colleges and universities should be urged to examine the transcript of a student's entire record rather than to rely on the misleading rank in class.

Recommendation 15: Academic Honors List

At the end of each marking period, a list should be published of the students who had elected courses recommended for the academically talented and had made an average grade of B. On graduation a notation might be made on the diploma if a student had placed on the academic honors list in all four years.

In order to provide an incentive for the election of a meaningful nonacademic sequence, those students whose achievement was outstanding in the courses that are usually labeled "commercial" or "vocational" should receive some special recognition. By such devices I believe the ambitions of students in various elective programs can be stimulated as much as by the granting of separate types of diploma.

153

Recommendation 16: Developmental Reading Program

A school should have the equipment for a developmental reading program. The program should be available on a voluntary basis for all the pupils in the school. The counselors and teachers of English should be asked to view this program sympathetically and to urge students to take advantage of the opportunity to increase reading speed and comprehension.

Developmental reading is not the remedial reading program designed for slow readers. Rather, it is a voluntary instructional program intended primarily to do three things: to help students acquire skill in different sorts of reading, from close and detailed reading to scanning; to increase reading speed; and to improve comprehension of the material read. Using equipment in a special room, students get a great deal of practice in reading and are able to test their speed. By appropriate tests, teachers check their comprehension.

Developmental reading programs have strong appeal for able students who understand the need for reading skills in subsequent college and university work. Teachers with whom I talked said that the ability of students in developmental reading classes had improved markedly. These teachers also insisted that enrollment in developmental reading should be on a voluntary basis since there seems to be a decided relationship between desire to improve and actual results.

Recommendation 17: Summer School

The school board should operate a tuition-free summer school in which courses are available not only for students who have to repeat a subject, but also for the bright and ambitious students who wish to use the summer to broaden the scope of their elective programs.

Summer sessions for bright students have increased in number during recent years. The sessions are usually six weeks long and in a few instances have become very popular among the brighter students. The importance of this development for the academically talented student is obvious. It is possible for such a student to use summer session to take either a practical course such as typing or an academic subject such as history. By the use of several summer sessions, a wider program can be elected than would otherwise be possible. Such is the case especially for students heavily engaged in extracurricular activities. The development of a summer session seems to me preferable to the lengthening of the school year.

Recommendation 18: Foreign Languages

The school board should be ready to offer a third and fourth year of a foreign language, no matter how few students enroll. The guidance officers should urge the completion of a four-year sequence of one foreign language if the student demonstrates ability in handling foreign languages. On the other hand, students who have real difficulty handling the first year of a language should be advised against continuing with the subject (Recommendation 13). The main purpose of studying a foreign language is to obtain something approaching a mastery of that language. And by a mastery is surely meant the ability to read the literature published in the language and, in the case of a modern language, to converse with considerable fluency and accuracy with an inhabitant of the country in question.

I have met no teachers of foreign language who felt that anything approaching mastery could be obtained by the study of a foreign language for only two years in high school, nor have the students felt that two years of study had given them any real working knowledge of the language. Four years of study, on the other hand, will yield dividends for those capable of handling foreign languages. This is the recommendation of the foreign language panel of the NEA Conference on the Identification and Education of the Academically Talented held in Washington in February, 1958.

Almost without exception, I found a deplorable state of affairs in regard to foreign languages. Too many students with limited ability were studying a foreign language for two years; too few able students were studying one language long enough. There appears to be a widespread feeling in the United States that there is considerable merit in a student's studying a language for two years — and only two years — in a high school.

Yet the foreign language teachers with whom I talked were almost unanimous in agreeing that two years were quite insufficient and that a very small residue, if any, was left in the student's mind after such an exposure. Even when a student's program included three or four years of a foreign language, it was very common to find that these three or four years were divided between the study of *two different* foreign languages.

Foreign language teachers complained of this situation, as did the bright students I interviewed when I met with the student leaders. Time and again I asked this question: "Why didn't you take three years of one language?" A frequent answer was: "Well, in their catalogues colleges only ask for two years." Or: "I wanted to take a third year, but there were only six or ten of us, and they will not give a third-year course unless there is a full class of at least twenty." I have found that students in general are interested in acquiring a real knowledge of a modern language and in many cases have felt frustrated by the failure of school authorities to offer a third and fourth year. Occasionally, I found a third year offered, but the students were placed in the same class-room with the second-year students. The teacher always reported that such an arrangement was highly unsatisfactory.

It is hardly necessary to argue the importance of a foreign language in a world which has been so constricted by the invention of the airplane. Since, however, I have met some resistance among school people to my recommendation that all the academically talented youth should study four years of one foreign language, it may be well to remind the reader of the arguments in favor of this recommendation.

In the first place, unless a person has acquired something approaching mastery of one foreign language, he has missed an educational experience of the first importance. Such people never know what it means to *know* another language. They either think

156

that acquiring mastery is an impossible hurdle to surmount, or else they believe that the ability to understand and speak a few words, perhaps enough to order a meal in a hotel, is a working knowledge. In short, a door is closed to them forever.

The second argument is the one usually put forward by foreign language teachers: that a real knowledge of a foreign language makes available a new approach to human problems. By reading the literature of another culture, one understands not only something of the culture, but realizes that ideas which English-speaking people accept as a matter of course may never have been formulated in a comparable way in another language and vice versa. It is particularly important for applied scientists to realize that, while mathematics is an international language, there are many words which are almost untranslatable from one language to another because the concepts they convey are somewhat alien. For example, I discovered in translating into German a book of mine on education with the aid of a bilingual collaborator that there is no German equivalent of "equality of opportunity."

The third and fourth arguments are practical ones and not unrelated to the highly constricted and deeply divided world in which we live. It is agreed by foreign language teachers that a person who has mastered one foreign language is in a position to learn a second with far greater ease than would otherwise be the case. This fact is true even if the second language is unrelated to the first. Therefore, a student who enters college with a considerable degree of mastery of one foreign language is able to pick up a second much more rapidly than he could otherwise. For example, one finds people in United States missions overseas who have the greatest difficulty learning the language of the country because they have never learned any foreign language.

Finally, it seems quite clear that a small fraction of our youth have those special talents which are needed for making rapid progress in the study of a foreign language. Unless such youth have an opportunity to find out that they are indeed highly gifted in this respect, their talents will never be developed. It is usually too late for such talents to be discovered and developed in the college years. Just as in the mathematics sequence in high school a few boys and girls are always discovered who are specially gifted in mathematics, so too if the foreign language sequence were as well developed as mathematics and science in our schools, those with equivalent linguistic talent would be discovered. One hardly need argue that such boys and girls will find fruitful and rewarding careers in the modern world. That the nation badly needs young people who can quickly master a foreign language for missions overseas, both official and private, is evident to all who read the daily news. The grim competition with the Soviet Union in newly developing countries turns quite as much on an adequate supply of competent linguists as on our ability to send competent engineers and businessmen to these nations.

One further word on the study of foreign languages. The movement is growing in the United States, sponsored by the leaders among the foreign language teachers, to start the instruction of the foreign languages in the lower grades. This instruction is to be given by teachers who speak the language in question fluently and with an acceptable accent. Speaking knowledge is developed before reading knowledge and without emphasis on grammar.

I do not venture to suggest the best method of teaching a foreign language. There is no doubt that very considerable progress has been made in developing new methods. Furthermore, there can be no question that children learn foreign languages more readily when they are young. Therefore, one can watch with interest the new developments which have started in a number of communities and which, it is hoped, will result in a considerable proportion of the eighth-grade students having a speaking knowledge and some degree of reading knowledge of a modern foreign language.

Thus far, I have seen only one school in which the transition from the lower grades to the high school level has been satisfactorily accomplished. That there are problems here, most of the experts in the field agree. And it is the final outcome with which a citizen must be concerned. In short, the question is whether a boy or girl ends his or her school years with something approaching a mastery of a foreign language.

It would be a great mistake if a school board put off making the necessary changes in the present high school offering with the excuse that foreign language instruction was to be developed in the grades. There is a time lag in education that must always be kept in mind. Development of foreign language instruction in the grades will not produce results for nine to fourteen years. This interval is too great. On the other hand, if a given high school adds a third and fourth year of a foreign language now, results will be evident in five or six years as college graduates take their place in national life as professional men and women.

Recommendation 19: Science Courses

All students should obtain some understanding of the nature of science and the scientific approach by a required course in physical science or biology. This course should be given in at least three sections grouped by ability (Recommendation 4).

To accommodate students who are interested in science but do not have the required mathematical ability, two types of chemistry courses should be offered. For entry into one, at least a C in algebra and tenth-grade mathematics should be required. The other course should be designed for pupils with less mathematical ability. The standards even in this second course, however, should be such that those with less than average ability (assuming a distribution of ability according to the national norm) will have difficulty passing the course.

In addition to the physics course given in the twelfth grade with mathematics as a prerequisite (Recommendation 13) another course in physics should be offered with some such designation as "practical physics." The standards in this second course should be such that students with less than average ability have difficulty passing the course.

Recommendation 20: Homerooms

For the purpose of developing an understanding between students of different levels of academic ability and vocational goals, homerooms should be organized in such a way as to make them significant social units in the school. To this end, students should be kept together in one homeroom for the entire senior high school course (three or four years), and care should be taken to have each homeroom a cross section of the school in terms of ability and vocational interest. The teachers in charge of the homerooms should be persuaded by the administration that their work as homeroom teachers is important. Sufficient time should be allotted to the homeroom so that students may use this period to develop a sense of community interest and to have practice in a small way in representative government. The homerooms should elect one or two representatives to the student council, and these representatives should report back after each meeting of the council. They should listen to the opinions of their constituents and be guided by their opinions in voting on matters before the student council. To be effective, the student council should be treated sympathetically by the school administrators so that there will be some important questions each year with which the student council can be concerned and which, in turn, can be presented to the homerooms by the representatives.

One of the highly important objectives of the comprehensive high school is the development of mutual respect and understanding between students with different abilities and different vocational interests. Indeed, in one school which I visited, the superintendent stated that one of his principal aims was to develop an attitude between the future manager of a factory and the future labor leader which would result in mutual respect and understanding. Such a strong democratic spirit, he said, was characteristic of his city. From my brief examination of the situation, I concluded he was right about the city and that his school was accomplishing the aim he had in mind.

Much as I believe in the importance of this aspect of public education, I should be quite unrealistic if I did not point out that in many communities there are blocks to the usefulness of the comprehensive high school as an instrument for developing a spirit of understanding between different groups. A school can make little progress against social pressures in a heavily polarized community.

Recommendation 21: Twelfth-grade Social Studies

In the twelfth grade a course on American problems or American government should be required. This course should include as much material on economics as the students can effectively handle at this point in their development. Each class in this course should be a cross section of the school: the class should be heterogeneously grouped. Teachers should encourage all students to participate in discussions. This course should develop not only an understanding of the American form of government and of the economic basis of our free society, but also mutual respect and understanding between different types of students. Current topics should be included; free discussion of controversial issues should be encouraged. This approach is one significant way in which our schools distinguish themselves from those in totalitarian nations. This course, as well as well-organized homerooms and certain student activities, can contribute a great deal to the development of future citizens of our democracy who will be intelligent voters, stand firm under trying national conditions, and not be beguiled by the oratory of those who appeal to special interests.

CONFUCIUS

CONFUCIUS (551-479 B. C.). China's most famous teacher was also a philosopher and a political theorist whose ideas have profoundly influenced all of eastern Asia. He taught his disciples a way of life but had no intention of being the founder of a great religion. Believing that his teaching had been ineffectual, he would today be astounded to find that he has been venerated in the East since his death and that his pronouncements are thought to embody infallible truth.

Kung Fu Tse, the Grand Master better known in the West by the Latinized name of Confucius, through his teachings and exemplary moral conduct effected a spiritual regeneration among the people of China. For some fourteen years he wandered throughout China, teaching poetry, history, music, and acceptance of traditional values — learning, wisdom, moral perfection, and correct deportment. As a high official he used his power to bring about reform and to punish evil-doers, even when they were mandarins.

As a scholar Confucius wrote little. His teachings were recalled and transcribed haphazardly by his disciples. The precepts that make up the following selection, "The Great Learning," are believed to be representative of his views on education. They are taken from James Legge's *The Texts of Confucianism.* The order has been changed and slight changes have been made in the wording and punctuation.

THE GREAT LEARNING*

A child should be obedient at home, modest away from home, attentive, faithful, benevolent, and interested in poetry and music.

A son should study the wishes of his father so long as his father is alive; after his father dies, the son should study his life and respect his memory.

*From *The Life and Teachings of Confucius,* by James Legge (London: N. Trübner and Company, 1867).

162

Mere study without thought is useless, but thought without study is dangerous.

A scholar's mind should be set on the search for truth; he should not be ashamed of his plain clothing or of his scant supply of food.

As long as a child's parents are alive, he should not desert them. If through necessity he must leave them, he should let them know where he is and be prepared to come to them in time of need.

On being asked, "What is wisdom?," the master replied, "To promote right thoughts and feelings among men; to honor the spirits of the dead.

"If my life could be lengthened out by a few years," the master said, "I would devote at least fifty years to the study of the Book of Changes."

The master used to teach five things: culture, ethics, good deportment, piety, and faithfulness.

Study as though you could never learn enough and as though you could never learn what is needed for good conduct in this life.

"Being of lowly birth," said the master, "I learned many trades when I was young, but there was nothing praiseworthy about that. The superior person may excel in one thing only, not in many things."

The highest class of men are those who are born wise; the next those who become wise by study; the next are those who have limited natural ability, yet learn much.

"My children," said the master once to his students, "Why do you not study the Book of Poetry? It would stimulate your mind, encourage introspection, teach you to love others and treat them with forbearance."

If a man fails to teach the members of his own family to be obedient and loyal to their head, how can he teach a nation to be united, obedient, and loyal?

Confucius said, "I won't teach a man who has no desire to learn, nor will I explain anything to a man who has no desire to seek his own explanation. And if I explain one-fourth of

163

something to a man, I won't bother to try to teach him again unless he reflects on what I have told him and tries to think out the implications in the other three-fourths."

Wake yourself up with poetry, build your character on *li* (moral discipline), and round out your education with music.

Knowing what you know and what you don't know is the mark of the sage.

Men are not too different at birth, but through their conduct they gradually set themselves apart from each other.

When you see a good man, imitate his example; when you see a bad man, ask yourself whether you share his faults.

A gentleman is ashamed for his words to be better than his deeds.

The kind of scholarship which stresses remembering things in order to be able to answer questions about them does not produce a good teacher.

What the Great Learning teaches is this: To illustrate illustrious virtue, to regenerate the people, and to rest in the highest excellence. The point of rest determines the object of pursuit, and determination of the object of pursuit leads to the attainment of perfect calm. That calm will be followed by repose marked by careful deliberation, and that deliberation will be followed by the attainment of the desired goal.

To know what is first and what is last will bring the scholar close to what is taught in the Great Learning.

From the emperor down to the mass of the people, all must consider the cultivation of the person the root of all else.

What heaven has conferred is called *Nature;* whatever accords with this nature is called *The Path of Duty;* the regulation of this path is called *Instruction.*

If a man keeps cultivating his old knowledge and adding to it, he is fit to be a teacher.

The superior man is broad-minded and unprejudiced. The mean man is biased and narrow.

A good man considers what is just, a bad man what is rewarding.

Perfect virtue consists in keeping to the Golden Mean. Whoever offends Heaven has no one to whom he can pray.

It is only the wisest and the most foolish who never change their opinions.

The master possessed great dignity, yet was gentle. He was majestic but did not inspire fear. He was gentlemanly but always at ease.

A man who is fond of learning is not a glutton or a lazy person. He is earnest and sincere in whatever he says or does. He seeks the company of good men and profits thereby.

At fifteen my whole mind was on study. At thirty I was able to stand on my own two feet. At forty I ceased to have doubts. At fifty I understand the will of heaven. At sixty I responded to higher instincts. At seventy my better nature ruled me altogether.

"There are three things about the superior man that have always eluded me," said Confucius. "The true man worries about nothing, the wise man is perplexed by nothing, and the brave man is afraid of nothing." Tse-Kung said, "But master, you are such a man." Confucius replied, "I am not so presumptuous as to assume that I am a true man, but I admit that I have tried to do my best to teach others. . . . I am afraid that I may fail to improve my character, that I may neglect my studies, that I may fail to advance when the right course is obvious to me, or that I may fail to correct myself when I see my mistake."

Tse-Kung once asked, "Is there one word that would serve as the guiding principle throughout life?" Confucius answered, "Perhaps that word is *shu* (altruism). Do not do unto others what you would not have others do unto you."

RENE DESCARTES

RENE DESCARTES (1596-1650). If the Age of Reason had a precise starting point it was the publication of the *Discourse on Method* (1637), in which René Descartes first elaborated the rational method that dominated European thought for the next century and a half. His revolt against scholasticism as it was reflected in the schools of his day was wholly in keeping with the Renaissance tradition, but the word "method," enhanced by the new philosophical insights set down in his treatise, became the motto of the age that was dawning.

The greatest of the French thinkers revealed his genius while still a child. Born at La Haye in Touraine on March 31, 1596, he was the third child of an affectionate father who referred to him as "my little philosopher" even before he began his formal schooling at the Jesuit college of La Fleche. Though he studied diligently, even to the point of undermining his health, he soon became thoroughly disillusioned with the scholastic method of instruction. Further study at Poitiers, a period of residence in Paris, and military service failed to modify his determination to "gain knowledge only from himself and the great book of the world."

It was in Germany that there came to him, on November 10, 1619, the idea which was the starting point of his whole system of thought: the idea "I think, therefore I exist," which clarified this purpose and showed him that the mathematical method of discovery might be applied to the whole field of knowledge. This idea, reinforced by three dreams, brought to a halt the philosophical doubt with which he had resolved to regard everything that he could conceivably doubt.

Descartes pursued his travels, investigations, and meditations until 1629, when he settled in Holland and began to articulate his ideas into a system. He was first of all a mathematician, and his contribution to intellectual history lay in applying the deductive method of mathematics to the physical world. Rejecting all ties to authority and tradition, he provided a theoretical structure for experiment and discovery, and he tried to extend man's knowledge of the physical world by interpreting the laws of nature as evidence of an all-pervading rationality. Though his life-long hope that his system would be incorporated in the curriculum of his old Jesuit school was never realized, as founder of the rational method of science he deserves to be called the first truly modern thinker. The method described in his famous four steps (intuition, analysis, synthesis, and review) is essentially that of the modern scientist.

THE RATIONAL METHOD*

I was then in Germany, to which country I had been attracted by the wars which have not yet been brought to a termination; and as I was returning to the army from the coronation of the Emperor, the setting in of winter arrested me in a locality where, as I found no society to interest me, and was besides fortunately undisturbed by any cares or passions, I remained the whole day in seclusion, with full opportunity to occupy my attention with my own thoughts. Of these one of the very first that occurred to me was, that there is seldom so much perfection in works composed of many separate parts, upon which different hands have been employed, as in those completed by a single master. Thus it is observable that the buildings which a single architect has planned and executed, are generally more elegant and commodious than those which several have attempted to improve, by making old walls serve for purposes for which they were not originally built. Thus also, those ancient cities which, from being at first only villages, have become, in course of time, large towns, are usually but ill laid out compared with the regularly constructed towns which a professional architect has freely planned on an open plain; so that although the several buildings of the former may often equal or surpass in beauty those of the latter, yet when one observes their indiscriminate juxtaposition, there a large one and here a small, and the consequent crookedness and irregularity of the streets, one is disposed to allege that chance rather than any human will guided by reason, must have led to such an arrangement. And if we consider that nevertheless there have been at all times certain officers whose duty it was to see that private buildings contributed to public ornament, the difficulty

*From *Discourse on Method,* reprinted in the Harvard Classics. Peter Eckler's translation of Part II has been revised by the editor.

of reaching high perfection with but the material of others to operate on, will be readily acknowledged. In the same way I fancied that those nations which, starting from a semi-barbarous state and advancing to civilisation by slow degrees, have had their laws successively determined, and, as it were, forced upon them simply by experience of the hurtfulness of particular crimes and disputes, would by this process come to be possessed of less perfect institutions than those which, from the commencement of their association as communities, have followed the appointments of some wise legislator. It is thus quite certain that the constitution of the true religion, the ordinances of which are derived from God, must be incomparably superior to that of every other. And, to speak of human affairs, I believe that the past pre-eminence of Sparta was due not to the goodness of each of its laws in particular, for many of these were very strange, and even opposed to good morals, but to the circumstance that, originated by a single individual, they all tended to a single end. In the same way I thought that the sciences contained in books, (such of them at least as are made up of probable reasonings, without demonstrations,) composed as they are of the opinions of many different individuals massed together, are farther removed from truth than the simple inferences which a man of good sense using his natural and unprejudiced judgment draws respecting the matters of his experience. And because we have all to pass through a state of infancy to manhood, and have been of necessity, for a length of time, governed by our desires and preceptors, (whose dictates were frequently conflicting, while neither perhaps always counselled us for the best,) I farther concluded that it is almost impossible that our judgments can be so correct or solid as they would have been, had our reason been mature from the moment of our birth, and had we always been guided by it alone.

It is true, however, that it is not customary to pull down all the houses of a town with the single design of rebuilding them differently, and thereby rendering the streets more handsome; but it often happens that a private individual takes down his own with the view of erecting it anew, and that people are even sometimes constrained to this when their houses are in danger of falling from age, or when the foundations are insecure. With this before me by way of example, I was persuaded that it would indeed be preposterous for a private individual to think of reforming a state by fundamentally changing it throughout, and overturning it in order to set it up amended; and the same I thought was true of any similar project for reforming the body of the sciences, or the order of teaching them established in the schools: but as for the opinions which up to that time I had embraced, I thought that I could not do better than resolve at once to sweep them wholly away, that I might afterwards be in a position to admit either others more correct, or even perhaps the same when they had undergone the scrutiny of reason. I firmly believed that in this way I should much better succeed in the conduct of my life, than if I built only upon old foundations, and leant upon principles which in my youth, I had taken upon trust. For although I recognised various difficulties in this understanding, these were not, however, without remedy, nor once to be compared with such as attend the slightest reformation in public affairs. Large bodies, if once overthrown, are with great difficulty set up again, or even kept erect when once seriously shaken, and the fall of such is always disastrous. Then if there are any imperfections in the constitutions of states, (and that many such exist the diversity of constitutions is alone sufficient to assure us,) custom has without doubt materially smoothed their inconveniencies, and has even managed to steer altogether clear of, or insensibly corrected a number which sagacity could not have provided against with equal effect; and, in fine, the defects are almost always more tolerable than the change necessary for their removal; in the same manner that highways which wind among mountains, by being much frequented, become gradually so smooth and commodious, that it is much better to follow them than to seek a straighter path by climbing over the tops of rocks and descending to the bottoms of precipices.

Hence it is that I cannot in any degree approve of those restless and busy meddlers who, called neither by birth nor fortune to take part in the management of public affairs, are yet always projecting reforms; and if I thought that this tract contained

169

anything which might justify the suspicion that I was a victim of such folly, I would by no means permit its publication. I have never contemplated anything higher than the reformation of my own opinions, and basing them on a foundation wholly my own. And although my own satisfaction with my work has led me to present here a draft of it, I do not by any means therefore recommend to every one else to make a similar attempt. Those whom God has endowed with a larger measure of genius will entertain, perhaps, designs still more exalted; but for the many I am much afraid lest even the present undertaking be more than they can safely venture to imitate. The single design to strip one's self of all past beliefs is one that ought not to be taken by every one. The majority of men is composed of two classes, for neither of which would this be at all a befitting resolution: in the *first* place, of those who with more than a due confidence in their own powers, are precipitate in their judgments and want the patience requisite for orderly and circumspect thinking; whence it happens, that if men of this class once take the liberty to doubt of their accustomed opinions, and quit the beaten highway, they will never be able to thread the byway that would lead them by a shorter course, and will lose themselves and continue to wander for life; in the *second* place, of those who, possessed of sufficient sense or modesty to determine that there are others who excel them in the power of discriminating between truth and error, and by whom they may be instructed, ought rather to content themselves with the opinions of such than trust for more correct to their own Reason.

For my own part, I should doubtless have belonged to the latter class, had I received instruction from but one master, or had I never known the diversities of opinion that from time immemorial have prevailed among men of the greatest learning. But I had become aware, even so early as during my college life, that no opinion, however absurd and incredible, can be imagined, which has not been maintained by some one of the philosophers; and afterwards in the course of my travels I remarked that all those whose opinions are decidedly repugnant to ours are not on that account barbarians and savages, but on the contrary that many of these nations make an equally good, if not a better, use of their reason than we do. I took into account also the very different character which a person brought up from infancy in France or Germany exhibits, from that which, with the same mind originally, this individual would have possessed had he lived always among the Chinese or with savages, and the circumstance that in dress itself the fashion which pleased us ten years ago, and which may again, perhaps, be received into favour before ten years have gone, appears to us at this moment extravagant and ridiculous. I was thus led to infer that the ground of our opinions is far more custom and example than any certain knowledge. And, finally, although such be the ground of our opinions, I remarked that a plurality of suffrages is no guarantee of truth where it is at all of difficult discovery, as in such cases it is much more likely that it will be found by one than by many. I could, however, select from the crowd no one whose opinions seemed worthy of preference, and thus I found myself constrained, as it were, to use my own reason in the conduct of my life.

But like one walking alone and in the dark, I resolved to proceed so slowly and with such circumspection, that if I did not advance far, I would at least guard against falling. I did not even choose to dismiss summarily any of the opinions that had crept into my belief without having been introduced by Reason, but first of all took sufficient time carefully to satisfy myself of the general nature of the task I was setting myself, and ascertain the true Method by which to arrive at the knowledge of whatever lay within the compass of my powers.

Among the branches of philosophy, I had, at an earlier period, given some attention to logic, and among those of mathematics to geometrical analysis and algebra, — three arts or sciences which ought, as I conceived, to contribute something to my design. But, on examination, I found that, as for logic, its syllogisms and the majority of its other precepts are of avail rather in the communication of what we already know, or even as the art of Lully, in speaking without judgment of things of which we are ignorant, than in the investigation of the unknown; and although this science contains indeed a number of correct and very excellent precepts, there are, nevertheless, so many others, and these either injurious or superfluous, mingled with the former, that it is almost quite as difficult to effect a severance of the true from the false as it is to extract a Diana or a Minerva from a rough block of marble. Then as to the Analysis of the ancients and the Algebra of the moderns, besides that they embrace only matters highly abstract, and, to appearance, of no use, the former is so exclusively restricted to the consideration of figures, that it can exercise the Understanding only on condition of greatly fatiguing the Imagination; and, in the latter, there is so complete a subjection to certain rules and formulas, that there results an art full of confusion and obscurity calculated to embarrass, instead of a science fitted to cultivate the mind. By these considerations I was induced to seek some other Method which would comprise the advantages of the three and be exempt from their defects. And as a multitude of laws often only hampers justice, so that a state is best governed when, with few laws, these are rigidly administered; in like manner, instead of the great number of precepts of which Logic is composed, I believe that the four following would prove perfectly sufficient for me, provided I took the firm and unwavering resolution never in a single instance to fail in observing them.

The *first* was never to accept anything for true which I did not clearly know to be such; that is to say, carefully to avoid precipitancy and prejudice, and to comprise nothing more in my judgment than what was presented to my mind so clearly and distinctly as to exclude all ground of doubt.

The *second*, to divide each of the difficulties under examination into as many parts as possible, and as might be necessary for its adequate solution.

The *third*, to conduct my thoughts in such order that, by commencing with objects the simplest and easiest to know, I might ascend little by little, and, as it were, step by step, to the knowledge of the more complex; assigning in thought a certain order even to those objects which in their own nature do not stand in a relation of antecedence and sequence.

And the *last*, in every case to make enumerations so complete, and reviews so general, that I might be assured that nothing was omitted.

The long chains of simple and easy reasonings by means of which geometers are accustomed to reach the conclusions of their most difficult demonstrations, had led me to imagine that all things, to the knowledge of which man is competent, are mutually connected in the same way, and that there is nothing so far removed from us as to be beyond our reach, or so hidden that we cannot discover it, provided only we abstain from accepting the false for the true, and always preserve in our thoughts the order necessary for the deduction of one truth from another. And I had little difficulty in determining the objects with which it was necessary to commence, for I was already persuaded that it must be with the simplest and easiest to know, and, considering that of all those who have hitherto sought truth in the Sciences, the mathematicians alone have been able to find any demonstrations, that is, any certain and evident reasons, I did not doubt but that such must have been the rule of their investigations. I resolved to commence, therefore, with the examination of the simplest objects, not anticipating, however, from this any other advantage than that to be found in accustoming my mind to the love and nourishment of truth, and to a distaste for all such reasonings as were unsound. But I had no intention on that account of attempting to master all the particular Sciences commonly denominated Mathematics: but observing that, however different their objects, they all agree in considering only the various relations or proportions subsisting among those objects, I thought it best for my purpose to consider these proportions in the most general form possible, without referring them to any objects in particular, except such as would most facilitate the knowledge of them, and without by any means restricting them to these, that afterwards I might thus be the better able to apply them to every other class of objects to which they are legitimately applicable. Perceiving further, that in order to understand these relations I should sometimes have to consider them one by one, and sometimes only to bear them in mind, or embrace them in the aggregate, I thought that, in order the better to consider them individually, I should view them as subsisting between straight lines, than which I could find no objects more simple, or capable of being more distinctly represented to my imagination and senses; and on the other hand, that in order to retain them in the memory, or embrace an aggregate of many, I should express them by certain characters the briefest possible. In this way I believe that I could borrow all that was best both in Geometrical Analysis and in Algebra, and correct all the defects of the one by help of the other.

And, in point of fact, the accurate observance of these few precepts gave me, I take the liberty of saying, such ease in unravelling all the questions embraced in these two sciences, that in the two or three months I devoted to their examination, not only did I reach solutions of questions I had formerly deemed exceedingly difficult, but even as regards questions of the solution of which I continued ignorant, I was enabled, as it appeared to me, to determine the means whereby, and the extent to which, a solution was possible; results attributable to the circumstance that I commenced with the simplest and most general truths, and that thus each truth discovered was a rule available in the discovery of subsequent ones. Nor in this perhaps shall I appear too vain if it be considered that, as the truth on any particular point is one, whoever apprehends the truth, knows all that on that point can be known. The child, for example, who has been instructed in the elements of arithmetic, and has made a particular addition, according to rule, may be assured that he has found, with respect to the sum of the numbers before him, all that in this instance is within the reach of human genius. Now, in conclusion, the method which teaches adherence to the true order, and an exact enumeration of all the conditions of the thing sought includes all that gives certitude to the rules of arithmetic.

But the chief ground of my satisfaction with this method, was the assurance I had of thereby exercising my reason in all matters, if not with absolute perfection, at least with the greatest attainable by me: besides, I was conscious that by its use my mind was becoming gradually habituated to clearer and more distinct conceptions of its objects; and I hoped also, from not having restricted this method to any particular matter, to apply it to the difficulties of the other sciences, with not less success than to those of algebra. I should not, however, on this account have ventured at once on the examination of all the difficulties of the Sciences which presented themselves to me, for this would have been contrary to the order prescribed in the Method, but observing that the knowledge of such is dependent on principles borrowed from philosophy, in which I found nothing certain, I thought it necessary first of all to endeavour to establish its principles. And because I observed, besides, that an inquiry of this kind was of all others of the greatest moment, and one in which precipitancy and anticipation in judgment were most to be dreaded, I thought that I ought not to approach it till I had reached a more mature age, (being at that time but twenty-three), and had first of all employed much of my time in preparation for the work, as well by eradicating from my mind all the erroneous opinions I had up to that moment accepted, as by amassing variety of experi-ence to afford materials for my reasonings, and by continually exercising myself in my chosen method with a view to increased skill in its application.

JOHN DEWEY

JOHN DEWEY (1859-1952). The unique influence of John Dewey on American education is rooted in his philosophy of instrumentalism and his life-long interest in the practical application of his theory in the classroom.

Born on a farm in Vermont on October 20, 1859, he credited his early surroundings with impressing upon him the importance of individual freedom in a democratic society. After graduating from the University of Vermont at the age of twenty, he taught at the universities of Michigan, Minnesota, and Chicago before going to Columbia, where he remained from 1904 until his retirement in 1930. At the time of his death on June 1, 1952, he was the most influential exponent of pragmatism or, in his own terminology, instrumentalism.

It was from the great philosophical streams of nineteenth-century Europe that Dewey first drew his inspiration. His doctoral dissertation was on Kant's psychology, and before the turn of the century he was strongly impressed by the writings of Hegel, Marx, and Darwin. Though never an orthodox Hegelian, he admired the German thinker for his ability to analyze and synthesize a plethora of discrete facts and to fit matter and mind, life and society into a coherent pattern; furthermore, he maintained "that there is greater richness and greater variety of insight in Hegel than in any other single systematic philosopher." From Hegel and Marx he received the incentive to investigate the complexity of the institutions in which human beings are enmeshed; from Darwin the evolutionary view that thought is an outgrowth of efforts on the part of a primitive organism to adapt to its environment as well as the concept that thinking may be interpreted in terms of the resolution of tension and conflict; from the great educators of the past the conviction that an effective system of public education is the heart of a democratic society.

His own distinctive views began to take shape at the turn of the century when, as the guiding spirit of the Laboratory School which he had founded with Mrs. Alice Chipman in 1896, he was able to test his ideas on education experimentally. Under the influence of William James he had abandoned the attempt to reinterpret Hegelian doctrine in naturalistic terms; now "experience" and "learning by doing" became the watchwords of his new pedagogical theory.

"My Pedagogic Creed," the first of the two essays that follow, was published in 1897, when he was directly exposed to the many problems then besetting the city of Chicago. A personal statement as well as a revolutionary manifesto, it typifies the reformist fervor of the period and is generally considered to be the prime force behind the Progressive movement in education.

It was to refute the charge that the Laboratory School was subversive and to encourage public support of his experiment that Dewey delivered in 1899 a lecture on "The School and Social Progress" and two other lectures published under the title *The School and Society*. Translated into many languages and widely read, these lectures were accepted as his justification of the new concept of education as an experimental, child-centered instrument for promoting social reform.

MY PEDAGOGIC CREED*

Article I — What Education Is

I believe that all education proceeds by the participation of the individual in the social consciousness of the race. This process begins unconsciously almost at birth, and is continually shaping the individual's powers, saturating his consciousness, forming his habits, training his ideas, and arousing his feelings and emotions. Through this unconscious education the individual gradually comes to share in the intellectual and moral resources which humanity has succeeded in getting together. He becomes an inheritor of the funded capital of civilization. The most formal and technical education in the world cannot safely depart from this general process. It can only organize it or differentiate it in some particular direction.

I believe that the only true education comes through the stimulation of the child's powers by the demands of the social situations in which he finds himself. Through these demands he is stimulated to act as a member of a unity, to emerge from his original narrowness of action and feeling, and to conceive of himself from the standpoint of the welfare of the group to which he belongs.

*From *The School Journal*, LIV (January 16, 1897), pp. 77-80.

Through the responses which others make to his own activities he comes to know what these mean in social terms. The value which they have is reflected back into them. For instance, through the response which is made to the child's instinctive babblings the child comes to know what those babblings mean; they are transformed into articulate language and thus the child is introduced into the consolidated wealth of ideas and emotions which are now summed up in language.

I believe that this educational process has two sides — one psychological and one sociological; and that neither can be subordinated to the other or neglected without evil results following. Of these two sides, the psychological is the basis. The child's own instincts and powers furnish the material and give the starting point for all education. Save as the efforts of the educator connect with some activity which the child is carrying on of his own initiative independent of the educator, education becomes reduced to a pressure from without. It may, indeed, give certain external results, but cannot truly be called educative. Without insight into the psychological structure and activities of the individual, the educative process will, therefore, be haphazard and arbitrary. If it chances to coincide with the child's activity it will get a leverage; if it does not, it will result in friction, or disintegration, or arrest of the child nature.

I believe that knowledge of social conditions, of the present state of civilization, is necessary in order properly to interpret the child's powers. The child has his own instincts and tendencies, but we do not know what these mean until we can translate them into their social equivalents. We must be able to carry them back into a social past and see them as the inheritance of previous race activities. We must also be able to project them into the future to see what their outcome and end will be. In the illustration just used, it is the ability to see in the child's babblings the promise and potency of a future social intercourse and conversation which enables one to deal in the proper way with that instinct.

I believe that the psychological and social sides are organically related and that education cannot be regarded as a compromise between the two, or a superimposition of one upon the other. We

178

are told that the psychological definition of education is barren and formal — that it gives us only the idea of a development of all the mental powers without giving us any idea of the use to which these powers are put. On the other hand, it is urged that the social definition of education, as getting adjusted to civilization, makes of it a forced and external process, and results in subordinating the freedom of the individual to a preconceived social and political status.

I believe that each of these objections is true when urged against one side isolated from the other. In order to know what a power really is we must know what its end, use, or function is; and this we cannot know save as we conceive of the individual as active in social relationships. But, on the other hand, the only possible adjustment which we can give to the child under existing conditions, is that which arises through putting him in complete possession of all his powers. With the advent of democracy and modern industrial conditions, it is impossible to foretell definitely just what civilization will be twenty years from now. Hence it is impossible to prepare the child for any precise set of conditions. To prepare him for the future life means to give him command of himself; it means so to train him that he will have the full and ready use of all his capacities; that his eye and ear and hand may be tools ready to command, that his judgment may be capable of grasping the conditions under which it has to work, and the executive forces be trained to act economically and efficiently. It is impossible to reach this sort of adjustment save as constant regard is had to the individual's own powers, tastes, and interests — say, that is, as education is continually converted into psychological terms.

In sum, I believe that the individual who is to be educated is a social individual and that society is an organic union of individuals. If we eliminate the social factor from the child we are left only with an abstraction; if we eliminate the individual factor from society, we are left only with an inert and lifeless mass. Education, therefore, must begin with a psychological insight into the child's capacities, interests, and habits. It must be controlled at every point by reference to these same considerations. These

powers, interests, and habits must be continually interpreted —
we must know what they mean. They must be translated into
terms of their social equivalents — into terms of what they are
capable of in the way of social service.

Article II — What the School Is

I believe that the school is primarily a social institution. Education being a social process, the school is simply that form of
community life in which all those agencies are concentrated that
will be most effective in bringing the child to share in the inherited
resources of the race, and to use his own powers for social ends.

I believe that education, therefore, is a process of living and
not a preparation for future living.

I believe that the school must represent present life — life as
real and vital to the child as that which he carries on in the home,
in the neighborhood, or on the playground.

I believe that education which does not occur through forms
of life, or that are worth living for their own sake, is always a
poor substitute for the genuine reality and tends to cramp and
to deaden.

I believe that the school, as an institution, should simplify existing social life; should reduce it, as it were, to an embryonic
form. Existing life is so complex that the child cannot be brought
into contact with it without either confusion or distraction; he is
either overwhelmed by the multiplicity of activities which are
going on, so that he loses his own power of orderly reaction, or
he is so stimulated by these various activities that his powers are
prematurely called into play and he becomes either unduly specialized or else disintegrated.

I believe that as such simplified social life, the school life should
grow gradually out of the home life; that it should take up and
continue the activities with which the child is already familiar
in the home.

I believe that it should exhibit these activities to the child, and
reproduce them in such ways that the child will gradually learn

the meaning of them, and be capable of playing his own part in relation to them.

I believe that this is a psychological necessity, because it is the only way of securing continuity in the child's growth, the only way of giving a back-ground of past experience to the new ideas given in school.

I believe that it is also a social necessity because the home is the form of social life in which the child has been nurtured and in connection with which he has had his moral training. It is the business of the school to deepen and extend his sense of the values bound up in his home life.

I believe that much of present education fails because it neglects this fundamental principle of the school as a form of community life. It conceives the school as a place where certain information is to be given, where certain lessons are to be learned, or where certain habits are to be formed. The value of these is conceived as lying largely in the remote future; the child must do these things for the sake of something else he is to do; they are mere preparation. As a result they do not become a part of the life experience of the child and so are not truly educative.

I believe that the moral education centers upon this conception of the school as a mode of social life, that the best and deepest moral training is precisely that which one gets through having to enter into proper relations with others in a unity of work and thought. The present educational systems, so far as they destroy or neglect this unity, render it difficult or impossible to get any genuine, regular moral training.

I believe that the child should be stimulated and controlled in his work through the life of the community.

I believe that under existing conditions far too much of the stimulus and control proceeds from the teacher, because of neglect of the idea of the school as a form of social life.

I believe that the teacher's place and work in the school is to be interpreted from this same basis. The teacher is not in the school to impose certain ideas or to form certain habits in the child, but is there as a member of the community to select the influences which shall affect the child and to assist him in properly responding to these influences.

I believe that the discipline of the school should proceed from the life of the school as a whole and not directly from the teacher.

I believe that the teacher's business is simply to determine on the basis of larger experience and riper wisdom, how the discipline of life shall come to the child.

I believe that all questions of the grading of the child and his promotion should be determined by reference to the same standard. Examinations are of use only so far as they test the child's fitness for social life and reveal the place in which he can be of the most service and where he can receive the most help.

Article III — The Subject-Matter of Education

I believe that the social life of the child is the basis of concentration, or correlation, in all his training or growth. The social life gives the unconscious unity and the background of all his efforts and of all his attainments.

I believe that the subject-matter of the school curriculum should mark a gradual differentiation out of the primitive unconscious unity of social life.

I believe that we violate the child's nature and render difficult the best ethical results, by introducing the child too abruptly to a number of special studies, of reading, writing, geography, etc., out of relation to this social life.

I believe, therefore, that the true center of correlation on the school subjects is not science, nor literature, nor history, nor geography, but the child's own social activities.

I believe that education cannot be unified in the study of science, or so called nature study, because apart from human activity, nature itself is not a unity; nature in itself is a number of diverse objects in space and time, and to attempt to make it the center of work by itself, is to introduce a principle of radiation rather than one of concentration.

I believe that literature is the reflex expression and interpretation of social experience; that hence it must follow upon and not precede such experience. It, therefore, cannot be made the basis, although it may be made the summary of unification.

182

I believe once more that history is of educative value in so far as it presents phases of social life and growth. It must be controlled by reference to social life. When taken simply as history it is thrown into the distant past and becomes dead and inert. Taken as the record of man's social life and progress it becomes full of meaning. I believe, however, that it cannot be so taken excepting as the child is also introduced directly into social life.

I believe accordingly that the primary basis of education is in the child's powers at work along the same general constructive lines as those which have brought civilization into being.

I believe that the only way to make the child conscious of his social heritage is to enable him to perform those fundamental types of activity which make civilization what it is.

I believe, therefore, in the so-called expressive or constructive activities as the center of correlation.

I believe that this gives the standard for the place of cooking, sewing, manual training, etc., in the school.

I believe that they are not special studies which are to be introduced over and above a lot of others in the way of relaxation or relief, or as additional accomplishments. I believe rather that they represent, as types, fundamental forms of social activity; and that it is possible and desirable that the child's introduction into the more formal subjects of the curriculum be through the medium of these activities.

I believe that the study of science is educational in so far as it brings out the materials and processes which make social life what it is.

I believe that one of the greatest difficulties in the present teaching of science is that the material is presented in purely objective form, or is treated as a new peculiar kind of experience which the child can add to that which he has already had. In reality, science is of value because it gives the ability to interpret and control the experience already had. It should be introduced, not as so much new subject-matter, but as showing the factors already involved in previous experience and as furnishing tools by which that experience can be more easily and effectively regulated.

I believe that at present we lose much of the value of literature and language studies because of our elimination of the social element. Language is almost always treated in the books of pedagogy simply as the expression of thought. It is true that language is a logical instrument, but it is fundamentally and primarily a social instrument. Language is the device for communication; it is the tool through which one individual comes to share the ideas and feelings of others. When treated simply as a way of getting individual information, or as a means of showing off what one has learned, it loses its social motive and end.

I believe that there is, therefore, no succession of studies in the ideal school curriculum. If education is life, all life has, from the outset, a scientific aspect, an aspect of art and culture, and an aspect of communication. It cannot, therefore, be true that the proper studies for one grade are mere reading and writing, and that at a later grade, reading, or literature, or science, may be introduced. The progress is not in the succession of studies but in the development of new attitudes towards, and new interests in, experience.

I believe finally, that education must be conceived as a continuing reconstruction of experience; that the process and the goal of education are one and the same thing.

I believe that to set up any end outside of education, as furnishing its goal and standard, is to deprive the educational process of much of its meaning and tends to make us rely upon false and external stimuli in dealing with the child.

Article IV — The Nature of Method

I believe that the question of method is ultimately reducible to the question of the order of development of the child's powers and interests. The law for presenting and treating material is the law implicit within the child's own nature. Because this is so I believe the following statements are of supreme importance as determining the spirit in which education is carried on:

1. I believe that the active side precedes the passive in the development of the child nature; that expression comes before

conscious impression; that the muscular development precedes the sensory; that movements come before conscious sensations; I believe that consciousness is essentially motor or impulsive; that conscious states tend to project themselves in action.

I believe that the neglect of this principle is the cause of a large part of the waste of time and strength in school work. The child is thrown into a passive, receptive, or absorbing attitude. The conditions are such that he is not permitted to follow the law of his nature; the result is friction and waste.

I believe that ideas (intellectual and rational processes) also result from action and devolve for the sake of the better control of action. What we term reason is primarily the law of orderly or effective action. To attempt to develop the reasoning powers, the powers of judgment, without reference to the selection and arrangement of means in action, is the fundamental fallacy in our present methods of dealing with this matter. As a result we present the child with arbitrary symbols. Symbols are a necessity in mental development, but they have their place as tools for economizing effort; presented by themselves they are a mass of meaningless and arbitrary ideas imposed from without.

2. I believe that the image is the great instrument of instruction. What a child gets out of any subject presented to him is simply the images which he himself forms with regard to it.

I believe that if nine tenths of the energy at present directed towards making the child learn certain things, were spent in seeing to it that the child was forming proper images, the work of instruction would be indefinitely facilitated.

I believe that much of the time and attention now given to the preparation and presentation of lessons might be more wisely and profitably expended in training the child's power of imagery and in seeing to it that he was continually forming definite, vivid, and growing images of the various subjects with which he comes in contact in his experience.

3. I believe that interests are the signs and symptoms of growing power. I believe that they represent dawning capacities. Accordingly the constant and careful observation of interests is of the utmost importance for the educator.

I believe that these interests are to be observed as showing the state of development which the child has reached.

I believe that they prophesy the stage upon which he is about to enter.

I believe that only through the continual and sympathetic observation of childhood's interests can the adult enter into the child's life and see what it is ready for, and upon what material it could work most readily and fruitfully.

I believe that these interests are neither to be humored nor repressed. To repress interest is to substitute the adult for the child, and so to weaken intellectual curiosity and alertness, to suppress initiative, and to deaden interest. To humor the interests is to substitute the transient for the permanent. The interest is always the sign of some power below; the important thing is to discover this power. To humor the interest is to fail to penetrate below the surface and its sure result is to substitute caprice and whim for genuine interest.

4. I believe that the emotions are the reflex of actions.

I believe that to endeavor to stimulate or arouse the emotions apart from their corresponding activities, is to introduce an unhealthy and morbid state of mind.

I believe that if we can only secure right habits of action and thought, with reference to the good, the true, and the beautiful, the emotions will for the most part take care of themselves.

I believe that next to deadness and dullness, formalism and routine, our education is threatened with no greater evil than sentimentalism.

I believe that this sentimentalism is the necessary result of the attempt to divorce feeling from action.

Article V — The School and Social Progress

I believe that education is the fundamental method of social progress and reform.

I believe that all reforms which rest simply upon the enactment of law, or the threatening of certain penalties, or upon changes in mechanical or outward arrangements, are transitory and futile.

I believe that education is a regulation of the process of coming to share in the social consciousness; and that the adjustment of individual activity on the basis of this social consciousness is the only sure method of social reconstruction.

I believe that this conception has due regard for both the individualistic and socialistic ideals. It is duly individual because it recognizes the formation of a certain character as the only genuine basis of right living. It is socialistic because it recognizes that this right character is not to be formed by merely individual precept, example, or exhortation, but rather by the influence of a certain form of institutional or community life upon the individual and that the social organism through the school, as its organ, may determine ethical results.

I believe that in the ideal school we have the reconciliation of the individualistic and the institutional ideals.

I believe that the community's duty to education is, therefore, its paramount moral duty. By law and punishment, by social agitation and discussion, society can regulate and form itself in a more or less haphazard and chance way. But through education society can formulate its own purposes, can organize its own means and resources, and thus shape itself with definiteness and economy in the direction in which it wishes to move.

I believe that when society once recognizes the possibilities in this direction, and the obligations which these possibilities impose, it is impossible to conceive of the resources of time, attention, and money which will be put at the disposal of the educator.

I believe that it is the business of every one interested in education to insist upon the school as the primary and most effective interest of social progress and reform in order that society may be awakened to realize what the school stands for, and aroused to the necessity of endowing the educator with sufficient equipment properly to perform his task.

I believe that education thus conceived marks the most perfect and intimate union of science and art conceivable in human experience.

I believe that the art of thus giving shape to human powers and adapting them to social service, is the supreme art; one calling into its service the best of artists; that no insight, sympathy, tact, executive power, is too great for such service.

I believe that with the growth of psychological service, giving added insight into individual structure and laws of growth; and with growth of social science, adding to our knowledge of the right organization of individuals, all scientific resources can be utilized for the purposes of education.

I believe that when science and art thus join hands the most commanding motive for human action will be reached; the most genuine springs of human conduct aroused and the best service that human nature is capable of guaranteed.

I believe, finally, that the teacher is engaged, not simply in the training of individuals, but in the formation of the proper social life.

I believe that every teacher should realize the dignity of his calling; that he is a social servant set apart for the maintenance of proper social order and the securing of the right social growth.

I believe that in this way the teacher always is the prophet of the true God and the usherer in of the true kingdom of God.

THE SCHOOL AND SOCIAL PROGRESS*

We are apt to look at the school from an individualistic standpoint, as something between teacher and pupil, or between teacher and parent. That which interests us most is naturally the progress made by the individual child of our acquaintance, his normal physical development, his advance in ability to read, write, and figure, his growth in the knowledge of geography and history, improvement in manners, habits of promptness, order, and industry — it is from such standards as these that we judge the work of the school. And rightly so. Yet the range of the outlook needs to be enlarged. What the best and wisest parent wants for his

*From *The School and Society* (Chicago: The University of Chicago Press, 1899).

188

own child, that must the community want for all of its children. Any other ideal for our schools is narrow and unlovely; acted upon, it destroys our democracy. All that society has accomplished for itself it puts, through the agency of the school, at the disposition of its future members. All its better thoughts of itself it hopes to realize through the new possibilities thus opened to its future self. Here individualism and socialism are at one. Only by being true to the full growth of all the individuals who make it up, can society by any chance be true to itself. And in the self-direction thus given nothing counts as much as the school, for, as Horace Mann said, "Where anything is growing, one former is worth a thousand re-formers."

Whenever we have in mind the discussion of a new movement in education, it is especially necessary to take the broader, or social view. Otherwise, changes in the school institution and tradition will be looked at as the arbitrary inventions of particular teachers, at the worst transitory fads, and at the best merely improvements in certain details — and this is the plane upon which it is too customary to consider school changes. It is as rational to conceive of the locomotive or the telegraph as personal devices. The modification going on in the method and curriculum of education is as much a product of the changed social situation, and as much an effort to meet the needs of the new society, that is forming, as are the changes in modes of industry and commerce.

It is to this, then, that I especially ask your attention: the effort to conceive what roughly may be termed the "New Education" in the light of larger changes in society. Can we connect this "New Education" with the general march of events? If we can, it will lose its isolated character, and will cease to be an affair which proceeds only from the over-ingenious minds of pedagogues dealing with particular pupils. It will be seen as part and parcel of the whole social evolution, and, in its more general features at least, as inevitable. . . .

A society is a number of people held together because they are working along common lines, in a common spirit, and with reference to common aims. The common needs and aims demand a growing interchange of thought and growing unity of sym-

189

pathetic feeling. The radical reason that the present school cannot organize itself as a natural social unit is because just this element of common and productive activity is absent. Upon the playground, in game and sport, social organization takes place spontaneously and inevitably. There is something to do, some activity to be carried on, requiring natural divisions of labor, selection of leaders and followers, mutual cooperation and emulation. In the schoolroom the motive and the cement of social organization are alike wanting. Upon the ethical side, the tragic weakness of the present school is that it endeavors to prepare future members of the social order in a medium in which the conditions of the social spirit are eminently wanting. . . .

Our whole conception of school discipline changes when we get this point of view. In critical moments we all realize that the only discipline that stands by us, the only training that becomes intuition, is that got through life itself. That we learn from experience, and from books or the sayings of others *only* in their vital relation to experience, are not mere phrases. But the school has been so set apart, so isolated from the ordinary conditions and motives of life, that the place where children are sent for discipline is the one place in the world where it is most difficult to get experience — the mother of all discipline worth the name. It is only where a narrow and fixed image of traditional school discipline dominates, that one is in any danger of overlooking that deeper and infinitely wider discipline that comes from having a part to do in constructive work, in contributing to a result which, social in spirit, is none the less obvious and tangible in form — and hence in a form with reference to which responsibility may be exacted and accurate judgment passed.

The great thing to keep in mind, then, regarding the introduction into the school of various forms of active occupation, is that through them the entire spirit of the school is renewed. It has a chance to affiliate itself with life, to become the child's habitat, where he learns through directed living, instead of being only a place to learn lessons having an abstract and remote reference to some possible living to be done in the future. It gets a chance to be a miniature community, an embryonic society. This is the

190

fundamental fact, and from this arise continuous and orderly sources of instruction. . . .

When occupations in the school are conceived in this broad and generous way, I can only stand lost in wonder at the objections so often heard, that such occupations are out of place in the school because they are materialistic, utilitarian, or even menial in their tendency. It sometimes seems to me that those who make these objections must live in quite another world. The world in which most of us live is a world in which everyone has a calling and occupation, something to do. Some are managers and others are subordinates. But the great thing for one as for the other is that each shall have had the education which shall enable him to see within his daily work all there is of large and human significance. How many of the employed are today mere appendages to the machines which they operate! This may be due in part to the machine itself, or to the *regime* which lays so much stress upon the products of the machine; but it is certainly due in large part to the fact that the worker has had no opportunity to develop his imagination and his sympathetic insight into the social and scientific values found in his work. At present, the impulses which lie at the basis of the industrial system are either practically neglected or positively distorted during the school period. Until the instincts of construction and production are systematically laid hold of in the years of childhood and youth, until they are trained in social directions, enriched by historical interpretation, controlled and illuminated by scientific methods, we certainly are in no position even to locate the sources of our economic evils, much less to deal with them effectively. . . .

But all this means a necessary change in the attitude of the school, one of which we are as yet far from realizing the full force. Our school methods, and to a very considerable extent our curriculum, are inherited from the period when learning and command of certain symbols, affording as they did the only access to learning, were all-important. The ideals of this period are still largely in control, even where the outward methods and studies have been changed. We sometimes hear the introduction of manual training, art and science into the elementary, and even

191

the secondary schools, deprecated on the ground that they tend toward the production of specialists — that they detract from our present scheme of generous, liberal culture. The point of this objection would be ludicrous if it were not often so effective as to make it tragic. It is our present education which is highly specialized, one-sided and narrow. It is an education dominated almost entirely by the mediaeval conception of learning. It is something which appeals for the most part simply to the intellectual aspect of our natures, our desire to learn, to accumulate information, and to get control of the symbols of learning; not to our impulses and tendencies to make, to do, to create, to produce, whether in the form of utility or of art. The very fact that manual training, art and science are objected to as technical, as tending toward mere specialism, is of itself as good testimony as could be offered to the specialized aim which controls current education. Unless education had been virtually identified with the exclusively intellectual pursuits, with learning as such, all these materials and methods would be welcome, would be greeted with the utmost hospitality. . . .

But why should I make this labored presentation? The obvious fact is that our social life has undergone a thorough and radical change. If our education is to have any meaning for life, it must pass through an equally complete transformation. This transformation is not something to appear suddenly, to be executed in a day by conscious purpose. It is already in progress. Those modifications of our school system which appear often (even to those most actively concerned with them, to say nothing of their spectator) as mere changes of detail, mere improvements within the school mechanism, are in reality signs and evidences of this change. The introduction of active occupations, of nature study, of elementary science, of art, of history; the relegation of the merely symbolic and formal to a secondary position; the change in the moral school atmosphere, in the relation of pupils and teachers — of discipline; the introduction of more active, expressive, and self-directing factors — all these are not mere accidents, they are necessities of the larger social evolution. It remains but to organize all these factors, to appreciate them in their fullness of meaning, and to put the ideas and ideals involved in complete, uncompromising possession of our school system. To do this means to make each one of our schools an embryonic community life, active with types of occupations that reflect the life of the larger society, and permeated throughout with the spirit of art, history, and science. When the school introduces and trains each child of society into membership within such a little community, saturating him with the spirit of service, and providing him with the instruments of effective self-direction, we shall have the deepest and best guarantee of a larger society which is worthy, lovely, and harmonious.

ALBERT EINSTEIN

ALBERT EINSTEIN (1879-1955). Apart from his formulation of the special and the general theory of relativity, Einstein is remembered as an unselfish man of the highest intellectual integrity, free of personal ambition, and as a passionate and active proponent of social justice and social responsibility. Most scientists agree that he has accomplished "one of the greatest generalizations" in the history of man and "has revolutionized our nineteenth century concepts . . . of the fundamental ideas of science."

He was born on March 14, 1879, at Ulm, Germany, but his family soon moved to Munich, where he began his schooling. He was generally bored with the pedantry of his teachers but, fortunately for humanity, had his interest in mathematics aroused by an uncle. Despite his indifference toward his formal studies, he read widely and received a Ph.D. degree from the University of Zurich (1905), where he became professor in 1909. His epoch-making paper on the general theory of relativity was published in 1916. As his fame spread, he became active in various causes and made many public appearances. He received the Nobel prize in physics in 1922. His famous letter to President Franklin D. Roosevelt resulted in the Manhattan project through which the atomic bomb was developed. By the time of his death on April 18, 1955, more than five thousand books and pamphlets had been published about him and his work.

On many occasions Einstein expressed his views on contemporary problems and issues. His conservative views on education, "founded upon *nothing but* his own personal experience," seem strikingly cogent in the turbulent world that has yet to adjust to the changes brought about by his discovery.

ON EDUCATION*

A day of celebration generally is in the first place dedicated to retrospect, especially to the memory of personages who have gained special distinction for the development of the cultural life.

*From *Out of My Later Years* (New York: Philosophical Library, 1950).

194

This friendly service for our predecessors must indeed not be neglected, particularly as such a memory of the best of the past is proper to stimulate the well-disposed of today to a courageous effort. But this should be done by someone who, from his youth, has been connected with this State and is familiar with its past, not by one who like a gypsy has wandered about and gathered his experiences in all kinds of countries.

Thus, there is nothing else left for me but to speak about such questions as, independently of space and time, always have been and will be connected with educational matters. In this attempt I cannot lay any claim to being an authority, especially as intelligent and well-meaning men of all times have dealt with educational problems and have certainly repeatedly expressed their views clearly about these matters. From what source shall I, as a partial layman in the realm of pedagogy, derive courage to expound opinions with no foundations except personal experience and personal conviction? If it were really a scientific matter, one would probably be tempted to silence by such considerations.

However, with the affairs of active human beings it is different. Here knowledge of truth alone does not suffice; on the contrary this knowledge must continually be renewed by ceaseless effort, if it is not to be lost. It resembles a statue of marble which stands in the desert and is continuously threatened with burial by the shifting sand. The hands of service must ever be at work, in order that the marble continue lastingly to shine in the sun. To these serving hands mine also shall belong.

The school has always been the most important means of transferring the wealth of tradition from one generation to the next. This applies today in an even higher degree than in former times for, through modern development of the economic life, the family as bearer of tradition and education has been weakened. The continuance and health of human society is therefore in a still higher degree dependent on the school than formerly.

Sometimes one sees in the school simply the instrument for transferring a certain maximum quantity of knowledge to the growing generation. But that is not right. Knowledge is dead; the school, however, serves the living. It should develop in the young individuals those qualities and capabilities which are of value for the welfare of the commonwealth. But that does not mean that individuality should be destroyed and the individual become a mere tool of the community, like a bee or an ant. For a community of standardized individuals without personal originality and personal aims would be a poor community without possibilities for development. On the contrary, the aim must be the training of independently acting and thinking individuals, who, however, see in the service of the community their highest life problem. As far as I can judge, the English school system comes nearest to the realization of this ideal.

But how shall one try to attain this ideal? Should one perhaps try to realize this aim by moralizing? Not at all. Words are and remain an empty sound, and the road to perdition has ever been accompanied by lip service to an ideal. But personalities are not formed by what is heard and said, but by labor and activity.

The most important method of education accordingly always has consisted of that in which the pupil was urged to actual performance. This applies as well to the first attempts at writing of the primary boy as to the doctor's thesis on graduation from the university, or as to the mere memorizing of a poem, the writing of a composition, the interpretation and translation of a text, the solving of a mathematical problem or the practice of physical sport.

But behind every achievement exists the motivation which is at the foundation of it and which in turn is strengthened and nourished by the accomplishment of the undertaking. Here there are the greatest differences and they are of greatest importance to the educational value of the school. The same work may owe its origin to fear and compulsion, ambitious desire for authority and distinction, or loving interest in the object and a desire for truth and understanding, and thus to that divine curiosity which every healthy child possesses, but which so often early is weakened. The educational influence which is exercised upon the pupil by the accomplishment of one and the same work may be widely different, depending upon whether fear of hurt, egoistic passion or desire for pleasure and satisfaction are at the bottom of this work. And nobody will maintain that the administration of the

196

school and the attitude of the teachers does not have an influence upon the molding of the psychological foundation for pupils.

To me the worst thing seems to be for a school principally to work with methods of fear, force and artificial authority. Such treatment destroys the sound sentiments, the sincerity and the self-confidence of the pupil. It produces the submissive subject. It is no wonder that such schools are the rule in Germany and Russia. I know that the schools in this country are free from this worst evil; this also is so in Switzerland and probably in all democratically governed countries. It is comparatively simple to keep the school free from this worst of all evils. Give into the power of the teacher the fewest possible coercive measures, so that the only source of the pupil's respect for the teacher is the human and intellectual qualities of the latter.

The second-named motive, ambition or, in milder terms, the aiming at recognition and consideration, lies firmly fixed in human nature. With absence of mental stimulus of this kind, human cooperation would be entirely impossible; the desire for the approval of one's fellowman certainly is one of the most important binding powers of society. In this complex of feelings, constructive and destructive forces lie closely together. Desire for approval and recognition is a healthy motive; but the desire to be acknowledged as better, stronger or more intelligent than a fellow being or fellow scholar easily leads to an excessively egoistic psychological adjustment, which may become injurious for the individual and for the community. Therefore the school and the teacher must guard against employing the easy method of creating individual ambition, in order to induce the pupils to diligent work.

Darwin's theory of the struggle for existence and the selectivity connected with it has by many people been cited as authorization of the encouragement of the spirit of competition. Some people also in such a way have tried to prove pseudo-scientifically the necessity of the destructive economic struggle of competition between individuals. But this is wrong, because man owes his strength in the struggle for existence to the fact that he is a socially living animal. As little as a battle between single ants of an ant hill

197

is essential for survival, just so little is this the case with the individual members of a human community.

Therefore one should guard against preaching to the young man success in the customary sense as the aim of life. For a successful man is he who receives a great deal from his fellowmen, usually incomparably more than corresponds to his service to them. The value of a man, however, should be seen in what he gives and not in what he is able to receive.

The most important motive for work in the school and in life is the pleasure in work, pleasure in its result and the knowledge of the value of the result to the community. In the awakening and strengthening of these psychological forces in the young man, I see the most important task given by the school. Such a psychological foundation alone leads to a joyous desire for the highest possessions of men, knowledge and artistlike workmanship.

The awakening of these productive psychological powers is certainly less easy than the practice of force or the awakening of individual ambition but is the more valuable for it. The point is to develop the childlike inclination for play and the childlike desire for recognition and to guide the child over to important fields for society; it is that education which in the main is founded upon the desire for successful activity and acknowledgment. If the school succeeds in working successfully from such points of view, it will be highly honored by the rising generation and the tasks given by the school will be submitted to as a sort of gift. I have known children who preferred schooltime to vacation.

Such a school demands from the teacher that he be a kind of artist in his province. What can be done that this spirit be gained in the school? For this there is just as little a universal remedy as there is for an individual to remain well. But there are certain necessary conditions which can be met. First, teachers should grow up in such schools. Second, the teacher should be given extensive liberty in the selection of the material to be taught and the methods of teaching employed by him. For it is true also of him that pleasure in the shaping of his work is killed by force and exterior pressure.

If you have followed attentively my meditations up to this

point, you will probably wonder about one thing. I have spoken fully about in what spirit, according to my opinion, youth should be instructed. But I have said nothing yet about the choice of subjects for instruction, nor about the method of teaching. Should language predominate or technical education in science?

To this I answer: In my opinion all this is of secondary importance. If a young man has trained his muscles and physical endurance by gymnastics and walking, he will later be fitted for every physical work. This is also analogous to the training of the mind and the exercising of the mental and manual skill. Thus the wit was not wrong who defined education in this way: "Education is that which remains, if one has forgotten everything he learned in school." For this reason I am not at all anxious to take sides in the struggle between the followers of the classical philologic-historical education and the education more devoted to natural science.

On the other hand, I want to oppose the idea that the school has to teach directly that special knowledge and those accomplishments which one has to use later directly in life. The demands of life are much too manifold to let such a specialized training in school appear possible. Apart from that, it seems to me, moreover, objectionable to treat the individual like a dead tool. The school should always have as its aim that the young man leave it as a harmonious personality, not as a specialist. This in my opinion is true in a certain sense even for technical schools, whose students will devote themselves to a quite definite profession. The development of general ability for independent thinking and judgment should always be placed foremost, not the acquisition of special knowledge. If a person masters the fundamentals of his subject and has learned to think and work independently, he will surely find his way and besides will better be able to adapt himself to progress and change than the person whose training principally consists in the acquiring of detailed knowledge.

Finally, I wish to emphasize once more that what has been said here in a somewhat categorical form does not claim to mean more than the personal opinion of a man, which is founded upon *nothing but* his own personal experience, which he has gathered as a student and as a teacher.

CHARLES W. ELIOT

CHARLES W. ELIOT (1834-1926). Almost a century ago Charles W. Eliot, the young president of Harvard, sponsored one of the most far-reaching innovations in the history of American education — the elective system which permits students to choose courses within certain limitations instead of adhering to a rigidly prescribed curriculum.

Born in Boston, Massachusetts, on March 20, 1834, Eliot graduated from Harvard in 1853 and returned to his alma mater as president in 1869, after he had studied in Europe and published papers dealing with the educational problems of Europe and America. He continued to serve as president of Harvard until 1909 and as president emeritus until his death on August 22, 1926. His influence on higher education was greater than that of any of his contemporaries, and he succeeded in raising the standards of secondary school education. His wide range of interests resulted in his lecturing extensively on educational and social issues and in his undertaking the preparation of the Harvard Classics, which was later known as "Dr. Eliot's five-foot shelf" and became a milestone in adult education by virtue of its widespread circulation.

"The New Education" was written for a popular magazine and stresses the superiority of American technology and organizing of education to meet new conditions. In the second essay reproduced here, Eliot offers his views on what democratic education should be.

THE NEW EDUCATION*

The American people are fighting the wilderness, physical and moral, on the one hand, and on the other are struggling to work out the awful problem of self-government. For this fight they must be trained and armed. No thoughtful American in active life reaches manhood without painfully realizing the deficiencies and shortcomings of his own early training. He knows how

*From *The Atlantic Monthly*, XXIII, (February and March, 1869), pp. 203-5 and 366-7.

200

ignorance balks and competition overwhelms, but he knows also the greatness of the material prizes to be won. He is anxious to have his boys better equipped for the American man's life than he himself was. It is useless to commend to him the good old ways, the established methods. He has a decided opinion that there are or ought to be better ways. He will not believe that the same methods which trained some boys well for the life of fifty or one hundred years ago are applicable to his son; for the reason, that the kind of man which he wants his son to make did not exist in all the world fifty years ago. So without any clear idea of what a practical education is, but still with some tolerably distinct notion of what it is not, he asks, "How can I give my boy a practical education?"

* * *

We wish to review the recent experience of this country in the attempt to organize a system of education based chiefly upon the pure and applied sciences, the living European languages, and mathematics, instead of upon Greek, Latin, and mathematics, as in the established college system. The history of education is full of stillborn theories; the literature of the subject is largely made up of theorizing; whoever reads it much will turn with infinite relief to the lessons of experience. But it should be observed that it is experience of a generation, and not individual experience, which is of value. To have been a schoolmaster or college professor thirty years only too often makes a man an unsafe witness in matters of education: there are flanges on his mental wheels which will only fit one gauge. On the other hand, it must be acknowledged that conservatism is never more respectable than in education, for nowhere are the risks of change greater. Our survey of the institutions which represent the new education in this country will be absolutely impersonal; the merits of different systems are to be discussed, not the characters or qualifications of the men who have invented, or worked under, these systems. This limitation of the discussion is judicious, from all points of view; for in no country is so little attention paid by parents and students to the reputation of teachers for genius and deep learning as in our own. Faradays, Rumfords, and Cuviers would get very few

201

pupils here, if their teachers were unmethodical and objectless, — if, in short, they taught under a bad general system. Spasmodic and ill-directed genius cannot compete in the American community with methodical, careful teaching by less inspired men.

* * *

But now some one may ask, To what good end all [the] discourse about the improvement of technical education? Are not Americans already the most ingenious people on the earth? Have we not invented mowers, and sewing-machines, and the best printing-press? Are we not doing countless things by machinery which other people do by hand? Is there really any need of instructing Americans in the application of science to the arts? The answers to these incredulous suggestions are not far to seek. In the first place, it is emphatically true that Americans have invented a large number of labor-saving machines of the greatest value. They are powerfully incited to this sort of invention by the dearness of labor in this country. Secondly, this same scarcity of laborers, and the consequent abundance of work for all willing hands, enable an American to pursue the precarious rewards of invention, perhaps for years, with the certainty that if, after all, he wins no prize in the lottery, he can readily find some steady employment to keep his old age from absolute want. But if a European once falls out of the ranks of industry, he has infinite trouble, in case he fails in his adventures, to recover any standing room whatever in society. An American may do with impunity, and without real wrong perhaps, what a European could only do in the spirit of the most reckless gambler or in the confidence of inspired genius. Freedom, and the newness and breadth of the land, explain this favored condition of the American. But it is to be noticed that the chief American successes in invention are of one sort, — machinery and mechanical appliances. In other departments of invention, which require greater knowledge, we are obviously borrowers, rather than lenders. How many millions of dollars are sunk every few years in mining enterprises, through sheer ignorance? Freiberg and Swansea have to be called upon to smelt American ores. The best managers of American printworks receive patterns of the latest French designs by every steamer. The aniline colors are not American discoveries. There are hardly twenty miles of good road, in the European sense, in the whole United States. The various chemical industries are chiefly foreign. American ingenuity has been of more limited range than is commonly imagined. Not a few reputed American inventions are really of European origin. But, however this may be, we may zealously endeavor to strengthen the scientific professions in this country without being a whit less proud of the undisputed achievements of American ingenuity. It is not a question of promoting fertility of invention by improving technical education. Inventors are a law unto themselves. What the country needs is a steady supply of men well trained in recognized principles of science and art, and well informed about established practice. We need engineers who thoroughly understand what is already known at home and abroad about mining, road and bridge building, railways, canals, water-power, and steam machinery; architects who have thoroughly studied their art; builders who can at least construct buildings which will not fall down; chemists and metallurgists who know what the world has done and is doing in the chemical arts, and in the extraction and working of metals; manufacturers who appreciate what science and technical skill can do for the works which they superintend.

Americans must not sit down contented with their position among the industrial nations. We have inherited civil liberty, social mobility, and immense native resources. The advantages we thus hold over the European nations are inestimable. The question is, not how much our freedom can do for us unaided, but how much we can help freedom by judicious education. We appreciate better than we did ten years ago that true progress in this country means progress for the world. In organizing the new education, we do not labor for ourselves alone. Freedom will be glorified in her works.

EDUCATION IN DEMOCRATIC SOCIETY*

What the function of education shall be in a democracy will depend on what is meant by democratic education.

Too many of us think of education for the people as if it meant only learning to read, write, and cipher. Now, reading, writing, and simple ciphering are merely the tools by the diligent use of which a rational education is to be obtained through years of well-directed labor. They are not ends in themselves, but means to the great end of enjoying a rational existence. Under any civilized form of government, these arts ought to be acquired by every child by the time it is nine years of age. Competent teachers, or properly conducted schools, now teach reading, writing, and spelling simultaneously, so that the child writes every word it reads, and, of course, in writing, spells the word. Ear, eye, and hand thus work together from the beginning in the acquisition of the arts of reading and writing. As to ciphering, most educational experts have become convinced that the amount of arithmetic which an educated person who is not some sort of computer needs to make use of, is but small, and that real education should not be delayed or impaired for the sake of acquiring a skill in ciphering, which will be of little use either to the child or to the adult. Reading, writing, and arithmetic, then, are not the goal of popular education.

The goal in all education, democratic or other, is always receding before the advancing contestant, as the top of a mountain seems to retreat before the climber, remoter and higher summits appearing successively as each apparent summit is reached. Nevertheless, the goal of the moment in education is always the acquisition of knowledge, the training of some permanent capacity for

*Published in *The World's Progress* (The Delphian Course, Vol. VI), pp. 295-303.

productiveness or enjoyment, and the development of character. Democratic education being a very new thing in the world, its attainable objects are not yet fully perceived. Plato taught that the laborious classes in a model commonwealth, needed no education whatever. That seems an extraordinary opinion for a great philosopher to hold; but, while we wonder at it, let us recall that only one generation ago, in some of our southern states, it was a crime to teach a member of the laborious class to read. In feudal society education was the privilege of some of the nobility and clergy, and was one source of the power of these two small classes. Universal education in Germany dates only from the Napoleonic wars; and its object has been to make intelligent soldiers and subjects, rather than happy freemen. In England the system of public instruction is but twenty-seven years old. Moreover, the fundamental object of democratic education — to lift the whole population to a higher plane of intelligence, conduct, and happiness — has not yet been perfectly apprehended even in the United States. Too many of our own people think of popular education as if it were only a protection against dangerous superstitions, or a measure of police, or a means of increasing the national productiveness in the arts and trades. Our generation may, therefore, be excused if it has but an incomplete vision of the goal of education in a democracy.

I proceed to describe briefly the main elements of instruction and discipline in a democratic school. As soon as the easy use of what I have called the tools of education is acquired, and even while this familiarity is being gained, the capacities for productiveness and enjoyment should begin to be trained through the progressive acquisition of an elementary knowledge of the external world. The democratic school should begin early — in the very first grades — the study of nature; and all its teachers should, therefore, be capable of teaching the elements of physical geography, meteorology, botany, and zoology, the whole forming in the child's mind one harmonious sketch of its complex environment. This is a function of the primary school teacher which our fathers never thought of, but which every passing year brings out more and more clearly as a prime function of every instructor of little children. Somewhat later in the child's progress towards maturity, the great sciences of chemistry and physics will find place in its course of systematic training. From the seventh or eighth year, according to the quality and capacity of the child, plane and solid geometry, the science of form, should find a place among the school studies, and some share of the child's attention that great subject should claim for six or seven successive years. The process of making acquaintance with external nature through the elements of these various sciences should be interesting and enjoyable for every child. It should not be painful, but delightful; and throughout the process the child's skill in the arts of reading, writing, and ciphering should be steadily developed.

There is another part of every child's environment with which he should early begin to make acquaintance, namely, the human part. The story of the human race should be gradually conveyed to the child's mind from the time he begins to read with pleasure. This story should be conveyed quite as much through biography as through history; and with the descriptions of facts and real events should be entwined charming and uplifting products of the imagination. . . .

Into the education of the great majority of children there enters as an important part their contribution to the daily labor of the household and the farm, or, at least, of the household. It is one of the serious consequences of the rapid concentration of population into cities and large towns, and of the minute division of labor which characterizes modern industries, that this wholesome part of education is less easily secured than it used to be when the greater part of the population was engaged in agriculture. Organized education must, therefore, supply in urban communities a good part of the manual and moral training which the co-operation of children in the work of father and mother affords in agricultural communities. Hence the great importance in any urban population of facilities for training children to accurate handwork, and for teaching them patience, forethought, and good judgment in productive labor.

Lastly, the school should teach every child, by precept, by example, and by every illustration its reading can supply, that the supreme attainment for any individual is vigor and loveliness of character. Industry, persistence, veracity in word and act, gentleness, and disinterestedness should be made to thrive and blossom during school life in the hearts of the children who bring these virtues from their homes well started, and should be planted and tended in the less fortunate children. Furthermore, the pupils should be taught that what is virtue in one human being is virtue in any group of human beings, large or small — a village, a city, or a nation; that the ethical principles which should govern an empire are precisely the same as those which should govern an individual; and that selfishness, greed, falseness, brutality, and ferocity are as hateful and degrading in a multitude as they are in a single savage.

The education thus outlined is what I think should be meant by democratic education. It exists today only among the most intelligent people, or in places singularly fortunate in regard to the organization of their schools; but though it be the somewhat distant ideal of democratic education, it is by no means an unattainable ideal. It is the reasonable aim of the public school in a thoughtful and ambitious democracy. It, of course, demands a kind of teacher much above the elementary school teacher of the present day, and it also requires a larger expenditure upon the public school than is at all customary as yet in this country. But that better kind of teacher and that larger expenditure are imperatively called for, if democratic institutions are to prosper, and to promote continuously the real welfare of the mass of the people. The standard of education should not be set at the now attained or the now attainable. It is the privilege of public education to press toward a mark remote.

From the total training during childhood there should result in the child a taste for interesting and improving reading, which should direct and inspire its subsequent intellectual life. That schooling which results in this taste for good reading, however unsystematic or eccentric the schooling may have been, has achieved a main end of elementary education; and that schooling which does not result in implanting this permanent taste has failed. Guided and animated by this impulse to acquire knowledge, and exercise his imagination through reading, the individual will continue to educate himself all through life. Without that deep-rooted impulsion he will soon cease to draw on the accumulated wisdom of the past and the new resources of the present, and, as he grows older, he will live in a mental atmosphere which is always growing thinner and emptier. Do we not all know many people who seem to live in a mental vacuum — to whom, indeed, we have great difficulty in attributing immortality, because they apparently have so little life except that of the body? Fifteen minutes a day of good reading would have given any one of this multitude a really human life. The uplifting of the democratic masses depends on this implanting at school of the taste for good reading.

Another important function of the public school in a democracy is the discovery and development of the gift or capacity of each individual child. This discovery should be made at the earliest practicable age, and, once made, should always influence, and sometimes determine, the education of the individual. It is for the interest of society to make the most of every useful gift or faculty which any member may fortunately possess; and it is one of the main advantages of fluent and mobile democratic society that it is more likely than any other society to secure the fruition of individual capacities. To make the most of any individual's peculiar power, it is important to discover it early, and then train it continuously and assiduously. It is wonderful that apparently small personal gifts may become the means of conspicuous service or achievement, if only they get discovered, trained, and applied. A quick eye for shades of color enables a blacksmith to earn double wages in sharpening drills for quarrymen. A delicate sense of touch makes the fortune of a wool buyer. An extraordinary perceptive forefinger gives a surgeon the advantage over all his competitors. A fine voice, with good elocution, and a strong memory for faces and parliamentary rules, may give striking political success to a man otherwise not remarkable. In the ideal democratic school no two children would follow the same course of study or have the same tasks, except that they would all need to learn the use of the elementary tools of education — reading, writing, and ciphering. The different children would hardly have any identical needs. There might be a minimum standard of attainment in every branch of study, but no maximum. The perception or discovery of the individual gift or capacity would often be effected in the elementary school, but more generally in the secondary; and the making of these discoveries should be held one of the most important parts of the teacher's work. The vague desire for equality in a democracy has worked great mischief in democratic schools. There is no such thing as equality of gifts, or powers, or faculties, among either children or adults. On the contrary, there is the utmost diversity; and education and all the experience of life increase these diversities, because school, and the earning of a livelihood, and the reaction of the individual upon his surroundings, all tend strongly to magnify innate diversities. The pretended democratic school with an inflexible programme is fighting not only against nature, but against the interests of democratic society. Flexibility of programme should begin in the elementary school, years before the period of secondary education is reached. There should be some choice of subjects of study by ten years of age, and much variety by fifteen years of age. On the other hand, the programmes of elementary, as well as of secondary schools, should represent fairly the chief divisions of knowledge, namely, language and literature, mathematics, natural science, and history, besides drawing, manual work, and music. If school programmes fail to represent the main varieties of intellectual activity, they will not afford the means of discovering the individual gifts and tendencies of the pupils. . . .

The next function of education in a democracy should be the firm planting in every child's mind of certain great truths which lie at the foundation of the democratic social theory. The first of these truths is the intimate dependence of each human individual on a multitude of other individuals, not in infancy alone, but at every moment of life — a dependence which increases with civilization and with the development of urban life. This sense of mutual dependence among multitudes of human beings can be brought home to children during school life so clearly and strongly that they will never lose it. By merely teaching children whence come their food, drink, clothing, and means of getting light and heat, and how these materials are supplied through the labors of many individuals of many races scattered all over the world, the school may illustrate and enforce this doctrine of intricate interdependence, which really underlies modern democracy — a doctrine never more clearly expressed than in these two Christian sentences: "No man liveth to himself," and "We are every one members one of another." The dependence of every family, and indeed every person, on the habitual fidelity of mechanics, purveyors, railroad servants, cooks and nurses, can be easily brought to children. Another mode of implanting this sentiment is to trace in history the obligations of the present generation to many former generations. These obligations can be easily pointed out in things material, such as highways, waterworks, fences, houses, and barns, and, in New England, at least, the stone walls and piles of stone gathered from the arable fields by the patient labor of predecessors on the family farm. But it may also be exhibited to the pupils of secondary schools, and, in some measure, to the pupils of elementary schools, in the burdens and sufferings which former generations have borne for the establishment of freedom of conscience and of speech, and of toleration in religion, and for the development of the institutions of public justice. Of course history is full of examples of the violation of this fundamental democratic doctrine of mutual help. Indeed, history, as commonly written, consists chiefly in the story of hideous violations of this principle, such as wars and oppressions, and the selfish struggles of class against class, church against church, and nation against nation. But these violations, with the awful sufferings that follow from them, may be made to point and emphasize the truth of the fundamental doctrine; and unless the teaching of history in our public schools does this, it were better that the subject should not be taught at all.

Another ethical principle which a democracy should teach to all its children is the familiar Christian doctrine that service rendered to others is the surest source of one's own satisfaction and happiness. This doctrine is a tap-root of private happiness among all classes and conditions of men; but in a democracy it is important to public happiness and well-being. In a democracy the public functionary is not a master, but a trusted servant. By excellence of service he earns not only a pecuniary consideration, but also respect and gratitude. This statement applies just as well to a letter-carrier, a fireman, or a village selectman, as it does to a high school teacher, a judge, or a governor. Democracy applies literally the precept: "If any man would be great among you, let him be your servant." The quality of this faithful service and its rewards should be carefully taught in school to all children of a democracy. The children should learn that the desire to be of great public service is the highest of all ambitions; and they should be shown in biography and in history how the men and women who, as martyrs, teachers, inventors, legislators, and judges, have rendered great service, have thereby won enduring gratitude and honor.

Since it is a fundamental object of a democracy to promote the happiness and well-being of the masses of the population, the democratic school should explicitly teach children to see and utilize the means of happiness which lie about them in the beauties and splendors of nature. The school should be a vehicle of daily enjoyment, and the teacher should be to the child a minister of joy. Democratic society has already learned how to provide itself, at least in the more intelligent communities, with open grounds in cities, and parks in suburbs, and has in these ways begun to provide directly for the wholesome pleasures of the population. It should be a recognized function of the democratic school to teach the children and their parents how to utilize all accessible means of innocent enjoyment.

Finally, the democratic school must teach its children what the democratic nobility is. The well-trained child will read in history and poetry about patricians, nobles, aristocrats, princes, kings, and emperors, some of them truly noble, but many vile; and he will also read with admiring sympathy of the loyalty and devotion which through all the centuries have been felt by generous men and women of humbler condition toward those of higher. He will see what immense virtues these personal loyalties have developed, even when the objects of loyalty have been unworthy; and he will ask himself: "What are to be the corresponding virtues in a

211

democracy?" The answer is: Fidelity to all forms of duty which demand courage, self-denial, and zeal, and loyal devotion to the democratic ideals of freedom, serviceableness, unity, toleration, public justice, and public joyfulness. The children should learn that the democratic nobility exists, and must exist if democracy is to produce the highest types of character; but that it will consist only of men and women of noble character, produced under democratic conditions by the combined influences of fine inherited qualities, careful education, and rich experience. They should learn to admire and respect persons of this quality, and to support them, on occasion, in preference to the ignoble. They should learn that mere wealth has no passport to the democratic nobility, and that membership in it can be transmitted to children only through the transmission of the sound mental and moral qualities which are its sole warrant. This membership should be the rightful ambition of parents for their children, and of children for their future selves. Every person of the true quality, no matter what his station or vocation, is admitted of right to this simple democratic nobility, which home, church, and school unite in recruiting; and there are, consequently, more real nobles under the democratic form of government than under any other.

THOMAS ELYOT

THOMAS ELYOT (c. 1490-1546). Sir Thomas Elyot's very popular *The Boke Named the Governour,* a plan for the education of those who were to wield authority, has been called the first book in English on the subject of education.

The date and place of Elyot's birth are unknown, and details of his education are uncertain. He was knighted in 1530, and the following year he published the celebrated work whose avowed purpose was "to instruct men in such vertues as shall be expedient to them which shall have authoritie in a weale publike." A friend of Sir Thomas More and holder of several public offices under Henry VIII, Elyot noted in his dedication to the king that he had "enterprised to describe in our vulgar tongue the form of a just public weal," and he cited Plato to prove that the state, if it is to flourish, must provide for the education of those who "hereafter may be deemed to be worthy of the public weal." As a Platonist he gave pre-eminence to the training of the governing class, and as a humanist he gave first place in his scheme to Latin and Greek, to the educational ideal of Cicero and Quintilian — the well-informed man who also possesses eloquence. He did not neglect the value of the fine arts, social studies, and physical training. His book therefore advanced an idea that soon became popular and influential: that of all-round education for the elite.

The selection that follows is a reproduction of the tenth chapter of the first volume of the two-volume work.

ORDER IN LEARNING*

Nowe lette us retourne to the ordre of lernyng apt for a gentyll man. Wherein I am of the opinion of Quintilian that I wolde haue hym lerne greke and latine autors bouth at one time: orels to begyn with greke, for as moche as that it is hardest to come by: by reason of the diursite of tonges, which be fyue in nombre: and all must be knowen, or elles uneth any poet can be well under-

*From *The Boke Named the Governour* (London, 1531).

213

stande. And if a childe do begyn therein at seuen yeres of age, he may continually lerne greke autours thre yeres, and in the meane tyme use the latin tonge as a familiar langage: whiche in a noble mannes sonne may well come to passe, hauynge none other persons to serue him or kepyng hym company, but suche as can speake latine elegantly. And what doubt is there but so may he as sone speake good latin, as he maye do pure frenche, whiche nowe is broughte in to as many rules and figures, and as longe a grammer as is latine or greke. I wyll nat contende who, amonge them that do write grammers of greke, (whiche nowe all most be innumerable,) is the beste: but that I referre to the discretion of a wyse mayster. Always I wolde aduyse hym nat to detayne the childe to longe in that tedious labours, eyther in the greke or latyne grammer. For a gentyll wytte is there with sone fatigate.

Grammer beinge but an introduction to the understanding of autors, if it be made to longe or exquisite to the lerner, hit in a maner mortifieth his corage: And by that time be cometh to the most swete and pleasant redinge of olde autours, the sparkes of feruent desire of lerynge is extincte with the burdone of grammer, lyke as a lyttel fyre is sone quenched with a great heape of small stickes: so that it can neuer come to the principall logges where it should longe bourne in a great pleasaunt fire.

Nowe to folowe my purpose: after a fewe and quicke rules of grammer, immediately, or interlasynge hit therwith, wolde be redde to the childe Esopes fables in greke: in whiche argument children moche do delite. And surely it is a moche pleasant lesson and also profitable, as well for that it is elegant and brefe, (and nat withstanding it hath moche variete in wordes, and therwith moche helpeth to the understandinge of greke) as also in those fables is included moche morall and politike wisedome. Wherfore, in the teaching of them, the maister diligently must gader to gyther those fables, whiche may be most accommodate to the aduauncement of some vertue, wherto he perceiueth the childe inclined: or to the rebuke of some vice, wherto he findeth his nature disposed. And therin the master ought to exercise his witte, as wel to make the childe plainly to understande the fable,

214

as also declarynge the signification therof compendiously and to the purpose, fore sene alwaye, that, as well this lesson, as all other autours whiche the childe shall lerne, either greke or latine, verse or prose, be perfectly had without the boke: wherby he shall nat only attaine plentie of the tongues called Copie, but also encrease and nourisshe remembrance wonderfully.

The nexte lesson wolde be some quicke and mery dialoges, elect out of Luciane, whiche be without ribawdry, or to moche skorning, for either of them is exactly to be eschewed, specially for a noble man, the one anoyeng the soule, the other his estimation concerning his grauitie. The comedies of Aristophanes may be in the place of Luciane, and by reason that they be in metre they be the sooner lerned by harte. I dare make none other comparison betwene them for offendinge the frendes of them both: but thus moche dare I say, that it were better that a childe shuld neuer rede any parte of Luciane than all Luciane.

I coulde reherce diuers other poetis whiche for mater and eloquence be very necessary, but I feare me to be to longe from noble Homere: from whom as from a fountaine proceded all eloquence and lernyng. For in his bokes be contained, and moste perfectly expressed, nat only the documentes marciall and discipline of armes, but also incomparable wisedomes, and instructions for politike gouernaunce of people: with the worthy commendation and laude of noble princis: where with the reders shall be so all inflamed, that they most feruently shall desire and coueite, by the imitation of their vertues, to acquire semblable glorie. For the whiche occasion, Aristotel, moost sharpest witted and excellent lerned Philosopher, as sone as he had receiued Alexander from kynge Philip his father, he before any other thynge taught hym the moost noble warkes of Homere: wherin Alexander founde suche swetenes and frute, that euer after had Homere nat onely with hym in all his iournayes, but also laide hym under his pillowe whan he went to reste: and often tymes wolde purposely wake some houres of the nyght, to take as it were his passe tyme with that mooste noble poete.

For by the redinge of his warke called *Iliados,* where the assembly of the most noble grekes agayne Troy is recited with theyr affaires, he gathered courage and strength agayne his ennemies, wysdome, and eloquence, for consultations, and persuations to his people and army. And by the other warke called *Odissea,* whiche recounteth the sondry aduentures of the wise Ulisses, he, by the example of Ulisses, apprehended many noble vertues, and also lerned to eskape the fraude and deceitfull imaginations of sondry and subtile crafty wittes. Also there shall he lerne to enserche and perceiue the maners and conditions of them that be his familiars, siftinge out (as I mought say) the best from the warst, wherby he may surely committee his affaires, and truste to euery persone after his vertues. Therfore I nowe conclude that there is no lesson for a yonge gentil man to be compared with Homere, if he be playnly and substantially expounded and declared by the mayster.

Nat withstandinge, for as moche as the saide warkes be very longe, and do require therfore a great time to be all lerned and kanned, some latine autour wolde be therwith myxte, and especially Virgile; whiche, in his warke called *Eneidos,* is most lyke to Homere, and all moste the same Homere in latine. Also, by the joynynge to gether of those autours, the one shall be the better understande by the other. And verily (as I before saide) none one autour serueth to so diuers witts as doth Virgile. For there is nat that affect or desire, wherto any childes fantasie is disposed, but in some of Virgils warkes may be founden matter therto apte and propise.

For what thinge can be more familiar than his bucolikes? nor no warke so nighe approacheth to the commune daliaunce and manners of children, and the praty controuerisies of the simple shepeherdes, therin contained, wonderfully reioyceth the childe that hereth hit well declared, as I knowe by myne owne experience. In his Georgikes lorde what pleasaunt varietie there is: the diuers graynes, herbes, and flowers that be there described, that, reding therin, hit semeth to a man to be in a delectable gardeine or paradise. What ploughe man knoweth so moche of husbandry as there is expressed? who, delitynge in good horsis, shall nat be therto more enflamed, reding there of the bredyng, chesinge,

216

and kepyng, of them? In the declaration whereof Virgile leauth farre behynde hym all breders, hakneymen, and skosers.

Is there any astronomer that more exactly setteth out the ordre and course of the celestiall bodies: or that more truely dothe deuine in his pronostications of the tymes of the yere, in their qualities, with the future astate of all thinges prouided by husbandry, than Virgile doth recite in that warke?

If the childe haue a delite in huntyng, what pleasure shall he take of the fable of Aristeus: semblably in the huntynge of Dido and Eneas, whiche is discriued moste elegantly in his boke of Eneidos. If he haue pleasure in wrastling, rennygn, or other lyke exercise, where shall he se any more plesant esbatementes, than that whiche was done by Eurealus and other troyans, whiche accompanyed Eneas? If he take solace in hearynge minstrelles, what minstrell may be compared to Jopas, whiche sange before Dido and Eneas? or to blinde Demodocus, that played and sange moste swetely at the dyner, that the kynge Alcinous made to Ulisses: whose dities and melodie excelled as farre the songes of our minstrelles, as Homere and Virgile excelle all other poetes.

If he be more desirous, (as the most parte of children be,) to here thinges marueilous and exquisite, whiche hath in it a visage of some thinges incredible, whereat shall he more wonder, than whan he shall beholde Eneas folowe Sibille in to helle? What shal he more drede, than the terrible visages of Cerberous, Gorgon, Megera, and other furies and monsters? Howe shall he abhorre tyranny, fraude, and auarice, whan he doth se the paynes of duke Theseus, Prometheus, Sisiphus, and suche other tourmented for their dissolute and vicious lyuyng? Howe glad soone after shall he be, whan he shall beholde, in the pleasant feldes of Elisius, the soules of noble princes and capitaines which, for their vertue, and labours in aduancing the publike weales of their countrayes, do yue eternally in pleasure inexplicable. And in the laste bokes of Eneidos shall he finde matter to ministre to hym audacite, valiaunt courage, and policie, to take and susteyne noble enterprises, if any shall be nedefull for the assailynge of his enemies.

Finally (as I haue saide) this noble Virgile, like to a good norise, giueth to a childe, if he wyll take it, euery thinge apte for

217

his witte and capacitie: wherfore he is in the ordre of lernyng to be preferred before any other author latine. I wolde set nexte unto hym two bokes of Ouid, the one called *Metamorphosios,* whiche is as moche to saye as, chaungynge of men in to other figure or fourme: the other is intitled *De fastis*: where the ceremonies of the gentiles, and specially the Romanes, be expressed: bothe right necessary for the understandynge of other poets. But by cause there is litell other lernyng in them, concernyng either vertuous maners or policie, I suppose it were better that as fables and ceremonies happen to come in a lesson, it were declared abundantly by the maister than that in the saide two bokes, a longe tyme shulde be spente and almost lost: which mought be better employed on suche autors that do minister both eloquence, ciuele policie, and exhortation to vertue. Wherfore in his place let us bringe in Horace, in whom is contayned moche varietie of lernynge and quickenesse of sentence.

This poet may be enterlaced with the lesson of *Odissea* of Homere, wherein is declared the wonderfull prudence and fortitude of Ulisses in his passage from Troy. And if the childe were induced to make versis by the initation of Virgile and Homere, it shulde ministre to hym moche dilectation and courage to studie: ne the making of versis is nat discommended is a noble man: sens the noble Augustus and almost all the olde emperours made bokes in versis.

The two noble poetis Silius, and Lucane, be very expedient to be lerned: for the one setteth out the emulation in qualities and prowesse of two noble and valiant capitaynes, one, enemy to the other, that is to says, Silius writeth of Scipio the Romane, and Haniball duke of Cartaginensis: Lucane declareth a semblable mater, but moche more lamentable: for as moche as the warres were ciuele, and, as it were, in the bowelles of the Romanes, that is to say, under the standerdes of Julius Cesar and Pompei.

Hesiodus, in greke, is more briefe than Virgile, where he writeth of husbandry, and doth nat rise so high in philosophie, but is fuller of fables: and therfore is more illecebrous.

And here I conclude to speke any more of poetis, necessary for the childehode of a gentil man: for as moche as these, I doubt nat, will suffice untill he passe the age of xiii yeres. In which time childhode declineth, and reason waxeth rype, and deprehendeth thinges with a more constant iugement. Here I wolde shulde be remembred, that I require nat that all these warkes shud be throughly radde of a childe in this tyme, whiche were almost impossible. But I only desire that they haue, in euery of the saide bokes, so moche instruction that they may take therby some profite.

Than the childes courage, inflamed by the frequent redynge of noble poetes, dayly more and more desireth to haue experience in those thinges, that they so vehemently do commende in them, that they write of.

Leonidas, the noble kynge of Spartanes, beinge ones demaunded, of what estimation in poetry Tirtaeus, (as he supposed,) was, it is writen that he answeryng saide, that, for sterynge the myndes of yonge men he was excellent, for as moche as they, being meued with his versis, do renne in to the bataile, regardying no perile, as men all inflamed in martiall courage.

And whan a man is comen to mature yeres, and that reason in him is confirmed with serious lerning and longe experience, than shall he, in redyng tragoedies, execrate and abhorre the intollerable life of tyrantes: and shall contemme the foly and dotage expressed by poetes lasciuious.

Here wyll I leaue to speake of the fyrste parte of a noble mannes studie: and nowe wyll I write of the seconde parte, which is more serious, and containeth in it sondry manners of lernynge.

DESIDERIUS ERASMUS

DESIDERIUS ERASMUS (c. 1466-1536). "Erasmus laid the eggs and Luther hatched the chickens," cried one Catholic preacher. The greatest of the humanists and one of the first great liberals in Europe, Desiderius Erasmus through his attacks on the abuses which he could not overlook lent support to the movement which became the Reformation even though he never left the Church and at length recoiled against the violence of Martin Luther. He was the embodiment of the best of the two great Renaissance trends — biblical scholarship and study of the ancient languages and literatures — and he believed that the education of humanity was the essential task of his life.

He was born at Rotterdam around 1466 and is believed to have died at Basel, Switzerland, in 1536. He traveled extensively, lecturing and teaching on the Continent and in England. One of the greatest philologists of all time, he produced critical editions of classical works and of the writings of the Church Fathers, wrote extensively, and translated the New Testament into Latin. He was an independent thinker, a fearless critic of narrowness and fanaticism, and a staunch defender of human reason. Always accompanied during his long tribulations by the figure of Christ, he was, in the words of Johan Huizinga, "the most profoundly serious advocate of that gentle state of spirit which the world needs so badly."

The Praise of Folly, from which the following selection is taken, was written in 1509 while Erasmus was traveling from Italy to England for the coronation of Henry VIII. In his treatise he attacks the superstitions and abuses of the Church and shows that the foolishness of the world is the wisdom of God. In the selection that follows he criticizes those who "seemingly pass for men of the soundest intellectuals" — grammarians, rhetoricians, logicians, sophisters, and the like — and who through "presumptuous imposture" manage to deceive the foolish.

THE PRAISE OF FOLLY*

I shall confine therefore my following discourse only to such as challenge the repute of wisdom, and seemingly pass for men of the soundest intellectuals. Among whom the Grammarians

*From *The Whole Familiar Colloquies of Erasmus* (London, 1877).

220

present themselves in the front, a sort of men who would be the most miserable, the most slavish, and the most hateful of all persons, if I did not in some way alleviate the pressures and miseries of their profession by blessing them with a bewitching sort of madness. For they are not only liable to those five curses, which they so oft recite from the first five verses of Homer, but to five hundred more of a worse nature; as always damned to thirst and hunger, to be choked with dust in their unswept schools. Schools, shall I term them, or rather elaboratories, nay, bridewells, and houses of correction.

To wear out themselves in fret and drudgery; to be deafened with the noise of gaping boys; and in short, to be stifled with heat and stench; and yet they cheerfully acquiesce in all these inconveniences, and, by the help of a fond conceit, think themselves as happy as any men living. Taking a great pride and delight in frowning and looking big upon the trembling urchins, in boxing, slashing, striking with the ferula, and in the exercise of all their other methods of tyranny. While thus lording it over a parcel of young, weak chits, they imitate the Cuman ass, and think themselves as stately as a lion, that domineers over all the inferior herd.

Elevated with this conceit, they can hold filth and nastiness to be an ornament; can reconcile their nose to the most intolerable smells; and finally, think their wretched slavery the most arbitrary kingdom, which they would not exchange for the jurisdiction of the most sovereign potentate. And they are yet more happy by a strong persuasion of their own parts and abilities; for thus when their employment is only to rehearse silly stories, and poetical fictions, they will yet think themselves wiser than the best experienced philosopher; nay, they have an art of making ordinary people, such as their school boys' fond parents, to think them as considerable as their own pride has made them.

Add hereunto this other sort of ravishing pleasure. When any of them has found out who was the mother of Anchises, or has lighted upon some old unusual word, such as *bubsequa bovinator, manticulator,* or other like obsolete cramp terms; or can, after a great deal of poring, spell out the inscription of some battered monument; Lord! what joy, what triumph, what congratulating their success, as if they had conquered Africa, or taken Babylon the Great! When they recite some of their frothy, bombast verses, if any happen to admire them, they are presently flushed with the least hint of commendation, and more devoutly than Pythagoras for his grateful hypotheses, whereby they are now become actuated with a descent of Virgil's poetic soul.

Nor is any divertissement more pleasant, than when they meet to flatter and curry another; yet they are so critical, that if any one hap to be guilty of the least slip, or seeming blunder, another shall presently correct him for it, and then to it they go in a tongue-combat with all the fervour, spleen, and eagerness imaginable. May Priscian himself be my enemy if what I am now going to say be not exactly true. I knew an old Sophister that was a Grecian, a latinist, a mathematician, a philosopher, a musician, and all to the utmost perfection, who, after threescore years' experience in the world, had spent the last twenty of them only in drudging to conquer the criticisms of grammar, and made it the chief part of his prayers, that his life might be so long spared till he had learned how rightly to distinguish betwixt the eight parts of speech, which no grammarian, whether Greek or Latin, had yet accurately done. If any chance to have placed that as a conjunction which ought to have been used as an adverb, it is a sufficient alarm to raise a war for doing justice to the injured word.

And since there have been as many several grammars, as particular grammarians, nay, more, for Aldus alone wrote five distinct grammars for his own share, the schoolmaster must be obliged to consult them all, sparing for no time nor trouble, though never so great, lest he should be otherwise posed in an unobserved criticism, and so by an irreparable disgrace lose the reward of all his toil. It is indifferent to me whether you call this folly or madness, since health, the weakening of their constitution, their contracting sore eyes, or perhaps turning stark blind; their poverty, their envy, their debarment from all pleasures, their hastening on old age, their untimely death, and what other inconveniences of a like or worse nature can be thought upon: and

222

yet the recompense for all this severe penance is at best no more than a mouthful or two of frothy praise.

These, as they are more laborious, so are they less happy than those, other hackney scribblers which I first mentioned, who never stand much to consider, but write what comes next at a venture, knowing that the more silly their composure, the more they will be bought up by the greater number of readers, who are fools and blockheads. And if they hap to be condemned by some few judicious persons, it is an easy matter by clamour to drown their censure, and to silence them by urging the more numerous commendations of others.

They are yet the wisest who transcribe whole discourses from others, and then reprint them as their own. By doing so they make a cheap and easy seizure to themselves of that reputation which cost the first author so much time and trouble to procure. If they are at any time pricked a little in conscience for fear of discovery, they feed themselves however with this hope, that if they be at last found plagiaries, yet at least for some time they have the credit of passing for the genuine authors.

It is pleasant to see how all these several writers are puffed up with the least blast of applause, especially if they walk along the streets, when their several pieces are laid open upon every bookseller's stall, when their names are embossed in a different character upon the title-page, sometime only with the two first letters, and sometime with fictitious cramp terms, which few shall understand the meaning of. And of those that do, all shall not agree in their verdict of the performance. Some censuring, others approving it, men's judgments being as different as their palates, that being toothsome to one which is unsavoury and nauseous to another. Though it is a sneaking piece of cowardice for authors to put feigned names to their works, as if, like bastards of their brain, they were afraid to own them. Thus one styles himself Telemachus, another Stelenus, a third Polycrates, another Thrasymachus, and so on. By the same liberty we may ransack the whole alphabet, and jumble together any letters that come next to hand.

It is farther very pleasant when these coxcombs employ their pens in writing congratulatory epistles, poems, and panegyricks, upon each other, wherein one shall be charactered for the incomparable Callimachus; this shall be commended for a completer orator than Tully himself; a fourth shall be told by his fellow-fool that the divine Plato comes short of him for a philosophic soul.

Sometime again they take up the cudgels, and challenge out an antagonist, and so get a name by a combat at dispute and controversy, while the unwary readers draw sides according to their different judgments. The longer the quarrel holds the more irreconcilable it grows; and when both parties are weary, they each pretend themselves the conquerors, and both lay claim to the credit of coming off with victory. These fooleries make sport for wise men, as being highly absurd, ridiculous and extravagant. True, but yet these paper-combatants, by my assistance, are so flushed with a conceit of their own greatness, that they prefer the solving of a syllogism before the sacking of Carthage; and upon the defeat of a poor objection carry themselves more triumphant than the most victorious Scipio.

Nay, even the learned and more judicious, that have wit enough to laugh at the other's folly, are very much beholden to my goodness; which, except ingratitude have drowned their ingenuity, they must be ready upon all occasions to confess. Among these I suppose the lawyers will shuffle in for precedence, and they of all men have the greatest conceit of their own abilities. They will argue as confidentially as if they spoke gospel instead of law; they will cite you six hundred several precedents, though not one of them come near to the case in hand. They will muster up the authority of judgments, deeds, glosses, and reports, and tumble over so many musty records, that they make their employ, though in itself easy, the greatest slavery imaginable; always accounting that the best plea which they have took most pains for.

To these, as bearing great resemblance to them, may be added Logicians and Sophisters, fellows that talk as much by rote as a parrot; who shall run down a whole gossiping of old women, nay, silence the very noise of a belfry, with louder clappers than those of the steeple. And if their unappeasable clamorousness were their only fault it would admit of some excuse; but they are at the same time so fierce and quarrelsome, that they will wrangle bloodily for the least trifle, and be so over intent and eager, that they many times lose their game in the chase and fright away that truth they are hunting for. Yet self-conceit makes these nimble disputants such doughty champions, that armed with three or four close-linked syllogisms, they shall enter the lists with the greatest master of reason, and not question the foiling of them in an irresistible baffle. Nay, their obstinacy makes them so confident of their being in the right, that all the arguments in the world shall never convince them to the contrary.

Next to these come the Philosophers in their long beards and short cloaks, who esteem themselves the only favourites of wisdom, and look upon the rest of mankind as the dirt and rubbish of the creation. Yet these men's happiness is only a frantic craziness of brain; they build castles in the air, and infinite worlds in a *vacuum*. They will give you to a hair's breadth the dimensions of the sun, moon, and stars, as easily as they would do that of a flagon or pipkin. They will give a punctual account of the rise of thunder, of the origin of winds, of the nature of eclipses, and of all the other obstrusest difficulties in physics, without the least demur or hesitation, as if they had been admitted into the cabinet council of nature, or had been eye-witnesses to all the accurate methods of creation; though alas nature does but laugh at all their puny conjectures. For they never yet made one considerable discovery, as appears in that they are unanimously agreed in no one point of the smallest moment; nothing so plain or evident but what by some or other is opposed and contradicted.

But though they are ignorant of the artificial contexture of the least insect, they vaunt however, and brag that they know all things, when indeed they are unable to construe the mechanism of their own body. Nay, when they are so purblind as not to be able to see a stone's cast before them, yet they shall be as sharp-sighted as possible in spying out ideas, universals, separate forms, first matters, quiddities, formalities, and a hundred such like niceties, so diminutively small, that were not their eyes extremely magnifying all the art of optics could never make them discernible.

But they then most despise the low grovelling vulgar when they bring out their parallels, triangles, circles, and other mathematical figures, drawn up in battalia, like to many spells and charms of conjuration in muster, with letters to refer to the explication of the several problems; hereby raising devils as it were, only to have the credit of laying them, and amusing the ordinary spectators into wonder, because they have not wit enough to understand the juggle. Of these some undertake to profess themselves judicial astrologers, pretending to keep correspondence with the stars, and so from their information can resolve any query. And though it is all but a presumptuous imposture, yet some to be sure will be so great fools as to believe them.

FENELON

FENELON (1651-1715). The first pedagogical work of François de Salignac de la Mothe-Fénelon, a theologian, mystic and educator, was written at the request of the Duc de Beauvilliers, father of eight daughters. Fénelon was a liberal in an age of absolutism, and the progressive ideas expressed in *Education of Girls* were influential throughout the eighteenth century.

Born at the Chateau de Fénelon in the province of Périgord on August 6, 1651, he manifested a thirst for knowledge at an early age. He studied first at home, then at Cahors, and finally at Paris, where he completed his course of instruction. He prepared for the priesthood at the Seminary of Saint Sulpice in Paris and was ordained in 1675. Three years later he was put in charge of the instruction of young women who had renounced Catholicism. In recognition of his outstanding ability and persuasiveness, he was appointed tutor to the grandson of Louis XIV in 1689 and was elevated to the archbishopric of Cambray in 1695. He died on January 7, 1715.

The Education of Girls, published in 1681, when he was directing the institution in Paris for the conversion of Protestant girls, has the distinction of being the first comprehensive and systematic exposition of the subject. He advocated the higher education of women but restricted their education to the practical needs of domestic life. His treatise evidences great wisdom and contains many general pedagogical principles, justifying the statement of Paroz in his *Histoire Universelle de la Pédagogie*: "Of all the Catholic clergy who have engaged in educational work, Fénelon has perhaps approached nearest to the rational principles which form the basis of modern pedagogy. This characteristic will always assign him a high rank among educators."

In the selections that follow are the first two chapters of Fénelon's treatise in thirteen chapters and representative passages from the remaining chapters.

227

THE EDUCATION OF GIRLS*

The Importance of the Education of Girls

1. Nothing is more neglected than the education of girls. Custom and the caprice of mothers frequently decide everything: people suppose that they ought to give but little instruction to this sex. The education of boys passes for one of the principal concerns of life through its relation to the public weal; and although scarcely fewer mistakes are made than in the education of girls, people are at least persuaded that much intelligence is needed to succeed in it. The cleverest people have endeavored to give rules in this matter. How many teachers and colleges we see! What expense for the printing of books, for the researches of science, for methods of learning the languages, for the choice of professors! All this great preparation often has more superficiality than solidity; but it indicates the high conception people have of the education of boys. As for girls, they say, it is not necessary that they be learned, curiosity renders them vain and affected; it is enough if they know how to govern some day their households, and to obey their husbands without question. People do not fail to refer to many women whom science has rendered ridiculous: after which they believe themselves justified in blindly abandoning girls to the management of ignorant and indiscreet mothers.

2. It is true that we should fear making ridiculous scholars. Women ordinarily have minds weaker and more inquisitive than men; thus it is not expedient to engage them in studies that might turn their heads. They are not to govern the state, make war, or enter the sacred ministry; accordingly they can dispense with certain branches of knowledge which belong to statecraft, the art of war, jurisprudence, philosophy, and theology. The greater

*From *Great Pedagogical Essays,* edited by F. V. N. Painter (New York: American Book Company, 1905).

228

part of the mechanic arts does not suit them: they are constituted for moderate exertion. Their bodies, as well as their minds, are less strong and robust than those of men; in return, nature has given them industry, neatness, and economy, to occupy them tranquilly in their homes.

3. But what follows from this natural weakness of women? The more they are weak, the more important is it to make them strong. Have they not duties to perform, even duties which form the foundation of all human life? Is it not women that ruin or uphold families, that regulate all the details of domestic life, and that decide, consequently, what touches most closely the whole human race? In that way they have the principal part in the good or the bad manners of almost the entire world. A judicious, diligent, and pious wife is the soul of a great household; she introduces order there for temporal welfare and future salvation. Even men, who have all authority in public, can not, by their deliberations, establish any efficient good, if women do not aid them to execute it.

4. The world is not a phantom; it is the union of all the families: and who can govern them with a nicer care than women who, besides their natural authority and their diligence in the household, have still the advantage of being born painstaking, attentive to details, industrious, winning, and persuasive? Can men themselves hope for any happiness in life, if their most intimate relation, which is that of marriage, turns to bitterness? And what will become of the children, who are later to constitute the human race, if their mothers spoil them from infancy?

5. These, then, are the occupations of women, which are scarcely less important to the public than those of men, since they have households to regulate, husbands to make happy, and children to bring up well. Add to this that virtue is no less for women than for men; without speaking of the good or ill they can do to the public, they are the half of the human race, redeemed by the blood of Jesus Christ, and destined to eternal life.

6. Finally, we must consider, besides the good which women do when they are well brought up, the evil which they cause in the world when they lack an education which inspires them with

virtue. It is unquestionable that the bad education of women does more harm than that of men, since the disorders of men often come both from the evil training which they have received from their mothers, and from the passions which other women have inspired in them at a more advanced age. What intrigues are presented to us in history, what overturnings of laws and manners, what bloody wars, what innovations in religion, what revolutions in the state, caused by the profligacy of women! These are the considerations that prove the importance of giving girls a good education: let us seek the means of doing so.

Defects of the Prevailing Education

7. A girl's ignorance is the cause that she grows weary, and that she does not know how to employ herself innocently. When she has reached a certain age without applying herself to solid things, she has neither a taste nor regard for them; all that is serious appears to her sad, all that demands sustained attention fatigues her; the inclination to pleasure, which is strong in youth, the examples of persons of the same age who are plunged in amusements — all serves to make her fear a regular and laborious life. At this early age she lacks the experience and authority to manage anything in the house of her parents; she does not even know the importance of applying herself to it, unless her mother has taken care to instruct her in detail. If she is of rank, she is exempt from the work of her hands: she will work therefore only some hour of the day, because people say, without knowing why, that it is proper for women to work; but often it will be only a pretense, and she will not become accustomed to continuous employment.

8. In this condition what will she do? The companionship of a mother who watches her, who scolds her, who thinks she is bringing her up properly by overlooking nothing, who is reconciled with her, who makes her endure her whims, and who always appears burdened with domestic cares, offends and repels her; she has around her flattering women, who seek to insinuate themselves into her regard by base and dangerous attentions, follow

all her idle fancies, and entertain her with all that can disgust her with the good: piety seems to her a tiresome business — a rule hostile to every pleasure. With what will she occupy herself? With nothing useful. This heedlessness will even turn into an incurable habit.

9. Meanwhile there is a great vacancy, which one can not hope to fill with solid things; it is necessary, therefore, that frivolous things take their place. In this inactivity a girl gives herself up to idleness; and idleness, which is a languor of the soul, is an inexhaustible source of weariness. She accustoms herself to sleep a third more than would be needful to keep her in perfect health; this large amount of sleep serves only to enervate her, to make her more delicate, more exposed to bodily ills: while moderate sleep, accompanied by regular exercise, renders a person cheerful, vigorous and strong — a thing which undoubtedly tends to the true perfection of the body, not to speak of its advantages to the mind. This effeminacy and indolence, being joined to ignorance, beget a pernicious desire for diversions and plays; they excite an inconsiderate and insatiable curiosity.

10. Persons who are educated and engaged in serious employments, have ordinarily only a moderate curiosity: what they know gives them a contempt for many things that they do not know; they see the uselessness and folly of most of the things which little minds that know nothing and have nothing to do, are eager to learn.

On the contrary, girls who are badly educated and indolent, always have a wandering imagination. For lack of solid nourishment, their curiosity ardently turns toward vain and dangerous objects. Those who have cleverness often become affected, and read all the books that can feed their vanity; they become passionately fond of novels, comedies, and fantastic adventures, in which sexual love has a place. They develop a visionary spirit of accustoming themselves to the magniloquent language of romantic heroes: they are even spoiled in that way for society; for all those beautiful, high-flown sentiments, all those generous passions, all those adventures which the author of the novel has invented for pleasure, have no connection with the true motives that operate in the world

231

and decide its affairs, nor with the disappointments that one finds in all that one undertakes.

A poor girl, full of the tender and marvelous incidents that have charmed her in her reading, is astonished not to find in society real persons resembling these heroes: she would like to live as imaginary princesses, who in novels are always charming, always adored, and always above every need. What disgust for her to descend from this heroism to the smallest details of housekeeping!

11. Some women push their inquisitiveness still further, and meddle in the decision of religious questions, although they lack the requisite knowledge. But those who have not sufficient openness of mind for these matters, have others that are suited to them: they ardently desire to know what is said, what is done, a song, a bit of news, an intrigue; to receive letters, to read those that others receive; they wish to be told all, and also to tell all; they are vain, and vanity talks a great deal; they are frivolous, and frivolity prevents the thoughtfulness which would often keep silent.

Various Principles and Recommendations.

12. It is necessary to be content with following and aiding nature. Children know but little, we should not urge them to talk: but since they do not know many things, they have many questions to ask. It is sufficient to answer them precisely, and to add sometimes little comparisons in order to render more intelligible the explanations that one is to give them. If they express a judgment of something without knowing it well, it is needful to embarrass them by some new question, in order to make them feel their error, without rudely putting them to confusion. At the same time we should let them see, not by vague praises, but by some practical mark of esteem, that we approve them much more when they doubt and when they ask what they do not know, than when they decide the best. This is the true means of imparting to their minds, with much politeness, a genuine modesty, and a great contempt for the wranglings that are so common with young people of little intelligence.

13. The curiosity of children is a natural inclination which goes

out to meet instruction; do not fail to take advantage of it. In the country, for example, they see a mill, and wish to know what it is; we should show them how the food that nourishes man is prepared. They observe some harvesters, and it is necessary to explain to them what they are doing, how grain is sowed, and how it multiplies in the earth. In the city they see shops where different arts are practiced, and where different articles of merchandise are sold. We should never be annoyed by their questions; these are openings which nature offers in order to facilitate instruction: express a pleasure in them; in that way you will gradually teach them how all the things are made which are of use to man, and with which commerce is concerned. Little by little, without special study, they will learn the best way to make everything they need, and the just value of it, which is the true foundation of economy. This knowledge, which ought to be despised by no one, since everybody has need to estimate his expense, is chiefly necessary to girls.

14. We have remarked that the brain of children is altogether warm and moist, a fact that gives them continual movement. By reason of this softness of the brain everything is easily impressed upon it, and the images of all sensible objects are very vivid: hence we should make haste to write on their minds while the characters are easily formed there. But we should choose well the images that we are to engrave there; for we should pour into so small and precious a receptacle only exquisite things: we should remember that we ought, at that age, to pour into minds only what we desire to remain there for life. The first impressions made while the brain is still soft, and nothing is written there, are the most profound. Besides they harden as age dries the brain; hence they become ineffaceable: whence it happens that when one is old, one distinctly remembers the things of youth, although far distant, while one recollects less clearly what has been seen at a more advanced age, because the impressions have been made upon the brain when it was hardened and full of other images.

15. At the same time it is necessary to seek every means to render agreeable to the child what you demand of her. If you have something unpleasant to propose, let her understand that the pain will be soon followed by pleasure; show her always the utility

of the things you teach her; make her see their use in relation to society and the duties of her station. Without that, study will seem to her an abstract, fruitless, and painful toil. Of what use is it, they will say to themselves, to learn all these things which people do not talk about in conversation, and which have no relation to what we are obliged to do? It is necessary, therefore, to give them a reason for what we teach them. It is to enable you, you will say to them, to do well what you will have to do some day; it is to form your judgment; it is to accustom you to reason correctly about all the affairs of life. We should always show them a substantial and agreeable end which will sustain them in their labor, and never pretend to bring them into subjection by a base and absolute authority.

16. Note a great fault in the prevailing education: we put all the pleasure on one side, and all the irksomeness on the other; all the irksomeness in study, and all the pleasure in amusement. What can a child do but bear this rule impatiently, and ardently run after games?

Let us endeavor then to change this order: let us render study agreeable, let us conceal it under the appearance of liberty and pleasure; let us allow children sometimes to interrupt their studies with little flights of amusement; they have need of these distractions in order to rest their minds.

17. Let us come now to the things in which a woman ought to be instructed. What are her employments? She is charged with the education of her children; with the boys up to a certain age, with the girls till they are married or enter a convent; with the management of servants, with their manners and duties; with the details of expense, with the means of doing everything economically and honorably; and ordinarily even with directing the estate and receiving its revenues.

The learning of women, as that of men, ought to be restricted to knowledge relating to their duties; the difference of their employments should make that of their studies. It is necessary therefore to limit the instruction of women to the things we have just mentioned. But an acquisitive woman will find that this is giving very narrow bounds to her desire for knowledge; she is mistaken;

it is because she does not know the importance and the extent of the things in which I propose to have her instructed.

18. Though the difficulty of finding governesses is great, we must confess that there is another still greater; it is that of the irregularity of parents: all the rest is useless, unless they are willing to coöperate themselves in the work. The foundation of all is that they give their children only correct maxims and edifying examples. It is what one can hope for only in a very small number of families. In most homes we see only confusion, change, a crowd of wrong-headed servants, and disagreement of master and mistress. What a frightful school for children! Often a mother who passes her life at cards, at the theater, and in unbecoming conversation, complains in a grave tone that she can not find a governess capable of educating her daughters. But what can the best education do with girls in view of such a mother?

BENJAMIN FRANKLIN

BENJAMIN FRANKLIN (1706-1790). The best known early American argument favoring advanced training in the things most useful and most ornamental is Benjamin Franklin's *Proposals Relating to the Education of Youth in Pensilvania*. Although his pragmatic ideas were not wholly adopted by the Academy of Philadelphia, remarkable contributions to professional education were made by the University of Pennsylvania, which grew out of the academy. His pre-eminence here as in a dozen other fields is undeniable, and it has been said that of all the founding fathers he would most readily adapt himself to the complexities of the modern world.

Born in Boston, Massachusetts, on January 17, 1706, Franklin achieved international renown and lived to see the inauguration of the government he had helped to bring to birth. The world mourned his passing on April 17, 1790. Statesman, scientist, philosopher, educator, printer, author, inventor, and diplomat, he labored constantly to improve his mind and character. He read widely, taught himself to write English by studying the best models, and mastered other languages as well — Latin, French, Italian, and Spanish. He attributed his many achievements to his industry and to his ability to write with simplicity and clarity. At the beginning of his famous autobiography he stated that if Providence gave him the choice, he "should have no objection to go over the same life from beginning to the end, requesting only the advantage authors have of correcting, in a second edition, the faults of the first."

The most remarkable characteristic of Franklin is his modernity. In 1956, on the occasion of the celebration of the 250th anniversary of his birth, the Franklin Institute of Philadelphia, in co-operation with other societies, defined ten areas in which his work or thought was believed to be relevant to the present. The first of these areas was education and science. In his life-time he was the living embodiment of a system which had enabled a common man to rise through self-education to pre-eminence in his country. Because he believed in the ideals of his democratic heritage, he advocated for the young and for adults training appropriate to their needs. Inasmuch as schools today are still faced with the problem of having much more to teach than can be assimilated, Franklin's criterion of practical selection seems even more appropriate to the organization of the modern high school than to the eighteenth-century academy.

PROPOSALS RELATING TO THE EDUCATION
OF YOUTH*

The good Education of Youth has been esteemed by wise Men in all Ages, as the surest Foundation of the Happiness both of private Families and of Commonwealths. Almost all Governments have therefore made it a principal Object of their Attention, to establish and endow with proper Revenues, such Seminaries of Learning, as might supply the succeeding Age with Men qualified to serve the Publick with Honour to themselves, and to their Country.

Many of the first Settlers of the Province were Men who had received a good Education in Europe, and to their Wisdom and good Management we owe much of our present Prosperity. But their Hands were full, and they could not do all Things. The present Race are not thought to be generally of equal Ability: For though the American Youth are allow'd not to want Capacity; yet the best Capacities require Cultivation, it being truly with them, as with the best Ground, which unless well tilled and sowed with profitable Seed, produces only ranker Weeds.

That we may obtain the Advantages arising from an Increase of Knowledge, and prevent as much as may be the mischievous Consequences that would attend a general Ignorance among us, the following *Hints* are offered towards forming a Plan for the Education of the Youth of Pennsylvania, viz.

It is propos'd.

That some Persons of Leisure and publick Spirit, apply for a Charter, by which they may be incorporated, with Power to erect an Academy for the Education of Youth, to govern the same, provide Masters, make Rules, receive Donations, purchase Lands, &c. and to add to their Number, from Time to Time such other Persons as they shall judge suitable.

*From the pamphlet *Proposals Relating to the Education of Youth in Pensilvania* (Philadelphia, 1751).

That the Members of the Corporation make it their Pleasure, and in some Degree their Business, to visit the Academy often, encourage and countenance the Youth, countenance and assist the Masters, and by all Means in their Power advance the Usefulness and Reputation of the Design; that they look on the Students as in some Sort their Children, treat them with Familiarity and Affection, and when they have behav'd well, and gone through their Studies, and are to enter the World, zealously unite, and make all the Interest that can be made to establish them, whether in Business, Offices, Marriages, or any other Thing for their Advantage, preferably to all other Persons whatsoever even of equal Merit.

And if Men may, and frequently do, catch such a Taste for cultivating Flowers, for Planting, Grafting, Inoculating, and the like, as to despise all other Amusements for their Sake, why may not we expect they should acquire a Relish for that *more useful* Culture of young Minds. Thompson says,

> 'Tis Joy to see the human Blossoms blow,
> When infant Reason grows apace, and calls
> For the kind Hand of an assiduous Care;
> Delightful Task! to rear the tender Thought,
> To teach the young Idea how to shoot,
> To pour the fresh Instruction o'er the Mind,
> To breathe th' enliv'ning Spirit, and to fix
> The generous Purpose in the glowing Breast.

That a House be provided for the Academy, if not in the Town, not many Miles from it; the Situation high and dry, and if it may be, not far from a River, having a Garden, Orchard, Meadow, and a Field or two.

That the House be furnished with a Library (if in the Country, if in the Town, the Town Libraries may serve) with Maps of all for Experiments in Natural Philosophy, and for Mechanics; Prints, Countries, Globes, some mathematical Instruments, an Apparatus of all Kinds, Prospects, Buildings, Machines, &c.

That the Rector be a Man of good Understanding, good Mor-

238

als, diligent and patient, learn'd in the Languages and Sciences, and a correct pure Speaker and Writer of the English Tongue; to have such Tutors under him as shall be necessary.

That the boarding Scholars diet together, plainly, temperately, and frugally.

That to keep them in Health, and to strengthen and render active their Bodies, they be frequently exercis'd in Running, Leaping, Wrestling, and Swimming, &c.

That they have peculiar Habits to distinguish them from other Youth, if the Academy be in or near the Town; for this, among other Reasons, that their Behaviour may be the better observed.

As to their Studies, it would be well if they could be taught *every Thing* that is useful, and *every Thing* that is ornamental: But Art is long, and their Time is short. It is therefore propos'd that they learn those Things that are likely to be most useful and most ornamental, Regard being had to the several Professions for which they are intended.

All should be taught to write a fair Hand, and swift, as that is useful to All. And with it may be learnt something of Drawing, by Imitation of Prints, and some of the first Principles of Perspective.

Arithmetick, Accounts, and some of the first Principles of *Geometry* and *Astronomy.*

The *English* Language might be taught by Grammar; in which some of our best Writers, as Tillotson, Addison, Pope, Algernon Sidney, Cato's Letters, &c. should be Classicks: The *Stiles* principally to be cultivated, being the *clear* and the *concise.* Reading should also be taught, and pronouncing, properly, distinctly, emphatically; not with an even Tone, which *under-does,* nor a theatrical, which *over-does* Nature.

To form their Stile, they should be put on Writing Letters to each other, making Abstracts of what they read; or writing the same Things in their own Words; telling or writing Stories lately read, in their own Expressions. All to be revis'd and corrected by the Tutor, who should give his Reasons, explain the Force and Import of Words, &c.

To form their Pronunciation, they may be put on making Declamations, repeating Speeches, delivering Orations, &c. The Tutor

239

assisting at the Rehearsals, teaching, advising, correcting their Accent, &c.

But if History be made a constant Part of their Reading, such as the Translations of the Greek and Roman Historians, and the modern Histories of antient Greece and Rome, &c. may not almost all Kinds of useful Knowledge be that Way introduc'd to Advantage, and with Pleasure to the Student? As

Geography, by reading with Maps, and being required to point out the Places *where* the greatest Actions were done, to give their old and new Names, with the Bounds, Situation, Extent of the Countries concern'd, &c.

Chronology, by the Help of Helvicus or some other Writer of the Kind, who will enable them to tell *when* those Events happened; what Princes were Contemporaries, what States or famous Men flourish'd about that Time &c. The several principal Epochas to be first well fix'd in their Memories.

Antient Customs, religious and civil, being frequently mentioned in History, will give Occasion for explaining them; in which the Prints of Medals, Basso Relievo's, and antient Monuments will greatly assist.

Morality, by descanting and making continual Observations on the Causes of the Rise or Fall of any Man's Character, Fortune, Power, &c. mention'd in History; the Advantages of Temperance, Order, Frugality, Industry, Perseverance, &c. &c. Indeed the general natural Tendency of Reading good History, must be, to fix in the Minds of Youth deep Impressions of the Beauty and Usefulness of Virtue of all Kinds, Publick Spirit, Fortitude, &c.

History will show the wonderful Effects of Oratory, in governing, turning and leading great Bodies of Mankind, Armies, Cities, Nations. When the Minds of Youth are struck with Admiration at this then is the Time to give them the Principles of that Art, which they will study with Taste and Application. Then they may be made acquainted with the best Models among the Antients, their Beauties being particularly pointed out to them. Modern Political Oratory being chiefly performed by the Pen and Press, its Advantages over the Antient in some Respects are to be shown; as that its Effects are more extensive, more lasting, &c.

History will also afford frequent Opportunities of showing the Necessity of a *Publick Religion,* from its Usefulness to the Publick; the Advantage of a Religious Character among private Persons; the Mischiefs of Superstition, &c. and the Excellency of the Christian Religion above all others antient or modern.

History will also give Occasion to expatiate on the Advantage of Civil Orders and Constitutions, how Men and their Properties are protected by joining in Societies and establishing Government; their Industry encouraged and rewarded, Arts invented, and Life made more comfortable: The Advantages of *Liberty,* Mischiefs of *Licentiousness,* Benefits arising from good Laws and a due Execution of Justice, &c. Thus may the first Principles of sound *Politicks* be fix'd in the Minds of Youth.

On *Historical* Occasions, Questions of Right and Wrong, Justice and Injustice, will naturally arise, and may be put to Youth, which they may debate in Conversation and in Writing. When they ardently desire Victory, for the Sake of the Praise attending it, they will begin to feel the Want, and be sensible of the Use of *Logic,* or the Art of Reasoning to *discover* Truth, and of Arguing to *defend* it, and *convince* Adversaries. This would be the Time to acquaint them with the Principles of that Art. Grotius, Puffendorff, and some other Writers of the same Kind, may be used on these Occasions to decide their Disputes. Publick Disputes warm the Imagination, whet the Industry, and strengthen the natural Abilities.

When Youth are told that the Great Men whose Lives and Actions they read in History spoke two of the best Languages that ever were, the most expressive, copious, beautiful; and that the finest Writings, the most correct Compositions, the most perfect Productions of human Wit and Wisdom, are in those Languages which have endured Ages and will endure while there are Men; that no Translation can do them Justice or give the Pleasure found in Reading the Originals; that those Languages contain all Science; that one of them is become almost universal, being the Language of Learned Men in all Countries; that to understand them is a distinguishing Ornament, &c. they may be thereby made desirous of learning those Languages, and their Industry sharpen'd in the

Acquisition of them. All intended for Divinity should be taught the Latin and Greek; for Physick, the Latin, Greek and French; for Law, the Latin and French; Merchants, the French, German, and Spanish: And though all should not be compell'd to learn Latin, Greek, or the modern foreign Languages; yet none that have an ardent Desire to learn them should be refused; their English, Arithmetick, and other Studies absolutely necessary, being at the same Time not neglected.

If the new *Universal History* were also read, it would give a *connected* Idea of human Affairs, so far as it goes, which should be follow'd by the best modern Histories, particularly of our Mother Country; then of these Colonies; which should be accompanied with Observations on their Rise, Encrease, Use to Great Britain, Encouragements, Discouragements, &c. the Means to make them flourish, secure their Liberties, &c.

With the History of Men, Times and Nations, should be read at proper Hours or Days, some of the best *Histories of Nature,* which would not only be delightful to Youth, and furnish them with Matter for their Letters, &c. as well as other History; but afterwards of great Use to them, whether they are Merchants, Handicrafts, or Divines; enabling the first the better to understand many Commodities, Drugs, &c. the second to improve his Trade or Handicraft by new Mixtures, Materials, &c, and the last to adorn his Discourses by beautiful Comparisons, and strengthen them by new Proofs of Divine Providence. The Conversation of all will be improved by it, as Occasions frequently occur of making Natural Observations, which are instructive, agreeable, and entertaining in almost all Companies. *Natural History* will also afford Opportunities of introducing many Observations relating to the Preservation of Health, which may be afterwards of great Use. Arbuthnot on Air and Aliment, Sanctorius on Perspiration, Lemery on Foods, and some others may now be read, and a very little Explanation will make them sufficiently intelligible to Youth.

While they are reading Natural History, might not a little *Gardening, Planting, Grafting, Inoculating,* &c. be taught and practiced; and now and then Excursions made to the neighbouring Plantations of the best Farmers, their Methods observ'd and reason'd upon for the Information of Youth. The Improvement of Agriculture being useful to all and Skill in it no Disparagement to any.

The History of *Commerce,* of the Invention of Arts, Rise of Manufactures, Progress of Trade, Change of its Seats, with the Reasons, Causes, &c. may also be made entertaining to Youth, and will be useful to all. And this, with the Accounts in other History of the prodigious Force and Effect of Engines and Machines used in War, will naturally introduce a Desire to be instructed in *Mechanicks* and to be inform'd of the Principles of that Art by which weak Men perform such Wonders, Labour is sav'd, Manufactures expedited, &c. This will be the Time to show them Prints of antient and modern Machines, to explain them, to let them be copied and to give Lectures in Mechanical Philosophy.

With the whole should be constantly inculcated and cultivated, that *Benignity of Mind,* which shows itself in *searching for* and *seizing* every Opportunity *to serve* and *to oblige;* and is the Foundation of what is called Good Breeding; highly useful to the Possessor, and most agreeable to all.

The Idea of what is *true Merit,* should also be often presented to Youth, explain'd and impress'd on their Minds, as consisting in an *Inclination* join'd with an *Ability* to serve Mankind, one's Country, Friends and Family; which *Ability* is (With the Blessing of God) to be acquir'd or greatly encreas'd by *true Learning* and should indeed be the great *Aim* and *End* of all Learning.

FRIEDRICH WILHELM FROEBEL

FRIEDRICH WILHELM FROEBEL (1782-1852). Pestalozzi's most illustrious disciple is credited with originating the kindergarten and with contributing to educational theory the concept of self-activity and play as essential factors in child development. At the grave of Friedrich Wilhelm Froebel one of his eulogists called attention to the sacrifices that he had made for his country in the wars of freedom and added that "he turned with the same enthusiasm which surrenders and sacrifices for the highest thought to the aim of cultivating the people and youth." It was one of his most enthusiastic disciples — Baroness Bertha von Marenholtz-Bülow — who introduced his teachings to educators in other nations of Europe, and it was the most influential of all American educators — John Dewey — who adopted his principles in the Laboratory School at the University of Chicago.

Froebel was born in the Thuringian village of Oberwiessbach on April 21, 1782. His mother died when he was very young, and his education suffered until he went to live with an uncle at the age of ten. His love of nature caused him to enter the University of Jena in 1799, but poverty cut short his studies. The turning point in his life came when he met Anton Gruner, a pupil of Pestalozzi, and decided to become a teacher. In 1808 he went to Yverdon, where he spent two years with Pestalozzi. He then attended the University of Göttingen until military service interrupted his studies. In 1816 he opened a school at Griesheim. Two years later he moved to Keilhau, where he put his theories into practice. Later he served as head of a new orphan asylum at Burgdorf, Switzerland. Convinced of the importance of the early stages of education and aware of certain weaknesses in Pestalozzi's work, he came to the conclusion that a thorough reform was in order. He saw that children use their senses, observe, invent, construct, delight in activity, and he resolved to found a kindergarten — a school which guides the interests and activities of children in such a way as to give order to their ideas, develop their faculties, and prepare them for a regular program of instruction. Today's "playway" in education owes a great debt to Froebel.

While he was directing the school at Keilhau, Froebel published *The Education of Man*, the great work on which his fame rests. Though not a great philosopher, he was profoundly influenced by the German thinkers of his day and by Rousseau. Believing in the underlying unity of all things

244

and in the importance of education in the process of evolution, he has been called a nature mystic. "His great word," according to W. T. Harris, "is *inner connection*. There must be an inner connection between the pupil's mind and the objects which he studies . . . an inner connection in those objects among themselves which determines their succession . . . an inner connection within the soul that unites the faculties of feeling, perception, phantasy, thought, and volition, and determines the law of their unfolding."

THE TEACHINGS OF PESTALOZZI*

The watchword of teaching and of education was at this time the name of Pestalozzi. It soon became evident to me that Pestalozzi was to be the watchword of my life also; for not only Gruner, but also a second teacher at the school, were pupils of Pestalozzi, and the first-named had even written a book on his method of teaching. The name had a magnetic effect upon me, the more so as during my self-development and self-education it had seemed to me an aspiration—a something perhaps never to be familiarly known, yet distinct enough, and at all events inspiriting. And now I recalled how in my early boyhood, in my father's house, I had got a certain piece of news out of some newspaper or another, or at least that is how the matter stood in my memory. I gathered that in Switzerland a man of forty, who lived retired from the world,—Pestalozzi by name,— had taught himself, alone and unaided, reading, writing, and arithmetic. Just at that time I was feeling the slowness and insufficiency of my own development, and this news quieted me, and filled me with the hope and trust that I, too, might, through my own endeavour, repair the deficiencies of my bringing-up. As I have grown older I have also found it consolatory to remark how the culture of vigorous, capable men has not seldom been acquired remarkably late in life. And in general I must acknowledge it as part of the groundwork

*From the *Autobiography*, translated by Emilie Michaelis and Keatley Moore.

underlying my life and the evolution of my character, that the contemplation of the actual existences of real men always wrought upon my soul, as it were, by a fruitful rain and the genial warmth of sunshine; while the isolated truths these lives enshrined, the principles those who lived them had thought out and embodied in some phrase or another, fell as precious seed-corn, as it were, or as solvent salt crystals upon my thirsty spirit. And while on this head I cannot help especially calling to mind how deep and lasting was the impression made upon me in my last year at school by the accounts in the Holy Scriptures of the lives of earnestly striving youths and men. I mention it here, but I shall have to return to the subject later on.

Now to return to the new life which I had begun. It was only to be expected that each thing and all things I heard of Pestalozzi seized powerfully upon me; and this more especially applies to a sketchy narrative of his life, his aims, and his struggles, which I found in a literary newspaper, where also was stated Pestalozzi's well-known desire and endeavour—namely, in some nook or corner of the world, no matter where, to build up an institution for the education of the poor, after his own heart. This narrative, especially the last point of it, was to my heart like oil poured on fire. There and then the resolution was taken to go and look upon this man who could so think and so endeavour to act, and to study his life and its work.

Three days afterwards (it was towards the end of August 1805) I was already on the road to Yverdon where Pestalozzi had not long before established himself. Once arrived there, and having met with the friendliest reception by Pestalozzi and his teachers, because of my introductions from Gruner and his colleagues, I was taken, like every other visitor, to the class-rooms, and there left more or less to my own devices. I was still very inexperienced, both in the theory and practice of teaching, relying chiefly in such things upon my memory of my own school-time, and I was therefore very little fitted for a rigorous examination into details of method and into the way they were connected to form a whole system. The latter point, indeed, was neither clearly thought out, nor was it worked out in practice. What I saw was to me at once elevating and depressing, arousing and also bewildering. My visit lasted only a fortnight. I worked away and tried to take in as much as I could; especially as, to help me in the duties I had undertaken, I felt impelled to give a faithful account in writing of my views on the whole system, and the effect it had produced upon me. With this idea I tried to hold fast in my memory all I heard. Nevertheless I soon felt that heart and mind would alike come to grief in a man of my disposition if I were to stay longer with Pestalozzi, much as I desired to do so. At that time the life there was especially vigorous; internally and externally it was a living, moving, stirring existence, for Prince Hardenberg, commissioned by the Austrian Government, had come to examine thoroughly into Pestalozzi's work.

The fruits of my short stay with Pestalozzi were as follows:—

In the first place, I saw the whole training of a great educational institution, worked upon a clear and firmly-settled plan of teaching. I still possess the "teaching-plan" of Pestalozzi's institution in use at that time. This teaching-plan contains, in my opinion, much that is excellent, somewhat also that is prejudicial. Excellent, I thought, was the contrivance of the so-called "exchange classes." In each subject the instruction was always given through the entire establishment at the same time. Thus the subjects for teaching were settled for every class, but the pupils were distributed amongst the various classes according to their proficiency in the subject in hand, so that the whole body of pupils was redistributed in quite a distinct division for each subject. The advantage of this contrivance struck me as so undeniable and so forcible that I have never since relinquished it in my educational work, nor could I now bring myself to do so. The prejudicial side of the teaching-plan, against which I intuitively rebelled, although my own tendencies on the subject were as yet so vague and dim, lay, in my opinion, in its incompleteness and its onesidedness. Several subjects of teaching and education highly important to the all-round harmonious development of a man seemed to me thrust far too much into the background, treated in step-motherly fashion, and superficially worked out.

The results of the arithmetical teaching astounded me, yet I

247

could not follow it into its larger applications and wider extent. The mechanical rules of this branch of instruction seemed to whirl me round and round as in a whirlpool. The teacher was Krüsi. The teaching, in spite of the brilliant results within its own circle, and in spite of the sharpness of the quickened powers of perception and comprehension in the children by which it attained those results, yet, to my personal taste, had something too positive in its setting forth, too mechanical in its reception. And Josias Schmid had already, even at that time, felt the imperfection of this branch of instruction. He imparted to me the first ground-principles of his later work on the subject, and his ideas at once commanded my approval, for I saw they possessed two important properties, many-sidedness and an exhaustive scientific basis.

The teaching of drawing was also very incomplete, especially in its first commencement; but drawing from right-angled prisms with equal sides, in various lengths, which was one of the exercises required at a later stage, and drawing other mathematical figures by means of which the comprehension of the forms of actual objects of every-day life might be facilitated were much more to my mind. Schmid's method of drawing had not yet appeared.

In physical geography, the usual school course, with its many-coloured maps, had been left far behind. Tobler, an active young man, was the principal teacher in this section. Still, even this branch had far too much positive instruction for me. Particularly unpleasant to me was the commencement of the course, which began with an account of the bottom of the sea, although the pupils could have no conception of their own as to its nature or dimensions. Nevertheless the teaching aroused astonishment, and carried one involuntarily along with it through the impression made by the lightning-quickness of the answers of the children.

In natural history I heard only the botany. The principal teacher, who had also prepared the plan of instruction in this subject for all the school, was Hopf, like the rest an active young man. The school course arranged and carried out by him had much that was excellent. In each separate instance — for example, the shape and position of leaves, flowers, etc. — he would first obtain all the possible varieties of form by question and answer between the class and himself, and then he would select from the results the form which was before them in nature. These lessons, which were in this way made so attractive, and whose merits spoke for themselves, showed, however, when it came to practical application, an unpractical, I had almost said, a self-contradictory aspect.

THE EDUCATION OF MAN*

In all things there lives and reigns an eternal law. To him whose mind, through disposition and faith, is filled, penetrated, and quickened with the necessity that this can not possibly be otherwise, as well as to him whose clear, calm mental vision beholds the inner in the outer and through the outer, and sees the outer proceeding with logical necessity from the essence of the inner, this law has been and is enounced with equal clearness and distinctness in nature (the external), in the spirit (the internal), and in life which unites the two. This all-controlling law is necessarily based on an all-pervading, energetic, living, self-conscious, and hence eternal Unity. This fact, as well as the Unity itself, is again vividly recognized, either through faith or through insight, with equal clearness and comprehensiveness; therefore, a quietly observant human mind, a thoughtful, clear human intellect, has never failed, and will never fail, to recognize this Unity.

This Unity is God. All things have come from the Divine Unity, from God, and have their origin in the Divine Unity, in God alone. God is the sole source of all things. In all things there lives and reigns the Divine Unity, God. All things live and have their being in and through the Divine Unity, in and through God. All things are only through the divine effluence that lives in them. The divine effluence that lives in each thing is the essence of each thing.

It is the destiny and life-work of all things to unfold their essence, hence their divine being, and, therefore, the Divine Unity itself — to reveal God in their external and transient being. It is the special destiny and life-work of man, as an intelligent and rational

*From *The Education of Man,* translated by W. N. Hailmann. Reprinted in the International Education Series.

being, to become fully, vividly, and clearly conscious of his essence, of the divine effluence in him, and, therefore, of God; to become fully, vividly, and clearly conscious of his destiny and life-work; and to accomplish this, to render it (his essence) active, to reveal it in his own life with self-determination and freedom.

Education consists in leading man, as a thinking, intelligent being, growing into self-consciousness, to a pure and unsullied conscious and free representation of the inner law of Divine Unity, and in teaching him ways and means thereto.

The knowledge of that eternal law, the insight into its origin, into its essence, into the totality, the connection, and intensity of its effects, the knowledge of life in its totality, constitute *science, the science of life;* and, referred by the self-conscious, thinking, intelligent being to representation and practice through and in himself, this becomes *science of education.*

The system of directions, derived from the knowledge and study of that law, to guide thinking, intelligent beings in the apprehension of their life-work and in the accomplishment of their destiny, is *the theory of education.*

The self-active application of this knowledge in the direct development and cultivation of rational beings toward the attainment of their destiny, is *the practice of education.*

The object of education is the realization of a faithful, pure, inviolate, and hence holy life.

Knowledge and application, consciousness and realization in life, united in the service of a faithful, pure, holy life, constitute the *wisdom of life,* pure wisdom.

To be wise is the highest aim of man, is the most exalted achievement of human self-determination.

To educate one's self and others, with consciousness, freedom, and self-determination, is a twofold achievement of wisdom: it *began* with the first appearance of man upon the earth; it *was manifest* with the first appearance of full self-consciousness in man; it *begins now* to proclaim itself as a necessary, universal requirement of humanity, and to be heard and heeded as such. With this achievement man enters upon the path which alone leads to life; which surely tends to the fulfillment of the inner, and thereby also to the fulfillment of the outer, requirement of humanity; which, through a faithful, pure, holy life, attains beatitude.

By education, then, the divine essence of man should be unfolded, brought out, lifted into consciousness, and man himself raised into free, conscious obedience to the divine principle that lives in him, and to a free representation of this principle in his life.

Education, in instruction, should lead man to see and know the divine, spiritual, and eternal principle which animates surrounding nature, constitutes the essence of nature, and is permanently manifested in nature; and, in living reciprocity and united with training, it should express and demonstrate the fact that the same law rules both (the divine principle and nature), as it does nature and man.

Education as a whole, by means of instruction and training, should bring to man's consciousness, and render efficient in his life the fact that man and nature proceed from God and are conditioned by him—that both have their being in God.

Education should lead and guide man to clearness concerning himself and in himself, to peace with nature, and to unity with God; hence, it should lift him to a knowledge of himself and of mankind, to a knowledge of God and of nature, and to the pure and holy life to which such knowledge leads.

In all these requirements, however, education is based on considerations of the innermost.

The inner essence of things is recognized by the innermost spirit (of man) in the outer and through outward manifestations. The inner being, the spirit, the divine essence of things and of man, is known by its outward manifestations. In accordance with this, all education, all instruction and training, all life as a free growth, start from the outer manifestations of man and things, and, proceeding from the outer, act upon the inner, and form its judgments concerning the inner. Nevertheless, education should not draw its inferences concerning the inner from the outer directly, for it lies in the nature of things that always in some relation inferences should be drawn inversely. Thus, the diversity and multiplicity in nature do not warrant the inference of multiplicity in the ultimate cause — a multiplicity of gods — nor does the unity of God warrant the inference of finality in nature; but, in both cases, the inference lies conversely from the diversity in nature to the oneness of its ultimate cause, and from the unity of God to an eternally progressing diversity in natural developments.

The failure to apply this truth, or rather the continual sinning against it, the drawing of direct inferences concerning the inner life of childhood and youth from certain external manifestations of life, is the chief cause of antagonism and contention, of the frequent mistakes in life and education. This furnishes constant occasion for innumerable false judgements concerning the motives of the young, for numberless failures in the education of children, for endless misunderstanding between parent and child, for so much needless complaint and unseemly arraignment of children, for so many unreasonable demands made upon them. Therefore, this truth, in its application to parents, educators, and teachers, is of such great importance that they should strive to render themselves familiar with its application in its smallest details. This would bring into the relations between parents and children, pupils and educators, teacher and taught, a clearness, a constancy, a serenity which are now sought in vain: for the child that seems good outwardly often is not good inwardly, i. e., does not desire the good spontaneously, or from love, respect, and appreciation; similarly, the outwardly rough, stubborn, self-willed child that seems outwardly not good, frequently is filled with the liveliest, most eager, strongest desire for spontaneous goodness in his actions; and the apparently inattentive boy frequently follows a certain fixed line of thought that withholds his attention from all external things.

Therefore, education in instruction and training, originally and in its first principles, should necessarily be *passive, following* (only guarding and protecting), *not prescriptive, categorical, interfering.*

The prescriptive, interfering education, indeed, can be justified only on two grounds; either because it teaches the clear, living thought, self-evident truth, or because it holds up a life whose ideal value has been established in experience. But, where self-evident, living, absolute truth rules, the eternal principle itself reigns, as it were, and will on this account maintain a passive, following character. For the living thought, the eternal divine principle as such demands and requires free self-activity and self-determination on the part of man, the being created for freedom in the image of God.

Again, a life whose ideal value has been perfectly established in experience never aims to serve as model in its form, but only in its essence, in its spirit. It is the greatest mistake to suppose that spiritual, human perfection can serve as model in its form. This accounts for the common experience that the taking of such external manifestations of perfection as examples, instead of elevating mankind, checks, nay, represses, its development.

In good education, in genuine instruction, in true training, necessity should call forth freedom; law, self-determination; external compulsion, inner free-will; external hate, inner love. Where hatred brings forth hatred; law, dishonesty and crime; compulsion, slavery; necessity, serviture; where oppression destroys and debases; where severity and harshness give rise to stubbornness and deceit — all education is abortive. In order to avoid the latter and to secure the former, all prescription should be adapted to the pupil's nature and needs, and secure his coöperation. This is the case when all education in instruction and training, in spite of its necessarily categorical character, bears in all details and ramifications the irrefutable and irresistible impress that the one who makes the demand is himself strictly and unavoidably subject to an eternally ruling law, to an unavoidable eternal necessity, and that, therefore, all despotism is banished.

All true education in training and instruction should, therefore, at every moment, in every demand and regulation, be simultaneously double-sided — giving and taking, uniting and dividing, prescribing and following, active and passive, positive yet giving scope, firm and yielding; and the pupil should be similarly conditioned; but between the two, between educator and pupil, between request and obedience, there should invisibly rule a third something, to which educator and pupil are equally subject. The third something is the *right*, the *best*, necessarily conditioned and expressed without arbitrariness in the circumstances. The calm recognition, the clear knowledge, and the serene, cheerful obedience to the rule of this third something is the particular feature that should be constantly and clearly manifest in the bearing and conduct of the educator and teacher, and often firmly and sternly emphasized by him. The child, the pupil, has a very keen feeling, a very clear apprehension, and rarely fails to distinguish whether what the educator, the teacher, or the father says or requests is personal or arbitrary, or whether it is expressed by him as a general law and necessity.

The representation of the infinite in the finite, of the eternal in the temporal, of the celestial in the terrestrial, of the divine in and through man, in the life of man by the *nursing* of his originally divine nature, confronts us unmistakably on every side as the only object, the only aim of all education, in all instruction and training. Therefore man should be viewed from this only true standpoint immediately with his appearance on earth; nay, as in the case of Mary, immediately with his annunciation, and he should be thus heeded and nursed while yet invisible, unborn.

The debasing illusion that man works, produces, creates only in order to preserve his body, in order to secure food, clothing, and shelter, may have to be endured, but should not be diffused and propagated. Primarily and in truth man works only that his spiritual, divine essence may assume outward form, and that thus he may be enabled to recognize his own spiritual, divine nature and the innermost being of God. Whatever food, clothing, and shelter he obtains thereby comes to him as an insignificant surplus. Therefore Jesus says, "Seek ye first the kingdom of heaven," that is, the realization of the divine spirit in your life and through your life, and whatever else your finite life may require, will be added unto you.

Yet human power should be developed, cultivated, and manifested, not only in inner repose, as religion and religious spirit; not only in outward efficiency, as work and industry; but also — withdrawing upon itself and its own resources — in abstinence, temperance, and frugality. Is it needful to do more than indicate this to a human being not wholly at variance with himself? Where *religion, industry and temperance,* the truly undivided trinity, rule in harmony, in true pristine unity, there, indeed, is heaven upon earth — peace, joy, salvation, grace, blessedness.

Play is the highest phase of child-development — of human development at this period; for *it is self-active representation of the inner — representation of the inner from inner necessity and impulse.* Play is the purest, most spiritual activity of man at this stage, and, at the same time, typical of human life as a whole — of the inner hidden natural life in man and all things. It gives, therefore, joy, freedom, contentment, inner and outer rest, peace with the world. It holds the sources of all that is good. A child that plays thoroughly, with self-active determination, perseveringly until physical fatigue forbids, will surely be a thorough, determined man, capable of self-sacrifice for the promotion of the welfare of himself and others. Is not the most beautiful expression of child-life at this time a playing child? — a child wholly absorbed in his play? — a child that has fallen asleep while so absorbed?...

The aim and object of parental care, in the domestic and family circle, is to awaken and develop, to quicken all the powers and natural gifts of the child, to enable all the members and organs of man to fulfill the requirements of the child's powers and gifts. The natural mother does all this instinctively, without instruction and direction; but this is not enough; it is needful that she should do it consciously, as a conscious being acting upon another being which is growing into consciousness, and consciously tending toward the continuous development of the human being, in a certain inner living connection.

The child—your child, ye fathers—follows you wherever you are, wherever you go, in whatever you do. Do not harshly repel him; show no impatience about his ever-recurring questions. Every harshly repelling word crushes a bud or shoot of his tree of life. Do not, however, tell him in words much more than he could find himself without your words. For it is, of course, easier to hear the answer from another, perhaps, to only half hear and understand it, than it is to seek and discover it himself. To have found one-fourth of the answer by his own efforts is of more value and importance to the child than it is to half hear and half understand it in the words of another; for this causes mental indolence. Do not, therefore, always answer your children's questions at once and directly; but as soon as they have gathered sufficient strength and experience, furnish them with the means to find the answers in the sphere of their own knowledge.

255

On the part of parents and educators the period of infancy demands chiefly *fostering care.* During the succeeding period of childhood which looks upon man predominantly as a unit, and would lead him to unity, *training prevails.* The period of boyhood leads man chiefly to the consideration of particular relationships and individual things, in order to enable him later on to discover their inner unity. The inner tendencies and relationships of individual things and conditions are sought and established.

Such a process constitutes the *school* in the widest sense of the word. The school, then, leads man to a knowledge of external things, and of their nature in accordance with the particular and general laws that lie in them; by the presentation of the external, the individual, the particular, it leads man to a knowledge of the internal, of unity, of the universal. Therefore, on entering the period of boyhood, man becomes at the same time a *schoolboy.* With this period, school begins for him, be it in the home or out of it, and taught by the father, the members of the family, or a teacher. School, then, means here by no means the schoolroom, nor schoolkeeping, but *the conscious communication of knowledge, for a definite purpose and in definite inner connection.*

On the other hand, as it has appeared and continues to appear in every aspect, the development and cultivation of man, for the attainment of his destiny, and the fulfillment of his mission, constitute an unbroken whole, steadily and continuously progressing, gradually ascending. The feeling of community, awakened in the infant, becomes in the child impulse, inclination; these lead to the formation of the disposition and of the heart and arouse in the boy his intellect and will. *To give firmness to the will, to quicken it, and to make it pure, strong, and enduring, in a life of pure humanity, is the chief concern, the main object in the guidance of the boy, in instruction and the school.*

Will is the mental activity, ever consciously proceeding from a definite point in a definite direction towards a definite object, in harmony with the man's nature as a whole. This statement contains everything, and indicates all that parent and educator, teacher and school, should be or should give to the boy in example and precept during these years. The starting point of all mental activity

256

in the boy should be energetic and sound; the source whence it flows, pure, clear, and ever flowing; the direction, simple, definite; the object, fixed, clear, living and life giving, elevating, worthy of the effort, worthy of the destiny and mission of man, worthy of his essential nature, and tending to develop it and give it full expression.

Instruction in example and in words, which later on become precept and example, furnishes the means for this. Neither example alone nor words alone will do; not example alone, for it is particular and special, and the word is needed to give to particular individual examples universal applicability; not words alone, for example is needed to interpret and explain the word which is general, spiritual, and of many meanings. But instruction and example alone and in themselves are not sufficient; they must meet a good, pure heart, and this is an outcome of proper educational influences in childhood.

In the family the child sees the parents, and other members at work, producing, doing something; the same he notices with adults generally in life and in those active interests with which his family is concerned. Consequently, the child, at this stage, would like himself to represent what he sees. He would like to represent— and tries to do so— all he sees his parents and other adults do and represent in work, all which he thus sees represented by human power and human skill.

What formerly the *child did only for the sake of the activity,* the *boy* now does *for the sake of result* or product of his activity; the child's instinct of activity has in the boy become a *formative instinct,* and this occupies the whole outward life, the outward manifestation of boy life at this period. How cheerfully and eagerly the boy and girl at this age begin to share the work of father and mother—not the easy work, indeed, but the difficult work, calling for strength and labor!

By no means, however, do all the plays and occupations of boys at this age aim at the representation of things; on the contrary many are predominantly mere practice and trials of strength, and many aim simply at display of strength. Nevertheless, the play of this period always bears a peculiar character, corresponding with

257

its inner life. For, while during the previous period of childhood the aim of play consisted simply in *activity* as such, its aim lies now in a *definite, conscious purpose;* it seeks *representation* as such, or the thing to be represented in the activity. This character is developed more and more in the free boyish games as the boys advance in age.

It is the sense of rare and reliable power, the sense of its increase, both as an individual and as a member of the group, that fills the boy with all-pervading, jubilant joy during these games. It is by no means, however, only the physical power that is fed and strengthened in these gains; intellectual and moral power, too, is definitely and steadily gained and brought under control. Indeed, a comparison of the relative gains of the mental and of the physical phases would scarcely yield the palm to the body. Justice, moderation, self-control, truthfulness, loyalty, brotherly love, and, again, strict impartiality — who, when he approaches a group of boys engaged in such games, could fail to catch the fragrance of these delicious blossomings of the heart and mind, and of a firm will; not to mention the beautiful, though perhaps less fragrant blossoms of courage, perseverance, resolution, prudence, together with the severe elimination of indolent indulgence? Whoever would inhale a fresh, quickening breath of life, should visit the playgrounds of such boys.

The existence of the present teaches man the existence of the past. This, too, which was before he was, he would know. Then there is developed in the boy at this age the desire and craving for tales, for legends, for all kinds of stories, and later on for historical accounts. This craving, especially in its first appearance, is very intense; so much so, that, when others fail to gratify it, the boys seek to gratify it themselves, particularly on days of leisure and in times when the regular employments of the day are ended.

Man is by no means naturally bad, nor has he originally bad or evil qualities or tendencies; unless, indeed, we consider as naturally evil, bad, and faulty, the *finite,* the *material,* the *transitory,* the *physical,* as such, and the logical consequences of the existing of these phenomena, namely, that man must have the possibility of failure in order to be good and virtuous, that he must be able to make himself a slave in order to be truly free. Yet these things are the necessary concomitants of the manifestation of the eternal in the temporal, of unity in diversity, and follow necessarily from man's destiny to become a conscious, reasonable, and free being.

A suppressed or perverted good quality—a good tendency, only repressed, misunderstood, or misguided—lies originally at the bottom of every shortcoming in man. Hence, the only and infallible remedy for counteracting any shortcomings and even wickedness is to find the originally good source, the originally good side of the human being that has been repressed, disturbed, or misled into the shortcoming, and then to foster, build up, and properly guide this good side. Thus the shortcoming will at last disappear, although it may involve a hard struggle *against habit, but not against original depravity* in man; and this is accomplished so much the more rapidly and surely because man himself tends to abandon his shortcomings, for man prefers right to wrong.

JOHANN FRIEDRICH HERBART

JOHANN FRIEDRICH HERBART (1776-1841). The chief legacy of Johann Friedrich Herbart, German philosopher, psychologist, and educational theorist, has been the development of a more scientific approach to the education of children. His educational theories were late in registering success but finally swept across Germany and the United States, where he is remembered as the exponent of the thesis that the chief aim of education is morality, meaning good character, and social adjustment.

Born at Oldenburg on May 4, 1776, he was professor at Göttingen from 1805 to 1809, taught at Königsberg from 1809 to 1833, then returned to Göttingen where he remained until his death on August 14, 1841. His collected works fill nineteen Volumes. Educational works available in English include *The Science of Education* (London, 1892), *Letters and Lectures on Education* (London, 1898), from which the following selection is taken, *A B C of Sense Perception and Minor Pedagogical Works* (New York, 1895), *The Application of Psychology to the Science of Education* (London, 1898), and *Outlines of Educational Doctrine* (New York, 1901). His educational theories are an integral part of his philosophy, which he defined as the analysis and elaboration of experience.

Rejecting the traditional doctrines of faculties and the doctrine of innate ideas, he conceived the process of education as beginning with the apperceptive masses acquired by the child through experience and social intercourse. Feelings, desires, and decisions are special states of consciousness created by mutual support or opposition of ideas. Since the will is a product of thought, instruction has to systematize the child's previously acquired knowledge and to arouse in addition all kinds of interests that can be derived from experience. Young people should be given the broadest possible range of experience so that they will develop "many-sidedness of interests." Morality (character) and many-sidedness of interests constitute the complete objectives of education, for they embrace the development of insight, maturity of judgement, and inner control, the cultivation of proper interests, and the introduction of the child to life in all its phases. Because they indicate the form in which the curriculum is acquired by the student, Ziller called his master's four stages of instruction — clarity, association, system, and method — the four formal stages. They are the formal foundations of all mental activities and are naturally applied in many and varied ways throughout the whole curriculum.

CHIEF CLASSES OF INTEREST*

Instruction must be joined to the knowledge furnished by experience, and to the disposition which is nourished by intercourse. Experience corresponds immediately with empirical, intercourse with sympathetic, interest. Progressive thought about the objects of experience develops speculative interest,—thought about the more complex relationships of intercourse develops social interest. To these we add on the one side aesthetic, on the other religious, interest. Both have their origin not so much in progressive thought, as in a quiet contemplation of things and their destiny.

It must not be expected that all these various kinds of interest will develop equally in each individual, but on the other hand we may expect to find them all more or less amongst a number of pupils. The required many-sidedness will be more perfectly attained, the more closely each individual approaches the standard of mental culture in which all these interests are aroused with equal energy.

That these six classes of interest naturally fall into two groups, has been already indicated when pointing out the historical and scientific divisions. This tallies with what has been generally observed in the Gymnasia (classical schools), that the pupils generally show a leaning either to the one side or the other. But it would be a great mistake to put for this reason, the historic interest in opposition to the scientific, or even to substitute in the place of these two the philological and mathematical, as is often done. This confusion of ideas must not be continued, otherwise entirely wrong views on instruction will be the result. This erroneousness will be most easily demonstrated, by a consideration of the many varieties of one-sidedness already occurring even *within* the two classes mentioned. In this way, at least, the many varieties

*From *Letters and Lectures on Education,* translated by Henry M. and E. Felkin (London, 1898).

261

it is necessary to distinguish here, will become more clearly separated. For the possible one-sided varieties of interest are much more widely differentiated from each other, than could be indicated by the previous six-fold classification.

Empirical interest will be in its way one-sided, if a certain class of objects of experience are dwelt on to the exclusion of others. So it will be, for instance, if a man desires to be a botanist only, or a mineralogist, or zoologist; or if he only cares for languages, perhaps only dead or only modern languages, or even but for one; or again, if a traveller (like many so-called tourists) only wishes to see certain celebrated districts during his journey, in order to be able to say he has seen them; or again, if as a collector he has only this or that particular hobby; or if as an historian he only cares for the annals of one country and one parish, and so on.

Speculative interest will be in its way one-sided, if it deals only with logic or mathematics, possibly with merely a branch of the latter, such as the geometry of the ancients, — or with metaphysics only, which again may be limited to the views of one school,—or with physics only, perhaps limited to the establishment of one hypothesis,—or finally, with pragmatic history alone.

Aesthetic interest tends to confine itself exclusively to painting or sculpture or poetry—perhaps the latter only of a lyric or dramatic class; or to music, or even only to a variety thereof, etc., etc.

Sympathetic interest will become one-sided, if an individual only cares to live with people of his own class, or with his compatriots, or only with members of his own family, and has no feeling for any others.

Social interest becomes one-sided, when a man is entirely devoted to his own political party, and measures all weal and woe by its interests alone.

Religious interest becomes one-sided, when it leads a man to adhere to certain sects and dogmas, and to despise those who think otherwise.

Many of these species of one-sidedness are brought about in later life, by the individual's vocation, but it ought not to isolate the man. It would certainly do so if such narrowness ruled him in earlier years.

262

It would be possible to analyze one-sided tendencies still further, but this is not necessary in order to determine what place the studies in the Gymnasia referred to, occupy amongst the subjects that serve to animate interest. Languages are the first on the list, as we know from experience, but why is the preference among so many given to Latin and Greek? Clearly because of their literature and history. Literature with the poets and orators belongs to aesthetic interest, history awakens sympathy for excellent men and for social weal and woe; through both channels it has a direct influence in developing religious interest. No better centre of unity for so many various stimuli can be found. Even speculative interest is not neglected, when the grammatical construction of these languages is added. But history does not stand still with the ancients; literary knowledge also widens, and aids in animating still more completely the interests before mentioned. The pragmatic treatment of history assists speculative interest from another side. In this respect however, mathematics have the preference, only, in order to gain a firmer footing and permanent influence, they must be combined with the natural sciences which arouse both empiric and speculative interest.

Now if these studies *co-operate* thoroughly, they achieve, conjoined with religious instruction, a good deal towards guiding the young mind in the direction conducive to many-sided interest. But were philology and mathematics to be separated, the connecting links removed, and every individual be left the choice of one or the other according to his own preference, the result would then show specimens of pure one-sidedness such as have been sufficiently characterized in the preceding remarks.

It is generally admitted now that the higher citizens' schools ought to introduce just this same many-sided education,—that is to say, they should make use of the very same main classes of interest as the Gymnasia, etc. The only difference is, that the pupils of the Gymnasia begin the exercise of their future calling later than do those of the citizens' schools. Consequently modern literature and history receive more consideration in the latter, and to those who are capable of going beyond these subjects, the higher ones necessary to complex mental activity can be given, but not *quite so fully* as in the Gymnasia. The same applies to all those lower schools which give a general education. It is different with technical schools and polytechnics, in short with such as presuppose that education is already finished, at least in so far as circumstances will allow.

Accordingly when a higher citizens' school has a correct curriculum, it will be seen from it, just, as from that of a Gymnasium, that an attempt has been made, through that curriculum, to avoid the *extreme* one-sidedness which results if one only of the *six main classes of interest* be disregarded.

But no instruction whatever is able to avoid those special one-sidednesses which occur within each main class. When once observation, reflection, taste for the beautiful, sympathy, social instincts, and religious feeling have been called into activity, though but in a narrow circle of subjects, it is chiefly left to the individual and opportunity to initiate further expansion, including a greater number and variety of subjects. To talented individuals, still more to geniuses, sufficient breadth of view may be given by instruction, to show them what has been done before by others of talent and genius; their idiosyncrasies however they must retain, and be responsible for themselves.

Nor are all these subordinate one-sided tendencies equally disadvantageous, for not all assert themselves exclusively to the same extent. Although all of them may become arrogant, yet they are not all equally liable to do so.

Under favorable conditions as regards time and opportunity, such as Gymnasia and higher citizens' schools have, the aim of instruction is not as is well known restricted to merely first efforts. The question then comes up, in what sequence should the interests which have been aroused be cultivated further? There is no lack of teaching matter; it is necessary to choose and systematize. For this purpose we must apply in general what has been said regarding the conditions of manysidedness and of interest. These conditions are, to proceed from the simple to the complex, and to provide suitable opportunities for the exercise of involuntary apperceptive attention. It is useless however to deceive ourselves about the difficulties and all that is required to carry this out.

264

Empirical subject-matter (in languages, history, geography, etc.) requires certain complications and series of presentations, together with their interconnections. To start with, the mere words consist of roots and those particles that pertain to modification and derivation, and these again of single articulate sounds. History has its periods in time, and geography its interconnections in space. The psychological laws of reproduction determine the acts of learning by memory, and of memory itself.

The mother-tongue serves as medium for the comprehension of foreign languages, but at the same time the child's mind struggles against foreign sounds and idioms. Besides this, a younger boy takes a long while to get accustomed to the idea, that at a remote time and place there were, and still are, human beings who speak and have spoken differently to himself—human beings who concern us here and now. The illusion also of many masters is very common and injurious, that because their expression (language) is clear, it must therefore be comprehended by the boy, whose child's language only grows slowly. These clogging influences can be overcome. Geography helps with respect to spatial distances, though the visible presentation of mountains is wanting to the inhabitants of a flat country, and that of plains to one who lives in a valley, and again of the sea to the majority of people. That the earth is a ball and turns on its axis, and revolves round the sun, sounds to children for a long time like a fairy-tale, and there are cultivated youths who doubt the theory of the planetary system, because they do not comprehend how it can be known. Such obstructions must be got rid of, and not multiplied unnecessarily. Old ruins might be made use of as a starting point for history, if they were not far too meagre and too near in time, when the young are to be introduced to Jewish, Greek and Roman antiquities. Recourse can only be had to stories to arouse a lively interest; these become the fulcrum of thought about a long vanished past, but the estimation of chronological distances leading up to our own time is still wanting, and can only be gradually realized by subsequent insertions.

Practice in thinking, and together with it, the animation of speculative interest, is stimulated by everything which reveals or

265

even only suggests connection by general laws in nature, in human affairs, in the structure of languages, in religious teaching. But everywhere, even in the things most commonly used, in general arithmetic and grammar, the pupil is confronted by general concepts, judgments and conclusions. He remains however attached to the single, familiar, sensuous. The abstract is strange to him; even geometrical figures drawn for the eye are but individual concrete things to him, and he only recognizes their general import with difficulty. The general notion ought to drive the special example out of his thoughts, but *vice versa* the special instance comes to the front in the usual series of presentations, and of the generalization, little remains to the boy but the words with which it is designated. If he is to draw a conclusion, he loses sight of one premise in dealing with the other, and the teacher must continually begin again, and illustrate the concepts and connect them, and gradually bring the premises together. When the middle terms in the premises have at last been correctly united, the union is still at first incomplete; the very same syllogisms are often forgotten, and afterwards too frequently repetitions have to be avoided, lest interest be extinguished instead of animated.

It is advisable to allow much of what has already been arrived at through conclusions to be for a time forgotten, as this cannot be prevented, and to return to the principal points later *by different routes*. The first preliminary exercises attain their purpose, if they give a glimpse of the general as revealed in the particular, before the concepts become the subjects of formulae, and before the propositions are formed into series of conclusions. Association must be made between the first demonstrations of the generalization and the systematic teaching of its interconnection.

Manifold external interests and also excited emotions may be the causes of aesthetic contemplation. But it only takes place spontaneously, when the spirit is sufficiently tranquil, to enable it to perfectly comprehend the simultaneously beautiful, and to follow the successively beautiful with answering rhythm. Comprehensible objects must be offered, contemplation must not be forced; but inappropriate remarks and, still more, damage done to objects of aesthetic value to which respect is due must certainly be forbidden. Frequently imitation, even if at first but roughly done, in drawing, singing, and reading aloud, and later on in translating, is a sign of attracted attention; such imitation may be encouraged, but certainly not praised. The true enthusiasm which grows spontaneously in aesthetic culture, is easily spoiled by being over-stimulated. To overburden is injurious; works of art that belong to a higher stage of culture must not be drawn down to a lower, and opinions and art criticisms should not be forced upon pupils.

The interests of sympathy are still more dependent on intercourse and home life than the former interests are on experience. If children are frequently moved from place to place, their attachment cannot take root anywhere. Even the change of masters and school is injurious. The pupils make comparisons of their own; an authority which is not permanent counts for little; on the contrary, efforts to obtain freedom act against it. Instruction cannot do away with such evils, the less because it is itself constantly obliged to change its form, which causes the master to appear different. It is consequently all the more necessary that in giving historical instruction, such warmth and sympathy should be expressed as is due to the personalities and events in question. For this reason, which is so important for the whole of education, we should carefully avoid making history a mere chronological skeleton. Specially should this be observed in the earlier instruction in history, as on it mainly depends what impression history as a whole will make later on.

It is needless to add, how much religious instruction should make the children feel their dependence, and how just are our expectations that it will not leave their souls untouched. In all this, historical must be combined with religious instruction, otherwise religious doctrine will occupy an isolated position, and will run the danger of not duly influencing the teaching and learning in all other subjects.

HRABANUS MAURUS

HRABANUS MAURUS (c. 776-856). One of the most learned men of his time, Hrabanus Maurus studied with Alcuin, the English churchman and scholar who figured prominently in the Carolingian renaissance, and he introduced the first teaching methods to come out of Germany.

He was born of noble parents at Mainz about 776 A. D. He was taught by his mother before he entered the monastery of Fulda, where he continued his education. As a young man he was privileged to study with Alcuin and to win the latter's confidence and affection. In 803 he was made head of the school at Fulda, which under his direction became the most famous monastery school in Germany. Exhibiting great zeal in his work, he won the proud distinction of *Preceptor Germaniae*. Ordained priest in 814, he became abbot of Fulda in 822. He died on February 4, 856.

His treatise on the education of clerics (*De doctrina christiana*) played an important part in the transmission of the educational ideal of St. Augustine to the Middle Ages. Significantly, it shows the subordination of education to religion and contains the most extensive discussion of the seven liberal arts that has survived from the Carolingian period.

EDUCATION OF THE CLERGY*

1. An ecclesiastical education should qualify the sacred office of the ministry for divine service. It is fitting that those who form an exalted station undertake the direction of the life of the Church, should acquire fulness of knowledge, and that they further should strive after rectitude of life and perfection of development. They should not be allowed to remain in ignorance about anything that appears beneficial for their own information or for the instruction of those entrusted to their care. Therefore they should endeavor to grasp and include in their knowledge the following

*From *Great Pedagogical Essays,* edited by F. V. N. Painter (New York: American Book Company, 1905).

things: An acquaintance with Holy Scripture, the unadulterated truth of history, the derivative modes of speech, the mystical sense of words, the advantages growing out of the separate branches of knowledge, the integrity of life that manifests itself in good morals, delicacy and good taste in oral discourse, penetration in the explanation of doctrine, the different kinds of medicine, and the various forms of disease. Any one to whom all this remains unknown, is not able to care for his own welfare, let alone that of others.

2. The foundation, the content, and the perfection of all wisdom is Holy Scripture, which has taken its origin from that unchangeable and eternal Wisdom, which streams from the mouth of the Most High, which was begotten before every other creature through the Holy Spirit, which is a light incessantly beaming from the words of Holy Scripture. And when anything else deserves the name of wisdom, it goes back in its origin to this one source of the wisdom of the Church. Every truth, which is discovered by any one, is recognized as true by the truth itself through the meditation of the truth; every good thing, which is in any way traced out, is recognized and determined as good by the good itself; all wisdom, which is brought to light by any one, is found to be wisdom by wisdom itself. And all that is found of truth and wisdom in the books of the philosophers of this world, dare be ascribed to nothing else than just to truth and wisdom; for it was not originally invented by those among whose utterances it is found; it has much rather been recognized as something present from eternity, so far as wisdom and truth, which bring illumination to all with their instruction, have granted the possibility of such recognition.

3. Now the Holy Scriptures, which come to the aid of the weakness of the human will, have, in dependence upon the one perfect language in which under favorable circumstances they might have spread over the whole globe, been widely circulated in the different languages of the translators, in order that they might be known to the nations unto salvation. Those who read them strive for nothing else than to grasp the thought and meaning of those who wrote them, in order thereby to fathom the will of God, at whose

bidding and under whose direction, as we believe, they were written. But those who read superficially allow themselves to be deceived through the manifold recurring passages, the sense of which is obscure, and the meaning of which is doubtful; they assign to what is read a meaning that does not belong to it; they seek errors where no errors are to be found; they surround themselves with an obscurity, in which they can not find the right path. I have no doubt that this has been so ordered by God's providence that the pride of man may be restrained through spiritual labor; in order that the knowledge of man may be divorced from pride, to which it easily falls a prey, and then loses its value entirely.

4. Above all it is necessary that he, who aims to attain the summit of wisdom, should be converted to the fear of the Lord, in order to know what the divine will bids us strive for and shun. The fear of the Lord fills us with the thought of our mortality and future death. With mortification of the flesh it nails, as it were, the movements of pride to the martyr cross of Christ. Then it is enjoined to be lowly in piety. Therefore we are not to raise any objection to the Holy Scriptures, either when we understand them and feel ourselves smitten by their words, or when we do not understand them, and give ourselves up to the thought that we can understand and grasp something better out of our own minds. We should remember that it is better and more conformable to truth, to believe what is written, even if the sense remains concealed from us, than to hold that for true which we are able to recognize by our own strength.

5. The first of the liberal arts is grammar, the second rhetoric, the third dialectic, the fourth arithmetic, the fifth geometry, the sixth music, the seventh astronomy.

Grammar takes its name from the written character, as the derivation of the word indicates. The definition of grammar is this: Grammar is the science which teaches us to explain the poets and historians; it is the art which qualifies us to write and speak correctly. Grammar is the source and foundation of the liberal arts. It should be taught in every Christian school, since the art of writing and speaking correctly is attained through it. How could one understand the sense of the spoken word or the meaning of letters and syllables, if one had not learned this before from grammar? How could one know about metrical feet, accent, and verses, if grammar had not given one knowledge of them? How should one learn to know the articulation of discourse, the advantages of figurative language, the laws of word formation, and the correct forms of words, if one had not familiarized himself with the art of grammar?

All the forms of speech, of which secular science makes use in its writings, are found repeatedly employed in the Holy Scriptures. Every one, who reads the sacred Scriptures with care, will discover that our (biblical) authors have used derivative forms of speech in greater and more manifold abundance than would have been supposed and believed. There are in the Scriptures not only examples of all kinds of figurative expressions, but the designations of some of them by name; as, allegory, riddle, parable. A knowledge of these things is proved to be necessary in relation to the interpretation of those passages of Holy Scripture which admit of a twofold sense; an interpretation strictly literal would lead to absurdities. Everywhere we are to consider whether that, which we do not at once understand, is to be apprehended as a figurative expression in some sense. A knowledge of prosody, which is offered in grammar, is not dishonorable, since among the Jews, as St. Jerome testifies, the Psalter resounds sometimes with iambics, sometimes with Alcaics, sometimes chooses sonorous Sapphics, and sometimes even does not disdain catalectic feet. But in Deuteronomy and Isaiah, as in Solomon and Job, as Josephus and Origen have pointed out, there are hexameters and pentameters. Hence this art, though it may be secular, has nothing unworthy in itself; it should rather be learned as thoroughly as possible.

6. According to the statements of teachers, rhetoric is the art of using secular discourse effectively in the circumstances of daily life. From this definition rhetoric seems indeed to have reference merely to secular wisdom. Yet it is not foreign to ecclesiastical instruction. Whatever the preacher and herald of the divine law, in his instruction, brings forward in an eloquent and becoming manner; whatever in his written exposition he knows how to

clothe in adequate and impressive language, he owes to his acquaintance with this art. Whoever at the proper time makes himself familiar with this art, and faithfully follows its rules in speaking and writing, needs not count it as something blameworthy. On the contrary, whoever thoroughly learns it so that he acquires the ability to proclaim God's word, performs a good work. Through rhetoric anything is proved true or false. Who would have the courage to maintain that the defenders of truth should stand weaponless in the presence of falsehood, so that those, who dare to represent the false, should know how by their discourse to win the favor and sympathy of the hearers, and that, on the other hand, the friends of truth should not be able to do this; that those should know how to present falsehood briefly, clearly, and with the semblance of truth, and that the latter, on the contrary, should clothe the truth in such an exposition, that listening would become a burden, apprehension of the truth a weariness, and faith in the truth an impossibility?

7. Dialectic is the science of the understanding, which fits us for investigations and definitions, for explanations, and for distinguishing the true from the false. It is the science of sciences. It teaches how to teach others; it teaches learning itself; in it the reason marks and manifests itself according to its nature, efforts, and activities; it alone is capable of knowing; it not only will, but can lead others to knowledge; its conclusions lead us to an apprehension of our being and of our origin; through it we apprehend the origin and activity of the good, of Creator and creature; it teaches us to discover the truth and to unmask falsehood; it teaches us to draw conclusions; it shows us what is valid in argument and what is not; it teaches us to recognize what is contrary to the nature of things; it teaches us to distinguish in controversy the true, the probable, and the wholly false; by means of this science we are able to investigate everything with penetration, to determine its nature with certainty, and to discuss it with circumspection.

Therefore the clergy must understand this excellent art and constantly reflect upon its laws, in order that they may be able keenly to pierce the craftiness of errorists, and to refute their fatal fallacies.

8. Arithmetic is the science of pure extension determinable by number; it is the science of numbers. Writers on secular science assign it, under the head of mathematics, to the first place, because it does not presuppose any of the other departments. Music, geometry, and astronomy, on the contrary, need the help of arithmetic; without it they cannot arise or exist. We should know, however, that the learned Hebrew Josephus, in his work on Antiquities, Chapter VIII, of Book I., makes the statement that Abraham brought arithmetic and astronomy to the Egyptians; but that they as a people of penetrating mind, extensively developed from these germs the other sciences. The holy Fathers were right in advising those eager for knowledge to cultivate arithmetic, because in large measure it turns the mind from fleshly desires, and furthermore awakens the wish to comprehend what with God's help we can merely receive with the heart. Therefore the significance of number is not to be underestimated. Its very great value for an interpretation of many passages of Holy Scripture is manifest to all who exhibit zeal in their investigations. Not without good reason is it said in praise of God, "Thou hast ordained all things by measure, number, and weight." (Book of Wisdom XI. 21.)

But every number, through its peculiar qualities, is so definite that none of the others can be like it. They are all unequal and different. The single numbers are different; the single numbers are limited; but all are infinite.

Those with whom Plato stands in especial honor will not make bold to esteem numbers lightly, as if they were of no consequence for the knowledge of God. He teaches that God made the world out of numbers. And among us the prophet says of God, "He forms the world by number." And in the Gospel the Savior says, "The very hairs of your head are all numbered." . . . Ignorance of numbers leaves many things unintelligible that are expressed in the Holy Scripture in a derivative sense or with a mystical meaning.

9. We now come to the discussion of geometry. It is an exposi-

tion of form proceeding from observation, it is also a very common means of demonstration among philosophers, who, to adduce at once the most full-toned evidence, declare that their Jupiter made use of geometry in his works. I do not know indeed whether I should find praise or censure in this declaration of the philosophers, that Jupiter engraved upon the vault of the skies precisely what they themselves draw in the sand of the earth.

When this in a proper manner is transferred to God, the Almighty Creator, this assumption may perhaps come near the truth. If this statement seems admissible, the Holy Trinity makes use of geometry in so far as it bestows manifold forms and images upon the creatures which up to the present day it has called into being, as in its adorable omnipotence it further determines the course of the stars, as it prescribes their course to the planets, and as it assigns to the fixed stars their unalterable position. For every excellent and well-ordered arrangement can be reduced to the special requirements of this science. . . .

This science found realization also at the building of the tabernacle and temple; the same measuring rod, circles, spheres, hemispheres, quadrangles, and other figures were employed. The knowledge of all this brings to him, who is occupied with it, no small gain for his spiritual culture.

10. Music is the science of time intervals as they are perceived in tones. This science is as eminent as it is useful. He who is a stranger to it is not able to fulfil the duties of an ecclesiastical office in a suitable manner. A proper delivery in reading and a lovely rendering of the Psalms in the church are regulated by a knowledge of this science. Yet it is not only good reading and beautiful psalmody that we owe to music; through it alone do we become capable of celebrating in the most solemn manner every divine service. Music penetrates all the activities of our life, in this sense namely, that we above all carry out the commands of the Creator and bow with a pure heart to his commands; all that we speak, all that makes our hearts beat faster, is shown through the rhythm of music united with the excellence of harmony; for music is the science which teaches us agreeably to change tones in duration and pitch. When we employ ourselves with good pur-

suits in life, we show ourselves thereby disciples of this art; so long as we do what is wrong, we do not feel ourselves drawn to music. Even heaven and earth, as everything that happens here through the arrangement of the Most High, is nothing but music, as Pythagoras testifies that this world was created by music and can be ruled by it. Even with the Christian religion music is most intimately united; thus it is possible that to him, who does not know even a little music, many things remain closed and hidden.

11. There remains yet astronomy which, as some one has said, is a weighty means of demonstration to the pious, and to the curious a grievous torment. If we seek to investigate it with a pure heart and an ample mind, then it fills us, as the ancients said, with great love for it. For what will it not signify, that we soar in spirit to the sky, that with penetration of mind we analyze that sublime structure, that we, in part at least, fathom with the keenness of our logical faculties what mighty space has enveloped in mystery! The world itself, according to the assumption of some, is said to have the shape of a sphere, in order that in its circumference it may be able to contain the different forms of things. Thus Seneca, in agreement with the philosophers of ancient times, composed a work under the title, "The Shape of the Earth."

Astronomy, of which we now speak, teaches the laws of the stellar world. The stars can take their place or carry out their motion only in the manner established by the Creator, unless by the will of the Creator a miraculous change takes place. Thus we read that Joshua commanded the sun to stand still in Gibeon, that in the days of King Josiah the sun went backward ten degrees, and that at the death of the Lord the sun was darkened for three hours. We call such occurrences miracles (*Wunder*), because they contradict the usual course of things, and therefore excite wonder. . . .

That part of astronomy, which is built upon the investigation of natural phenomena, in order to determine the course of the sun, of the moon, and stars, and to effect a proper reckoning to time, the Christian clergy should seek to learn with the utmost diligence, in order through the knowledge of laws brought to light and through the valid and convincing proof of the given means of evidence, to place themselves in a position, not only to determine the course of past years according to truth and reality, but also for further times to draw confident conclusions, and to fix the time of Easter and all other festivals and holy days, and to announce to the congregation the proper celebration of them.

12. The seven liberal arts of the philosophers, which Christians should learn for their utility and advantage, we have, as I think, sufficiently discussed. We have this yet to add. When those, who are called philosophers, have in their expositions or in their writings, uttered perchance some truth, which agrees with our faith, we should not handle it timidly, but rather take it as from its unlawful possessors and apply it to our own use.

THOMAS HUXLEY

THOMAS HUXLEY (1825-1895). Thomas Henry Huxley, usually remembered as "Darwin's bulldog" and the leading spokesman for the Darwinian theory of evolution, was an indefatigable educator, a prolific writer, a popular speaker, and a dedicated humanitarian. Like Voltaire he fought ignorance and superstition, and like Rousseau he decried the scholastic methods of instruction which thwarted true learning by overtaxing the memory. His vast erudition, his ready adaptability to the audience before him, and his recognition of the urgency of his mission made him one of the most influential men of his generation. Largely through his efforts, Darwinism became the most important element in the climate of opinion that characterized the last years of the nineteenth century.

Born on May 4, 1825, he was the son of a poor schoolmaster in Ealing. Largely self-educated, he earned a medical degree from the University of London and served as assistant surgeon on H. M. S. *Rattlesnake*. The scientific papers which he prepared during his four-year sea voyage established his reputation in science. He taught, lectured, and served on several governmental commissions before he was finally accorded the crowning honor of his life — election to the presidency of the Royal Society. He died in Eastbourne on June 29, 1895.

Between 1862 and 1883 Huxley served on ten royal commissions. During a brief two-year period of service as a member of the newly constituted London school board (1870-1872), he is said to have exerted a stronger influence on the foundations of national elementary education than any other man. Children were to be trained for worthy citizenship, and aesthetic development through drawing and singing was to have a place in the program. The three R's were the essential tools for the acquisition of knowledge, and intellectual discipline was to be inculcated through the study of basic principles of physical science. Although the law prescribed that science should be taught in the schools, it did not provide for teachers. Huxley established courses for teachers in general biology, and these were widely adopted in the United States. During his course he would lecture for an hour and have his students dissect specimens and draw for an hour — a procedure still widely followed.

A clear idea of his views on education may be gained from his address on "Science and Culture," which is a forcible plea for the importance of natural science in the education of modern man.

SCIENCE AND CULTURE*

Six years ago, as some of my present hearers may remember, I had the privilege of addressing a large assemblage of the inhabitants of this city, who had gathered together to do honor to the memory of their famous townsman, Joseph Priestley; and, if any satisfaction attaches to posthumous glory, we may hope that the manes of the burned-out philosopher were then finally appeased.

No man, however, who is endowed with a fair share of common-sense, and not more than a fair share of vanity, will identify either contemporary or posthumous fame with the highest good; and Priestley's life leaves no doubt that he, at any rate, set a much higher value upon the advancement of knowledge, and the promotion of that freedom of thought which is at once the cause and the consequence of intellectual progress.

Hence I am disposed to think that, if Priestley could be among us to-day, the occasion of our meeting would afford him even greater pleasure than the proceedings which celebrated the centenary of his chief discovery. The kindly heart would be moved, the high sense of social duty would be satisfied, by the spectacle of well-earned wealth, neither squandered in tawdry luxury and vainglorious show, nor scattered with the careless charity which blesses neither him that gives nor him that takes, but expended in the execution of a well-considered plan for the aid of present and future generations of those who are willing to help themselves.

We shall all be of one mind thus far. But it is needful to share Priestley's keen interest in physical science; and to have learned, as he had learned, the value of scientific training in fields of in-

*Originally delivered as an address, in 1880, at the opening of Mason College, now the University of Birmingham. Reprinted in *Science and Education* (New York: Philosophical Library, 1964).

quiry apparently far remote from physical science; in order to appreciate, as he would have appreciated, the value of the noble gift which Sir Josiah Mason has bestowed upon the inhabitants of the Midland district.

For us children of the nineteenth century, however, the establishment of a college under the conditions of Sir Josiah Mason's Trust, has a significance apart from any which it could have possessed a hundred years ago. It appears to be an indication that we are reaching the crisis of the battle, or rather of the long series of battles, which have been fought over education in a campaign which began long before Priestley's time, and will probably not be finished just yet.

In the last century, the combatants were the champions of ancient literature on the one side, and those of modern literature on the other; but, some thirty years ago, the contest became complicated by the appearance of a third army, ranged round the banner of Physical Science.

I am not aware that any one has authority to speak in the name of this new host. For it must be admitted to be somewhat of a guerrilla force, composed largely of irregulars, each of whom fights pretty much for his own hand. But the impressions of a full private, who has seen a good deal of service in the ranks, respecting the present position of affairs and the conditions of a permanent peace, may not be devoid of interest; and I do not know that I could make a better use of the present opportunity than by laying them before you.

From the time that the first suggestion to introduce physical science into ordinary education was timidly whispered, until now, the advocates of scientific education have met with opposition of two kinds. On the one hand, they have been pooh-poohed by the men of business who pride themselves on being the representatives of practicality; while, on the other hand, they have been excommunicated by the classical scholars, in their capacity of Levites in charge of the ark of culture and monopolists of liberal education.

The practical men believed that the idol whom they worship — rule of thumb — has been the source of the past prosperity, and will suffice for the future welfare of the arts and manufactures.

They were of opinion that science is speculative rubbish; that theory and practice have nothing to do with one another; and that the scientific habit of mind is an impediment, rather than an aid, in the conduct of ordinary affairs.

I have used the past tense in speaking of the practical men — for although they were very formidable thirty years ago, I am not sure that the pure species has not been extirpated. In fact, so far as mere argument goes, they have been subjected to such a *feu d'enfer* that it is a miracle if any have escaped. But I have remarked that your typical practical man has an unexpected resemblance to one of Milton's angels. His spiritual wounds, such as are inflicted by logical weapons, may be as deep as a well and as wide as a church door, but beyond shedding a few drops of ichor, celestial or otherwise, he is no whit the worse. So, if any of these opponents be left, I will not waste time in vain repetition of the demonstrative evidence of the practical value of science; but knowing that a parable will sometimes penetrate where syllogisms fail to effect an entrance, I will offer a story for their consideration.

Once upon a time, a boy, with nothing to depend upon but his own vigorous nature, was thrown into the thick of the struggle for existence in the midst of a great manufacturing population. He seems to have had a hard fight, inasmuch as, by the time he was thirty years of age, his total disposable funds amounted to twenty pounds. Nevertheless, middle life found him giving proof of his comprehension of the practical problems he had been roughly called upon to solve, by a career of remarkable prosperity.

Finally, having reached old age with its well-earned surroundings of "honor, troops of friends," the hero of my story bethought himself of those who were making a like start in life, and how he could stretch out a helping hand to them.

After long and anxious reflection, this successful practical man of business could devise nothing better than to provide them with the means of obtaining "sound, extensive, and practical scientific knowledge." And he devoted a large part of his wealth and five years of incessant work to this end.

I need not point the moral of a tale which, as the solid and specious fabric of the Scientific College assures us, is no fable, nor can anything which I could say intensify the force of this practical answer to practical objections.

We may take it for granted then that, in the opinion of those best qualified to judge, the diffusion of thorough scientific education is an absolutely essential condition of industrial progress; and that the College which has been opened to-day will confer an inestimable boon upon those whose livelihood is to be gained by the practice of the arts and manufactures of the district.

The only question worth discussion is, whether the conditions, under which the work of the College is to be carried out, are such as to give it the best possible chance of achieving permanent success.

Sir Josiah Mason, without doubt most wisely, has left very large freedom of action to the trustees, to whom he proposes ultimately to commit the administration of the College, so that they may be able to adjust its arrangements in accordance with the changing conditions of the future. But, with respect to three points he has laid most explicit injunctions upon both administrators and teachers.

Party politics are forbidden to enter into the minds of either, so far as the work of the College is concerned; theology is as sternly banished from its precincts; and finally, it is especially declared that the College shall make no provision for "mere literary instruction and education."

It does not concern me at present to dwell upon the first two injunctions any longer than may be needful to express my full conviction of their wisdom. But the third prohibition brings us face to face with those other opponents of scientific education, who are by no means in the moribund condition of the practical man, but alive, alert, and formidable.

It is not impossible that we shall hear this express exclusion of "literary instruction and education" from a College which, nevertheless, professes to give a high and efficient education, sharply criticised. Certainly the time was that the Levites of culture would have sounded their trumpets against its walls as against an educational Jericho.

281

How often have we not been told that the study of physical science is incompetent to confer culture; that it touches none of the higher problems of life; and, what is worse, that the continual devotion to scientific studies tends to generate a narrow and bigoted belief in the applicability of scientific methods to the search after truth of all kinds? How frequently one has reason to observe that no reply to a troublesome argument tells so well as calling its author a "mere scientific specialist." And, as I am afraid it is not permissible to speak of this form of opposition to scientific education in the past tense, may we not expect to be told that this, not only omission, but prohibition, of "mere literary instruction and education" is a patent example of scientific narrow-mindedness?

I am not acquainted with Sir Josiah Mason's reasons for the action which he has taken; but if, as I apprehend is the case, he refers to the ordinary classical course of our schools and universities by the name of "mere literary instruction and education," I venture to offer sundry reasons of my own in support of that action.

For I hold very strongly by two convictions — The first is, that neither the discipline nor the subject-matter of classical education is at least as effectual as an exclusively literary education.

I need hardly point out to you that these opinions, especially the latter, are diametrically opposed to those of the great majority of educated Englishmen, influenced as they are by school and university traditions. In their belief, culture is obtainable only by a liberal education; and a liberal education is synonymous, not merely with education and instruction in literature, but in one particular form of literature, namely, that of Greek and Roman antiquity. They hold that the man who has learned Latin and Greek, however little, is educated; while he who is versed in other branches of knowledge, however deeply, is a more or less respectable specialist, not admissible into the cultured caste. The stamp of the educated man, the University degree, is not for him.

I am too well acquainted with the generous catholicity of spirit, the true sympathy with scientific thought, which pervades the writings of our chief apostle of culture to identify him with these opinions; and yet one may cull from one and another of those epistles to the Philistines, which so much delight all who do not answer to that name, sentences which lend them some support.

Mr. Arnold tells us that the meaning of culture is "to know the best that has been thought and said in the world." It is the criticism of life contained in literature. That criticism regards "Europe as being, for intellectual and spiritual purposes, one great confederation, bound to a joint action and working to a common result; and whose members have, for their common outfit, a knowledge of Greek, Roman, and Eastern antiquity, and of one another. Special, local, and temporary advantages being put out of account, that modern nation will in the intellectual and spiritual sphere make most progress which most thoroughly carries out this programme. And what is that but saying that we too, all of us, as individuals, the more thoroughly we carry it out, shall make the more progress?"

We have here to deal with two distinct propositions. The first, that a criticism of life is the essence of culture; the second, that literature contains the materials which suffice for the construction of such a criticism.

I think that we must all assent to the first proposition. For culture certainly means something quite different from learning or technical skill. It implies the possession of an ideal, and the habit of critically estimating the value of things by comparison with a theoretic standard. Perfect culture should supply a complete theory of life, based upon a clear knowledge alike of its possibilities and of its limitations.

But we may agree to all this, and yet strongly dissent from the assumption that literature alone is competent to supply this knowledge. After having learned all that Greek, Roman, and Eastern antiquity have thought and said, and all that modern literatures have to tell us, it is not self-evident that we have laid a sufficiently broad and deep foundation for that criticism of life, which constitutes culture.

Indeed, to any one acquainted with the scope of physical science, it is not at all evident. Considering progress only in the "intellectual and spiritual sphere," I find myself wholly unable to admit that either nations or individuals will really advance, if their common outfit draws nothing from the stores of physical science. I should say that an army, without weapons of precision and with no particular base of operations, might more hopefully enter upon a campaign on the Rhine, than a man, devoid of a knowledge of what physical science has done in the last century, upon a criticism of life.

When a biologist meets with an anomaly, he instinctively turns to the study of development to clear it up. The rationale of contradictory opinions may with equal confidence be sought in history.

It is, happily, no new thing that Englishmen should employ their wealth in building and endowing institutions for educational purposes. But, five or six hundred years ago, deeds of foundation expressed or implied conditions as nearly as possible contrary to those which have been thought expedient by Sir Josiah Mason. That is to say, physical science was practically ignored, while a certain literary training was enjoined as a means to the acquirement of knowledge which was essentially theological.

The reason of this singular contradiction between the actions of men alike animated by a strong and disinterested desire to promote the welfare of their fellows, is easily discovered.

At that time, in fact, if any one desired knowledge beyond such as could be obtained by his own observation, or by common conversation, his first necessity was to learn the Latin language, inasmuch as all the higher knowledge of the western world was contained in works written in that language. Hence, Latin grammar, with logic and rhetoric, studied through Latin, were the fundamentals of education. With respect to the substance of the knowledge imparted through this channel, the Jewish and Christian Scriptures, as interpreted and supplemented by the Romish Church, were held to contain a complete and infallibly true body of information.

Theological dicta were, to the thinkers of those days, that which the axioms and definitions of Euclid are to the geometers of these. The business of the philosophers of the Middle Ages was to deduce, from the data furnished by the theologians, conclusions in accordance with ecclesiastical decrees. They were allowed the high privilege of showing, by logical process, how and why that which the Church said was true, must be true. And if their demonstrations fell short of or exceeded this limit, the Church was maternally ready to check their aberrations; if need were by the help of the secular arm.

Between the two, our ancestors were furnished with a compact and complete criticism of life. They were told how the world began and how it would end; they learned that all material existence was but a base and insignificant blot upon the fair face of the spiritual world, and that nature was, to all intents and purposes, the playground of the devil; they learned that the earth is the centre of the visible universe, and that man is the cynosure of things terrestrial; and more especially was it inculcated that the course of nature had no fixed order, but that it could be, and constantly was, altered by the agency of innumerable spiritual beings, good and bad, according as they were moved by the deeds and prayers of men. The sum and substance of the whole doctrine was to produce the conviction that the only thing really worth knowing in this world was how to secure that place in a better world which, under certain conditions, the Church promised.

Our ancestors had a living belief in this theory of life, and acted upon it in their dealings with education, as in all other matters. Culture meant saintliness — after the fashion of the saints of those days; the education that led to it was, of necessity, theological; and the way to theology lay through Latin.

That the study of nature — further than was requisite for the satisfaction of every-day wants — should have any bearing on human life was far from the thoughts of men thus trained. Indeed, as nature had been cursed for man's sake, it was an obvious conclusion that those who meddled with nature were likely to come into pretty close contact with Satan. And, if any born scientific investigator followed his instincts, he might safely reckon upon earning the reputation, and probably upon suffering the fate, of a sorcerer.

Had the western world been left to itself in Chinese isolation, there is no saying how long this state of things might have en-

285

dured. But, happily, it was not left to itself. Even earlier than the thirteenth century, the development of Moorish civilization in Spain and the great movement of the Crusades had introduced the leaven which, from that day to this, has never ceased to work. At first, through the intermediation of Arabic translations, afterward by the study of the originals, the western nations of Europe became acquainted with the writings of the ancient philosophers and poets, and, in time, with the whole of the vast literature of antiquity.

Whatever there was of high intellectual aspiration or dominant capacity in Italy, France, Germany and England, spent itself for centuries in taking possession of the rich inheritance left by the dead civilizations of Greece and Rome. Marvellously aided by the invention of printing, classical learning spread and flourished. Those who possessed it prided themselves on having attained the highest culture then within the reach of mankind.

And justly. For, saving Dante on his solitary pinnacle, there was no figure in modern literature at the time of the Renascence to compare with the men of antiquity; there was no art to compete with their sculpture; there was no physical science but that which Greece had created. Above all, there was no other example of perfect intellectual freedom — of the unhesitating acceptance of reason as the sole guide to truth and the supreme arbiter of conduct.

The new learning necessarily soon exerted a profound influence upon education. The language of the monks and schoolmen seemed little better than gibberish to scholars fresh from Virgil and Cicero, and the study of Latin was placed upon a new foundation. Moreover, Latin itself ceased to afford the sole key to knowledge. The student who sought the highest thought of antiquity found only a second-hand reflection of it in Roman literature, and turned his face to the full light of the Greeks. And after a battle, not altogether dissimilar to that which is at present being fought over the teaching of physical science, the study of Greek was recognized as an essential element of all higher education.

Thus the Humanists, as they were called, won the day; and

the great reform which they effected was of incalculable service to mankind. But the Nemesis of all reformers is finality; and the reformers of education, like those of religion, fell into the profound, however common, error of mistaking the beginning for the end of the work of reformation.

The representatives of the Humanists, in the nineteenth century, take their stand upon classical education as the sole avenue to culture, as firmly as if we were still in the age of Renascence. Yet, surely, the present intellectual relations of the modern and the ancient worlds are profoundly different from those which obtained three centuries ago. Leaving aside the existence of a great and characteristically modern literature, of modern painting, and, especially, of modern music, there is one feature of the present state of the civilized world which separates it more widely from the Renascence, than the Renascence was separated from the Middle Ages.

This distinctive character of our own times lies in the vast and constantly increasing part which is played by natural knowledge. Not only is our daily life shaped by it, not only does the prosperity of millions of men depend upon it, but our whole theory of life has long been influenced, consciously or unconsciously, by the general conceptions of the universe, which have been forced upon us by physical science.

In fact, the most elementary acquaintance with the results of scientific investigation shows us that they offer a broad and striking contradiction to the opinion so implicitly credited and taught in the Middle Ages.

The notions of the beginning and the end of the world entertained by our forefathers are no longer credible. It is very certain that the earth is not the chief body in the material universe, and that the world is not subordinated to man's use. It is even more certain that nature is the expression of a definite order with which nothing interferes, and that the chief business of mankind is to learn that order and govern themselves accordingly. Moreover, this scientific "criticism of life" presents itself to us with different credentials from any other. It appeals not to authority, nor to what anybody may have thought or said, but to Nature. It admits

287

that all our interpretations of natural fact are more or less imperfect and symbolic, and bids the learner seek for truth not among words but among things. It warns us that the assertion which outstrips evidence is not only a blunder but a crime.

The purely classical education advocated by the representatives of the Humanists in our day, gives no inkling of all this. A man may be a better scholar than Erasmus, and know no more of the chief causes of the present intellectual fermentation than Erasmus did. Scholarly and pious persons, worthy of all respect, favor us with allocutions upon the sadness of the antagonism of science to their medieval way of thinking, which betray an ignorance of the first principles of scientific investigation, an incapacity for understanding what a man of science means by veracity, and an unconsciousness of the weight of established scientific truths, which is almost comical.

There is no great force in the *tu quoque* argument, or else the advocates of scientific education might fairly enough retort upon the modern Humanists that they may be learned specialists, but that they possess no such sound foundation for a criticism of life as deserves the name of culture. And, indeed, if we were disposed to be cruel, we might urge that the Humanists have brought this reproach upon themselves, not because they are too full of the spirit of the ancient Greek, but because they lack it.

The period of the Renascence is commonly called that of the "Revival of Letters," as if the influences then brought to bear upon the mind of Western Europe had been wholly exhausted in the field of literature. I think it is very commonly forgotten that the revival of science, effected by the same agency, although less conspicuous, was not less momentous.

In fact, the few and scattered students of nature of that day picked up the clew to her secrets exactly as it fell from the hands of the Greeks a thousand years before. The foundations of mathematics were so well laid by them that our children learn their geometry from a book written for the schools of Alexandria two thousand years ago. Modern astronomy is the natural continuation and development of the work of Hipparchus and of Ptolemy; modern physics of that of Democritus and of Archimedes; it was long before modern biological science outgrew the knowledge bequeathed to us by Aristotle, by Theophrastus, and by Galen.

We cannot know all the best thoughts and sayings of the Greeks unless we know what they thought about natural phenomena. We cannot fully apprehend their criticism of life unless we understand the extent to which that criticism was affected by scientific conceptions. We falsely pretend to be the inheritors of their culture, unless we are penetrated, as the best minds among them were, with an unhesitating faith that the free employment of reason, in accordance with scientific method, is the sole method of reaching truth.

Thus I venture to think that the pretensions of our modern Humanists to the possession of the monopoly of culture and to the exclusive inheritance of the spirit of antiquity must be abated, if not abandoned. But I should be very sorry that anything I have said should be taken to imply a desire on my part to depreciate the value of classical education, as it might be and as it sometimes is. The native capacities of mankind vary no less than their opportunities; and while culture is one, the road by which one man may best reach it is widely different from that which is most advantageous to another. Again, while scientific education is yet inchoate and tentative, classical education is thoroughly well organized upon the practical experience of generations of teachers. So that, given ample time for learning and destination for ordinary life, or for a literary career, I do not think that a young Englishman in search of culture can do better than follow the course usually marked out for him, supplementing its deficiencies by his own efforts.

But for those who mean to make science their serious occupation; or who intend to follow the profession of medicine; or who have to enter early upon the business of life; for all these, in my opinion, classical education is a mistake; and it is for this reason that I am glad to see "mere literary education and instruction" shut out from the curriculum of Sir Josiah Mason's College, seeing that its inclusion would probably lead to the introduction of the ordinary smattering of Latin and Greek.

Nevertheless, I am the last person to question the importance of genuine literary education, or to suppose that intellectual culture can be complete without it. An exclusively scientific training will bring about a mental twist as surely as an exclusively literary training. The value of the cargo does not compensate for a ship's being out of trim; and I should be very sorry to think that the Scientific College would turn out none but lopsided men.

There is no need, however, that such a catastrophe should happen. Instruction in English, French and German is provided, and thus the three greatest literatures of the modern world are made accessible to the student.

French and German, and especially the latter language, are absolutely indispensable to those who desire full knowledge in any department of science. But even supposing that the knowledge of these languages acquired is not more than sufficient for purely scientific purposes, every Englishman has, in his native tongue, an almost perfect instrument of literary expression; and, in his own literature, models of every kind of literary excellence. If an Englishman cannot get literary culture out of his Bible, his Shakespeare, his Milton, neither, in my belief, will the profoundest study of Homer and Sophocles, Virgil and Horace, give it to him.

Thus, since the constitution of the College makes sufficient provision for literary as well as for scientific education, and since artistic instruction is also contemplated, it seems to me that a fairly complete culture is offered to all who are willing to take advantage of it.

But I am not sure that at this point the "practical" man, scotched but not slain, may ask what all this talk about culture has to do with an Institution, the object of which is defined to be "to promote the prosperity of the manufactures and the industry of the country." He may suggest that what is wanted for this end is not culture, nor even a purely scientific discipline, but simply a knowledge of applied science.

I often wish that this phrase, "applied science," had never been invented. For it suggests that there is a sort of scientific knowledge of direct practical use, which can be studied apart from another sort of scientific knowledge, which is of no practical utility, and which is termed "pure science." But there is no more complete

290

fallacy than this. What people call applied science is nothing but the application of pure science to particular classes of problems. It consists of deductions from those general principles, established by reasoning and observation, which constitute pure science. No one can safely make these deductions until he has a firm grasp of the principles; and he can obtain that grasp only by personal experience of the operations of observation and of reasoning on which they are founded.

Almost all the processes employed in the arts and manufactures fall within the range either of physics or of chemistry. In order to improve them, one must thoroughly understand them; and no one has a chance of really understanding them, unless he has obtained that mastery of principles and that habit of dealing with facts which is given by long-continued and well-directed purely scientific training in the physical and the chemical laboratory. So that there really is no question as to the necessity of purely scientific discipline, even if the work of the College were limited by the narrowest interpretation of its stated aims.

And, as to the desirableness of a wider culture than that yielded by science alone, it is to be recollected that the improvement of manufacturing processes is only one of the conditions which contribute to the prosperity of industry. Industry is a means and not an end; and mankind work only to get something which they want. What that something is depends partly on their innate, and partly on their acquired, desires.

If the wealth resulting from prosperous industry is to be spent upon the gratification of unworthy desires, if the increasing perfection of manufacturing processes is to be accompanied by an increasing debasement of those who carry them on, I do not see the good of industry and prosperity.

Now it is perfectly true that men's views of what is desirable depend upon their characters; and that the innate proclivities to which we give that name are not touched by any amount of instruction. But it does not follow that even mere intellectual education may not, to an indefinite extent, modify the practical manifestation of the characters of men in their actions, by supplying them with motives unknown to the ignorant. A pleasure-loving character

291

will have pleasure of some sort; but, if you give him the choice, he may prefer pleasures which do not degrade him to those which do. And this choice is offered to every man who possesses in literary or artistic culture a never-failing source of pleasures, which are neither withered by age, nor staled by custom, nor imbittered in the recollection by the pangs of self-reproach.

If the Institution opened to-day fulfils the intention of its founder, the picked intelligences among all classes of the population of this district will pass through it. No child born in Birmingham, henceforward, if he have the capacity to profit by the opportunities offered to him, first in the primary and other schools, and afterward in the Scientific College, need fail to obtain, not merely the instruction, but the culture most appropriate to the conditions of his life.

Within these walls, the future employer and the future artisan may sojourn together for a while, and carry, through all their lives, the stamp of the influences then brought to bear upon them. Hence, it is not beside the mark to remind you that the prosperity of industry depends not merely upon the improvement of manufacturing processes, not merely upon the ennobling of the individual character, but upon a third condition, namely, a clear understanding of the conditions of social life, on the part of both the capitalist and the operative, and their agreement upon common principles of social action. They must learn that social phenomena are as much the expression of natural laws as any others; that no social arrangements can be permanent unless they harmonize with the requirements of social statics and dynamics; and that, in the nature of things, there is an arbiter whose decisions execute themselves.

But this knowledge is only to be obtained by the application of the methods of investigation adopted in physical researches to the investigation of the phenomena of society. Hence, I confess, I should like to see one addition made to the excellent scheme of education propounded for the College, in the shape of provision for the teaching of Sociology. For though we are all agreed that party politics are to have no place in the instruction of the College; yet in this country, practically governed as it is now by universal suffrage, every man who does his duty must exercise political functions. And, if the evils which are inseparable from the good of political liberty are to be checked, if the perpetual oscillation of nations between anarchy and despotism is to be replaced by the steady march of self-restraining freedom; it will be because men will gradually bring themselves to deal with political, as they now deal with scientific questions; to be as ashamed of undue haste and partisan prejudice in the one case as in the other; and to believe that the machinery of society is at least as delicate as that of a spinning-jenny, and as little likely to be improved by the meddling of those who have not taken the trouble to master the principles of its action.

In conclusion, I am sure that I make myself the mouthpiece of all present in offering to the venerable founder of the Institution, which now commences its beneficent career, our congratulations on the completion of his work; and in expressing the conviction that the remotest posterity will point to it as a crucial instance of the wisdom which natural piety leads all men to ascribe to their ancestors.

THOMAS JEFFERSON

THOMAS JEFFERSON (1743-1826). More than any other national figure of his time, Thomas Jefferson saw the crucial role of education in the life of a free people. Realizing that a free society must rely on education in its pursuit of social justice and enlightenment, he tried to establish a universal and free system of public instruction in his native state of Virginia. Though his dream fell short of realization, he championed more fruitfully than anyone of his time the quest for intellectual goals and the utilization of the fruits of enlightenment for the betterment of mankind.

The liberty championed throughout his lifetime by Jefferson was essentially freedom of belief. In education as in politics, he advocated the disestablishment of religion. His campaign culminated in the adoption by the Assembly of Virginia of his proposal for establishing religious freedom — a statement which he regarded as one of his supreme achievements and which brilliantly delineates the theory of the separation of church and state in a representative republican government.

The second selection presented here — "The Administration of Justice and the Description of the Laws" — stresses the importance of diffusing knowledge throughout society and "prescribes the selection of our youths of genius from among the classes of the poor" so as "to avail the state of those talents which nature has shown as liberally among the poor as the rich, but which perish without use, if not sought out and cultivated."

In his "Correspondence" Jefferson pursues the theme of separation of church and state (in his letters to Dodge, Miller, and Wendover) and shows the practical meaning of the principle of separation. In the letter to John Adams he pleads for the establishment of an institution of higher learning "where every branch of science, useful at this day, may be taught in its highest degree." It has been said that while popular education was uppermost in his head, higher education was closest to his heart. Convinced that the advancement of science was man's noblest undertaking, he asked to have inscribed on his tomb these words: "Author of the Declaration of Independence; of the Statute for Religious Liberty in Virginia; and Founder of the University of Virginia." The last letter reproduced here (letter to Ticknor) recapitulates Jefferson's views on a general system of education and restates the belief that "knowledge is power, knowledge is safety, knowledge is happiness."

A BILL FOR ESTABLISHING RELIGIOUS FREEDOM*

Well aware that Almighty God hath created the mind free;
that all attempts to influence it by temporal punishments or burdens, or by civil incapacitations, tend only to beget habits of
hypocrisy and meanness, and are a departure from the plan of
the Holy Author of our religion, who being Lord both of body
and mind, yet chose not to propagate it by coercions on either,
as was in his Almighty power to do; that the impious presumption
of legislators and rulers, civil as well as ecclesiastical, who, being
themselves but fallible and uninspired men, have assumed dominion over the faith of others, setting up their own opinions and
modes of thinking as the only true and infallible, and as such en-
deavoring to impose them on others, hath established and maintained false religions over the greatest part of the world, and
through all time; that to compel a man to furnish contributions
for money for the propagation of opinions which he disbelieves,
is sinful and tyrannical; that even the forcing him to support this
or that teacher of his own religious persuasion, is depriving him
of the comfortable liberty of giving his contributions to the particular pastor whose morals he would make his pattern, and whose
powers he feels most persuasive to righteousness, and is withdrawing from the ministry those temporal rewards, which, proceeding from an approbation of their personal conduct, are an additional incitement to earnest and unremitting labors for the instruction of mankind; that our civil rights have no dependence on
our religious opinions, more than our opinions in physics or
geometry; that, therefore, the proscribing any citizen as unworthy
the public confidence by laying upon him an incapacity of being
called to the offices of trust and emolument, unless he profess or

*Passed by the Assembly of Virginia in 1780. Reprinted in *Three Thou-
sand Years of Educational Wisdom,* edited by Robert Ulich (Cambridge,
Mass.: Harvard University Press, 1961).

renounce this or that religious opinion, is depriving him injuriously of those privileges and advantages to which in common with his fellow citizens he has a natural right; that it tends also to corrupt the principles of that very religion it is meant to encourage, by bribing, with a monopoly of worldly honors and emoluments, those who will externally profess and conform to it; that though indeed these are criminal who do not withstand such temptation, yet neither are those innocent who lay the bait in their way; that to suffer the civil magistrate to intrude his powers into the field of opinion and to restrain the profession or propagation of principles, on the supposition of their ill tendency, is a dangerous fallacy, which at once destroys all religious liberty, because he being of course judge of that tendency, will make his opinions the rule of judgment, and approve or condemn the sentiments of others only as they shall square with or differ from his own; that it is time enough for the rightful purposes of civil government, for its officers to interfere when principles break out into overt acts against peace and good order; and finally, that truth is great and will prevail if left to herself, she is the proper and sufficient antagonist to error, and has nothing to fear from the conflict, unless by human interposition disarmed of her natural weapons, free argument and debate, errors ceasing to be dangerous when it is permitted freely to contradict them.

We the General Assembly of Virginia do enact that no man shall be compelled to frequent or support any religious worship, place, or ministry whatsoever, nor shall be enforced, restrained, molested, or burdened in his body or goods, nor shall otherwise suffer on account of his religious opinions or beliefs; but that all men shall be free to profess, and by argument to maintain, their opinions in matters of religion, and that the same shall in nowise diminish, enlarge, or affect their civil capacities.

And though we well know this Assembly, elected by the people for the ordinary purposes of legislation only, have no power to restrain the acts of succeeding assemblies, constituted with the powers equal to our own, and that therefore to declare this act irrevocable would be of no effect in law, yet we are free to declare, and do declare, that the rights hereby asserted are of the natural rights of mankind, and that if any act shall be hereafter passed to repeal the present or to narrow its operation, such act will be an infringement of natural right.

THE ADMINISTRATION OF JUSTICE AND THE DESCRIPTION OF THE LAWS*

Many of the laws which were in force during the monarchy being relative merely to that form of government, or inculcating principles inconsistent with republicanism, the first assembly which met after the establishment of the commonwealth, appointed a committee to revise the whole code, to reduce it into proper form and volume, and report it to the assembly. . . .

The plan of the revisal was this. The common law of England, by which is meant that part of the English law which was anterior to the date of the oldest statutes extant, is made the basis of the work. It was thought dangerous to attempt to reduce it to a text: it was therefore left to be collected from the usual monuments of it. . . .

Another object of the revisal is, to diffuse knowledge more generally through the mass of the people. This bill proposes to lay off every county into small districts of five or six miles square, called hundreds and in each of them to establish a school for teaching, reading, writing, and arithmetic. The tutor to be supported by the hundred, and every person in it entitled to send their children three years gratis, and as much longer as they please, paying for it. These schools to be under a visitor who is annually to chuse the boy of best genius in the school, of those whose parents are too poor to give them further education, and to send him forward to one of the grammar schools, of which twenty are proposed to be erected in different parts of the country, for teaching Greek, Latin, geography, and the higher branches of numerical arithmetic. Of the boys thus sent in any one year, trial is to be

*From *The Writings of Thomas Jefferson*, edited by Paul L. Ford (New York, 1899).

made at the grammar schools one or two years, and the best genius of the whole selected, and continued six years, and the residue dismissed. By this means twenty of the best geniuses will be raked from the rubbish annually, and be instructed, at the public expence, so far as the grammar schools go. At the end of six years instruction, one half are to be discontinued (from among whom the grammar schools will probably be supplied with future masters); and the other half, who are to be chosen for the superiority of their parts and disposition, are to be sent and continued three years in the study of such sciences as they shall chuse, at William and Mary college, the plan of which is proposed to be enlarged, as will be hereafter explained, and extended to all the useful sciences. The ultimate result of the whole scheme of education would be the teaching all the children of the State reading, writing, and common arithmetic; turning out ten annually, of superior genius, well taught in Greek, Latin, geography, and the higher branches of arithmetic; turning out ten others annually, of still superior parts, who to those branches of learning, shall have added such of the sciences as their genius shall have led them to; the furnishing to the wealthier part of the people convenient schools at which their children may be educated at their own expence. — The general objects of this law are to provide an education adapted to the years, to the capacity, and the condition of every one, and directed to their freedom and happiness. Specific details were not proper for the law. These must be the business of the visitors entrusted with its execution. The first stage of this education being the schools of the hundreds, wherein the great mass of the people will receive their instruction, the principal foundations of future order will be laid here. Instead, therefore, of putting the Bible and Testament into the hands of the children at an age when their judgements are not sufficiently matured for religious inquiries, their memories may here be stored with the most useful facts from Grecian, Roman, European, and American history. The first elements of morality too may be instilled into their minds; such as, when further developed as their judgments advance in strength, may teach them how to work out their own greatest happiness, by shewing them that it does not depend on the condition of life in which chance has placed them, but is always the result of a good conscience, good health, occupation, and freedom in all just pursuits. — Those whom either the wealth of their parents or the adoption of the state shall destine to higher degrees of learning, will go on to the grammar schools, which constitute the next stage, there to be instructed in the languages. The learning Greek and Latin, I am told, is going into disuse in Europe. I know not what their manners and occupations may call for: but it would be very ill-judged in us to follow their example in this instance. There is a certain period of life, say from eight to fifteen or sixteen years of age, when the mind like the body is not yet firm enough for laborious and close operations. If applied to such, it falls an early victim to premature exertion; exhibiting, indeed, at first, in these young and tender subjects, the flattering appearance of their being men while they are yet children, but ending in reducing them to be children when they should be men. The memory is then most susceptible and tenacious of impressions: and the learning of languages being chiefly a work of memory, it seems precisely fitted to the powers of this period, which is long enough too for acquiring the most useful languages, antient and modern. I do not pretend that language is science. It is only an instrument for the attainment of science. But that time is not lost which is employed in providing tools for future operation: more especially as in this case the books put into the hands of the youth for this purpose may be such as will at the same time impress their minds with useful facts and good principles. If this period be suffered to pass in idleness, the mind becomes lethargic and impotent, as would the body it inhabits if unexercised during the same time. The sympathy between body and mind during their rise, progress and decline, is too strict and obvious to endanger our being misled while we reason from the one to the other. — As soon as they are of sufficient age, it is supposed they will be sent on from the grammar schools to the university, which constitutes our third and last stage, there to study those sciences which may be adapted to their views. — By that part of our plan which prescribes the selection of the youths of genius from among the classes of the poor, we hope to avail the state of those talents which nature has sown as liberally among the poor as the rich, but which perish without use, if not sought for and cultivated. — But of all the views of this law none is more important, none more legitimate, than that of rendering the people the safe, as they are the ultimate, guardians of their own liberty. For this purpose the reading in the first stage where *they* will receive their whole education, is proposed, as has been said, to be chiefly historical. History, by apprising them of the past, will enable them to judge of the future; it will avail them of the experience of other times and other nations; it will qualify them as judges of the actions and designs of men; it will enable them to know ambition under every disguise it may assume; and knowing it, to defeat its views.

CORRESPONDENCE*

TO MESSRS. NEHEMIAH DODGE, EPHRAIM ROBBINS, AND STEPHEN S. NELSON, A COMMITTEE OF THE DANBURY BAPTIST ASSOCIATION, IN THE STATE OF CONNECTICUT

Washington, January 1, 1802.

Believing with you that religion is a matter which lies solely between man and his God, that he owes account to none other for his faith or his worship, that the legislative powers of government reach actions only, and not opinions, I contemplate with sovereign reverence that act of the whole American people which declared that their legislature should "make no law respecting an establishment of religion, or prohibiting the free exercise thereof," thus

*The letters to Dodge *et al.* and to Wendover are from *The Writings* of Thomas Jefferson, edited by A. Lipscomb and A. Bergh (Washington, D.C., 1903); those to Miller, Adams, and Ticknor are from *The Writings of Thomas Jefferson,* edited by Paul L. Ford (New York, 1899). All are reprinted in *Crusade Against Ignorance,* edited by Gordon C. Lee (*Classics in Education,* No. 6, New York: Teachers College Bureau of Publications, 1961).

building a wall of separation between Church and State. Adhering to this expression of the supreme will of the nation in behalf of the rights of conscience, I shall see with sincere satisfaction the progress of those sentiments which tend to restore to man all his natural rights, convinced he has no natural right in opposition to his social duties.

I reciprocate your kind prayers for the protection and blessing of the common Father and Creator of man, and tender you for yourselves and your religious association, assurances of my high respect and esteem.

TO REV. SAMUEL MILLER

Washington, Jan. 23, 1808.

I consider the government of the U.S. as interdicted by the Constitution from intermeddling with religious institutions, their doctrines, discipline, or exercises. This results not only from the provision that no law shall be made respecting the establishment, or free exercise, of religion, but from that also which reserves to the states the powers not delegated to the U.S. Certainly no power to prescribe any religious exercise, to assume authority in religious discipline, has been delegated to the general government. It must then rest with the states, as far as it can be in any human authority. But it is only proposed that I should *recommend*, not prescribe a day of fasting & prayer. That is, that I should *indirectly* assume to the U. S. an authority over religious exercises which the Constitution has directly precluded them from. It must be meant too that this recommendation is to carry some authority, and to be sanctioned by some penalty on those who disregard it; not indeed of fine and imprisonment, but of some degree of proscription perhaps in public opinion. And does the change in the nature of the penalty make the recommendation the less *a law* of conduct for those to whom it is directed? I do not believe it is for the interest of religion to invite the civil magistrate to direct its exercises, its discipline, or its doctrines; nor of the religious societies that the general government should be invested with the power of effecting any uniformity of time or matter among them. Fasting

301

& prayer are religious exercises. The enjoining them an act of discipline. Every religious society has a right to determine for itself the times for these exercises, & the objects proper for them, according to their own particular tenets; and this right can never be safer than in their own hands, where the constitution has deposited it.

I am aware that the practice of my predecessors may be quoted. But I have ever believed that the example of state executives led to the assumption of that authority by the general government, without due examination, which would have discovered that what might be a right in a state government, was a violation of that right when assumed by another. Be this as it may, every one must act according to the dictates of his own reason, & mine tells me that civil powers alone have been given to the President of the U.S. and no authority to direct the religious exercises of his constituents.

I again express my satisfaction that you have been so good as to give me an opportunity of explaining myself in a private letter, in which I could give my reasons more in detail than might have been done in a public answer: and I pray you to accept assurances of my high esteem & respect.

TO P. H. WENDOVER

Monticello, March 13, 1815.

Sir, — Your favor of January the 30th was received after long delay on the road, and I have to thank you for the volume of discourses which you have been so kind as to send me. I have gone over them with great satisfaction, and concur with the able preacher in his estimate of the character of the belligerents in our late war, and lawfulness of defensive war. I consider the war, with him, as "made on good advice," that is for just causes, and its dispensation as providential. . . .

The mass of human concerns, moral and physical, is so vast, the field of knowledge requisite for man to conduct them to the best advantage is so extensive, that no human being can acquire the whole himself, and much less in that degree necessary for the instruction of others. It has of necessity, then, been distributed into different departments, each of which, singly, may give occupation enough to the whole time and attention of a single individual. Thus we have teachers of Languages, teachers of Mathematics, of Natural Philosophy, of Chemistry, of Medicine, of Law, of History, of Government, etc. Religion, too, is a separate department, and happens to be the only one deemed requisite for all men, however high or low. Collections of men associate together, under the name of congregations, and employ a religious teacher of the particular sect of opinions of which they happen to be, and contribute to make up a stipend as a compensation for the trouble of delivering them, at such periods as they agree on, lessons in the religion they profess. If they want instruction in other sciences or arts, they apply to other instructors; and this is generally the business of early life. But I suppose there is not an instance of a single congregation which has employed their preacher for the mixed purposes of lecturing them *from the pulpit* in Chemistry, in Medicine, in Law, in the science and principles of Government, or in anything but Religion exclusively. Whenever, therefore, preachers, instead of a lesson in religion, put them off with a discourse on the Copernican system, on chemical affinities, on the construction of government, or the characters or conduct of those administering it, it is a breach of contract, depriving their audience of the kind of service for which they are salaried, and giving them, instead of it, what they did not want, or, if wanted, would rather seek from better sources in that particular art or science. In choosing our pastor we look to his religious qualifications, without inquiring into his physical or political dogmas, with which we mean to have nothing to do. I am aware that arguments may be found, which may twist a thread of politics into the cord of religious duties. So may they for every other branch of human art or science. Thus, for example, it is a religious duty to obey the laws of our country; the teacher of religion, therefore, must instruct us in those laws, that we may know how to obey them. It is a religious duty to assist our sick neighbors;

303

the preacher must, therefore, teach us medicine, that we may do it understandingly. It is a religious duty to preserve our own health; our religious teacher, then, must tell us what dishes are wholesome, and give us recipes in cookery, that we may learn how to prepare them. And so, ingenuity, by generalizing more and more, may amalgamate all the branches of science into any one of them, and the physician who is paid to visit the sick, may give a sermon instead of medicine, and the merchant to whom money is sent for a hat, may send a handkerchief instead of it. But notwithstanding this possible confusion of all sciences into one, common sense draws lines between them sufficiently distinct for the general purposes of life, and no one is at a loss to understand that a recipe in medicine or cookery, or a demonstration in geometry, is not a lesson in religion. I do not deny that a congregation may, if they please, agree with their preacher that he shall instruct them in Medicine also, or Law, or Politics. Then lectures in these, from the pulpit, become not only a matter of right, but of duty also. But this must be with the consent of every individual; because the association being voluntary, the mere majority has no right to apply the contributions of the minority to purposes unspecified in the agreement of the congregation. I agree, too, that on all other occasions, the preacher has the right, equally with every other citizen, to express his sentiments, in speaking or writing, on the subjects of Medicine, Law, Politics, etc., his leisure time being his own, and his congregation not obliged to listen to his conversation or to read his writings; and no one would have regretted more than myself, had any scruple as to this right withheld from us the valuable discourses which have led to the expression of an opinion as to the true limits of the right. I feel my portion of indebtment to the reverend author for the distinguished learning, the logic and the eloquence with which he has proved that religion, as well as reason, confirms the soundness of those principles on which our government has been founded and its rights asserted.

These are my views on this question. They are in opposition to those of the highly respected and able preacher, and are, therefore, the more doubtingly offered. Difference of opinion leads to inquiry, and inquiry to truth; and that, I am sure, is the ultimate and sincere object of us both. We both value too much the freedom of opinion sanctioned by our Constitution, not to cherish its exercise even where in opposition to ourselves.

TO JOHN ADAMS

Monticello, July 5, 1814

I am just returned from one of my long absences, having been at my other home for five weeks past. Having more leisure there than here for reading, I amused myself with reading seriously Plato's Republic. I am wrong, however, in calling it amusement, for it was the heaviest task-work I ever went through. I had occasionally before taken up some of his other works, but scarcely ever had patience to go through a whole dialogue. While wading through whimsies, the puerilities, and unintelligible jargon of this work, I laid it down often to ask myself how it could have been, that the world should have so long consented to give reputation to such nonsense as this? How the *soi-disant* Christian world, indeed, should have done it, is a piece of historical curiosity. But how could the Roman good sense do it? And particularly, how could Cicero bestow such eulogies on Plato! Although Cicero did not wield the dense logic of Demosthenes, yet he was able, learned, laborious, practised in the business of the world, and honest. He could not be the dupe of mere style, of which he was himself the first master in the world. With the moderns, I think, it is rather a matter of fashion and authority. Education is chiefly in the hands of persons who, from their profession, have an interest in the reputation and the dreams of Plato. They give the tone while at school, and few in their after years have occasion to revise their college opinions. But fashion and authority apart, and bringing Plato to the test of reason, take from him his sophisms, futilities and incomprehensibilities, and what remains? In truth, he is one of the race of genuine sophists, who has escaped the oblivion of his brethren, first, by the elegance of his diction, but chiefly, by the adoption and incorporation of his whimsies into the body of artificial Christianity. His foggy mind is forever presenting the semblances of objects which, half seen through a mist, can be defined neither in form nor dimensions. Yet this, which should have consigned him to early oblivion, really procured him immortality of fame and reverence. The Christian priesthood, finding the doctrines of Christ levelled to every understanding, and too plain to need explanation, saw in the mysticism of Plato materials with which they might build up an artificial system, which might, from its indistinctness, admit everlasting controversy, give employment for their order, and introduce it to profit, power and pre-eminence. The doctrines which flowed from the lips of Jesus himself are within the comprehension of a child; but thousands of volumes have not yet explained the Platonisms engrafted on them; and for this obvious reason, that nonsense can never be explained. Their purposes, however, are answered. Plato is canonized; and it is now deemed as impious to question his merits as those of an Apostle of Jesus. He is peculiarly appealed to as an advocate of the immortality of the soul; and yet I will venture to say, that were there no better arguments than his in proof of it, not a man in the world would believe it. It is fortunate for us, that Platonic republicanism has not obtained the same favor as Platonic Christianity; or we should now have been all living, men, women and children, pell mell together, like beasts of the field or forest. Yet "Plato is a great philosopher," said La Fontaine. But, says Fontenelle, "Do you find his ideas very clear?" "Oh no! he is of an obscurity impenetrable." "Do you not find him full of contradictions?" "Certainly," replied La Fontaine, "he is but a sophist." Yet immediately after he exclaims again, "Oh, Plato was a great philosopher." Socrates had reason, indeed, to complain of the mis-representations of Plato; for in truth, his dialogues are libels on Socrates.

But why am I dosing you with these antediluvian topics? Because I am glad to have some one to whom they are familiar, and who will not receive them as if dropped from the moon. Our post-revolutionary youth are born under happier stars than you and I were. They acquire all learning in their mother's womb, and bring it into the world ready made. The information of books

306

is no longer necessary; and all knowledge which is not innate, is in contempt, or neglect at least. Every folly must run its round; and so, I suppose, must that of self-learning and self-sufficiency; of rejecting the knowledge acquired in past ages, and starting on the new ground of intuition. When sobered by experience, I hope our successors will turn their attention to the advantages of education. I mean of education on the broad scale, and not that of the petty *academies,* as they call themselves, which are starting up in every neighborhood, and where one or two men, possessing Latin and sometimes Greek, a knowledge of the globe, and the first six books of Euclid, imagine and communicate this as the sum of science. They commit their pupils to the theatre of the world, with just taste enough of learning to be alienated from industrious pursuits, and not enough to do service in the ranks of science. We have some exceptions, indeed. I presented one to you lately, and we have some others. But the terms I use are general truths. I hope the necessity will, at length, be seen of establishing institutions here, as in Europe, where every branch of science, useful at this day, may be taught in its highest degree. Have you ever turned your thoughts to the plan of such an institution? I mean to a specification of the particular sciences of real use in human affairs, and how they might be so grouped as to require so many professors only as might bring them within the views of a just but enlightened economy? I should be happy in a communication of your ideas on this problem, either loose or digested.

TO GEORGE TICKNOR

Poplar Forest near Lynchburg, Nov. 25, 1817.

Dear Sir, — Your favor of Aug. 14. was delivered to me as I was setting out for the distant possession from which I now write, & to which I pay frequent & long visits. On my arrival here I make it my first duty to write the letter you request to Mr. Erving, and to inclose it in this under cover to your father that you may get it in time. My letters are always letters of thanks because you are always furnishing occasion for them. I am very glad you have been so kind as to make the alteration you mention in the Herodotus & Livy I had asked from the Messrs. Desbures. I have not yet heard from them, but daily expect to do so, and to learn the arrival of my books. I shall probably send them another catalogue early in spring; every supply from them furnishing additional materials for my happiness. . . .

I am now entirely absorbed in endeavours to effect the establishment of a general system of education in my native state, on the triple basis, 1, of elementary schools which shall give to the children of every citizen gratis, competent instruction in reading, writing, common arithmetic, and general geography. 2. Collegiate institutions for antient & modern languages, for higher instruction in arithmetic, geography & history, placing for these purposes a college within a day's ride of every inhabitant of the state, and adding a provision for the full education at the public expence of select subjects from among the children of the poor, who shall have exhibited at the elementary schools the most prominent indications of aptness of judgment & correct disposition. 3. An University in which all the branches of science deemed useful at this day, shall be taught in their highest degree. This would probably require ten or twelve professors, for most of whom we shall be obliged to apply to Europe, and most likely to Edinburg, because of the greater advantage the students will receive from communications made in their native language. This last establishment will probably be within a mile of Charlottesville, and four from Monticello, if the system should be adopted at all by our legislature who meet within a week from this time. My hopes however are kept in check by the ordinary character of our state legislatures, the members of which do not generally possess information enough to perceive the important truths, that knowledge is power, that knowledge is safety, and that knowledge is happiness.

THE JESUIT ORDER

The Society of Jesus, or the Jesuit Order, was founded by Ignatius of
Loyola in 1539 and soon became the principal weapon of the papacy in
its counter-attack against the Protestant reformers. Renouncing the glory
of a soldier's career to become a warrior of Christ, Loyola attracted to
his cause a group of able men. The first Jesuits — eight in number — took
their vows of poverty, chastity, and obedience at the church of Montmartre
in Paris in 1534, and six years later they received official papal approval.
The first Jesuit college was opened at Coimbra, Portugal, in 1542, and soon
such colleges were offering both secondary and university education in all
parts of Europe.

The Jesuit plan of education was systematic, highly organized, and
dependent for its success on the discipline, zeal, and devotion of a select
group of Jesuit Fathers whose ideal was the militant life for Christ and
whose two great principles — love of Christ and concern for the salvation
of souls — were brought together in their motto: *Ad Majorem Dei Gloriam*
("All for the greater glory of God"). The general character of the educational mission of the Jesuits was expressed in the Constitution of the
order, which were begun by Ignatius himself in 1541. The plan is set
out fully in the fourth part of the Constitution, the *Ratio Studiorum,* or
system of studies, completed in 1599. Based upon years of educational
experiment (a commission of experts had drawn up a provisional scheme
which was put into practice, observed, modified, and used again in
practice before being adopted for universal application), the *Ratio
Studiorum* has proven to be the most enduring of all educational regulations, for in a slightly modified form it continues to serve as the directive
for modern Jesuit schools.

The *Ratio Studiorum* covers something more than a hundred pages
and concentrates on the prescription of the duties of the officers of the
order and the subjects and methods of the various teachers. The Catholic
tradition and selected classics constitute the heart of the subject matter,
and emphasis is on inculcating a spirit of obedience and a strong sense of
competition. The success of the Jesuits was remarkable. In the words
of F. Paulsen, the German Protestant historian, "From the mouth of the
Rhine to the mouth of the Vistula the Jesuits encircled the seat of heresy
with a chain of colleges, as if by a belt of fortresses." Their schools
were reputed to be the best in Europe and even drew praise from their

enemies. Francis Bacon remarked that "concerning human learning and moral matters, I may say . . . 'they are so good that I wish they were on our side.'"

The following selections from the *Ratio Studiorum* provide a general insight into the pedagogical principles of the Jesuits.

SYSTEM AND PLAN OF STUDIES*

1. Since it is one of the weightiest duties of our society to teach men all the branches of knowledge in keeping with our organization in such a manner, that they may be moved thereby to a knowledge and love of our Creator and Redeemer, let the Provincial hold it as his duty, to provide with all zeal, that the results, which the grace of our vocation demands, abundantly answer to our manifold labors in education.

2. Long before let him [the Provincial] consider whom he can take as professors in each department, and take heed to those who seem to be best fitted for the place, who are learned, diligent, and assiduous, and are zealous for the progress of their students in their lectures as well as in their other literary exercises.

3. Let him promote with great care the study of the Holy Scriptures; in which he will succeed, if he selects for this office men who are not only proficient in the languages (for that is especially necessary), but also well versed in theology and the other sciences, in history and in general learning, and also, as far as possible, in eloquence.

4. But he must especially remember that only men who are well disposed to St. Thomas are to be promoted to theological chairs. Whoever is indifferent to him or is not studious of him shall be removed from the office of teaching.

5. The professors of philosophy, except when the gravest necessity calls for an exception, must not simply complete the course in theology, but also repeat it for two years, in order that their teaching may be the safer and more serviceable to theology.

*From *Great Pedagogical Essays,* edited by F. V. N. Painter (New York: American Book Company, 1905).

310

Should any, however, be inclined to innovating opinions or exhibit too liberal a spirit, they must undoubtedly be removed from the office of teaching.

6. When students have entered upon the philosophical course, they must undergo a rigid examination at the end of the year given by the appointed examiners in the presence of the rector, and if possible, of the Provincial himself. No one may pass from the first to the second year of philosophy, unless he has reached mediocrity, that is so that he understands well what he hears and can give an account of it. But no one shall be admitted to scholastic theology who has not risen above mediocrity in the philosophical course, so that he can defend and maintain philosophical theses with applause; except in the case that such mediocrity displays a distinguished talent for administration or preaching, on which account the Provincial may dispose of his case otherwise, though in other things he has no power to grant dispensations.

7. These examinations, in which it is decided whether the students of philosophy or theology shall pass to the following years, shall take place by secret ballot; and the decision arrived at, together with the judgement of the examiners, shall be entered in a book designed for that purpose; and all who were present at the examination shall maintain silence about it.

8. Schools for lower studies must not exceed five in number, namely, one for rhetoric, the second for humanity, and three for grammar. For these are five grades so intimately connected that they must not be confused or increased in number.

9. Furthermore, care must be exercised that where there are too few schools, always the higher classes, so far as possible, must be retained, and the lower classes given up.

10. In order to preserve a knowledge of classical literature and to establish a sort of nursery for gymnasium teachers, let him [the Provincial] endeavor to have in his province at least two or three men distinguished in these services and in eloquence. To this end, from the number of those who are capable and inclined to these studies, he shall set apart for that work alone a few who are sufficiently instructed in the other departments, in order

that through their efforts and activity a body of good teachers my be maintained and provided for the future.

11. Let him procure as many life-long teachers of grammar and rhetoric as possible. This he will be able to do, if at the close of ethical or even theological studies he earnestly directs and exhorts to the teacher's vocation some, from whose help he can expect in the Lord greater results in this office than in any other, that they may wholly dedicate themselves to so salutary a work for the greater service of God.

12. With all diligence let him watch and esteem it a matter of the highest importance that all books of the poets and other writings, which might prove injurious to character and good manners, be kept from our schools, until they have been purged of impure passages and words; and should this expurgation not be possible, the books shalt rather not be read, in order that their contents may not contaminate the purity of the soul.

13. Let still greater care be exercised in the case of native writers, where the reading of such authors is customary in the schools. These authors shall be carefully selected, and none shall ever be read or praised, in whom the young may not take an interest without danger to their faith and morals. Therefore, men well versed in the native literature shall be consulted, in order to determine what may be done in this matter without injury, and then see to it that what has been determined, be also conscientiously observed by the prefects and teachers of the schools.

14. Let him [the Rector] see to it that the use of the Latin language is diligently maintained among the students; from this requirement of speaking Latin only holidays and recreation hours are to be excepted, unless the Provincial finds it advisable in certain localities to retain the use of Latin also on such days. He may also insist that our students, who have not yet completed their course of study, write their letters to other brethren of the order in Latin. Besides this our philosophical and theological students, two or three times a year, at the opening of a session or the renewal of their vows, shall compose and publicly post some poetical production.

15. The subject-matter of tragedies and comedies, which how-

ever shall be only in Latin and seldom acted, shall be of a sacred and pious character; the interludes also shall be in Latin and of due decorum; female roles and costumes are prohibited.

16. Prizes may be publicly distributed once a year, provided they be of moderate cost, according to the number of students and the grade of the college. But if any one provides the necessary cost for this purpose, his name must be honorably mentioned at the distribution of prizes.

17. The lower schools shall have a weekly recess of a whole day or a half day, according to the custom of the locality.

18. At all disputations, at which the professors of theology or philosophy are present, the Prefect must preside; he must give the disputants the sign to begin, and divide the time in such a manner that each one may have his turn in the discussion. He must let no difficulty which comes into the discussion be bandied about so that it remains just as obscure afterwards as it was before; but when it has been sufficiently discussed on both sides, let him have it carefully explained by the first defendant. For he himself shall not answer objections, but rather direct the advocates and defendants; an office which he will fulfil with more dignity, if he helps, not through arguments (which however he may sometimes make) but through questions, to solve the difficulty.

19. Nothing shall be publicly delivered in the House or out of it, either by those who are promoted to degrees or by those who hold general or particular disputations or by the students of rhetoric, unless it has first been examined and approved.

20. Let him [the Prefect] exercise care that the students have neither a lack of useful books nor a superfluity of useless books. Therefore, he shall early remind the rector, that our students, and those residing out of the House, may not suffer a lack of the books which they need daily or for the coming year.

21. He shall not grant to the students of theology and philosophy all the books they may desire, but with the knowledge of the rector and the advice of the teachers, suitable books: namely, to the theologues, besides the author read in the school, the *Summa* of St. Thomas [Aquinas] and a commentary thereto or another select author, further the Council of Trent together with a Bible,

in the reading of which he shall be at home. Whether they shall have a holy Father or a writer of Church history, he may consider with the rector.

To the students of philosophy, besides the text-book he may assign, if it seems good to him, another approved author. Besides, let him give to every theological and philosophical student a book from classic literature, and admonish them not to neglect the reading of the same at certain suitable hours.

22. The special aim of the teacher, in his lectures on suitable occasion and elsewhere, should be to inspire his pupils to the service and love of God and to the exercise of the virtues through which we may please him, and to lead them to recognize this as the sole end of their studies.

23. In those questions which are left free to personal judgment, let him defend his own opinion in such a manner as modestly and benevolently to consider the reputation of the other party and still more of his predecessor in case the latter taught differently. If the different authors can be brought into agreement, it is desirable that this should not be neglected. Finally, let him be modest in naming or confuting authors.

24. Even when no danger to faith and piety is involved, no one, in subjects of any importance, shall bring forward, without previous consultation with the authorities, new questions or any opinion which is not held by some reputable author, nor present any views contrary to the teachings of the doctors and against the general view of the existing schools. Rather shall they all follow carefully the approved teachers, and cling to that which through long years has been especially accepted in Catholic academies.

25. Let him not bring forward useless, obsolete, absurd, or manifestly false opinions, nor continue too long in mentioning and refuting them. Let him seek to establish his conclusions not so much by the number as by the weight of his arguments. Let him not digress to foreign materials nor use his own too diffusely or in a wrong connection. Let him not heap up a mass of possible objections, but only bring forward briefly the weightiest of them, unless their refutation is easily manifest from the fundamental principles already laid down.

26. In quoting learned authorities he shall not go to excess; but if he adduces the testimony of distinguished authors to confirm his position, let him briefly and faithfully cite, if possible, the very words; this he must do especially in passages from the Sacred Scriptures, Councils, and the holy Fathers. But for the sake of his dignity hardly any author is to be cited that he has not read himself.

27. Let him often question his pupils about the lecture, and insist on repetition. But after the lecture let him remain in or near the school, that his hearers may be able to question him.

28. Also in the House, except on Saturdays, holidays, and festival days, an hour must be assigned our students for repetition and disputation in order that in this manner the mind may be exercised and the occurring difficulties cleared up. Therefore, one or two should be designated to repeat the lesson by heart in not more than a quarter of an hour; then one or two shall assail the conclusion, while just as many defend it; and if afterwards there is sufficient time, all sorts of doubts may be proposed. But in order that there may be time, the professor must insist strenuously upon the syllogistic form in disputation, and when nothing new is any longer brought forward, he must at once cut off the discussion.

29. Toward the end of the school year reviews are to be so arranged that, if possible, all the lessons may be repeated before the beginning of vacation.

30. Finally let him [the professor] with the help of divine grace be diligent and assiduous in all things, and seek the progress of his students not only in their lessons but also in their other exercises; and let him not be more familiar with one student than with another; let him despise none, and let him care for the studies of the poor as of the rich; let him promote the progress of each student individually.

31. Let him [the professor of Holy Scripture] recognize it as his principal duty, piously, learnedly, and thoroughly to explain the books given of God, according to their genuine and liberal sense, which confirms the right faith in God and the principles of good morals. Among other ends which he is to pursue, let this

315

stand as chief, that he is to defend the translation (Vulgate) approved by the Church.

32. As to other translations, whether later Latin or vernacular... let him undertake the refutation only of weighty and easily corrupting errors; on the other hand let him not pass over what is favorable to the Latin Vulgate and the mysteries of our faith, especially, when it is found in the Septuagint, which is always to be spoken of reverently.

33. When the canons of the popes or councils, especially the general councils, indicate the literal sense of a passage of Scripture as the true one, let him also by all means defend it and adduce no other literal sense, except where special reasons exist. When they employ a text expressly as proof of an article of faith, let him teach likewise that this is the indubitable sense, whether literal or mystical.

34. Let him reverently follow in the footsteps of the holy Fathers; when they are agreed about the literal or allegorical sense of a passage, especially when they expressly say so and purposely treat of passages of Scripture or articles of faith, let him not depart from that sense; but where they are not agreed, let him choose from their different expositions what the Church for years and with great unanimity has preferred.

35. When he comes upon a text, over which we are in controversy with heretics, or which is quoted on both sides in theological discussions, let him expound it simply, yet thoroughly and vigorously, especially against heretics, and point out what weight is in the passage for deciding the question at issue; all the rest let him lay aside, in order that he, mindful of his vocation, may be simply an expounder of the Holy Scriptures.

36. Let him [the professor of theology] regard it as his function so to unite through subtlety of investigation with the true faith and with piety, that it may be subordinated and serviceable to them.

37. In scholastic theology our members shall follow the doctrine of St. Thomas, consider him as their true teacher, and take great pains that our students develop the utmost fondness for him. Yet it must not be thought that they are so bound to St. Thomas,

that they may not deviate from him in any point; for even those who especially profess to be followers of St. Thomas, sometimes deviate from him; and it would not be right to bind our people to St. Thomas more strictly than the Thomists themselves.

38. In teaching, confirmation of faith and growth in piety must above all be considered. Therefore in questions, which St. Thomas has not expressly handled, no one shall teach anything that does not well harmonize with the views of the Church and the generally received traditions, and that in any way disturbs the foundation of genuine piety.

39. If it is known that certain views of any author would seriously offend the Catholics in a province or academy, let them not be taught and defended there. For where neither the doctrine of faith nor the purity of morals is in danger, a wise charity demands that our people accommodate themselves to those with whom they dwell.

40. Let him [the professor of Church history] treat the history of the Church with the view and with such skill, that he may render the study of theology more easy for his students, and more deeply impress upon their minds the dogmas of faith and the canons.

41. Let him clearly demonstrate that the rights of the Church and of its head rest upon antiquity, and let him show that the statements of innovators about the late origin of such rights are pure inventions.

42. Let him draw his exposition of history from unadulterated sources, and when it can be easily done, let him use the words of the authors themselves; let him show how the innovators have often corrupted the original statements.

43. Questions of doctrine and ecclesiastical law he must not treat himself, but hand them over to the proper professors; but at the same time he must consider it his duty to go over them historically and to establish them by facts themselves.

44. Inasmuch as philosophy prepares the mind for theology and other departments of study, contributes to their perfect comprehension and practical application, and promotes in itself the culture of the understanding and consequently the perfection of the

317

will, let the teacher present it with due clearness, and honestly seek in all things the honor and glory of God, so that he may prepare his students for other sciences, but especially for theology, equip them with the weapons of truth against the errors of the innovators, and encourage them above all to a recognition of their Creator.

45. In all important questions he must not deviate from the teaching everywhere accepted in the academies. Let him defend the orthodox faith with his might, and seek thoroughly to refute the philosophical systems and arguments directed against it. Finally let him not forget in the choice of different opinions that theology must light the way.

46. Those philosophers who have been unfriendly to the Christian religion he must not read without great discrimination or discuss them in the school; let him beware lest his pupils conceive an affection for them. If he quotes anything good from them, let him do so without praise, and show, if possible, that they have borrowed it elsewhere.

47. On the contrary let him always speak reverently of St. Thomas; let him follow him gladly, as often as possible, and deviate from him only unwillingly and respectfully, when he finds less pleasure in him.

48. Monthly disputations shall be held, at which the defendant shall briefly and philosophically establish one or two theses, and besides a professor invited to advocate the affirmative, the students of the higher class shall debate with those of the lower class, and then the students of the same class shall debate with one another.

49. From the beginning of logic on, the students shall be so instructed that in their disputations they may be ashamed of nothing more than of a departure from syllogistic form. The teacher shall insist on nothing more than on an observance of the laws of disputation and the proper alternation between attack and defense. Therefore, let the defendant first repeat the whole argumentation without any reply to the separate propositions; then let him repeat again the propositions, and add to each one "I grant it," or "I deny the major or minor premise or the conclusion." Let him also sometimes draw distinctions, but not urge upon any

318

one against his will the explanation or reason which one is accustomed to introduce.

50. Finally he [the professor of physics] shall not forget that he is to pursue the secular sciences in a religious manner, in order that "the invisible things of God may be made known through those things which are made" [Rom. 1:20]; therefore let him seek, as occasion presents itself, to confirm the truths of faith also through physical science, yet without going aside to theological, metaphysical, or Scriptural exposition.

51. There shall be three examiners [in the lower gymnasium studies]: one of them must ordinarily be the Prefect; the other two must be learned in the humanities, and be appointed by the rector together with the Prefect. A majority of the three shall decide. But where the number of students is large, two or more such triumvirates may be appointed.

52. The order of the examination is as follows: first each student, when he is called on, shall read a part of his composition; then let him correct his mistakes and explain them, with a citation of the rule which he has failed to observe. Afterwards the grammar students shall immediately translate into Latin an exercise assigned them in the vernacular; all shall be interrogated about the rules and subjects of their class. Finally, when it is necessary, a brief interpretation of any passage from those books, which have been read in class, may be required of them.

53. When three students have been examined, and while the recollection of the examiners is still clear, the vote shall be taken, in which the composition, the notes of the teacher, and the oral examination shall all be considered.

54. The list of promoted students shall be announced publicly either in the separate classes or in the assembly room. When any students have greatly distinguished themselves, they shall first receive honorable mention; with the rest the order of the alphabet or of studies must be observed.

55. Let him [the Prefect] have great care that the students give public proof of their progress and of the good standing of our schools with due solemnity; to this end let him timely admonish

319

the teachers and personally examine those students who are to appear publicly before they are allowed to do so.

56. In every class, according to the custom of the place, let him appoint a student as public censor, or if this name is displeasing, an upper decurion or praetor; who, that he may be in honor among his fellow-students, must be distinguished through some privilege, and have the right, with the approval of the teacher, of petitioning in behalf of his fellow-students for the remission of lighter punishments. Let him observe whether any of his fellow-pupils before the signal for school wanders around in the yard or enters another school, or leaves his own school or place. He must also inform the Prefect every day, who has been absent from school, whether any one not a student has entered the classroom, and finally whether in the presence or absence of the teacher any fault has been committed in the school.

57. On account of those who are lacking in diligence and good morals, and for whom kind words and admonitions are not alone sufficient, a corrector must be appointed who does not belong to the Society. Where such a person can not be had, another way should be devised (either through one of the students themselves or otherwise), by which the guilty may receive proper chastisement.

58. When neither words nor the office of the corrector is sufficient, when no improvement in the student is to be hoped for, and moral contamination for others is to be feared, it is better to remove him from the school than to keep him there, where he makes no progress himself and injures others. But that all may be done, as is fitting, to the glory and service of God, the decision of the matter must be left to the rector.

59. Christian doctrine must be learned by heart in all the classes; and in the three grammar classes, and if necessary, in the other classes, it must be repeated Fridays or Saturdays. According to the grade of each class more ample explanations shall be given and required.

60. On Friday or Saturday let him [the Professor of the lower classes] deliver for half an hour a pious exhortation or explanation of the catechism; but especially let him exhort to daily prayer to

320

God, to a daily reciting of the rosary or office of the Blessed Virgin, to an examination of the conscience every evening, to a frequent and worthy reception of the sacraments of penance and the altar, to an avoidance of evil habits, to a detestation of vice, and finally to a practice of all the virtues becoming a Christian.

61. Especial care must be exercised that the students acquire the habit of speaking Latin. Therefore the teacher, at least from the upper grammar grade, must speak in Latin, and require also that the students speak Latin, especially in the explanation of rules, the correction of Latin exercises, in disputation of authors he must himself have great regard for the purity and correct pronunciation of the mother tongue, and strictly require the same from the students.

62. The class-match (concertatio) is usually so arranged that either the teacher questions and the contestants (æmuli) correct the answers, or the contestants question one another. This exercise is to be highly esteemed and, as often as possible, engaged in, in order that a proper emulation (honesta æmulatio), which is a great incentive to study, may be cultivated.

IMMANUEL KANT

IMMANUEL KANT (1724-1804). The most illustrious German philosopher of the modern period was born on April 22, 1724 in Königsberg, where he lived until his death on February 12, 1804. The acute logic of his critical philosophy had a purifying effect on his contemporaries and made his contribution to educational theory an achievement of the highest order.

The son of a saddler who belonged to the Lutheran sect of Pietists in Königsberg, Immanuel Kant received his education at the Collegium Fredericianum and at the University of Königsberg, where he finally completed the doctorate (1755) and was made professor of logic and metaphysics (1770). He never married and is said always to have remained within the confines of the province in which he was born. He gave his life to study and meditation, and the fame that attended his lectures and writings made his native city a mecca for students of philosophy.

The philosophic system which he formulated, known as the *critical philosophy,* overwhelmed the shallow worship of reason of the men of the Enlightenment, and the purity and nobility of his ethics permeated the lectures (edited by his pupil Rink and published in 1803 under the title *Immanuel Kant über Pädagogik*) in which he expressed his belief in the unlimited powers of education.

The task of education is to make mankind ever more perfect. The highest purpose of education is the formation of a moral character which will enable the student to do his duty and to perform good deeds in the absence of considerations of reward and punishment. The four means of achieving this end are discipline, cultivation of the necessary skills, acquisition of knowledge of the world about us, and formation of a character that acts only according to the categorical imperative: "Act only on that maxim whereby thou canst at the same time will that it should become a universal law." Mankind can be made ever more perfect only if each generation educates the succeeding one to a higher level of achievement.

The first selection that follows is from Kant's *Fundamental Principles of Morals.* The last two selections are from the lectures on education which he was required to deliver as professor of philosophy. These three selections give a fairly complete accounting of his system of education.

322

ETHICS IN EDUCATION*

If then there is a supreme practical principle or, in respect of the human will, a categorical imperative, it must be one which, being drawn from the conception of that which is necessarily an end for every one because it is *an end in itself,* constitutes an *objective* principle of will, and can therefore serve as a universal practical law. The foundation of this principle is: *rational nature exists as an end in itself.* Man necessarily conceives his own existence as being so; so far then this is a *subjective* principle of human actions. But every other rational being regards its existence similarly, just on the same rational principle that holds for me: so that it is at the same time an objective principle, from which as a supreme practical law all laws of the will must be capable of being deduced. Accordingly the practical imperative will be as follows: *So act as to treat humanity, whether in thine own person or in that of any other, in every case as an end withal, never as means only.*

Looking back now on all previous attempts to discover the principle of morality, we need not wonder why they all fail. It was seen that man was bound to laws by duty, but it was not observed that the laws to which he is subject are *only those of his own giving,* though at the same time they are *universal,* and that he is only bound to act in conformity with his own will; a will, however, which is designed by nature to give universal laws. For when one has conceived man only as subject to a law (no matter what), then this law required some interest, either by way of attraction or constraint, since it did not originate as a law from *his own* will, but this will was according to a law obliged by *something else* to act in a certain manner. Now by this necessary consequence all the labour spent in finding a supreme principle of *duty* was irrevocably lost. . . .

*From *Fundamental Principles of Morals* (New York, 1910).

The practical necessity of acting on this principle, *i.e.*, duty, does not rest at all on feelings, impulses, or inclinations, but solely on the relation of rational beings to one another, a relation in which the will of a rational being must always be regarded as *legislative*, since otherwise it could not be conceived as *an end in itself*. Reason then refers every maxim of the will, regarding it as legislating universally, to every other will and also to every action towards oneself; and this not on account of any other practical motive or any future advantage, but from the idea of the *dignity* of a rational being, obeying no law but that which he himself also gives.

PEDAGOGICAL PRINCIPLES*

Man is the only creature that needs to be educated. By education we understand *nurture* (attention, food), *discipline*, and *instruction* together with *culture*. Accordingly man is infant, child, and pupil.

Animals use their powers, as soon as they are possessed of then, according to a regular plan, that is, in a way not to injure themselves. It is indeed wonderful, for example, that young swallows, newly hatched and still blind, are careful not to defile their nest. Animals therefore need no nurture, but at the most food, warmth, and guidance, or a kind of protection. It is true most animals need feeding, but they do not require nurture. For by nurture we mean the tender care that parents exercise in order to prevent their children from using their powers in a way to be harmful to them. For instance, should an animal cry at birth, as children do, it would surely fall a prey to wolves and other wild animals, which would be attracted by its cry.

Discipline or training transforms animal nature into human nature. An animal is by instinct all that it ever can be; some other reason has already provided everything for it. But man needs a reason of his own. Having no instinct, he has to work

---

*From *Great Pedagogical Essays*, edited by F. V. N. Painter (New York, American Book Company, 1905).

out a plan of conduct himself. Since, however, he is not able to do this at once, but comes into the world undeveloped, others must do it for him.

Through its own efforts the human race is by degrees to develop all the natural endowments of man. One generation educates the next. The beginning of this process may be looked for either in a rude and unformed, or in a perfect and cultivated condition. If we assume the latter, man must afterwards have degenerated and lapsed into barbarism.

Discipline prevents man from being turned aside by his animal impulses from humanity, his appointed end. It must restrain him, for example, from venturing wildly and thoughtlessly into danger. Discipline thus is merely negative, namely, the process by which man is deprived of his brutality. Instruction, on the contrary, is the positive part of education.

Brutality is independence of law. Discipline subjects man to the laws of mankind, and lets him feel their constraint. But this must take place early. Thus children are at first sent to school, not so much to learn anything, as to become accustomed to sitting still and obeying promptly what they are told, to the end that later in life they may not actually and instantly follow all their impulses.

* * *

The love of freedom is naturally so strong in man that when he has once grown accustomed to it he will sacrifice everything for it. For this very reason discipline must be brought into exercise early; for when this has not been done, it is difficult afterwards to change the character. He will then follow every caprice. We see this also among savage nations which, though they may live in subjection to Europeans a long time, yet never adopt European customs. With them, however, this is not a noble love of freedom, as Rousseau and others imagine, but a kind of savagery, in which the animal, so to speak, has not yet developed its humanity. Man should therefore accustom himself early to submit to the dictates of reason. If a man in his youth is allowed to follow his own will without opposition, he will retain a certain

325

lawlessness through life. And it is no advantage to such a man to be spared in his youth through a superabundant motherly tenderness, for later on he will meet with all the more opposition on every side and everywhere encounter rebuffs, when he enters into the business of the world.

It is a common mistake in the education of the great that, because they are destined to rule, they should never meet with opposition in their youth. Owing to his love of freedom, man needs to have his native roughness smoothed down; but with animals instinct renders this unnecessary.

*　*　*

Man needs *nurture* and *culture*. Culture includes discipline and instruction. These, so far as we know, no animal needs; for none of them learn anything from their elders, except the birds, which are taught by them to sing. It is a touching sight to watch the mother bird singing with all her might to her young ones, which like children at school, try to produce the same tones out of their tiny throats.

Man can become man only by education. He is nothing but what education makes him. It is to be noted that man is educated only by men who have themselves been educated. Hence lack of discipline and instruction on the part of some men makes them in turn bad educators of their pupils. Were some being of a higher nature than man to undertake our education, we should then be able to see what man might become. Since some things are imparted to man by education, and others only developed, it is difficult for us to estimate accurately his native capabilities. If, by the help of the great and the cooperative efforts of many persons, the experiment were made, we might gain some idea of the eminence which it is possible for man to attain. But it is just as important for the philosopher, as it is sad for the philanthropist, to see how the great generally care only for their own interests, and take no part in the weighty experiments of education, which might bring our nature one step nearer to perfection.

*　*　*

326

A theory of education is a glorious ideal, and it matters little, if we are not able to realize it at once. Only we must not look upon the idea as chimerical, nor decry it as a beautiful dream, though difficulties stand in the way of its realization.

An idea is nothing else than the conception of a perfection that has not yet been realized. For instance, the idea of a perfect republic governed by the principles of justice — is it impossible because it has never existed? First of all our idea must be corrected, and then, in spite of all the hindrances that stand in the way of its realization, it is by no means impossible. If, for example, lying became universal, would veracity on that account be merely a whim? And the idea of an education which will develop all man's natural gifts is certainly a true one.

* * *

Under the present system of education man does not fully attain the object of his being. For how differently men live! Uniformity can prevail among them, only when they act according to the same principles, which have become to them a second nature. We can work out a better system of education, and hand down to posterity such directions as will enable them by degrees to bring it to realization.

There are many undeveloped powers in man; and it is our task to unfold these natural gifts in due proportion, to develop humanity from its germinal state, and to lead man to a realization of his destiny. Animals unconsciously fulfil their destiny themselves. Man must strive to attain it, but this he can not do, unless he has a conception as to the object of his existence. The fulfilment of his destiny is absolutely impossible to the individual. In times past men had no conception of the perfection to which human nature might attain. We ourselves have not yet become perfectly clear on the subject. This much, however, is certain: no individual man, whatever may be the culture of his pupils, can insure the fulfilment of their destiny. To succeed in this high end, not the work of individuals, but that of the whole human race, is necessary.

* * *

327

Education is an art, the practice of which can become perfect only through many generations. Each generation, provided with the knowledge of the preceding one, can more and more bring about an education, which will develop man's natural gifts in due proportion and relation to their end, and thus advance the whole human race towards its destiny. Providence has willed that man shall develop the good that lies hidden in his nature, and has spoken, as it were, thus to him: "Go forth into the world, I have equipped thee with all the potencies of good. It is for thee to develop them, and thus thy happiness and unhappiness depend upon thyself alone."

Man must develop his talents for the good; Providence has not placed a fully formed goodness in him, but merely capabilities without moral distinction. Man's duty is to improve himself; to cultivate his mind, and when he is evil, to develop moral character. Upon reflection we shall find this very difficult. Hence education is the greatest and most difficult problem to which man can devote himself. For insight depends on education, and education in its turn depends on insight. Hence it follows that education can advance only by degrees, and that a true conception of the method of education can arise only when one generation transmits its stores of experience and knowledge to the following one, which in turn adds something of its own before handing them down to its successor. What vast culture and experience does not this conception presuppose! Accordingly it can originate only at a remote period, and we ourselves have not fully realized it. The question arises whether the education of the individual should be conformed to the education of the human race through its successive generations?

There are two inventions of man which may be regarded as the most difficult of all, namely, the art of government and the art of education; and people are still divided as to their true idea.

* * *

Since the development of man's natural gifts does not take place of itself, all education is an art. Nature has placed no instinct in him for that purpose. The origin as well as the progress of this

328

art is either mechanical and without plan, ordered according to given circumstances, or it involves the exercise of intelligent judgment. Education is mechanical when on only chance occasions we learn by experience whether anything is useful or harmful to man. All education which is merely mechanical must carry with it many mistakes and deficiencies because it rests on no basal principle. If education is to develop human nature so that it may attain its destiny, it must involve the exercise of judgment. Educated parents are models which children use for imitation. But if children are to progress beyond their parents, pedagogy must become a study; otherwise we can hope for nothing from it, and men of defective education will become the educators of others. Mechanism in education must be changed into a science; otherwise it will never become a consistent pursuit, and one generation may pull down what another had built up.

* * *

One principle of education which those men especially who form educational schemes should keep before their eyes is this — children ought to be educated, not for the present, but for a possibly improved condition of man in the future; that is, in a manner which is adapted to the idea of humanity and the whole destiny of man. This principle is of great importance. Parents usually educate their children in such a manner that they may be adapted to the present conditions, however degenerate the world may be. But they ought to give them a better education, in order that a better condition of things may thereby be brought about in the future.

* * *

Here, however, we encounter two difficulties: (1) Parents usually care only that their children make their way in the world, and (2) Princes consider their subjects only as instruments for their own purposes. Parents care for the home, princes for the state. Neither have as their aim the universal good and the perfection to which man is destined and for which he has also the natural gifts. But the basis of a scheme of education must be

329

cosmopolitan. And is, then, the idea of the universal good hurtful to us as individuals? Never! for though it may appear that something must be sacrificed with this idea, nevertheless it furthers the best interests of the individual under his present conditions. And then what splendid results follow! It is through good education that all the good in the world arises. The germs which lie hidden in man need only to be more and more developed. For the elements of evil are not to be found in the natural endowments of man. The failure to bring nature under control — this is the cause of evil. In man there are only germs of good.

But by whom is this better condition of the world to be brought about? By rulers, or by their subjects? Shall the latter improve themselves so that they meet a good government half way? If this better condition is to be established by princes, then their own education must first be improved, for their training has long suffered the great mistake of not allowing them to meet with opposition in their youth.

Accordingly the management of schools should entirely depend upon the judgment of the most enlightened experts. All culture begins with the individual, and radiates from him as a center. It is only through the efforts of people of broader views, who take an interest in the general good, and who are capable of entertaining the idea of a better condition of things in the future, that the gradual progress of human nature towards its goal is possible.

Thus, in education, man must in the first place, be made the subject of *discipline*. Discipline means the effort to restrain the animal side of our nature, in the individual as well as in social life, from working harm. It is thus nothing but the subjugation of our brutality. In the second place, man must acquire *culture*. Culture includes information and instruction. It is culture that brings out ability. Ability is the possession of a faculty which is capable of being adapted to all desired ends. It does not determine ends, but leaves that to subsequent circumstances. On account of the multitude of ends, ability is in some sense infinite. In the third place, man must acquire *discretion* and be able to conduct himself in society so that he may be esteemed, and possess influence. To

330

this end there is needed a kind of culture which we call *refinement*. This includes manners, courtesy, and a certain discretion, which will enable their possessor to use all men for his own ends. This refinement changes according to the varying taste of successive ages. Thus, some decades ago, ceremonies were the fashion in social intercourse. In the fourth place, *moral training* must form a part of education. It is not enough that a man be fitted for any end, but he must also acquire the disposition to choose only good ends. Good ends are those which are necessarily approved by everyone, and which may at the same time be the aim of everyone.

* * *

Man may be either broken in, trained, and mechanically taught, or he may be really enlightened. Horses and dogs are broken in, and man, too, may be broken in. But it is not enough that children should be merely broken in; it is eminently important that they learn to think. That leads to the principle from which all transactions proceed. Thus we see that a real education involves a great deal. But as a rule, in private education, the fourth and most important point is still too much neglected, for children are substantially educated in such a way that moral training is left to the preacher. And yet how infinitely important it is that children be taught from youth up to detest vice, not merely on the ground that God has forbidden it, but because it is in itself detestable.

* * *

Experimental schools must be established before we can establish normal schools. Education and instruction must not be merely mechanical; they must be based on fixed principles. Yet education must be not entirely theoretical, but at the same time, in a certain sense, mechanical.

People commonly imagine that experiments in education are not necessary, and that we can judge from our reason whether anything is good or not. But this is a great mistake, and experience teaches that the results of our experiments are often entirely

331

different from what we expected. Thus we see that, since we must be guided by experiments, no one generation can set forth a complete scheme of education.

EDUCATION FOR FREEDOM*

The child should be left perfectly free, from earliest childhood, in everything (except in such instances where he might injure himself; as, for example, when he reaches for an open knife), unless the manner of his freedom interferes with that of others; as, or example, when he screams, or is merry in too noisy a way, he discommodes others.

The child must be shown that he can attain his aims only as he permits others to reach theirs; as, for example, he will be granted no pleasure if he does not do what others desire, that he must learn, etc.

It must also be shown to the child that he is under such constraint as will lead him to the use of his own freedom; that he is cultivated, so that one day he may be free — that is, not dependent upon the foresight of others. That is the child's latest acquisition. For the consideration that each must rely upon himself for his own sustenance comes to the child very late. They fancy it will always be as it is in the parental home; that food and drink will come without any thought on their part. Without such treatment, children, and especially those of rich parents and princes, become like the inhabitants of Tahiti, who remain children their whole life long.

Here public education has the most evident advantage, since in it one learns to measure his powers and the limitations which the rights of others impose upon him. In this form of education no one has prerogatives, since opposition is felt everywhere, and merit becomes the only standard of preferment. This education produces the best prototype of the future citizen.

*From E. F. Buchner, *Kant's Educational Theory*, Philadelphia, 1904.

WILLIAM H. KILPATRICK

WILLIAM H. KILPATRICK (1871-1965). As a leader of the Progressive movement, as a dynamic and frequently controversial teacher, and as a popular lecturer and writer, William Heard Kilpatrick has had a considerable influence on educational developments during the past-half century. He defended the dignity of the individual and his right to arrive independently at his own opinions and beliefs on both sectarian and non-sectarian issues, popularized the educational theories of John Dewey and the project method, stressed the role of meaningful activities and the reconstruction of experience in the lives of students, and built an educational philosophy around the concept of learning as living.

Born at White Plains, Georgia, on November 20, 1871, he graduated from Mercer University in 1891, studied at Johns Hopkins, taught in the public schools of Georgia, and joined the faculty of Teachers College, Columbia University, in 1909. He received his doctorate in philosophy in 1912. He continued as professor of the philosophy of education until 1938, when he became emeritus professor. His numerous books include *The Montessori System Examined* (1914), *Foundations of Method* (1925), *Education for a Changing Civilization* (1926), *Education and the Social Crisis* (1932), *Remaking the Curriculum* (1936), *Selfhood and Civilization* (1941), and *Philosophy of Education* (1951).

The address that follows was delivered to a group of German educators who were visiting America in 1928. In it he explains the background and source of American educational attitudes, states five hypotheses for "understanding and ordering life," and outlines a system of education to satisfy the demands of American life. Significantly, the curriculum he proposes "is not properly conceived in terms of the subject matter to be acquired but as a life process, a succession of experiences, each growing out of the preceding experiences in such a way as to continue most fruitfully the reconstruction of experience."

THE PHILOSOPHY OF AMERICAN EDUCATION*

There is, of course, no one philosophy of education to be ascribed to America. There are, however, certain tendencies more or less consistent with each other which, taken together, may with reasonable accuracy be said to characterize the dominant American attitude in educational matters. Such tendencies the philosophy of education should sense and criticize with a view to securing a more defensible unity of outlook and endeavor. Beyond these characteristic trends there will thus result individual philosophies. One such is here presented.

The account here given is necessarily but sketchy. At the outset a glance is taken at the background and source of American educational problems and attitudes. Then follows an outline of the basic philosophy of education with a correlative discussion of certain more fundamental problems in the educational situation. It is but fair in connection with this to say two things — first, that the author of these lines is but one of a group, of which Professor Dewey is the most distinguished member, to hold in general to this position, and, second, that to various aspects of the position herein taken there is opposition from certain other groups in American thought. The reader will understand that the writer speaks then only for himself.

What is the background of American thought and attitude? A hasty glance at this will serve to orientate our thinking and at the same time to set before us some of the more insistent problems confronting American education.

Perhaps the most characteristic factor in American history has been the influence of frontier life, the necessity of subduing a

*From an address made at Teachers College on April 16, 1928. Published in *Teachers College Record*, XXX (1928-1929), pp. 13-22. Reprinted by permission of Mrs. Marian Kilpatrick and the editor of *Teachers College Record*.

wilderness on its own terms. For this European tradition did not suffice. New ways must be found. Strong individual self-direction was needed, a reliance on self and on small group cooperation. Through successive generations characteristics of initiative, self-reliance, and face-to-face cooperation were built into the folkways, along with an impatience at restraint of practically any sort. These characteristics meant a ready acceptance of the conscious doctrines of liberty and of the more doctrinaire theory of laissez-faire. The last-named might almost be said to be the sophistication of all the rest, a principle, however, from which America now increasingly departs. Religiously, the early settlement was in outlook almost entirely Protestant and even Puritan, a fact which has given the national outlook a definite tendency toward external regulation of morals and conduct.

It is easy to see democracy as the political outlook natural to the Protestant and the frontiersman, and this in spite of the contradiction between moral regulation and frontier freedom.

The later half of American national life has seen great changes, possibly more sweeping than any hitherto found within the range of European culture. Streams of foreign immigration have poured in from many diverse sources, breaking up the older uniformity of outlook and introducing a new need for social integration. Industrialization has come almost as a flood, with an unparalleled mass production. A popular faith in scientific thought has spread over the country, partly as cause and partly as effect of industrialization. The mingling of different national cultures, the changes introduced into living by great industry and its products, the opportunities at indulgence from increasing wealth and leisure, the popular faith in science and its criticisms — all have united to shift old folkways and to question traditional outlooks. The resulting problems cut deep.

Amid all these changes, one faith of America stands firm with even clearer idealism — that in popular education, secondary no less than primary. In favored sections practically all adolescent population is enrolled in secondary schools. Popular education is almost pathetically the hope for directing civilization along right and better lines.

In facing thus its task, American education sees a people buoyant in the faith that effort counts and willing perhaps beyond all others to try the new. The situation is plastic to thought. Ideas, at least within a certain range, spread more rapidly here than in any other part of the world. The opportunity of the school to influence life is real and great.

No less real or great is the demand. The loosening of tradition, here as elsewhere in the world, raises serious questions. Youth increasingly rejects external authority. Our only hope seems internal authority based on an inherent "Why?" Still further, increasing change in general social life makes it increasingly impossible to conduct education on the old basis of specific preparation to meet foreknown situations. The future is too largely unknown. We of the older generations must acknowledge our lack of foreknowledge and somehow prepare the rising generation to face its own problems as these shall arise. To fix our present ideas in the young may prove hurtful disservice. Education must remake its ways to meet these new demands.

In the face of the insistent need for an intelligent re-thinking of our social tradition, we have nevertheless in this country many who exactly fear this re-thinking and wish to prevent it. They rightly fear that thinking may not justify and retain all they have hitherto held. These opponents of progress are able to mobilize a certain herd-mindedness and with it seriously to oppose the free and impartial weighing of questioned doctrines and institutions. It has even been proposed to maintain the old by legal prescription. Education is thus threatened in its own house. Democracy has been tempted to hamper teaching.

The task of the school is thus increased. But there is yet more. A civilization loosed from its old moorings, industrially efficient and wealth-producing beyond compare, faces the ever old, ever new problem of life itself. What is the life we should intelligently seek? If we do not know an answer to this problem or if the majority will not recognize the best answer thus far found, what shall the school do? What can the school do, seeing that it is controlled by this same majority? This is perhaps the most difficult of all the problems facing American education.

336

The general attack upon these problems here presented and defended may be stated in two parts; first, the more fundamental assumptions taken to underlie a defensible outlook on life, and, second, the educational superstructure built upon these assumptions specifically to meet the problems of American life as set out above.

These as fundamental assumptions are here stated in brief, even dogmatic fashion. They are to be counted as hypotheses for understanding and ordering life.

a. Criticized experience is the final test of all things — experience criticized in its bearing on other experience. From this point of view, knowledge and "principles" are hypotheses for guiding experience.

b. The universe is fundamentally precarious. But effort produces real effect. Thinking is past experience guiding present effort. Through thought man is self-directive and effective in a sense and degree true of no other organism.

c. No principle is absolute but each such is to be applied only in the light of all other principles involved in the situation under consideration.

d. The self is an organization effected through continued experience in the social situation, the beginning being in biologic heredity, communication playing an essential part. The individual is thus inherently social in origin and nature.

e. The good life is one of activity of the varied capacities of the person so managed as to continue and increase such activity, both individual and shared, in the self and in others. We seek then the maximum development of each in relation to all, each as an end in himself and never a means merely.

From the foregoing, particularly the last two, we get definitions and guiding conceptions of development, ethics, and democracy. Development is no mere unfolding of latency, but an ever-extending process (stopped only by senile decay), taking continually more and more adequate account of meanings disclosed through experience. Such growing is of the very nature of the good life. Ethics gets its definition in the effort to bring this good life in the highest possible degree to all together. Democracy, much more than mere government, is the kind of society built to favor this good life and the maximum development.

With these as the more fundamental conceptions, what shall be the system of education reared on this foundation to take adequate care of the demands of American life?

In describing the proposed scheme of education, it is perhaps well to warn the reader that certain older terms as method and curriculum have been re-defined for use here that they may the better carry the new burdens placed upon them. The new definitions appear more or less explicitly in the descriptions given below.

In the resulting scheme of education, method takes a leading part, possibly the dominant part. Method is the *how* side of the educative process, but is far more than *how* to teach arithmetic or the other subjects. Rather it is *how* to deal with children, *how* to help steer the whole life of the learner that all aspects of life may be more adequately called into play and more adequately directed so that integration will result, internal integration of the self, external integration of the self with the environment.

The psychology we follow tells us that learning is essentially active. Behavior is responding and we learn only the responses that we make, no others. We cannot learn what we do not practice. If this be so, then the schoolroom environment must be such as to evoke from the learner the varied desirable characteristics which he is to build. To accomplish this school must be actual life, not a mere learning about life. It is selected life, yes; but so selected and steered as to have in it all the riches of real living, its stimulations, its opportunities, and its responsibilities. On no other basis can the child build the kind of self demanded by the highest conception of the good life.

But our psychology tells us further that we do not learn all the responses that we make. There is a selective effect on learning, as the outcome does or does not satisfy our endeavor. In any actual instance we learn *to do* what meets the case for us, we learn *not to do* what fails to meet the case. The learner's attitude is thus an essential factor to determine the direction of his learning, whether he shall learn *to do* or learn *not to do*.

It is from this point of view that the factor of purpose comes

338

to be stressed in the educative experience. When the learner has a purpose of his own which he himself wishes to effect, whether, for example, to make a boat, or to write a poem expressive of a certain emotion or idea, or to join with others in presenting a play, he has not only an impulse which efficiently calls out his endeavors along the line of his purpose, he has besides (in the aim held thus in view) a criterion for telling success from failure, and even more he has (in his willed purpose) the inner attitude which identifies the objective success of the enterprise with inner success to him. So that all the psychology of learning discussed above is through purpose automatically put to work in behalf of better learning.

Nor is this yet all. A study of the psychology of behavior discloses that behavior and effort arise when some equilibrium is disturbed within the self or organism. This disturbance creates an organic urge or "mind-set" to straighten out the difficulty, to set matters straight. This urge or "set" involves the whole organism. When through thought the self sets up in imagination an end or aim the attainment of which defines satisfaction and the re-establishment of equilibrium, then the whole organism being involved all its resources pertinent to the attainment of the end are thereby rendered "ready" for action. The eye is quicker to see anything pertinent to the quest, the ear quicker to hear, the hand quicker to act. Action is thus facilitated in detail and learning quickened. In this, purpose again helps.

And there is yet more: Always many learnings are simultaneously in process. While any extended experience is under way, attention is directed now to this factor and now to that, especially as these factors help or hinder the aims that the experiencer has. Where any element or factor in the experience is thus such as to arouse conscious attention and consideration, with consequent like or dislike, for each such factor at least two learnings and generally three are in process: first, an attitude of like or dislike is being built (and if sufficiently keen or sufficiently prolonged or sufficiently repeated an abiding attitude will be built); second, an idea of the factor at work and how it acts is being built (or strengthened or weakened if such has already existed); and, third, there is

339

generally being built also an ideal as to what should be the character and action of this factor. With such an attitude and idea or ideal always being built with regard to each outstanding factor involved in the experience, and with the admitted significance of attitudes and ideas for life, it needs no argument to prove that such accompanying learnings are in the aggregate often more important than the learnings more obviously in the mind of teacher and pupil. In this way through infinitely many small effects children come to build their abiding attitudes and ideals towards the various significant aspects of life. Fortunate are they if the resulting ideals are clear and good and the attitudes sound. And here again purposing may greatly help. It requires little thought to see that when the purpose is itself sound and wholesome and intelligently sought, ideals will the more likely be intelligently built and attitudes favorable to them be built in accord.

So in order to build self-directing characters that can be relied upon to act intelligently and efficiently, the method of purposeful activity is stressed. Properly guided it makes for efficient learning and for efficient organization of learning and builds at the same time the kind of character needed to cope with the changing life that confronts. This is what is often called the "project method" or the "project idea." The essence of the idea is that the unit element of the educative process is to be conceived as an enterprise (or instance of purposeful experience) felt by the learner to be his own so that he of himself assumes responsibility for carrying it forward to successful completion.

The terms "free" and "freedom" are often used in connection with such purposeful activity. It is at once clear that freedom is here desired as a condition necessary for such prosecution of the enterprise as best fosters good learning conditions. The function that freedom thus plays tells us not only why we wish freedom but tells us equally how much and what kind we need. The test is always: What is being learned?

Such a conception of method as the purposeful and responsible pursuit by pupils of enterprises characteristic of all the varied aspects of life will mean that subjects such as geography or history will no longer be learned separately. This method recognizes what

340

is in fact true, that our various separate school subjects are adult sophistications, abstractions of and from life, not units in life. Genuine instances of living seldom remain long at a time within the artificial confines of such abstractions. Typically then we as teachers will ignore such boundaries, as we help our pupils to live in our schools.

We are thus led to consider the curriculum. It is but fair to say that there is at this point even less agreement among our people than on method. The position here presented is not the traditional one but one so chosen as to place education more inherently in the life process. It is, of course, true that in the history of the race education long preceded the school. If we consider out-of-school living, say of a child before going to school or of any man of affairs as he faces a novel situation, it is easy to see how learning is inherent in each forward step made in such living. Take, for instance, a child first attempting to feed himself with a spoon. Five steps are distinguishable: (1) he starts to feed himself; (2) he meets (typically) a difficulty, he lacks the needed behavior-skill; (3) he tries under the direction of nurse or mother to get the needed way-of-behaving; (4) at length, he finds, gets, and applies the hitherto lacking behavior-skill, the needed new way-of-behaving; (5) the activity begun under (1) and balked under (2) now goes forward. These steps are typical wherever life takes a step forward. We see then (*a*) how the demand for learning is inherent in progressive living; (*b*) how study, item (3) above, is for each individual an effort at the finding of a new way of behaving in the light of the demands of the situation and possibly under the guidance of one who can help steer the process; (*c*) how learning when thus got is essentially a creative act, even though the act is in part guided by another; and (*d*) how the actual situation tests whether the learning has in fact taken place by whether the balked activity really goes forward, whether the proposed new step is really taken.

We can at once say of such life learning that it is *intrinsic* in life, having a real function to play in the development of life. In comparison we can say that much, if not most, of ordinary school learning is *extrinsic* to the life of the learner, not having been called

341

for by the present demands of his life as he now lives that life nor, when learned, functioning in any full sense in that life as it now is. This distinction between "intrinsic" and "extrinsic" learning is crucial to the present discussion. The position here taken is that school learning is good and wholesome, other things being equal, to the degree that it is intrinsic.

It is well to see further how learning functions inherently in the on-going and developing life. Consider a baby that has just learned to crawl. Clearly he has added a new way-of-behaving to his previous repertoire of behavior patterns. But the effect is far more and other than this mere addition. Before times when he has been placed on a rug, for example, he has necessarily stayed where he was placed. His active experiences were then limited to what was within reach of the fixed spot where he had been placed. But now that he can crawl he has greatly increased the range of his possible experiences. And each new experience brings with it new things to be learned. This he may touch, that he may not; this he may put in his mouth, that he may not. When he does put this in his mouth, it calls for thus-and-such behavior. All of these new learnings — facts, sense experiences, appropriate reactions, social obligations — all have been made possible and even called out by the single added learning of how to crawl.

Not all new learnings are so prolific of new experiences and new learnings, but in general each new thing learned opens in some measure new possibilities. The remaking of experience from such learnings is what Professor Dewey has called the "reconstruction of experience." We are then prepared for his definition of the aim of education as such a reconstruction of experience as yields ever new meanings and gives to the learner continually increasing control over the process.

From this point of view the curriculum is not properly conceived in terms of the subject matter to be acquired but as a life process, a succession of experiences, each growing out of the preceding experiences in such a way as to continue most fruitfully the reconstruction of experience. At any point taken as a beginning, the teacher will then help his pupils to choose as their next experience one that is both rich as present living and pregnant with promise for the future. While this experience is being lived, the teacher will help so to steer it that it will mean most in continuous succession for rich living thereafter.

Space does not allow a detailed discussion of criteria for choosing experiences nor of immediate aims as we try to steer any present experience. Besides these are also many other matters to be considered, as how to secure sufficient skill and techniques, and how to avoid one-sided growth. Important as these are they are minor to the revised conception of the curriculum here outlined. Such a revision is as the shift from Ptolemy to Copernicus. The center of attention is shifted from subject-matter to life, from inertness to dynamic life and its remaking. Such a conception puts the emphasis on life and personality, on the increasing self-direction of life in the light of an ever-broadening outlook and deepening insight.

One concluding word about morals and religion. Many of us in this country, most I think of those who speak most authoritatively in education, feel that morals has no need of support in dogmatic theology. For my part what is said above, properly understood, will care inherently for morals and religion better than will any scheme of separate lessons in either or both. Surely morals and religion in any defensible sense lie at the heart of the life process. When we care properly for life and its education we care properly for them. The name of either need then not appear as a separate item in the school program. If we take pains that life's meanings are got as best we can from each succeeding experience, all is done that man can do.

Such seems the American situation. Such is the philosophy proposed for its understanding. Such is the education suggested for meeting the situation. If merit it has, this lies exactly in its being throughout experimental. On this basis only dare we face our changing future.

JOHN LOCKE

JOHN LOCKE (1632-1704). Generally revered as the founding father of the English Enlightenment, John Locke was its most important champion in the field of education. Like Montaigne he considered the acquisition of knowledge the least important part of education, and like the members of the English ruling class he stressed the importance of respect for independent thinking, preparation for a practical life, common sense, and respect for established moral standards and values. His influence on modern education was far-reaching: he was largely responsible for the establishment of the worldly ideal of the "gentleman" as the dominant social pattern in England, for bringing about the adoption of the individual tutorial method (recommended earlier by Montaigne), and for giving a utilitarian turn to eighteenth-century education.

Locke was born at Wrighton on August 29, 1632, attended Oxford, served for years as tutor of the third Earl of Shaftesbury, lived in various cities outside England as a voluntary political exile, and finally returned to England and won high favor with the court before his death on October 28, 1704. It was during his last fifteen years that he published the works on which his fame rests, including *Some Thoughts concerning Education* (1695).

Continuing the work of Bacon, Locke referred all cognition to experience and maintained that nine-tenths of all men are what their education has made them since the human soul is at birth a smoothed tablet (*tabula rasa*) and can therefore be molded at will by education. The most important task of education is for Locke the development of a sense of moral responsibility. He starts with a discussion of the care of bodily health as a preliminary to intellectual and spiritual education. He treats in some details the selection and character of the right tutor and offers valuable advice on education in general. He holds that every man should leave to his children four great treasures: virtue, wisdom, knowledge, and the right way of life. He would like to replace superfluous stylistic exercises in Latin, a common device of his time, with translation into English, and to give primary attention to those subjects which have some practical application in the lives of students. Some kind of manual skill, such as gardening or carpentry, has a place in his system. To the extent that he rejected scholarship as an educational ideal, emphasized the study of modern languages, practical knowledge and manual skills, his views correspond to the prevailing spirit of mercantilism.

The following selections from Locke's *Thoughts* give a detailed account of his system.

SOME THOUGHTS CONCERNING EDUCATION*

(1) A sound mind in a sound body, is a short but full description of a happy state in this world: he that has these two, has little more to wish for; and he that wants either of them, will be but little the better for any thing else. Men's happiness or misery is most part of their own making. He whose mind directs not wisely, will never take the right way; and he whose body is crazy and feeble, will never be able to advance in it.

(27) As the strength of the body lies chiefly in being able to endure hardship, so also does that of the mind. And the great principle and foundation of all virtue and worth is placed in this, that a man is able to deny himself his own desires, cross his own inclinations, and purely follow what reason directs as best, though the appetite lean the other way.

(28) The great mistake I have observed in people's breeding their children has been, that this has not been taken care enough of in its due season; that the mind has not been made obedient to discipline, and pliant to reason, when at first it was most tender, most easy to be bowed. Parents being wisely ordained by nature to love their children, are very apt, if reason watch not that natural affection very warily; are apt, I say, to let it run into fondness.

(30) For if the child must have grapes, or sugar-plums, when he has a mind to them, rather than make the poor baby cry, or be out of humour; why, when he is grown up, must he not be satisfied too, if his desires carry him to wine or women? They are objects as suitable to the longing of twenty-one or more years, as what he cried for, when little, was to the inclinations of a child. The having desires accommodated to the apprehensions and relish of those several ages, is not the fault; but the not having them

*Sections 1-50 are from the edition of Locke's essay published in the Library of Education; the remaining sections are from that published in the Harvard Classics.

subject to the rules and restraints of reason: the difference lies not in the having or not having appetites, but in the power to govern, and deny ourselves in them. He that is not used to submit his will to the reason of others, when he is young, will scarce hearken or submit to his own reason, when he is of an age to make use of it. And what kind of a man such a one is like to prove, is easy to foresee.

(40) On the other side, if the mind be curbed, and humbled too much in children; if their spirit be abased and broken much, by too strict an hand over them; they lose all their vigour and industry, and are in a worse state than the former. For extravagant young fellows, that have liveliness and spirit, come sometimes to be set right, and so make able and great men: but dejected minds, timorous and tame, and low spirits, are hardly ever to be raised, and very seldom attain to any thing. To avoid the danger that is on either hand is the great art: and he that has found a way how to keep up a child's spirit, easy, active, and free; and yet, at the same time, to restrain him from many things that are uneasy to him; he, I say, that knows how to reconcile these seeming contradictions, has, in my opinion, got the true secret of education.

(50) The rewards and punishments, then, whereby we should keep children in order are quite of another kind; and of that force, that when we can get them once to work, the business, I think, is done, and the difficulty is over. Esteem and disgrace are, of all others, the most powerful incentives to the mind, when once it is brought to relish them. If you can once get into children a love of credit, and an apprehension of shame and disgrace, you have put into them the true principle, which will constantly work, and incline them to the right. But, it will be asked, How shall this be done?

I confess, it does not, at first appearance, want some difficulty; but yet I think it worth our while to seek the ways, (and practise them when found,) to attain this, which I look on as the great secret of education.

(53) I say not this, that I would have children kept from the conveniences or pleasures of life, that are not injurious to their

346

health or virtue. On the contrary, I would have their lives made as pleasant and as agreeable to them as may be, in a plentiful enjoyment of whatsoever might innocently delight them; provided it be with this caution, that they have those enjoyments, only as the consequences of the state of esteem and acceptation they are in with their parents and governors; but they should never be offer'd or bestow'd on them, as the *rewards of this or that particular performance* that they show an aversion to, or to which would not have apply'd themselves without that temptation.

(54) But if you take away the rod on one hand, and these little encouragements which they are taken with, on the other, how then (will you say) shall children be govern'd? Remove hope and fear, and there is an end of all discipline. I grant that good and evil, *reward* and *punishment,* are the only motives to a rational creature: these are the spur and reins whereby all mankind are set on work, and guided, and therefore they are to be made use of to children too. For I advise their parents and governors always to carry this in their minds, that children are to be treated as rational creatures.

(55) *Rewards,* I grant, and *punishments* must be proposed to children, if we intend to work upon them. The mistake I imagine is, that those that are generally made use of, are *ill chosen.* The pains and pleasures of the body are, I think, of ill consequence, when made the rewards and punishments whereby men would prevail on their children; for, as I said before, they serve but to increase and strengthen those inclinations, which 'tis our business to subdue and master. What principle of virtue do you lay in a child, if you will redeem his desires of one pleasure, by the proposal of another? This is but to enlarge his appetite, and instruct it to wander. If a child cries for an unwholesome and dangerous fruit, you purchase his quiet by giving him a less hurtful sweetmeat. This perhaps may preserve his health, but spoils his mind, and sets that farther out of order. For here you only change the object, but flatter still his *appetite,* and allow that must be satisfy'd, wherein, as I have shew'd, lies the root of the mischief; and till you bring him to be able to bear a denial of that satisfaction, the child may at present be quiet and orderly, but the disease is not

cured. By this way of proceeding, you foment and cherish in him that which is the spring from whence all the evil flows, which will be sure on the next occasion to break out again with more violence, give him stronger longings, and you more trouble.

(56) The *rewards* and *punishments* then, whereby we should keep children in order, are quite of another kind, and of that force, that when we can get them once to work, the business, I think, is done, and the difficulty is over. *Esteem* and *disgrace* are, of all others, the most powerful incentives to the mind, when once it is brought to relish them. If you can once get into children a love of credit, and an apprehension of shame and disgrace, you have put into 'em the true principle, which will constantly work and incline them to the right. But it will be ask'd, How shall this be done?

I confess it does not at first appearance want some difficulty; but yet I think it worth our while to seek the ways (and practise them when found) to attain this, which I look on as the great secret of education.

(57) *First,* children (earlier perhaps than we think) are very sensible of *praise* and commendation. They find a pleasure in being esteem'd and valu'd, especially by their parents and those whom they depend on. If therefore the father *caress and commend them when they do well, shew a cold and neglectful countenance to them upon doing ill,* and this accompany'd by a like carriage of the mother and all others that are about them, it will, in a little time, make them sensible of the difference; and this, if constantly observ'd, I doubt not but will of itself work more than threats or blows, which lose their force when once grown common, and are of no use when shame does not attend them; and therefore are to be forborne, and never to be us'd, but in the case hereafter-mention'd, when it is brought to extremity.

(58) But *secondly,* to make the sense of *esteem* or *disgrace* sink the deeper, and be of the more weight, *other agreeable or disagreeable things should constantly accompany these different states;* not as particular rewards and punishments of this or that particular action, but as necessarily belonging to, and constantly attending one, who by his carriage has brought himself into a

state of disgrace or commendation. By which way of treating them, children may as much as possible be brought to conceive, that those that are commended, and in esteem for doing well, will necessarily be belov'd and cherish'd by every body, and have all other good things as a consequence of it; and on the other side, when any one by miscarriage falls into disesteem, and cares not to preserve his credit, he will unavoidably fall under neglect and contempt; and in that state, the want of whatever might satisfy or delight him will follow. In this way the objects of their desires are made assisting to virtue, when a settled experience from the beginning teaches children that the things they delight in, belong to, and are to be enjoy'd by those only who are in a state of reputation. If by these means you can come once to shame them out of their faults, (for besides that, I would willingly have no punishment) and make them in love with the pleasure of being well thought on, you may turn them as you please, and they will be in love with all the ways of virtue.

(61) Concerning *reputation*, I shall only remark this one thing more of it, that though it be not the true principle and measure of virtue, (for that is the knowledge of a man's duty, and the satisfaction it is to obey his maker, in following the dictates of that light God has given him, with the hopes of acceptation and reward) yet it is that which comes nearest to it: and being the testimony and applause that other people's reason, as it were by a common consent, gives to virtuous and well-order'd actions, it is the proper guide and encouragement, of children, 'till they grow able to judge for themselves, and to find what is right by their own reason.

(64) And here give me leave to take notice of one thing I think a fault in the ordinary method of education; and that is, the charging of children's memories, upon all occasions, with *rules* and precepts, which they often do not understand, and constantly as soon forget as given. If it be some action you would have done, or done otherwise, whenever they forget, or do it awkwardly, make them do it over and over again, 'till they are perfect, whereby you will get these two advantages. *First,* to see whether it be an action they can do, or is fit to be expected of them:

for sometimes children are bid to do things which upon trial they are found not able to do, and had need be taught and exercis'd in before they are requir'd to do them. But it is much easier for a tutor to command than to teach. *Secondly,* another thing got by it will be this, that by repeating the same action 'till it be grown habitual in them, the performance will not depend on memory or reflection, the concomitant of prudence and age, and not of childhood, but will be natural in them. Thus bowing to a gentleman, when he salutes him, and looking in his face, when he speaks to him, is by constant use as natural to a well-bred man, as breathing; it requires no thought, no reflection. Having this way cured in your child any fault, it is cured for ever: and thus one by one you may weed them out all, and plant what habits you please.

(65) I have seen parents so heap *rules* on their children, that it was impossible for the poor little ones to remember a tenth part of them, much less to observe them. However, they were either by words or blows corrected for the breach of those multiply'd and often very impertinent precepts. Whence it naturally follow'd that the children minded not what was said to them, when it was evident to them that no attention they were capable of was sufficient to preserve them from transgression, and the rebukes which follow'd it.

Let therefore your *rules* to your son be as few as possible, and rather fewer than more that seem absolutely necessary. For if you burden him with many *rules,* one of these two things must necessarily follow; that either he must be very often punish'd, which will be of ill consequence, by making punishment too frequent and familiar; or else you must let the transgressions of some of your rules go unpunish'd, whereby they will of course grow contemptible, and your authority become cheap to him. Make but few *laws,* but see they be well observ'd when once made. Few years require but few laws, and as his age increases, when one rule is by practice well establish'd, you may add another.

(66) But pray remember, children are *not* to be *taught by rules* which will be always slipping out of their memories. What you think necessary for them to do, settle in them by an indispensable

practice, as often as the occasion returns; and if it be possible, make occasions. This will beget *habits* in them which being once establish'd, operate of themselves easily and naturally without the assistance of the memory. But here let me give two cautions. 1. The one is, that you keep them to the practice of what you would have grow into a habit in them, by kind words, and gentle admonitions, rather as minding them of what they forget, than by harsh rebukes and chiding, as if they were wilfully guilty. 2. Another thing you are to take care of, is, not to endeavor to settle too many *habits* at once, lest by variety you confound them, and so perfect none. When constant custom has made any one thing easy and natural to 'em, and they practise it without reflection, you may then go on to another.

This method of teaching children by a repeated *practice*, and the same action done over and over again, under the eye and direction of the tutor, 'till they have got the habit of doing it well, and not by relying on *rules* trusted to their memories, has so many advantages, which way soever we consider it, that I cannot but wonder (if ill customs could be wondered at in any thing) how it could possibly be so much neglected. I shall name one more that comes now in my way. By this method we shall see whether what is requir'd of him be adapted to his capacity, and any way suited to the child's natural genius and constitution; for that too must be consider'd in a right education. We must not hope wholly to change their original tempers, nor make the gay pensive and grave, nor the melancholy sportive, without spoiling them. God has stamp'd certain characters upon men's minds, which like their shapes, may perhaps be a little mended, but can hardly be totally alter'd and transform'd into the contrary.

He therefore that is about children should well study their natures and aptitudes, and see by often trial what turn they easily take, and what becomes them; observe what their native stock is, how it may be improv'd, and what it is fit for: he should consider what they want, whether they be capable of having it wrought into them by industry, and incorporated there by practice; and whether it be worth while to endeavour it. For in many cases, all that we can do, or should aim at, is, to make the best of what

351

nature has given, to prevent the vices and faults to which such a constitution is most inclin'd, and give it all the advantages it is capable of. . . .

(93) The *tutor* therefore ought in the first place to be well-bred: and a young gentleman, who gets this one qualification from his *governor,* sets out with great advantage, and will find that this one accomplishment will more open his way to him, get him more friends, and carry him farther in the world, than all the hard words or real knowledge he has got from the liberal arts, or his *tutor's* learned *encyclopaedia*: not that those should be neglected, but by no means preferr'd, or suffer'd to thrust out the other.

(94) Besides being well-bred, the *tutor* should know the world well; the ways, the humours, the follies, the cheats, the faults of the age he is fallen into, and particularly of the country he lives in. These he should be able to shew to his pupil, as he finds him capable; teach him skill in men, and their manners; pull off the mask which their several callings and pretences cover them with, and make his pupil discern what lies at the bottom under such appearances, that he may not, as unexperienc'd young men are apt to do if they are unwarn'd, take one thing for another, judge by the outside, and give himself up to shew, and the insinuation of a fair carriage, or an obliging application. A governor should teach his scholar to guess at and beware of the designs of men he hath to do with, neither with too much suspicion, nor too much confidence; but as the young man is by nature most inclin'd to either side, rectify him, and bend him the other way. He should accustom him to make, as much as is possible, a true judgment of men by those marks which serve best to shew what they are, and give a prospect into their inside, which often shows itself in little things, especially when they are not in parade, and upon their guard. He should acquaint him with the true state of the world, and dispose him to think no man better or worse, wiser or foolisher, than he really is. Thus, by safe and insensible degrees, he will pass from a boy to a man; which is the most hazardous step in all the whole course of life. . . .

The shewing him the world as really it is, before he comes wholly into it, is one of the best means, I think, to prevent this mischief. He should by degrees be informed of the vices in fashion, and warned of the applications and designs of those who will make it their business to corrupt him.

I know it is often said, that to discover to a young man the vices of the age is to teach them him. That, I confess, is a good deal so, according as it is done; and therefore requires a discreet man of parts, who knows the world, and can judge of the temper, inclination, and weak side of his pupil. This farther is to be remember'd, that it is not possible now (as perhaps formerly it was) to keep a young gentleman from vice by a total ignorance of it, unless you will all his life mew him up in a closet, and never let him go into company. The longer he is kept thus hoodwink'd, the less he will see when he comes abroad into open daylight, and be the more expos'd to be a prey to himself and others. And an old boy, at his first appearance, with all the gravity of his ivy-bush about him, is sure to draw on him the eyes and chirping of the whole town volery; amongst which there will not be wanting some birds of prey, that will presently be on the wing for him.

The only fence against the world, is, a thorough knowledge of it, into which a young gentleman should be enter'd by degrees, as he can bear it; and the earlier the better, so he be in safe and skilful hands to guide him. The scene should be gently open'd, and his entrance made step by step, and the dangers pointed out that attend him from the several degrees, tempers, designs, and clubs of men. He should be prepar'd to be shock'd by some, and caress'd by others; warn'd who are like to oppose, who to mislead, who to undermine him, and who to serve him. He should be instructed how to know and distinguish them; where he should let them see, and when dissemble the knowledge of them and their aims and workings. And if he be too forward to venture upon his own strength and skill, the perplexity and trouble of a misadventure now and then, that reaches not his innocence, his health, or reputation, may not be an ill way to teach him more caution.

This, I confess, containing one great part of wisdom, is not the product of some superficial thoughts, or much reading; but the effect of experience and observation in a man who has liv'd in the world with his eyes open, and convers'd with men of all sorts.

And therefore I think it of most value to be instill'd into a young man upon all occasions which offer themselves, that when he comes to launch into the deep himself, he may not be like one at sea without a line, compass or sea-chart; but may have some notice before-hand of the rocks and shoals, the currents and quicksands, and know a little how to steer, that he sink not before he get experience. He that thinks not this of more moment to his son, and for which he more needs a governor, than the languages and learned sciences, forgets of how much more use it is to judge right of men, and manage his affairs wisely with them, than to speak *Greek* and *Latin*, or argue in mood and figures or to have his head fill'd with the abstruse speculations of natural philosophy and metaphysicks. . . .

(139) Having laid the foundations of virtue in a true notion of a God, such as the creed wisely teaches, as far as his age is capable, and by accustoming him to pray to Him; the next thing to be taken care of is to keep him exactly to speaking of *truth*, and by all the ways imaginable inclining him to be *good-natur'd*. Let him know that twenty faults are sooner to be forgiven than the *straining of truth* to cover any one *by an excuse*. And to teach him betimes to love and be *good-natur'd* to others is to lay early the true foundation of an honest man; all injustice generally springing from too great love of ourselves and too little of others.

This is all I shall say of this matter in general, and is enough for laying the first foundations of virtue in a child: as he grows up, the tendency of his natural inclination must be observed; which, as it inclines him more than is convenient on one or t'other side from the right path of virtue, ought to have proper remedies applied.

(147) You will wonder, perhaps, that I put *learning* last, especially if I tell you I think it the least part. This may seem strange in the mouth of a bookish man; and this making usually the chief, if not only bustle and stir about children, this being almost that alone which is thought on, when people talk of education, makes it the greater paradox. When I consider, what ado is made about a little *Latin* and *Greek*, how many years are spent in it, and what a noise and business it makes to no purpose, I can hardly

354

forbear thinking that the parents of children still live in fear of the school-master's rod, which they look on as the only instrument of education; as a language or two to be its whole business. How else is it possible that a child should be chain'd to the oar seven, eight, or ten of the best years of his life, to get a language or two, which, I think, might be had at a great deal cheaper rate of pains and time, and be learn'd almost in playing?

Forgive me therefore if I say, I cannot with patience think, that a young gentleman should be put into the herd, and be driven with a whip and scourge, as if he were to run the gantlet through the several classes, *ad capiendum ingenii cultum.* What then? say you, would you not have him write and read? Shall he be more ignorant than the clerk of our parish, who takes *Hopkins* and *Sternhold* for the best poets in the world, whom yet he makes worse than they are by his ill reading? Not so, not so fast, I beseech you. Reading and writing and *learning* I allow to be necessary, but yet not the chief business. I imagine you would think him a very foolish fellow, that should not value a virtuous or a wise man infinitely before a great scholar. Not but that I think *learning* a great help to both in well-dispos'd minds; but yet it must be confess'd also, that in others not so dispos'd, it helps them only to be the more foolish, or worse men. I say this, that when you consider the breeding of your son, and are looking out for a school-master or a tutor, you would not have (as is usual) Latin and *logick* only in your thoughts. *Learning* must be had, but in the second place, as subservient only to greater qualities. Seek out somebody that may know how discreetly to frame his manners: place him in hands where you may, as much as possible, secure his innocence, cherish and nurse up the good, and gently correct and weed out any bad inclinations, and settle in him good habits. This is the main point, and this being provided for, *learning* may be had into the bargain, and that, as I think, at a very easy rate, by methods that may be thought on.

(215) I confess, the knowledge of men is so great a skill, that it is not to be expected a young man should presently be perfect in it. But yet his *going abroad* is to little purpose, if *travel* does not sometimes open his eyes, make him cautious and wary, and ac-

355

custom him to look beyond the outside, and, under the inoffensive
guard of a civil and obliging carriage, keep himself free and safe
in his conversation with strangers and all sorts of people without
forfeiting their good opinion. He that is sent out to *travel* at the
age, and with the thoughts of a man designing to improve himself,
may get into the conversation and acquaintance of persons of
condition where he comes; which, tho' a thing of most advantage
to a gentleman that travels, yet I ask, amongst our young men
that go abroad under tutors, what one is there of an hundred, that
ever visits any person of quality? Much less makes an acquaintance with such, from whose conversation he may learn what is
good breeding in that country, and what is worth observation in
it; tho' from such persons it is, one may learn more in one day,
than in a year's rambling from one inn to another. Nor indeed,
is it to be wondered; for men of worth and parts will not easily
admit the familiarity of boys who yet need the care of a tutor;
tho' a young gentleman and stranger, appearing like a man, and
shewing a desire to inform himself in the customs, manners, laws,
and government of the country he is in, will find welcome assistance and entertainment amongst the best and most knowing
persons every where, who will be ready to receive, encourage and
countenance, an ingenuous and inquisitive foreigner.

(216) This, how true soever it be, will not I fear alter the custom,
which has cast the time of travel upon the worst part of a man's
life; but for reasons not taken from their improvement. The young
lad must not be ventured abroad at eight or ten, for fear of what
may happen to the tender child, tho' he then runs ten times less
risque than at sixteen or eighteen. Nor must he stay at home till
that dangerous, heady age be over, because he must be back
again by one and twenty, to marry and propagate. The father
cannot stay any longer for the portion, nor the mother for a new
set of babies to play with; and so my young master, whatever
comes on it, must have a wife look'd out for him by that time he
is of age; tho' it would be no prejudice to his strength, his parts,
or his issue, if it were respited for some time, and he had leave to
get, in years and knowledge, the start a little of his children, who
are often found to tread too near upon the heels of their fathers,

to the no great satisfaction either of son or father. But the young gentleman being got within view of matrimony, 'tis time to leave him to his mistress.

(217) Tho' I am now come to a conclusion of what obvious remarks have suggested to me concerning education, I would not have it thought that I look on it as a just treatise on this subject. There are a thousand other things that may need consideration; especially if one should take in the various tempers, different inclinations, and particular defaults, that are to be found in children, and prescribe proper remedies. The variety is so great that it would require a volume; nor would that reach it. Each man's mind has some peculiarity, as well as his face, that distinguishes him from all others; and there are possibly scarce two children who can be conducted by exactly the same method. Besides that, I think a prince, a nobleman, and an ordinary gentleman's son, should have different ways of breeding. But having had here only some general views in reference to the main end and aims in education, and those designed for a gentleman's son, whom, being then very little, I considered only as white paper, or wax, to be moulded and fashioned as one pleases; I have touched little more than those heads which I judged necessary for the breeding of a young gentleman of his condition in general; and have now published these my occasional thoughts with this hope, that tho' this be far from being a complete treatise on this subject, or such as that every one may find what will just fit his child in it, yet it may give some small light to those, whose concern for their dear little ones makes them so irregularly bold, that they dare venture to consult their own reason in the education of their children, rather than wholly to rely upon old custom.

MARTIN LUTHER

MARTIN LUTHER (1483-1546). Martin Luther, the greatest of the Protestant reformers, probably did more than any man of his century to promote universal education and to make governments aware of their needs and responsibilities in this respect.

Born at Eisleben, Saxony, on November 10, 1483, he attended the Latin schools of Magdeburg and Eisenach, obtained the degree of bachelor of arts (1502) and that of master of arts (1505) at the University of Erfurt, then entered the cloister of the Augustinian hermits of Erfurt. In 1507 he was ordained a priest, and in 1508 he was called to Wittenberg, where he lectured on Aristotle and on Scripture. In 1512 he obtained the highest academic rank, having earned the doctorate in theology, and succeeded Johann Stuapitz in the theological faculty as professor of Biblical theology. While still serving in this capacity five years later he tacked his famous ninety-five academic theses to the door of the Castle Church at Wittenberg, hoping that some scholar would debate with him the relation of penance and indulgences. The event is generally regarded as initiating the Reformation. The tremendous burden of work and responsibility which he carried thereafter resulted in his premature death on February 18, 1546.

Luther, although he attached the utmost importance to religion and considered everything else secondary, realized through his own studies that education was the key to the Scriptures. His profound patriotism as well as his devotion is reflected in his German hymns and in his translation of the New Testament, through which his countrymen could be instructed in the new Protestant faith. He seems to have grasped the idea of education as a means of preparing children not only for scholarship but also for a productive life in a Christian community. The city is obliged to see to the education of the young. Universal education is necessary for the perpetuation of society, though only superior minds require the special training that will enable them to be preachers, physicians, and so on.

The classic statement of Luther's convictions regarding the establishment of schools is his "Letter to the Mayors and Aldermen of All the Cities of Germany in Behalf of Christian Schools." In it he condemns existing institutions ("What have men learned hitherto in the universities and monasteries, except to be asses and blockheads?"), praises the liberal education available to the sons of Roman citizens ("Thus they became

358

. . . excellent men . . . so that all the bishops, priests, and monks in Germany put together would not equal a Roman soldier"), and calls on the mayors and aldermen to exercise the greatest care over the young ("For since the happiness, honor, and life of the city are committed to their hands, they would be held recreant before God and the world if they did not, day and night, seek its welfare and improvement"). His letter marks the beginning of the movement that culminated in the establishment of the public schools of Europe and America.

LETTER TO THE MAYORS AND ALDERMEN*

Grace and peace from God our Father and the Lord Jesus Christ. Honored and dear Sirs: Having three years ago been put under the ban and outlawed, I should have kept silent, had I regarded the command of men more than that of God. Many persons in Germany both of high and low estate assail my discourses and writings on that account, and shed much blood over them. But God who has opened my mouth and bidden me speak, stands firmly by me, and without any counsel or effort of mine strengthens and extends my cause the more, the more they rage, and seems, as the second Psalm says, to "have them in derision." By this alone any one not blinded by prejudice may see that the work is of God; for it exhibits the divine method, according to which God's cause spreads most rapidly when men exert themselves most to oppose and suppress it.

Therefore, as Isaiah says, I will not hold my peace until the righteousness of Christ go forth as brightness, and his salvation as a lamp that burneth. And I beseech you all, in the name of God and of our neglected youth, kindly to receive my letter and admonition, and give it thoughtful consideration. For whatever I may be in myself, I can boast with a clear conscience before God that I am not seeking my own interest, (which would be best served by silence,) but the interest of all Germany, according to the mission, (doubt it who will,) with which God has honored me. And I wish to declare to you frankly and confidently that if

*From *Luther on Education,* by F. V. N. Painter (Philadelphia, Concordia Publishing House, 1890).

you hear me, you hear not me but Christ; and whoever will not hear me, despises not me but Christ. For I know the truth of what I declare and teach; and every one who rightly considers my doctrine will realize its truth for himself.

First of all we see how the schools are deteriorating throughout Germany. The universities are becoming weak, the monasteries are declining, and, as Isaiah says, "The grass withereth, the flower fadeth, because the spirit of the Lord bloweth upon it," through the Gospel. For through the word of God the unchristian and sensual character of these institutions is becoming known. And because selfish parents see that they can no longer place their children upon the bounty of monasteries and cathedrals, they refuse to educate them. "Why should we educate our children," they say, "if they are not to become priests, monks, and nuns, and thus earn a support?"

The hollow piety and selfish aims of such persons are sufficiently evident from their own confession. For if they sought anything more than the temporal welfare of their children in monasteries and the priesthood, if they were deeply in earnest to secure the salvation and blessedness of their children, they would not lose interest in education and say, "if the priestly office is abolished, we will not send our children to school." But they would speak after this manner: "if it is true, as the Gospel teaches, that such a calling is dangerous to our children, teach us another way in which they may be pleasing to God and become truly blessed; for we wish to provide not alone for the bodies of our children, but also for their souls." Such would be the language of faithful Christian parents.

It is no wonder that the devil meddles in the matter, and influences groveling hearts to neglect the children and the youth of the country. Who can blame him for it? He is the prince and god of this world, and with extreme displeasure sees the Gospel destroy his nurseries of vice, the monasteries and priesthood, in which he corrupts the young beyond measure, a work upon which his mind is especially bent. How could he consent to a proper training of the young? Truly he would be a fool if he permitted such a thing in his kingdom, and thus consented to its overthrow: which indeed

360

would happen, if the young should escape him, and be brought up to the service of God.

Hence he acted wisely at the time when Christians were educating and bringing up their children in a Christian way. Inasmuch as the youth of the land would have thus escaped him, and inflicted an irreparable injury upon his kingdom, he went to work and spread his nets, established such monasteries, schools, and orders, that it was not possible for a boy to escape him without the miraculous intervention of God. But now that he sees his snares exposed through the Word of God, he takes an opposite course, and dissuades men from all education whatever. He thus pursues a wise course to maintain his kingdom and win the youth of Germany. And if he secures them, if they grow up under his influence and remain his adherents, who can gain any advantage over him? He retains an easy and peaceful mastery over the world. For any fatal wound to his cause must come through the young, who, brought up in the knowledge of God, spread abroad the truth and instructed others.

Yet no one thinks of this dreadful purpose of the devil, which is being worked out so quietly that it escapes observation; and soon the evil will be so far advanced that we can do nothing to prevent it. People fear the Turks, wars, and floods, for in such matters they can see what is injurious or beneficial; but what the devil has in mind no one sees or fears. Yet where we would give a florin to defend ourselves against the Turks, we should give a hundred florins to protect us against ignorance, even if only one boy could be taught to be a truly Christian man; for the good such a man can accomplish is beyond all computation.

Therefore I beg you all, in the name of God and of our neglected youth, not to think of this subject lightly, as many do who see not what the prince of this world intends. For the right instruction of youth is a matter in which Christ and all the world are concerned. Thereby are we all aided. And consider that great Christian zeal is needed to overcome the silent, secret, and artful machinations of the devil. If we must annually expend large sums on muskets, roads, bridges, dams, and the like, in order that the city may have temporal peace and comfort, why should we not apply as much to our poor, neglected youth, in order that we may have a skillful school-master or two?

There is one consideration that should move every citizen, with devout gratitude to God, to contribute a part of his means to the support of schools — the consideration that if divine grace had not released him from exactions and robbery, he would still have to give large sums of money for indulgences, masses, vigils, endowments, anniversaries, mendicant friars, brotherhoods, and other similar impositions. And let him be sure that where turmoil and strife exist, there the devil is present, who did not writhe and struggle so long as men blindly contributed to convents and masses. For Satan feels that his cause is suffering injury. Let this, then, be the first consideration to move you, — that in this work we are fighting against the devil, the most artful and dangerous enemy of men.

Another consideration is found in the fact that we should not, as St. Paul says, receive the grace of God in vain, and neglect the present favorable time. For Almighty God has truly granted us Germans a gracious visitation, and favored us with a golden opportunity. We now have excellent and learned young men, adorned with every science and art, who, if they were employed, could be of great service as teachers. Is it not well known that a boy can now be so instructed in three years, that at the age of fifteen or eighteen he knows more than all the universities and convents have known heretofore? Yea, what have men learned hitherto in the universities and monasteries, except to be asses and blockheads? Twenty, forty years, it has been necessary to study, and yet one has learned neither Latin nor German! I say nothing of the shameful and vicious life in those institutions, by which our worthy youth have been so lamentably corrupted.

I should prefer, it is true, that our youth be ignorant and dumb rather than that the universities and convents should remain as the only sources of instruction open to them. For it is my earnest intention, prayer and desire that these schools of Satan either be destroyed or changed into Christian schools. But since God has so richly favored us, and given us a great number of persons who are competent thoroughly to instruct and train our young people, it is

362

truly needful that we should not disregard His grace and let Him knock in vain. He stands at the door; happy are we if we open to Him. He calls us; happy is the man who answers Him. If we disregard His call, so that He passes by, who will bring Him back? Let us consider the wretchedness of our former condition and the darkness in which we were enveloped. I believe Germany has never heard so much of the Word of God as at the present time; history reveals no similar period. If we let the gracious season pass without gratitude and improvement, it is to be feared that we shall suffer still more terrible darkness and distress. My dear country-men, buy while the market is at your door; gather the harvest while the sun shines and the weather is fair: use the grace and Word of God while they are near. For know this, that the Word and grace of God are like a passing shower, which does not return where it has once been. The Divine favor once rested upon the Jews, but it has departed. Paul brought the Gospel into Greece; but now they have the Turks. Rome and Italy once enjoyed its blessings; but now they have the Pope. And the German people should not think that they will always have it; for ingratitude and neglect will banish it. Therefore seize it and hold it fast, whoever can; idle hands will have an evil year.

The third consideration is the highest of all, namely, God's command, which through Moses so often urges and enjoins that parents instruct their children, that the seventy-eighth Psalm says: "He established a testimony in Jacob and appointed a law in Israel, which he commanded our fathers that they should make them known to their children." And the fourth commandment also shows this, where he has so strictly enjoined children to obey their parents, that disobedient children were to be put to death. And why do old people live, except to care for, teach, and bring up the young? It is not possible for inexperienced youth to instruct and care for themselves; and for that reason God has commended them to us who are older and know what is good for them, and He will require a strict account at our hands. Therefore Moses gives this injunction: "Ask thy father, and he will show thee; thy elders, and they will tell thee."

It is indeed a sin and shame that we must be aroused and incited to the duty of educating our children and of considering their highest interests, whereas nature itself should move us thereto, and the example of the heathen affords us varied instruction. There is no irrational animal that does not care for and instruct its young in what they should know, except the ostrich, of which God says; "She leaveth her eggs in the earth, and warmeth them in the dust; and is hardened against her young ones, as though they were not hers." And what would it avail if we possessed and performed all else, and became perfect saints, if we neglect that for which we chiefly live, namely, to care for the young? In my judgment there is no other outward offense that in the sight of God so heavily burdens the world, and deserves such heavy chastisement, as the neglect to educate children.

In my youth this proverb was current in the schools: "It is no less a sin to neglect a pupil than to do violence to a woman." It was used to frighten teachers. But how much lighter is this wrong against woman (which as a bodily sin may be atoned for), than to neglect and dishonor immortal souls, when such a sin is not recognized and can never be atoned for? O eternal woe to the world! Children are daily born and grow up among us, and there are none, alas! who feel an interest in them; and instead of being trained, they are left to themselves. The convents and cathedral schools are the proper agencies to do it; but to them we may apply the words of Christ: "Woe unto the world because of offenses! Whoso shall offend one of these little ones which believe in me, it were better for him that a mill-stone were hanged about his neck, and that he were drowned in the depth of the sea." They are nothing but destroyers of children.

But all that, you say, is addressed to parents; what does it concern the members of the council and the mayors? That is true; but how, if parents neglect it? Who shall attend to it then? Shall we therefore let it alone, and suffer the children to be neglected? How will the mayors and council excuse themselves, and prove that such a duty does not belong to them?

Parents neglect this duty from various causes.

In the first place, there are some who are so lacking in piety and uprightness that they would not do it if they could, but like the ostrich, harden themselves against their own offspring, and do nothing for them. Nevertheless these children must live among us and with us. How then can reason and, above all, Christian Charity, suffer them to grow up ill-bred, and to infect other children, till at last the whole city be destroyed, like Sodom, Gomorrah, and some other cities?

In the second place, the great majority of parents are unqualified for it, and do not understand how children should be brought up and taught. For they have learned nothing but to provide for their bodily wants; and in order to teach and train children thoroughly, a separate class is needed.

In the third place, even if parents were qualified and willing to do it themselves, yet on account of other employments and household duties they have no time for it, so that necessity requires us to have teachers for public schools, unless each parent employ a private instructor. But that would be too expensive for persons of ordinary means, and many a bright boy, on account of poverty, would be neglected. Besides, many parents die and leave orphans; and how they are usually cared for by guardians, we might learn, even if observation were not enough, from the sixty-eighth Psalm, where God calls himself the "Father of the fatherless," as of those who are neglected by all others. Also there are some who have no children, and therefore feel no interest in them.

Therefore it will be the duty of the mayors and council to exercise the greatest care over the young. For since the happiness, honor, and life of the city are committed to their hands, they would be held recreant before God and the world, if they did not, day and night, with all their power, seek its welfare and improvement. Now the welfare of a city does not consist alone in great treasures, firm walls, beautiful houses, and munitions of war; indeed, where all these are found, and reckless fools come into power, the city sustains the greater injury. But the highest welfare, safety, and power of a city consists in able, learned, wise, upright, cultivated citizens, who can secure, preserve, and utilize every treasure and advantage.

In ancient Rome the boys were so brought up that at the age of fifteen, eighteen, twenty, they were masters not only of the choicest Latin and Greek, but also of the liberal arts, as they are called; and immediately after this scholastic training, they entered the army or held a position under the government. Thus they became intelligent, wise, and excellent men, skilled in every art and rich in experience, so that all the bishops, priests, and monks in Germany put together would not equal a Roman soldier. Consequently their country prospered; persons were found capable and skilled in every pursuit. Thus, in all the world, even among the heathen, school-masters and teachers have been found necessary where a nation was to be elevated. Hence in the Epistle to the Galatians Paul employs a word in common use when he says, "The law was our *school-master.*"

Since, then, a city must have well-trained people, and since the greatest need, lack, and lament is that such are not to be found, we must not wait till they grow up of themselves; neither can they be hewed out of stones nor cut out of wood; nor will God work miracles, so long as men can attain their object through means within their reach. Therefore we must see to it, and spare no trouble or expense to educate and form them ourselves. For whose fault is it that in all the cities there are at present so few skillful people except the rulers, who have allowed the young to grow up like trees in the forest, and have not cared how they were reared and taught? The growth, consequently, has been so irregular that the forest furnishes no timber for building purposes, but like a useless hedge, is good only for fuel.

Yet there must be civil government. For us, then, to permit ignoramuses and blockheads to rule when we can prevent it, is irrational and barbarous. Let us rather make rulers out of swine and wolves, and set them over people who are indifferent to the manner in which they are governed. It is barbarous for men to think thus: "We will now rule; and what does it concern us how those fare who shall come after us?" Not over human beings, but over swine and dogs should such people rule, who think only of their own interests and honor in governing. Even if we exercise the greatest care to educate able, learned and skilled rulers, yet much care and effort are necessary in order to secure prosperity. How can a city prosper, when no effort is made?

But, you say again, if we shall and must have schools, what is the use to teach Latin, Greek, Hebrew, and the other liberal arts? Is it not enough to teach the Scriptures, which are necessary to salvation, in the mother tongue? To which I answer: I know, alas! that we Germans must always remain irrational brutes, as we are deservedly called by surrounding nations. But I wonder why we do not also say: of what use to us are silk, wine, spices, and other foreign articles, since we ourselves have an abundance of wine, corn, wool, flax, wood, and stone in the German states, not only for our necessities, but also for embellishment and ornament? The languages and other liberal arts, which are not only harmless, but even a greater ornament, benefit, and honor than these things, both for understanding the Holy Scriptures and carrying on the civil government, we are disposed to despise; and the foreign articles which are neither necessary nor useful, and which besides greatly impoverish us, we are unwilling to dispense with. Are we not rightly called German dunces and brutes?

Indeed, if the languages were of no practical benefit, we ought still to feel an interest in them as a wonderful gift of God, with which he has now blessed Germany almost beyond all other lands. We do not find many instances in which Satan has fostered them through the universities and cloisters; on the contrary, these institutions have fiercely inveighed and continue to inveigh against them. For the devil scented the danger that would threaten his kingdom, if the languages should be generally studied. But since he could not wholly prevent their cultivation, he aims at least to confine them within such narrow limits, that they will of themselves decline and fall into disuse. They are to him no welcome guest, and consequently he shows them scant courtesy in order that they may not remain long. This malicious trick of Satan is perceived by very few.

Therefore, my beloved countrymen, let us open our eyes, thank God for this precious treasure, and take pains to preserve it, and to frustrate the design of Satan. For we cannot deny that, although the Gospel has come and daily comes through the Holy Spirit, it has come by means of the languages, and through them must increase and be preserved. For when God wished through the apostles to spread the Gospel abroad in all the world, he gave the languages for that purpose; and by means of the Roman empire he made Latin and Greek the language of many lands, that his Gospel might speedily bear fruit far and wide. He has done the same now. For a time no one understood why God had revived the study of the languages; but now we see that it was for the sake of the Gospel, which he wished to bring to light and thereby expose and destroy the reign of Antichrist. For the same reason he gave Greece a prey to the Turks, in order that Greek scholars, driven from home and scattered abroad, might bear the Greek tongue to other countries, and thereby excite an interest in the study of languages.

In the same measure that the Gospel is dear to us, should we zealously cherish the languages. For God had a purpose in giving the Scriptures only in two languages, the Old Testament in the Hebrew, and the New Testament in the Greek. What God did not despise, but chose before all others for His Word, we should likewise esteem above all others. St. Paul, in the third chapter of Romans, points out, as a special honor and advantage of the Hebrew language, that God's Word was given in it: "What profit is there of circumcision? Much every way; chiefly because that unto them were committed the oracles of God." Likewise King David boasts in the one hundred and forty-seventh Psalm: "He showeth his word unto Jacob, his statutes and his judgments unto Israel. He hath not dealt so with any nation: and as for his judgments, they have not known them." Hence the Hebrew language is called sacred. And St. Paul, in Romans i. 2, speaks of the Hebrew Scriptures as holy, no doubt because of the Word of God which they contain. In like manner the Greek language might well be called holy, because it was chosen, in preference to others, as the language of the New Testament. And from this language, as from a fountain, the New Testament has flowed through translations into other languages, and sanctified them also.

And let this be kept in mind, that we will not preserve the Gospel without the languages. The languages are the scabbard in which the Word of God is sheathed. They are the casket in which this jewel is enshrined; the cask in which this wine is kept; the chamber in which this food is stored. And, to borrow a figure from the Gospel itself, they are the baskets in which this bread, and fish, and fragments are preserved. If through neglect we lose the languages (which may God forbid), we will not only lose the Gospel, but it will finally come to pass that we will lose also the ability to speak and write either Latin or German. Of this let us take as proof and warning the miserable and shocking example presented in the universities and cloisters, in which not only the Gospel has been perverted, but also the Latin and German languages have been corrupted, so that the wretched inmates have become like brutes, unable to speak and write German or Latin, and have almost lost their natural reason.

The apostles considered it necessary to embody the New Testament in the Greek language, in order, no doubt, that it might be securely preserved unto us as in a sacred shrine. For they foresaw what has since taken place, namely, that when the divine revelation is left to oral tradition, much disorder and confusion arise from conflicting opinions and doctrines. And there would be no way to prevent this evil and to protect the simple-minded, if the New Testament was not definitely recorded in writing. Therefore it is evident that where the languages are not preserved, there the Gospel will become corrupted.

Experience shows this to be true. For immediately after the age of the apostles, when the languages ceased to be cultivated, the Gospel, and the true faith, and Christianity itself, declined more and more, until they were entirely lost under the Pope. And since the time that the languages disappeared, not much that is noteworthy and excellent has been seen in the Church; but through ignorance of the languages very many shocking abominations have arisen. On the other hand, since the revival of learning, such a light has been shed abroad, and such important changes have taken place, that the world is astonished, and must acknowledge that we have the Gospel almost as pure and unadulterated as it was in the times of the apostles, and much purer than it was in the days of St. Jerome and St. Augustine. In a word, since the Holy Ghost, who does nothing foolish or useless, has often bestowed the gift of tongues, it is our evident duty earnestly to cultivate the languages, now that God has restored them to the world through the revival of learning.

But many of the church fathers, you say, have become saints and have taught without a knowledge of the languages. That is true. But to what do you attribute their frequent misunderstanding of the Scriptures? How often is St. Augustine in error in the Psalms and in other expositions, as well as Hilary, and indeed all those who have undertaken to explain the Scriptures without an acquaintance with the original tongues? And if perchance they have taught correct doctrine, they have not been sure of the application to be made of particular passages. For example, it is truly said that Christ is the Son of God. But what mockery does it seem to adversaries when as proof of that doctrine Psalm cx. 3 is adduced: *"Tecum principium in die virtutis,"* since in the Hebrew no reference is made in that verse to the Deity. When the faith is thus defended with uncertain reasons and proof-texts, does it not seem a disgrace and mockery in the eyes of such adversaries as are acquainted with the Greek and the Hebrew? And they are only rendered the more obstinate in their error, and with good ground hold our faith as a human delusion.

What is the reason that our faith is thus brought into disgrace? It is our ignorance of the languages; and the only remedy is a knowledge of them. Was not St. Jerome forced to make a new translation of the Psalms from the Hebrew, because the Jews, when quotations were made from the Latin version, derided the Christians, affirming that the passages adduced were not found in the original? The comments of all the ancient fathers who, without a knowledge of the languages, have treated of the Scriptures (although they may teach nothing heretical), are still of such a character that the writers often employ uncertain, doubtful, and inappropriate expressions, and grope like a blind man along a wall, so that they often miss the sense of the text and mould it according to their pious fancy, as in the example mentioned in the last paragraph. St. Augustine himself was obliged to confess that the Christian teacher, in addition to Latin, should be acquainted with Hebrew and Greek. Without this knowledge, the expositor will

370

inevitably fall into mistakes; and even when the languages are understood, he will meet with difficulties.

With a simple preacher of the faith it is different from what it is with the expositor of the Scriptures, or prophet, as St. Paul calls him. The former has so many clear passages and texts in translations, that he is able to understand and preach Christ, and lead a holy life. But to explain the Scriptures, to deal with them independently, and oppose heretical interpreters, such a one is too weak without a knowledge of the languages. But we need just such expositors, who will give themselves to the study and interpretation of the Scriptures, and who are able to controvert erroneous doctrines; for a pious life and orthodox teaching are not alone sufficient. Therefore the languages are absolutely necessary, as well as prophets or expositors; but it is not necessary that every Christian or preacher be such a prophet, according to the diversity of gifts of which St. Paul speaks in I Corinthians xii. 8, 9, and in Ephesians iv. 11.

This explains why, since the days of the apostles, the Scriptures have remained in obscurity, and no reliable and enduring expositions have anywhere been written. For even the holy fathers, as we have said, are often in error, and because they were not versed in the languages, they seldom agree. St. Bernard was a man of great ability, so that I am inclined to place him above all other distinguished teachers, whether ancient or modern; but how often he trifles with the Scriptures, in a spiritual manner to be sure, and wrests them from their true meaning! For the same reason the Papists have said that the Scriptures are of obscure and peculiar import. But they do not perceive that the trouble lies in ignorance of the languages; but for this, nothing simpler has ever been spoken than the Word of God. A Turk must indeed speak unintelligibly to me, although a Turkish child of seven years understands him, because I am unacquainted with the language.

Hence it is foolish to attempt to learn the Scriptures through the comments of the fathers and the study of many books and glosses. For that purpose we ought to give ourselves to the languages. For the beloved fathers, because they were not versed in the languages, have often failed, in spite of their verbose expositions, to give the meaning of the text. You peruse their writings with great toil; and yet with a knowledge of the languages you can get the meaning of Scripture better than they do. For in comparison with the glosses of the fathers, the languages are as sunlight to darkness.

Since, then, it behooves Christians at all times to use the Bible as their only book and to be thoroughly acquainted with it, especially is it a disgrace and sin at the present day not to learn the languages, when God provides every facility, incites us to study, and wishes to have His word known. O how glad the honored fathers would have been, if they could have learned the languages, and had such access to the Holy Scriptures! With what pain and toil they scarcely obtained crumbs, while almost without effort we are able to secure the whole loaf! O how their industry shames our idleness, yea, how severely will God punish our neglect and ingratitude.

St. Paul, in 1 Corinthians xiv. 29, enjoins that there be judgment upon doctrine — a duty that requires a knowledge of the languages. For the preacher or teacher may publicly read the whole Bible as he chooses, right or wrong, if there be no one present to judge whether he does it correctly or not. But if one is to judge, there must be an acquaintance with the languages; otherwise, the judging will be in vain. Hence, although faith and the Gospel may be preached by ordinary ministers without the languages, still such preaching is sluggish and weak, and the people finally become weary, and fall away. But a knowledge of the languages renders it lively and strong, and faith finds itself constantly renewed through rich and varied instruction. In the first Psalm the Scriptures liken such study to "a tree planted by the rivers of water, that bringeth forth its fruit in its season; its leaf also shall not wither."

We should not allow ourselves to be deceived because there are some who, while setting little store by the Scriptures, boast of the Spirit. Some also, like the Waldenses, do not regard the languages useful. But, dear friend, whatever such persons may say, I have also been in the Spirit, and have seen more of His power (if it is allowable to boast of one's self), than they will see in a year, however much they may vaunt themselves. I have also been able to accomplish somewhat, while they have remained without influence, and done little more than boast. I know full well that the Spirit does almost everything. Still I should have failed in my work, if the languages had not come to my aid, and made me strong and immovable in the Scriptures. I might without them have been pious, and preached the Gospel in obscurity; but I could not have disturbed the Pope, his adherents, and all the reign of Antichrist. The devil cares less for the Spirit within me than for my pen and linguistic knowledge. For while the Spirit takes nothing but myself away from him, the Holy Scriptures and the languages drive him from the world and break up his kingdom.

I can not praise the Waldenses for depreciating the languages. For although they taught no heresies, yet they often necessarily failed in their proof-texts, and remained unqualified and unskilled to contend against error for the true faith. Besides, their teaching is so unenlightened, and presented in such peculiar forms, not following the language of Scripture, that I fear it will not continue pure. For it is dangerous to speak of divine things in a manner or in words different from those employed in the Scriptures. In brief, they may lead holy lives and teach among themselves; but because they are without the languages, they will lack what others have lacked, namely, an assured and thorough handling of the Scriptures, and the ability to be useful to other nations. And because they could have done this, and would not, they will have an account to render before God for their neglect.

So much for the utility and necessity of the languages, and of Christian schools for our spiritual interests and the salvation of the soul. Let us now consider the body and inquire: though there were no soul, nor heaven, nor hell, but only the civil government, would not this require good schools and learned men more than do our spiritual interests? Hitherto the Papists have taken no interest in civil government, and have conducted the schools so entirely in the interests of the priesthood, that it has become a matter of reproach for a learned man to marry, and he has been forced to hear remarks like this: "Behold, he has become a man of the world, and cares nothing for the clerical state," just as if the priestly order were alone acceptable to God, and the secular classes, as they are called, belonged to Satan, and were unchristian. But in the sight of God, the former rather belong to Satan, while the despised masses (as happened to the people of Israel in the Babylonian captivity) remain in the land and in right relations with God.

It is not necessary to say here that civil government is a divine institution; of that I have elsewhere said so much, that I hope no one has any doubts on the subject. The question is, how are we to get able and skillful rulers? And here we are put to shame by the heathen, who in ancient times, especially the Greeks and Romans, without knowing that civil government is a divine ordinance, yet instructed to boys and girls with such earnestness and industry that, when I think of it, I am ashamed of Christians, and especially of our Germans, who are such blockheads and brutes that they can say: "Pray, what is the use of schools, if one is not to become a priest?" Yet we know, or ought to know, how necessary and useful a thing it is, and how acceptable to God, when a prince, lord, counsellor, or other ruler, is well-trained and skillful in discharging, in a Christian way, the functions of his office.

Even if there were no soul, (as I have already said,) and men did not need schools and the languages for the sake of Christianity and the Scriptures, still, for the establishment of the best schools everywhere, both for boys and girls, this consideration is of itself sufficient, namely, that society, for the maintenance of civil order and the proper regulation of the household, needs accomplished and well-trained men and women. Now such men are to come from boys, and such women from girls; hence it is necessary that boys and girls be properly taught and brought up. As I have before said, the ordinary man is not qualified for this task, and can not, and will not do it. Princes and lords ought to do it; but they spend their time in pleasure-driving, drinking, and folly, and are burdened with the weighty duties of the cellar, kitchen and bedchamber. And though some would be glad to do it, they must stand in fear of the rest, lest they be taken for fools or heretics. Therefore, honored members of the city councils, this work must remain in your hands; you have more time and better opportunity for it than princes and lords.

But each one, you say, may educate and discipline his own sons and daughters. To which I reply: We see indeed how it goes with this teaching and training. And where it is carried to the highest point, and is attended with success, it results in nothing more than that the learners, in some measure, acquire a forced external propriety of manner; in other respects they remain dunces, knowing nothing, and incapable of giving aid or advice. But were they instructed in schools or elsewhere by thoroughly qualified male or female teachers, who taught the languages, other arts, and history, then the pupils would hear the history and maxims of the world, and see how things went with each city, kingdom, prince, man, and woman; and thus, in a short time, they would be able to comprehend, as in a mirror, the character, life, counsels, undertakings, successes, and failures, of the whole world from the beginning. From this knowledge they could regulate their views, and order their course of life in the fear of God, having become wise in judging what is to be sought and what avoided in this outward life, and capable of advising and directing others. But the training which is given at home is expected to make us wise through our own experience. Before that can take place, we shall die a hundred times, and all through life act injudiciously; for much time is needed to give experience.

Now since the young must leap and jump, or have something to do, because they have a natural desire for it which should not be restrained, (for it is not well to check them in everything,) why should we not provide for them such schools, and lay before them such studies? By the gracious arrangement of God, children take delight in acquiring knowledge, whether languages, mathematics, or history. And our schools are no longer a hell or purgatory, in which children are tortured over cases and tenses, and in which with much flogging, trembling, anguish and wretchedness they learn nothing. If we take so much time and pains to teach our children to play cards, sing, and dance, why should we not take as much time to teach them reading and other branches of knowledge, while they are young and at leisure, are quick at

375

learning, and take delight in it? As for myself, if I had children and were able, I would have them learn not only the languages and history, but also singing, instrumental music, and the whole course of mathematics. For what is all this but mere child's play, in which the Greeks in former ages trained their children, and by this means became wonderfully skillful people, capable for every undertaking? How I regret that I did not read more poetry and history, and that no one taught me in these branches. Instead of these I was obliged with great cost, labor, and injury, to read Satanic filth, the Aristotelian and Scholastic philosophy, so that I have enough to do to get rid of it.

But you say, who can do without his children and bring them up, in this manner, to be young gentlemen? I reply: it is not my idea that we should establish schools as they have been heretofore, where a boy has studied Donatus and Alexander twenty or thirty years, and yet has learned nothing. The world has changed, and things go differently. My idea is that boys should spend an hour or two a day in school, and the rest of the time work at home, learn some trade and do whatever is desired, so that study and work may go on together, while the children are young and can attend to both. They now spend tenfold as much time in shooting with crossbows, playing ball, running, and tumbling about.

In like manner, a girl has time to go to school an hour a day, and yet attend to her work at home; for she sleeps, dances, and plays away more than that. The real difficulty is found alone in the absence of an earnest desire to educate the young, and to aid and benefit mankind with accomplished citizens. The devil much prefers blockheads and drones, that men may have more abundant trials and sorrows in the world.

But the brightest pupils, who give promise of becoming accomplished teachers, preachers, and workers, should be kept longer at school, or set apart wholly for study, as we read of the holy martyrs, who brought up St. Agnes, St. Agatha, St. Lucian, and others. For this purpose also the cloisters and cathedral schools were founded, but they have been perverted into another and accursed use. There is great need for such instruction; for the

376

tonsured crowd is rapidly decreasing, and besides, for the most part, the monks are unskilled to teach and rule, since they know nothing but to care for their stomachs, the only thing they have been taught. Hence we must have persons qualified to dispense the Word of God and the Sacraments, and to be pastors of the people. But where will we obtain them, if schools are not established on a more Christian basis, since those hitherto maintained, even if they do not go down, can produce nothing but depraved and dangerous corrupters of youth?

There is consequently an urgent necessity, not only for the sake of the young, but also for the maintenance of Christianity and of civil government, that this matter be immediately and earnestly taken hold of, lest afterwards, although we would gladly attend to it, we shall find it impossible to do so, and be obliged to feel in vain the pangs of remorse forever. For God is now graciously present, and offers his aid. If we despise it, we already have our condemnation with the people of Israel, of whom Isaiah says: "I have spread out my hands all the day unto a rebellious people." And Proverbs i. 24-26: "I have stretched out my hand, and no man regarded: but ye have set at naught all my counsel, and would none of my reproof: I also will laugh at your calamity; I will mock when your fear cometh." Let us then take heed. Consider for example what great zeal Solomon manifested; for he was so much interested in the young that he took time, in the midst of his imperial duties, to write a book for them called Proverbs. And think how Christ himself took the little children in His arms! How earnestly He commends them to us, and speaks of their guardian angels, in order that He may show us how great a service it is, when we rightly bring them up: on the other hand, how His anger kindles, if we offend the little ones, and let them perish.

Therefore, dear Sirs, take to heart this work, which God so urgently requires at your hands, which pertains to your office, which is necessary for the young, and which neither the world nor the Spirit can do without. We have, alas! lived and degenerated long enough in darkness; we have remained German brutes too long. Let us use our reason, that God may observe in us gratitude for His mercies, and that other lands may see that we are human beings, capable both of learning and of teaching, in order that through us, also, the world may be made better. I have done my part; I have desired to benefit the German states, although some have despised me and set my counsel at naught as knowing better themselves, — to all which I must submit. I know indeed that others could have accomplished it better; but because they were silent, I have done the best I could. It is better to have spoken, even though imperfectly, than to have remained silent. And I have hope that God will rouse some of you to listen to any counsel, and that instead of considering the adviser, you will let yourselves be moved by the great interest at stake.

Finally, this must be taken into consideration by all who earnestly desire to see such schools established and the languages preserved in the German states: that no cost nor pains should be spared to procure good libraries in suitable buildings, especially in the large cities, which are able to afford it. For if a knowledge of the Gospel and of every kind of learning is to be preserved, it must be embodied in books, as the prophets and apostles did, as I have already shown. This should be done, not only that our spiritual and civil leaders may have something to read and study, but also that good books may not be lost, and that the arts and languages may be preserved, with which God has graciously favored us. St. Paul was diligent in this matter, since he lays the injunction upon Timothy: "Give attendance to reading;" and directs him to bring the books, but especially the parchments left at Troas.

All the kingdoms that have been distinguished in the world have bestowed care upon this matter, and particularly the Israelites, among whom Moses was the first to begin the work, who commanded them to preserve the book of the law in the ark of God, and put it under the care of the Levites, that any one might procure copies from them. He even commanded the king to make a copy of this book in the hands of the Levites. Among other duties, God directed the Levitical priesthood to preserve and attend to the books. Afterwards Joshua increased and improved this library, as did subsequently Samuel, David, Solomon, Isaiah, and many kings and prophets. Hence have come to us the Holy Scriptures of the Old Testament, which would not otherwise have been collected and preserved, if God had not required such diligence in regard to it.

After this example the collegiate churches and convents formerly founded libraries, although with few good books. And the injury resulting from the neglect to procure books and good libraries, when there were men and books enough for that purpose, was afterwards perceived in the decline of every kind of knowledge; and instead of good books, the senseless, useless, and hurtful books of the monks, the Catholicon, Florista, Graecista, Labyrinthus, Dormi Secure, and the like were introduced by Satan, so that the Latin language was corrupted, and neither good schools, good instruction, nor good methods of study remained. And as we see, the languages and arts are, in an imperfect manner, recovered from fragments of old books rescued from the worms and dust; and every day men are seeking these literary remains, as people dig in the ashes of a ruined city after treasures and jewels.

Therein we have received our just due, and God has well recompensed our ingratitude, in that we did not consider His benefits, and lay up a supply of good literature when we had time and opportunity, but neglected it, as if we were not concerned. He in turn, instead of the Holy Scriptures and good books, suffered Aristotle and numberless pernicious books to come into use, which only led us further from the Bible. To these were added the progeny of Satan, the monks and the phantoms of the universities, which we founded at incredible cost, and many doctors, preachers, teachers, priests and monks that is to say, great, coarse, fat asses, adorned with red and brown caps, like swine led with a golden chain and decorated with pearls; and we have burdened ourselves with them, who have taught us nothing useful, but have made us more and more blind and stupid, and as a reward have consumed all our property, and filled all the cloisters, and indeed every corner, with the dregs and filth of their unclean and noxious books, of which we can not think without horror.

Has it not been a grievous misfortune that a boy has hitherto been obligated to study twenty years or longer, in order to learn enough miserable Latin to become a priest and to read the mass? And whoever has succeeded in this, has been called blessed, and blessed the mother that has borne such a child! And yet he has remained a poor ignorant man all through life, and has been of no real service whatever. Everywhere we have had such teachers and masters, who have known nothing themselves, who have been able to teach nothing useful, and who have been ignorant even of the right methods of learning and teaching. How has it come about? No books have been accessible but the senseless trash of the monks and sophists. How could the pupils and teachers differ from the books they studied? A jackdaw does not hatch a dove, nor a fool make a man wise. That is the recompense of our ingratitude, in that we did not use diligence in the formation of libraries, but allowed good books to perish, and bad ones to survive.

But my advice is, not to collect all sort of books indiscriminately, thinking only of getting a vast number together. I would have discrimination used, because it is not necessary to collect the commentaries of all the jurists, the productions of all the theologians, the discussions of all the philosophers, and the sermons of all the monks. Such trash I would reject altogether, and provide my library only with useful books; and in making the selection, I would advise with learned men.

In the first place, a library should contain the Holy Scriptures in Latin, Greek, Hebrew, German, and other languages. Then the best and most ancient commentators in Greek, Hebrew, and Latin.

Secondly, such books as are useful in acquiring the languages, as the poets and orators, without considering whether they are heathen of Christian, Greek or Latin. For it is from such works that grammar must be learned.

Thirdly, books treating of all the arts and sciences.

Lastly, books on jurisprudence and medicine, though here discrimination is necessary.

A prominent place should be given to chronicles and histories, in whatever languages they may be obtained; for they are wonderfully useful in understanding and regulating the course of the world, and in disclosing the marvelous works of God. O how many noble deeds and wise maxims produced on German soil have been forgotten and lost, because no one at the time wrote them down; or if they were written, no one preserved the books: hence we Germans are unknown in other lands, and are called brutes that know only how to fight, eat, and drink. But the Greeks and Romans, and even the Hebrews, have recorded their history with such particularity, that even if a woman or child did any thing noteworthy, all the world was obliged to read and know it; but we Germans are always Germans, and will remain Germans.

Since God has so graciously and abundantly provided us with art, scholars, and books, it is time for us to reap the harvest and gather for future use the treasures of these golden years. For it is to be feared, (and even now it is beginning to take place,) that new and different books will be produced, until at last, through the agency of the devil, the good books which are being printed will be crowded out by the multitude of ill-considered, senseless, and noxious works. For Satan certainly designs that we should torture ourselves again with Catholicons, Floristas, Modernists, and other trash of the accursed monks and sophists, always learning, yet never acquiring knowledge.

Therefore, my dear Sirs, I beg you to let my labor bear fruit with you. And though there be some who think me too insignificant to follow my advice, or who look down upon me as one condemned by tyrants: still let them consider that I am not seeking my own interest, but that of all Germany. And even if I were a fool, and should yet hit upon something good, no wise man should think it a disgrace to follow me. And even if I were a Turk and heathen, and it should yet appear that my advice was advantageous, not for myself, but for Christianity, no reasonable person would despise my counsel. Sometimes a fool has given better advice than a whole company of wise men. Moses received instruction from Jethro.

Herewith I commend you all to the grace of God. May He soften your hearts, and kindle therein a deep interest in behalf of the poor, wretched, and neglected youth; and through the blessing of God may you so counsel and aid them as to attain to a happy Christian social order in respect to both body and soul, with all fullness and abounding plenty, to the praise and honor of God the Father, through Jesus Christ our Saviour. Amen.

LU TING-YI

LU TING-YI (1907-   ). Educational policy in China strongly reflects the political objectives of the Chinese Communist Party. As chief of the Propaganda Department of the Central Committee of the C. C. P. and Vice Premier of the State Council, Lu Ting-yi is the highest party official concerned with educational policy. Under his direction strong emphasis has been placed on compulsory "socialist" education at all levels, and for all citizens, under a special curriculum prescribed by the Propaganda Department. Especially after 1958, students and teachers at all levels of instruction were required to work in factories, on farms, or in other productive enterprises.

In the article from which the following excerpt is taken, the author states that since the founding of the People's Republic of China in 1949 a socialist educational system has been established, that "ideological remolding has been conducted among the teachers and students," that great strides have been taken toward the elimination of illiteracy, and that the principle of combining education with productive labor will wipe out "the survival of all the systems of exploitation that have existed in history, so that humanity may enter into communist society." It is interesting to note that according to official statistics, almost ninety-four per cent of all school age children were attending schools in the early 1960s, and that the school population had increased since 1949 from 350,000 to approximately 100,-000,000. The militancy of the new leadership is reflected in the foregoing statements and in the assertion that "a struggle has to be waged" to destroy traditions "that have persisted for thousands of years."

EDUCATION MUST BE COMBINED WITH PRODUCTIVE LABOR*

We are Marxists and so we maintain that it is necessary to proceed from objective reality. Therefore we must first study our own condition seriously and take to it with enthusiasm. We also study the experiences of our fraternal countries seriously, and we study history seriously, but our purpose is not to copy or transplant but to understand history, understand historical materialism in

*From the article published in 1958 by the Foreign Language Press, Peking.

383

the field of education, so as to have examples for study with the aid of which we can do our work satisfactorily in accordance with our own conditions. Whatever work we do, we must rely closely on the leadership of the Party because it is none but the Communist Party that understands our conditions best and knows Marxism best. The Communist Party is the highest form of organization of the working class; it must and can give leadership in everything. From the Central Committee down to the basic organizations, the Communist Party is the organized, disciplined vanguard of the working class. . . .

In the final analysis, the debate on education that has been going on in recent years boils down to the question of "what is all-round development." Marxists believe in "producing fully developed human beings" and in achieving this through education. It is well that our educationalists often talk about all-round development.

The essence of all-round development is that the students should acquire comparatively broader knowledge, become versatile people capable of "going over in sequence from one branch of production to another, depending on the requirements of society or their own inclinations" (F. Engels: *Principles of Communism*). We maintain that civilians should take up military service and retired military men go back to production. We maintain that cadres should participate in physical labor and productive workers in administration. All these propositions are already being put into practice gradually. Measures such as these which involve both the division of labor and change of work conform to the needs of society. They are more reasonable than the division of labor under the capitalist system. They not only increase production but enable the state to carry out reasonable readjustment of the productive forces when this becomes socially necessary, without causing social upheaval.

Our leap forward in industry and agriculture is already giving rise to the problem of the partial transfer of producers to other branches of production when what they are making grows in output to the point where it meets the current maximum demands of the people and there is even a surplus. Without such transfer

384

there would be failure to meet the demands of the people, to develop the productive forces of society continuously and raise the people's living standards continuously. Our educational and other relevant spheres of work must prepare the ground for such transfers. Education should enable the students to acquire broad knowledge. But how broad depends on concrete objective and subjective conditions. In the future, when communist society is fully consolidated, developed and mature, men will be trained in many kinds of work and be able to undertake many professions while specializing in selected fields. This is what we aim at. We must march to this goal.

In our country's present condition, we can train people to do many kinds of work, but cannot yet train "people to be capable of undertaking any profession." The essence of all-round development is also that the knowledge imparted to the students must be not one-sided and fragmentary, but comparatively complete knowledge. This requires that education should serve politics and be combined with productive labor. Speaking of his ideal of education in the future Karl Marx referred to "an education that will, in the case of every child over a given age, combine productive labor with instruction and gymnastics, not only as one of the methods of adding to the efficiency of production, but as the only method of producing fully developed human beings" (*Capital*, volume I). That is, he urged that students acquire comparatively complete knowledge and be able to engage not only in mental labor but manual labor as well. . . .

In brief, the all-round development we stand for is this: Students should be enabled to acquire comparatively complete, broader knowledge, grow up physically fit, and acquire communist morals. In his "On the Correct Handling of Contradictions Among the People," Comrade Mao Tse-tung said: "Our educational policy must enable everyone who gets an education to develop morally, intellectually, and physically and become a cultured, socialist-minded worker." This is our educational principle of all-round development. "A cultured, socialist-minded worker" is a man who is both politically conscious and educated. He is able to understand both mental and manual work. He is what we

regard as developed in an all-round way, both politically and professionally qualified. He is a worker-intellectual and an intel-
lectual-worker.

We insist on the educational principle of all-round development. We consider that the only method to train human beings
in all-round development is to educate them to serve working-
class politics and combine education with productive labor. We
say the only method, because there is no other way to achieve
this aim. . . .

Great achievements have been made in our educational work,
under the leadership of the Chinese Communist Party, in the past
nine years since the founding of the People's Republic of China.
These are — the recovery of the right to run education, a right
formerly usurped by the imperialists; the satisfactory taking over
of the schools all over the country; the abolition of the fascist
system of school management practiced by the Kuomintang reactionary clique; the abolition of its fascist education and domination of the students by its special agents; the setting up of a
socialist educational system; and the wiping out, in the main, of
the counter-revolutionaries and other bad elements hidden in educational circles. In addition, courses in Marxism-Leninism have
been opened in the schools; ideological remolding has been conducted among the teachers and students; the universities and departments have been reorganized and teaching systems reformed;
and struggles have been waged against the bourgeois rightists.
The number of students in institutions of higher learning, middle
schools, and primary schools has in all cases increased severalfold;
big advances have been made in the campaign against illiteracy
and in spare-time cultural and technical education; the policy of
working while studying has begun to be applied in all schools;
organizations of the Chinese Communist Party have been established among the educational workers; and large numbers of
people have been trained as cadres for socialist construction.

But the struggle between working-class and bourgeois ideas
proceeds continuously on the educational front. This is in the
nature of a struggle between the socialist and the capitalist roads.
Bourgeois thinking has hampered the development of education.

When the bourgeois rightists made their ferocious attacks, they even attempted to use the students as a stepping stone for the restoration of capitalism. This was at one time the dream of Chang Po-chun, Lo Lung-chi, Tseng Chao-lun, Chien Wei-chang, and other of their ilk. Our victory in the antirightist struggle and the great leap forward in industry and agriculture have turned bad things to good account and enabled people to understand better the danger and baneful consequences of bourgeois thinking in educational work. The work in the past nine years has given us experience and enabled us to explain our Party's policy of educational work more clearly and systematically.

The chief mistake or defect in our educational work has been the divorce of education from productive labor. The policy of combining education with productive labor was put forward by our Party early in 1934. Comrade Mao Tse-tung already then said: "What is the general policy for the Soviet culture and education? It is to educate the broad masses of the toiling people in the spirit of communism, to make culture and education serve the revolutionary war and the class struggle, to combine education with labor, and to enable the broad masses of the Chinese people to enjoy civilization and happiness." In 1954 when the period of economic rehabilitation was over and the First Five-Year Plan was already in operation, the Central Committee of the Party raised the question of adding productive labor to the curricula of the schools. But the proposal encountered obstruction and was not carried through at that time. The Central Committee of the Party repeatedly stressed its policy that education must be combined with productive labor — at the national conference on propaganda work in March 1957, in the editorial of *Renmin Ribao* (*People's Daily*) on April 8 of the same year, and at the Nanking meeting in January 1958. It is only now that this policy of the Party has been carried out on a nationwide scale. Education must serve politics, must be combined with productive labor, and must be led by the Party — these three things are interrelated. Education divorced from productive labor is bound to lead, to a degree, to the neglect of politics and of Party leadership in educational work, thus divorcing education from the realities of our country and eventually causing right deviationist and doctrinaire mistakes.

The combination of education with productive labor is required by our country's socialist revolution and socialist construction, by the great goal of building a communist society, and by the need to develop our education with greater, faster, better, and more economical results.

The aim of our socialist revolution is to wipe out all exploiting classes, all systems of exploitation, including their remnants. Basic victory has now been won in the socialist revolution on the economic front. On the political and ideological fronts, too, the socialist revolution has achieved decisive victory. As the Second Session of the Eighth National Congress of the Communist Party of China has pointed out in its resolution, our task is "to carry out actively the technical and cultural revolutions while continuing with the socialist revolution on the economic, political, and ideological fronts."

The cultural revolution is to enable all 600 million Chinese people, except for those who are incapable, to do productive work and to study. This means to make the masses of our workers and peasants intellectuals as well and our intellectuals laborers too. Only when the masses of the workers and peasants and the intellectuals alike develop along the line of making up what they lack is it possible to change thoroughly the irrational legacy of the old society and eradicate the backwardness of each, i.e., eliminate the cultural deficiency of the masses of workers and peasants and eliminate the bourgeois thinking of the intellectuals. This is, therefore, a very far-reaching revolution which demands that education must serve working-class politics, that is, be combined with productive labor. . . .

Our socialist construction demands the utmost effort and consistent pressing ahead; it demands building the country industriously and thriftily; it also demands technique and culture and the training of large numbers of socialist-minded and professionally proficient technicians in conformity with the principle of achieving greater, faster, better, and more economical results. These needs of socialist construction also demand the combination

388

of education with productive labor. Lenin said: "It is impossible to visualize the ideal of future society without combining the training and education of the young generation with productive labor. Neither training and education without productive labor, nor productive labor without parallel training and education could have been raised to the height demanded by present-day technique and the state of scientific knowledge." The policy of combining education with productive labor will certainly raise the quality of education. This holds true for intellectual and for moral and physical education. The educational policy of divorcing mental and manual labor cannot meet the needs of socialist construction.

The future communist society will be one of "from each according to his ability and to each according to his needs," a society in which the differences between town and country and between mental and manual labor are eliminated. Our big leap forward in industry and agriculture has made the attainment of communism no longer a far distant prospect. One hundred and ten years ago Marx and Engels in the *Communist Manifesto* formulated ten measures to establish a communist society, which "will be pretty generally applicable . . . in the most advanced countries." Of these, the first eight have already been carried out in China, through the adoption of methods suitable to the actual conditions of our country; and the last two, namely "the combination of agriculture with manufacturing industries; the gradual abolition of the distinction between town and country" and "the combination of education with industrial production," are beginning to be carried out.

It is clear to everyone that because of the application, in the course of industrial development, of the policy "to develop industry and agriculture simultaneously while giving priority to heavy industry; and, with centralized leadership, over-all planning, proper division of labor, and coordination to develop national and local industries, and large, small, and medium-sized enterprises simultaneously," industry has appeared in the rural areas and, with it, the phenomenon of workers who are simultaneously peasants and peasants who are simultaneously workers. This phenomenon has the embryo of communist society.

Because the principle of combining education with productive labor is beginning to go into operation, with schools setting up their own factories and farms, and factories and agricultural cooperatives establishing their own schools on a large scale, the phenomenon of students who are at the same time workers and peasants and of workers and peasants who are students at the same time is beginning to appear. This, too, has the embryo of communist society. It can be imagined that when China enters into communism, our basic social organizations will be many communist communes. With few exceptions, each basic unit will have workers, peasants, traders, students, and militia. In the field of education, each basic unit will have its own primary and secondary schools and institutions of higher learning; at the same time everybody will have the time to acquire education as both laborer and intellectual. In *The Housing Question* Engels anticipated this situation when he said: "And it is precisely this industrial revolution which has raised the productive power of human labor among all, of producing not only enough for the plentiful consumption of all members of society and for an abundant reserve fund, but also of leaving each individual sufficient leisure so that what is really worth preserving in historically inherited culture — science, art, forms of intercourse — may not only be preserved but converted from a monopoly of the ruling class into common property of the whole of society, and may be further developed." To attain this prospect, our educational work must not go in the direction of divorcing mental and manual labor but in the direction of combining mental with manual labor and education with productive labor.

To the bourgeois educationalists it seems impossible to get greater, faster, better, and more economical results in education. But the tremendous growth in educational work can make it develop with greater, faster, better, and more economical results. The combination of education with labor, making education an activity that is warmly welcomed by the workers and peasants, is an important way of arousing mass initiative in the setting up of schools. The principles of running schools by applying the mass line under Communist Party leadership are: First, to combine unity with diversity. The purpose of the training is unified, that is, to train socialist-minded, educated workers; but the schools can be run by the central or local authorities, factories and mines, enterprises and agricultural cooperatives, and the forms the schools can take are varied. They may be full-time or part-work, part-study, or spare-time schools; they may collect fee or be free of charge. As production grows further and working hours can be shortened, the present spare-time school will be similar to part-work part-study schools. When production develops considerably and public accumulation rises greatly, the schools that now charge fees will similarly become free.

Second, to combine the spreading of education widely with the raising of educational levels. The level of education must be raised on the basis of popularization and popularization must be so guided as to raise the level of education. Some of the full-time, the part-work part-study, and the spare-time schools undertake the task of raising educational levels at the same time as education is being spread extensively through part-work part-study and spare-time courses. Since the schools that popularize education are part-work part-study or spare-time schools, they can meet the whole or the greater part of their expenditures themselves, and can find teachers locally in accordance with the principle that "every capable person can teach." They can develop gradually by perfecting their curricula, equipment and teaching staff with aid from the government. In schools where courses in labor are lacking, the stress should be on introducing them, and in schools where the deficiency is in the basic courses the stress should be on introducing these, so that both kinds of schools go forward to fill in what they lack and apply the principle of combining theory with practice more effectively.

Third, to combine over-all planning with decentralization, to bring into play the initiative of both the various central government departments and the local authorities, guided by the Party committees, to develop education as fast as possible and enable this development to benefit, not hamper, the growth of production.

Fourth, to apply the mass line in the political, administrative, pedagogic, and research work in the schools. In all such work, it is necessary, guided by the Party committees, to adopt the method of open and free airing of views, and *tatsepao* and the method of the "three combinations" (for instance, in working out teaching plans and programs, the method can be adopted of combining the efforts of the teachers and the students under the leadership of the Party committee, and so on), and to establish democratic relations of equality — changing the old irrational relations — between the teachers and the students. Experience shows that remarkable achievements have been made where these methods have been adopted.

A struggle has to be waged before the combination of education with labor is effected, and this struggle will be a protracted one. Why? Because this is a revolution upsetting old traditions in educational work that have persisted for thousands of years. The principle of divorcing mental from manual labor has dominated educational work for thousands of years. All the exploiting classes in history have adhered firmly to this principle. More than two thousand years ago, Confucius took a stand against combining education with productive labor. . . .

Fourier and Owen, the Utopian socialists of the eighteenth century, were the first to put forward the idea of combining education with productive labor. Marx, Engels, and Lenin all endorsed this idea. In volume I of *Capital* Marx expressed the view that a part-work part-study system of schooling was more suitable for children than full-time study. In "The Directive to the Delegates of the Provisional Central Council on Some Questions" he suggested: "In a reasonable social order every child must become a productive worker starting at the age of nine."

He maintained that children from the age of nine to twelve should do two hours' work every day in a work-shop or at home, children from thirteen to fifteen years of age four hours, and from sixteen to seventeen years of age six hours. He believed that "the combination of remunerative productive labor, mental education, physical exercise, and polytechnical training elevates the working class considerably above the level of the higher and middle classes." Marx once foretold that "there can be no doubt that when the working class comes into power, as inevitably it must, technical instruction, both theoretical and practical, will take its proper place in the working-class schools" (*Capital*, volume I). Only in a socialist country led by the working class and the Communist Party can the principle of combining education with productive labor be carried into effect and play a great role in revolution and construction. Marx's prophecy will come true in our country.

We must realize that to carry the combination of education with productive labor into effect means a fight with the old traditions that have persisted for thousands of years. Without the communist style of toppling down the old idols, burying doctrinairism, and daring to think, speak, and do, without the creative spirit of combining the universal truths of Marxism with the concrete realities of our country, we cannot succeed. Today, in our educational work, vigorous efforts are being made to pull down the outdated and set up the new. Bourgeois and doctrinaire ideas are being broken down and new, Marxist educational theories, systems and methods, curricula and school systems suited to our country are being created. This educational revolution has solid economic foundations. The Marxist doctrine of historical materialism teaches that the superstructure must conform to the economic base. The political system is superstructure, the concentrated expression of economic life. Education comes into the category of ideology and is also super-structure; it serves politics. Class society which has existed for thousands of years has had ownership by slave-owners, landlords, or capitalists as its economic base. The political systems that conform to these types of education that serve these dictatorships are those of the slave-owners, the landlords, and the bourgeoisie. These types of education differ from each other, but all have this in common, that education is divorced from productive labor, mental from manual labor, and manual labor and laborers are despised. The divorce of mental from manual labor is needed by all the exploiting classes, including the bourgeoisie.

Our society has socialist ownership as its economic base. The political system suited to socialist ownership is proletarian dictatorship. Our education serves the proletarian dictatorship. Therefore, contrary to the old traditions that persisted for thousands of years, it must apply the principle of combining education with productive labor so as to eliminate the difference between mental and manual labor; and this also means wiping out the survivals of all the systems of exploitation that have existed in history, so that humanity may enter into communist society.

The principle of combining education with productive labor is needed by the working class and all other working people. This principle, which conforms to the people's desires, will certainly prevail. On the other hand, the principle of divorcing mental from manual labor, since it does not conform to the socialist economic base and the people's requirements, will sooner or later be discarded by the people even though it has a tradition of thousands of years. With politics in command, with leadership by the Communist Party, and with the rallying of the entire Party and all educational workers who can be rallied to fight against bourgeois educational policy and for the application of the Party's educational policy, we can so carry through our cultural revolution that all of our 600 million people are able to do productive work and all are able to study, changing them into new men who are both laborers and intellectuals.

ANTON MAKARENKO

ANTON MAKARENKO (1888-1939). In a letter dated January 30, 1933, Maxim Gorky praised Anton Makarenko in these words: "For twelve years you have labored, and the results of those labors are priceless. Your revolutionary and astonishingly successful pedagogical experiment is, in my opinion, of world-wide significance."

Makarenko was born on March 13, 1888, in the Ukraine, attended the municipal school in Kryukov for six years, graduated from a one-year course for teachers in 1905, and began teaching at a large two-class railway school. The first years of his pedagogical activities were coincident with the first Russian revolution. He entered the Poltava Teachers Institute in 1914, graduated from the Institute in 1917, and returned to Kryukov to serve as headmaster. Already searching for new forms and methods of education, he welcomed the Revolution of 1917 "with great hopes." It was as organizer and director of colonies for juvenile delinquents that he achieved fame in the field of education. By setting bold tasks, by personal example and tact, by skillful method of approach to each colonist, by organizing groups of teachers devoted to their work, he laid the foundation for the education and rehabilitation of the members of the groups known as the Gorky Labor Colony, the Kuryazh Colony, and the Dzerzhinsky Commune (composed of destitute children). These experiences provided him with the raw materials from which he was to construct his theories of education and the literary works on which his fame rests (*The Road to Life — an Epic of Education, 1930 Marches On, Learning to Live*).

Makarenko credited his concern for honesty, self-respect, and a sense of duty to the examples set by his father and mother. Details of his early life and experience in working with delinquent children appear in *The Road to Life,* praised by the Communist press as a classic work of socialist realism. Begun in 1925 and published in 1933, the book was described by its author as "a book about my own life, my mistakes, and my little struggle." Its publication brought a flood of letters from all over the U.S.S.R., from teachers and especially from parents seeking his advice on what was then one of the most neglected topics in pedagogics — the upbringing of children in the home — and Makarenko considered it his civic duty to explore this field of education. The results of his exploration are reflected in the selections which follow. "From My Own Practice" is reprinted in full. The other selections, considerably abridged, are intended to show Makarenko's views on specific issues relating to the pre-school education of children.

FROM MY OWN PRACTICE*

Comrades, in giving this talk I think perhaps you will say something too, since my experience — and I speak only from experience — will be different to yours. But I am also a teacher, a railwaymen's teacher and the son of a railwayman, so I should be pedagogically minded, just as you are, although I dare say I have been more fortunate than you have.

In 1920 the Soviet authorities put me in charge of a Colony of delinquents. I took the job not because I considered myself proficient as an educator. After the Revolution I worked in a school in Poltava, and had to use the premises of the Gubernia Economic Council for the purpose after office hours. Whenever I came there I found dirty office desks and cigarette-ends lying about on the floor, and the air, as a rule, was compounded of nicotine and smoke. It was very difficult to conduct a school there under such conditions, and naturally I was prepared to run anywhere to escape it. And that is how I came to take this Colony job. I worked at it for sixteen years, and in that respect I have been lucky. Few people have had the good fortune to manage one and the same collective in the course of sixteen years.

In 1935, however, this work came to an end, through no fault of mine.**

During all those years I worked with a single collective. True, people came and went, but these changes were gradual, and traditions, continuity between the generations, were preserved. As

*This is a paper which A. S. Makarenko read in Moscow at a conference of schoolteachers of the Yaroslavl Railway on March 29, 1931. This and the following extracts are from *Makarenko, His Life and Work*, translated by Bernard Isaacs (Moscow: Foreign Language Publishing House, n. d.).

**In July 1935 Makarenko was appointed Assistant Manager of the Labour Colonies Department of the People's Commissariat for Internal Affairs in Kiev.

a result of my work in this collective I have been led to certain conclusions, which I am inclined to apply to the ordinary school as well. I say this because during the last eight years of its existence the Dzerzhinsky Commune in the Ukraine differed very little from the ordinary school as far as the nature of the children's society was concerned.

The Commune had a complete secondary school, and the children very quickly — approximately in 3 or 4 months — became normal children, super-normal, if you like, compared with the average schoolboy. I have no grounds, therefore, for presuming that the population at my school was more of a problem than anywhere else. If anything, it was easier than in some schools. I could allow myself such freedom of action, for instance, as to do away with my tutor staff at the Commune after two years' work. My charges no longer needed special supervisory aid in their domestic life.

My school was a more difficult problem than yours because the children I got were more or less backward. Ten-and twelve-year-olds could barely read or write, and some of them could not write at all. It was therefore more difficult for them to complete the ten-year course at the age of 18.

There was an old intellectualist illusion that a street arab was more precocious and smarter. As a matter of fact he was in some respects inferior to the normal child. He was not trained to do systematic school work. This made it more difficult for him to master the course of secondary education. But these waifs had something that enabled them and me to overcome these great odds. They could not count on the help of parents, and could rely only on themselves. They realised this. Another thing they soon realised was that the school was a road leading to the university and higher schools. This became clear to them when the first communard undergraduates made their appearance, and these undergraduates visited the Commune.

The communards saw that the road to higher education was the finest road, the most interesting. Another of its attractions was the hostel and the stipend that went with it.

The urge towards knowledge among my communards was

stronger than it is with the average schoolboy. It was this urge that helped them to conquer laziness and all difficulties.

We had better facilities for educative work in the Commune than you have, because the communards were in my hands twenty-four hours a day for five, six, and seven years. You use a terminology like "this method is educative, that method is non-educative". Your educative method, by the way, is not one that pursues an object, but one that involves less rows, less noise. (*Laughter.*) It is a method of playing safe. As to what such a method leads to, no one really seems to care, for no one checks results.

An educative method to me was something that pursued a definite object, even if this meant rows. In this respect I was in a better position and quicker on the move. Another thing that made for easier work was the fact that the Commune ran a factory.

I was once an adherent of the "labour-processes" idea. We all believed that a child's work instincts found an outlet in labour processes. I even believed that the labour process was essential in order to give a child the labour touch. Eventually I realised that a child should be taught some productive work, should acquire a work skill.

We educators soared very high theoretically, but were very low practically. We thought we could give our child a good skill, but actually we gave him one that did not enable him to make anything better than a poor stool. We trained a dressmaker who could sew only shorts. I even experienced a glow of feeling myself when my boots were well mended, when a pair of shorts were sewn for me, or when a poor stool was made. Later I shed this pedagogical illusion. You probably remember that illusion about the labour process having to be "tied up" with the school syllabus. How hard we racked our brains over that accursed question. The children were making a stool, say, and this had to be linked up somehow with geography or mathematics. (*Laughter.*) I felt pretty bad when an inspection committee came down and failed to discover any co-ordination between a stool and the Russian language. (*Laughter.*) In the end I just gave it up, and flatly denied that there was any connection here at all.

I know my arguments now, after the Commune had organised

a splendid factory, organised it with our own hands. A factory that made Leica-type cameras. This camera has three hundred parts machined to within 0.001 mm, high precision lenses, and its manufacture is a most intricate process such as Russia had never known in the old days.

When I watched that factory at work — and that work meant an exact, detailed plan, standards of tolerance, standards of quality, servicing by dozens of engineers, a design office, etc., etc. — only then did I realise what such production meant. And how pitiful all that prattle was about tying up the school syllabus with labour processes. I discovered that the teaching process at school and the production process were strong personality builders, because they tended to eliminate the distinction between manual and mental labour and turned out highly skilled people.

One of our girls I recently met in Kharkov is shortly graduating from the institute. She is a high-grade lens polisher, and although she is now studying at an institution of higher education, she still retains her skill, has not forgotten it. When boys and girls with a secondary education and high work qualifications left the Commune I saw that their school studies had done them good. The factory, real production, provided the very conditions which facilitated pedagogical work. I shall now endeavour to have these facilities introduced in our Soviet school. I shall work for this all the harder since children's productive work opens up many educational vistas.

Finally, another aspect of the case — and by no means one to be despised — is the profitableness of such a business. The Dzerzhinsky Commune turned down the government subsidy it had been receiving and began to pay its own way. Lately, it not only covered the cost of maintaining the factory, the hostel, all living requirements such as meals, clothes, including the school, but gave the state an annual net profit of five million rubles. And that was only because we ran things on a self-supporting basis.

You can imagine what a power of instrumentation was wielded by the teachers. We decide that five hundred of us are to take a trip down the Volga, to the Caucasus. For that we need two hundred thousand rubles. And so a resolution is passed to work half an hour extra every day in the course of a month, and this gives us the two hundred thousand we need.

We were able to clothe the boys in cloth suits and the girls in silk and woollen dresses. We are able to spend forty thousand rubles on the theatre. And when this is done by way of work discipline, by way of wealth-earning effort, when the whole collective is out to achieve this aim, then we have a pedagogical agency of incomparable force.

I say nothing of the other minor merits of such a system. Wages, for instance. Wages are an excellent thing not because they give the pupil money, but because they put him on his own budget and are a means of cultivating thrift and industry. Every graduating member of the Commune had two thousand rubles to his account in the savings bank.

I am convinced that the object we pursue in education is not only to bring up a creator and a citizen capable of effectual participation in the development of the state. We should rear a person who is obliged to be a happy man. Money in the Soviet Union can serve as an excellent educator, an excellent teacher. I can speak on pedagogical questions from my own experience, and I was more fortunate in the conditions of that experience than you are.

I will urge that similar conditions be created in our schools. It may seem a bit terrifying at first, but it isn't in reality. If I were given a school today I would speak at the pedagogical meeting about what ideas I intended to put into effect, and at the same time I would be thinking where I could get the necessary money from. At the Dzerzhinsky Commune I looked for a man who could buy and sell things, and make himself generally useful. And I found such a person. He said, "Fancy complaining, when you have two hundred work hands." "What can we do with them?" I asked. "I tell you what," he says, "we'll make cotton thread." "Where will we get the money?" "We don't need money. We'll sign a contract and buy cheap home-made machines." And so we did. We started making thread. Six years later we had the best lens factory in the U.S.S.R. worth several million rubles.

And so we started with cotton thread and stools: How do you

400

make a stool? Some said that to make a stool the pupil had to make all the parts himself, then he would become a good craftsman. Others said, on the contrary, one pupil makes this part, another that part, a third does the polishing, and so on. And that is correct. But when the "pious teacher" saw this work, he paled and swooned. Whoever heard of such maltreatment of a poor boy. All he does is to saw off that thing. Yes, the boy only had that thing to handle, but he sawed off two hundred pieces in several minutes, he was working as part of a collective.

Division of labour is necessary. Today we do not so much need a craftsman who can make a stool all by himself as we do a joiner who is able to operate a machine. This is the kind of collective, this is the kind of production we had in my practice.

You shouldn't think from what I have told you that I am only an economy worker. I have always remained an educator, I have always been interested in questions of upbringing, and I have arrived at certain conclusions which may possibly run counter to current theoretical opinion. I have always been opposed to the view that pedagogy is based on a study of the child and a study of isolated, abstract educative methods. I consider education to be the expression of a teacher's political credo, his knowledge being a contributing factor. You can pump me as full as you like with methodology, but I shall never be able to rear a whiteguard. Nor will you. Only a person who is himself a whiteguard at heart can do that.

Pedagogical skill can be developed to a high degree of perfection, almost to that of technique. That is my belief, and all my life I have sought evidence in support of this belief. I contend that questions of education, methods of education, cannot be restricted to questions of teaching, all the more as the educative process takes place not only in the classroom but literally on every square yard of our land. Pedagogy should master the resources of influence potent and universal enough to nullify any harmful influences that your pupil is likely to meet. Hence, under no circumstances can we imagine this educative work as something confined to the classroom. Educative work governs the whole life of the pupil.

My second emphatic point is that I stand for active education, that is to say, I am for educating a person with definite qualities, and I do everything I can, I exert all the powers of my mind and body towards achieving that end. I must find the means towards that end, and must always see the goal before me, see the model, the ideal, towards which I am striving. The fact that the "personality will start squeaking" does not worry me. Let it squeak — I shall go on trying to achieve my aim. This does not mean that I stand for suffering. On the contrary, I am convinced that many shortcomings, especially in discipline, tone, and style, are due to the fact that we do not attach sufficient importance to a very important circumstance. This circumstance — I saw it better when dealing with my waifs and strays — is bad children's nerves. I used to think, this one is a disorganizer, that one is a thief or a lazybones, but in most cases they were simply children with ragged nerves. Every word of yours, every impulse, met with resistance. Their nerves cried out when you approached them. And sometimes our most cunning pedagogical devices are simply a strain on their nerves.

People say a child should shout after lessons (this is not done in your school); sometimes he feels like breaking windows. They say it's in the child's nature. They believe he should be diverted from the window-breaking urge to something else, that his nerves should be irritated in some other direction. He should be made to sing, or dance, or have the radio switched on for him.

I visit many schools, and my nerves are as hard as steel ropes, but when I come into a noisy school like that I get a nervous tic. And mind you, children go to school for ten years.

We are asked to be "pedagogic" and not show our feelings. Only our lips quiver sometimes and we don't sleep at nights, or else we take it out on our near ones. At one time there was even a profound conviction that a teacher's work was nervous work, and that a teacher was bound to be a neurasthenic.

I gave my thoughts to this a long time ago. And then I saw what a blessing it was to have a well-ordered school, with no screaming, no running about. If you wanted to run about, there was the playground for you outside. If you wanted to scream, then you were not to. You have to think of us too. We teachers are useful servants of the state and you children must spare our nerves.

As for windows, there can be only one solution — you dare not break any windows, I shall put no radio or music on for you, and I shall not allow you to destroy public property. I'm not going to divert you in any way.

And when a school community takes a conscientious attitude towards such an arrangement, you will get peace and orderliness in that community, you will get that degree of strict and well-defined bounds which are essential to calm nerves. It took me some time to reach this conclusion. But you could visit the Commune at any time and never see the children engaged in rough horseplay, or breaking windows, etc. It was a cheerful, happy community, and nobody hit anyone. I am absolutely convinced that the child's urge to run about in a disorderly fashion and shout can easily be channelled into calmer waters. Very often we are asked to believe in the pedagogical wisdom of things that really should be questioned, because it is highly doubtful whether this is pedagogical wisdom or wisdom at all.

Another important question: the school should be much more demanding than it is. I am grateful to the communards — they appreciated the importance of demandingness and taught me a great deal in this respect.

Take emulation, for instance. I demanded a lot, and so did the whole community. This emulation was organised without contracting parties. There was a general ruling for all classes and detachments on all occasions, and that was to be polite, to behave well, and so on. I had a card index and kept a record. The best detachment, winner of the monthly competition, received a bonus in the shape of six tickets to the theatre every day until all thirty members of the detachment had received theirs, and was granted the right of cleaning the non-living quarters.

The logic of demand developed into very curious forms. Thus, the most unpleasant work was assigned by merit and preference. Our 4th Detachment was a fine detachment. It fell to its lot to clean the lavatory in the course of a month. Its members cleaned

403

the lavatory with alkali and acid and then sprinkled eau-de-Cologne around. Everyone knew that they made a thorough job of it. The detachment won preferential right. After the month's work, the detachment declared, "We reserve the right of cleaning the lavatory." Two months later they did the same. On the third month preference was won by the 3rd Detachment, who declared, "No, we've won preference this time and the lavatory cleaning job is ours now."

It is amusing today to think of this. At first lavatory cleaning, like all other cleaning jobs, was assigned by drawing lots, and afterwards it was assigned by merit.

This logic, comrades, was not my invention, it was a natural logic arising from demands.

You cannot be demanding if you have no single well-knit collective. If I were put in charge of a school the first thing I would do would be to get the teachers together and tell them, "My dear friends, I want you to do things this way." If any teacher did not agree, I would tell him, however high his qualifications, "Go to another school." To a girl of eighteen, if I saw that she agreed with me, I would say, "You are inexperienced, but I can tell from the sparkle in your eyes that you are keen to work. So please remain and work, and we shall show you how."

A real collective is a very difficult thing to achieve. Whether a man is right or wrong, these questions should be decided not as a matter of personal prestige or personal interests, but in the interests of the collective. To always maintain discipline, to do what has to be done however unpleasant it may be — is the highest degree of discipline.

I believe that the teachers of a single school should be on good terms with one another, should be friends in and out of school.

The last subject is the handling of parents. Here my previous experience in the railwaymen's school is supplemented by my work in the Commune. During the last five years pupils were sent to me whom their teachers had given up as a bad job, as a disruptive influence.

These children, of course, were more difficult than the waifs. With a waif all roads led to the Commune, to me and to my teaching staff. But this one has a Father and a Mother. Papa sometimes has a car, a stripe, a gramophone, and money. Try and tackle a fellow like that. He's more difficult. And so I decided that close contact with the parents was necessary.

You know the old, stereotyped pattern, when you send for the parents and tell them, "Your boy has done this and that." You look them in the face and think: "Now what are the parents going to do with him?" Your own face wears a virtuous expression, and you say, "There's no need to beat him, of course." The Father goes away, you don't say a word to anybody, but deep down in your heart, hidden even from your wife, you think: "It wouldn't be a bad thing after all if he gave the rascal a good hiding." With us, this kind of hypocrisy is intolerable.

Another form of handling parents is this. It is clear to the class-teacher and the headmaster that this particular family is unable to bring up the child. And what do they do? Convinced though they are that the family is incapable of bringing up the child, they usually go to that family and begin to teach the parents how to bring up the child. The family that has spoilt the child will not be able, as a rule, to grasp your instructions. Re-education is a very difficult job, and if you start teaching the rudiments of pedagogics to such a family you are likely to make things worse.

This does not mean, however, that there is no way of influencing the family. It is your duty to help it. And the best way of doing this is through the child.

This influence on the family through the pupil can be increased. I worked in the Kryukov Railway School. The pupils lived in families. I organised teams of pupils on a territorial basis. Every morning all the team-leaders reported what was going on in the house yards, and how the pupils, the members of the teams, behaved. Periodically I gave the order for a review to be held. This was attended by the class monitors besides myself. I came to the yard where the team was drawn up, and I and other members of the team made a round of the homes where the pupils of my school lived.

Such teams, answerable through their team-leaders to the

405

headmaster, and obliged to report back to the general meeting, are an excellent method of influencing the family. I believe the question of what forms this influence should take, should be decided according to the following logic: the school is a state organisation, the family a domestic organisation, and the best way of influencing the family is through the pupil.

LECTURES ON THE EDUCATION OF CHILDREN

Play

Play is of great importance in the life of a child; it means as much to him as work, activity, and employment mean to a grown-up person. What a child is in play will largely show itself in work when that child grows up. Therefore it is in play that the future citizen first begins his training.

In order to guide a child's play and educate him through play the parent should give serious thought to the question: What is play, and in what way does it differ from work? Unless the parents ponder this question and work it out for themselves they will not be able to guide their child, they will always find themselves at a loss, and will spoil the child rather than educate him.

For one thing, there is not such a great difference between play and work as most people think. Good play resembles good work, bad play resembles bad work. This resemblance is very great. In fact, bad work is more like bad play than good work. . . .

A child's play passes through several stages of development, each of which requires a special method of guidance. The first stage is the period of indoor games, the period of toys. It begins to pass into the second stage at the age of five or six. The first stage is characterised by the fact that the child prefers to play alone, rarely allowing one or two companions to join him. During these years the child likes to play with his own toys and is reluctant to play with somebody else's. It is at this stage that the child develops his individual abilities. . . .

The second stage of a child's play does not lend itself so well to guidance, since at this stage children no longer play within sight of the parents, but step out into a wider social field. The second stage lasts up to 11 or 12 years and covers part of the school period.

The school brings with it a wider society, a wider circle of interests and a more difficult field, notably that of games, but it also brings a ready-made and more efficient organisation, a definite and more systematised routine, and, most important of all, the assistance of qualified teachers. In this second stage the child now acts as a member of society, but a society still of children, which lacks strict discipline and social control. The school gives both of these things. It is likewise a form of transition to the third stage of play.

In this third stage of play we now find the child acting as a member of the collective body, not only the play collective, but the practical studying community as well. Therefore play at this age assumes more rigid collective forms and gradually becomes a sport, that is to say, games with definite physical-culture aims, rules, and — most important of all — notions of collective interest and collective discipline.

In all three stages of game development the influence of parents is of tremendous importance. Of course, first in importance comes the influence during the first stage, when the child is not yet a member of any collective body other than the family, and when the parents are often the only guides he has. But in the other stages, too, the influence of the parents can be very important and useful.

In all three stages of play you should cultivate an urge towards more valuable satisfactions than mere staring or simple enjoyment; you should cultivate grit, the ability to cope with difficulties, develop imagination, and mental alertness. At the second and third stages you should always bear in mind that your child has already become a member of society, that what is required of him is not only an ability to play, but an ability to adopt the right attitude to people.

407

One of the first things parents should always remember is this. Your child is going to be a member of a working community. Consequently, his significance in that community, his value as a citizen, will depend solely on the extent to which he is able to participate in the work of the community, the extent to which he is fitted for that work. His well-being, his standard of living will also depend upon this, for the Soviet Constitution, among other things, says, "From each according to his ability, to each according to his work". We know very well that all people are endowed by nature with approximately similar work capacities, but in life some people are able to work better than others, some are capable only of the simplest form of work, while others are able to do more intricate work, consequently, more valuable work. These different work capacities are not a gift of nature, but are cultivated in a person throughout his life, and especially in his youth. . . .

In training a child in habits of work, the most important aspect of the method is this. The child should be given a certain task which he is able to perform with the aid of one or another work device. This task need not necessarily be of short duration, one or two days, say. It can last a long time, for months or even years. The important thing is to let the child have a certain freedom in the choice of ways and means, and to bear a certain responsibility for the performance and quality of the work. It is no good telling the child, "Here's a broom, go and sweep that room, do it like this or like that."

The best thing is to charge a child with keeping a definite room clean and leave it to him to decide how he is going to do it and to be responsible for his own decision. In the first instance you have set the child only a manual task, in the second you have set him an organisational task, which is definitely more superior and useful. Consequently, the more intricate and independent a work task is, the better will it be from the point of view of educative conditioning. Many parents fail to take this circumstance into account. They tell their children to do one or another job, but the only effect of this is a dispersion among minor errands. They

408

send a boy or girl to the shop to buy a certain article but it would be much better if they imposed upon the child a definite and regular chore, for instance, that of keeping the family supplied with soap or tooth-paste.

Work participation of children in the home life should start very early. It should start with play. The child should be told that he is responsible for looking after the toys, and seeing that the places where the toys are kept and where he plays with them are kept clean and tidy. This work should be explained to him in a general way: things should be kept clean, and not left lying about, you must not spill things, or let the toys get dusty. Naturally, certain ways of tidying up can be shown to the child, but on the whole it is a good thing if the child discovers for himself that for dusting things a clean cloth is required, if he asks his mother for that cloth himself, if he sets certain sanitary standards of his own to that cloth, if he demands a better duster, and so on. Similarly, he should be left to his own devices in the matter of mending broken toys, in so far, of course, as he is able to cope with the task. For this purpose he should be given the necessary materials.

Work tasks should become more complicated as the child grows older and should be separated from play. We shall list certain chores for children, which each family can rectify or supplement according to its living conditions and the age of the children.

1. Watering plants in the room or in the whole flat.
2. Dusting the window-sills.
3. Laying the table.
4. Looking after the salt-cellars and mustard-pots.
5. Looking after Father's writing-desk. . . .

A few words concerning the quality of work. Quality should always be a decisive factor, and a high standard should be demanded always and in all seriousness. Naturally a child has no experience and often he is physically incapable of performing a job that would be perfect in all respects. The standard of workmanship demanded of him should be something that is within his powers of performance and understanding.

A child should not be reproved, shamed or scolded for poor

409

work. You should say simply and calmly that the job has not been done satisfactorily, that it needs redoing or rectifying. Parents should never, in such cases, do the work for the child, but they may, on rare occasions, do part of that work when it is obviously beyond the child's powers and when its object is to correct the original mistake of giving such an assignment.

We emphatically disapprove of the use of any forms of encouragement or punishment in the sphere of labour. The work task itself and its performance should give the child the satisfaction to make it enjoyable. The mere fact that his work is acknowledged to be good should be the best reward for his labour. A similar reward will be your approval of his inventiveness, his resourcefulness, and his techniques. But this verbal approval, too, should not be abused, and care should be taken not to praise a child for his work in the presence of your friends or acquaintances. Still less should a child be punished for work done poorly or not done at all. The important thing in this case is to get the work done in spite of everything.

Sex Education

Sex education is considered one of the most difficult of pedagogical problems. Indeed, in no other question has there been so much confusion and misconception. Practically speaking, however, this problem is not so difficult at all and in many families it has been dealt with very simply and without painful misgivings. It only becomes difficult when it is treated on its own, when too much importance is attached to it by singling it out from the general mass of educational questions.

The problem of sex education in the family can be correctly dealt with only when the parents have a clear idea of the purpose they are pursuing in their children's sex education. If this purpose is clear to the parents the way it is to be achieved will be clear to them too.

What are the requirements of social morality in matters of sex life? It requires that the sexual life of every person, every man and woman, should be in constant harmonious relation with two

410

spheres of life, namely, with the family and with love. The only kind of sexual life that it recognises as normal and morally legitimate is that which is based on mutual love and finds expression in the family, that is, in an open civil union between a man and a woman, a union that pursues two aims — that of human happiness and the birth and upbringing of children.

In this light the aims of sex education are clear. We must educate our children in such a way that only in love could they enjoy sexual life and that this enjoyment, this love, could be realised in the family. . . .

How should such sex education be carried out? Example here is better than precept. Genuine love between the Father and Mother, their respect for each other, help and care, openly permissible manifestations of affection and tenderness, if all this takes place in front of children from the first year of their lives, are a powerful educative factor which cannot but compel the attention of the children towards such serious and beautiful relations between a man and a woman.

Another important factor is the general cultivation of a feeling of love in the child. If the child, in growing up, has not learned to love his parents, his brothers and sisters, his school, his country, if the germ of gross selfishness has been allowed to develop in his character, he will hardly have a deep love for the woman of his choice. Such men often display strong sexual feeling, but are always inclined to show lack of respect for the woman who attracts them. They care nothing for the qualities of the woman's mind and are not even interested in it. They therefore change their affections lightly and are only a step removed from plain debauchery. Of course, this happens not only with men, but with women too.

Non-sexual love-friendship, experience of this love-friendship gained in childhood, experience of lasting attachments formed for individuals, love of country cultivated from childhood — all this is the best method for cultivating a future highly social attitude towards woman as a friend. Unless such an attitude is cultivated it is very difficult to discipline the sexual sphere and keep it within bounds.

411

HORACE MANN

HORACE MANN (1796-1859). The indefatigable efforts of Horace Mann to advance "the supremest welfare of mankind upon earth" earned him the title, "the father of American public education." His view of a system of common schools as the great bulwark of democratic citizenship is reflected in each of his twelve annual reports to the Massachusetts State Board of Education, and most modern educators would agree that before his death he had fulfilled a pledge expressed earlier in the form of a valedictory address: "Be ashamed to die until you have won some victory for humanity." For although Massachusetts had been the first of the colonies to establish public schools and to found a college, the quality of education had steadily deteriorated as control had slipped into the hands of local districts concerned more with economy than with efficiency, and it was due principally to the efforts of Horace Mann that the public school system was unified and vastly improved.

Born in Franklin, Massachusetts, on May 4, 1796, he overcame deficiencies in his childhood education and won entrance to Brown University, from which he graduated with highest honors in 1819. He interrupted a promising career in law and politics to become secretary to the state board of education and devote his time to the reorganization of the public school system. He visited all parts of the state, delivered moving and eloquent addresses, established *The Common School Journal* for the discussion of educational questions, and left as an enduring monument his *Annual Reports,* in which he treated practically and in detail the various issues relating to the performance of his duties.

Toward the end of his life he accepted the presidency of Antioch College and devoted his time thereafter to higher education. His death on August 2, 1859, cut short a career which promised to add a new dimension to his greatness by extending his influence into the field of higher education.

The following extracts from his *Reports,* his "Rejoinder" to those who objected to his *Seventh Report,* and his remarks on the "Code of Honor," particularly as it relates to Antioch College, present his basic views and give an indication of the moderation and restraint characteristic of his handling of controversial issues.

412

DEFECTS OF THE DISTRICT SYSTEM*

The most important of these defects is *the want of that kind of teaching which really educates;* which imparts a *knowledge of things* as well as of the forms and sounds of words; and which duly develops the various faculties of the mind — training the pupils to rich *habits* of thought, feeling, and action. . . In place of it we have what is called the "rote system." The memory is almost the only faculty regarded, and only one element of that, namely, the memory of words, while the memory of the understanding is seldom called into exercise.

In my visits, it was very uncommon to hear, in any of these schools, a single question or remark by the teacher which had any reference to the understanding of the children. In many cases the reading was little more than the mechanical pronunciation of an unknown tongue. There is a textbook in daily use in all these schools, entitled, "Spelling and Thinking Combined"; but in all the exercises in this book, I never saw the slightest evidence of any attempt at the combination indicated in the title.

Go into any of these schools at any time of day, and in nine cases out of ten, if not in forty-nine out of fifty, three fourths of the pupils will be found without profitable employment. Thus the time of these children is wasted for precious months and years in succession. But this great waste of time is not the only evil arising from this defect. Many bad habits are formed. The strength of the teacher, which should be expended in teaching, is necessarily taxed to a great extent by the incessant vigilance and care requisite to keep these idlers out of mischief, and to procure some reasonable degree of stillness.

I am clearly of the opinion that a great advance in the *amount* and *quality* of education in these schools is not only desirable but

*From the *First Annual Report to the Massachusetts State Board of Education* (1857). Reprinted in *Readings in Public Education,* edited by Ellwood P. Cubberley (Boston: Houghton Mifflin Company, 1934).

practicable, and that they might be and ought to be brought nearer to that standard of perfection which causes every pupil, by the influence of right motives, to do the right things at the right time and in the right manner.

ON PRUSSIAN SCHOOL CLASSIFICATION*

I do not hesitate to say that there are many things abroad which we at home should do well to imitate — things, some of which are here as yet mere matters of speculation and theory, but which, there, have long been in operation and are now producing a harvest of rich and abundant blessings. Among the nations of Europe, Prussia has long enjoyed the most distinguished reputation for the excellence of its schools. In reviews, in speeches, in tracts, and even in graver works devoted to the cause of education, its schools have been exhibited as models for the imitation of the rest of Christendom. . . .

The first element of superiority in a Prussian school, and one whose influence extends throughout the whole subsequent course of instruction, consists in the proper classification of the scholars. In all places where the numbers are sufficiently large to allow it the children are divided according to ages and attainments, and a single teacher has the charge only of a single class or of as small a number of classes as is practicable. I have before adverted to the construction of the schoolhouses, by which, as far as possible, a room is assigned to each class. Let us suppose a teacher to have charge of but one class, and to have talent and resources sufficient properly to engage and occupy its attention, and we suppose a perfect school. But how greatly are the teacher's duties increased and his difficulties multiplied if he have four, five, or half a dozen classes under his personal inspection. While attending to the recitation of one his mind is constantly called off to attend to the studies and the conduct of all the others. For this very few teachers amongst us have the requisite capacity, and hence the idleness and

*From the *Seventh Annual Report* (1843). *Ibid.*

414

disorder that reign in so many of our schools, excepting in cases where the debasing motive of fear puts the children in irons. All these difficulties are at once avoided by a suitable classification, by such a classification as enables the teacher to address his instructions at the same time to all the children who are before him, and to accompany them to the playground at recess or intermission without leaving any behind who might be disposed to take advantage of his absence. All this will become more and more obvious as I proceed with a description of exercises. There is no obstacle whatever, save prescription, and that *vis inertiae* of mind which continues in the beaten track because it has not vigor enough to turn aside from it, to the introduction at once of this mode of dividing and classifying scholars in all our large towns. . . .

Whatever may be the especial object of an American citizen in going abroad, still, if his mind is imbued with the true spirit of the institutions of his own country, he cannot fail, in travelling through the different nations of Europe, to find material for the most profound and solemn reflection. There is no earthly subject, in its own nature, of higher intrinsic dignity and interest than a contemplation of the different forms into which humanity has been shaped by different institutions. The interest deepens when we compare our own condition with the contemporaneous condition of other great families of mankind. . .

Whatever now is, whether of weal or of woe, is the effect of causes that have pre-existed; in like manner, what is to be, whether of glory or debasement, will result from the causes put in operation by ourselves or others. The past is a unit, fixed, irrevocable, about which there is no longer either option or alternative; but the future presents itself to us as an infinite of possibilities. For the great purpose of duty and happiness, tomorrow is in the control of the weakest of men; but yesterday is beyond the dominion of the mightiest prince or potentate — it is no longer changeable by human or divine power. The future, then, is our field of action; the past is only valuable as furnishing lights by which that field can be more successfully entered and cultivated. . . .

The experience of the ages that are past, the hopes of the ages that are to come unite their voices in an appeal to us: they implore us to think more of the character of our people than of its numbers; to look upon our vast natural resources, not as tempters to ostentation and pride, but as means to be converted, by the refining alchemy of education, into mental and spiritual treasures; they supplicate us to seek for whatever complacency or self-satisfaction we are disposed to indulge, not in the extent of our territory or the products of our soil, but in the expansion and perpetuation of the means of human happiness; they beseech us to exchange the luxuries of sense for the joys of charity, and thus give to the world the example of a nation whose wisdom increases with its prosperity, and whose virtues are equal to its power. For these ends, they enjoin upon us a more earnest, a more universal, a more religious devotion of our exertions and resources to the culture of the youthful mind and heart of the Nation. Their gathered voices assert the eternal truth that, *in a Republic, Ignorance is a Crime; and that Private Immorality is not less an Opprobrium to the State than it is a Guilt to the Perpetrator.*

REPLY TO THE BOSTON SCHOOLMASTER*

After acquainting myself with the different school systems in the United States, and visiting schools in a large portion of the States of our Union, I went abroad. In European schools I saw many things, good, bad, and indifferent. The good I attempted to describe for imitation, and the bad for warning. Of the indifferent there is no lack of specimens in our own country. In some instances, what has been seen abroad was compared with what existed at home; but no particular teacher, or town, or class of schools, was designated for special approval or disapproval. I left the good sense of the community to make the application. Before that tribunal all good schools and good teachers would be safe; nay, would obtain commendation...

*From Mann's *Answer to The "Rejoinder" of Twenty-Nine Boston School Masters* (Boston, 1845). Reprinted in *Readings in Public Education in the United States,* edited by Ellwood P. Cubberley (Boston: Houghton Mifflin Company, 1934).

416

The Report of my tour, being prepared under the most adverse circumstances, was very far from being what I desired. Although it contains not a single assertion which I would wish to retract, yet I would have had it, in some respects more full, in others more explicit. But one thing is certain: That Report contained no special allusion to, or comparison with, any class of the Boston schools. It has had, judging from the number of copies disposed of, more than a hundred thousand readers in this country, and not one of them, that I have ever heard of, out of the city of Boston, ever surmised that it contained any attack, either open or covert, upon the Boston Masters. Nay, some of the Masters did not discern it, until their vision was aided by sharper-sighted eyes; and subsequently to their having expressed a favorable opinion. From the number of copies which have been sold, and the selections made from it by the public press, it must have been deemed to contain some useful information respecting school systems and modes of instruction and discipline; and it has been acknowledged to do so in the countries to which it refers. . . .

It was this Report which the Boston Masters saw fit so virulently to assail. And what were its sins; or rather, — to put the question more broadly and therefore more favorably for them, — what were the supposed errors in my philosophy of instruction and discipline? On their own showing, they were four, and these only:

1. I was supposed to lean too far to the side of oral instruction, as contra-distinguished from the study of textbooks.

2. I was — mistakenly however, — supposed to approve the intense activity and excitement of some of the Scotch schools.

3. I was charged with error in advocating the method of teaching children to read, by beginning with words, instead of letters; and

4. It was numbered among my sins that I indulged the hope of seeing corporal punishment more and more disused in our schools, as its necessity might be gradually superseded, by substituting the pleasures of knowledge and high motives of action in its stead, until, at some future period (which I never attempted to fix), it might be dispensed with, except, as I was accustomed to express it, "in most extraordinary cases."

417

The above were proper subjects for discussion; and, in the *Common School Journal*, I had published whatever had been offered me, adverse to my own views on these points, as readily as I had published my own opinions. But, though proper subjects for discussion, they furnished no provocation for hostile attack... They furnished no pretext or shadow of excuse for holding me up before the public as having been ignorant of, and indifferent to, the cause of education before my appointment as Secretary; or for attempting to array the whole State in arms against me, by the false accusation of my "great disparagement of committees, teachers, and the condition of the school system of Massachusetts"; or for assailing the Normal Schools, because I was friendly to them, or their Principals, because they were friendly to me; or for accusing me and my friends of a base collusion for most unworthy objects; or for comparing me, personally, with some of the most offensive of the English tourists who have ever visited this country; or, in fine, for the imputation of many other most dishonorable motives and actions with which the *Remarks* abound.

THE GROUND OF THE FREE-SCHOOL SYSTEM*

The Pilgrim Fathers amid all their privations and dangers conceived the magnificent idea, not only of a universal, but of a free education for the whole people. To find the time and the means to reduce this grand conception to practice, they stinted themselves, amid all their poverty, to a still scantier pittance; amid all their toils, they imposed upon themselves still more burdensome labors; and, amid all their perils, they braved still greater dangers. Two divine ideas filled their great hearts, — their duty to God and to posterity. For the one they built the church, for the other they opened the school. Religion and knowledge, — two attributes of the same glorious and eternal truth, and that truth the only one on which immortal or mortal happiness can be securely founded!

*Extracts from the *Tenth Annual Report,* reprinted in *Readings in American Education,* edited by William H. Lucio (Chicago: Scott Foresman and Co., 1963).

418

It is impossible for us adequately to conceive the boldness of the measure which aimed at universal education through the establishment of free schools. As a fact, it had no precedent in the world's history; and, as a theory, it could have been refuted and silenced by a more formidable array of argument and experience than was ever marshalled against any other institution of human origin. But time has ratified its soundness. Two centuries of successful operation now proclaim it to be as wise as it was courageous, and as beneficent as it was disinterested. Every community in the civilized world awards it the meed of praise; and states at home and nations abroad, in the order of their intelligence, are copying the bright example. What we call the enlightened nations of Christendom are approaching, by slow degrees, to the moral elevation which our ancestors reached at a single bound. . . .

The alleged ground upon which the founders of our free-school system proceeded when adopting it did not embrace the whole argument by which it may be defended and sustained. Their insight was better than their reason. They assumed a ground, indeed, satisfactory and convincing to Protestants; but at that time only a small portion of Christendom was Protestant, and even now only a minority of it is so. The very ground on which our free schools were founded, therefore, if it were the only one, would have been a reason with more than half of Christendom for their immediate abolition.

In later times, and since the achievement of American independence, the universal and ever-repeated argument in favor of free schools has been that the general intelligence which they are capable of diffusing, and which can be imparted by no other human instrumentality, is indispensable to the continuance of a republican government. This argument, it is obvious, assumes, as a *postulatum,* the superiority of a republican over all other forms of government; and, as a people, we religiously believe in the soundness both of the assumption and of the argument founded upon it. But, if this be all, then a sincere monarchist, or a defender of arbitrary power, or a believer in the divine right of kings, would oppose free schools for the identical reasons we offer in their behalf. . . .

Again, the expediency of free schools is sometimes advocated on

419

grounds of political economy. An educated people is always a more industrious and productive people. Intelligence is a primary ingredient in the wealth of nations. . . . The moralist, too, takes up the argument of the economist. He demonstrates that vice and crime are not only prodigals and spendthrifts of their own, but defrauders and plunderers of the means of others, that they would seize upon all the gains of honest industry and exhaust the bounties of Heaven itself without satiating their rapacity; and that often in the history of the world whole generations might have been trained to industry and virtue by the wealth which one enemy to his race has destroyed.

And yet, notwithstanding these views have been presented a thousand times with irrefutable logic, and with a divine eloquence of truth which it would seem that nothing but combined stolidity and depravity could resist, there is not at the present time, with the exception of the States of New England and a few small communities elsewhere, a country or a state in Christendom which maintains a system of free schools for the education of its children. . . .

I believe in the existence of a great, immortal, immutable principle of natural law, or natural ethics, — a principle antecedent to all human institutions, and incapable of being abrogated by any ordinance of man, — a principle of divine origin, clearly legible in the ways of Providence as those ways are manifested in the order of nature and in the history of the race, which proves the *absolute right* to an education of every human being that comes into the world, and which, of course, proves the correlative duty of every government to see that the means of that education are provided for all.

CODE OF HONOR*

A moment's consideration must convince the most simple minded that the idea of a natural hostility between teachers and pupils is

*From "Report on the 'Code of Honor,' Falsely So Called." Reprinted in *Horace Mann at Antioch,* edited by Joy Elmer Mortan (The Horace Mann Centennial Fund, National Education Association: Washington, D.C., 1938).

420

not merely wrong, but ruinous. Without sympathy, without mutual affection, between instructors and instructed, many of the noblest purposes of education are wholly baffled and lost. No student can ever learn even the most abstract science from a teacher whom he dislikes as well as from one whom he loves. Affection is an element in which all the faculties of the mind as well as all the virtues of the heart flourish.

Springing from this deplorable sentiment of a natural antagonism between teachers and students, an actual belligerent condition ensues between them. One party promulgates laws: the other disobeys them when it dares; or, what is an evil only one degree less in magnitude than actual disobedience, it renders but a formal or compulsory compliance — there being, in strictness, no obedience but that of the heart. One party enjoins duties: the other evades or grudgingly performs them. Prohibitions are clandestinely violated. A rivalry grows up between the skill and vigilance that would detect, and the skill and vigilance that would evade detection. Authority on the one side, and fear on the other, usurp the place of love. Aggression and counter-aggression, not friendship and cooperation, become the motives of conduct; and the college or the school is a house divided against itself. . . .

Though all students do not partake of this feeling of hostility towards teachers, or in the practice of disobedience to their requirements, yet, as a matter of fact, the wrong-doers have inspired the right-doers with something of their sentiments and coerced them as auxiliaries into their service. A feeling almost universally prevails throughout the colleges and schools of our country that the students in each institution constitute of themselves a kind of corporation, and that this corporation is bound to protect and defend, with the united force of the whole body, any individual member who may be in peril of discipline, although that peril may have been incurred by his own misconduct. If, then, there is a corporation bound together by supposed collective interests, it is certain that this body will have its laws; and as laws will be inefficacious without penalties, it will have its penalties also. These laws, by those who are proud to uphold and prompt to vindicate them, are called the *code of honor* — a name which at once arouses

421

the attention and attracts the sympathies of ardent and ingenuous youth. . . .

The requisitions of this code are different in different places and at different times. Sometimes they are simply negative, demanding that a student shall take care to be absent when anything culpable is to be committed, or silent when called on as a witness for its exposure. Sometimes they go farther and demand evasion, misrepresentation, or even falsehood, in order to screen a fellow-student or a fellow-conspirator from the consequences of his misconduct; and sometimes anyone who exposes not merely a violator of college regulations, but an offender against the laws of morality and religion, in order that he may be checked in his vicious and criminal career, is stigmatized as an "informer," is pursued with the shafts of ridicule or the hisses of contempt, or even visited with some form of wild and savage vengeance.

It is impossible not to see that, when such a sentiment becomes the "common law" of a literary institution, offenders will be freed from all salutary fear of detection and punishment. Where witnesses will not testify, or will testify falsely, of course the culprit escapes. This security from exposure becomes a premium on transgression. Lawlessness runs riot when the preventive police of virtuous sentiment and of allegiance to order is blinded and muzzled. Thus, at the very outset, this code of honor inaugurates the reign of dishonor and shame. Judged, then, by its fruits, what condemnation of such a code can be too severe? . . .

As set forth in the resolutions, a college is a community. Like other communities, it has its objects which are among the noblest; it has its laws indispensable for accomplishing those objects; and these laws, as usually framed, are salutary and impartial. The laws are for the benefit of the community to be governed by them; and without the laws, and without a general observance of them, this community, like any other, would accomplish its ends imperfectly, perhaps come to ruin.

Now, in any civil community, what class of persons is it which arrays itself in opposition to wise and salutary laws? Of course, it never is the honest, the virtuous, the exemplary. They regard good laws as friends and protectors. But horse-thieves, counterfeiters, defrauders of the custom-house or post-office — these, in their several departments, league together and form conspiracies to commit crimes beforehand and to protect each other from punishment afterwards. But honest farmers, faithful mechanics, upright merchants, the high-toned professional man — these have no occasion for plots and perjuries, for they have no offences to hide and no punishments to fear. The first aspect of the case, then, shows the paternity of this false idea of "honor" among students. It was borrowed from rogues and knaves and peculators and scoundrels generally, and not from men of honor, rectitude, and purity. As it regards students, does not the analogy hold true?...

The student who would inform me if he saw a cut-purse purloining the money from my pocket, is bound, by reasons still more cogent, to inform me if he sees any culprit or felon destroying that capital, that stock-in-trade, which consists in the fair name or reputation of the college over which I preside.

And what is the true relation which the protecting student holds to the protected offender? Is it that of a real friend, or that of the worst enemy? An offender tempted onward by the hope of impunity is almost certain to repeat his offence. If repeated, it becomes habitual, and will be repeated, not only with aggravation in character, but with rapidity of iteration; unless, indeed, it be abandoned for other offences of a higher type. A college-life filled with the meannesses of clandestine arts, first spotted, and then made black all over with omissions and commissions, spent in shameful escapes from duty, and in enterprises of positive wrong still more shameful, is not likely to culminate in a replenished, dignified, and honorable manhood. Look for such wayward students after twenty years, and you would not go to the high places of society to find them, but to gaming-house or prison or some place of infamous resort; or if reformation has intervened, and and an honorable life falsifies the auguries of a dishonorable youth, nowhere will you hear the voice of repentance and sorrow more sad or more sincere than from the lips of the moral wanderer himself. Now, let us ask what kind of a friend is he to another, who, when he sees him just entering on the high road to destruction, instead of summoning natural or official guardians to save him, refuses to give the alarm, and thus clears away all the obstacles, and supplies all the facilities for his speedy passage to ruin?

If one student sees another just stepping into deceitful waters where he will probably be drowned, or proceeding along a pathway which has a pitfall in its track or a precipice at its end, is it not the impulse of friendship to shout his danger in his ear? Or if I am nearer than he, or can for any reason more probably rescue the imperilled from his danger, ought he not to shout to me? But a student just entering the outer verge of the whirlpool of temptation, whose narrowing circle and accelerating current will soon ingulf him in the vortex of sin, is in direr peril than any danger of drowning, of pitfall, or precipice, because the spiritual life is more precious than the bodily. It is a small thing to die, but a great one to be depraved. If a student will allow me to cooperate with him to save a fellow-student from death, why not from calamities which are worse than death? He who saves one's character is a greater benefactor than he who saves his life. Who, then, is the true friend — he who supplies the immunity which a bad student *desires,* or the saving warning or coercion which he *needs?*

But young men are afraid of being ridiculed if they openly espouse the side of progress, and of good order as one of the essentials to progress. But which is the greater evil — the ridicule of the wicked, or the condemnation of the wise?...

But again: look at the parties that constitute a college. A faculty is selected from the community at large for their supposed competency for teaching and training youth. Youth are committed to their care to be taught and trained. The two parties are now together, face to face — the one ready and anxious to impart and to mold, the other in a receptive and growing condition. . . .

Such is the whole philosophy of that miserable and wicked doctrine, that it is a *point of honor* not to "report" — though from the most humane and Christian motives — the misconduct of a fellow-student to the faculty that has legitimate jurisdiction over the case, and is bound by every obligation of affection, of honor, and of religion to exercise that jurisdiction with a single eye to the good of the offender and of the community over which it presides. It is a foul doctrine. It is a doctrine which every parent ought to denounce wherever he hears it advanced, at his table, his fireside, or in public. It is a doctrine which every community of students ought, for their own peace, safety, and moral progress, to abolish. It is a doctrine which every college faculty ought to banish from its halls, first by extracting it from its possessor and expelling it alone; or, if that severance be impossible, by expelling the possessor with it.

The practicability of carrying out the views above presented is not an untried experiment. In an institution with which one of your committee is officially connected (Antioch College), the doctrines above set forth were announced at its opening, and have now been practiced upon for a period of more than three years; and they have been attended with the happiest results. Such a degree of order, of regularity, and of exemplariness of conduct has been secured, that for more than fourteen months last past, and with between three and four hundred students in attendance, not a single serious case for discipline has occurred.

In some respects, the experiment here referred to has been tried under more than an average of favoring circumstances; in other respects, under less. The institution was new. There was no traditionary sentiment in regard to the so called code of honor to break down. In that organism the distemper was not chronic. And further: a large portion of its early members were of mature age — persons who *came* to college instead of being *sent* there — whose head and hands were alike unsullied by idea or implement of rowdyism, and who looked with a high-minded disdain upon all those brainless exploits which cluster under the name of college "pranks" or "tricks" or "practical jokes." We call them *brainless,* because there has scarcely been a new one for centuries; the professors in these arts being compelled to imitate, because they have too little genius to invent. Indeed, their best palliation is that they are too witless to know better, or that they suffer under the misfortune of having silly fathers and silly mothers who have permitted their minds to remain in that *simia* stage of development through which they were passing up towards manhood; for at this stage *quadrumana* and *bimana* will act alike.

425

Another point in which the college referred to has enjoyed a great advantage in regard to the motive-power actuating its students, has been the presence of both sexes. Each sex has exercised a salutary influence upon the other. Intellectually they have stimulated, morally they have restrained, one another; and it is the opinion of those who have administered the institution that no other influence could, in so short a time, have produced so beneficial an effect. To this, perhaps, it should also be added that this college discards all artificial systems of emulation by prizes, parts, or honors, as they are called; so that one of the most powerful temptations to degrade the standing of a fellow-student in the hope of advancing one's own is removed.

But, on the other hand, it is obvious that an attempt by a single college to revolutionize a public sentiment so widespread, so deep-seated, and so fortified by wicked purposes acting under the disguises of honor and magnanimity, must be an arduous and a perilous enterprise. So true is this that a hundred individual attempts successively made, though followed by a hundred discomfitures, would supply no argument against the triumphant success of a combined and simultaneous assault, by all our literary institutions, upon the flagitious doctrines of the "code of honor." For while the virus of the code exists in other seminaries and in the public mind generally, every new student must be placed, as it were, *in quarantine;* and even this could afford no adequate security that he would not introduce the contagion. It is only when moral health prevails in the place from which he comes that we can be sure of maintaining it in the place he enters.

In the experiment here spoken of, the general doctrines set forth in the resolutions, though announced and vindicated on all proper occasions, were not incorporated into the college statutes nor were they presented to new students for signature or pledge; but when any student fell under censure, he was then required, under penalty of dismission, to yield an affirmative acquiescence to the soundness of these doctrines and to make an express promise to abide by them. Only a single case of contumacy under this requirement has occurred for more than three years; and, so far as known, not a case of nonfulfilment of the promise. Indeed, but few cases are left for the promise to act upon.

In conclusion, the committee would express a confident opinion that the proposed revolution in public sentiment is entirely practicable. The evil to be abolished is an enormous one. The reform would be not only relatively, but positively, beneficent. The precedent already established, if it does not enforce conviction, at least affords encouragement.

MAO TSE-TUNG

MAO TSE-TUNG (1893-   ). Article 41 of the *Common Programme,* which was adopted by the Chinese People's Political Consultative-Conference and functioned as the law of the land from the time the Communists seized power in 1949 until the adoption of a constitution in 1954, prescribed that a new system of education should be created and that it should be "nationalistic, scientific and popular." Mao Tse-tung asserted in 1957: "Not to have a correct political point of view is like having no soul. . . . Our educational policy must enable everyone who gets an education to become a cultured, socialist-minded worker." And in 1958, in launching "The Great Leap Forward," Mao himself reaffirmed the thesis that party control of all education is an absolute necessity.

The leader and founder of the Chinese Communist state was born into a moderately prosperous peasant family of Shao Shan, in Huan Province, on November 19, 1893. After receiving his degree from the Hunan Normal School in 1918, he worked briefly in the library of Peking University and as a teacher in Hunan. Converted by his own studies of Marx and Engels, he devoted himself to organizing the Chinese Communist Party (1921), and by 1923 his local successes had earned him a place in the national leadership of the party. In 1928 he helped to organize the Chinese Red Fourth Army, and six years later, as chairman of the Soviet Republic of China, he set up headquarters and prepared the foundations of the new Communist state. Reverses proved only temporary, and by 1949 his forces had won control of continental China. After Stalin's death (1953) Mao's influence throughout the Communist world grew. By the time he gave up his leadership of the nation in 1959 (though he retained his chairmanship of the party), he had gone far toward making China the most Communist of all nations and the most influential in the eyes of the emergent nations. In view of the influence which it is likely to exert on less-developed nations, his educational experiment in transforming the nation along the lines laid down by the party assumes considerable significance.

The two selections that follow have received much attention inside and outside China. "On the New Democracy" shows the revolutionary nature of his plan for creating a new national culture. "On the Correct Handling of Contradictions among the People," widely used as a text for socialist education, presents Mao's views on many problems inherent in a transitional society. In the selection presented here he deals mainly with the question of intellectuals.

ON THE NEW DEMOCRACY*

New democratic culture is national. It opposes imperialist oppression and upholds the dignity and independence of the Chinese nation. It belongs to our own nation, and bears our national characteristics. It unites with the socialist and new-democratic cultures of all other nations, and establishes with them the relations whereby we can absorb something from each other and help each other to develop, and form together the new culture of the world; but it can never unite with the reactionary imperialist culture of any nation, for it is a revolutionary national culture. China should absorb on a large scale the progressive cultures of foreign countries as an ingredient for her own culture; in the past we did not do enough work of this kind. We must absorb whatever we find useful today, not only from the present socialist or new-democratic cultures of other nations, but also from the older cultures of foreign countries, such as those of the various capitalist countries in the age of enlightenment. However, we must treat these foreign materials as we do our food, which should be chewed in the mouth, submitted to the working of the stomach and intestines, mixed with saliva, gastric juice, and intestinal secretions, and then separated into essence to be absorbed and waste matter to be discarded — only thus can food benefit our body; we should never swallow anything raw or absorb it uncritically. So-called "wholesale Westernization" is a mistaken viewpoint. China has suffered a great deal in the past from the formalist absorption of foreign things. Likewise, in applying Marxism to China, Chinese Communists must fully and properly unite the universal truth of Marxism with the specific practice of the Chinese revolution; that is to say, the truth of Marxism must be in-

*Extract from an essay that has appeared under the same title in various publications. Published in *Chinese Education under Communism*, edited by Chang-Tu Hu (New York: Bureau of Publications, Teachers College, Columbia University, 1962).

429

tegrated with the characteristics of the nation and given a definite national form before it can be useful; it must not be applied subjectively as a mere formula. Formula-Marxists are only fooling with Marxism and the Chinese revolution, and there is no place for them in the ranks of the Chinese revolution. China's culture should have its own form, namely, a national form. National in form, new-democratic in content — such is our new culture today.

New-democratic culture is scientific. It is opposed to all feudal and superstitious ideas; it stands for seeking truth from facts; it stands for objective truth and for the unity between theory and practice. On this point, the scientific thought of the Chinese proletariat can form an anti-imperialist, antifeudal, and antisuperstitious united front with the still progressive bourgeois materialists and natural scientists, but it can never form a united front with any reactionary idealism. Communists may form an anti-imperialist and antifeudal united front for political actions with certain idealists and even with religious followers, but we can never approve of their idealism or religious doctrines. A splendid ancient culture was created during the long period of China's feudal society. To clarify the process of development of this ancient culture, to throw away its feudal dross and to absorb its democratic essence is a necessary condition for the development of our new national culture and for the increase of our national self-confidence; but we should never absorb anything and everything uncritically. We must separate all the rotten things of the ancient feudal ruling class from the fine ancient popular culture that is more or less democratic and revolutionary in character. As China's present new politics and new economy have developed out of her old politics and old economy, and her new culture has also developed out of her old culture, we must respect our own history and should not cut ourselves adrift from it. However, this respect for history simply means giving history a definite place among the sciences, respecting its dialectical development, but not eulogizing the ancient while disparaging the modern, or praising any noxious feudal element. As to the masses of the people and the young students, the essential thing is to direct them not to look backward, but to look forward.

New-democratic culture belongs to the broad masses, hence it is democratic. It should be in the service of the toiling masses of workers and peasants who constitute more than 90 per cent of the nation's population, and it should gradually become their culture. The knowledge to be imparted to the revolutionary cadres and the knowledge to be imparted to the broad revolutionary masses must be qualitatively different from each other but still also linked to each other; elevation and popularization must be distinguished from each other but linked to each other. Revolutionary culture is a powerful revolutionary weapon for the broad masses of the people. Before the revolution comes, revolutionary culture prepares for it in the ideological field; during the revolution, it is a necessary and important sector in the general revolutionary front. Revolutionary cultural workers are the commanders of various ranks on this cultural front. "Without a revolutionary theory, there can be no revolutionary movement," thus one can see how important the revolutionary cultural movement is to the practical revolutionary movement. And the cultural movement and practical movement are both of a mass character. Therefore all progressive cultural workers should have their own cultural army in the Anti-Japanese War, and this army is the broad mass of the people themselves. A revolutionary cultural worker who does not get close to the people is merely "a general without an army," and his firing power cannot bring the enemy down. For the realization of this aim, our written language must be reformed in certain ways, and our spoken language must be brought close to that of the people; we must know that the people are the inexhaustibly rich source of our revolutionary culture.

National, scientific and mass culture is the anti-imperialist, anti-feudal culture of the broad masses of the people; it is new-democratic culture and the new culture of the Chinese nation.

The combination of new-democratic politics, new-democratic economy, and new-democratic culture is precisely a republic of New Democracy, a republic of China in name and in fact and the new China we want to build.

This New China stands before every Chinese; we should welcome her.

The mast of the ship *New China* is appearing above the horizon; we should clap our hands and hail her.

Raise both your hands; new China is ours!

ON THE CORRECT HANDLING OF CONTRADICTIONS AMONG THE PEOPLE*

Contradictions within the ranks of the people in our country also find expression among our intellectuals. Several million intellectuals who worked for the old society have come to serve the new society. The question that now arises is how they can best meet the needs of the new society and how we can help them do so. This is also a contradiction among the people.

Most of our intellectuals have made marked progress during the past seven years. They express themselves in favor of the socialist system. Many of them are diligently studying Marxism, and some have become Communists. Their number, though small, is growing steadily. There are, of course, still some intellectuals who are skeptical of socialism or who do not approve of it, but they are in a minority.

China needs as many intellectuals as she can get to carry through the colossal task of socialist construction. We should trust intellectuals who are really willing to serve the cause of socialism, radically improve our relations, with them, and help them solve whatever problems that have to be solved, so that they can give full play to their talents. Many of our comrades are not good at getting along with intellectuals. They are stiff with them, lack respect for their work, and interfere in scientific and cultural matters in a way that is uncalled for. We must do away with all such shortcomings.

Our intellectuals have made some progress, but they should not be complacent. They must continue to remold themselves, gradual-

*Extract from a speech delivered on February 27, 1957. Reprinted in *Chinese Education under Communism*, edited by Chang-Tu Hu (New York: Bureau of Publications, Teachers College, Columbia University, 1962).

ly shed their bourgeois world outlook, and acquire a proletarian, communist world outlook so that they can fully meet the needs of the new society and closely unite with the workers and peasants. This change in world outlook is a fundamental one, and up to now it cannot be said that most of our intellectuals have accomplished it. We hope that they will continue making progress, and, in the course of work and study, gradually acquire a communist outlook, get a better grasp of Marxism-Leninism, and identify themselves with the workers and peasants. We hope they will not stop halfway, or, what is worse, slip back; for if they do they will find themselves in a blind alley.

Since the social system of our country has changed and the economic basis of bourgeois ideology has in the main been destroyed, it is not only necessary but also possible for large numbers of our intellectuals to change their world outlook. But a thorough change in world outlook takes quite a long time, and we should go about it patiently and not be impetuous. Actually, there are bound to be some who continue to be reluctant, ideologically, to accept Marxism-Leninism and communism. We should not be too exacting in what we expect of them; as long as they comply with the requirements of the state and engage in legitimate pursuits, we should give them opportunities for suitable work.

There has been a falling off recently in ideological and political work among students and intellectuals, and some unhealthy tendencies have appeared. Some people apparently think that there is no longer any need to concern themselves about politics, the future of their motherland, and the ideals of mankind. It seems as if the Marxism that was once all the rage is not so much in fashion now. If this is true, we must improve our ideological and political work.

Both students and intellectuals should study hard. In addition to specialized subjects, they should study Marxism-Leninism, current events, and political affairs in order to progress both ideologically and politically. Not to have a correct political point of view is like having no soul. Ideological remolding in the past was necessary and has yielded positive results. But it was carried on in a somewhat rough and ready way and the feelings of some people

433

were hurt — this was not good. We must avoid such shortcomings in the future. All departments and organizations concerned should take up their responsibilities with regard to ideological and political work. This applies to the Communist Party, the Youth League, government departments responsible for this work, and especially the heads of educational institutions and teachers.

Our educational policy must enable everyone who gets an education to develop morally, intellectually and physically and become cultured, socialist-minded workers. We must spread the idea of building our country through hard work and thrift. We must see to it that all our young people understand that ours is still a very poor country, that we cannot change this situation radically in a short time, and that only through the united hands can our country be made strong and prosperous within a period of several decades. It is true that the establishment of our socialist system has opened the road leading to the ideal state of the future, but we must work hard, very hard indeed, if we are to make that ideal a reality. Some of our young people think that everything ought to be perfect once a socialist society is established and that they should be able to enjoy a happy life, ready-made, without working for it. This is unrealistic.

JOHN MILTON

JOHN MILTON (1608-1674). For modern readers the two best known pamphlets of John Milton, both published in 1644, are the *Areopagitica,* a plea "for the liberty of unlicensed liberty of printing," cast in the form of a classical oration, and *Of Education,* a systematic statement of his ideas on the proper education of an English gentleman. As one of the last in a long line of expositions of the humanistic ideal, it stresses the traditional aim of molding boys into cultured, responsible citizens.

Milton was born in London on December 9, 1608, and died there on November 8, 1674. Remembered for his verse, he was important in his own day as a Latin writer, Puritan pamphleteer, and Commonwealth secretary for foreign languages. Studious from early childhood, he probably learned to read and write at home and entered St. Paul's at the age of seven. Here and at Oxford, from which he received his B. A. in 1629 and his M. A. in 1632, he learned to imitate the best classical authors and to express himself orally and in writing.

Of Education, presumably written at the request of his friend Mr. Samuel Hartlib, with whom he had touched on his ideas on the education of a gentleman during the course of their conversations, outlines a program which seems strenuous only in comparison with modern schools. Viewed against the background of the programs of his day and those urged by earlier humanists such as Rabelais and Erasmus, it suggests that Milton was looking forward rather than backward, especially with respect to his inclusion of history, geography, and natural science. Milton begins by defining a "complete and generous education" as one "which fits a man to perform justly, skilfully, and magnanimously all the offices, both public and private, of peace and war." The program of his proposed academy places the Bible and Christian teaching first, the ancient classics second. Since Greek and Latin were the keys to a storehouse of learning, the inclusion of these languages was to be expected, but only a scholar endowed with Milton's aptitude for language would have insisted on the addition of Syrian, Chaldean, and Hebrew. Languages were only means to an end: for him the elements of education were not words but things. He objected to a premature excess of logic and planned instead a graduated advance from sense perception to abstract ideas. His suggestions for physical exercise also had a practical end. Though he did not accept the Puritan attitude of hostility toward the classics, he gave poetry and music a place in his academy because of their influence on character as well as for their recreative value. As Milton himself notes, his scheme is "not a bow for every man to shoot it," but as an ideal it is provocative and stimulating.

OF EDUCATION*

I am long since persuaded, that to say, or do aught worth
memory and imitation, no purpose or respect should sooner move
us, than simply the love of God, and of mankind. Nevertheless to
write now the reforming of education, though it be one of the
greatest and noblest designs that can be thought on, and for the
want whereof this nation perishes, I had not yet at this time been
induced, but by your earnest entreaties, and serious conjurements;
as having my mind for the present half diverted in the pursuance
of some other assertion, the knowledge and the use of which, can
not but be a great furtherance both to the enlargement of truth,
and honest living, with much more peace. Nor should the laws
of any private friendship have prevailed with me to divide thus, or
transpose my former thoughts, but that I see those aims, those
actions which have won you with me the esteem of a person sent
hither by some good providence from a far country to be the
occasion and the incitement of great good to this island. And, as
I hear, you have obtained the same repute with men of most approved wisdom, and some of highest authority among us. Not to
mention the learned correspondence which you hold in foreign
parts, and the extraordinary pains and diligence which you have
used in this matter both here, and beyond the seas; either by the
definite will of God so ruling, or the peculiar sway of nature,
which also is God's working. Neither can I think that so reputed,
and so valued as you are, you would to the forfeit of your own
discerning ability, impose upon me an unfit and over-ponderous
argument, but that the satisfaction which you profess to have received from those incidental discourses which we have wandered
into, hath pressed and almost constrained you into a persuasion,
that what you require from me in this point, I neither ought, nor
can in conscience defer beyond this time both of so much need
at once, and so much opportunity to try what God hath deter-

*Published in 1673.

mined. I will not resist therefore, whatever it is either of divine, or human obligement that you lay upon me; but will forthwith set down in writing, as you request me, that voluntary *Idea*, which hath long in silence presented itself to me, of a better education, in extent and comprehension far more large, and yet of time far shorter, and of attainment far more certain, than hath been yet in practise.

Brief I shall endeavor to be; for that which I have to say, assuredly this nation hath extreme need should be done sooner than spoken. To tell you therefore what I have benefited herein among old renowned authors, I shall spare; and to search what many modern *Januas* and *Didactics* more than ever I shall read, have projected, my inclination leads me not. But if you can accept of these few observations which have flowered off, and are, as it were, the burnishing of many studious and contemplative years altogether spent in the search of religious and civil knowledge, and such as pleased you so well in the relating, I here give you them to dispose of.

The end then of learning is to repair the ruins of our first parents by regaining to know God aright, and out of that knowledge to love him, to imitate him, to be like him, as we may the nearest by possessing our souls of true virtue, which being united to the heavenly grace of faith makes up the highest perfection. But because our understanding can not in this body found itself but on sensible things, nor arrive so clearly to the knowledge of God and things invisible, as by orderly conning over the visible and inferior creature, the same method is necessarily to be followed in all discreet teaching. And seeing every nation affords not experience and tradition enough for all kind of learning, therefore we are chiefly taught the languages of those people who have at any time been most industrious after wisdom; so that language is but the instrument conveying to us things useful to be known. And though a linguist should pride himself to have all the tongues that *Babel* cleft the world into, yet if he have not studied the solid things in them as well as the words and lexicons, he were nothing so much to be esteemed a learned man, as any yeoman or tradesman competently wise in his mother dialect only. Hence appear

the many mistakes which have made learning generally so un-
pleasing and so unsuccessful; first we do amiss to spend seven
or eight years merely in scraping together so much miserable
Latin and Greek, as might be learned other wise easily and delight-
fully in one year. And that which casts our proficiency therein
so much behind, is our time lost partly in too oft idle vacancies
given both to schools and universities, partly in a preposterous
exaction, forcing the empty wits of children to compose themes,
verses and orations, which are the acts of ripest judgment and
the final work of a head filled by long reading and observing,
with elegant maxims, and copious invention. These are not matters
to be wrung from poor striplings, like blood out of the nose, or the
plucking of untimely fruit: besides the ill habit and Greek *idiom*,
with their untutored *Anglicisms*, odious to be read, yet not to be
avoided without a well continued and judicious conversing among
pure authors digested, which they scarce taste, whereas, if after
some preparatory grounds of speech by their certain forms got
into memory, they were led to the praxis thereof in some chosen
short books lessoned thoroughly to them, they might then forthwith proceed to learn the substance of good things, and arts in
due order, which would bring the whole language quickly into
their power. This I take to be the most rational and most profitable
way of learning languages, and whereby we may best hope to give
account to God of our youth spent herein: and for the usual
method of teaching arts, I deem it to be an old error of universities not yet well recovered from the scholastic grossness of
barbarous ages, that instead of beginning with arts most easy,
and those be such as are most obvious to the sense, they present
their young unmatriculated novices at first coming with the most
intellective abstractions of logic and metaphysics; so that they
having but newly left those grammatic flats and shallows where
they stuck unreasonably to learn a few words with lamentable
construction, and now on the sudden transported under another
climate to be tossed and turmoiled with their unballasted wits
in fathomless and unquiet deeps of controversy, do for the most
part grow into hatred and contempt of learning, mocked and
deluded all this while with ragged notions and babblements, while

they expected worthy and delightful knowledge; till poverty or youthful years call them importunately their several ways, and hasten them with the sway of friends either to an ambitious and mercenary, or ignorantly zealous divinity; some allured to the trade of law, grounding their purposes not on the prudent and heavenly contemplation of justice and equity which was never taught them, but on the promising and pleasing thoughts of litigious terms, fat contentions and flowing fees; others betake them to State affairs, with souls so unprincipled in virtue and true generous breeding, that flattery, and court shifts and tyrannous aphorisms appear to them the highest points of wisdom; instilling their barren hearts with a conscientious slavery, if, as I rather think, it be not feigned. Others lastly of a more delicious and airy spirit, retire themselves knowing no better, to the enjoyments of ease and luxury, living out their days in feast and jollity; which indeed is the wisest and the safest course of all these, unless they were with more integrity undertaken. And these are the fruits of misspending our prime youth at the schools and universities as we do, either in learning mere words or such things chiefly, as were better unlearned.

I shall detain you no longer in the demonstration of what we should not do, but straight conduct ye to a hill side where I will point ye out the right path of a virtuous and noble education; laborious indeed at the first ascent, but else so smooth, so green, so full of good prospect, and melodious sounds on every side, that the harp of *Orpheus* was not more charming. I doubt not but ye shall have more ado to drive our dullest and laziest youth, our stocks and stubs from the infinite desire of such a happy nurture, than we have not to hale and drag our choicest and hope-fulest wits to that asinine feast of sowthistles and brambles which is commonly set before them, as all the food and entertainment of their tenderest and most docible age. I call therefore a complete and generous education that which fits a man to perform justly, skilfully and magnanimously all the offices both private and public, of peace and war. And how all this may be done between twelve, and one and twenty, less time than is now bestowed in pure trifling at grammar and *sophistry*, is to be thus ordered.

First to find out a spacious house and ground about it fit for an academy, and big enough to lodge a hundred and fifty persons, whereof twenty or thereabout may be attendants, all under the government of one, who shall be thought of desert sufficient, and ability either to do all, or wisely to direct, and oversee it done. This place should be at once both school and university, not heeding a remove to any other house of scholarship, except it be some peculiar College of Law, or Physic, where they mean to be practitioners; but as for those general studies which take up all our time from *Lilly* to the commencing, as they term it, Master of Art, it should be absolute. After this pattern, as many Edifices may be converted to this use, as shall be needful in every city throughout this land, which would tend much to the increase of learning and civility everywhere. This number, less or more thus collected, to the convenience of a foot company, or interchangeably two troops of cavalry, should divide their day's work into three parts, as it lies orderly. Their studies, their exercise, and their diet.

For the studies, first they should begin with the chief and necessary rules of some good grammar, either that now used, or any better: and while this is doing, their speech is to be fashioned to a distinct and clear pronunciation, as near as may be to the *Italian,* especially in the vowels. For we *Englishmen* being far northerly, do not open our mouths in the cold air, wide enough to grace a southern tongue; but are observed by all other nations to speak exceeding close and inward: So that to smatter Latin with an English mouth, is as ill a hearing as Law-French. Next to make them expert in the usefulest points of grammar, and withal to season them, and win them early to the love of virtue and true labor, ere any flattering seducement, or vain principle seize them wandering, some easy and delightful book of education would be read to them; whereof the Greeks have store, as *Cebes, Plutarch,* and other Socratic discourses. But in Latin we have none of classic authority extant except the two or three first books of *Quintilian,* and some select pieces elsewhere. But here the main skill and groundwork will be, to temper them such lectures and explanations upon every opportunity as may lead

440

and draw them in willing obedience, inflamed with the study of learning, and the admiration of virtue; stirred up with high hopes of living to be brave men, and worthy patriots, dear to God, and famous to all ages. That they may despise and scorn all their childish, and ill-taught qualities, to delight in manly, and liberal exercises: which he who hath the art, and proper eloquence to catch them with, what with mild and effectual persuasions, and what with the intimation of some fear, if need be, but chiefly by his own example, might in a short space gain them to an incredible diligence and courage: infusing into their young breasts such an ingenuous and noble ardor, as would not fail to make many of them renowned and matchless men. At the same time, some other hour of the day, might be taught them the rules of arithmetic, and soon after the elements of geometry even playing, as the old manner was. After evening repast, till bed-time their thoughts will be best taken up in the easy grounds of religion, and the story of Scripture. The next step would be to the authors on *agriculture, Cato, Varro, and Columella,* for the matter is most easy, and if the language be difficult, so much the better, it is not a difficulty above their years. And here will be an occasion of inciting and enabling them hereafter to improve the tillage of their country, to recover the bad soil, and to remedy the waste that is made of good; for this was one of *Hercules'* praises. Ere half these authors be read (which will soon be with plying hard, and daily) they can not choose but be masters of any ordinary prose. So that it will be the reasonable for them to learn in any modern author, the use of the globes, and all the maps; first with the old names, and then with the new: or they might be then capable to read any compendious method of natural philosophy. And at the same time might be entering into the Greek tongue, after the same manner as was before prescribed in the Latin; whereby the difficulties of grammar being soon overcome, all the historical physiology of *Aristotle* and *Theophrastus* are open before them, and as I may say, under contribution. The like access will be to *Vitruvius,* to *Seneca's* natural questions, to *Mela, Celsus, Pliny,* or *Solinus.* And having thus passed the principles of *arithmetic, geometry, astronomy,* and *geography* with a general compact of physics, they may descend in *mathematics* to the instrumental science of *trigonometry* and from thence to fortification, architecture, engineering, or navigation. And in natural philosophy they may proceed leisurely from the history of meteors, minerals, plants and living creatures as far as anatomy. Then also in course might be read to them out of some not tedious writer the institution of physics; that they may know the tempers, the humors, the seasons, and how to manage a crudity; which he who can wisely and timely do, is not only a great physician to himself, and to his friends, but also may at some time or other, save an army by this frugal and expenseless means only; and not let the healthy and stout bodies of young men rot away under him for want of this discipline; which is a great pity, and no less a shame to the commander. To set forward all these proceedings in nature and mathematics, what hinders, but that they may procure, as often as shall be needful, the helpful experiences of hunters, fowlers, fishermen, shepherds, gardeners, apothecaries; and in the other sciences, architects, engineers, mariners, anatomists; who doubtless would be ready some for reward, and some to favor such a hopeful seminary. And this will give them such a real tincture of natural knowledge, as they shall never forget, but daily augment with delight. Then also those poets which are now counted most hard, will be both facile and pleasant, *Orpheus, Hesiod, Theocritus, Aratus, Nicander, Oppian, Dionysius,* and in Latin *Lucretius, Manilius,* and the rural part of *Virgil.*

By this time, years and good general precepts will have furnished them more distinctly with that act of reason which in *ethics* is called *proairesis* that they may with some judgment contemplate upon moral good and evil. Then will be required a special reenforcement of constant and sound indoctrinating to set them right and firm, instructing them more amply in the knowledge of virtue and the hatred of vice: while their young and pliant affections are led through all the moral works of *Plato, Xenophon, Cicero, Plutarch, Laertius* and those *Locrian* remnants; but still to be reduced in their nightward studies wherewith they close the day's work, under the determinate sentence of *David* or *Solomon,* or the evangels and apostolic scriptures. Being perfect in the knowledge of personal duty, they may then begin the study of economics. And either now, or before this, they may have easily learned at any odd hour the *Italian tongue*. And soon after, but with wariness and good antidote, it would be wholesome enough to let them taste some choice comedies, Greek, Latin, or *Italian*: Those tragedies also that treat of household matters, as Trachiniae, Alcestis and the like. The next remove must be to the study of politics; to know the beginning, end, and reasons of political societies; that they may not in a dangerous fit of the commonwealth be such poor, shaken, uncertain reeds, of such a tottering conscience, as many of our great counselors have lately shown themselves, but steadfast pillars of the state. After this they are to dive into the ground of law and legal justice; delivered first, and with best warrant by *Moses;* and as far as human prudence can be trusted, in those extolled remains of Grecian lawgivers, *Lycurgus, Solon, Zaleucus, Charondas,* and thence to all the Roman *edicts* and tables with their *Justinian;* and so down to the *Saxon* and common laws of *England,* and the statutes. Sundays also and every evening may be now understandingly spent in the highest matters of *theology,* and church history ancient and modern: and ere this time the Hebrew tongue at a set hour might have been gained, that the Scriptures may be now read in their own original; whereto it would be no impossibility to add the *Chaldean,* and the *Syrian* dialect. When all these employments are well conquered, then will the choice histories, *heroic poems,* and *Attic* tragedies of stateliest and most regal argument, with all the famous political orations offer themselves; which if they were not only read; but some of them got by memory, and solemnly pronounced with right accent, and grace, as might be taught, would endow them even with the spirit and vigor of *Demosthenes* or *Cicero, Euripides,* or *Sophocles.* And now lastly will be the time to read with them those organic arts which enable men to discourse and write perspicuously, elegantly, and according to the fitted style of lofty, mean, or lowly. Logic therefore so much as is useful, is to be referred to this due place with all her well couched heads and topics, until to be time to open her contracted palm into a graceful and ornate rhetoric taught out of the rule of *Plato, Aristotle, Phalereus, Cicero, Hermogenes, Longinus.* To which poetry would be made subsequent, or indeed rather precedent, as being less subtle and fine, but more simple, sensuous and passionate. I mean not here the prosody of a verse, which they could not have hit on before among the rudiments of grammar; but that sublime art which in *Aristotle's Poetics,* in *Horace,* and the *Italian commentaries* of *Castelvetro, Tasso, Mazzoni,* and others, teaches what the laws are of a true *epic* poem, what of a *dramatic,* what of a *lyric,* what decorum is, which is the grand masterpiece to observe. This would make them soon perceive what despicable creatures our common rimers and playwriters be, and show them, what religious, what glorious and magnificent use might be made of poetry both in divine and human things. From hence and not till now will be the right season of forming them to be able writers and composers in every excellent matter, when they shall be thus fraught with an universal insight into things. Or whether they be to speak in Parliament or council, honor and attention would be waiting on their lips. There would then also appear in pulpits other visages, other gestures, and stuff otherwise wrought than what we now sit under, ofttimes to as great a trial of our patience as any other that they preach to us. These are the studies wherein our noble and our gentle youth ought to bestow their time in a disciplinary way from twelve to one and twenty; unless they rely more upon their ancestors dead, than upon themselves living. In which methodical course it is so supposed they must proceed by the steady pace of learning onward, as at convenient times for memories' sake to retire back into the middle ward, and sometimes into the rear of what they have been taught, until they have confirmed, and solidly united the whole body of their perfected knowledge, like the last embattling of a Roman legion. Now will be worth the seeing what exercises and recreations may best agree, and become these studies.

Their Exercise

The course of study hitherto briefly described, is, what I can

444

guess by reading, likest to those ancient and famous schools of *Pythagoras, Plato, Isocrates, Aristotle* and such others, out of which were bred up such a number of renowned philosophers, orators, historians, poets and princes all over *Greece, Italy,* and *Asia,* besides the flourishing studies of *Cyrene* and *Alexandria.* But herein it shall exceed them, and supply a defect as great as that which *Plato* noted in the commonwealth of *Sparta,* whereas that city trained up their youth most for war, and these in their Academies and *Lycaeum,* all for the gown, this institution of breeding which I here delineate, shall be equally good both for peace and war. Therefore about an hour and a half ere they eat at noon should be allowed them for exercise and due rest afterward: but the time for this may be enlarged at pleasure, according as their rising in the morning shall be early. The exercise which I commend first, is the exact use of their weapon, to guard and to strike safely with edge, or point; this will keep them healthy, nimble, strong, and well in breath, is also the likeliest means to make them grow large and tall, and to inspire them with a gallant and fearless courage, which being tempered with seasonable lectures and precepts to them of true fortitude and patience, will turn into a native and heroic valor, and make them hate the cowardise of doing wrong. They must be also practised in all the locks and grips of wrestling, wherein Englishmen were wont to excel, as need may often be in fight to tug or grapple, and to close. And this perhaps will be enough, wherein to prove and heat their single strength. The interim of unsweating themselves regularly, and convenient rest before meat may both with profit and delight be taken up in recreating and composing their travailed spirits with the solemn and divine harmonies of music heard or learned; either while the skilful *organist plies his grave* and fancied descant, in lofty fugues, or the whole symphony with artful and unimaginable touches adorn and grace the well studied chords of some choice composer, sometimes the lute, or soft organ stop waiting on elegant voices either to religious, martial or civil ditties; which if wise men and prophets be not extremely out, have a great power over dispositions and manners, to smooth and make them gentle from rustic harshness and distempered passions. The like also

445

would not be unexpedient after meat to assist and cherish Nature in her first concoction, and send their minds back to study in good tune and satisfaction. Where having followed it closer under vigilant eyes till about two hours before supper, they are by a sudden alarum or watchword, to be called out to their military motions, under sky or covert, according to the season, as was the Roman wont: first on foot, then as their age permits, on horseback, to all the art of cavalry; that having in sport, but with much exactness, and daily muster, served out the rudiments of their soldiership in all the skill of embattling, marching, encamping, fortifying, besieging and battering, with all the helps of ancient and modern stratagems, *tactics* and warlike maxims, they may as it were out of a long war come forth renowned and perfect commanders in the service of their country. They would not then, if they were trusted with fair and hopeful armies, suffer them for want of just and wise discipline to shed away from about them like sick feathers, though they never so oft supplied: they would not suffer their empty and unrecruitable colonels of twenty men in a company to quaff out, or convey, into secret hoards, the wages of a delusive list, and a miserable remnant: yet in the meanwhile to be overmastered with a score or two of drunkards, the only soldiery left about them, or else to comply with all rapines and violences. No certainly, if they knew aught of that knowledge that belongs to good men or good governors, they would not suffer these things. But to return to our own institute, besides these constant exercises at home, there is another opportunity of gaining experience to be won from pleasure itself abroad; in those vernal seasons of the year, when the air is calm and pleasant, it were an injury and sullenness against nature not to go out, and see her riches, and partake in her rejoicing with heaven and earth. I should not therefore be a persuader to them of studying much then, after two or three years that they have well laid their grounds, but to ride out in companies with prudent and staid guides, to all the quarters of the land: learning and observing all places of strength, all commodities of building and of soil, for towns and tillage, harbors and ports for trade. Sometimes taking sea as far as to our navy, to learn there also what they can

446

in the practical knowledge of sailing and of sea-fight. These ways would try all their peculiar gifts of nature, and if there were any secret excellence among them, would fetch it out, and give it fair opportunities to advance itself by, which could not but mightily redound to the good of this nation, and bring into fashion again those old admired virtues and excellencies, with far more advantage now in this purity of Christian knowledge. Nor shall we then need the monsieurs of *Paris,* to take our hopeful youth into their slight and prodigal custodies and send them over back again transformed into mimics, apes, and kickshaws. But if they desire to see other countries at three or four and twenty years of age, not to learn principles but to enlarge experience, and make wise observation, they will by that time be such as shall deserve the regard and honor of all men where they pass, and the society and friendship of those in all places who are best and most eminent. And perhaps then other nations will be glad to visit us for their breeding, or else to imitate us in their own country.

Now lastly for their diet there can not be much to say, save only that it would be best in the same house; for much time else would be lost abroad, and many ill habits got; and that it should be plain, healthful, and moderate I suppose is out of controversy. Thus Mr. *Hartlib,* you have a general view in writing, as your desire was, of that which at several times I had discoursed with you concerning the best and noblest way of education; not beginning as some have done from the cradle, which yet might be worth many considerations, if brevity had not been my scope, many other circumstances also I could have mentioned, but this to such as have the worth in them to make trial, for light and direction may be enough. Only I believe that this is not a bow for every man to shoot in that counts himself a teacher; but will require sinews almost equal to those which *Homer* gave *Ulysses,* yet I am withal persuaded that it may prove much more easy in the essay, than it now seems at distance, and much more illustrious: howbeit not more difficult than I imagine, and that imagination presents me with nothing but very happy and very possible according to best wishes; if God have so decreed, and this age have spirit and capacity enough to apprehend.

447

MICHEL DE MONTAIGNE

MICHEL DE MONTAIGNE (1533-1592). One of the most learned men of his time, Michel de Montaigne had the advantage of receiving the kind of education described in his *Essays*. Though the aristocratic emphasis of his writings now makes some passages seem outmoded, his work as a whole is suffused with fundamental insights which make them of great worth to all those interested in the conditions of human development. Francis Bacon and John Locke borrowed freely from his writings, and many of his views on educational theories and techniques — for instance, the emphasis on spontaneity and pleasurable assimilation of practical knowledge — seem quite modern.

Montaigne was born in Perigord on February 28, 1533, the son of a self-made man of prominence who filled, among other offices, that of mayor of Bordeaux. The father chose peasant godparents for Michel, the oldest of nine children, in order that he might not lose touch with the simple life of earthy people. Montaigne was awakened in the morning by the sound of chamber music rather than by the alarming noise of a gong. Corporal punishment was outlawed as injurious to his nervous system. He learned Latin from a German tutor who knew no French. By the remarkably early age of thirteen he had completed the course of instruction at the College of Guienne in Bordeaux. He studied law but lacked the inclination to take an active part in courtly service or martial affairs and, on reaching the age of thirty-eight, resolved to devote the rest of his life to study and meditation. After eight years of retirement he published the first two volumes of his *Essays* (1580), then ventured forth as a traveler. During his absence in Italy Montaigne was elected mayor of Bordeaux, an office which he accepted out of a sense of civic duty and filled effectively, though he still managed to find time to add to his *Essays*. Montaigne was the first to use the term "essay" to describe the literary form he helped to establish. He died on September 13, 1592.

The essay *Of the Education of Children* advocates liberal views of education and probably was more effective than any other single piece of writing in turning opinion against the harsh discipline and restricted course of study prevalent in his day. Written in the form of a letter addressed to his friend, the Countess of Gurson, it contains the essence of his thinking on the subject of education.

OF THE EDUCATION OF CHILDREN*

A friend of mine the other day told me that I should a little farther have extended my discourse on the education of children. Now, madam, if I had any sufficiency in this subject, I could not possibly better employ it than to present my best instructions to the little gentleman that threatens you shortly with a happy birth (for you are too generous to begin otherwise than with a male); for having had so great a hand in the treaty of your marriage, I have a certain particular right and interest in the greatness and prosperity of the issue that shall spring from it; besides that, your having had the best of my services so long in possession sufficiently obliges me to desire to honour and advantage of all wherein you shall be concerned. But, in truth, all I understand as to that particular is only this, that the greatest and most important difficulty of human science is the education of children. For as in agriculture, the husbandry that is to precede planting, as also planting itself, is certain, plain, and well known; but after that which is planted comes to life, there is a great deal more to be done, more art to be used, more care to be taken, and much more difficulty to cultivate and bring it to perfection: so it is with men; it is no hard matter to get children; but after they are born, then begins the trouble, solicitude, and care rightly to train, principle, and bring them up. The symptoms of their inclinations in that tender age are so obscure and the promises so uncertain and fallacious that it is very hard to establish any solid judgment or conjecture upon them. . . . Whence it comes to pass that, for not having chosen the right course, we often take very great pains and consume a good part of our times in training up children to things for which, by their natural constitution, they are totally unfit. In this difficulty, nevertheless, I am clearly of opinion that they ought to be elemented in the best

*Extract from Charles Cotton's translation.

449

and most advantageous studies, without taking too much notice of, or being too superstitious in, those light prognostics they give of themselves in their tender years, and to which Plato in his "Republic" gives, methinks, too much authority.

Madam, science is a very great ornament, and a thing of marvellous use, especially in persons raised to that degree of fortune in which you are. And, in truth, in persons of mean and low condition it cannot perform its true and genuine office, being naturally more prompt to assist in the conduct of war, in the government of peoples, in negotiating the leagues and friendships of princes and foreign nations, than in forming a syllogism in logic, in pleading a process in law, or in prescribing a dose of pills in physic. . . .

For a boy of quality, then, who pretends to letters not upon the account of profit (for so mean an object as that is unworthy of the grace and favour of the Muses, and moreover, in it a man directs his service to and depends upon others), nor so much for outward ornament, as for his own proper and peculiar use, and to furnish and enrich himself within, having rather a desire to come out an accomplished cavalier than a mere scholar or learned man; for such a one, I say, I would also have his friends solicitous to find him out a tutor who has rather a well-made than a well-filled head; seeking, indeed, both the one and the other, but rather of the two to prefer manners and judgment to mere learning, and that this man should exercise his charge after a new method.

'Tis the custom of pedagogues to be eternally thundering in their pupil's ears, as they were pouring into a funnel, whilst the business of the pupil is only to repeat what the others have said. Now I would have a tutor to correct this error, and that at the very first he should, according to the capacity he has to deal with, put it to the test, permitting his pupil himself to taste things and of himself to discern and choose them, sometimes opening the way to him, and sometimes leaving him to open it for himself; that is, I would not have him alone to invent and speak, but that he should also hear his pupil speak in turn. Socrates, and since him Arcesilaus, made first their scholars speak, and then they spoke to them. "The authority of those who teach, is very often an impediment to those who desire to learn." It is good to make him, like a young horse, trot before him, that he may judge of his going and how much he is to abate of his own speed to accommodate himself to the vigour and capacity of the other. For want of which due proportion we spoil all; which also to know how to adjust, and to keep within an exact and due measure, is one of the hardest things I know, and 'tis the effect of a high and well-tempered soul to know how to condescend to such puerile motions and to govern and direct them. I walk firmer and more secure up hill than down. . . .

To know by rote is no knowledge, and signifies no more but only to retain what one has intrusted to our memory. That which a man rightly knows and understands, he is the free disposer of at his own full liberty, without any regard to the author from whence he had it or fumbling over the leaves of his book. A mere bookish learning is a poor, paltry learning; it may serve for ornament, but there is yet no foundation to the opinion of Plato, who says that constancy, faith, and sincerity are the true philosophy, and the other sciences, that are directed to other ends, mere adulterate paint. I could wish that Paluel or Pompey, those two noted dancers of my time, could have taught us to cut capers by only seeing them do it, without stirring from our places, as these men pretend to inform the understanding without ever setting it to work; or that we could learn to ride, handle a pike, touch a lute, or sing without the trouble of practice, as these attempt to make us judge and speak well without exercising us in judging or speaking. Now in this initiation of our studies and in their progress, whatsoever presents itself before us is book sufficient; a roguish trick of a page, a sottish mistake of a servant, a jest at the table are so many new subjects.

And for this reason, conversation with men is of very great use and travel into foreign countries; not to bring back (as most of our young monsieurs do) an account only of how many paces Santa Rotonda is in circuit; or of the richness of Signora Livia's petticoats; or, as some others, how much Nero's face, in a statue in such an old ruin, is longer and broader than that made for him on some medal; but to be able chiefly to give an account of the

451

humours, manners, customs, and laws of those nations where he has been, and that we may whet and sharpen our wits by rubbing them against those of others. I would that a boy should be sent abroad very young, and first, so as to kill two birds with one stone, into those neighbouring nations whose language is most differing from our own, and to which, if it be not formed betimes, the tongue will grow too stiff to bend.

And also 'tis the general opinion of all that a child should not be brought up in his mother's lap. Mothers are too tender, and their natural affection is apt to make the most discreet of them all so overfond that they can neither find in their hearts to give them due correction for the faults they commit, nor suffer them to be inured to hardships and hazards, as they ought to be. They will not endure to see them return all dust and sweat from their exercise, to drink cold drink when they art hot, nor see them mount an unruly horse, nor take a foil in hand against a rude fencer, or so much as to discharge a carbine. And yet there is no remedy; whoever will breed a boy to be good for anything when he comes to be a man must by no means spare him when young and must very often transgress the rules of physic: — "Let him live in the open air, and ever in movement about something." It is not enough to fortify his soul; you are also to make his sinews strong; for the soul will be oppressed if not assisted by the members and would have too hard a task to discharge two offices alone. I know very well to my cost how much mine groans under the burden from being accommodated with a body so tender and indisposed as eternally leans and presses upon her; and often in reading perceive that our masters in their writings makes examples pass for magnanimity and fortitude of mind, which really are rather toughness of skin and hardness of bones; for I have seen men, women, and children naturally born of so hard and insensible a constitution of body that a sound cudgelling has been less to them than a flirt with a finger would have been to me, and that would neither cry out, wince, nor shrink for a good swinging beating; and when wrestlers counterfeit the philosophers in patience, 'tis rather strength of nerves than stoutness of heart.

Now to be inured to undergo labour is to be accustomed to endure pain: "Labour hardens us against pain." . . .

I have observed this vice, that instead of gathering observations from others we make it our whole business to lay ourselves upon them, and are more concerned how to expose and set out our own commodities than how to increase our stock by acquiring new. Silence, therefore, and modesty are very advantageous qualities in conversation. One should, therefore, train up this boy to be sparing and a husband of his knowledge when he has acquired it; and to forbear taking exceptions at or reproving every idle saying or ridiculous story that is said or told in his presence; for it is a very unbecoming rudeness to carp at everything that is not agreeable to our own palate. Let him be satisfied with correcting himself and not seem to condemn everything in another he would not do himself, nor dispute it as against common customs. "Let him be wise without ostentation, without envy." Let him be taught to be curious in the election and choice of his reasons, to abominate impertinence, and, consequently, to affect brevity; but, above all, let him be lessoned to acquiesce and submit to truth so soon as ever he shall discover it, whether in his opponent's argument or upon better consideration of his own, for he shall never be preferred to the chair for a mere clatter of words and syllogisms and is no further engaged to any argument whatever than as he shall in his own judgment approve it: nor yet is arguing a trade, where the liberty of recantation and getting off upon better thoughts are to be sold for ready money: "Neither is there any necessity upon him that he should defend all things that are recommended to and enjoined him." . . .

Let him examine every man's talent; a peasant, a bricklayer, a passenger: one may learn something from every one of these in their several capacities, and something will be picked out of their discourse whereof some use may be made at one time or another; nay, even the folly and impertinence of others will contribute to his instruction. By observing the graces and manners of all he sees, he will create to himself an emulation of the good and a contempt of the bad.

Let an honest curiosity be suggested to his fancy of being inquisitive after everything; whatever there is singular and rare near the place where he is, let him go and see it; a fine house, a noble fountain, an eminent man, the place where a battle has been anciently fought, the passages of Caesar and Charlemagne: "What country is bound in frost, what land is friable with heat, what wind serves fairest for Italy." Let him inquire into the manners, revenues, and alliances of princes, things in themselves very pleasant to learn, and very useful to know.

In this conversing with men, I mean also, and principally, those who only live in the records of history; he shall, by reading those books, converse with the great and heroic souls of the best ages. 'Tis an idle and vain study to those who make it so by doing it after a negligent manner, but to those who do it with care and observation, 'tis a study of inestimable fruit and value; and the only study, as Plato reports, that the Lacedaemonians reserved to themselves. What profit shall he not reap as to the business of men by reading the lives of Plutarch? But, withal, let my governor remember to what end his instructions are principally directed, and that he do not so much imprint in his pupil's memory the date of the ruin of Carthage as the manners of Hannibal and Scipio; nor so much where Marcellus died as why it was unworthy of his duty that he died there. Let him not teach him so much the narrative parts of history as to judge them. . . .

Human understanding is marvellously enlightened by daily conversation with men, for we are, otherwise, compressed and heaped up in ourselves and have our sight limited to the length of our own noses. One asking Socrates of what country he was, he did not make answer, of Athens, but of the world; he whose imagination was fuller and wider, embraced the whole world for his country, and extended his society and friendship to all mankind; not as we do, who look no further than our feet. When the vines of my village are nipped with the frost, my parish priest presently concludes that the indignation of God is gone out against all the human race and that the cannibals have already got the pip. Who is it that, seeing the havoc of these civil wars of ours, does not cry out that the machine of the world is near dissolution and that the day of judgment is at hand; without considering that many

454

worse things have been seen and that, in the meantime, people are very merry in a thousand other parts of the earth for all this? . . .

This great world which some do yet multiply as several species under one genus, is the mirror wherein we are to behold ourselves, to be able to know ourselves as we ought to do in the true bias. In short, I would have this to be the book my young gentleman should study with the most attention. So many humours, so many sects, so many judgments, opinions, laws, and customs teach us to judge aright of our own and inform our understanding to discover its imperfection and natural infirmity, which is no trivial speculation. So many mutations of states and kingdoms and so many turns and revolutions of public fortune will make us wise enough to make no great wonder of our own. So many great names, so many famous victories and conquests drowned and swallowed in oblivion render our hopes ridiculous of eternising our names by the taking of half-a-score of light horse, or a henroost, which only derives its memory from its ruin. The pride and arrogance of so many foreign pomps and ceremonies, the tumorous majesty of so many courts and grandeurs accustom and fortify our sight without astonishment or winking to behold the lustre of our own; so many millions of men, buried before us, encourage us not to fear to go seek such good company in the other world: and so of all the rest. Pythagoras was wont to say that our life resembles the great and populous assembly of the Olympic games, wherein some exercise the body, that they may carry away the glory of the prize, others bring merchandise to sell for profit; there are also some (and those none of the worst sort) who pursue no other advantage than only to look on, and consider how and why everything is done, and to be spectators of the lives of other men, thereby the better to judge of and regulate their own.

To examples may fitly be applied all the profitable discourses of philosophy, to which all human actions, as to their best rule, ought to be especially directed: a scholar shall be taught to know — "Learn what it is right to wish; what is the true use of coined money; how much it becomes us to give in liberality to our country and our dear relations; whom and what the Deity commanded thee to be; and in what part of the human system thou art placed; what we are and to what purpose engendered"; what it is to know, and what to be ignorant; what ought to be the end and design of study; what valor, temperance, and justice are; the difference betwixt ambition and avarice, servitude and subjection, licence and liberty; by what token a man may know true and solid contentment; how far death, affliction, and disgrace are to be apprehended: "And how you may shun or sustain every hardship"; by what secret springs we move and the reason of our various agitations and irresolutions: for, methinks, the first doctrine with which one should season his understanding ought to be that which regulates his manners and his sense; that teaches him to know himself and how both well to die and well to live. Amongst the liberal sciences, let us begin with that which makes us free; not that they do not all serve in some measure to the instruction and use of life, as all other things in some sort also do; but let us make choice of that which directly and professedly serves to that end. If we are once able to restrain the offices of human life within their just and natural limits, we shall find that most of the sciences in use are of no great use to us, and even in those that are, that there are many very unnecessary cavities and dilations which we had better let alone, and following Socrates' direction, limit the course of our studies to those things only where is a true and real utility: "Dare to be wise; begin: he who defers the hour of living well is like the clown, waiting till the river shall have flowed out; but the river still runs on, and will run on, with constant course, to ages without end." 'Tis a great foolery to teach our children — "What influence Pisces have, or the sign of angry Leo, or Capricorn laving in the Hesperian wave." . . .

After having taught him what will make him more wise and good, you may then entertain him with the elements of logic, physics, geometry, rhetoric, and the science which he shall then himself most incline to, his judgment being beforehand formed and fit to choose, he will quickly make his own. The way of instructing him ought to be sometimes by discourse and sometimes by reading; sometimes his governor shall put the author himself, which he shall think most proper for him, into his hands, and sometimes only the marrow and substance of it; and if himself be not conversant enough in books to turn to all the fine discourses the books contain for his purpose, there may some man of learning be joined to him that upon every occasion shall supply him with what he stands in need of, to furnish it to his pupil. And who can doubt but that this way of teaching is much more easy and natural than that of Gaza, in which the precepts are so intricate and so harsh and the words so vain, lean, and insignificant that there is no hold to be taken of them, nothing that quickens and elevates the wit and fancy, whereas here the mind has what to feed upon and to digest. This fruit, therefore, is not only without comparison much more fair and beautiful, but will also be much more early ripe. . . .

But the governor that I would have, that is such a one as knows it to be his duty to possess his pupil with as much or more affection than reverence to virtue, will be able to inform him that the poets have evermore accommodated themselves to the public humour, and make him sensible that the gods have planted more toil and sweat in the avenues of the cabinets of Venus than in those of Minerva. And when he shall once find him begin to apprehend and shall represent to him a Bradamante or an Angelica for a mistress, a natural, active, generous, and not a viragoish, but a manly beauty, in comparison of a soft, delicate, artificial, simpering, and affected form; the one in the habit of a heroic youth, wearing a glittering helmet, the other tricked up in curls and ribbons like a wanton minx; he will then look upon his own affection as brave and masculine when he shall choose quite contrary to that effeminate shepherd of Phrygia.

Such a tutor will make a pupil digest this new lesson, that the height and value of true virtue consists in the facility, utility, and pleasure of its exercise; so far from difficulty that boys as well as men and the innocent as well as the subtle may make it their own; it is by order, and not by force, that it is to be acquired. Socrates, her first minion, is so averse to all manner of violence, as totally to throw it aside, to slip into the more natural facility of her own progress. 'Tis the nursing mother of all human pleasures, who in rendering them just, renders them also pure and permanent; in interdicting those which she herself refuses, whets our desire to those that she allows; and, like a kind and liberal mother, abundantly allows all that nature requires, even to satiety, if not to lassitude: unless we mean to say that the regimen which stops the toper before he has drunk himself drunk, the glutton before he has eaten to a surfeit, and the lecher before he has got the pox is an enemy to pleasure. If the ordinary fortune fail, she does without it and forms another, wholly her own, not so fickle and unsteady as the other. She can be rich, be potent and wise, and knows how to lie upon soft perfumed beds: she loves life, beauty, glory, and health; but her proper and peculiar office is to know how to regulate the use of all these good things, and how to lose them without concern: an office much more noble than troublesome, and without which the whole course of life is unnatural, turbulent, and deformed, and there it is indeed, that men may justly represent those monsters upon rocks and precipices.

If this pupil shall happen to be of so contrary a disposition that he had rather hear a tale of a tub than the true narrative of some noble expedition or some wise and learned discourse; who at the beat of drum that excites the youthful ardour of his companions leaves that to follow another that calls to a morris dance or the bears; who would not wish, and find it more delightful and more excellent, to return all dust and sweat victorious from a battle than from tennis or from a ball, with the prize of those exercises; I see no other remedy but that he be bound prentice in some good town to learn to make minced pies, though he were the son of a duke; according to Plato's precept that children are to be placed out and disposed of, not according to the wealth, qualities, or condition of the father, but according to the faculties and the capacity of their own souls.

Since philosophy is that which instructs us to live, and that infancy has there its lessons as well as other ages, why is it not communicated to children betimes? "The clay is moist and soft: now, now make haste, and form the pitcher on the rapid wheel." They begin to teach us to live when we have almost done living.

A hundred students have got the pox before they have come to read Aristotle's lecture on temperance. Cicero said that though he should live two men's ages, he should never find leisure to study the lyric poets; and I find these sophisters yet more deplorably unprofitable. The boy we would breed has a great deal less time to spare; he owes but the first fifteen or sixteen years of his life to education; the remainder is due to action. Let us, therefore, employ that short time in necessary instruction. Away with the thorny subtleties of dialectics; they are abuses, things by which our lives can never be amended. Take the plain philosophical discourses, learn how rightly to choose, and then rightly to apply them; they are more easy to be understood than one of Boccaccio's novels; a child from nurse is much more capable of them than of learning to read or to write. Philosophy has discourses proper for childhood as well as for the decrepit age of men.

I am of Plutarch's mind that Aristotle did not so much trouble his great disciple with the knack of forming syllogisms or with the elements of geometry as with infusing into him good precepts concerning valor, prowess, magnanimity, temperance, and the contempt of fear; and with this ammunition sent him, whilst yet a boy, with no more than thirty thousand foot, four thousand horse, and but forty-two thousand crowns to subjugate the empire of the whole earth. For the other arts and sciences, he says, Alexander highly indeed commended their excellence and charm and had them in very great honour and esteem, but not ravished with them to that degree as to be tempted to affect the practice of them in his own person. "Young men and old men derive hence a certain end to the mind, and stores for miserable grey hairs."

Epicurus, in the beginning of his letter to Meniceus, says, "That neither the youngest should refuse to philosophize nor the oldest grow weary of it." Who does otherwise seems tacitly to imply that either the time of living happily is not yet come or that it is already past. And yet, for all that, I would not have this pupil of ours imprisoned and made a slave to his book; nor would I have him given up to the morosity and melancholic humour of a sour, ill-natured pedant; I would not have his spirit cowed and subdued by applying him to the rack and tormenting him, as some

459

do, fourteen or fifteen hours a day and so make a packhorse of him. Neither should I think it good when, by reason of a solitary and melancholic complexion, he is discovered to be overmuch addicted to his book, to nourish that humour in him; for that renders him unfit for civil conversation, and diverts him from better employments. And how many have I seen in my time totally brutified by an immoderate thirst after knowledge? Carneades was so besotted with it that he would not find time so much as to comb his head or to pare his nails. Neither would I have his generous manners spoiled and corrupted by the incivility and barbarism of those of another. The French wisdom was anciently turned into proverb: "Early, but of no continuance." And, in truth, we yet see that nothing can be more ingenious and pleasing than the children of France; but they ordinarily deceive the hope and expectation that have been conceived of them; and grown up to be men, have nothing extraordinary or worth taking notice of: I have heard men of good understanding say, these colleges of ours to which we send our young people (and of which we have but too many) make them such animals as they are.

But to our little monsieur, a closet, a garden, the table, his bed, solitude and company, morning and evening, all hours shall be the same, and all places to him a study; for philosophy, who, as the formatrix of judgment and manners, shall be his principal lesson, has that privilege to have a hand in everything. The orator Isocrates, being at a feast entreated to speak of his art, all the company were satisfied with and commended his answer: "It is not now a time," said he, "to do what I can do; and that which it is now time to do, I cannot do." For to make orations and rhetorical disputes in a company met together to laugh and make good cheer had been very unseasonable and improper, and as much might have been said of all the other sciences. But as to what concerns philosophy, that part of it at least that treats of man and of his offices and duties, it has been the common opinion of all wise men that, out of respect to the sweetness of her conversation, she is ever to be admitted in all sports and entertainments. And Plato, having invited her to his feast, we see after how gentle and obliging a manner, accommodated both to time and place, she entertained the company, though in a discourse of the highest and most important nature. "It profits poor and rich alike, but, neglected, equally hurts old and young." By this method of instruction, my young pupil will be much more and better employed than his fellows of the college are. But as the steps we take in walking to and fro in a gallery, though three times as many, do not tire a man so much as those we employ in a formal journey, so our lesson, as it were accidentally occurring without any set obligation of time or place and falling naturally into every action, will insensibly insinuate itself. By which means our very exercises and recreations, running, wrestling, music, dancing, hunting, riding, and fencing, will prove to be a good part of our study. I would have his outward fashion and mien and the disposition of his limbs formed at the same time with his mind. 'Tis not a soul, 'tis not a body that we are training up, but a man, and we ought not to divide him. And, as Plato says, we are not to fashion one without the other, but make them draw together like two horses harnessed to a coach. By which saying of his, does he not seem to allow more time for, and to take more care of, exercises for the body, and to hold that the mind, in a good proportion, does her business at the same time too?

As to the rest, this method of education ought to be carried on with a severe sweetness, quite contrary to the practice of our pedants, who, instead of tempting and alluring children to letters by apt and gentle ways, do in truth present nothing before them but rods and ferules, horror and cruelty. Away with this violence! away with this compulsion! than which, I certainly believe nothing more dulls and degenerates a well-descended nature. If you would have him apprehend shame and chastizement, do not harden him to them: inure him to heat and cold, to wind and sun, and to dangers that he ought to despise; wean him from all effeminacy and delicacy in clothes and lodging, eating and drinking; accustom him to everything, that he may not be a Sir Paris, a carpet-knight, but a sinewy, hardy, and vigorous young man. I have ever, from a child to the age wherein I now am, been of this opinion, and am still constant to it. But amongst other things, the

461

strict government of most of our colleges has evermore displeased me; peradventure they might have erred less perniciously on the indulgent side. 'Tis a real house of correction of imprisoned youth. They are made debauched by being punished before they are so. Do but come in when they are about their lesson and you shall hear nothing but the outcries of boys under execution, with the thundering noise of their pedagogues drunk with fury. A very pretty way this, to tempt these tender and timorous souls to love their book, with a furious countenance and a rod in hand! A cursed and pernicious way of proceeding! Besides what Quintilian has very well observed, that this imperious authority is often attended by very dangerous consequences, and particularly our way of chastising. How much more decent would it be to see their classes strewed with green leaves and fine flowers than with the bloody stumps of birch and willows? Were it left to my ordering, I should paint the school with the pictures of joy and gladness; Flora and the Graces, as the philosopher Speusippus did his. Where their profit is, let them there have their pleasure too. Such viands as are proper and wholesome for children should be sweetened with sugar, and such as are dangerous to them embittered with gall. 'Tis marvellous to see how solicitous Plato is in his *Laws* concerning the gaiety and diversion of the youth of his city, and how much and often he enlarges upon their races, sports, songs, leaps, and dances: of which, he says, that antiquity has given the ordering and patronage particularly to the gods themselves, to Apollo, Minerva, and the Muses. He insists long upon, and is very particular in, giving innumerable precepts for exercises; but as to the lettered sciences, says very little, and only seems particularly to recommend poetry upon the account of music.

All singularity in our manners and conditions is to be avoided as inconsistent with civil society. Who would not be astonished at so strange a constitution as that of Demophoon, steward to Alexander the Great, who sweated in the shade, and shivered in the sun? I have seen those who have run from the smell of a mellow apple with greater precipitation than from a harquebuss shot; others afraid of a mouse; others vomit at the sight of cream; others ready to swoon at the making of a feather bed; Germanicus

462

could neither endure the sight nor the crowing of a cock. I will not deny but that there may, peradventure, be some occult cause and natural aversion in these cases; but, in my opinion, a man might conquer it if he took it in time. Precept has in this wrought so effectually upon me, though not without some pains on my part, I confess, that beer excepted, my appetite accommodates itself indifferently to all sorts of diet.

Young bodies are supple; one should, therefore, in that age bend and ply them to all fashions and customs: and provided a man can contain the appetite and the will within their due limits, let a young man, in God's name, be rendered fit for all nations and all companies, even to debauchery and excess, if need be; that is, where he shall do it out of complacency to the customs of the place. Let him be able to do everything, but love to do nothing but what is good. . . .

The lad will not so much get his lesson by heart as he will practise it: he will repeat it in his actions. We shall discover if there be prudence in his exercises, if there be sincerity and justice in his deportment, if there be grace and judgment in his speaking, if there be constancy in his sickness, if there be modesty in his mirth, temperance in his pleasures, order in his domestic economy, indifference in his palate, whether what he eats or drinks be flesh or fish, wine or water. "Who considers his own discipline, not as a vain ostentation of science, but as a law and rule of life; and who obeys his own decrees, and the laws he has prescribed to himself." The conduct of our lives is the true mirror of our doctrine. Zeuxidamus, to one who asked him why the Lacedaemonians did not commit their constitutions of chivalry to writing and deliver them to their young men to read, made answer that it was because they would inure them to action and not amuse them with words. With such a one, after fifteen or sixteen years' study, compare one of our college Latinists, who has thrown away so much time in nothing but learning to speak. The world is nothing but babble; and I hardly ever yet saw that man who did not rather prate too much than speak too little. And yet half of our age is embezzled this way: we are kept four or five years to learn words only, and to tack them together into clauses; as many more

463

to form them into a long discourse, divided into four or five parts; and other five years at least to learn succinctly to mix and interweave them after a subtle and intricate manner: let us leave all this to those who make a profession of it. . . .

Let but our pupil be well furnished with things, words will follow but too fast; he will pull them after him if they do not voluntarily follow. I have observed some to make excuses that they cannot express themselves and pretend to have their fancies full of a great many very fine things which yet, for want of eloquence, they cannot utter; 'tis a mere shift, and nothing else. Will you know what I think of it? I think they are nothing but shadows of some imperfect images and conceptions that they know not what to make of within, nor consequently bring out. They do not yet themselves understand what they would be at, and if you but observe how they haggle and stammer upon the point of parturition, you will soon conclude that their labour is not to delivery, but about conception, and that they are but licking their formless embryo. For my part, I hold, and Socrates commands it, that whoever has in his mind a sprightly and clear imagination will express it well enough in one kind of tongue or another, and, if he be dumb, by signs. "Once a thing is conceived in the mind, the words to express it soon present themselves."

And as another as poetically says in his prose, "When things are once in the mind, the words offer themselves readily:" and this other, "The things themselves force words to express them." He knows nothing of ablative, conjunctive, substantive, or grammar, no more than his lackey or a fishwife of the Petit Pont; and yet these will give you a bellyful of talk, if you will hear them, and peradventure shall trip as little in their language as the best masters of art in France. He knows no rhetoric, nor how in a preface to bribe the benevolence of the courteous reader; neither does he care to know it. Indeed, all this fine decoration of painting is easily effaced by the lustre of a simple and blunt truth: these fine flourishes serve only to amuse the vulgar, of themselves incapable of more solid and nutritive diet. . . .

No doubt but Greek and Latin are very great ornaments, and of very great use, but we buy them too dear. I will here discover one way, which has been experimented in my own person, by which they are to be had better cheap, and such may make use of it as will. My late father, having made the most precise inquiry that any man could possibly make amongst men of the greatest learning and judgment, of an exact method of education, was by them cautioned of this inconvenience then in use, and made to believe that the tedious time we applied to the learning of the tongues of them who had them for nothing was the sole cause we could not arrive to the grandeur of soul and perfection of knowledge of the ancient Greeks and Romans. I do not, however, believe that to be the only cause. However, the expedient my father found out for this was that in my infancy, and before I began to speak, he committed me to the care of a German, who since died a famous physician in France, totally ignorant of our language, but very fluent, and a great critic in Latin. This man, whom he had fetched out of his own country, and whom he entertained with a great salary for this only end, had me continually with him: to him there were also joined two others, of inferior learning, to attend me and to relieve him; who all of them spoke to me in no other language but Latin. As to the rest of his family, it was an inviolable rule that neither himself, nor my mother, man nor maid, should speak anything in my company but such Latin words as every one had learned only to gabble with me. It is not to be imagined how great an advantage this proved to the whole family; my father and my mother by this means learned Latin enough to understand it perfectly well and to speak it to such a degree as was sufficient for any necessary use; as also those of the servants did who were most frequently with me. In short we Latined it at such a rate, that it overflowed to all the neighbouring villages, where there yet remain, that have established themselves by custom, several Latin appellations of artisans and their tools. As for what concerns myself, I was above six years of age before I understood either French or Perigordin, any more than Arabic; and without art, book, grammar, or precept, whipping, or the expense of a tear, I had, by that time, learned to speak as pure Latin as my master himself, for I had no means of mixing it up with any other. . . .

As to Greek, of which I have but a mere smattering, my father also designed to have it taught me by a device, but a new one, and by way of sport; tossing our declensions to and fro, after the manner of those who, by certain games at tables and chess, learn geometry and arithmetic. For he, amongst other rules, had been advised to make me relish science and duty by an unforced will and of my own voluntary motion and to educate my soul in all liberty and delight without any severity or constraint; which he was an observer of to such a degree, even of superstition, if I may say so, that some being of opinion that it troubles and disturbs the brains of children suddenly to wake them in the morning and to snatch them violently and over-hastily from sleep (wherein they are much more profoundly involved than we), he caused me to be wakened by the sound of some musical instrument and was never unprovided of a musician for that purpose. By this example you may judge of the rest, this alone being sufficient to recommend both the prudence and the affection of so good a father, who is not to be blamed if he did not reap fruits answerable to so exquisite a culture. Of this, two things were the cause: first, a sterile and improper soil; for, though I was a strong and healthful constitution, and of a disposition tolerably sweet and tractable, yet I was, withal, so heavy, idle, and indisposed that they could not rouse me from my sloth, not even to get me out to play. What I saw, I saw clearly enough, and under this heavy complexion nourished a bold imagination and opinions above my age. I had a slow wit, that would go no faster than it was led; a tardy understanding, a languishing invention, and, above all, incredible defect of memory; so that it is no wonder if from all these nothing considerable could be extracted. Secondly, like those who, impatient of a long and steady cure, submit to all sorts of prescriptions and recipes, the good man being extremely timorous of any way failing in a thing he had so wholly set his heart upon, suffered himself at last to be overruled by the common opinions, which always follow their leader as a flight of cranes, and complying with the method of the time, having no more those persons he had brought out of Italy and who had given him the first model of education about him, he sent me at six years of age to the College of Guienne, at that time the best and most flourishing in France. And there it was not possible to add anything to the care he had to provide me the most able tutors, with all other circumstances of education, reserving also several particular rules contrary to the college practice; but so it was, that with all these precautions it was a college still. My Latin immediately grew corrupt, of which also by discontinuance I have since lost all manner of use; so that this new way of education served me to no other end than only at my first coming to prefer me to the first forms; for at thirteen years old, that I came out of the college, I had run through my whole course (as they call it), and in truth, without any manner of advantage that I can honestly brag of in all this time. . . .

To return to my subject, there is nothing like alluring the appetite and affections; otherwise you make nothing but so many asses laden with books; by dint of the lash, you give them their pocketful of learning to keep; whereas, to do well, you should not only lodge it with them, but make them espouse it.

MONTESQUIEU

MONTESQUIEU (1689-1755). Charles Louis de Secondat, Baron de la Brède de Montesquieu, born into a noble family at the chateau La Brède on January 18, 1689, did not live to see his great work on *The Spirit of Laws* become a veritable textbook of the American revolutionaries. He died at Paris on February 10, 1755, but his fame continued long after his death, and for more than a century he was the guiding spirit of reformers not only in France but abroad.

He received an excellent education designed to prepare him for the family traditional profession, but he soon tired of his legal work and turned to study, travel and writing. He achieved great fame and opened the wide field of the philosophy of history with his work on the grandeur and decline of Rome (*Considerations sur les causes de la grandeur et de la decadence des Romains,* 1734). Continuing his original researches for a still greater work, he became the most eminent literary man of France with the publication, in 1748, of *The Spirit of Laws,* generally conceded to be the outstanding political work of the eighteenth century and the most original work of its time.

In the selection that follows, Montesquieu's remarks on education should be considered in their context. Abandoning the traditional division of governments into aristocracy and democracy, Montesquieu assigns an animating principle to each of three forms of government identified through his analysis: the republic, based on virtue; the monarchy, based on honor; and despotism, based on fear. Also important in assessing his ideas on education is his celebrated doctrine of the political influence of climate, for he insists that climate and many other factors influence the intellectual outlook and requirements of society. Like Thomas Jefferson, he asserts that "it is in a republican government that the whole power of education is required."

THE LAWS OF EDUCATION*

1. *Of the Laws of Education*. The laws of education are the first impressions we receive; and as they prepare us for civil life, every private family ought to be governed by the plan of that great household which comprehends them all.

If the people in general have a principle, their constituent parts, that is, the several families, will have one also. The laws of education will be therefore different in each species of government: in monarchies they will have honour for their object; in republics, virtue; in despotic governments, fear.

2. *Of Education in Monarchies*. In monarchies the principal branch of education is not taught in colleges or academies. It commences, in some measure, at our setting out in the world; for this is the school of what we call honour, that universal preceptor which ought everywhere to be our guide.

Here it is that we constantly hear three rules or maxims, viz., that we should have a certain nobleness in our virtues, a kind of frankness in our morals, and a particular politeness in our behaviour.

The virtues we are here taught are less what we owe to others than to ourselves; they are not so much what draws us towards society, as what distinguishes us from our fellow-citizens.

Here the actions of men are judged, not as virtuous, but as shining; not as just, but as great; not as reasonable, but as extraordinary. . . .

Honour allows of gallantry when united with the idea of sensible affection, or with that of conquest; this is the reason why we never meet with so strict a purity of morals in monarchies as in republican governments.

*From Thomas Nugent's translation of *The Spirit of Laws* (1748), Book IV: "That the Laws of Education Ought to Be in Relation to the Principles of Government." Reprinted in the Harvard Classics.

It allows of cunning and craft, when joined with the notion of greatness of soul or importance of affairs; as, for instance, in politics, with finesses of which it is far from being offended.

It does not forbid adulation, save when separated from the idea of a large fortune, and connected only with the sense of our mean condition.

With regard to morals, I have observed that the education of monarchies ought to admit of a certain frankness and open carriage. Truth, therefore, in conversation is here a necessary point. But is it for the sake of truth? By no means. Truth is requisite only because a person habituated to veracity has an air of boldness and freedom. And indeed a man of this stamp seems to lay a stress only on the things themselves, not on the manner in which they are received.

Hence it is that in proportion as this kind of frankness is commended, that of the common people is despised, which has nothing but truth and simplicity for its object.

In fine, the education of monarchies requires a certain politeness of behavior. Man, a sociable animal, is formed to please in society; and a person that would break through the rules of decency, so as to shock those he conversed with, would lose the public esteem, and become incapable of doing any good.

But politeness, generally speaking, does not derive its origin from so pure a source. It arises from a desire of distinguishing ourselves. It is pride that renders us polite; we are flattered with being taken notice of for behaviour that shows we are not of a mean condition, and that we have not been bred with those who in all ages are considered the scum of the people.

Politeness, in monarchies, is naturalised at court. One man excessively great renders everybody else little. Hence that regard which is paid to our fellow-subjects; hence that politeness, equally pleasing to those by whom, as to those towards whom, it is practised, because it gives people to understand that a person actually belongs, or at least deserves to belong, to the court.

A courtly air consists in quitting a real for borrowed greatness. The latter pleases the courtier more than the former. It inspires him with a certain disdainful modesty, which shows itself externally, but whose pride insensibly diminishes in proportion to its distance from the source of this greatness.

At court we find a delicacy of taste in everything — a delicacy arising from the constant use of the superfluities of life, from the variety, and especially the satiety, of pleasures, from the multiplicity and even confusion of fancies, which, if they are but agreeable, are sure of being well received.

These are the things which properly fall within the province of education, in order to form what we call a man of honour, a man possessed of all the qualities and virtues requisite in this kind of government.

Here it is that honour interferes with everything, mixing even with people's manner of thinking, and directing their very principles.

To this whimsical honour it is owing that the virtues are only just what it pleases; it adds rules of its own invention to everything prescribed to us; it extends or limits our duties according to its own fancy, whether they proceed from religion, politics, or morality.

There is nothing so strongly inculcated in monarchies, by the laws, by religion and honour, as submission to the prince's will; but this very honour tells us that the prince never ought to command a dishonourable action, because this would render us incapable of serving him.

Crillon refused to assassinate the Duke of Guise, but offered to fight him. After the massacre of St. Bartholomew, Charles IX, having sent orders to the governors in the several provinces for the Huguenots to be murdered, Viscount Dorte, who commanded at Bayonne, wrote thus to the king: "Sire, among the inhabitants of this town, and your majesty's troops, I could not find so much as one executioner; they are honest citizens and brave soldiers. We jointly, therefore, beseech your majesty to command our arms and lives in things that are practicable." This great and generous soul looked upon a base action as a thing impossible.

There is nothing that honour more strongly recommends to the nobility than to serve their prince in a military capacity. And, indeed, this is their favourite profession, because its dangers, its successes, and even its miscarriages are the road to grandeur. Yet

471

this very law of its own making honour chooses to explain: and in case of any affront, it requires or permits us to retire.

It insists also that we should be at liberty either to seek or to reject employments, a liberty which it prefers even to an ample fortune.

Honour therefore has its supreme laws, to which education is obliged to conform. The chief of these are that we are permitted to set a value upon our fortune, but are absolutely forbidden to set any upon our lives.

The second is that, when we are raised to a post or preferment, we should never do or permit anything which may seem to imply that we look upon ourselves as inferior to the rank we hold.

The third is that those things which honour forbids are more rigorously forbidden, when the laws do not concur in the prohibition; and those it commands are more strongly insisted upon, when they happen not to be commanded by law.

3. *Of Education in a Despotic Government.* As education in monarchies tends to raise and ennoble the mind, in despotic governments its only aim is to debase it. Here it must necessarily be servile; even in power such an education will be an advantage, because every tyrant is at the same time a slave.

Excessive obedience supposes ignorance in the person that obeys: the same it supposes in him that commands, for he has no occasion to deliberate, to doubt, to reason; he has only to will.

In despotic states, each house is a separate government. As education, therefore, consists chiefly in social converse, it must be here very much limited; all it does is to strike the heart with fear, and to imprint on the understanding a very simple notion of a few principles of religion. Learning here proves dangerous, emulation fatal; and as to virtue, Aristotle cannot think that there is any one virtue belonging to slaves; if so, education in despotic countries is confined within a very narrow compass.

Here, therefore, education is in some measure needless: to give something, one must take away everything, and begin with making a bad subject in order to make a good slave.

For why should education take pains in forming a good citizen, only to make him share in the public misery? If he loves his country, he will strive to relax the springs of government; if he miscarries he will be undone; if he succeeds, he must expose himself, the prince, and his country to ruin.

4. Difference between the Effects of Ancient and Modern Education. Most of the ancients lived under governments that had virtue for their principle; and when this was in full vigour they performed actions unusual in our times, and at which our narrow minds are astonished.

Another advantage their education possessed over ours was that it never could be effaced by contrary impressions. Epaminondas, the last year of his life, said, heard, beheld, and performed the very same things as at the age in which he received the first principles of his education.

In our days we receive three different or contrary educations, namely, of our parents, of our masters, and of the world. What we learn in the latter effaces all the ideas of the former. This, in some measure, arises from the contrast we experience between our religious and worldly engagements, a thing unknown to the ancients.

5. Of Education in a Republican Government. It is in a republican government that the whole power of education is required. The fear of despotic governments naturally arises of itself amidst threats and punishments; the honour of monarchies is favoured by the passions, and favours them in its turn; but virtue is a self-renunciation, which is ever arduous and painful.

This virtue may be defined as the love of the laws and of our country. As such love requires a constant preference of public to private interest, it is the source of all private virtues; for they are nothing more than this very preference itself.

This love is peculiar to democracies. In these alone the government is entrusted to private citizens. Now a government is like everything else: to preserve it we must love it.

Has it ever been known that kings were not fond of monarchy, or that despotic princes hated arbitrary power?

Everything therefore depends on establishing this love in a re-

473

public; and to inspire it ought to be the principal business of education: but the surest way of instilling it into children is for parents to set them an example.

People have it generally in their power to communicate their ideas to their children; but they are still better able to transfuse their passions.

If it happens otherwise, it is because the impressions made at home are effaced by those they have received abroad.

It is not the young people that degenerate; they are not spoiled till those of maturer age are already sunk into corruption.

6. *Of some Institutions among the Greeks.* The ancient Greeks, convinced of the necessity that people who live under a popular government should be trained up to virtue, made very singular institutions in order to inspire it. Upon seeing in the life of Lycurgus the laws that legislator gave to the Lacedaemonians, I imagine I am reading the history of the Sevarambes. The laws of Crete were the model of those of Sparta; and those of Plato reformed them.

Let us reflect here a little on the extensive genius with which those legislators must have been endowed, to perceive that by striking at received customs, and by confounding all manner of virtues, they should display their wisdom to the universe. Lycurgus, by blending theft with the spirit of justice, the hardest servitude with excess of liberty, the most rigid sentiments with the greatest moderation, gave stability to his city. He seemed to deprive her of all resources, such as arts, commerce, money, and walls; ambition prevailed among the citizens without hopes of improving their fortune; they had natural sentiments without the tie of a son, husband, or father; and chastity was stripped even of modesty and shame. This was the road that led Sparta to grandeur and glory; and so infallible were these institutions, that it signified nothing to gain a victory over that republic without subverting her polity.

By these laws Crete and Laconia were governed. Sparta was the last that fell a prey to the Macedonians, and Crete to the Romans. The Samnites had the same institutions, which furnished those very Romans with the subject of four-and-twenty triumphs.

A character so extraordinary in the institutions of Greece has shown itself lately in the dregs and corruptions of modern times. A very honest legislator has formed a people to whom probity seems as natural as bravery to the Spartans. Mr. Penn is a real Lycurgus: and though the former made peace his principal aim, as the latter did war, yet they resemble one another in the singular way of living to which they reduced their people, in the ascendant they had over free men, in the prejudices they overcame, and in the passions which they subdued.

Another example we have from Paraguay. This has been the subject of an invidious charge against a society that considers the pleasure of commanding as the only happiness in life: but it will be ever a glorious undertaking to render a government subservient to human happiness.

It is glorious indeed for this society to have been the first in pointing out to those countries the idea of religion joined with that of humanity. By repairing the devastations of the Spaniards, she has begun to heal one of the most dangerous wounds that the human species ever received.

An exquisite sensibility to whatever she distinguishes by the name of honour, joined to her zeal for a religion which is far more humbling in respect to those who receive than to those who preach its doctrines, has set her upon vast undertakings, which she has accomplished with success. She has drawn wild people from their woods, secured them a maintenance, and clothed their nakedness; and had she only by this step improved the industry of mankind, it would have been sufficient to eternise her fame.

They who shall attempt hereafter to introduce like institutions must establish the community of goods as prescribed in Plato's republic; that high respect he required for the gods; that separation from strangers, for the preservation of morals; and an extensive commerce carried on by the community, and not by private citizens: they must give our arts without our luxury, and our wants without our desires.

They must proscribe money, the effects of which are to swell people's fortunes beyond the bounds prescribed by nature; to learn to preserve for no purpose what has been idly hoarded up; to multiply without end our desires; and to supply the sterility of nature, from whom we have received very scanty means of inflaming our passions, and of corrupting each other.

"The Epidamnians, perceiving their morals depraved by conversing with barbarians, chose a magistrate for making all contracts and sales in the name and behalf of the city." Commerce then does not corrupt the constitution, and the constitution does not deprive society of the advantages of commerce.

7. *In what Cases these singular Institutions may be of Service.* Institutions of this kind may be proper in republics, because they have virtue for their principle; but to excite men to honour in monarchies, or to inspire fear in despotic governments, less trouble is necessary.

Besides, they can take place but in a small state, in which there is a possibility of general education, and of training up the body of the people like a single family.

The laws of Minos, of Lycurgus, and of Plato suppose a particular attention and care, which the citizens ought to have over one another's conduct. But an attention of this kind cannot be expected in the confusion and multitude of affairs in which a large nation is entangled.

In institutions of this kind, money, as we have above observed, must be banished. But in great societies, the multiplicity, variety, embarrassment, and importance of affairs, as well as the facility of purchasing, and the slowness of exchange, require a common measure. In order to support or extend our power, we must be possessed of the means to which, by the unanimous consent of mankind, this power is annexed.

8. *Explanation of a Paradox of the Ancients in respect to Manners.* That judicious writer, Polybius, informs us that music was necessary to soften the manners of the Arcadians, who lived in a cold, gloomy country; that the inhabitants of Cynete, who slighted music, were the cruellest of all the Greeks, and that no other town was so immersed in luxury and debauchery. Plato is not afraid to affirm that there is no possibility of making a change in music without altering the frame of government. Aristotle, who seems to have written his *Politics* only in order to contradict Plato, agrees with him, notwithstanding, in regard to the power and influence

of music over the manners of the people. This was also the opinion of Theophrastus, of Plutarch, and of all the ancients — an opinion grounded on mature reflection; being one of the principles of their polity. Thus it was they enacted laws, and thus they required that cities should be governed.

This I fancy must be explained in the following manner. It is observable that in the cities of Greece, especially those whose principal object was war, all lucrative arts and professions were considered unworthy of a freeman. "Most arts," says Xenophon, "corrupt and enervate the bodies of those that exercise them; they oblige them to sit in the shade, or near the fire. They can find no leisure, either for their friends or for the republic." It was only by the corruption of some democracies that artisans became freemen. This we learn from Aristotle, who maintains that a well-regulated republic will never give them the right and freedom of the city.

Agriculture was likewise a servile profession, and generally practised by the inhabitants of conquered countries, such as the Helotes among the Lacedaemonians, the Periecians among the Cretans, the Penestes among the Thessalians, and other conquered people in other republics.

In fine, every kind of low commerce was infamous among the Greeks; as it obliged a citizen to serve and wait on a slave, on a lodger, or a stranger. This was a notion that clashed with the spirit of Greek liberty; hence Plato in his *Laws* orders a citizen to be punished if he attempts to concern himself with trade.

Thus in the Greek republics the magistrates were extremely embarrassed. They would not have the citizens apply themselves to trade, to agriculture, or to the arts, and yet they would not have them idle. They found, therefore, employment for them in gymnastic and military exercises; and none else were allowed by their institution. Hence the Greeks must be considered as a society of wrestlers and boxers. Now, these exercises having a natural tendency to render people hardy and fierce, there was a necessity for tempering them with others that might soften their manners. For this purpose, music, which influences the mind by means of the corporeal organs, was extremely proper. It is a kind of medium

477

between manly exercises, which harden the body, and speculative sciences, which are apt to render us unsociable and sour. It cannot be said that music inspired virtue, for this would be inconceivable: but it prevented the effects of a savage institution, and enabled the soul to have such a share in the education as it could never have had without the assistance of harmony.

Let us suppose among ourselves a society of men so passionately fond of hunting as to make it their sole employment; they would doubtless contract thereby a kind of rusticity and fierceness. But if they happen to imbibe a taste for music, we should quickly perceive a sensible difference in their customs and manners. In short, the exercises used by the Greeks could raise but one kind of passions, viz., fierceness, indignation, and cruelty. But music excites all these; and is likewise able to inspire the soul with a sense of pity, lenity, tenderness, and love. Our moral writers, who declaim so vehemently against the stage, sufficiently demonstrate the power of music over the mind.

If the society above mentioned were to have no other music than that of drums, and the sound of the trumpet, would it not be more difficult to accomplish this end than by the more melting tones of softer harmony? The ancients were therefore in the right when, under particular circumstances, they preferred one mode to another in regard to manners.

But some will ask, why should music be pitched upon as preferable to any other entertainment? It is because of all sensible pleasures there is none that less corrupts the soul. We blush to read in Plutarch that the Thebans, in order to soften the manners of their youth, authorised by law a passion which ought to be proscribed by all nations.

478

MARIA MONTESSORI

MARIA MONTESSORI (1870-1952). Born in Chiaravalle on August 31, 1870, Maria Montessori was the first Italian woman to earn a medical degree. She is also credited by Henry W. Holmes, who wrote the introduction to *The Montessori Method,* with being the first woman to elaborate an original educational system.

While practicing medicine at the psychiatric clinic of the University of Rome, Dr. Montessori became interested in the education of children. After founding the Orthophrenic School for feeble-minded and defective children in Rome, (1898), she was able to apply the methods and principles of Edouard Séquin with such success that idiot children under her tutelage passed the state examinations in reading and writing. Turning her attention to another field, she proved that her principles were equally valuable when applied to the teaching of normal children. Her *Casa dei Bambini* ("children's house") in Rome became the prototype of many schools in Europe and America based on the "Montessori Method." She was appointed state inspector of schools in Italy, and before her death on May 6, 1952, had taught and supervised courses in Spain, India, England, and Holland.

The fundamental idea of Dr. Montessori's system is that even tiny children should be allowed freedom of movement, provided their behavior does not violate good manners and social order and harmony, that children are eager to educate themselves under appropriate conditions realized through self-discipline, and that their remarkable powers of concentration only require release (she found that young children are happiest when learning and that eight-year-olds learn algebra faster than adolescents). An equally important contribution to pedagogy is the "educational apparatus" or "didactic material" to engage the learner's interest and attention. To her own amazement, the founder of progressive education — who amazed Roman society by going about the streets unchaperoned as a girl — discovered that young children would repeat exercises with an air of complete absorption generally associated only with men of genius.

The following selections are from *The Montessori Method,* the first of Dr. Montessori's books to appear in English. In "Nature in Education" she explains the five steps in the moral education of the child through nature study; in "Conclusions and Impressions" she summarizes her thinking on various aspects of the education of young children.

NATURE IN EDUCATION*

We must prepare man, who is one among the living creatures and therefore belongs to nature, for social life, because social life being his own peculiar work, must also correspond to the manifestation of his natural activity. . . .

To soften this transition in education by giving a large part of the educative work to nature itself is as necessary as it is not to snatch the little child suddenly and violently from its mother and to take him to school; and precisely this is done in the "Children's Houses," which are situated within the tenements where the parents live, where the cry of the child reaches the mother and the mother's voice answers it. . . .

But in all this progress of modern child education, we have not freed ourselves from the prejudice which denies children spiritual expression and spiritual needs, which makes us consider them only as amiable vegetating bodies to be cared for, kissed, and set in motion. . . .

But if for the physical life it is necessary to have the child exposed to the vivifying forces of nature, it is also necessary for his psychical life to place the soul of the child in contact with creation, in order that he may lay up for himself treasure from the directly educating forces of living nature. The method for arriving at this end is to set the child at agricultural labour, guiding him to the cultivation of plants and animals, and so to the intelligent contemplation of nature. . . . In this method, which is a progressive ascent, several gradations can be distinguished: I mention here the principal ones:

First. The child is initiated into observation of the phenomena of life. He stands with respect to the plants and animals in rela-

*This extract and the selection which follows are from *The Montessori Method,* translated by Anne E. George (London: William Heinemann, 1912).

tions analogous to those in which the *observing* teacher stands towards him. Little by little, as interest and observation grow, his zealous care for the living creatures grows also, and in this way, the child can logically be brought to appreciate the care which the mother and the teacher take of him.

Second. The child is initiated into *foresight* by way of *auto-education;* when he knows that the life of the plants that have been sown depends upon his care in watering them, and that of the animals, upon his diligence in feeding them, without which the little plant dries up and the animals suffer hunger, the child becomes vigilant, as one who is beginning to feel a mission in life. Moreover, a voice quite different from that of his mother and his teacher calling him to his duties, is speaking here, exhorting him never to forget the task he has undertaken. It is the plaintive voice of the needy life which lives by his care. Between the child and the living creatures which he cultivates there is born a mysterious correspondence which induces the child to fulfil certain determinate acts without the intervention of the teacher, that is, leads him to an *auto-education.*

The rewards which the child reaps also remain between him and nature: one fine day after long patient care in carrying food and straw to the brooding pigeons, behold the little ones! behold a number of chickens peeping about the setting hen which yesterday sat motionless in her brooding place! behold one day the tender little rabbits in the hutch where formerly dwelt in solitude the pair of big rabbits to which he had not a few times lovingly carried the green vegetables left over in his mother's kitchen!

I have not yet been able to institute in Rome the breeding of animals, but in the "Children's Houses" at Milan there are several animals, among them a pair of pretty little white American fowl that live in a diminutive and elegant *chalet,* similar in construction to a Chinese pagoda: in front of it, a little piece of ground inclosed by a rampart is reserved for the pair. The little door of the *chalet* is locked at evening, and the children take care of it in turn. With what delight they go in the morning to unlock the door, to fetch water and straw, and with what care they watch during the day, and at evening lock the door after having made sure that the fowl lack nothing! The teacher informs me that among all the educative exercises this is the most welcome, and seems also the most important of all. Many a time when the children are tranquilly occupied in tasks, each at the work he prefers, one, two, or three, get up silently, and go out to cast a glance at the animals to see if they need care. Often it happens that a child absents himself for a long time and the teacher surprises him watching enchantedly the fish gliding ruddy and resplendent in the sunlight in the waters of the fountain.

One day I received from the teacher in Milan a letter in which she spoke to me with great enthusiasm of a truly wonderful piece of news. The little pigeons were hatched. For the children it was a great festival. They felt themselves to some extent the parents of these little ones, and no artificial reward which had flattered their vanity would ever have provoked such a truly fine emotion. Not less great are the joys which vegetable nature provides. In one of the "Children's Houses" at Rome, where there was no soil that could be cultivated, there have been arranged through the efforts of Signora Talamo, flower-pots all around the large terrace, and climbing plants near the walls. The children never forget to water the plants with their little watering-pots.

One day I found them seated on the ground, all in a circle, around a splendid red rose which had bloomed in the night; silent and calm, literally immersed in mute contemplation.

Third. The children are initiated into the virtue of *patience and into confident expectation,* which is a form of faith and of philosophy of life.

When the children put a seed into the ground, and wait until it fructifies, and see the first appearance of the shapeless plant, and wait for the growth and the transformations into flower and fruit, and see how some plants sprout sooner and some later, and how the deciduous plants have a rapid life, and the fruit-trees a slower growth, they end by acquiring a peaceful equilibrium of conscience, and absorb the first germs of that wisdom which so characterised the tillers of the soil in the time when they still kept their primitive simplicity.

Fourth. The children are inspired with a feeling for nature, which is maintained by the marvels of creation — that creation which *rewards* with a generosity not measured by the labour of those who help it to evolve the life of its creatures.

Even while at the work, a sort of correspondence arises between the child's soul and the lives which are developed under his care. The child loves naturally the manifestations of life: Mrs. Latter tells us how easily little ones are interested even in earthworms and in the movement of the larvae of insects in manure, without feeling that horror which we, who have grown up isolated from nature, experience towards certain animals. It is well then, to develop this feeling of trust and confidence in living creatures, which is, moreover, a form of love, and of union with the universe.

But what most develops a feeling of nature is the *cultivation* of the *living* things, because they by their natural development give back far more than they receive, and show something like infinity in their beauty and variety. When the child has cultivated the iris or the pansy, the rose or the hyacinth, has placed in the soil a seed or a bulb and periodically watered it, or has planted a fruit-bearing shrub, and the blossomed flower and the ripened fruit offer themselves as a *generous gift* of nature, a rich reward for a small effort; it seems almost as if nature were answering with her gifts to the feeling of desire, to the vigilant love of the cultivator, rather than striking a balance with his material efforts.

It will be quite different when the child has to gather the *material* fruits of his labour: motionless, uniform objects, which are consumed and dispersed rather than increased and multiplied.

The difference between the products of nature and those of industry, between divine products and human products — it is this that must be born spontaneously in the child's conscience, like the determination of a fact.

But at the same time, as the plant must give its fruit, so man must give his labour.

Fifth. The child follows the natural way of development of the human race. In short, such education makes the evolution of the individual harmonise with that of humanity. Man passed from the natural to the artificial state through agriculture: when he

483

discovered the secret of intensifying the production of the soil, he obtained the reward of civilisation.

The same path must be traversed by the child who is destined to become a civilised man.

The action of educative nature so understood is very practically accessible. Because, even if the vast stretch of ground and the large courtyard necessary for physical education are lacking, it will always be possible to find a few square yards of land that may be cultivated, or a little place where pigeons can make their nest, things sufficient for spiritual education. Even a pot of flowers at the window can, if necessary, fulfil the purpose.

In the first "Children's House" in Rome we have a vast court-yard, cultivated as a garden, where the children are free to run in the open air — and, besides, a long stretch of ground, which is planted on one side with trees, has a branching path in the middle, and on the opposite side, has broken ground for the cultivation of plants. This last, we have divided into so many portions, reserving one for each child.

While the smaller children run freely up and down the paths, or rest in the shade of the trees, the *possessors of the earth* (children from four years of age up), are sowing, or hoeing, watering or examining, the surface of the soil watching for the sprouting of plants. It is interesting to note the following fact: the little reservations of the children are placed along the wall of the tenement, in a spot formerly neglected because it leads to a blind road; the inhabitants of the house, therefore, had the habit of throwing from those windows every kind of offal, and at the beginning our garden was thus contaminated.

But, little by little, without any exhortation on our part, solely through the respect born in the people's mind for the children's labour, nothing more fell from the windows, except the loving glances and smiles of the mothers upon the soil which was the beloved possession of their little children.

In the "Children's Houses," the old-time teacher, who wore himself out maintaining discipline of immobility, and who wasted her breath in loud and continual discourse, has disappeared.

For this teacher we have substituted the *dialectic material,* which contains within itself the control of errors and which makes auto-education possible to each child. The teacher has thus become a *director* of the spontaneous work of the children. She is not a *passive* force, a *silent* presence.

The children are occupied each one in a different way, and the directress, watching them, can make psychological observations which, if collected in an orderly way and according to scientific standards, should do much toward the reconstruction of child psychology and the development of experimental psychology. I believe that I have by my method established the conditions necessary to the development of scientific pedagogy; and whoever adopts this method opens, in doing so, a laboratory of experimental pedagogy.

From such work, we must await the positive solution of all those pedagogical problems of which we talk to-day. For through such work there has already come the solution of some of these very questions: that of the liberty of the pupils; auto-education; the establishment of harmony between the work and activities of home life and school tasks, making both work together for the education of the child.

The problem of religious education, the importance of which we do not fully realise, should also be solved by positive pedagogy. If religion is born with civilisation, its roots must lie deep in human nature. We have had most beautiful proof of an instinctive love of knowledge in the child, who has too often been misjudged in that he has been considered addicted to meaningless play, and games void of thought. The child who left the game in his eagerness for knowledge, has revealed himself as a true son of that humanity which has been throughout centuries the creator of scientific and civil progress. We have belittled the son of man by giving him foolish and degrading toys, a world of idleness where he is suffocated by a badly conceived discipline. Now, in his liberty, the child should show us, as well, whether man is by nature a religious creature.

To deny, *a priori,* the religious sentiment in man, and to deprive humanity of the education of this sentiment, is to commit a pedagogical error similar to that of denying, *a priori,* to the child, the love of learning for learning's sake. This ignorant assumption led us to dominate the scholar, to subject him to a species of slavery, in order to render him apparently disciplined.

The fact that we assume that religious education is only adapted to the adult, may be akin to another profound error existing in education to-day, namely, that of overlooking the education of the senses at the very period when this education is possible. The life of the adult is practically an application of the senses to the gathering of sensations from the environment. A lack of preparation for this, often results in inadequacy in practical life, in that lack of poise which causes so many individuals to waste their energies in purposeless effort. Not to form a parallel between the education of the senses as a guide to practical life, and religious education as a guide to the moral life, but for the sake of illustration, let me call attention to how often we find inefficiency, instability, among irreligious persons, and how much precious individual power is miserably wasted.

How many men have had this experience! And when that spiritual awakening comes late, as it sometimes does, through the softening power of sorrow, the mind is unable to establish an equilibrium, because it has grown too much accustomed to a life deprived of spirituality. We see equally piteous cases of religious fanaticism, or we look upon intimate dramatic struggles between the heart, ever seeking its own safe and quiet port, and the mind that constantly draws it back to the sea of conflicting ideas and emotions, where peace is unknown. These are all psychological phenomena of the highest importance; they present, perhaps, the gravest of all our human problems. We Europeans are still filled with prejudices and hedged about with preconceptions in regard to these matters. We are very slaves of thought. We believe that liberty of conscience and of thought consists in denying certain sentimental beliefs, while liberty never can exist where one struggles to stifle some other thing, but only where unlimited expansion is granted; where life is left free and untrammelled. He who really does not believe, does not fear that which he does not believe, and does not combat that which for him does not exist. If he believes and fights, he then becomes an enemy to liberty.

In America, the great positive scientist, William James, who expounds the physiological theory of emotions, is also the man who illustrates the psychological importance of religious "conscience." We cannot know the future of the progress of thought: here, for example, in the "Children's House" the triumph of *discipline* through the conquest of liberty and independence marks the foundation of the progress which the future will see in the matter of pedagogical methods. To me it offers the greatest hope for human redemption through education.

Perhaps, in the same way, through the conquest of liberty of thought and of conscience, we are making our way toward a great religious triumph. Experience will show, and the psychological observations made along this line in the "Children's Houses" will undoubtedly be of the greatest interest.

This book of methods compiled by one person alone, must be followed by many others. It is my hope that, starting from the *individual study of the child* educated with our method, other educators will set forth the results of their experiments. These are the pedagogical books which await us in the future.

From the practical side of the school, we have with our methods the advantage of being able to teach in one room, children of very different ages. In our "Children's Houses" we have little ones of two years and a half, who cannot as yet make use of the most simple of the sense exercises, and children of five and a half who because of their development might easily pass into the third elementary. Each one of them perfects himself through his own powers, and goes forward guided by that inner force which distinguishes him as an individual.

One great advantage of such a method is that it will make instruction in the rural schools easier, and will be of great advantage in the schools in the small provincial towns where there

487

are few children, yet where all the various grades are represented. Such schools are not able to employ more than one teacher. Our experience shows that one directress may guide a group of children varying in development from little ones of three years old to the third elementary. Another great advantage lies in the extreme facility with which written language may be taught, making it possible to combat illiteracy and to cultivate the national tongue.

As to the teacher, she may remain for a whole day among children in the most varying stages of development, just as the mother remains in the house with children of all ages, without becoming tired.

The children work by themselves, and, in doing so, make a conquest of active discipline, and independence in all the acts of daily life, just as through daily conquests they progress in intellectual development. Directed by an intelligent teacher, who watches over their physical development as well as over their intellectual and moral progress, children are able with our methods to arrive at a splendid physical development, and, in addition to this, there unfolds within them, in all its perfection, the soul, which distinguishes the human being.

We have been mistaken in thinking that the natural education of children should be purely physical; the soul, too, has its nature, which it was intended to perfect in the spiritual life, — the dominating power of human existence throughout all time. Our methods take into consideration the spontaneous psychic development of the child, and help this in ways that observation and experience have shown us to be wise.

If physical care leads the child to take pleasure in bodily health, intellectual and moral care make possible for him the highest spiritual joy, and send him forward into a world where continual surprises and discoveries await him; not only in the external environment, but in the intimate recesses of his own soul.

It is through such pleasures as these that the ideal man grows, and only such pleasures are worthy of a place in the education of the infancy of humanity.

Our children are noticeably different from those others who have grown up within the grey walls of the common schools. Our little pupils have the serene and happy aspect and the frank and open friendliness of the person who feels himself to be master of his own actions. When they run to gather about our visitors, speaking to them with sweet frankness, extending their little hands with gentle gravity and well-bred cordiality, when they thank these visitors for the courtesy they have paid us in coming, the bright eyes and the happy voices make us feel that they are, indeed, unusual little men. When they display their work and their ability, in a confidential and simple way, it is almost as if they called for a maternal approbation from all those who watch them. Often, a little one will seat himself on the floor beside some visitor silently writing his name, and adding a gentle word of thanks. It is as if they wished to make the visitor feel the affectionate gratitude which is in their hearts.

When we see all these things and when, above all, we pass with these children from the busy activity of the schoolroom at work, into the absolute and profound silence which they have learned to enjoy so deeply, we are moved in spite of ourselves and feel that we have come in touch with the very souls of these little pupils.

The "Children's House" seems to exert a spiritual influence upon everyone. I have seen here, men of affairs, great politicians preoccupied with problems of trade and of state, cast off like an uncomfortable garment the burden of the world, and fall into a simple forgetfulness of self. They are affected by this vision of the human soul growing in its true nature, and I believe that this is what they mean when they call our little ones, wonderful children, happy children — the infancy of humanity in a higher stage of evolution than our own. I understand how the great English poet Wordsworth, enamoured as he was of nature, demanded the secret of all her peace and beauty. It was at last revealed to him — the secret of all nature lies in the soul of a little child. He holds there the true meaning of that life which exists throughout humanity. But this beauty which "lies about us in our infancy" becomes obscured; "shades of the prison house, begin to close about the growing boy . . . at last the man perceives it die away, and fade into the light of common day."

Truly our social life is too often only the darkening and the death of the natural life that is in us. These methods tend to guard that spiritual fire within man, to keep his real nature unspoiled and to set it free from the oppressive and degrading yoke of society. It is a pedagogical method informed by the high concept of Immanuel Kant: "Perfect art returns to nature."

GEORGE HERBERT PALMER

GEORGE HERBERT PALMER (1842-1933). At the beginning of the twentieth century the chairman of the Department of Philosophy at Harvard University wrote the classic statement of the four qualifications of the ideal teacher. In his essay he points up the close relation between teaching and living, the necessity of "invigorating life through knowledge," and the contradiction inherent in the very term "the ideal teacher."

Born in Boston, Massachusetts, on March 19, 1842, George Herbert Palmer graduated from Harvard in 1864 and, after studying at the University of Tubingen and at Andover Theological Seminary, joined the faculty of Harvard (1870), where he remained until 1913. He died on May 7, 1933. As a member of the most distinguished group of philosophers ever associated with an American University, he produced some important original works (among them *The Field of Ethics,* in which he attempted to synthesize the teachings of Georg W. F. Hegel and the Puritan tradition), edited the works of the poet for whom he was named, and produced a classic translation of *The Odyssey.* Teaching, however, is his life blood, and his concept of the ideal teacher is that of a brilliantly successful practitioner of the art with first-hand knowledge of its true rewards.

THE IDEAL TEACHER*

In America, a land of idealism, the profession of teaching has become one of the greatest of human employments. In 1903-04 half a million teachers were in charge of sixteen million pupils. Stating the same facts differently, we may say that a fifth of our entire population is constantly at school; and that wherever one hundred and sixty men, women, and children are gathered, a teacher is sure to be among them.

But figures fail to express the importance of the work. If each year an equal number of persons should come in contact with as

*From *The Teacher*: *Essays and Addresses on Education* by George Herbert Palmer and Alice Freeman Palmer (Boston: Houghton Mifflin Co., 1908).

many lawyers, no such social consequences would follow. The touch of the teacher, like that of no other person, is formative. Our young people are for long periods associated with those who are expected to fashion them into men and women of an approved type. A charge so influential is committed to nobody else in the community, not even to the ministers; for though these have a more searching aim, they are directly occupied with it but one day instead of six, but one hour instead of five. Accordingly, as the tract of knowledge has widened, and the creative opportunities involved in conducting a young person over it have correspondingly become apparent, the profession of teaching has risen to a notable height of dignity and attractiveness. It has moved from a subordinate to a central place in social influence, and now undertakes much of the work which formerly fell to the church. Each year divinity schools attract fewer students, graduate and normal schools more. On school and college instruction the community now bestows its choicest minds, its highest hopes, and its largest sums. During the year 1903-04 the United States spent for teaching not less than $350,000,000.

Such weighty work is ill adapted for amateurs. Those who take it up for brief times and to make money usually find it unsatisfactory. Success is rare, the hours are fixed and long, there is repetition and monotony, and the teacher passes his days among inferiors. Nor are the pecuniary gains considerable. There are few prizes, and neither in school nor in college will a teacher's ordinary income carry him much above want. College teaching is falling more and more into the hands of men of independent means. The poor can hardly afford to engage in it. Private schools, it is true, often show large incomes; but they are earned by the proprietors, not the teachers. On the whole, teaching as a trade is poor and disappointing business.

When, however, it is entered as a profession, as a serious and difficult fine art, there are few employments more satisfying. All over the country thousands of men and women are following it with a passionate devotion which takes little account of the income received. A trade aims primarily at personal gain; a profession at the exercise of powers beneficial to mankind. This prime aim of

492

the one, it is true, often properly becomes a subordinate aim of the other. Professional men may even be said to offer wares of their own — cures, conversions, court victories, learning — much as traders do, and to receive in return a kind of reward. But the business of the lawyer, doctor, preacher, and teacher never squares itself by equivalent exchange. These men do not give so much for so much. They give in lump and they get in lump, without precise balance. The whole notion of bargain is inapplicable in a sphere where the gains of him who serves and him who is served coincide; and that is largely the case with the professions. Each of them furnishes its special opportunity for the use of powers which the possessor takes delight in exercising. Harvard College pays me for doing what I would gladly pay it for allowing me to do. No professional man, then, thinks of giving according to measure. Once engaged, he gives his best, gives his personal interest, himself. His heart is in his work, and for this no equivalent is possible; what is accepted is in the nature of a fee, gratuity, or consideration, which enables him who receives it to maintain a certain expected mode of life. The real payment is the work itself, this and the chance to join with other members of the profession in guiding and enlarging the sphere of its activities.

The idea, sometimes advanced, that the professions might be ennobled by paying them powerfully, is fantastic. Their great attraction is their removal from sordid aims. More money should certainly be spent on several of them. Their members should be better protected against want, anxiety, neglect, and bad conditions of labor. To do his best work one needs not merely to live, but to live well. Yet in that increase of salaries which is urgently needed, care should be used not to allow the attention of the professional man to be diverted from what is important, — the outgo of his work, — and become fixed on what is merely incidental, — his income. When a professor in one of our large universities, angered by the refusal of the president to raise his salary on his being called elsewhere, impatiently exclaimed, "Mr. President, you are banking on the devotion of us teachers, knowing that we do not willingly leave this place," the president properly replied, "Certainly, and no college can be managed on any other principle."

Professional men are not so silly as to despise money; but after all, it is interest in their work, and not the thought of salary, which predominantly holds them.

Accordingly in this paper I address those only who are drawn to teaching by the love of it, who regard it as the most vital of the Fine Arts, who intend to give their lives to mastering its subtleties, and who are ready to meet some hardships and to put up with moderate fare if they may win its rich opportunities.

But supposing such a temper, what special qualifications will the work require? The question asked thus broadly admits no precise answer; for in reality there is no human excellence which is not useful for us teachers. No good quality can be thought of which we can afford to drop. Some day we shall discover a disturbing vacuum in the spot which it left. But I propose a more limited problem: what are those characteristics of the teacher without which he must fail, and what those which, once his, will almost certainly insure him success? Are there any such essentials, and how many? On this matter I have pondered long; for, teaching thirty-nine years in Harvard College, I have each year found out a little more fully my own incompetence. I have thus been forced to ask myself the double question, through what lacks do I fail, and in what direction lie the roots of my small successes? Of late years I think I have hit on these roots of success and have come to believe that there are four of them, —four characteristics which every teacher must possess. Of course he may possess as many more as he likes, — indeed, the more the better. But these four appear fundamental. I will briefly name them.

First, a teacher must have an aptitude for vicariousness; and second, an already accumulated wealth; and third, an ability to invigorate life through knowledge; and fourth, a readiness to be forgotten. Having these, any teacher is secure. Lacking them, lacking even one, he is liable to serious failure. But as here stated they have a curiously cabalistic sound and show little relation to the needs of any profession. They have been stated with too much condensation, and have become unintelligible through being too exact. Let me repair the error by successively expanding them.

The teacher's art takes its rise in what I call an aptitude for vicariousness. As year by year my college boys prepare to go forth into life, some laggard is sure to come to me and say, "I want a little advice. Most of my classmates have their minds made up about what they are going to do. I am still uncertain. I rather incline to be a teacher, because I am fond of books and suspect that in any other profession I can give them but little time. Business men do not read. Lawyers only consult books. And I am by no means sure that ministers have read all the books they quote. On the whole it seems safest to choose a profession in which books will be my daily companions. So I turn toward teaching. But before settling the matter I thought I would ask how you regard the profession." "A noble profession," I answer, "but quite unfit for you. I would advise you to become a lawyer, a car conductor, or something equally harmless. Do not turn to anything so perilous as teaching. You would ruin both it and yourself; for you are looking in exactly the wrong direction."

Such an inquirer is under a common misconception. The teacher's task is not primarily the acquisition of knowledge, but the impartation of it, — an entirely different matter. We teachers are forever taking thoughts out of our minds and putting them elsewhere. So long as we are content to keep them in our possession, we are not teachers at all. One who is interested in laying hold on wisdom is likely to become a scholar. And while no doubt it is well for a teacher to be a fair scholar, — I have known several such, — that is not the main thing. What constitutes the teacher is the passion to make scholars; and again and again it happens that the great scholar has no such passion whatever.

But even that passion is useless without aid from imagination. At every instant of the teacher's life he must be controlled by this mighty power. Most human beings are contented with living one life and delighted if they can pass that agreeably. But this is far from enough for us teachers. We incessantly go outside ourselves and enter into the many lives about us, — lives dull, dark, and unintelligible to any but an eye like ours. And this is imagination, the sympathetic creation in ourselves of conditions which belong to others. Our profession is therefore a double ended one. We inspect truth as it rises fresh and interesting before our eager sight.

495

But that is only the beginning of our task. Swiftly we then seize the lines of least intellectual resistance in alien minds and, with perpetual reference to these, follow our truth till it is safely lodged beyond ourselves. Each mind has its peculiar set of frictions. Those of our pupils can never be the same as ours. We have passed far on and know all about our subject. For us it wears an altogether different look from that which it has for beginners. It is their perplexities which we must reproduce and — as if a rose should shut and be a bud again — we must reassume in our developed and accustomed souls something of the innocence of childhood. Such is the exquisite business of the teacher, to carry himself back with all his wealth of knowledge and understand how his subject should appear to the meagre mind of one glancing at it for the first time.

And what absurd blunders we make in the process! Becoming immersed in our own side of the affair, we blind ourselves and readily attribute to our pupils modes of thought which are not in the least theirs. I remember a lesson I had on this point, I who had been teaching ethics half a lifetime. My nephew, five years old, was fond of stories from the Odyssey. He would creep into bed with me in the morning and beg for them. One Sunday, after I had given him a pretty stiff bit of adventure, it occurred to me that it was an appropriate day for a moral. "Ulysses was a very brave man," I remarked. "Yes," he said, "and I am very brave." I saw my opportunity and seized it. "That is true," said I. "You have been gaining courage lately. You used to cry easily, but you don't do that nowadays. When you want to cry now, you think how like a baby it would be to cry, or how you would disturb mother and upset the house; and so you conclude not to cry." The little fellow seemed hopelessly puzzled. He lay silent a minute or two and then said, "Well no, Uncle, I don't do that. I just go sh-sh-sh, and I don't." There the moral crisis is stated in its simplicity; and I had been putting off on that holy little nature sophistications borrowed from my own battered life.

But while I am explaining the blunders caused by self-engrossment and lack of imagination, let me show what slight adjustments will sometimes carry us past depressing difficulties. One year when

I was lecturing on some intricate problems of obligation, I began to doubt whether my class was following me, and I determined that I would make them talk. So the next day I constructed an ingenious ethical case and, after stating it to the class, I said, "Supposing now the state of affairs were thus and thus, and the interests of the persons involved were such and such, how would you decide the question of right, — Mr. Jones." Poor Jones rose in confusion. "You mean," he said, "if the case were as you have stated it? Well, hm, hm, hm, — yes, — I don't think I know, sir." And he sat down. I called on one and another with the same result. A panic was upon them, and all their minds were alike empty. I went home disgusted, wondering whether they had comprehended anything I had said during the previous fortnight, and hoping I might never have such a stupid lot of students again. Suddenly it flashed upon me that it was I who was stupid. That is usually the case when a class fails; it is the teacher's fault. The next day I went back prepared to begin at the right end. I began, "Oh, Mr. Jones." He rose, and I proceeded to state the situation as before. By the time I paused he had collected his wits, had worked off his superfluous flurry, and was ready to give me an admirable answer. Indeed in a few minutes the whole class was engaged in an eager discussion. My previous error had been in not remembering that they, I, and everybody, when suddenly attacked with a big question, are not in the best condition for answering. Occupied as I was with my end of the story, the questioning end, I had not worked in that double-ended fashion which alone can bring the teacher success; in short, I was deficient in vicariousness, — in swiftly putting myself in the weak one's place and bearing his burden.

Now it is in this chief business of the artistic teacher, to labor imaginatively himself in order to diminish the labors of his slender pupil, that most of our failures occur. Instead of lamenting the imperviousness of our pupils, we had better ask ourselves more frequently whether we have neatly adjusted our teachings to the conditions of their minds. We have no right to tumble out in a mass whatever comes into our heads, leaving to that feeble folk the work of finding in it what order they may. Ours it should be to see that every beginning, middle, and end of what we say is helpfully shaped for readiest access to those less intelligent and interested than we. But this is vicariousness. *Noblesse oblige.* In this profession any one who will be great must be a nimble servant, his head full of others' needs.

Some discouraged teacher, glad to discover that his past failures have been due to the absence of sympathetic imagination, may resolve that he will not commit that blunder again. On going to his class to-morrow he will look out upon his subject with his pupils' eyes, not with his own. Let him attempt it, and his pupils will surely say to one another, "What is the matter to-day with teacher?" They will get nothing from that exercise. No, what is wanted is not a resolve, but an aptitude. The time for using vicariousness is not the time for acquiring it. Rather it is the time for dismissing all thoughts of it from the mind. On entering the classroom we should leave every consideration of method outside the door, and talk simply as interested men and women in whatever way comes most natural to us. But into that nature vicariousness should long ago have been wrought. It should be already on hand. Fortunate we if our great-grandmother supplied us with it before we were born. There are persons who, with all good will, can never be teachers. They are not made in that way. Their business it is to pry into knowledge, to engage in action, to make money, or to pursue whatever other aim their powers dictate; but they do not readily think in terms of the other person. They should not, then, be teachers.

The teacher's habit is well summed in the Apostle's rule, "Look not every man on his own things, but every man also" — it is double — "on the things of others." And this habit should become as nearly as possible an instinct. Until it is rendered instinctive and passes beyond conscious direction, it will be of little worth. Let us then, as we go into society, as we walk the streets, as we sit at table, practice altruistic limberness and learn to escape from ourselves. A true teacher is always meditating his work, disciplining himself for his profession, probing the problems of his glorious art, and seeing illustration of them everywhere. In only one place is he freed from such criticism, and that is in his classroom.

Here in the moment of action he lets himself go, unhampered by theory, using the nature acquired elsewhere, and uttering as simply as possible the fulness of his mind and heart. Direct human intercourse requires instinctive aptitudes. Till altruistic vicariousness has become our second nature, we shall not deeply influence anybody.

But sympathetic imagination is not all a teacher needs. Exclusive altruism is absurd. On this point too I once got instruction from the mouths of babes and sucklings. The children of a friend of mine, children of six and four, had just gone to bed. Their mother overheard them talking when they should have been asleep. Wondering what they might need, she stepped into the entry and listened. They were discussing what they were here in the world for. That is about the size of problems commonly found in infant minds. The little girl suggested that we are probably in the world to help others. "Why, no indeed, Mabel," said her big brother, "for then what would others be here for?" Precisely! If anything is only fit to give away, it is not fit for that. We must know and prize its goodness in ourselves before generosity is even possible.

Plainly, then, beside his aptitude for vicariousness, our ideal teacher will need the second qualification of an already accumulated wealth. These hungry pupils are drawing all their nourishment from us, and have we got it to give? They will be poor, if we are poor; rich if we are wealthy. We are their source of supply. Every time we cut ourselves off from nutrition, we enfeeble them. And how frequently devoted teachers make this mistake! dedicating themselves so to the immediate needs of those about them that they themselves grow thinner each year. We all know the "teacher's face." It is meagre, worn, sacrificial, anxious, powerless. That is exactly the opposite of what it should be. The teacher should be the big bounteous being of the community. Other people may get along tolerably by holding whatever small knowledge comes their way. A moderate stock will pretty well serve their private turn. But that is not our case. Supplying a multitude, we need wealth sufficient for a multitude. We should then be clutching at knowledge on every side. Nothing must escape us. It is a mistake to reject a bit of truth because it lies outside our province. Some day we shall need it. All knowledge is our province.

In preparing a lecture I find I always have to work hardest on the things I do not say. The things I am sure to say I can easily get up. They are obvious and generally accessible. But they, I find, are not enough. I must have a broad background of knowledge which does not appear in speech. I have to go over my entire subject and see how the things I am to say look in their various relations, tracing out connections which I shall not present to my class. One might ask what is the use of this? Why prepare more matter than can be used? Every successful teacher knows. I cannot teach right up to the edge of my knowledge without a fear of falling off. My pupils discover this fear, and my words are ineffective. They feel the influence of what I do not say. One cannot precisely explain it; but when I move freely across my subject as if it mattered little on what part of it I rest, they get a sense of assured power which is compulsive and fructifying. The subject acquires consequence, their minds swell, and they are eager to enter regions of which they had not previously thought.

Even, then, to teach a small thing well we must be large. I asked a teacher what her subject was, and she answered, "Arithmetic in the third grade." But where is the third grade found? In knowledge, or in the schools? Unhappily it is in the schools. But if one would be a teacher of arithmetic, it must be arithmetic she teaches and not third grade at all. We cannot accept these artificial bounds without damage. Instead of accumulated wealth they will bring us accumulated poverty, and increase it every day. Years ago at Harvard we began to discuss the establishment of a Graduate School; and I, a young instructor, steadily voted against it. My thought was this: Harvard College, in spite of what the public imagines, is a place of slender resources. Our means are inadequate for teaching even undergraduates. But graduate instruction is vastly more expensive; courses composed of half a dozen students take the time of the ablest professors. I thought we could not afford this. Why not leave graduate instruction to a university which gives itself entirely to that task? Would it not be wiser to

500

spend ourselves on the lower ranges of learning, covering these adequately, than to try to spread ourselves over the entire field?

Doubting so, I for some time opposed the coming of a Graduate School. But a luminous remark of our great President showed me the error of my ways. In the course of debate he said one evening, "It is not primarily for the graduates that I care for this school; it is for the undergraduates. We shall never get good teaching here so long as our instructors set a limit to their subjects. When they are called on to follow these throughout, tracing them far off toward the unknown, they may become good teachers; but not before."

I went home meditating. I saw that the President was right, and that I was myself in danger of the stagnation he deprecated. I changed my vote, as did others. The Graduate School was established; and of all the influences which have contributed to raise the standard of scholarship at Harvard, both for teachers and taught, that graduate work seems to me the greatest. Every professor now must be the master of a field of knowledge, and not of a few paths running through it.

But the ideal teacher will accumulate wealth, not merely for his pupils' sake, but for his own. To be a great teacher one must be a great personality, and without ardent and individual tastes the roots of our being are not fed. For developing personal power it is well, therefore, for each teacher to cultivate interests unconnected with his official work. Let the mathematician turn to the English poets, the teacher of classics to the study of birds and flowers, and each will gain a lightness, a freedom from exhaustion, a mental hospitality, which can only be acquired in some disinterested pursuit. Such a private subject becomes doubly dear because it is just our own. We pursue it as we will; we let it call out our irresponsible thoughts; and from it we ordinarily carry off a note of distinction lacking in those whose lives are too tightly organized.

To this second qualification of the teacher, however, I have been obliged to prefix a condition similar to that which was added to the first. We need not merely wealth, but an already accumulated wealth. At the moment when wealth is wanted it cannot be acquired. It should have been gathered and stored before the occasion arose. What is more pitiable than when a person who desires to be a benefactor looks in his chest and finds it empty? Special knowledge is wanted, or trained insight, or professional skill, or sound practical judgement; and the teacher who is called on has gone through no such discipline as assures these resources. I am inclined to think that women are more liable to this sort of bankruptcy than men. Their sex is more sympathetic than ours and they spend more hastily. They will drop what they are doing and run if a baby cries. Excellence requires a certain hardihood of heart, while quick responsiveness is destructive of the larger giving. He who would be greatly generous must train himself long and tenaciously, without much attention to momentary calls. The plan of the Great Teacher, by which he took thirty years for acquisition and three for bestowal, is not unwise, provided that we too can say, "For their sakes I sanctify myself."

But the two qualifications of the teacher already named will not alone suffice. I have known persons who were sympathetically imaginative, and who could not be denied to possess large intellectual wealth, who still failed as teachers. One needs a third something, the power to invigorate life through learning. We do not always notice how knowledge naturally buffets. It is offensive stuff, and makes young and wholesome minds rebel. And well it may; for when we learn anything, we are obliged to break up the world, inspect it piecemeal, and let our minds seize it bit by bit. Now about a fragment there is always something repulsive. Any one who is normally constituted must draw back in horror, feeling that what is brought him has little to do with the beautiful world he has known. Where was there ever a healthy child who did not hate the multiplication table? A boy who did not detest such abstractions as seven times eight would hardly be worth educating. By no ingenuity can we relieve knowledge of this unfortunate peculiarity. It must be taken in disjointed portions. That is the way attention is made. In consequence each of us must be to some extent a specialist, devoting himself to certain sides of the world and neglecting others quite as important. These are the conditions under which we imperfect creatures work. Our sight is not world-wide. When we give our attention to one object, by that very act we withdraw it from others. In this way our children must learn and have their expansive natures subdued to pedagogic exigencies.

Because this belittlement through the method of approach is inevitable, it is all-important that the teacher should possess a supplemental dignity, replacing the oppressive sense of pettiness with stimulating intimations of high things in store. Partly on this account a book is an imperfect instructor. Truth there, being impersonal, seems untrue, abstract, and insignificant. It needs to shine through a human being before it can exert its vital force on a young student. Quite as much for vital transmission as for intellectual elucidation, is a teacher employed. His consolidated character exhibits the gains which come from study. He need not point them out. If he is a scholar, there will appear in him an augustness, accuracy, fulness of knowledge, a buoyant enthusiasm even in drudgery, and an unshakable confidence that others must soon see and enjoy what has enriched himself; and all this will quickly convey itself to his students and create attention in his classroom. Such kindling of interest is the great function of the teacher. People sometimes say, "I should like to teach if only pupils cared to learn." But then there would be little need of teaching. Boys who have made up their minds that knowledge is worth while are pretty sure to get it, without regard to teachers. Our chief concern is with those who are unawakened. In the Sistine Chapel Michael Angelo has depicted the Almighty moving in clouds over the rugged earth where lies the newly created Adam, hardly aware of himself. The tips of the fingers touch, the Lord's and Adam's, and the huge frame loses its inertness and rears itself into action. Such may be the electrifying touch of the teacher.

But it must be confessed that not infrequently, instead of invigorating life through knowledge, we teachers reduce our classes to complete passivity. The blunder is not altogether ours, but is suggested by certain characteristics of knowledge itself: for how can a learner begin without submitting his mind, accepting facts, listening to authority, in short becoming obedient? He is called on to put aside his own notions and take what truth dictates. I have said that knowledge buffets, forcing us into an almost slavish attitude, and that this is resented by vigorous natures. In almost every school some of the most original, aggressive, and independent boys stand low in their classes, while at the top stand "grinds," — objects of horror to all healthy souls.

Now it is the teacher's business to see that the onslaught of knowledge does not enfeeble. Between the two sides of knowledge, information and intelligence, he is to keep the balance true. While a boy is taking in facts, facts not allowed to be twisted by any fancy or carelessness, he is all the time to be made to feel that these facts offer him a field for critical and constructive action. If they leave him inactive, docile, and plodding, there is something wrong with the teaching. Facts are pernicious when they subjugate and do not quicken the mind that grasps them. Education should unfold us and truth together; and to enable it to do so the learner must never be allowed to sink into a mere recipient. He should be called on to think, to observe, to form his own judgments, even at the risk of error and crudity. Temporary one-sidedness and extravagance is not too high a price to pay for originality. And this development of personal vigor, emphasized in our day by the elective system and independent research, is the great aim of education. It should affect the lower ranges of study as truly as the higher. The mere contemplation of truth is always a deadening affair. Many a dull class in school and college would come to life if simply given something to do. Until the mind reacts for itself on what it receives, its education is hardly begun.

The teacher who leads it so to react may be truly called "productive," productive of human beings. The noble word has recently become Germanized and corrupted, and is now hardly more than a piece of educational slang. According to the judgments of to-day a teacher may be unimaginative, pedantic, dull, and may make his students no less so; he will still deserve a crown of wild olive as a "productive" man if he neglects his classroom for the printing press. But this is to put first things second and second things first. He who is original and fecund, and knows how to beget a similar spirit in his students, will naturally wish to express himself beyond his classroom. By snatching the fragments of time which his arduous work allows he may accomplish much worthy writing and probably increase too his worth for his college, his students, and himself. But the business of book-making is, after all, collateral with us teachers. Not for this are we employed, desirable though it is for showing the kind of mind we bear. Many of my most productive colleagues have printed little or nothing, though they have left a deep mark on the life and science of our time. I would encourage publication. It keeps the solitary student healthy, enables him to find his place among his fellows, and more distinctly to estimate the contributions he is making to his subject. But let him never neglect his proper work for that which must always have in it an element of advertising.

Too long I have delayed the fourth, the disagreeable, section of my paper. Briefly it is this: a teacher must have a readiness to be forgotten. And what is harder? We may be excellent persons, may be daily doing kindnesses, and yet not be quite willing to have those kindnesses overlooked. Many a man is ready to be generous, if by it he can win praise. The love of praise, — it is almost our last infirmity; but there is no more baffling infirmity for the teacher. If praise and recognition are dear to him, he may as well stop work. Dear to him perhaps they must be, as a human being; but as a teacher, he is called on to rise above ordinary human conditions. Whoever has followed me thus far will perceive the reason. I have shown that a teacher does not live for himself, but for his pupil and for the truth which he imparts. His aim is to be a colorless medium through which that truth may shine on opening minds. How can he be this if he is continually interposing himself and saying, "Instead of looking at the truth, my children, look at me and see how skilfully I do my work. I thought I taught you admirably to-day. I hope you thought so too." No, the teacher must keep himself entirely out of the way, fixing young attention on the proffered knowledge and not on anything so small as the one who brings it. Only so can he be vicarious, whole-hearted in invigorating the lives committed to his charge.

Moreover, any other course is futile. We cannot tell whether those whom we are teaching have taken our best points or not. Those best points, what are they? We shall count them one thing, our pupils another. We gather what seems to us of consequence and pour it out upon our classes. But if their minds are not fitted to receive it, the little creatures have excellent protective arrange-ments which they draw down, and all we pour is simply shed as if nothing had fallen; while again we say something so slight that we hardly notice it, but, happening to be just the nutritive element which that small life then needs, it is caught up and turned into human fibre. We cannot tell. We work in the dark. Out upon the waters our bread is cast, and if we are wise we do not attempt to trace its return.

On this point I received capital instruction from one of my pupils. In teaching a course on English Empiricism I undertook a line of exposition which I knew was abstruse. Indeed, I doubted if many of the class could follow; but there on the front seat sat one whose bright eyes were ever upon me. It seemed worth while to teach my three or four best men, that man in particular. By the end of the term there were many grumblings. My class did not get much out of me that year. They graduated, and a couple of years later this young fellow appeared at my door to say that he could not pass through Cambridge without thanking me for his work on Locke, Berkeley, and Hume. Pleased to be assured that my questionable methods were justified, and unwilling to drop a subject so agreeable, I asked if he could tell precisely where the value of the course lay. "Certainly," he answered. "It all centred in a single remark of Locke's. Locke said we ought to have clear and distinct ideas. I don't think I got anything else out of the course."

Well, at first I was inclined to think the fellow foolish, so to mistake a bit of commonplace for gospel truth. Why did he not listen to some of the profound things I was saying? But on reflec-tion I saw that he was right and I wrong. That trivial saying had come to him at a critical moment as a word of power; while the deep matters which interested me, and which I had been offering him so confidently day by day, being unsuited to him, had passed him by. He had not heard them.

To such proper unthankfulness we teachers must accustom our-selves. We cannot tell what are our good deeds, and shall only plague ourselves and hinder our classes if we try to find out. Let us display our subjects as lucidly as possible, allow our pupils considerable license in apprehension, and be content ourselves to escape observation. But though what we do remains unknown, its results often awake deep affection. Few in the community receive love more abundantly than we. Wherever we go, we meet a smiling face. Throughout the world, by some good fortune the period of learning is the period of romance. In those halcyon days of our boys and girls we have a share, and the golden lights which flood the opening years are reflected on us. Though our pupils cannot follow our efforts in their behalf, and indeed ought not, — it being our art to conceal our art, — yet they perceive that in the years when their happy expansion occurred we were their guides. To us, therefore, their blind affections cling as to few beside their parents. It is better to be loved than to be understood.

Perhaps some readers of this paper will begin to suspect that it is impossible to be a good teacher. Certainly it is. Each of the four qualifications I have named is endless. Not one of them can be fully attained. We can always be more imaginative, wealthy, stimulating, disinterested. Each year we creep a little nearer to our goal, only to find that finished teacher is a contradiction in terms. Our reach will forever exceed our grasp. Yet what a delight in approximation! Even in our failures there is comfort, when we see that they are generally due not to technical but to personal defects. We have been putting ourselves forward, or have taught in mechanical rather than vital fashion, or have not undertaken betimes the labor of preparation, or have declined the trouble of vicariousness.

Evidently, then, as we become better teachers we also become in some sort better persons. Our beautiful art, being so largely personal, will at last be seen to connect itself with nearly all other employments. Every mother is a teacher. Every minister. The lawyer teaches the jury, the doctor his patient. The clever salesman might almost be said to use teaching in dealing with his customer, and all of us to be teachers of one another in daily intercourse. As teaching is the most universal of the professions, those are fortunate who are able to devote their lives to its enriching study.

CHARLES S. PEIRCE

CHARLES S. PEIRCE (1839-1914). Before men like William James and John Dewey made his name famous, Charles Saunders Peirce could say: "I am a man of whom critics never found anything good to say." As the initiator and exponent of the philosophical movement of pragmatism (first defined in the *Popular Science Monthly* for January 1878 and first used in print in his article in Baldwin's *Dictionary of Philosophy,* published in 1901), he exerted a profound influence on the climate of opinion from which pedagogical trends arose. His reflections on educational issues therefore are still of considerable interest.

The son of Benjamin Peirce, the great mathematician, he was born in Cambridge, Massachusetts, on September 10, 1839, and graduated from Harvard in 1859. He worked for many years with the United States Coast and Geodetic Survey, taught at Harvard during the periods 1864-1865 and 1869-1870 and at Johns Hopkins from 1879-1884, and contributed largely to the *Century Dictionary* and to Baldwin's *Dictionary.* He died at Milford, Pennsylvania, on April 14, 1914. His *Collected Papers* fill six volumes.

In the extracts that follow Peirce expresses the opinion that Clark University, "in recognizing the pursuit of science as its first object . . . has perhaps the most elevated ideal of any university in the world," and he invites criticism by stating that "a liberal education . . . means *logic.* That is indispensable to it, and no other one thing is."

THE FUNCTION OF A UNIVERSITY*

Of the three verbs to *be,* to *do,* and to *know,* the great majority of young men unhesitatingly regard the second as expressing the ultimate purpose and end of life. This is, as a matter of course, the idea of the practical man, who knows what he wants, and does not desire to want anything else. The average trustee of an Amer-

*Excerpts from Peirce's review of *Clark University 1889-1899: Decennial Celebration* (Worcester, Mass., 1899), in *Science* (April 20, 1900), pp. 620-22.

ican college will think it a commendable thing for a professor to employ all the time he can possibly save in making money; but if he devotes much energy to any purely theoretical research, the trustees will look upon him askance, as a barely respectable squanderer of his opportunities. In England, this notion takes a turn that really makes it a little less gross; yet, being foreign, perhaps we can discern its error more easily than in its more familiar guise. Thus, Dr. Karl Pearson, in the introduction to his *Grammar of Science*, deliberately lays down the principle that no end whatever is to be approved without a reason, except the end of the preservation of society; and applying this rule, declares that the only valid excuse for the encouragement of scientific activity lies in its tending to maintain "the stability of society." This is truly a British phrase, meaning the House of Lords and vested rights and all that. Only recently we have seen an American man of science and of weight discuss the purpose of education, without once alluding to the only motive that animates the genuine scientific investigator. I am not guiltless in this matter myself, for in my youth I wrote some articles to uphold a doctrine I called Pragmatism, namely, that the meaning and essence of every conception lies in the application that is to be made of it. That is all very well, when properly understood. I do not intend to recant it. But the question arises, *what is* the ultimate application; at that time I seem to have been inclined to subordinate the *conception* to the *act*, knowing to doing. Subsequent experience of life has taught me that the only thing that is really desirable without a reason for being so, is to render ideas and things reasonable. One cannot well demand a reason for reasonableness itself. Logical analysis shows that reasonableness consists in association, assimilation, generalization, the bringing of items together into an organic whole — which are so many ways of regarding what is essentially the same thing. In the emotional sphere this tendency towards union appears as Love; so that the Law of Love and the Law of Reason are quite at one.

There was a simple fellow who, in a benighted age and land, wandered about uttering appreciations of the elements of human life which have made an extraordinary impression upon most of us. Of all his sayings there is none whose truth has been brought

509

home to me more strongly by what I have been able to detect in successful men and women than this: Whoever makes his own welfare his object will simply ruin it utterly.

American education, for the most part, is directed to no other object than the welfare of individual scholars; and thereby incites *them* to pursue that object exclusively. A great university bears upon its seal the remark of its founder: "I wish to found an institution where any man can learn anything." It was a noble idea; and it would be mean to pick flaws in it! especially as he did not say what ulterior purpose he might have in view. But the university which parades this casual remark as its motto seems to proclaim to its students that their individual well-being is its only aim. Our scientific schools distribute circulars which dwell chiefly upon the handsome incomes their alumni are making, thereby calling up such images as a handsomely laid table with a pair of Havre de Grace ducks and a bottle of Château Margaux. What comes of such a conception of education and of life, for surely the purpose of education is not different from the purpose of life? The result is that, notwithstanding all the devices and tricks of the American teachers' art, it may be doubted whether any teaching ever anywhere did less to make happy men and women. At any rate, the spiritual meagreness of the typical American school-book is extreme. The great mediæval universities, the modern German universities, the new science colleges of England, which did, and do, great things for their students personally, were never in the least founded for their students' individual advantage, but, on the contrary, because of the expectation that the truths that would be brought to light in such institutions would benefit the state. This end was, and is, so constantly in view that the scholars are led to regard their own lives as having a purpose beyond themselves.

Yet even this is a low view of learning and science. No reader of this Journal is likely to be content with the statement that the searching out of the ideas that govern the universe has no other value than that it helps human animals to swarm and feed. He will rather insist that the only thing that makes the human race worth perpetuation is that thereby rational ideas may be developed, and the rationalization of things furthered.

510

No other occupation of man is so purely and immediately directed to the one end that is alone intrinsically rational as scientific investigation. It so strongly influences those who pursue it to subordinate all motives of ambition, fame, greed, self-seeking of every description, that other people, even those who have relatively high aspirations, such as theologians and teachers, altogether fail, in many cases, to divine the scientific man's simple motives. The Clark University, in recognizing the pursuit of science as its first object, with teaching — of course, an indispensable means of securing continuity of work — as only a subordinate, or at most a secondary object, has perhaps the most elevated ideal of any university in the world; and I believe it to be so much the better for the individual students.

LOGIC AND A LIBERAL EDUCATION*

This is the age of Methods; and the university which is to be exponent of the living condition of the human mind must be the university of methods.

Now I grant you that to say this is the age of the development of new methods of research is so far from saying it is the age of the theory of methods that it is almost to say the reverse. Unfortunately practice generally precedes theory, and it is the usual fate of mankind to get things done in some boggling way first, and find out afterwards how they could have done them much more easily and perfectly. And it must be confessed that we students of modern methods are as yet but a voice crying in the wilderness, and saying prepare ye the way for this lord of the sciences which is to come. . . .

The theory of any act in no wise aids the doing of it, so long as what is to be done is of a narrow description, so that it can be

*From the Johns Hopkins University Circulars (Nov. 1882). Excerpted by Max H. Fisch and Jackson I. Cope, "Peirce at the Johns Hopkins University," in Studies in the Philosophy of C. S. Peirce, ed. Philip P. Wiener and Frederic H. Young (Cambridge: Harvard University Press, 1952).

governed by the unconscious part of our organism. . . . But when new paths have to be struck out, a spinal cord is not enough; a brain is needed, and that brain an organ of mind, and that mind perfected by a liberal education. And a liberal education — so far as its relation to the understanding goes — means *logic*. That is indispensable to it, and no other one thing is. . . .

Now although a man needs not the theory of a method in order to apply it as it has been applied already, yet in order to adapt to his own science the method of another with which he is less familiar, and to properly modify it so as to suit it to its new use, an acquaintance with the principles upon which it depends will be of the greatest benefit. For that sort of work a man needs to be more than a specialist; he needs such a general training of his mind and such knowledge as shall show him how to make his powers most effective in a new direction. That knowledge is logic.

In short, if my view is the true one, a young man wants a physical education and an aesthetic education, an education in the ways of the world and a moral education, and with all these logic has nothing in particular to do; but so far as he wants an intellectual education, it is precisely logic that he wants; and whether it be in one lecture-room or another, his ultimate purpose is to improve his logical power and his knowledge of methods. To this great end a young man's attention ought to be directed when he first comes to the university; he ought to keep it steadily in view during the whole period of his studies; and finally, he will do well to review his whole work in the light which an education in logic throws upon it.

JOHANN HEINRICH PESTALOZZI

JOHANN HEINRICH PESTALOZZI (1746-1827). Johann Heinrich Pestalozzi, the greatest educational reformer of his era, called the home the origin and model of all education and maintained that "the upward development of the inner forces of human nature into a pure human wisdom is the general purpose of all education, even of the lowliest of men." In opposition to Rousseau, he characterized man as a social being whose innate tendencies are unfolded in a natural fashion within the frame of the living community represented by the family. He used simple terms and simple images to communicate profound insights concerning values, liberal and vocational education, and basic psychological truths. Among his notable followers were Friedrich Froebel and Johann Friedrich Herbart, each of whom exerted a strong influence on the development of modern education. The gradual transfer of the school from a church-dominated to a state-supported institution for the training of future citizens is an important by-product of his activity.

Johann Heinrich Pestalozzi, revered in his native country because of his tireless efforts to help poor, orphaned children, was born at Zurich, Switzerland, on January 12, 1746. Educated at the University of Zurich, he was active in social and political reform. He studied for the ministry and for a legal career, thinking that he could help the poor through political action. Impressed by *Emile,* he tried Rousseau's educational system on his own child, only to find it imperfect. Determined to learn more about the nature of education for himself, he took a group of under-privileged children into his home in 1774 and combined their study with remunerative labor. He was aided by an illiterate peasant woman, the prototype of Gertrude in his later writings. An impractical man all his life, Pestalozzi was unable to operate his enterprise profitably and had to close the Neuhof School after five years and turn to writing as a means of earning a living. In 1798 he took charge of almost a hundred destitute children at Stanz and with almost superhuman zeal devoted himself to the task of improving their lot. In 1805 he founded at Yverdon his famous boarding school, which developed into a model teacher training institute. Yverdon became a place of pilgrimage for educators and philanthropists, and the school was attended by students from every country in Europe. Convinced that society could be regenerated through education, he spent the next twenty years testing and developing his philosophy. He died on February 17, 1827.

Leonard and Gertrude (1781-1787), from which the first of the following extracts is taken, represents the culmination of Pestalozzi's influence on the development of modern educational theory. It is the story of a humble peasant woman who through her devotion and lofty purpose transformed the life of her whole village. It is a tale of deep, unselfish love, not for an individual, but for the weak, the impoverished, the helpless. The plot is simple: Gertrude, the mason's wife, went to the magistrate to ask for work for her husband and to complain about the wicked bailiff whose beer had made her husband drunk; the husband obtained the job of building a new church, the bailiff was duly punished, and Gertrude's children learned domestic industries and good moral precepts; an idler witnessed her feat and decided to become a teacher himself; even the preacher was influenced by her work, for he realized that his sermons should be more meaningful; in short, the whole spirit of the hamlet was regenerated, and the royal cabinet became interested, studied the situation, and concluded that the other ministries of the realm might profitably imitate the example of Bonnal, the fictional hamlet.

The second selection presented here is extracted from a report made by Pestalozzi in 1800 to a Society of Friends of Education, which had been formed to support his work. In his report (posthumously published in 1828 under the title *The Method*) he gives a general outline of his method of instruction.

LEONARD AND GERTRUDE*

In the village of Bonnal there lived a mason named Leonard. His trade would have enabled him to support his family of a wife and seven children, if he could have resisted the temptation to frequent the tavern, where there were always enough idle loafers to entice him in, and induce the good-natured, easy-going man to squander his earnings in drink and gambling. Leonard always repented his weakness when he saw his children want for bread, yet was not strong enough to reform. He was blest with a good, pious wife, who was overwhelmed with sorrow at the ruin which seemed to stare them in the face.

Gertrude had always contrived to conceal her sadness from the children, but one day, when her husband remained away from home longer than usual, she was so overcome with anxiety and grief that the little ones saw her weep. "You are crying, mother!" they exclaimed in chorus, and crowding about her, added their tears to hers. Even the baby in her arms seemed to feel a premonition of sorrow, and looked up in her face for the first time without a smile. This was too much for the afflicted mother, who now wept aloud, accompanied by the sobs of the children. Their grief was at its height when the door opened, and Leonard entered. Gertrude's face was hidden, and the children were clinging about her, too much engrossed with their mother's distress to notice the approach of their father.

"Merciful heavens, what is it?" he cried, turning pale as death. They looked up at the sound of his voice, and the violence of their lamentation ceased. "Gertrude, what dreadful sorrow is this?" he asked again.

"Dear husband, heavy cares oppress my heart, and when you are away, my misery is still greater."

*From *Leonard and Gertrude*, translated and abridged by Eva Channing (Boston: D. C. Heath and Company, 1898).

515

"Gertrude," said Leonard; "I know why you weep, — wretch that I am!"

She led the children away, and Leonard laid his head in her lap without speaking. The quiet was broken only by his sobs, for Gertrude was praying silently. Finally she spoke: "Leonard, trust in God's mercy, and take courage to do right!"

"O Gertrude!" was all he could say amid his tears.

"Take courage, dear," she repeated, "and trust in your Father in heaven. I would not willingly grieve you, and you well know that I do not ask for more than bread and water at your side; and that I often work uncomplainingly till long past midnight for you and the children. But, husband, I should not feel I was true to you or our dear ones if I concealed my cares from you. Our children are loving and dutiful now; but they will not remain so if we do not fulfil our obligation as parents. Think how you would feel if all our little ones should lose their gratitude and respect for us through our fault! And could you bear to see your Nicholas, your Jonas, your Lizzie and Annie, homeless and forced to seek their bread among strangers? It would kill me!" and her tears flowed as she spoke.

Leonard wept also. "O Gertrude, what shall I do? It breaks my heart to make you miserable, but I cannot help it. I owe the Bailiff Hummel thirty florins, and if I stay away from his tavern, he threatens me with the law; yet if I go, he gets possession of all my wages."

"Can you not go to Arner, the people's father? All the widows and orphans praise him, and I think he would give you advice and protection."

"Gertrude, I dare not! How could I, a poor miserable drunkard, complain of the Bailiff, who has a thousand ways of blackening me in the eyes of his superior? And think how he would revenge himself if I should try it and fail!"

"But he will ruin you in any case. Leonard, think of your children, and go. If you do not, I shall!"

"I dare not! But, Gertrude, if you have the courage, go to Arner in Heaven's name, and tell him all."

"I will!" she answered. She prayed throughout the sleepless

night, and the next morning took her blooming baby and walked two long hours to the Castle.

The nobleman was sitting under a linden-tree at the gate, and saw her as she approached, with tears in her eyes and the infant on her arm. "Who are you, my daughter, and what do you wish?" he asked, in so kind a tone that she took heart to answer: "I am Gertrude, wife of the mason Leonard in Bonnal."

"You are a good woman," said Arner. "I have noticed that your children behave better than all the others in the village, and they seem better fed, although I hear you are very poor. What can I do for you, my daughter?"

"O gracious Sir, for a long time my husband has owed thirty florins to the Bailiff Hummel, a hard man, who leads him into all sorts of temptation. Leonard is in his power: so he dares not keep away from the tavern, where day after day he spends the wages which ought to buy bread for his family. We have seven little children, Sir, and unless something is done we shall all be beggars. I ventured to come to you for help, because I know that you have compassion for the widowed and fatherless. I have brought the money I have laid aside for my children, to deposit with you, if you will be so good as to make some arrangement so that the Bailiff shall not torment my husband any more until he is paid."

Arner took up a cup which stood near, and said to Gertrude: "Drink this tea, and give your pretty baby some of this milk." She blushed, and was moved even to tears by his fatherly kindness.

The nobleman now requested her to relate her causes of complaint against the Bailiff, and listened attentively to her story of the cares and troubles of many years. Suddenly he asked her how it had been possible to lay aside money for her children in the midst of her distress.

"It was very hard, gracious Sir; yet I could not help feeling as if the money were not mine, but had been given me by a dying man on his death-bed, in trust for his children. So when in the hardest times I had to borrow from it to buy bread for the family, I gave myself no rest till by working late and early I had paid it back again."

Gertrude laid seven neat packages on the table, each of which had a ticket attached, saying whose it was; and if she had taken anything from it, the fact was noted, and likewise when she had replaced it. She saw him read these tickets through attentively, and said blushing: "I ought to have taken those papers away, gracious Sir."

Arner only smiled, and admired the modesty which shrank from even merited praise. He added something to each parcel, saying: "Carry back your children's money, Gertrude; I will lay aside thirty florins until the Bailiff is paid. Now go home; I shall be in the village to-morrow, at all events, and will settle the matter with Hummel."

"God reward you, gracious Sir!" she faltered; and started joyfully with her baby on the long homeward way. Leonard saw her as she approached the house. "Already back again?" he cried. "You have been successful with Arner."

"How do you know?"

"I can see it in your face, my dear wife, — you cannot deceive me."

From this time forward, when the mason's children said their prayers at morning and evening, they prayed not only for their father and mother, but also for Arner, the people's father.

XXV. — *Gertrude's Method of Instruction.*

It was quite early in the morning when Arner, Glülphi and the pastor went to the mason's cottage. The room was not in order when they entered, for the family had just finished breakfast, and the dirty plates and spoons still lay upon the table. Gertrude was at first somewhat disconcerted, but the visitors reassured her, saying kindly: "This is as it should be; it is impossible to clear the table before breakfast is eaten!"

The children all helped wash the dishes, and then seated themselves in their customary places before their work. The gentlemen begged Gertrude to let everything go on as usual, and after the first half hour, during which she was a little embarrassed, all proceeded as if no stranger were present. First the children sang their morning hymns, and then Gertrude read a chapter of the Bible aloud, which they repeated after her while they were spinning, rehearsing the most instructive passages until they knew them by heart. In the mean time, the oldest girl had been making the children's beds in the adjoining room, and the visitors noticed through the open door that she silently repeated what the others were reciting. When this task was completed, she went into the garden and returned with vegetables for dinner, which she cleaned while repeating Bible-verses with the rest.

It was something new for the children to see three gentlemen in the room, and they often looked up from their spinning toward the corner where the strangers sat. Gertrude noticed this, and said to them: "Seems to me you look more at these gentlemen than at your yarn." But Harry answered: "No, indeed! We are working hard, and you'll have finer yarn to-day than usual."

Whenever Gertrude saw that anything was amiss with the wheels or cotton, she rose from her work, and put it in order. The smallest children, who were not old enough to spin, picked over the cotton for carding, with a skill which excited the admiration of the visitors.

Although Gertrude thus exerted herself to develop very early the manual dexterity of her children, she was in no haste for them to learn to read and write. But she took pains to teach them early how to speak; for, as she said, "of what use is it for a person to be able to read and write, if he cannot speak? — since reading and writing are only an artificial sort of speech." To this end she used to make the children pronounce syllables after her in regular succession, taking them from an old A-B-C book she had. This exercise in correct and distinct articulation was, however, only a subordinate object in her whole scheme of education, which embraced a true comprehension of life itself. Yet she never adopted the tone of instructor toward her children; she did not say to them: "Child, this is your head, your nose, your hand, your finger;" or: "Child, this is your head, your eye, your ear?" — but instead, she would say: "Come here, child, I will wash your little hands," "I will comb your hair," or: "I will cut your finger-nails." Her verbal instruction seemed to vanish in the spirit of her real activity, in which it always had its source. The result of her system was that each child was skilful, intelligent and active to the full extent that its age and development allowed.

The instruction she gave them in the rudiments of arithmetic was intimately connected with the realities of life. She taught them to count the number of steps from one end of the room to the other, and two of the rows of five panes each, in one of the windows, gave her an opportunity to unfold the decimal relations of numbers. She also made them count their threads while spinning, and the number of turns on the reel, when they wound the yarn into skeins. Above all, in every occupation of life she taught them an accurate and intelligent observation of common objects and the forces of nature.

All that Gertrude's children knew, they knew so thoroughly that they were able to teach it to the younger ones; and this they often begged permission to do. On this day, while the visitors were present, Jonas sat with each arm around the neck of a smaller child, and made the little ones pronounce the syllables of the A-B-C book after him; while Lizzie placed herself with her wheel between two of the others, and while all three spun, taught them the words of a hymn with the utmost patience.

When the guests took their departure, they told Gertrude they would come again on the morrow. "Why?" she returned; "You will only see the same thing over again." But Glülphi said: "That is the best praise you could possibly give yourself." Gertrude blushed at this compliment, and stood confused when the gentlemen kindly pressed her hand in taking leave.

The three could not sufficiently admire what they had seen at the mason's house, and Glülphi was so overcome by the powerful impression made upon him, that he longed to be alone and seek counsel of his own thoughts. He hastened to his room, and as he crossed the threshold, the words broke from his lips: "*I* must be schoolmaster in Bonnal!" All night visions of Gertrude's schoolroom floated through his mind, and he only fell asleep toward morning. Before his eyes were fairly open, he murmured: "I will be schoolmaster!" — and hastened to Arner to acquaint him with his resolution.

XXXI. — *The Organization of a New School.*

Glülphi was full of the idea of his school, and could speak of nothing else with Arner and the pastor. He used all his spare time in visiting Gertrude, in order to talk it over with her; but she seemed quite unable to explain her method in words, and usually deprecated the idea of her advice being necessary. Occasionally, however, she would let drop some significant remark which the lieutenant felt went to the root of the whole matter of education. For example, she said to him one day: "You should do for your children what their parents fail to do for them. The reading, writing and arithmetic are not, after all, what they most need; it is all well and good for them to learn something, but the really important thing is for them to *be* something, — for them to become what they are meant to be, and in becoming which they so often have no guidance or help at home."

Finally, the day arrived on which the new schoolmaster was to be formally presented to the village. Arner and the pastor led him solemnly between them to the church, which was crowded with the inhabitants of Bonnal. The good clergyman preached a sermon on the ideal function of the school in its relation to the home, and to the moral development of the community; after which Arner led Glülphi forward to the railing of the choir, and introducing him to the people, made a short but earnest plea in his behalf. The lieutenant was much affected, but mastered his emotion sufficiently to express in a few words his sense of the responsibility conferred upon him, and his hope that the parents would cooperate with him in his undertaking.

Arner was anxious to make the occasion of Glülphi's installation a festival for the school-children, so after the services at the church, he invited all the little folks to the parsonage, where, with the help of the pastor's wife, preparations had been made to receive them. It was a time-honored custom that every year, at Christmas and Easter, eggs and rolls should be distributed among the children of Bonnal. On this day, on entering the parsonage, the young people beheld even more beautifully painted eggs than they had seen at Easter; and beside each child's portion lay a bright nosegay.

The lieutenant, who knew nothing of the whole matter, was in an adjoining room, when suddenly the door was thrown open, and the children, at a sign from Theresa, struck up with one accord their prettiest song, and Glülphi found himself surrounded by the lively throng of his future charges. He was much moved, and when the song was concluded, he greeted them kindly, shaking many of them by the hand, and chatting pleasantly with them. Arner ordered some of his own wine to be brought, and the children drank the health of their schoolmaster.

On the following morning the lieutenant began his school, and Gertrude helped him in the arrangement of it. They examined the children with regard to their previous studies, and seated those together who were equally advanced. First there were those who had not learned their letters, then those who could read separate words, and finally, those who already knew how to read. Beside reading, all were to learn writing and arithmetic, which previously had only been taught to the more wealthy, in private lessons.

At first Glülphi found it harder than he had expected; but every day, as he gained in experience, his task became easier and more delightful. A good and capable woman, named Margaret, who came to take charge of the sewing, spinning etc., proved a most valuable and conscientious helper in the work. Whenever a child's hand or wheel stopped, she would step up and restore things to their former condition. If the children's hair was in disorder, she would braid it up while they studied and worked; if there was a hole in their clothes, she would take a needle and thread, and mend it; and she showed them how to fasten their shoes and stockings properly, beside many other things they did not understand.

The new master was anxious, above all, to accustom his charges to strict order, and thus lead them to the true wisdom of life. He began school punctually on the stroke of the clock, and did not allow any one to come in late. He also laid great stress on good habits and behavior. The children were obliged to come to

522

school clean in person and apparel, and with their hair combed. While standing, sitting, writing and working, they always were taught to keep the body erect as a candle. Glülphi's schoolroom must be clean as a church, and he would not suffer a pane of glass to be missing from the window, or a nail to be driven crooked in the floor. Still less did he allow the children to throw the smallest thing upon the floor, or to eat while they were studying; and it was even arranged that in getting up and sitting down they should not hit against each other.

Before school began, the children came up to their teacher one by one, and said: "God be with you!" He looked them over from head to foot, so that they knew by his eye if anything was wrong. If this glance was not sufficient, he spoke to them, or sent a message to their parents. A child would not infrequently come home with the word: "The schoolmaster sends greeting, and wants to know whether you have no needles and thread," or "whether water is dear," etc. At the close of school, those who had done well went up to him first, and said: "God be with you!" He held out his hand to each one, replying: "God be with you, my dear child!" Then came those who had only done partly well, and to these he merely said: "God be with you!" without giving them his hand. Finally, those who had not done well at all had to leave the room without even going to him.

The lieutenant's punishments were designed to remedy the faults for which they were inflicted. An idle scholar was made to cut fire-wood, or to carry stones for the wall which some of the older boys were constructing under the master's charge; a forgetful child was made school-messenger, and for several days was obliged to take charge of all the teacher's business in the village. Disobedience and impertinence he punished by not speaking with him only in private, after school. Wickedness and lying were punished with the rod, and any child thus chastised was not allowed to play with the others for a whole week; his name was registered in a special record-book of offences, from which it was not erased until plain evidence of improvement was given. The schoolmaster was kind to the children while punishing them, talking with them more then than at any other time, and trying to help them correct their faults.

XXXII. — A Good Pastor and Schoolmaster. — The Opening of a New Era.

In his instruction, Glülphi constantly sought to lay the foundation of that equanimity and repose which man can possess in all circumstances of life, provided the hardships of his lot have early become a second nature to him. The success of this attempt soon convinced the pastor that all verbal instruction, in so far as it aims at true human wisdom, and at the highest goal of this wisdom, true religion, ought to be subordinated to a constant training in practical domestic labor. The good man, at the same time, became aware that a single word of the lieutenant's could accomplish more than hours of his preaching. With true humility, he profited by the superior wisdom of the schoolmaster, and remodelled his method of religious instruction. He united his efforts to those of Glülphi and Margaret, striving to lead the children, without many words, to a quiet, industrious life, and thus to lay the foundations of a silent worship of God and love of humanity. To this end, he connected every word of his brief religious teachings with their actual, every-day experience, so that when he spoke of God and eternity, it seemed to them as if he were speaking of father and mother, house and home, in short, of the things with which they were most familiar. He pointed out to them in their books the few wise and pious passages which he still desired them to learn by heart, and completely ignored all questions involving doctrinal differences. He no longer allowed the children to learn any long prayers by rote, saying that this was contrary to the spirit of Christianity, and the express injunctions of their Saviour.

The lieutenant often declared that the pastor was quite unable to make a lasting impression on men, because he spoiled them by his kindness. Glülphi's own principles in regard to education were very strict, and were founded on an accurate knowledge of the world. He maintained that love was only useful in the education of men when in conjunction with fear; for they must learn to root out thorns and thistles, which they never do of their own accord, but only under compulsion, and in consequence of training.

He knew his children better in eight days than their parents did in eight years, and employed this knowledge to render deception difficult, and to keep their hearts open before his eyes. He cared for their heads as he did for their hearts, demanding that whatever entered them should be plain and clear as the silent moon in the sky. To insure this, he taught them to see and hear with accuracy, and cultivated their powers of attention. Above all, he sought to give them a thorough training in arithmetic; for he was convinced that arithmetic is the natural safeguard against error in the pursuit of truth.

Despite the children's rapid progress in their school, the lieutenant did not please everybody in the village, and a rumor soon spread abroad that he was too proud for a schoolmaster. It was in vain that the children contradicted this report; their parents only answered: "Even if he is good to you, he may be proud all the same." It was not until three weeks after the beginning of the school, that an event occurred which accomplished for him what the children's defence had been unable to do.

For the last twenty years the old rotten foot-bridge opposite the schoolhouse had been out of repair, so that in a rainy season the children must get wet above their ankles in crossing the lane to school. The first time the road was in this condition, Glülphi planted himself in the middle of the street in all the rain, and as the children came, lifted them, one after the other, across the brook. Now it happened that some of the very persons who had complained most of the lieutenant's pride, lived just across the way. It amused them greatly to see him get wet through and through in his red coat, and they fancied it would not be many minutes before he would call to them for help. When, however, he kept on patiently lifting the children over, until his hair and clothes were dripping wet, they began to say behind the window-panes: "He must be a good-natured fool, and we were certainly mistaken; if he were proud, he would have given it up long ago."

525

Finally, they came out, and offered to relieve him from his task, while he went home and dried himself. But this was not all; when school was out that day, the children found a foot-bridge built, over which they could go home dry-shod. And from that day forth, not a word more was heard of the schoolmaster's pride.

The school was still not without enemies, the bitterest among them being the old schoolmaster, whose envy and rage at its success would have known no bounds, had he not feared to lose the pension which had been granted him by Arner, on condition that he should not set himself against the new order of things. But the schoolmaster was not the only man in the village who looked back with regret to bygone days. Half of the villagers had been accustomed to spend their evenings at the tavern, and the bitterest complaints were heard on all sides, because, after the affair with Hummel, Arner had caused this house to be closed. As soon as he learned the state of things, and found that many of the former loafers were making their homes miserable by their idle discontent, Arner opened the peat swamps in the vicinity of Bonnal, and at once supplied more than fifty men with good employment.

The condition of the poor people of the village was much improved in various ways. The prospect of tithe-free land brought order and thrift into the houses of many of the spinners, and the poor in general were no longer so servile in their obedience to the whims and exactions of the rich. Renold's wife, who had always been noted for her charity, began to see that more good could be done by leading the people to help themselves, than by all her alms-giving; and now, whenever her aid was asked, her first answer was: "I must go home with you, and see what you really need, and how I can best help you."

Every evening the lieutenant had a half dozen young people at his house, to whom he talked for hours of what Arner and the pastor intended, and showed how their designs had been misunderstood. Among his hearers was one young man, Lindenberger by name, who seemed to comprehend it all at a single word, and whose clear and forcible language served to set things in their true light before many of the villagers.

526

It was only the old generation, who were hardened in vice, for whom the new era that was opening contained no prospect of anything better. The quack doctor Treufaug, who had promised the parson to abstain from his evil practices, could not resolve to leave his old life and lead a good and useful one; the former Bailiff Hummel, when freed from the pressure which had been brought to bear upon him in the time of his great humiliation, and deprived of his daily intercourse with the pastor, fell back into his old ways, so far as his changed circumstances would allow; and Hartknopf, after a brief season of repentance, became the same canting hypocrite as ever.

THE METHOD*

I am trying to psychologize the instruction of mankind; I am trying to bring it into harmony with the nature of my mind, with that of my circumstances and my relations to others. I start from no positive form of teaching, as such, but simply ask myself: —

"What would you do, if you wished to give a single child all the knowledge and practical skill he needs, so that by wise care of his best opportunities he might reach inner content?"

I think to gain this end the human race needs exactly the same thing as the single child.

I think, further, the poor man's child needs a greater refinement in the methods of instruction than the rich man's child.

Nature, indeed, does much for the human race, but we have strayed away from her path. The poor man is thrust away from her bosom, and the rich destroy themselves both by rioting and by lounging on her overflowing breast.

The picture is severe. But ever since I have been able to see I have seen it so; and it is from this view that the impulse arises within me, not merely to plaster over the evils in schools which are enervating the people of Europe, but to cure them at their root.

*From *The Method, A Report by Pestalozzi* (Aix-la-Chapelle, 1828). Extract reprinted in *Readings in Public Education in the United States*, edited by Ellwood P. Cubberley (Boston: Houghton Mifflin Company, 1934).

But this can never be done without subordinating all forms of instruction to those eternal laws by which the human mind is raised from physical impressions on the senses to clear ideas.

I have tried to simplify the elements of all human knowledge according to these laws, and to put them into a series of typical examples that shall result in spreading a wide knowledge of Nature, general clearness of the most important ideas in the mind, and vigorous exercises of the chief bodily powers, even among the lowest classes.

I know what I am undertaking; but neither the difficulties in the way, nor my own limitations in skill and insight, shall hinder me from giving my mite for a purpose which Europe needs so much. And, gentlemen, in laying before you the results of those labors on which my life has been spent, I beg of you but one thing. It is this: — Separate those of my assertions that may be doubtful from those that are indisputable. I wish to found my conclusions entirely upon complete convictions, or at least upon perfectly recognized premises.

The most essential point from which I start is this: —

Sense-impression of Nature is the only true foundation of human instruction, because it is the only true foundation of human knowledge.

All that follows is the result of this sense-impression, and the process of abstraction from it. Hence in every case where this is imperfect, the result also will be neither certain, safe, nor positive; and in any case, where the sense-impression is inaccurate, deception and error follow.

I start from this point and ask: — "What does Nature itself do in order to present the world truly to me, so far as it affects me? That is, — By what means does she bring the sense-impressions of the most important things around me to a perfection that contents me?" And I find, — She does this through my surroundings, my wants and my relations to others.

Through my surroundings she determines the kinds of sense-impressions I receive. Through my wants she stimulates my activities. Through my relations to others she widens my observation and raises it to insight and forethought. Through my surroundings, my wants, my relations to others, she lays the foundations of my knowledge, my work, and my right-doing.

And now I ask myself: — "What general method of the Art of Teaching has the experience of ages put into the hands of humanity to strengthen this influence of Nature in developing intelligence, energy, and virtue in our race?" And I find these methods are speech, the arts of drawing, writing, reckoning, and measuring.

And when I trace back all these elements of the human Art to their origin, I find it in the common basis of our mind, by means of which our understanding combines those impressions which the senses have received from Nature, and represents them as wholes, that is, as concepts.

Then the problem I have to solve is this: — How to bring the elements of every art into harmony with the very nature of my mind, by following the psychological mechanical laws by which my mind rises from physical sense-impressions to clear ideas.

PLATO

PLATO (c. 427-347 B. C.). The first systematic method of teaching and the first systematic treatise on education in the history of Western civilization have come down to us by way of Plato. Though not everyone would agree on the superiority of the Socratic method (using questions to elicit a clear and coherent expression of something assumed to be implicitly known by all men), everyone would probably concede that Plato's *Republic* is the most profound treatise ever written on the subject of education.

Socrates was already in his sixties when Aristocles (nicknamed Plato, from the Greek word for "broad," probably referring to his shoulders) came to him for instruction as a young man not yet twenty. For ten years Plato absorbed the wisdom of Socrates, and he perfected the dialogue, the most charming of literary forms, to record his master's question-and-answer teachings. In his hands the dialogue became the ideal medium for examining issues and ideas, and he put it to such exemplary use that Emerson wrote in his *Representative Men*: "Out of Plato come all things that are still written and debated among men of thought."

Plato was born in Athens about 427 B. C. and probably received the best education obtainable before coming under the influence of Socrates. He was related through his mother to Solon and through his father to Codrus, once king of Athens. After he became acquainted with the teachings of Socrates and decided to devote his life to philosophy, he traveled extensively, going first to Megara, where he resided for a time with Euclid, then to Italy, where he was influenced by the Pythagorean school. He began to teach philosophy at the Academy at Athens in 386 B. C., and for nearly half a century pupils came from all parts of Greece to hear his lectures.

In *The Republic,* from which the first of the following selections is taken, Plato defines an aristocratic utopia in which the common people are ruled over by an enlightened minority, carefully chosen and trained to serve the state. The seventh book of the dialogue begins with the allegory of the cave, and the tenth begins with the investigation of the question of art as imitation. Plato holds that the material objects revealed to us by the senses are forever changing, that true knowledge consists in grasping divine Ideas, and that the highest Idea is the moving principle of the world — Goodness. All education therefore has an ethical purpose, for it is by understanding moral ideas — courage, beauty, love —

that men are led to virtue. Plato's famous conclusion that all art is imitation means that art can have no place in the education of the philosopher who is to serve the republic.

In the last two selections, from *Laws* and *Symposium*, he further elaborates his views on education. In *Laws*, written in his old age, he discusses gymnastics and music, the two main branches of education in the prevailing system at Athens. In Symposium he returns to the idea of beauty and to the "life above all others which man should live, in the contemplation of beauty absolute."

THE REPUBLIC*

VII. — And now, I said, let me show in a figure how far our nature is enlightened or unenlightened: — Behold! human beings living in an underground den, which has a mouth open towards the light and reaching all along the den; here they have been from their childhood, and have their legs and necks chained so that they cannot move, and can only see before them, being prevented by the chains from turning round their heads. Above and behind them a fire is blazing at a distance, and between the fire and the prisoners there is a raised way; and you will see, if you look, a low wall built along the way, like the screen which marionette players have in front of them, over which they show the puppets.

I see.

And do you see, I said, men passing along the wall carrying all sorts of vessels, and statues and figures of animals made of wood and stone and various materials, which appear over the wall? Some of them are talking, others silent.

You have shown me a strange image, and they are strange prisoners.

Like ourselves, I replied; and they see only their own shadows, or the shadows of one another, which the fire throws on the opposite wall of the cave?

*From *The Republic*, translated by Benjamin Jowett, 3rd edition (Oxford: Clarendon Press, 1892).

True, he said; how could they see anything but the shadows if they were never allowed to move their heads?

And of the objects which are being carried in like manner they would only see the shadows?

Yes, he said.

And if they were able to converse with one another, would they not suppose that they were naming what was actually before them?

Very true.

And suppose further that the prison had an echo which came from the other side, would they not be sure to fancy when one of the passers-by spoke that the voice which they heard came from the passing shadow?

No question, he replied.

To them, I said, the truth would be literally nothing but the shadows of the images.

That is certain.

And now look again, and see what will naturally follow if the prisoners are released and disabused of their error. At first, when any of them is liberated and compelled suddenly to stand up and turn his neck round and walk and look towards the light, he will suffer sharp pains; the glare will distress him, and he will be unable to see the realities of which in his former state he had seen the shadows; and then conceive some one saying to him, that what he saw before was an illusion, but that now, when he is approaching nearer to being and his eye is turned towards more real existence, he has a clearer vision, — what will be his reply? And you may further imagine that his instructor is pointing to the objects as they pass and requiring him to name them, — will he not be perplexed? Will he not fancy that the shadows which he formerly saw are truer than the objects which are now shown to him?

Far truer.

And if he is compelled to look straight at the light, will he not have a pain in his eyes which will make him turn away to take refuge in the objects of vision which he can see, and which he will conceive to be in reality clearer than the things which are now being shown to him?

True, he said.

And suppose once more, that he is reluctantly dragged up a steep and rugged ascent, and held fast until he is forced into the presence of the sun himself, is he not likely to be pained and irritated? When he approaches the light his eyes will be dazzled, and he will not be able to see anything at all of what are now called realities.

Not all in a moment, he said.

He will require to grow accustomed to the sight of the upper world. And first he will see the shadows best, next the reflections of men and other objects in the water, and then the objects themselves; then he will gaze upon the light of the moon and the stars and the spangled heaven; and he will see the sky and the stars by night better than the sun or the light of the sun by day?

Certainly.

Last of all he will be able to see the sun, and not mere reflections of him in the water, but he will see him in his own proper place, and not in another; and he will contemplate him as he is.

Certainly.

He will then proceed to argue that this is he who gives the season and the years, and is the guardian of all that is in the visible world, and in a certain way the cause of all things which he and his fellows have been accustomed to behold?

Clearly, he said, he would first see the sun and then reason about him.

And when he remembered his old habitation, and the wisdom of the den and his fellow-prisoners, do you not suppose that he would felicitate himself on the change, and pity them?

Certainly, he would.

And if they were in the habit of conferring honours among themselves on those who were quickest to observe the passing shadows and to remark which of them went before, and which followed after, and which were together; and who were therefore best able to draw conclusions as to the future, do you think that he would care for such honours and glories, or envy the possessors of them? Would he not say with Homer,

'Better to be the poor servant of a poor master,'

and to endure anything, rather than think as they do and live after their manner?

Yes, he said, I think that he would rather suffer anything than entertain these false notions and live in this miserable manner.

Imagine once more, I said, such a one coming suddenly out of the sun to be replaced in his old situation; would he not be certain to have his eyes full of darkness?

To be sure, he said.

And if there were a contest, and he had to compete in measuring the shadows with the prisoners who had never moved out of the den, while his sight was still weak, and before his eyes had become steady (and the time which would be needed to acquire this new habit of sight might be very considerable), would he not be ridiculous? Men would say of him that up he went and down he came without his eyes; and that it was better not even to think of ascending; and if any one tried to loose another and lead him up to the light, let them not catch the offender, and they would put him to death.

No question, he said.

This entire allegory, I said, you may now append, dear Glaucon, to the previous argument; the prison-house is the world of sight, the light of the fire is the sun, and you will not misapprehend me if you interpret the journey upwards to be the ascent of the soul into the intellectual world according to my poor belief, which, at your desire, I have expressed — whether rightly or wrongly God knows. But, whether true or false, my opinion is that in the world of knowledge the idea of good appears last of all, and is seen only with an effort; and, when seen, is also inferred to be the universal author of all things beautiful and right, parent of light and of the lord of light in this visible world, and the immediate source of reason and truth in the intellectual; and that this is the power upon which he who would act rationally either in public or private life must have his eye fixed.

I agree, he said, as far as I am able to understand you.

Moreover, I said, you must not wonder that those who attain to this beatific vision are unwilling to descend to human affairs; for their souls are ever hastening into the upper world where they desire to dwell; which desire of theirs is very natural, if our allegory may be trusted.

Yes, very natural.

And is there anything surprising in one who passes from divine contemplations to the evil state of man, misbehaving himself in a ridiculous manner; if, while his eyes are blinking and before he has become accustomed to the surrounding darkness, he is compelled to fight in courts of law, or in other places, about the images or the shadows of images of justice, and is endeavouring to meet the conceptions of those who have never yet seen absolute justice?

Anything but surprising, he replied.

Anyone who has common sense will remember that the bewilderments of the eyes are of two kinds, and arise from two causes, either from coming out of the light or from going into the light, which is true of the mind's eye, quite as much as of the bodily eye; and he who remembers this when he sees any one whose vision is perplexed and weak, will not be too ready to laugh; he will first ask whether that soul of man has come out of the brighter life, and is unable to see because unaccustomed to the dark, or having turned from darkness to the day is dazzled by excess of light. And he will count the one happy in his condition and state of being, and he will pity the other; or, if he have a mind to laugh at the soul which comes from below into the light, there will be more reason in this than in the laugh which greets him who returns from above out of the light into the den.

That, he said, is a very just distinction.

But then, if I am right, certain professors of education must be wrong when they say that they can put a knowledge into the soul which was not there before, like sight into blind eyes.

Then undoubtedly say this, he replied.

Whereas, our argument shows that the power and capacity of learning exists in the soul already; and that just as the eye was unable to turn from darkness to light without the whole body, so too the instrument of knowledge can only by the movement of the whole soul be turned from the world of becoming into that of being, and learn by degrees to endure the sight of being, and of the brightest and best of being, or in other words, of the good.

Very true.

And must there not be some art which will effect conversion in the easiest and quickest manner; not implanting the faculty of sight, for that exists already, but has been turned in the wrong direction, and is looking away from the truth?

Yes, he said, such an art may be presumed.

And whereas the other so-called virtues of the soul seem to be akin to bodily qualities, for even when they are not originally innate they can be implanted later by habit and exercise, the virtue of wisdom more than anything else contains a divine element which always remains, and by this conversion is rendered useful and profitable; or, on the other hand, hurtful and useless.

Did you never observe the narrow intelligence flashing from the keen eye of a clever rogue — how eager he is, how clearly his paltry soul sees the way to his end; he is the reverse of blind, but his keen eyesight is forced into the service of evil, and he is mischievous in proportion to his cleverness?

Very true, he said.

But what if there had been a circumcision of such natures in the days of their youth; and they had been severed from those sensual pleasures, such as eating and drinking, which, like leaden weights, were attached to them at their birth, and which drag them down and turn the vision of their souls upon the things that are below — if, I say, they had been released from these impediments and turned in the opposite direction, the very same faculty in them would have seen the truth as keenly as they see what their eyes are turned to now.

Very likely.

Yes, I said; and there is another thing which is likely, or rather a necessary inference from what has preceded, that neither the uneducated and uninformed of the truth, nor those who never make an end of their education, will be able ministers of State; not the former, because they have no single aim of duty which is the rule of all their actions, private as well as public; nor the latter, because they will not act at all except upon compulsion, fancying that they are already dwelling apart in the islands of the blest.

Very true, he replied.

Then, I said, the business of us who are founders of the State will be to compel the best minds to attain that knowledge which we have already shown to be the greatest of all — they must continue to ascend until they arrive at the good; but when they have ascended and seen enough we must not allow them to do as they do now.

What do you mean?

I mean that they remain in the upper world: but this must not be allowed; they must be made to descend again among the prisoners in the den, and partake of their labours and honours. . . .

And so, Glaucon, I said, we have at last arrived at the hymn of dialectic. This is that strain which is of the intellect only, but which the faculty of sight will nevertheless be found to imitate; for sight, as you may remember, was imagined by us after a while to behold the real animals and stars, and last of all the sun himself. And so with dialectic; when a person starts on the discovery of the absolute by the light of reason only, and without any assistance of sense, and perseveres until by pure intelligence he arrives at the perception of the absolute good, he at last finds himself at the end of the intellectual world, as in the case of sight at the end of the visible.

Exactly, he said.

Then this is the progress which you call dialectic?

True.

But the release of the prisoners from chains, and their translation from the shadows to the images and to the light, and the ascent from the underground den to the sun, while in his presence they are vainly trying to look on animals and plants and the light of the sun, but are able to perceive even with their weak eyes the images in the water [which are divine], and are the

537

shadows of true existence (not shadows of images cast by a light of fire, which compared with the sun is only an image) — this power of elevating the highest principle in the soul to the contemplation of that which is best in existence, with which we may compare the raising of that faculty which is the very light of the body to the sight of that which is brightest in the material and visible world — this power is given, as I was saying, by all that study and pursuit of the arts which has been described.

I agree in what you are saying, he replied, which may be hard to believe, yet, from another point of view, is harder still to deny. This however is not a theme to be treated of in passing only, but will have to be discussed again and again. And so, whether our conclusion be true or false, let us assume all this, and proceed at once from the prelude or preamble to the chief strain, and describe that in like manner. Say, then, what is the nature and what are the divisions of dialectic, and what are the paths which lead thither; for these paths will also lead to our final rest.

Dear Glaucon, I said, you will not be able to follow me here, though I would do my best, and you should behold not an image only but the absolute truth, according to my notion. Whether what I told you would or would not have been a reality I cannot venture to say; but you would have seen something like reality; of that I am confident.

Doubtless, he replied.

But I must also remind you, that the power of dialectic alone can reveal this, and only to one who is a disciple of the previous sciences.

Of that assertion you may be as confident as of the last.

And assuredly no one will argue that there is any other method of comprehending by any regular process all true existence or of ascertaining what each thing is in its own nature; for the arts in general are concerned with the desires or opinions of men, or are cultivated with a view to production and construction, or for the preservation of such productions and constructions; and as to the mathematical sciences which, as we were saying, have some apprehension of true being — geometry and the like — they only dream about being, but never can they behold the waking reality so long as they leave the hypotheses which they use unexamined, and are unable to give an account of them. For when a man knows not his own first principle, and when the conclusion and intermediate steps are also constructed out of he knows not what, how can he imagine that such a fabric of convention can ever become science?

Impossible, he said.

Then dialectic, and dialectic alone, goes directly to the first principle and is the only science which does away with hypotheses in order to make her ground secure; the eye of the soul, which is literally buried in an outlandish slough, is by her gentle aid lifted upwards; and she uses as handmaids and helpers in the work of conversion, the sciences which we have been discussing. Custom terms them sciences, but they ought to have some other name, implying greater clearness than opinion and less clearness than science: and this, in our previous sketch, was called understanding. But why should we dispute about names when we have realities of such importance to consider?

Why, indeed, he said, when any name will do which expresses the thought of the mind with clearness?

At any rate, we are satisfied, as before, to have four divisions; two for intellect and two for opinion, and to call the first division science, the second understanding, the third belief, and the fourth perception of shadows, opinion being concerned with becoming, and intellect with being; and so as to make a proportion: —

As being is to becoming, so is pure intellect to opinion. And as intellect is to opinion, so is science to belief, and understanding to the perception of shadows.

But let us defer the further correlation and subdivision of the subjects of opinion and of intellect, for it will be a long inquiry, many times longer than this has been.

As far as I understand, he said, I agree.

And do you also agree, I said, in describing the dialectician as one who attains a conception of the essence of each thing? And he who does not possess and is therefore unable to impart this conception, in whatever degree he fails, may in that degree also be said to fail in intelligence? Will you admit so much?

Yes, he said; how can I deny it?

And you would say the same of the conception of the good? Until the person is able to abstract and define rationally the idea of good, and unless he can run the gauntlet of all objections, and is ready to disprove them, not by appeals to opinion, but to absolute truth, never faltering at any step of the argument — unless he can do all this, you would say that he knows neither the idea of good nor any other good: he apprehends only a shadow, if anything at all, which is given by opinion and not by science; — dreaming and slumbering in this life, before he is well awake here, he arrives at the world below, and has his final quietus.

In all that I should most certainly agree with you.

And surely you would not have the children of your ideal State, whom you are nurturing and educating — if the ideal ever becomes a reality — you would not allow the future rulers to be like posts, having no reason in them, and yet to be set in authority over the highest matters?

Certainly not.

Then you will make a law that they shall have such an education as will enable them to attain the greatest skill in asking and answering questions?

Yes, he said, you and I together will make it.

Dialectic, then, as you will agree, is the coping-stone of the sciences, and is set over them; no other science can be placed higher — the nature of knowledge can no further go?

I agree, he said.

But to whom we are to assign these studies, and in what way they are to be assigned, are questions which remain to be considered.

Yes, clearly.

You remember, I said, how the rulers were chosen before?

Certainly, he said.

The same natures must still be chosen, and the preference again given to the surest and the bravest, and, if possible, to the fairest; and, having noble and generous tempers, they should also have the natural gifts which will facilitate their education.

And what are these?

Such gifts as keenness and ready powers of acquisition; for the mind more often faints from the severity of study than from the severity of gymnastics: the toil is more entirely the mind's own, and is not shared with the body.

Very true, he replied.

Further, he of whom we are in search should have a good memory, and be an unwearied solid man who is a lover of labour in any line; or he will never be able to endure the great amount of bodily exercise and to go through all the intellectual discipline and study which we require of him. . . .

X. — Of the many excellences which I perceive in the order of our State, there is none which upon reflection pleases me better than the rule about poetry.

To what do you refer?

To the rejection of imitative poetry, which certainly ought not to be received; as I see far more clearly now that the parts of the soul have been distinguished.

What do you mean?

Speaking in confidence, for I should not like to have my words repeated to the tragedians and the rest of the imitative tribe — but I do not mind saying to you, that all poetical imitations are ruinous to the understanding of the hearers, and that the knowledge of their true nature is the only antidote to them.

Explain the purpose of your remark.

Well, I will tell you, although I have always from my earliest youth had an awe and love of Homer, which even now makes the words falter on my lips, for he is the great captain and teacher of the whole of that charming tragic company; but a man is not to be reverenced more than the truth, and therefore I will speak out.

Very good, he said.

Listen to me then, or rather, answer me.

Put your question.

Can you tell me what imitation is? for I really do not know.

A likely thing, then, that I should know.

Why not? for the duller eye may often see a thing sooner than the keener.

Very true, he said; but in your presence, even if I had any faint notion, I could not muster courage to utter it. Will you inquire yourself?

Well then, shall we begin the inquiry in our usual manner: Whenever a number of individuals have a common name, we assume them to have also a corresponding idea of form: — do you understand me?

I do.

Let us take any common instance; there are beds and tables in the world — plenty of them, are there not?

Yes.

But the maker of either of them makes a bed or he makes a table for our use, in accordance with the idea — that is our way of speaking in this and similar instances — but no artificer makes the ideas themselves: how could he?

Impossible.

And there is another artist, — I should like to know what you would say of him.

Who is he?

One who is the maker of all the works of all other workmen.

What an extraordinary man!

Wait a little, and there will be more reason for your saying so. For this is he who is able to make not only vessels of every kind, but plants and animals, himself and all other things — the earth and heaven, and the things which are in heaven or under the earth; he makes the gods also.

He must be a wizard and no mistake.

Oh! you are incredulous, are you? Do you mean that there is no such maker or creator, or that in one sense there might be a maker of all these things but in another not? Do you see that there is a way in which you could make them all yourself?

What way?

An easy way enough; or rather, there are many ways in which the feat might be quickly and easily accomplished, none quicker than that of turning a mirror round and round — you would soon enough make the sun and the heavens, and the earth and yourself, and other animals and plants, and all the other things of which we were just now speaking, in the mirror.

Yes, he said; but they would be appearances only.

Very good, I said, you are coming to the point now. And the painter too is, as I conceive, just such another — a creator of appearances, is he not?

Of course.

But then I suppose you will say that what he creates is untrue. And yet there is a sense in which the painter also creates a bed?

Yes, he said, but not a real bed.

And what of the maker of the bed? were you not saying that he too makes, not the idea which, according to our view, is the essence of the bed, but only a particular bed?

Yes, I did.

Then if he does not make that which exists he cannot make true existence, but only some semblance of existence; and if any one were to say that the work of the maker of the bed, or of any other workman, has real existence, he could hardly be supposed to be speaking the truth.

At any rate, he replied, philosophers would say that he was not speaking the truth.

No wonder, then, that his work too is an indistinct expression of truth.

No wonder.

Suppose now that by the light of the examples just offered we inquire who this imitator is?

If you please.

Well, then, here are three beds: one existing in nature, which is made by God, as I think that we may say — for no one else can be the maker?

No.

There is another which is the work of the carpenter?

Yes.

And the work of the painter is a third?

Yes.

543

Beds, then, are of three kinds, and there are three artists who superintend them: God, the maker of the bed, and the painter?

Yes, there are three of them.

God, whether from choice or from necessity, made one bed in nature and one only; two or more such ideal beds neither ever have been nor ever will be made by God.

Why is that?

Because even if He had made but two, a third would still appear behind them which both of them would have for their idea, and that would be the ideal bed and not the two others.

Very true, he said.

God knew this, and He desired to be the real maker of a real bed, not a particular maker of a particular bed, and therefore He created a bed which is essentially and by nature one only.

So we believe.

Shall we, then, speak of Him as the natural author or maker of the bed?

Yes, he replied; inasmuch as by the natural process of creation He is the author of this and of all other things.

And what shall we say of the carpenter — is not he also the maker of the bed?

Yes.

But would you call the painter a creator and maker?

Certainly not.

Yet if he is not the maker, what is he in relation to the bed?

I think, he said, that we may fairly designate him as the imitator of that which the others make.

Good, I said; then you call him who is third in the descent from nature an imitator?

Certainly, he said.

And the tragic poet is an imitator, and therefore, like all other imitators, he is thrice removed from the king and from the truth?

That appears to be so.

Then about the imitator we are agreed. And what about the painter? — I would like to know whether he may be thought to imitate that which originally exists in nature, or only the creation of artists?

The latter.

As they are or as they appear? you have still to determine this.

What do you mean?

I mean, that you may look at a bed from different points of view, obliquely or directly from any other point of view, and the bed will appear different, but there is no difference in reality. And the same of all things.

Yes, he said, the difference is only apparent.

Now let me ask you another question: Which is the art of painting designed to be — an imitation of things as they are, or as they appear — of appearance or of reality?

Of appearance.

Then the imitator, I said, is a long way off the truth, and can do all things because he lightly touches on a small part of them, and that part an image. For example: A painter will paint a cobbler, carpenter, or any other artist, though he knows nothing of their arts; and, if he is a good artist, he may deceive children or simple persons, when he shows them his picture of a carpenter from a distance, and they will fancy that they are looking at a real carpenter.

Certainly.

THE LAWS*

Ath. Up to the age of three years, whether of boy or girl, if a person strictly carries out our previous regulations and makes them a principal aim, he will do much for the advantage of the young creatures. But at three, four, five, and six years the childish nature will require sports; now is the time to get rid of self-will in him, punishing him, not so as to disgrace him. As we were saying about slaves, that we ought neither to punish them in hot blood or so as to anger them, nor yet to leave them unpunished lest they become self-willed, a like rule is to be observed in the

*Extracts from the seventh book of *The Laws,* translated by Jowett. The persons of the dialogue are an Athenian stranger, Cleinias (a Cretan), and Megillus (a Lacedaemonian).

case of the free-born. Children at that age have certain natural modes of amusement which they find out for themselves when they meet. And all the children who are between the ages of three and six ought to meet at the temples of the villages, several families of a village uniting on one spot, and the nurses seeing that the children behave properly and orderly, — they themselves and their whole company being under the care of one of the twelve women aforesaid annually appointed out of their number by the guardians of the law to inspect and order each company. Let the twelve be appointed by the women who have authority over marriage, one out of each tribe and all of the same age; and when appointed, let them hold office and go to the temples every day, punishing all offenders, male or female, who are slaves or strangers, by the help of some of the public servants; but if any citizen disputes the punishment, let her bring him before the wardens of the city; or, if there be no dispute, let her punish him herself. After the age of six years the time has arrived for the separation of the sexes, — let boys live with boys, and girls in like manner with girls. Now they must begin to learn — the boys going to teachers of horsemanship and the use of the bow, the javelin, and sling; and if they do not object, let women go to learn if not to practice; above all, they ought to know the use of arms; for I may note, that the practice which now almost universally prevails is due to ignorance.

Cle. In what respect?

Ath. In this respect, that the right and left hand are supposed to differ by nature when we use them; whereas no difference is found in the use of the feet and the lower limbs; but in the use of the hands we are in a manner lame, by reason of the folly of nurses and mothers; for although our several limbs are by nature balanced, we create a difference in them by bad habit. In some cases this is of no consequence, as, for example, when we hold the lyre in the left hand, and the plectrum in the right, but it is downright folly to make the same distinction in other cases. The custom of the Scythians proves our error; for they not only hold the bow from them with the left hand and draw the arrow to then with their right, but use either hand for both purposes. And there are many similar examples in charioteering and other things, from which we may learn that those who make the left side weaker than the right act contrary to nature. In the case of the plectrum, which is of horn only, and similar instruments, as I was saying, it is of no consequence, but makes a great difference, and may be of very great importance to the warrior who has to use iron weapons, bows and javelins, and the like. . . .

Ath. Education has two branches, — one of gymnastic, which is concerned with the body, and the other of music, which is designed for the improvement of the soul. And gymnastics has also two parts — dancing and wrestling; and one sort of dancing imitates musical recitation, and aims at preserving dignity and freedom; the other aims at producing health, agility, and beauty of the limbs and parts of the body, giving the proper flexion and extension to each of them, diffusing and accompanying the harmonious motion of the dance everywhere. As regards wrestling, the tricks which Antaeus and Cercyon devised in their systems out of a vain spirit of competition, or the tricks of boxing which Epeius or Amycus invented, are useless for war, and do not deserve to have much said about them; but the art of wrestling erect and keeping free the neck and hands and sides, working with energy and constancy, with a composed strength, and for the sake of health — these are always useful, and are not to be neglected, but to be enjoined alike on masters and scholars, when we reach that part of legislation; and we will desire the one to give their instructions freely, and the others to receive them thankfully. Nor, again, must we omit suitable imitations of war in our dances; in Crete there are the armed sports of the Curetes, and in Lacedaemon of the Dioscori. And our virgin lady, delighting in the sports of the dance, thought it not fit to dance with empty hands; she must be clothed in a complete suit of armor, and in this attire go through the dance; and youths and maidens should in every respect imitate her example, honoring the Goddess both with a view to the actual necessities of war, and to festive amusements; it will be right also for the boys until such time as they go out to war to make processions and supplications to the Gods in goodly array, armed and on horseback, in dances and marches, fast or slow, offering up prayers to the Gods and to the sons of Gods; and also engaging in contests and preludes of contests, if at all, with these objects. For this sort of exercises, and no others, are useful both in peace and war, and are beneficial both to states and to private houses. But other labors and sports and excessive training of the body are unworthy of freemen, O Megillus and Cleinias.

I have now completely described the kind of gymnastic which I said at first ought to be described; if you know of any better, will you communicate your thoughts?

Cle. It is not easy, Stranger, to put these principles of gymnastic aside and to enunciate better ones.

Ath. Next in order follow the gifts of the Muses and of Apollo: before, we fancied that we had said all, and that gymnastics alone remained to be discussed; but now we see clearly what points have been omitted, and should be first proclaimed; of these, then, let us proceed to speak.

Cle. By all means.

Ath. Hear me once more, although you have heard me say the same before — that caution must be always exercised, both by the speaker and by the hearer, about anything that is singular and unusual. For my tale is one which many a man would be afraid to tell, and yet I have a confidence which makes me go on.

Cle. What have you to say, Stranger?

Ath. I say that in states generally no one has observed that the plays of childhood have a great deal to do with the permanence or want of permanence in legislation. For when plays are ordered with a view to children having the same plays and amusing themselves after the same manner, and finding delight in the same playthings, the more solemn institutions of the state are allowed to remain undisturbed. Whereas if sports are disturbed and innovations are made in them, and they constantly change, and the young never speak of their having the same likings, or the same established notions of good and bad taste, either in the bearing of their bodies or in their dress, but he who devises something new and out of the way in figures and colors and the like is held in special honor, we may truly say that no greater evil

548

can happen in a state; for he who changes the sports is secretly changing the manners of the young, and making the old to be dishonored among them and the new to be honored. . . .

There ought to be no bye-work interfering with the greater work of providing the necessary exercise and nourishment for the body, and instruction and education for the soul. Night and day are not long enough for the accomplishment of their perfection and consummation; and therefore to this end all freemen ought to arrange the time of their employments during the whole course of the twenty-four hours, from morning to evening and from evening to the morning of the next sunrise. . . .

Now, neither sheep nor any other animals can live without a shepherd, nor can children be left without tutors, or slaves without masters. And of all animals the boy is the most unmanageable, inasmuch as he has the fountain of reason in him not yet regulated; he is the most insidious, sharp-witted, and insubordinate of animals. Wherefore he must be bound with many bridles; in the first place, when he gets away from mother and nurses, he must be under the control of tutors on account of his childishness and foolishness; then, again, being a freeman, he must have teachers and be educated by them in anything which they teach, and must learn what he has to learn; but he is also a slave, and in that regard any freeman who comes in his way may punish him and his tutor and his instructor, if any of them does anything wrong; and he who comes across him and does not inflict upon him the punishment which he deserves, shall incur the greatest disgrace; and let the guardian of the law, who is the director of education, see to him who coming in the way of the offenses which we have mentioned, does not chastise them when he ought, or chastises them in a way which he ought not; let him keep a sharp lookout, and take especial care of the training of our children, directing their natures, and always turning them to good according to the law.

And how can our law sufficiently train the director of education himself; for as yet all has been imperfect, and nothing has been said either clear or satisfactory? Now, as far as possible, the law ought to leave nothing to him, but to explain everything, that

549

he may be the interpreter and tutor of others. About dances and music and choral strains, I have already spoken both as to the character of the selection of them, and the manner in which they are to be improved and consecrated. . . . Attend, then, to what I am now going to say: We were telling, you, in the first place, that you were not sufficiently informed about letters, and the objection made was to this effect, — "That you were never told whether he who was meant to be a respectable citizen should apply himself in detail to that sort of learning, or not apply himself at all;" and the same remark was made about the lyre. But now we say that he ought to attend to them. A fair time for a boy of ten years old to spend in letters is three years; at thirteen years he should begin to handle the lyre, and he may continue at this for another three years, neither more nor less, and whether his father or himself like or dislike the study, he is not to be allowed to spend more or less time in learning music than the law allows. . . .

When I reflected upon all these words of ours, I naturally felt pleasure, for of all the discourses which I have ever learnt or heard, either in poetry or prose, this seemed to me to be the justest, and most suitable for young men to hear; I cannot imagine any better pattern than this which the guardian of the law and the educator can have. They cannot do better than advise the teachers to teach the young these and the like words, and if they should happen to find writings, either in poetry or prose, or even unwritten discourses like these of ours, and of the same family, they should certainly preserve them, and commit them to writing. And, first of all, they shall constrain the teachers themselves to learn and approve them, and any of them who will not, shall not be employed by them, but those whom they find agreeing in their judgment, they shall make use of and shall commit to them the instruction and education of youth. And here and on this wise let my fanciful tale about letters and teachers of letters come to an end.

SYMPOSIUM*

I will do my utmost to inform you, and do you follow if you can. For he who would proceed aright in this matter should begin in youth to visit beautiful forms; and first, if he be guided by his instructor aright, to love one such form only — out of that he should create fair thoughts; and soon he will of himself perceive that the beauty of one form is akin to the beauty of another; and then if beauty of form in general is his pursuit, how foolish would he be not to recognize that the beauty in every form is one and the same! And when he perceives this he will abate his violent love of the one, which he will despise and deem a small thing, and will become a lover of all beautiful forms; in the next stage he will consider that the beauty of the mind is more honourable than the beauty of the outward form. So that if a virtuous soul have but a little comeliness, he will be content to love and tend him, and will search out and bring to the birth thoughts which may improve the young, until he is compelled to contemplate and see the beauty of institutions and laws, and to understand that the beauty of them all is of one family, and that personal beauty is a trifle; and after laws and institutions he will go on to the sciences, that he may see their beauty, being not like a servant in love with the beauty of one youth or man or institution, himself a slave mean and narrow-minded, but drawing towards and contemplating the vast sea of beauty, he will create many fair and noble thoughts and notions in boundless love of wisdom; until on that shore he grows and waxes strong, and at last the vision is revealed to him of a single science, which is the science of beauty everywhere. . . .

He who has been instructed thus far in the things of love, and who has learned to see the beautiful in due order and succession, when he comes toward the end will suddenly perceive a nature of wondrous beauty. . . . a nature which in the first place is everlasting, not growing and decaying, or waxing and waning; secondly, not fair in one point of view and foul in another, or

*Extract from *Symposium,* translated by Jowett.

at one time or in one relation or at one place fair, at another time or in another relation or at another place foul, as if fair to some and foul to others, or in the likeness of a face or hands or any other part of the bodily frame, or in any form of speech or knowledge, or existing in any other being, as for example, in an animal, or in heaven, or in earth, or in any other place; but beauty absolute, separate, simple, and everlasting, which without diminution and without increase, or any change, is imparted to the ever-growing and perishing beauties of all other things. He who from these ascending under the influence of true love, begins to perceive that beauty, is not far from the end. And the true order of going, or being led by another, to the things of love, is to begin from the beauties of earth and mount upwards for the sake of that other beauty, using these as steps only, and from one going on to two, and from two to all fair forms, and from fair forms to fair practices, and from fair practices to fair notions, until from fair notions he arrives at the notion of absolute beauty, and at last knows what the essence of beauty is. This . . . is that life above all others which man should live, in the contemplation of beauty absolute; a beauty which if you once beheld, you would see not to be after the measure of gold, and garments, and fair boys and youths, whose presence now entrances you; and you and many a one would be content to live seeing them only and conversing with them without meat or drink, if that were possible — you only want to look at them and to be with them. But what if man had eyes to see the true beauty — the divine beauty, I mean, pure and clear and unalloyed, not clogged with the pollutions of mortality and all the colours and vanities of human life — thither looking, and holding converse with the true beauty simple and divine? Remember how in that communion only, beholding beauty with the eye of the mind, he will be enabled to bring forth, not images of beauty, but realities (for he has hold not of an image but of a reality), and bringing forth and nourishing true virtue to become the friend of God and be immortal, if mortal man may.

PLUTARCH

PLUTARCH (c. 50-120 A.D.). Plutarch of Chaeronea was considered "the true Philanthropist" in the ancient world, and in his *Moralia* he recorded his thoughts on everything that might interest, educate, or edify his contemporaries. Emerson summed up the opinion of many when he called Plutarch the embodiment of the highest ideal of humanity.

Born in Boeotia in 50 A.D., he studied philosophy under Ammonius, resided in Rome, where he lectured on philosophy and gathered material for his *Parallel Lives,* and later served as a magistrate in his native city of Chaeronea, where he was able to realize his ideal of perfect manhood: "serving the state in a public capacity, and living the calm and tranquil life of philosophy." A knowledge of his works, particularly his monumental study of the lives of the outstanding Greeks and Romans, was long considered indispensable to culture.

The following selection, "On Education," is from *Moralia,* a collection of Plutarch's essays on philosophy and practical subjects. The modernity of the views expressed in his famous treatise gives him clear title to a place among the most important educational thinkers of all time.

ON EDUCATION*

If anyone thinks that those who have not good natural ability cannot to some extent make up for the deficiencies of nature by right training and practice, let such a one know that he is very wide of the mark, if not out of it altogether. For good natural parts are impaired by sloth; while inferior ability is mended by training: and while simple things escape the eyes of the careless, difficult things are reached by painstaking. The wonderful efficacy and power of long and continuous labor you may see indeed every day in the world around you. . . . By toil what is contrary to nature becomes stronger than even nature itself. . . .

*From *Morals,* translated by Philemon Holland. Revised and reprinted in Bohn's Classical Library.

In my opinion mothers ought to nurse and suckle their own children. For they will bring them up with more sympathy and care, if they love them so intimately and, as the proverb puts it, "from their first growing their nails." Whereas the affection of wet or dry nurses is spurious and counterfeit, being merely for pay. And nature itself teaches that mothers ought themselves to suckle and rear those they have given birth to. . . . For infancy is supple and easily molded, and what children learn sinks deeply into their souls while they are young and tender, whereas everything hard is softened only with great difficulty. For just as seals are impressed on soft wax, so instruction leaves its permanent mark on the minds of those still young. . . . Phocylides the poet also seems to give admirable advice when he says, "We must teach good habits while the pupil is still a boy." . . .

The schoolmasters we ought to select for our boys should be of blameless life, of pure character, and of great experience. For a good training is the source and root of gentlemanly behavior. And just as farmers prop up their trees, so good schoolmasters prop up the young by good advice and suggestions, that they may become upright. . . . Were they not then wise words that the time-honored Socrates used to utter and say that he would proclaim, if he could, climbing up to the highest part of the city, "Men, what can you be thinking of, who move heaven and earth to make money while you bestow next to no attention on the sons you are going to leave that money to?" I would add to this that such fathers act very similarly to a person who should be very careful about his shoe but care nothing about his foot. Many persons also are so niggardly about their children, and indifferent to their interests, that for the sake of a paltry saving, they prefer worthless teachers for their children, practicing a vile economy at the expense of their children's ignorance. *Apropos* of this, Aristippus on one occasion rebuked an empty-headed parent neatly and wittily. For being asked how much money a parent ought to pay for his son's education, he answered, "A thousand drachmae." And he replying, "Hercules, what a price! I could buy a slave for as much;" Aristippus answered, "You shall have two slaves then, your son and the slave you buy." And is it not altogether strange that you accustom your son to take his food in his right hand, and chide him if he offers his left, whereas you care very little about his hearing good and sound discourses? I will tell you what happens to such admirable fathers, when they have educated and brought up their sons so badly: when the sons grow to man's estate, they disregard a sober and well-ordered life, and rush headlong into disorderly and low vices; then at the last the parents are sorry they have neglected their education, bemoaning bitterly when it is too late their sons' debasement.

I say, then, to speak comprehensively (and I might be justly considered in so saying to speak as an oracle, not to be delivering a mere precept), that a good education and sound bringing-up is of the first and middle and last importance; and I declare it to be most instrumental and conducive to virtue and happiness. . . . Education is of all our advantages the only one immortal and divine. And two of the most powerful agencies in man's nature are mind and reason. And mind governs reason, and reason obeys mind; and mind is irremovable by fortune, cannot be taken away by informers, cannot be destroyed by disease, cannot have inroads made into it by old age. For the mind alone flourishes in age; and while time takes away everything else, it adds wisdom to old age. Even war, that sweeps away everything else like a winter torrent, cannot take away education.

And as I advise parents to think nothing more important than the education of their children, so I maintain that it must be a sound and healthy education, and that our sons must be kept as far as possible from vulgar twaddle. For what pleases the vulgar displeases the wise. . . .

Next our freeborn lad ought to go in for a course of what is called general knowledge, but a smattering of this will be sufficient, a taste as it were (for perfect knowledge of all subjects would be impossible); but he must seriously cultivate philosophy. I borrow an illustration to show my meaning: it is well to sail round many cities, but advantageous to live in the best. Philosophy, therefore, ought to be regarded as the most important branch of study. For as regards the cure of the body, men have found two branches, medicine and exercise: the former of which gives health, and the latter good condition of body; but philosophy is the only cure for the maladies and disorders of the soul. For with her as ruler and guide we can know what is honorable, what is disgraceful; what is just, what unjust; generally speaking, what is to be sought after, what to be avoided; how we ought to behave to the gods, to parents, to elders, to the laws, to foreigners, to rulers, to friends, to women, to children, to slaves: viz., that we ought to worship the gods, honor parents, reverence elders, obey the laws, submit ourselves to rulers, love our friends, be chaste in our relations with women, kind to our children, and not to treat our slaves badly; and, what is of the greatest importance, to be neither over elated in prosperity nor over depressed in adversity, nor to be dissolute in pleasures, nor fierce and brutish in anger. These I regard as the principal blessings that philosophy teaches. For to enjoy prosperity nobly shows a man; and to enjoy it without exciting envy shows a moderate man; and to conquer the passions by reason argues a wise man; and it is not everybody who can keep his temper in control. And those who can unite political ability with philosophy I regard as perfect men, for I take them to attain two of the greatest blessings, serving the state in a public capacity, and living the calm and tranquil life of philosophy. For, as there are three kinds of life, the practical, the contemplative, and the life of enjoyment, and of these three the one devoted to enjoyment is a paltry and animal life, and the practical without philosophy an unlovely and harsh life, and the contemplative without the practical a useless life, so we must endeavor with all our power to combine public life with philosophy as far as circumstances will permit. Such was the life led by Pericles, by Archytas of Tarentum, by Dion of Syracuse, by Epaminondas the Theban, one of whom was a disciple of Plato (viz., Dion).

And as to education, I do not know that I need dwell any more on it. But in addition to what I have said, it is useful, if not necessary, not to neglect to procure old books, and to make a collection of them, as is usual in agriculture. For the use of books is an instrument in education, and it is profitable in learning to go to the fountain head.

Exercise also ought not to be neglected, but we ought to send our boys to the master of the gymnasium to train them duly, partly with a view to carrying the body well, partly with a view to strength. For good habit of body in boys is the foundation of a good old age. For as in fine weather we ought to lay up for winter, so in youth one ought to form good habits and live soberly so as to have a reserve stock of strength for old age. Yet ought we to husband the exertions of the body, so as not to be wearied out by them and rendered unfit for study. For, as Plato says, excessive sleep and fatigue are enemies to learning.

But why dwell on this? For I am in a hurry to pass to the most important point. Our lads must be trained for warlike encounters, making themselves efficient in hurling the javelin and darts, and in the chase. For the possessions of those who are defeated in battle belong to the conquerors as booty of war; and war is not the place for delicately brought up bodies: it is the spare warrior that makes the best combatant, who as an athlete cuts his way through the ranks of the enemies. Supposing anyone objects: "How so? As you undertook to give advice on the education of freeborn children, do you now neglect the poor and plebeian ones, and give instructions only suitable to the rich?" It is easy enough to meet such critics. I should prefer to make my teaching general and suitable to all; but if any, through their poverty, shall be unable to follow up my precepts, let them blame fortune, and not the author of these hints. We must try with all our might to procure the best education for the poor as well as the rich, but if that is impossible, then we must put up with the practicable. . . .

We ought to try to draw our boys to good pursuits by entreaties and exhortation, but certainly not by blows or abusive language. For that seems to be more fitting for slaves than the freeborn. For slaves try to shirk and avoid their work, partly because of the pain of blows, partly on account of being reviled. But praise or censure are far more useful than abuse to the freeborn, praise pricking them on to virtue, censure deterring them from vice. But one must censure and praise alternately: when they are too saucy we must censure them and make them ashamed of themselves, and again encourage them by praise.

SIDNEY L. PRESSEY

SIDNEY L. PRESSEY (1888-   ). Sidney Leavitt Pressey exhibited and described the first teaching machine, which he described modestly as "a simple apparatus which gives tests and scores — and teaches." Already a fairly sophisticated design, it was the prototype of present-day devices associated with programed instruction or automated learning. B. F. Skinner justly credits him with initiating a new educational technology — one which Pressey himself looked upon as the means of effecting an "industrial revolution" in education.

Born in Brooklyn, New York, on December 28, 1888, Pressey received his undergraduate training at Williams College and his graduate training at Harvard, where he earned his doctorate in psychology in 1917. After teaching at Indiana University from 1917 to 1921, he went to Ohio State University, where he was professor of educational psychology until 1959. Upon his retirement he went to the University of California at Los Angeles as visiting professor (1959-1960). For years he has been active in accelerated programs of learning. He has written more than a hundred articles and books on educational, normal, and abnormal psychology, the psychology of genius, and gerontology.

His fundamental concepts regarding automated instruction, elaborated in a series of articles, are presented in their earliest form in the article reproduced here.

A SIMPLE APPARATUS WHICH GIVES TESTS AND SCORES — AND TEACHES*

For a number of years the writer has had it in mind that a simple machine for automatic testing of intelligence or information was entirely within the realm of possibility. The modern objective test, with its definite systematization of procedure and objectivity of scoring, naturally suggests such a development. Further, even with the modern objective test the burden of scor-

*From the article in *School and Society*, XXIII (1926), pp. 373-6. Reprinted by permission of the editor of *School and Society*.

ing (with the present very extensive use of such tests) is nevertheless great enough to make insistent the need for labor-saving devices in such work.

The writer has also felt that the procedures in mastery of drill and informational material were in many instances simple and definite enough to permit handling of much routine teaching by mechanical means. The average teacher is woefully burdened by such routine of drill and information-fixing. It would seem highly desirable to lift from her shoulders as much as possible of this burden and make her freer for those inspirational and thought-stimulating activities which are, presumably, the real function of the teacher.

The present brief paper deals with a simple apparatus which automatically gives *and* scores a test, and which will also, automatically, teach — and teach informational and drill material more efficiently, in certain respects, than the "human machine."

Using the Apparatus

The apparatus is about the size of an ordinary portable typewriter — though much simpler. A schematic front view is shown in Chart I. The person who is using the machine finds presented

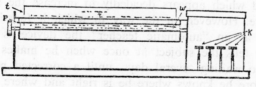

CHART I

to him in a little window (w) a typewritten or mimeographed question of the ordinary selective answer type — for instance:

To help the poor debtors of England James Oglethorpe founded the colony of (1) Connecticut, (2) Delaware, (3) Maryland, (4) Georgia.

To one side of the apparatus are four keys (k). Suppose now that the person taking the test considers answer number 4 to be the correct answer. He then presses key 4, and so indicates his reply to the question. The pressing of the key operates to turn up a new question, to which the subject responds in the same fashion. The apparatus counts the number of his correct responses on a little counter to the back of the machine. . . . All the person taking the test has to do, then, is to read each question as it appears, and press a key to indicate his answer. And the labor of the person giving and scoring the test is confined simply to slipping the test sheet into the device, at the beginning (this is done exactly as one slips a sheet of paper into a typewriter), and noting on the counter the total score, after the subject has finished.

The above paragraph describes the operation of the apparatus if it is being used simply to test. If it is to be used also to teach then a little lever to the back is raised. This automatically shifts the mechanism so that a new question is not rolled up until the correct answer to the question to which the subject is responding is found. However, the counter counts all trys.

It should be emphasized that, for most purposes, this second set is by all odds the most valuable and interesting. With this second set the device is exceptionally valuable for testing, since it is possible for the subject to make more than one mistake on a question — a feature which is, so far as the writer knows, entirely unique, and which appears decidedly to increase the significance of the score. However, in the way in which it functions at the same time as an "automatic teacher" the device is still more unusual. It tells the subject at once when he makes a mistake (there is no waiting several days, until a corrected paper is returned, before he knows where he is right and where wrong). It keeps each question on which he makes an error before him until he finds the right answer; he *must* get the correct answer to each question before he can go on to the next. When he does give the right answer the apparatus informs him, immediately, to that effect. If he runs the material through the little machine again it measures for him his progress in mastery of the topics dealt with. In short, the apparatus provides, in very interesting ways, for efficient learning.

The Mechanism

The general nature of the mechanism is shown in the schematic drawing below (Chart II), which should be studied in relation to Chart I. As shown in Chart I, the paper (t) on which the test question appears is carried by a typewriter platen (p) — and in exactly the same manner as paper is carried in a typewriter. The keys which the subject presses in taking the test appear at (k) in both charts. The "inner workings," which bring about the various operations mentioned in the previous section of the paper, are shown in Chart II.

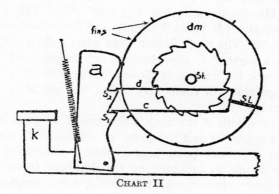

CHART II

The fundamental principle is simple. The shaft on which the platen is carried carries also a drum (dm). On this drum are rows of little projecting fins — one row for each question, and four fins in each row (one for each possible answer). These fins can easily, with a finger nail, be turned in so that they are almost flush with the drum, or turned out so that they project slightly. What the experimenter does, in setting the apparatus for a particular test sheet, is simply to "gear" this drum to the test by turning in the fin corresponding to each right answer.

When now the key (k) is pressed (Chart II shows the key pressed down) the shoulders sl and s2 on the activating upright (a) will, in the return movement, engage with the ends of the platen drive arm (d) and counter drive arm (c). That is, the platen will roll up a new question, and the counter (an ordinary Vidor counter, not shown in the charts) will count. . . . All this will happen if the "correct" key was pressed. Suppose the subject had pressed the wrong key. The activating upright of that key would have been held back by a fin — back far enough so that shoulder s2 would have missed the end of the platen drive arm (d). However, shoulder s1 would have still engaged the end of the counter drive arm (c). Thus no new question would be turned up, but the counter would count a try (the description is for operation with the more important set 2, for testing *and* teaching).

Suppose now the experimenter wishes to shift the apparatus to set 1. He simply raises the shift lever (SL). This pushes the platen drive arm (d) forward slightly, and draws back the counter drive arm (c). The result is that, even when a fin holds back the activating upright (a), shoulders, s1 will engage and the drum will be turned; but the counter drive arm (a) will not engage. That is, the apparatus will count only rights, but will always turn up a new question.

The exact details of the construction are of no great importance here; as a matter of fact a number of alternative forms are possible. The important point here is that a mechanism as comparatively simple as indicated by the drawings (quite as simple as the ordinary alarm clock) will do the things mentioned under "Using the Apparatus" above.

Labor-saving Devices in Education

Now briefly as to the larger significance of the device. It raises the fundamental question as to whether labor-saving mechanisms may not be used in education as in other work. The writer has seen somewhere the statement that education was at present the most inefficiently carried on of any large scale undertaking in this country. In so far as this is true, it is due in large measure, the writer believes, to lack of any consistent application of *ingenuity* to the teacher's problems. Education is, of course, almost always conservative, and comparatively, a teacher's time is cheap.

The result is that there are at present many things now done in our schools and colleges in very unnecessarily labored and enthusiasm-killing fashion. The writer is convinced that mechanical aids are possible which would do much to relieve the situation. These aids would probably do their particular work better (just as a calculating machine is more accurate than the old-time bank clerk). More important — they would leave the teacher more free time for her most important work, for developing in her pupils fine enthusiasms, clear thinking and high ideals.

Now an illustration to show, concretely, what might be done. The writer is in immediate charge of a first course in educational psychology which is handled by a number of instructors. In this course it has been the custom to give each week a short quiz — usually of the objective answer type. These quizzes take about five hours per section to score. There are an average of five sections per quarter, for the four quarters of the year. The total time cost of scoring these tests is thus, for the year, about 1,000 hours, or 125 eight-hour days — about five months (twenty-one weeks) of one person's full time. Thirty-five of the above-described simple machines would have halved practically all this labor. Further, mistakes would be eliminated. The students would profit much more by the quizzes since (with the second set of the apparatus) they would have, always, to obtain the right answer to each question. As a result of this last fact, little if any time would need to be given in class to going over the questions after the quiz. And the instructors could do very much more than at present in the way of class discussion, special help on difficulties, and so on. That is, in actual practice such mechanical aids would seem likely to prove of real and by no means negligible value.

Summary

(1) It is pointed out that objective tests naturally suggest the possibility of a simple mechanism for testing. There are also some reasons for supposing that some of the teaching of drill material might be done by machine.

(2) An apparatus is described which gives and scores tests, and informs the subject with regard to the right answers (an attachment will reward the subject after any given number of right answers has been made).

(3) It is emphasized that teachers are now heavily burdened with routine and clerical tasks which might well be handled mechanically — thus freeing the teacher for much more real teaching, of the thought-stimulating and ideal-developing type, than is now possible.

QUINTILIAN

QUINTILIAN (c. 35-95 A. D.). The ideal of Graeco-Roman culture and education found its classical expression under the Empire in the *Institutio Oratoria*. Though its author lacked the high political purpose of men like Aristotle, Plato, and Plutarch, he showed a better understanding of the importance of method, penetrated more deeply into the problems of teaching, and respected the qualities peculiar to childhood. Through his influence, following discovery of the lost manuscript of the *Institutes of Oratory* in the Monastery of St. Gallen, harshness and punishment were discredited by Renaissance schoolmen and teaching gradually was changed from an act of imposition to a process of self-development.

Quintilian was born in Spain about 35 A. D., but he was educated in Rome, where he achieved distinction as a teacher of eloquence and numbered among his pupils the younger Pliny. Honored with the title of "professor of eloquence," he was the first teacher in Rome to be paid a salary from the public treasury. Upon his retirement from teaching, he devoted his last years to the writing of his great textbook of oratory, the most systematic and comprehensive treatise on education that has survived from antiquity. Though his conclusion that oratory deserves a place equal to that of philosophy is wholly unfounded, the process through which he would conduct his pupil "from the cradle to the utmost heights of the oratorical art" (the words are those of his translator), commands our admiration.

The following selection presents Quintilian's ideas on the aims and methods of primary education in "a science which is necessary to the young, pleasing to the old, and an agreeable companion in retirement, and which alone, of all departments of learning, has in it more service than show."

THE EDUCATION OF THE ORATOR*

I. Before all things, let the talk of the child's nurses not be ungrammatical. Chrysippus wished them, if possible, to be women of some knowledge; at any rate he would have the best, as far

*From *Quintilian's Institutes of Oratory*, edited and translated by J. S. Watson (London: George Bell and Sons, 1875). Extracts are from Chapters I, II, and III.

as circumstances would allow, chosen. To their morals, doubtless, attention is first to be paid; but let them also speak with propriety. It is they that the child will hear first; it is their words that he will try to form by imitation. We are by nature most tenacious of what we have imbibed in our infant years; as the flavor, with which you scent vessels when new, remains in them; nor can the colors of wool, for which its plain whiteness has been exchanged, be effaced; and those very habits, which are of a more objectionable nature, adhere with the greater tenacity; for good ones are easily changed for the worse, but when will you change bad ones into good? Let the child not be accustomed, therefore, even while he is yet an infant, to phraseology which must be unlearned. . . .

I prefer that a boy should begin with the Greek language, because he will acquire Latin, which is in general use, even though we tried to prevent him, and because, at the same time, he ought first to be instructed in Greek learning, from which ours is derived. Yet I should not wish this rule to be so superstitiously observed that he should for a long time speak or learn only Greek, as is the custom with most people; for hence arise many faults of pronunciation, which is viciously adapted to foreign sounds, and also of language, in which when Greek idioms have become inherent by constant usage, they keep their place most pertinaciously even when we speak a different tongue. The study of Latin ought therefore to follow at no long interval and soon after to keep pace with the Greek; and thus it will happen, that, when we have begun to attend to both tongues with equal care, neither will impede the other.

Some have thought that boys, as long as they are under seven years of age, should not be set to learn, because that is the earliest age that can understand what is taught, and endure the labor of learning. . . . Those, however, advise better, who, like Chrysippus think that no part of a child's life should be exempt from tuition; for Chrysippus, though he has allowed three years to the nurses, yet is of opinion that the minds of children may be imbued with excellent instruction even by them. And why should not that age be under the influence of learning, which is now confessedly subject to moral influences? I am not indeed ignorant that, during the whole time of which I am speaking, scarcely as much can be done as one year may afterwards accomplish, yet those who are of the opinion which I have mentioned, appear with regard to this part of life to have spared not so much the learners as the teachers. What else, after they are able to speak, will children do better, for they must do something? Or why should we despise the gain, how little soever it be, previous to the age of seven years? For certainly, small as may be the proficiency which an earlier age exhibits, the child will yet learn something greater during the very year in which he would have been learning something else. This advancement extended through each year, is a profit on the whole; and whatever is gained in infancy is an acquisition to youth. The same rule should be prescribed as to the following years, so that what every boy has to learn, he may not be too late in beginning to learn. Let us not then lose even the earliest period of life, and so much the less, as the elements of learning depend on the memory alone, which not only exists in children, but is at that time of life even most tenacious.

Yet I am not so unacquainted with differences of age, as to think that we should urge those of tender years severely, or exact a full complement of work from them; for it will be necessary, above all things, to take care lest the child should conceive a dislike to the application which he cannot yet love, and continue to dread the bitterness which he has once tasted, even beyond the years of infancy. Let his instruction be an amusement to him; let him be questioned, and praised; and let him never feel pleased that he does not know a thing; and sometimes, if he is unwilling to learn, let another be taught before him, of whom he may be envious. Let him strive for victory now and then, and generally suppose that he gains it; and let his powers be called forth by rewards, such as that age prizes. . . .

II. But let us suppose that the child now gradually increases in size, and leaves the lap, and applies himself to learning in earnest. In this place, accordingly, must be considered the question, whether it be more advantageous to confine the learner at home, and within the walls of a private house, or to commit him to the large numbers of a school, and, as it were, to public teach-ers. The latter mode, I observe, has had the sanction of those by whom the polity of the most eminent states was settled, as well as that of the most illustrious authors.

Yet it is not to be concealed, that there are some who, from certain notions of their own, disapprove of this almost public mode of instruction. These persons appear to be swayed chiefly by two reasons: one, that they take better precautions for the morals of the young, by avoiding a concourse of human beings of that age which is most prone to vice (from which cause I wish it were falsely asserted that provocations to immoral conduct arise); the other, that whoever may be the teacher, he is likely to bestow his time more liberally on one pupil, than if he has to divide it among several. The first reason indeed deserves great consideration; for if it were certain that schools, though ad-vantageous to studies, are pernicious to morals, a virtuous course of life would seem to me preferable to one even of the most distinguished eloquence. But in my opinion, the two are com-bined and inseparable; for I am convinced that no one can be an orator who is not a good man! and, even if any one could, I should be unwilling that he should be. On this point, therefore, I shall speak first.

People think that morals are corrupted in schools; for indeed they are at times corrupted; but such may be the case even at home. Many proofs of this fact may be adduced; proofs of character having been vitiated, as well as preserved with the ut-most purity, under both modes of education. It is the disposition of the individual pupil, and the care taken of him, that make the whole difference. Suppose that his mind be prone to vice, sup-pose that there be neglect in forming and guarding his morals in early youth, seclusion would afford no less opportunity for immorality than publicity; for the private tutor may be himself of bad character; nor is intercourse with vicious slaves at all safer than that with immodest free-born youths. But if his disposition be good, and if there be not a blind and indolent negligence on the part of his parents, it will be possible for them to select a tutor of irreproachable character, (a matter to which the utmost attention is paid by sensible parents,) and to fix on a course of instruction of the very strictest kind; while they may at the same time place at the elbow of their son some influential friend or faithful freedman, whose constant attendance may improve even those of whom apprehensions may be entertained. . . .

But as emulation is of use to those who have made some advancement in learning so, to those who are but beginning, and are still of tender age, to imitate their school-fellows is more pleasant than to imitate their master, for the very reason that it is more easy; for they who are learning the first rudiments will scarcely dare to exalt themselves to the hope of attaining that eloquence which they regard as the highest; they will rather fix on what is nearest to them, as vines attached to a tree gain the top by taking hold of the lower branches first. This is an observation of such truth, that it is the care even of the master himself, when he has to instruct minds that are still unformed, not (if he prefer at least the useful to the showy) to overburden the weakness of his scholars, but to moderate his strength, and to let himself down to the capacity of the learned. For as narrow-necked vessels reject a great quantity of the liquid that is poured upon them, but are filled by that which flows or is poured into them by degrees, so it is for us to ascertain how much the minds of boys can receive, since what is too much for their grasp of intellect will not enter their minds, as not being sufficiently expanded to admit it. It is of advantage therefore for a boy to have school-fellows whom he may first imitate, and afterwards try to surpass. Thus will he gradually conceive hope of higher excellence.

To these observations I shall add, that masters themselves, when they have but one pupil at a time with them, cannot feel the same degree of energy and spirit in addressing him, as when they are excited by a large number of hearers. Eloquence depends in a great degree on the state of the mind, which must conceive images of objects, and transform itself, so to speak, to the nature of the things of which we discourse. Besides, the more noble and lofty a mind is, by the more powerful springs, as it were, it is moved, and accordingly is both strengthened by praise, and enlarged by effort, and is filled with joy at achieving something great. But a certain secret disdain is felt at lowering the power of eloquence, acquired by so much labor, to one auditor; and the teacher is ashamed to raise his style above the level of ordinary conversation. . . .

III. Let him that is skilled in teaching, ascertain first of all, when a boy is entrusted to him, his ability and disposition. The chief symptom of ability in children is memory, of which the excellence is twofold, to receive with ease and retain with fidelity. The next symptom is imitation; for that is an indication of a teachable disposition, but with this provision, that it express merely what it is taught, and not a person's manner or walk, for instance, or whatever may be remarkable for deformity. The boy who shall make it his aim to raise a laugh by his love of mimicry, will afford me no hope of good capacity; for he who is possessed of great talent will be well disposed; else I should think it not at all worse to be of a dull, than of a bad, disposition; but he who is honorably inclined will be very different from the stupid or idle. Such a pupil as I would have, will easily learn what is taught him, and will ask questions about some things, but will still rather follow than run on before. That precocious sort of talent scarcely ever comes to good fruit. Such are those who do little things easily, and, impelled by impudence, show at once all that they can accomplish in such matters. But they succeed only in what is ready to their hand; they string words together, uttering them with an intrepid countenance, not in the least discouraged by bashfulness; and do little but do it readily. There is no real power behind, or any that rests on deeply fixed roots; but they are like seeds which have been scattered on the surface of the ground and shoot up prematurely, and like grass that resembles corn, and grows yellow, with empty ears, before the time of harvest. Their efforts give pleasure, as compared with their years; but their progress comes to a stand and our wonder diminishes.

When a tutor has observed these indications, let him next consider how the mind of his pupil is to be managed. Some boys are indolent, unless you stimulate them; some are indignant at being commanded; fear restrains some, and unnerves others;

continued labor forms some; with others, hasty efforts succeed better. Let the boy be given to me, whom praise stimulates, whom honor delights, who weeps when he is unsuccessful. His powers must be cultivated under the influence of ambition; reproach will sting him to the quick; honor will incite him, and in such a boy I shall never be apprehensive of indifference.

Yet some relaxation is to be allowed to all; not only because there is nothing that can bear perpetual labor, (and even those things that are without sense and life are unbent by alternate rest, as it were, in order that they may preserve their vigor), but because application to learning depends on the will, which cannot be forced. Boys, accordingly, when re-invigorated and refreshed, bring more sprightliness to their learning, and a more determined spirit, which for the most part spurns compulsion. Nor will play in boys displease me; it is also a sign of vivacity; and I cannot expect that he who is always dull and spiritless will be of an eager disposition in his studies, when he is indifferent even to that excitement which is natural to his age. There must however be bounds set to relaxation, lest the refusal of it beget an aversion to study, or too much indulgence in it a habit of idleness. There are some kinds of amusement, too, not unserviceable for sharpening the wits of boys, as when they contend with each other by proposing all sorts of questions in turn. In their plays, also, their moral dispositions show themselves more plainly, supposing that there is no age so tender that it may not readily learn what is right and wrong; and the tender age may best be formed at a time when it is ignorant of dissimulation, and most willingly submits to instructors; for you may break, sooner than mend, that which has hardened into deformity. A child is as early as possible, therefore, to be admonished that he must do nothing too eagerly, nothing dishonestly, nothing without self-control; and we must always keep in mind the maxim of Virgil, *Adeo in teneris consuescere multum est,* "of so much importance is the acquirement of habit in the young."

But that boys should suffer corporal punishment, though it be a received custom, and Chrysippus makes no objection to it, I by no means approve; first, because it is a disgrace, and a punishment for slaves, and in reality (as will be evident if you imagine the age changed) an affront; secondly, because, if a boy's disposition be so abject as not to be amended by reproof, he will be hardened, like the worst of slaves, even to stripes and lastly, because, if one who regularly exacts his tasks be with him, there will not be the least need of any such chastisement. At present, the negligence of *paedagogi* seems to be made amends for in such a way that boys are not obliged to do what is right, but are punished whenever they have not done it. Besides, after you have coerced a boy with stripes, how will you treat him when he becomes a young man, to whom such terror cannot be held out, and by whom more difficult studies must be pursued? Add to these considerations, that many things unpleasant to be mentioned, and likely afterwards to cause shame, often happen to boys while being whipped, under the influence of pain or fear; and such shame enervates and depresses the mind, and makes them shun people's sight and feel a constant uneasiness. If, moreover, there has been too little care in choosing governors and tutors of reputable character, I am ashamed to say how scandalously unworthy men may abuse their privilege of punishing, and what opportunity also the terror of the unhappy children may sometimes afford to others. I will not dwell upon this point; what is already understood is more than enough. It will be sufficient therefore to intimate, that no man should be allowed too much authority over an age so weak and so unable to resist ill-treatment. . . .

In regard to the boy who has attained facility in reading and writing, the next object is instruction from the grammarians. Nor is it of importance whether I speak of the Greek or Latin grammarian, though I am inclined to think that the Greek should take the precedence. Both have the same method. This profession, then, distinguished as it is, most compendiously, into two parts, the art *of speaking correctly* and the *illustration of the poets,* carries more beneath the surface than it shows on its front. For not only is the *art of writing* combined with that of speaking, but *correct reading* also precedes illustration, and with all these is joined the exercise of *judgment,* which the old grammarians, indeed, used with such severity, that they not only allowed themselves to distinguish certain verses with a particular mark of censure, and to remove, as spurious, certain books which had been inscribed with false titles, from their sets, but even brought some authors within their canon, and excluded others altogether from classification. Nor is it sufficient to have read the poets only; every class of writers must be studied, not simply for matter, but for words, which often receive their authority from writers. Nor can grammar be complete without a knowledge of music, since the grammarian has to speak of meter and rhythm; nor if he is ignorant of astronomy, can he understand the poets, who, to say nothing of other matters, so often allude to the rising and setting of the stars in marking the seasons; nor must he be unacquainted with philosophy, both on account of numbers of passages, in almost all poems, drawn from the most abstruse subtleties of physical investigation, and also on account of Empedocles among the Greeks, and Varro and Lucretius among the Latins, who have committed the precepts of philosophy to verse. The grammarian has also need of no small portion of eloquence, that he may speak aptly and fluently on each of those subjects which are here mentioned. Those therefore are by no means to be regarded who deride this science as trifling and empty, for unless it lays a sure foundation for the future orator, whatever superstructure you raise will fall; it is a science which is necessary to the young, pleasing to the old, and an agreeable companion in retirement, and which alone, of all departments of learning, has in it more service than show.

FRANCOIS RABELAIS

FRANÇOIS RABELAIS (c. 1495-1553). The two most famous French writers of the sixteenth century were equally dissatisfied with the impractical and antiquated character of the prevalent system of education. Like the essayist Montaigne, the creator of *Gargantua and Pantagruel* proposed a wider curriculum related to life rather than to books alone and advocated freedom rather than restraint, gentleness rather than harshness. His satire on the degraded schools of his time and his forceful promotion of the best and noblest ideas of the humanist Renaissance reflect his strong belief in the essential goodness of man. His view that a new kind of education will call forth the basic goodness of man influenced such reformers as Rousseau and Pestalozzi.

Born near Chinon in Touraine, probably between 1482 and 1495, François Rabelais was trained as a novice in the Franciscan order. Later he busied himself especially with the "new learning" (Greek and other humanistic studies), studied law and medicine, traveled extensively, maintained close ties with other prominent humanists and jurists, and held a minor post in the retinue of Francis I. The tradition is that he died in Paris in 1553.

Demanding complete freedom throughout his life to pursue his whims, he illustrates better than any other writer the lusty individualism of the Renaissance — the spirit now implied by the word "rabelaisian." Throughout the reckless, bawdy humor of his tale of *Gargantua and Pantagruel,* from which the following selection is taken, runs his boundless faith in human nature. It underlies his attack on the stultifying character of medieval education and motivates his praise of the fictional Abbey of Theleme, in which humanistic learning is stimulated and governed by the single rule, "Do what thou wilt."

GARGANTUA AND PANTAGRUEL*

Chapter XXI

The Study of Gargantua, according to the discipline of his School-masters and Sophisters.

The first day being thus spent, and the bells put up again in their own place, the citizens of Paris, in acknowledgment of this courtesy, offered to maintain and feed his mare as long as he pleased, which Gargantua took in good part, and they sent her to graze in the forest of Biere. I think she is not there now. This done, he with all his heart submitted his study to the discretion of Ponocrates; who for the beginning appointed that he should do as he was accustomed, to the end he might understand by what means, in so long time, his old masters had made him so sottish and ignorant. He disposed therefore of his time in such fashion, that ordinarily he did awake between eight and nine a clock, whether it was day or not, for so had his ancient governors ordained, alleging that which David saith, Vanum est vobis ante lucem surgere. Then did he tumble and toss, wag his legs, and wallow in the bed some time, the better to stir up and rouse his vital spirits, and appareled himself according to the season: but willingly he would wear a great long gown of thick frieze, furred with fox skins. Afterwards he combed his head with an Alman comb, which is the four fingers and the thumb. For his preceptor said, that to comb himself other ways, to wash and make himself neat, was to lose time in this world. Then he dunged, pist, spued, belched, cracked, yawned, spitted, coughed, yexed, sneezed, and snotted himself like an arch-deacon, and to suppress the dew and bad air, went to breakfast, having some good fried tripe, fair rashers on the coals, excellent gammons of bacon,

*From *Gargantua and Pantagruel*, translated by Sir Thomas Urquhart. Reprinted in *The World in Literature*, edited by Robert Warnock and George K. Anderson (Chicago: Scott, Foresman and Company, 1950).

store of fine minced meat, and a great deal of sippit brewis, made-up of the fat of the beef-pot, laid upon bread, cheese, and chopped parsley stewed together. Ponocrates showed him, that he ought not eat so soon after rising out of his bed, unless he had performed some exercise beforehand. Gargantua answered, what! have not I sufficiently well exercised myself? I have wallowed and rolled myself six or seven turns in my bed, before I rose. Is not that enough? Pope Alexander did so, by the advice of a Jew his physician, and lived till his dying day in despite of his enemies. My first masters have used me to it, saying that to breakfast made a good memory, and therefore they drank first. I am very well after it, and dine but the better. And Master Tubal, who was the first licenciate at Paris, told me, that it was not enough to run a pace, but to set forth betimes: so doth not the total welfare of our humanity depend upon perpetual drinking in a ribble rabble, like ducks, but on drinking early in the morning; unde versus,

> To rise betimes is no good hour,
> To drink betimes is better sure.

After he had thoroughly broke his fast, he went to church, and they carried him in a great basket, a huge impantoufled or thick covered breviary, weighing, what in grease, clasps, parchment, and cover, little more or less than eleven hundred and six pounds. There he heard six and twenty or thirty masses. This while, to the same place came his orison-mutterer impaletocked, or lapped up about the chin, like a tufted whoop, and his breath antidoted with the store of the vine-tree-sirup. With him he mumbled all his kiriels, and dunsicals breborions, which he so curiously thumbed and fingered, that there fell not so much as one grain to the ground. As he went from the church, they brought him, upon a dray drawn with oxen, a confused heap of pater-nosters and aves of Sanct Claude, every one of them being of the bigness of a hat-block; and thus walking through the cloisters, galleries or garden, he said more in turning them over, than sixteen hermits would have done. Then did he study some paltry half four with his eyes fixed upon his book; but as the comic saith, his mind was in the kitchen. He sat down at table; and because he was naturally phlegmatic, he began his meal with some dozens of gammons, dried neat's tongues, hard rows of mullet, called botargos, andouilles, or sausages, and such other forerunners of wine. In the mean while, four of his folks did cast into his mouth one after another continually mustard by whole shovels full. Immediately after that, he drank a horrible draught of white-wine for the ease of his kidneys. When that was done, he ate according to the season meat agreeable to his appetite, and then left off eating when his belly began to strout, and was like to crack for fulness. As for his drinking, he had neither end nor rule. For he was wont to say that the limits and bounds of drinking were, when the cork of the shoes of him that drinketh swelleth up half a foot high.

Chapter XXIII

How Gargantua was instructed by Ponocrates, and in such sort disciplinated, that he lost not one hour of the day.

When Ponocrates knew Gargantua's vicious manner of living, he resolved to bring him up in another kind; but for a while he bore with him, considering that nature cannot endure such a change, without great violence. Therefore to begin his work the better, he requested a learned physician of that time, called Master Theodorus, seriously to perpend, if it were possible, how to bring Gargantua unto a better course. The said physician purged him canonically with Anticyrian-hellebore, by which medicine he cleansed all the alteration, and perverse habitude of his brain. By this means also Ponocrates made him forget all that he had learned under his ancient preceptors, as Timotheus did to his disciples, who had been instructed under other musicians. To do this better, they brought him into the company of learned men, which were there, in whose imitation he had a great desire and affection to study otherwise, and to improve his parts. Afterwards he put himself into such a road and way of studying that he lost not any one hour in the day, but employed all his time in learning, and honest knowledge. Gargantua awak'd them about four o'clock in the morning. Whilst they were in rubbing of him, there was read unto him some chapter of the Holy Scripture aloud and clearly, with a pronunciation fit for the matter, and hereunto was appointed a young page born in Basché, named Anagnostes. According to the purpose and argument of that lesson, he oftentimes gave himself to worship, adore, pray, and send up his supplications to that good God, whose word did show his majesty and marvellous judgment. Then went he into the secret places to make excretion of his natural digestions. There his master repeated what had been read, expounding unto him the most obscure and difficult points. In returning, they considered the face of the sky, if it was such as they had observed it the night before, and into what signs the sun was entering, as also the moon for that day. This done, he was appareled, combed, curled, trimmed and perfumed, during which time they repeated to him the lessons of the day before. He himself said them by heart, and upon them would ground some practical cases concerning the estate of man, which he would prosecute sometimes two or three hours, but ordinarily they ceased as soon as he was fully clothed. Then for three good hours he had a lecture read unto him. This done, they went forth, still conferring of the substance of the lecture, either unto a field near the university called the Brack, or unto the meadows where they played at the ball, the long-tennis, and at the pile trigone, most gallantly exercising their bodies, as formerly they had done their minds. All their play was but in liberty, for they left off when they pleased, and that was commonly when they did sweat over all their body, or were otherwise weary. Then were they very well wiped and rubbed, shifted their shirts, and walking soberly, went to see if dinner was ready. Whilst they stayed for that, they did clearly and eloquently pronounce some sentences that they had retained of the lecture. In the meantime Master Appetite came, and then very orderly sat they down at table. At the beginning of the meal, there was read some pleasant history of the warlike actions of former times, until he had taken a glass of wine. Then, if they thought good, they continued reading, or began to discourse merrily together; speaking first of the virtue, propriety, efficacy and nature of all that was served in at that table; of bread, of wine, of water, of salt, of fleshes, fishes, fruits, herbs, roots, and of their dressing. By means whereof, he learned in a little time all the passages competent for this, that were to be found in Pliny, Athenaeus, Dioscorides, Julius Pollux, Galen, Porphyrius, Oppian, Polybius, Heliodorus, Aristotle, Aelian and others. Whilst they talked of these things, many times, to be the more certain, they caused the very books to be brought to the table, and so well and perfectly did he in his memory retain the things above said, that in that time there was not a physician that knew half so much as he did. Afterwards they conferred of the lessons read in the morning, and, ending their repast with some conserve or marmalade of quinces, he picked his teeth with mastic tooth-pickers, washed his hands and eyes with fair fresh water, and gave thanks unto God in some fine canticks, made in praise of the divine bounty and munificence. This done, they brought in cards, not to play, but to learn a thousand pretty tricks, and new inventions, which were all grounded upon arithmetic. By this means he fell in love with that numerical science, and every day after dinner and supper he passed his time in it as pleasantly, as he was wont to do at cards and dice: so that at last he understood so well both the theory and practical part thereof, that Tunstal the Englishman, who had written very largely of that purpose, confessed that verily in comparison of him he had no skill at all. And not only in that, but in the other mathematical sciences, as geometry, astronomy, music, &c. For in waiting on the concoction, and attending the digestion of his food, they made a thousand pretty instruments and geometrical figures, and did in some measure practice the astronomical canons.

After this they recreated themselves with singing musically, in four or five parts, or upon a set theme or ground at random, as it best pleased them. In matter of musical instruments, he learned to play upon the lute, the virginals, the harp, the Allman flute with nine holes, the violin, and the sackbut. This hour thus spent, and digestion finished, he did purge his body of natural excre-

579

ments, then betook himself to his principal study for three hours together, or more, as well to repeat his matutinal lectures, as to proceed in the book wherein he was, as also to write handsomely, to draw and form the antique and Roman letters. This being done, they went out of their house, and with them a young gentleman of Touraine, named the Esquire Gymnast, who taught him the art of riding. Changing then his clothes, he rode a Naples courser, Dutch roussin, a Spanish gennet, a barbed or trapped steed, then a light fleet horse, unto whom he gave a hundred carieres, made him go to the high saults, bounding in the air, free a ditch with a skip, leap over a stile or pale, turn short in a ring both to the right and left hand. There he broke not his lance; for it is the greatest foolery in the world to say, I have broken ten lances at tilts or in fight. A carpenter can do even as much. But it is a glorious and praiseworthy action, with one lance to break and overthrow ten enemies. Therefore with a sharp, stiff, strong, and well-steeled lance, would he usually force up a door, pierce a harness, beat down a tree, carry away the ring, lift up a cuirassier saddle, with the mail-coat and gauntlet. All this he did in complete arms from head to foot. As for the prancing flourishes, and smacking popisms, for the better cherishing of the horse, commonly used in riding, none did them better than he. The voltiger of Ferrara was but as an ape compared to him. He was singularly skilful in leaping nimbly from one horse to another without putting foot to ground, and these horses were called desultories. He could likewise from either side, with a lance in his hand, leap on horseback without stirrups, and rule the horse at his pleasure without a bridle, for such things are useful in military engagements. Another day he exercised the battle-axe, which he so dexterously wielded, both in the nimble, strong, and smooth management of that weapon, and that in all the feats practiceable by it, that he passed knight of arms in the field, and at all essays.

Then tossed he the pike, played with the two-handed sword, with the back sword, with the Spanish tuck, the dagger, poniard, armed, unarmed, with a buckler, with a cloak, with a target. Then would he hunt the hart, the roebuck, the bear, the fallow deer, the wild boar, the hare, the pheasant, the partridge and the bustard. He played at the balloon, and made it bound in the air, both with fist and foot. He wrestled, ran, jumped, not at three steps and a leap, called the hops, nor at clochepied, called the hare's leap, nor yet at the Almanes; for, said Gymnast, these jumps are for the wars altogether unprofitable, and of no use: but at one leap he would skip over a ditch, spring over a hedge, mount six paces upon a wall, ramp and grapple after this fashion up against a window, of the full height of a lance. He did swim in deep waters on his belly, on his back, sideways, with all his body, with his feet only, with one hand in the air, wherein he held a book, crossing thus the breadth of the River Seine, without wetting, and dragging along his cloak with his teeth, as did Julius Caesar; then with the help of one hand he entered forcibly into a boat, from whence he cast himself again headlong into the water, sounded the depths, hollowed the rocks, and plunged into the pits and gulfs. Then turned he the boat about, governed it, led it swiftly or slowly with the stream and against the stream, stopped it in his course, guided it with one hand, and with the other laid hard about him with a huge great oar, hoisted the sail, hied up along the mast by the shrouds, ran upon the edge of the decks, set the compass in order, tackled the bowlines, and steered the helm. Coming out of the water, he ran furiously up against a hill, and with the same alacrity and swiftness ran down again. He climbed up trees like a cat, leaped from the one to the other like a squirrel. He did pull down the great boughs and branches, like another Milo; then with two sharp well-steeled daggers, and two tried bodkins, would he run up by the wall to the very top of a house like a rat; then suddenly come down from the top to the bottom with such an even composition of members, that by the fall he would catch no harm.

He did cast the dart, throw the bar, put the stone, practise the javelin, the boar spear or partisan, and the halbert. He broke the strongest bows in drawing, bended against his breast the greatest cross-bows of steel, took his aim by the eye with the hand-gun, and shot well, traversed and planted the cannon, shot at but-marks, at the papgay from below upwards, or to a height from above downwards, or to a descent; then before him side-wise, and behind him, like the Parthians. They tied a cable-rope to the top of a high tower, by one end whereof hanging near the ground he wrought himself with his hands to the very top; then upon the same tract came down so sturdily and firm that you could not on a plain meadow have run with more assurance. They set up a great pole fixed upon two trees. There would he hang by his hands, and with them alone, his feet touching at nothing, would go back and fore along the aforesaid rope with so great swiftness, that hardly could one overtake him with running; and then, to exercise his breast and lungs, he would shout like all the devils in hell. I heard him once call Eudemon from St. Victor's gate to Montmartre. Stentor never had such a voice at the siege of Troy. Then for the strengthening of his nerves or sinews, they made him two great sows of lead, each of them weighing eight thousand and seven hundred quintals, which they called Alteres. Those he took up from the ground, in each hand one, then lifted them up over his head, and held them so without stirring three quarters of an hour or more, which was an inimitable force. He fought at barriers with the stoutest and most vigorous champions; and when it came to the cope, he stood so sturdily on his feet, that he abandoned himself unto the strongest, in case they could remove him from his place, as Milo was wont to do of old. In whose imitation likewise he held a pomegranate in his hand, to give it unto him that could take it from him. The time being thus bestowed, and himself rubbed, cleansed, wiped, and refreshed with other clothes, he returned fair and softly; and passing through certain meadows, or other grassy places, beheld the trees and plants, comparing them with what is written of them in the books of the ancients, such as Theophrast, Dioscorides, Marinus, Pliny, Nicander, Macer, and Galen, and carried home to the house great handfuls of them, whereof a young page called Rizotomos had charge; together with little mattocks, pickaxes, grubbing hooks, cabbies, pruning knives, and other instruments requisite for herborising. Being come to their lodging, whilst supper was making ready, they repeated certain passages of that which had been read, and then sat down at table. Here remark, that

582

his dinner was sober and thrifty, for he did then eat only to prevent the gnawings of his stomach, but his supper was copious and large; for he took then as much as was fit to maintain and nourish him; which indeed is the true diet prescribed by the art of good and sound physic, although a rabble of logger-headed physicians, muzzled in the brabbling shop of sophisters, counsel the contrary. During that repast was continued the lesson read at dinner as long as they thought good: the rest was spent in good discourse, learned and profitable. After that they had given thanks, he set himself to sing vocally, and play upon harmonious instruments, or otherwise passed his time at some pretty sports, made with cards and dice, or in practising the feats of legerdemain with cups and balls. There they staid some nights in frolicking thus, and making themselves merry till it was time to go to bed; and on other nights they would go make visits unto learned men, or to such as had been travellers in strange and remote countries. When it was full night before they retired themselves, they went unto the most open place of the house to see the face of the sky, and there beheld the comets, if any were, as likewise the figures, situations, aspects, oppositions and conjunctions of both the fixed stars and planets.

Then with his master did he briefly recapitulate, after the manner of the Pythagoreans, that which he had read, seen, learned, done and understood in the whole course of that day.

Then prayed they unto God the Creator, in falling down before him, and strengthening their faith towards him, and glorifying him for his boundless bounty; and, giving thanks unto him for the time that was past, they recommended themselves to his divine clemency for the future. Which being done, they went to bed, and betook themselves to their repose and rest.

Chapter LVII

How the Thelemites were governed, and of their manner of living.

All their life was spent not in laws, statutes, or rules, but according to their own free will and pleasure. They rose out of their beds when they thought good: they did eat, drink, labour, sleep, when they had a mind to it, and were disposed for it. None did awake them, none did offer to constrain them to eat, drink, nor to do any other thing; for so had Gargantua established it. In all their rule, and strictest tie of their order, there was but this one clause to be observed,

Do What Thou Wilt.

Because men that are free, well-born, well-bred, and conversant in honest companies, have naturally an instinct and spur that prompteth them unto virtuous actions, and withdraws them from vice, which is called honour. Those same men, when by base subjection and constraint they are brought under and kept down, turn aside from that noble disposition, by which they formerly were inclined to virtue, to shake off and break that bond of servitude, wherein they are so tyrannously enslaved; for it is agreeable with the nature of man to long after things forbidden, and to desire what is denied us.

By this liberty they entered into a very laudable emulation, to do all of them what they saw did please one. If any of the gallants or ladies should say, Let us drink, they would all drink. If any one of them said, Let us play, they all played. If one said, Let us go a walking into the fields, they went all. If it were to go a hawking or a hunting, the ladies mounted upon dainty well-paced nags, seated in a stately palfrey saddle, carried on their lovely fists, miniardly begloved every one of them, either a sparhawk, or a laneret, or a merlin, and the young gallants carried the other kinds of hawks. So nobly were they taught, that there was neither he nor she amongst them, but could read, write, sing, play upon several musical instruments, speak five or six several languages, and composed in them all very quaintly, both in verse and prose. Never were seen so valiant knights, so noble and worthy, so dexterous and skilful both on foot and a horseback, more brisk and lively, more nimble and quick, or better handling all manner of weapons than were there. Never were seen ladies so proper and handsome, so miniard and dainty, less forward, or more ready with their hand, and with their needle, in every honest and free action belonging to that sex, than were there. For this reason, when the time came, that any man of the said abbey, either at the request of his parents, or for some other cause, had a mind to go out of it, he carried along with him one of the ladies, namely her whom he had before that chosen for his mistress, and they were married together. And if they had formerly in Theleme lived in good devotion and amity, they did continue therein and increase it to a greater height in their state of matrimony: and did entertain that mutual love till the very last day of their life, in no less vigour and fervency, than at the very day of their wedding.

JEAN JACQUES ROUSSEAU

JEAN JACQUES ROUSSEAU (1712-1788). The greatest contribution to the development of modern educational theory in the eighteenth century came from the erratic and fascinating genius who diagnosed the symptoms of the crisis of modern civilization and for whom education was to be the moving force in a revolution that would eliminate oppression and establish freedom for mankind.

Jean Jacques Rousseau, the most influential figure in modern French philosophy and literature, was born in Geneva, Switzerland, on June 27, 1712. His mother died when he was born, causing him to state that his birth was the first of his misfortunes. Alternately pampered and neglected by his eccentric father, he developed a taste for reading early in life and devoured a number of worthless romances as well as the works of Plutarch, Ovid, and Bossuet. At the age of sixteen he left Geneva and soon fell under the influence of Mme. de Warens, a widow who accepted him as her lover and encouraged his study of literature, religion, and philosophy. His errant life continued after he quarreled with his mistress and returned to Paris in 1741. Fame came to him in 1750, when he received a prize for a composition in which he advanced the theory that progress in the arts and sciences, far from being a beneficent influence on society, had brought about its corruption. The theme of the "return to Nature" was also the substructure of his two educational novels (*The New Heloise*, published in 1761, and *Emile*, published in 1762) and of his *Social Contract* (1762), which generated such excitement that he was (erroneously) held responsible for the French revolution. He died in Paris on June 28, 1778, and his *Confessions*, one of the most celebrated biographies ever written, were published six years later.

Emile, from which the following selection is taken, was condemned by the *parlement* of Paris in 1762, and the Archbishop of Paris forbade its reading: "We condemn the said book as containing an abominal doctrine, ready to subvert natural law and to destroy the foundations of the Christian religion, setting up maxims contrary to the morality of the Gospels; tending to trouble the peace of states, to cause subjects to revolt against their sovereigns." His romanticized treatise on education is, as he himself says, "a collection of thoughts and observations, without order and almost without connection." Abounding in mingled truth and falsehood, it must be read critically. The two basic principles which have most influenced educational practice are probably these: (1) we should study and follow nature; (2) the continuum of education extends from early childhood to maturity. Many of Rousseau's incidental suggestions for reform have now become standard practices in contemporary schools. He takes his fictional hero through five periods of development and devotes to each period one book in which he outlines appropriate methods and precepts. Pestalozzi and Froebel on the Continent and Herbert Spencer in England caught much of their inspiration from this revolutionary work by Rousseau.

TREATISE ON EDUCATION*

We are born weak, we have need of help; we are born destitute of every thing, we stand in need of assistance; we are born stupid, we have need of understanding. All that we are not possessed of at our birth, and which we require when grown up, is bestowed on us by education.

This education we receive from nature, from men, or from circumstances. The constitutional exertion of our organs and faculties is the education of nature: the uses we are taught to make of that exertion, constitute the education given us by men; and in the acquisitions made by our own experience, on the objects that surround us, consists our education from circumstances.

We are formed, therefore, by three kinds of masters. The pupil, in whom the effects of their different lessons are contradictory, is badly educated and can never be consistent with himself. He in whom they are perfectly consonant, and always tend to the same point, hath only attained the end of a complete education. His life and actions demonstrate this, and that he alone is well brought up.

Of these three different kinds of education, that of nature depends not on ourselves; and but in a certain degree that of circum-

*From *Selections from Emilius, or, a Treatise of Education, translated from the French of J. J. Rousseau, Citizen of Geneva,* 3 vols. (Edinburgh, 1773). Reprinted in *Three Thousand Years of Educational Wisdom,* edited by Robert Ulich (Cambridge, Mass.: Harvard University Press, 1961).

stances: the third, which belongs to men, is that only we have in our power: and even of this we are masters only in imagination; for who can flatter himself, he will be able entirely to govern the discourse and actions of those who are about a child?

No sooner, then, doth education become an art, or profession, than it is almost impossible it should succeed, as the concurrent circumstances necessary to its success are not to be depended on. All that can be done with our utmost solicitude, is to approach as near as possible the end we aim at, attributing it to good fortune if it be attained.

If it be asked, what is this end? it may be answered, that of nature, which has been already proved. For, since the concurrence of three kinds of education is necessary to its perfection, it is by that one, which is entirely independent of us, we must regulate the two others. . . .

It must be observed, I do not esteem, as public institutions, those ridiculous establishments that go by the name of Universities. I regard just as little the education acquired by an intercourse with the world, because that experience, aiming at two contrary ends, falls short of both. It is only calculated to make men deceitful, appearing always to interest themselves in the good of others, and being never interested in any thing but what relates to their own. As these pretensions are also become general, there is no one deceived by them; so that it is only to much pains thrown away.

From these contradictions arises that which we constantly experience in ourselves. Impelled by nature and custom to contrary ways, and forced to yield in a degree to both impulses, we take a route in the mean direction of both, that leads us neither to the end of one or the other. Thus held in suspense, and wavering, during the whole course of our lives, we end our days without being able to render ourselves consistent and without ever being good for any thing to ourselves or others.

There remains then only a private education, or that of nature. But of what use to others, it may be said, would a man be, educated only for himself? Perhaps, if the twofold object proposed could be reduced to a single one, in taking from man his contradictory motives of action, we should remove a great obstacle to his happiness. To judge of this, we should see him quite formed; should have observed his inclinations and propensities, have traced their progress, and attended them throughout; in a word, we should be made acquainted with the natural man. I flatter myself the reader will have made some advance in these researches, after having perused this treatise. . . .

According to the order of society, in which the respective places of individuals are fixed, every one ought to be educated for that which he is to fill. A man formed for one place, if taken out of it, would be fit for no other, and consequently good for nothing. In this state, education is useful only as fortune seconds the intentions of parents; in every other case it would be hurtful to the pupil, were it only on account of the prejudices it might instil. In Egypt, where the son was obliged to follow the occupation or profession of his father, education had at least a determinate end; but among us, where rank and profession are only permanent, and persons continually changing, a father would not know whether, in bringing up his child to his own profession, he might be doing him good or ill.

According to the order of nature, all men being equal, their common vocation is the profession of humanity; and whoever is well educated to discharge the duties of a man, cannot be badly prepared to fill up any of those offices that have a relation to him. . . .

In general, little more is thought of in the education of a child, than to preserve his being; this is not enough: he ought to learn how to preserve himself when he is grown up to manhood; to support the shocks of fortune, to bear riches or poverty; and to live, if occasion require, either amidst mountains of ice in Greenland, or on the burning rocks of Malta. You may take what precaution you will to preserve his life; he must inevitably die; and though his death may not be justly charged to your solicitude, your pains will be in a great measure thrown away. It is less needful to preserve your child from death, than to teach him how to live. To live is not merely to breathe; it is to act, to make a proper use of our organs, our senses, our faculties, and of all those parts of the human frame which contribute to the consciousness of our existence. The man who has lived most, is not he who hath survived the greatest number of years, but he who has experienced most of life. A man may be buried at an hundred years of age, who died in his cradle. Such a one would have been a gainer by dying young, at least if he had lived, in our sense of the word, till the time of his decease.

All our wisdom consists in servile prejudice; all our customs are nothing but subjection, confinement, and restraint. Civilized man is born, lives, and dies in slavery: at his birth he is bound up in swaddling-cloths, and at his death nailed down in his coffin. As long as he wears the appearance of the human form, he is confined by our institutions. . . .

The poor stand in no need of education; that of their station is confined, and they cannot attain any other. On the contrary, the education of those who are in a wealthy station, is that which is the least adapted to their own good, or to the good of society. Add to this, that an education adapted to the nature of things, ought to qualify a man for all conditions of life: now it is certainly less reasonable to educate the poor for a high station, than the rich for a low one; for, in proportion to the number of both, there are much fewer persons who become rich, than there are who become poor, as it is much easier to spend a fortune than to acquire one. Our pupil therefore shall be rich: thus we are sure at least of forming one man the more; a poor one may become a man of himself.

It is for the same reason, I shall not be sorry that Emile should be also of noble birth; as we are sure of snatching one victim from the absurdities of prejudice.

Emile is an orphan. It is to no purpose he should have a father or mother. As I charge myself with their obligations, I succeed to their rights and authority. He ought indeed to honour his parents, but complacence is all that is due to me. This is the first, or rather the only condition I make with him. . . .

I say it again, the education of a man commences at his birth: before he can speak, before he can understand, he is already instructed. Experience is the forerunner of precept; the moment he knows the features of his nurse, he may be said to have acquired considerable knowledge. Trace the progress of the most ignorant of mortals, from his birth to the present hour, and you will be astonished at the knowledge he has acquired. If we divide all human science into two parts, the one consisting of that which is common to all men, and the other of what is peculiar to the learned, the latter will appear insignificant and trifling in comparison with the other. . . .

As it grows up, a child acquires strength, and becomes less active and restless; it contracts its powers more within itself. The body and soul, if I may so say, keep each other in aequilibrio; and nature requires no greater quantity of motion than is necessary to our preservation. But the desire of command doth not cease with the motives that gave rise to it; the notion of superiority is flattering to self-love, and is increased by habit: thus caprice succeeds to necessity, and the force of prejudice and opinion takes root in the mind.

The principle once known, we see clearly the track wherein we began to deviate from nature: let us inquire then, what must be done, in order to prevent our going astray. So far from being endued with superfluous abilities, children have at first hardly sufficient for the purposes nature requires; it is requisite therefore to leave them at full liberty to employ those she hath given them, and which they cannot abuse: this is my first maxim.

It is our duty to assist them, and supply their deficiencies, whether of body or mind, in every circumstance of physical necessity. Second maxim.

Every assistance afforded them should be confined to real utility, without administering any thing to the indulgence of their caprice or unreasonable humours; for they will never be capricious unless through neglect, or in some particular circumstance depending on their constitution. Third maxim.

The meaning of their language and signs ought to be carefully studied, in order to be able to distinguish, in an age when they know not how to dissemble, between those inclinations that arise immediately from nature, and what are only fantastical. Fourth maxim.

The design and tendency of these rules are, to give children more real liberty and less command; to leave them more to do of themselves than to require of others. Thus, by being early accustomed to confine their desire to their abilities, they will be little affected with the want of what is out of their power. . . .

II. What can we think, then, of that barbarous method of education, by which the present is sacrificed to an uncertain future; by which a child is laid under every kind of restraint, and is made miserable, by way of preparing him for we know not what pretended happiness, which there is reason to believe he may never live to enjoy? Supposing it not unreasonable in its design, how can we see, without indignation, the unhappy innocents subjected to a yoke of insupportable rigour, and condemned like galley-slaves to continual labour, without being assured that such mortifications and restrictions will ever be of any service to them? The age of cheerfulness and gaiety is spent in the midst of tears, punishments, threats, and slavery. . . .

To prevent our running into chimeras, let us never lose sight of what is befitting our situation. Humanity has its place in the order and constitution of things; the state of infancy in those of human life; men should be considered as men, and children as children. To assign both their separate places, and regulate the human passions, agreeable to the constitution of man, are all that can be done for his happiness. The rest depends on circumstances which are not in our power. . . .

In what then consists human wisdom, or the means of acquiring happiness? To diminish our desires is certainly not the method; for if these were less than our abilities, part of our faculties would remain useless and inactive, and we should enjoy but half of our being. Nor is it, on the other hand, to extend our natural capacity for enjoyment; for if our desires, at the same time, be extended in a greater proportion, we should only become thereby the more miserable.

It must consist, therefore, in lessening the disproportion between our abilities and our desires; and in reducing our inclinations and our powers to a perfect equilibrium. It is in such a situation, and that only, that all our faculties may be employed;

and yet the mind preserve its tranquillity, and the body its due regularity and ease. . . .

Confine, O man, thy existence within thyself, and thou wilt be no longer miserable. Remain in the place nature hath assigned you in the scale of beings: spurn not against the hard law of necessity, nor waste, by our opposition, that strength which heaven hath bestowed on you, not to extend and prolong your existence, but only to preserve it during its own time and in its own manner. Your liberty, your power, extend as far as your natural faculties, and no farther; all the rest is only slavery, illusion, and deceit. Authority itself is servile, when it is founded on opinion; for you depend on the prejudices of those whom you govern by the force of prejudice. To govern them according to your own pleasure, you must govern them agreeable to theirs. They have only to change their mode of thinking, and you will be obliged to change yours of acting. . . .

Excessive severity, as well as excessive indulgence, should be equally avoided. If you leave children to suffer, you expose their health, endanger their lives, and make them actually miserable; on the other hand, if you are too anxious to prevent their being sensible of any kind of pain and inconvenience, you only pave their way to feel much greater; you enervate their constitutions, make them tender and effeminate; in a word, you remove them out of their situation as men, into which they must hereafter return in spite of all your solicitude. In order not to expose them to the few evils nature would inflict on them, you provide for them many which they would otherwise never have suffered. . . .

It is very strange, that, ever since mankind have taken it into their heads to trouble themselves so much about the education of children, they should never have thought of any other instruments to effect their purpose than those of emulation, jealousy, envy, pride, covetousness, and servile fear; all passions, the most dangerous, the most apt to ferment, and the most proper to corrupt the soul, even before the body is formed. With every premature instruction we instill into the head, we implant a vice in the bottom of the heart. Senseless preceptors, those, who think they work wonders, by making children actually vicious, in order to instruct them in the theory of virtue, and then gravely tell us, Such is man. Yes, such, indeed, is the man of your making.

Almost every method has been tried but one, and that the only one which can succeed, natural liberty duly regulated. No one ought to undertake the education of a child who cannot conduct him at pleasure, merely by the maxims of possibility and impossibility. The sphere of both being equally unknown to infancy, it may be extended or contracted as we please. A child may be equally excited or restrained, by the single plea of necessity, without murmuring: he may be rendered pliant and docile by the force of circumstance only, without ever giving occasion to sow the seeds of vice in his heart: for the passions will never be irritated so long as they must be exerted without effect. Give your pupil no kind of verbal instructions; he should receive none but from experience: inflict on him no kind of punishment, for he knows not what it is to be in fault: require him never to ask pardon, for he cannot offend you. As he is insensible of all moral obligation, he cannot do any thing morally evil, or that is deserving of punishment or reprimand. . . .

Let us lay down as an incontestable maxim, That the first emotions of nature are always right: there is no original perversity in the human heart. I will venture to say, there is not a single vice to be found there, that one could not say how and which way it entered. The only passion natural to man is the love of himself, or self-love taken in an extensive sense. This passion considered in itself, or as relative to us, is good and useful; and, as it has no necessary relation to any one else, it is in that respect naturally indifferent: it becomes good or evil, therefore, from our application of it, and the several relations we give it. Till the guide of self-love, then, which is reason, appears, a child should do nothing merely because he is seen or heard, nothing from causes merely relative to others, but only those things which nature requires and infligates; and then he will never do wrong. . . .

May I venture here to lay down the greatest, most important, and most useful rule of education? It is this, Not to gain time, but to lose it. The generality of readers will be so good as to excuse my paradoxes; there is an absolute necessity for them in

594

making reflections: and, say what you will, I had rather be remarkable for hunting after a paradox, than for being misled by prejudice. The most critical interval of human life is that between the hour of our birth and twelve years of age. This is the time wherein vice and error take root, without our being possessed of any instrument to destroy them: and when the implement is found, they are so deeply grounded, that they are no longer to be eradicated. If children took a leap from their mother's breast, and at once arrived at the age of reason, the methods of education now usually taken with them would be very proper; but according to the progress of nature, they require those which are very different. We should not tamper with the mind, till it has acquired all its faculties: for it is impossible it should perceive the light we hold out to it while it is blind; or that it should pursue, over an immense plain of ideas, that route which reason hath so slightly traced as to be perceptible only to the sharpest sight.

The first part of education, therefore, ought to be purely negative. It consists, neither in teaching virtue nor truth; but in guarding the heart from vice, and the mind from error. If you could be content to do nothing yourself, and could prevent any thing being done by others; if you could bring up your pupil healthy and robust to the age of twelve years, without his being able to distinguish his right hand from his left, the eyes of his understanding would be open to reason at your first lesson; void both of habit and prejudice, his passions would not operate against your endeavours, and he would become, under proper instructions, the wisest of men. It is thus, by attempting nothing in the beginning, you might produce a prodigy of education.

Take the road directly opposite to that which is in use, and you will almost always do right. As we think it not enough children should be children, but it is expected they should be masters of arts; so fathers and preceptors think they can never have too many checks, corrections, reprimands, menaces, promises, instructions, fair speeches, and fine arguments. You will act wiser than all this, by being reasonable yourself, and never arguing with your child, particularly in striving to reconcile him to what he dislikes: for to use him to reason only upon disagreeable subjects,

595

is the way to disgust him, and bring argument early into discredit with a mind incapable of understanding it. Exercise his corporeal organs, senses, and faculties, as much as you please; but keep his intellectual ones inactive as long as possible. . . .

Emilius shall never be set to learn any thing by heart, not even fables, not even the fables of Fontaine, simple and beautiful as they are; for the words of a fable are no more the fable itself, than those of a history are the history. How is it possible men can be so blind as to call fables the moral lectures for children, without reflecting that the apologue, in amusing, only deceives them; and that, seduced by the charms of falsehood, the truth couched underneath it escapes their notice? Yet so it is; and the means which are thus taken to render instruction agreeable prevents their profiting by it. Fables may instruct grown persons, but the naked truth should ever be presented to children: for if we once spread over it a veil, they will not take the trouble to draw it aside in order to look at it.

Children universally read the fables of Fontaine, and yet there is not one who understands them. It would be still worse, however, if they did understand them; for the moral is so complicated and disproportionate to their capacities, that it would rather induce them to vice than virtue. . . .

It has been made a matter of great importance, to find out the best method of teaching children to read; to this end cards and other implements have been invented, so various and numerous, that they made the nursery resemble the workshop of a printer. Mr. Locke would have a child taught to read by means of letters carved on dice. Is not this an excellent invention! A more certain method than any of these, and that which is nevertheless always neglected, is to excite in children a desire to learn. Give a child this desire, and do as you will with your cards and dice; any method will then be sufficient.

The grand motive, indeed the only one that is certain and effectual, is present interest. Émile sometimes receives written invitations from his father, mother, and other friends, to dinner, to go on a party of pleasure, or to see some public entertainment. These invitations are short, plain, precise, and well written. When received, it is necessary for him to find somebody to read them to him: such a person is not always at hand, or complaisant enough to comply with his request. Thus the opportunity is lost: the billet, indeed, is read to him afterwards, but then it is too late to obey the summons. How ardently must he wish on such an occasion to be able to read himself! He receives others, equally short and interesting: he sets immediately about deciphering them; sometimes receiving assistance, and at others denied it. By dint of study, he at length hammers out that he is invited to go to-morrow to eat cream; but where or with whom he cannot discover. How many efforts will he not make to find out the rest: Émile will learn to read by such means as these, without standing in need of horn-books, cards, or dice. I might here speak of teaching him to write; but I am ashamed of descending to such trifling objects in a treatise on education. . . .

III. Although, till the age of puberty, the whole course of life be one continued series of imbecility, there is a certain period in this first age of life, in which the progress of his passions exceeding that of his necessities, the growing animal, though absolutely weak, becomes relatively strong. His wants not being wholly displayed, his actual abilities are more than sufficient to provide for those which he really feels. Considered as a man, he is very weak; but as a child, he is abundantly strong. Whence proceeds the weakness of man? From the disproportion he finds between his faculties and his desires. It is our passions that render us feeble; because, to gratify them, requires greater powers than nature has furnished us with. Diminish, then, the number, check the extravagance, of our desires, and you increase your powers of gratification. He who can compass more than he requires, hath ability to spare, and is certainly a powerful being. Here begins the third stage of infancy, of which I am now about to treat; it being that state of childhood which approaches nearly to puberty, without being quite arrived at the term. . . .

Let us convert our sensations into ideas; but let us not fly at once from sensible to intellectual objects. It is by a due and rational attention to the former we can only attain the latter. In the first operations of the understanding, let our senses then always be our guide, the world our only book, and facts our sole preceptors. Children, when taught to read, learn that only; they never think; they gain no information; all their learning consists in words.

Direct the attention of your pupil to the phaenomena of nature, and you will soon awaken his curiosity; but to keep that curiosity alive, you must be in no haste to satisfy it. Put questions to him adapted to his capacity, and leave him to resolve them. Let him take nothing on trust from his preceptor, but on his own comprehension and conviction: he should not learn, but invent the sciences. If ever you substitute authority in the place of argument, he will reason no longer; he will be ever afterwards bandied like a shuttlecock between the opinions of others.

. . . Talk not to children in a language they do not comprehend; make use of no pompous descriptions, no flowers of speech, no tropes and figures, no poetry; taste and sentiment are at present quite out of the question: simplicity, gravity, and precision are all that are yet required; the time will come but too soon when we must assume a different style.

A pupil educated agreeable to these maxims, and accustomed to receive no assistance till he has discovered his own inabilities, will examine every new object with a long and silent attention. He will be thoughtful without asking questions. Content yourself, therefore, with presenting proper objects opportunely to his notice, and when you see they have sufficiently excited his curiosity, drop from leading laconic questions, which may put him in the way of discovering the truth. . . .

To accustom a child to give attention to objects, and to make sensible truths appear striking to his imagination, it is necessary to keep him some time in suspense before they are explained or discovered to him. If he should not sufficiently comprehend the nature of the present question by the means proposed, it may be rendered still more obvious by diversifying the terms of it. If he cannot comprehend in what manner the sun proceeds from its setting to its rising, he knows at least how it proceeds from its rising to its setting; he hath ocular information of this. Explain the first question, then, by the second; and if your pupil be not extremely dull indeed, the analogy is too obvious to escape him.

The sciences are connected together by a series of propositions, all dependent on some general and common principles, which are gradually displayed. The philosophers make use of these; with us they are as yet out of the question. There is another chain of reasoning, of a different construction, by which every particular object is connected to some other, and points out that which succeeds it. This order of succession, which, from our natural curiosity, keeps alive our attention, is generally made use of by grown persons, and is peculiarly adapted to children. . . .

We acquire, without doubt, notions more clear and certain, or things we thus learn of ourselves, than of those we are taught by others. Another advantage also resulting from this method is, that we do not accustom ourselves to a servile submission to the authority of others; but, by exercising our reason, grow every day more ingenious in the discovery of the relations of things, in connecting our ideas, and in the contrivance of machines. . . .

I have already observed, that the mere speculative part of science is by no means adapted to children, even when they approach adolescency; it is proper, nevertheless, though you do not enter with them too profoundly into the depth of physical theory, to connect their experiments by some chain of deduction, that they may arrange them in some order in their minds, for the sake of remembering them: for it is very difficult to retain separate and independent facts and conclusions long in the memory, without some leading clue for occasional recollection.

In your researches into the laws of nature, begin always with the most common and obvious phænomena; accustoming your pupil to look upon them always as mere facts. . . .

As soon as we are so far advanced as to give our pupil an idea of the word *useful,* we have attained a considerable influence over his future conduct; this term being very striking, provided the sense annexed to it be adapted to his years, and he see clearly its relation to his present welfare. Ordinary children are not affected by this term, because no care has been taken to affix to it an idea conformable to their understandings, and because others taking upon them to provide for them what is useful, they have no need to think of it themselves, and therefore remain ignorant of the meaning of utility.

What is the use of that? shall, for the future, be the determinate question between my pupil and me, on all occasions. On my part, I shall infallibly make use of it in answer to all his interrogatories; which may serve as a check to that multiplicity of silly, troublesome questions, with which children are incessantly teazing those about them, more for the sake of indulging themselves in a kind of imperiousness, than out of a desire of information. The child who is taught, as the most important lesson, to know nothing but what is useful to him, will interrogate with the views of a Socrates: he will not put a question, without having an answer ready to that which he knows will be put to him before his own is resolved. . . .

Never point out any thing to a child which is beyond his views. While he is a stranger to the relations and duties of humanity, as you cannot raise his comprehension to the state of manhood, you should bring down the state of manhood to a level with his capacity. In projecting what may be useful to him hereafter, speak to him directly only of what is apparently useful to him at present. Beware, also, in general, of making comparisons between your pupil and other children; let him have no rival, no competitor, not even in his corporeal exercises, as soon as he begins to reason. I had much rather should not learn at all whatever must be taught him by means of vanity or jealousy. I would content myself, in this respect, with remarking his annual progress, and comparing his situation and exploits in the present year with those of the past. I would say to him, you are grown so much since such a time; here is the ditch you leaped, the weight you lifted, the distance you threw a stone, so far you run without fetching breath; let us see what you can do more at present. Thus would I excite him to emulation, without making him jealous or envious of a rival: he would be desirous indeed to excel himself, and so he ought to be; I see no inconvenience in this kind of emulation.

I hate books; they only teach people to talk about what they do not understand. It is said that Hermes engraved the elements of the sciences on columns, to secure his discoveries from being

600

lost in the time of a general deluge. Had he imprinted them on the minds of men, they had been better preserved by tradition. The organs of the memory, duly prepared, are the monuments on which human science would be most indelibly engraven. . . .

All things duly considered, the trade I should like best my pupil should have a taste for, is that of a joiner. This is neat, useful, and may be carried on within doors: it is sufficiently laborious to keep the body in exercise, and requires both diligence and dexterity: at the same time, taste and elegance are not excluded from being displayed on the form and contrivance of the work.

If it should so happen, indeed, that your pupil has a natural turn for the speculative sciences, I should not blame you for teaching him a mechanic art conformable to his inclinations; let him learn, for example, to design and construct mathematical instruments, quadrants, telescopes, and the like.

When Émile learns a trade, I also will learn it with him; for I am convinced he will never learn, as should be, what we do not learn together. We will, therefore, both serve an apprenticeship; not affecting to be treated as gentlemen, but as real apprentices who are not trifling with a profession: nay, why should we not be so in reality? Czar Peter worked as a common ship-carpenter in the yard, and served as a drummer in his own troops: do you think that prince was not your equal, at least either in birth or merit? The reader will observe, I do not ask Émile this question, but put it to every one, of whatever rank he may happen to be.

If I have hitherto made myself understood, the reader will perceive, that, while I have accustomed my pupil to corporeal exercise and manual labour, I have given him insensibly a taste for reflection and meditation; in order to counterbalance that indolence which would be the natural result of his indifference for the opinions of mankind and the tranquility of his passions, it is necessary that he work like a peasant, and think like a philosopher, lest he become as idle as a savage. The great secret of education is, to make the exercises of the body and the mind serve as a relaxation to each other.

IV. Our passions are the principal instruments of our preservation: therefore, to endeavour to destroy them is equally vain and absurd; it is to find fault with nature, to attempt to reform the works of God. Should the Almighty require man to annihilate those passions which he had given him, he would not know his own mind, he would contradict himself: but the Almighty never gave such a ridiculous command; the heart of man has received no such injunction; and whatever is required of him, is not made known to him by the mouth of another, God himself imprints it on his heart.

To suppress the passions, in my opinion, is almost as absurd as entirely to destroy them; whoever imagines this to have been my intention, has grossly mistaken my meaning.

But because it is in the nature of man to have passions, is it therefore rational to conclude, that all the passions which we feel within ourselves, and which we perceive in others, are natural? Their source indeed is natural, but that source is increased by a thousand adventitious streams; it is a great river continually augmenting, in which it would be very difficult to find one drop of the original spring. Our natural passions are extremely limited; they are, however, the instruments of our liberty, and tend to our preservation. Such passions as are prejudicial, and by which our reason is subdued, spring from some other source; nature does not give them to us, we adopt them to the prejudice of nature. . . .

If the period when man becomes conscious of his sex is as much determined by education as by nature, consequently this period may be accelerated or retarded: and if the body gains or loses solidity, in proportion as this progress is forwarded or delayed, it follows, that the longer it is retarded the stronger we grow. . . .

A total ignorance of certain things were perhaps the most to be wished; but they should learn betimes what it is impossible always to conceal from them. Either their curiosity should not be at all excited, or it should be satisfied before the time of danger. Your conduct with regard to your pupil greatly depends on his particular situation, the people by whom he is surrounded, and many other circumstances. It is of importance to leave nothing to chance; and if you are not positively certain that you can keep him ignorant of the difference of sex till the age of sixteen, be careful to let him know it before the age of ten.

I cannot approve of speaking to children in a language too refined, nor of palpable circumlocution only to avoid calling things by their proper names. Virtuous innocence knows no disguise; but an imagination polluted by vice, renders the ear delicate, and obliges us to a continual refinement of expression. Mere words can be of no consequence; lascivious ideas are what we should guard against.

Though modesty is natural to the human species, yet children have it not from nature. A sense of shame proceeds only from the knowledge of evil; and how can children who neither have, nor ought to have this knowledge, shew its effects? To read them lectures on shame and decency, is to teach them that there are things shameful and immodest; it is inspiring them with a secret desire of knowing these things. Sooner or later they arrive at this knowledge; and the first spark which catches the imagination, is sure to set the passions in a flame. Whoever blushes, is already culpable; real innocence can never be ashamed. . . .

The first sentiment of which a youth, carefully educated, is susceptible, is not love, but friendship. The first act of his youthful imagination is to inform him that there are beings similar to himself, and the species affects him before the sex. Another advantage arising from prolonging his innocence is, that it enables us, by means of his growing sensibility, to sow the first seeds of humanity in his heart: an advantage of infinite importance, because it is the only time of his life when this care will be attended with equal success. . . .

Our instructors complain, that the natural fire of this age renders youth ungovernable. Very true; but is it not entirely their own fault? Can they be ignorant, that when they have once suffered this fire to make its way through the senses, it is not in their power to divert its course? Will the tedious, frigid sermons of a pedant, efface from the mind of his pupil the idea of pleasure which he has conceived? Will they banish from his heart the desires which torment him? Will they quench the ardor of a flame of which he already knows the use? Will he not be enraged at those obstacles which oppose the only happiness of which he has any idea? and in the severe law prescribed without explanation, what can he

603

discover except the caprice and hatred of a man who chuses to torment him? Is it therefore wonderful that he should oppose and hate the pedagogue in his turn?

It is easy to conceive, that, by relaxing his severity, a tutor may render himself less disagreeable to his pupil, and yet preserve an apparent authority: but I cannot perceive the use of that authority which serves only to foment the vices which it ought to repress; it is much the same as if a rider, in order to tame an unruly horse, were to leap him down a precipice.

This fire of youth, so far from being an obstacle in his education, is the proper instrument of its accomplishment; it is that which gives you an advantage over the heart of your pupil, when he ceases to be less powerful than yourself. His first affections are the reins with which you should direct all his motions. He was before at liberty; but now he is enslaved. Whilst he was incapable of affection, he was dependent only on himself and his necessities; but the moment he loves, he depends on his attachments. Thus are formed the first bonds which unite him to his species; but we are not to suppose that his new born sensibility will be universal, or that he will conceive any meaning in the word *mankind*. No; that sensibility will be first confined to his equals; and his equals are those only with whom he is acquainted; those whom custom has rendered dear to him, or useful; those in whom he perceives a similitude of ideas and sensation; those who are exposed to the pains, and are sensible of the pleasures, which he has experienced; in a word, those in whom the manifest identity of nature increases his disposition to self-love. It is not till after having cultivated his disposition in a thousand forms, after much reflection on his own sentiments as well as those of others, that he will be able to generalize his notions under the abstract idea of humanity, and add to his particular affections those which are to unite him to the whole species.

In becoming capable of attachment, he becomes sensible of it in others and therefore attentive to the signs of this attachment. Thus you see what a new empire you acquire over him; you enslave his heart before he is aware of it. What must be his sensations, when, turning his eyes upon himself, he discovers the services you have done for him; when he compares himself with other young people of his own age, and you with other tutors? I say, when he discovers, for let it never be urged: if you once hint the obligation, from that instant he will cease to perceive it. If you exact obedience in return for your services, he will suspect that he has been deceived; he will conclude, that, under pretence of serving him, you have bound him in a contract to which he never consented. In vain you will urge, that what you exact is entirely for his own good; it is sufficient that it is exacted, and that in return for what was done without his consent.

When an unhappy wretch accepts a shilling, supposing it to be a gift, and afterwards finds himself to be enlisted, do we not exclaim against the injustice? And are you not equally unjust to demand a return for obligations which your pupil never accepted?

Ingratitude would be more rare, if benefits upon usury were less common. Nothing can be more natural than to love those who do us service. The heart of man is self-interested, but never ungrateful; and the obliged are less to be charged with ingratitude than their benefactors with self-interest. If you sell me your favours, let us settle the price; but if you pretend to give, and afterwards expect to make terms with me, you are guilty of fraud; it is their being given *gratis* which renders them inestimable. The heart will receive laws only from itself; by endeavouring to enslave it you give it liberty, and by leaving it at liberty it becomes your slave.

History is generally defective in recording only those facts which are rendered conspicuous by name, place, or date; but the slow progressive causes of those facts, not being thus distinguished, remain for ever unknown. How frequently do we find a battle lost or won, mentioned as the cause of a revolution which was become inevitable before the battle was fought? War is generally nothing more than a manifestation of events already determined by moral causes, of which historians are ignorant.

The spirit of philosophy has, in like manner, infected many of the writers in this age; but I am in doubt whether truth gains any thing by their labours. A madness for system having got possession of them all, they best agree with their favourite hypotheses.

605

To these reflections we may add, that history is a representation of actions rather than of men, who are shown only at certain intervals, in their vestments of parade; we see man only in public life, after he has put himself in a proper position for being viewed. History follows him not into his house, into his closet, among his family and friends: it paints him only when he makes his appearance; it exhibits his dress, and not his person.

I should rather chuse to begin the study of the human heart by reading the lives of particular men; for there it is impossible for the hero to conceal himself a moment. The biographer pursues him into his most secret recesses, and exposes him to the piercing eye of the spectator; he is best known when he believes himself most concealed. "I like," say Montaigne, "those biographers who give us the history of counsels, rather than events; who shew us what passes within, rather than without; therefore Plutarch is the writer after my own heart."

*　　*　　*

I foresee how much my readers will be surprised to find I have attended my pupil throughout the whole first age of life, without once speaking to him of religion. He hardly knows at fifteen years of age whether or not he hath a soul, and perhaps it will not be time to inform him of it when he is eighteen; for, if he learns it too soon, he runs a risk of never knowing it at all.

If I were to design a picture of the most deplorable stupidity, I would draw a pedant teaching children their catechism: and were I resolved to crack the brain of a child, I would oblige him to explain what he said when he repeated his catechism. It may be objected, that the greater part of the dogmas of Christianity being mysterious, to expect the human mind should be capable of conceiving them, is not so much to expect children should be men, but that man should be something more. To this I answer, in the first place, that there are mysteries, which it is not only impossible for man to comprehend, but also believe; and I do not see what we get by teaching them to children. . . .

Reason tells us, that man is punishable only for his wilful errors, and that invincible ignorance can never be imputed to him as a crime. Hence it should follow, that in the eyes of Eternal Justice every man who would have believed had he had the opportunities of information, will appear as a believer; and that none will be punished for infidelity but those whose hearts refuse to admit the truth.

Let us beware of divulging the truth to those who are incapable of understanding it: for this is the way to substitute error in the room of it. It were better to have no idea of God at all, than to entertain those which are mean, fantastical, injurious, and unworthy a divine object; it is a less crime to be ignorant of, than insult, him. . . .

Custom and prejudice triumph particularly in matters of religion. But how shall we, who on all occasions pretend to shake off its yoke; we, who pay no regard to the authority of opinion; who would teach our pupil nothing but what he might have learned himself, in any country; in what religion shall we educate Émile? To what sect shall we unite the man of nature? The answer appears to me very simple; we shall unite him neither to one nor another; but place him in a proper situation, and qualify him to make choice of that which the best use of his reason may induce him to adopt.

DAGOBERT D. RUNES

DAGOBERT D. RUNES (1902-   ). In his writings on education Dagobert D. Runes takes issue with the methods practiced in both the East and the West. Counterposing the teachings of earlier generations with contemporary systems, he attributes many of the tragic mistakes of today to the inadequacy of yesteryear's learnings.

Dr. Runes, former director of the Institute for Advanced Education, received his degree of Doctor of Philosophy from the University of Vienna. Among the numerous books he has written or edited are *The Ethics of Plato and Spinoza, Twentieth Century Philosophy, On the Nature of Man, Encyclopedia of the Arts, Treasury of Philosophy,* and *The Hebrew Impact on Western Civilization.* He has served as editor of a number of learned journals, among them *Journal of Aesthetics, Philosophical Abstracts,* and *The Modern Thinker.* Concerning his writings on the theory and practice of education, Albert Schweitzer wrote: "We both travel the same path, to bring to mankind a deeply ethical, deeply spiritual consciousness, with the purpose of leading the people back from the mentality of indifference in which they are living, to a new and higher manner of thinking." Albert Einstein observed that the opinions expressed by Dr. Runes "are closely akin to those I hold."

In the following selections from *Letters to My Teacher,* Dr. Runes raises vital questions and offers some common-sense answers based on his knowledge of the world of books and men and on what he terms "self-thinking, the prime object of all teaching."

*ROSES UPON THE ROGUES**

Quite a few decades have passed since I left your classroom in that little Austrian university town. Time has traveled at quickstep, with infinite misery stumbling close behind.

You ask me if your lessons of old have stood up under the tests of a new era and a new hemisphere. Yours is not a single query; it involves a flock of questions. Which am I to answer first? I hardly know where to begin. I look at the portrait you sent me

*From *Letters to My Teacher* (New York: Philosophical Library, 1961).

and I see a withered, spare old man with a sorrowful face, living in a country that was once an empire and now is not much more than a highlight on the international tourist map.

I saw the Empire yet in flower — and I saw it crumble and fall apart. And, in melancholy analogy, so very many of the pedagogical structures which you erected before my intent eyes shared the fate of the Austrian Empire.

When I was a boy you looked mighty tall to me. You were insistent and voluble and set paragraph upon paragraph like bricks of cement. I felt myself traveling on the train of progress and enlightenment toward a not too distant goal of perfection, from a promising present of accomplishment to a jubilant era of tomorrow's civilization.

I take another look at your portrait, and your wistful demeanor betrays that you share my feeling of disappointment. During those few years that we were given to watch history instead of slipping into it, man may have taken a step or two forward, but the Lord only knows how disastrously far back into barbarism man's boots were marching most of the time.

Our generation has massacred 40 million people in that many years. Of these only a minority died in warfare; the others were put to death — men, women and children — in so-called lawful manner by malevolent usurpers of power and with the consent of the citizens.

No one can deny that Hitler, Stalin and Mao, to name just three of the executioners anointed by the Devil himself, were enjoying enthusiastic popularity among their fellow-men; and that at no time did they fail to receive ecstatic approval of their respective genocides.

There are many smaller examples of present-day man's inhumanity to man. Their great number prohibits enumeration. But the sordid deeds are known to all. Be it that opposing gangsters are assassinated in front of television sets in Cuba with the entire city population of Havana cheering every detail of the butchery; be it that an oil-guided satyr of Araby sits on the throne of a realm where every fifth person is a bound slave, kidnaped from the plains of Africa and sold in the market place — for the favor of such dastardly creatures these things are viewed by the leaders of the West with a benevolent smile and by those of the East with brotherly embrace.

The most disturbing element in this sad panorama is the fact that the masses of the world, eagerly as well as gingerly, place garlands of roses upon the shoulders of the evildoers.

What is wrong with education that makes 100 million Germans cheer Hitler; or 200 million Russians mummify Stalin so that the next thousand years may behold him; or 600 million Chinese bow daily before Mao's picture; or 400 million Indians hail Nehru's forked tongue? And, finally, what's wrong with education in some segments of our own country where men will invite a manure-sniffing dog to sleep on their cot and women will place an evil-smelling cat on their bed pillow, but none would permit a colored man to live in the same block or eat at the same counter?

There must be something wrong with education, fundamentally wrong. Let us get down to fundamentals.

LEARNING AND THE COMMON MAN*

One of the reasons, perhaps the major reason, why education has made so little progress in comparison with other cultural endeavors over the last thousand years is that much of it has been, and is still, aloof from practical, or even intelligent, purpose.

The study, for instance, of botany and zoology, except for a more detailed and unified systematization of nomenclature, still hangs on the rote learning of hundreds of assorted terms germane to plant structure and animal anatomy, physiology and histology. The so-called major problems in biology, heredity and evolution, are passed over rather lightly with pat responses of Darwinian hypotheses which a ten-year-old, if he were made to think instead of recite, could disprove by such primitive processes of reasoning as: if man, "the highest form of present-day existence," could trace his origin to lower species, e.g. mammals, amphibian creatures, protozoa, even a quorum of gases, the question would arise — who created those gases out of which these trillions of trillions of tons of matter evolved? *Ex nihilo nihilum.*

*From *Letters to My Teacher* (New York: Philosophical Library, 1961).

610

A sixteen-year-old could reduce many of the so-called theorems in Darwinism to weak-legged hypotheses. As it is, sweating his memory cells into temporary absorption of hundreds of *termini technici* adds little to his understanding, and blocks the latter from getting beneath the skin-wisdom of rote learning. The acquisition of modern categorization in biology encourages as little true research as the medieval memorizing of old-fashioned Aristotelian biological categories.

What generally the schools fail to realize is that the status of a particular body of science in a particular era is, educationally speaking, only a means of encouraging scientific thinking in the student, and it is not an aim in itself. The important thing is to examine and comprehend the processes by which science was deepened and widened. The mere memorization of scientific data is of quite secondary significance; undue stress on the memorizing of parts and particles of animal and plant bodies, with their ancient Latin or Greek surnames, will elevate no mind, but burden many.

Let us look at this situation in retrospect and see of what was dished out in school how much was really wheat and how much was chaff that the winds of worldly life blew away.

How many of those you ask in their mature years can remember the hundred odd names attached to the anatomy of the reptile or the structures of the seemingly endless masses of plant life? How many remember the manifold math problems they had to carry through with little or no understanding of broad mathematical principles? How much use did any of them have of the multiple language courses on which they wasted thousands of hours of their time, instead of reading in easily available, splendid translations the literature of these foreign countries? Some quote the 18th-Century adage: "A gentleman is one who has learned and forgotten his Latin and French." I think this is too heavy a price to pay for being a gentleman.

At this time I should also like to mention again the absurdity of our history teaching, concentrating on rote learning of the lives and loves of the great European kings and conquerors; the miserable manner in which they carried on a blood-spattered existence, made possible only by Church-upheld laws of heredity which allegedly applied to these yellow-hearted princelings of blue blood.

Of what little merit this kind of historic battle report and court gossip is can be deduced from the fact that we in the Western world study not and know not, school-wise, the corresponding history of India, China or Siam while by the same token their peoples know not ours. And they get along fine without it, just as we do.

We would get along much better with our own people, and with others, if we would reinterpret history as the knowledge of the people's events, and not their usurpers' and black knights'; and relegate the study of military and kingly tyrants, bastard or legitimate, to the criminal records for those to examine who have reason or desire to search in the black books of the underworld. If nowhere else, as it seems, history should at least find its true judge in the young and the studious. How is the youth to know what will be right for tomorrow, if the wrong remains hidden in yesterday?

If the present-day unhappy competition with the East is to be taken seriously, it isn't a greater number of mediocre people that will tip the balance, but rather a greater number of original minds. It is this self-thinking that should be prime object of all teaching, in which program the science data are never a goal, but only a means. After all data have been recounted and copied, nothing has been accomplished of significance. Nearly all of it remains shelf wisdom — and not self-improvement. In science the processes of discovery and research are the proper subject of attention, and nothing else.

In the humanities the evaluation of deeds and concepts is of import, and not the cold presentation of figures and foibles. With few exceptions the so-called historic personages, be they Caesars or Alexanders, Napoleons or Stalins, are monsters of this earth which they drenched with the blood of its people. Where are the historians who write of the people, and the events that molded their fate for the better? And how much do those who went through our present-day schools know of the life and work and the struggle of the common man, the end of which is still afar?

612

BENJAMIN RUSH

BENJAMIN RUSH (1745-1813). Deeply involved in the struggle for independence, Benjamin Rush was also a fiery proponent of educational reform, of higher education for women, and of the establishment of free public schools in every township in order to create unified systems of state education. He was a prolific writer on many issues and was continually active in the support of institutions and organizations concerned with the advancement of human learning.

The physician and pioneering medical educator, called the "Hippocrates of Pennsylvania," was born of a Quaker family on a farm north of Philadelphia on December 24, 1745. After graduating from Princeton College at the age of fifteen, he spent six years in medical apprenticeship before completing the degree of Doctor of Medicine in 1768. Following a brief trip to France, he was appointed professor of chemistry in the College of Philadelphia, the first medical school in America. He introduced clinical instruction at the Philadelphia dispensary and, convinced that medical science was in its infancy, stressed research. As a member of the Continental Congress he was among the signers of the Declaration of Independence, and he served briefly as surgeon general of the army. From 1799 until his death on April 19, 1813, he served as treasurer of the United States Mint. He was a founder of Dickinson College, an advocate of the abolition of slavery, an active supporter of various religious, scientific, and educational societies, and the author of many volumes of medical studies, essays, addresses, and of the first American textbook on chemistry.

In the two essays reproduced here, Rush outlines a course of study in keeping with the needs of the young republic. After pointing out the necessity of making public instruction secular, he adds that "from the combined and reciprocal influence of religion, liberty and learning . . . it is impossible to measure the degrees of happiness and perfection to which mankind can be raised."

OF THE MODE OF EDUCATION PROPER IN A REPUBLIC*

The business of education has acquired a new complexion by the independence of our country. The form of government we have assumed, has created a new class of duties to every American. It becomes us, therefore, to examine our former habits upon this subject, and in laying the foundations for nurseries of wise and good men, to adapt our modes of teaching to the peculiar form of our government.

The first remark that I shall make upon this subject is, that an education in our own, is to be preferred to an education in a foreign country. The principle of patriotism stands in need of the reinforcement of prejudice, and it is well known that our strongest prejudices in favour of our country are formed in the first one and twenty years of our lives. The policy of the Lacedemonians is well worthy of our imitation. When Antipater demanded fifty of their children as hostages for the fulfillment of a distant engagement, those wise republicans refused to comply with his demand, but readily offered him double the number of their adult citizens, whose habits and prejudices could not be shaken by residing in a foreign country. Passing by, in this place, the advantages to the community from the early attachment of youth to the laws and constitution of their country, I shall only remark, that young men who have trodden the paths of science together, or have joined in the same sports, whether of swimming, skating, fishing, or hunting, generally feel, thro' life, such ties to each other, as add greatly to the obligations of mutual benevolence.

I conceive the education of our youth in this country to be peculiarly necessary in Pennsylvania, while our citizens are composed of the natives of so many different kingdoms in Europe. Our schools of learning, by producing one general, and uniform

*From *The Selected Writings of Benjamin Rush,* edited by Dagobert D. Runes (New York: Philosophical Library, 1947).

system of education, will render the mass of the people more homogeneous and thereby fit them more easily for uniform and peaceable government.

I proceed in the next place, to enquire, what mode of education we shall adopt so as to secure to the state all the advantages that are to be derived from the proper instruction of youth; and here I beg leave to remark, that the only foundation for a useful education in a republic is to be laid in Religion. Without this there can be no virtue, and without virtue there can be no liberty, and liberty is the object and life of all republican governments.

Such is my veneration for every religion that reveals the attributes of the Deity, or a future state of rewards and punishments, that I had rather see the opinions of Confucius or Mahomed inculcated upon our youth, than see them grow up wholly devoid of a system of religious principles. But the religion I mean to recommend in this place, is that of the New Testament.

It is foreign to my purpose to hint at the arguments which establish the truth of the Christian revelation. My only business is to declare, that all its doctrines and precepts are calculated to promote the happiness of society, and the safety and well being of civil government. A Christian cannot fail of being a republican. The history of the creation of man, and of the relation of our species to each other by birth, which is recorded in the Old Testament, is the best refutation that can be given to the divine right of kings, and the strongest argument that can be used in favor of the original and natural equality of all mankind. A Christian, I say again, cannot fail of being a republican, for every precept of the Gospel inculcates those degrees of humility, self-denial, and brotherly kindness, which are directly opposed to the pride of monarchy and the pageantry of a court. A Christian cannot fail of being useful to the republic, for his religion teacheth him, that no man "liveth to himself." And lastly, a Christian cannot fail of being wholly inoffensive, for his religion teacheth him, in all things to do to others what he would wish, in like circumstances, they should do to him.

I am aware that I dissent from one of those paradoxical opinions with which modern times abound; and that it is improper to fill the minds of youth with religious prejudices of any kind, and that they should be left to choose their own principles, after they have arrived at an age in which they are capable of judging for themselves. Could we preserve the mind in childhood and youth a perfect blank, this plan of education would have more to recommend it; but this we know to be impossible. The human mind runs as naturally into principles as it does after facts. It submits with difficulty to those restraints or partial discoveries which are imposed upon it in the infancy of reason. Hence the impatience of children to be informed upon all subjects that relate to the invisible world. But I beg leave to ask, why should we pursue a different plan of education with respect to religion, from that which we pursue in teaching the arts and sciences? Do we leave our youth to acquire systems of geography, philosophy, or politics, till they have arrived at an age in which they are capable of judging for themselves? We do not. I claim no more then for religion, than for the other sciences, and I add further, that if our youth are disposed after they are of age to think for themselves, a knowledge of one system, will be the best means of conducting them in a free enquiry into other systems of religion, just as an acquaintance with one system of philosophy is the best introduction to the study of all the other systems in the world.

Next to the duty which young men owe to their Creator, I wish to see a regard to their country, inculcated upon them. When the Duke of Sully became prime minister to Henry the IVth of France, the first thing he did, he tells us, "Was to subdue and forget his own heart." The same duty is incumbent upon every citizen of a republic. Our country includes family, friends and property, and should be preferred to them all. Let our pupil be taught that he does not belong to himself, but that he is public property. Let him be taught to love his family, but let him be taught, at the same time, that he must forsake, and even forget them, when the welfare of his country requires it. He must watch for the state, as if its liberties depended upon his vigilance alone, but he must do this in such a manner as not to defraud his creditors, or neglect his family. He must love private life, but he must decline no station, however public or responsible it may be, when called to it by the suffrages of his fellow citizens. He must love popularity, but he must despise it when set in competition with the dictates of his judgement, or the real interest of his country. He must love character, and have a due sense of injuries, but he must be taught to appeal only to the laws of the state, to defend the one, and punish the other. He must love family honor, but he must be taught that neither the rank nor antiquity of his ancestors, can command respect, without personal merit. He must avoid neutrality in all questions that divide the state, but he must shun the rage, and acrimony of party spirit. He must be taught to love his fellow creatures in every part of the world, but he must cherish with a more intense and peculiar affection, the citizens of Pennsylvania and of the United States. I do not wish to see our youth educated with a single prejudice against any nation or country; but we impose a task upon human nature, repugnant alike to reason, revelation and the ordinary dimensions of the human heart, when we require him to embrace, with equal affection, the whole family of mankind. He must be taught to amass wealth, but it must be only to encrease his power of contributing to the wants and demands of the state. He must be indulged occasionally in amusements, but he must be taught that study and business should be his principal pursuits in life. Above all he must love life, and endeavor to acquire as many of its conveniences as possible by industry and economy, but he must be taught that this life "is not his own," when the safety of his country requires it. These are practicable lessons, and the history of the commonwealths of Greece and Rome show, that human nature, without the aids of Christianity, has attained these degrees of perfection.

While we inculcate these republican duties upon our pupil, we must not neglect, at the same time, to inspire him with republican principles. He must be taught that there can be no durable liberty but in a republic, and that government, like all other sciences, is of a progressive nature. The chains which have bound this science in Europe are happily unloosed in America. Here it is open to investigation and improvement. While philosophy has protected us by its discoveries from a thousand natural evils, government has unhappily followed with an unequal pace. It would be to dishonor human genius, only to name the many defects which still exist in the best systems of legislation. We daily see matter of a perishable nature rendered durable by certain chemical operations. In like manner, I conceive, that it is possible to combine power in such a way as not only to encrease the happiness, but to promote the duration of republican forms of government far beyond the terms limited for them by history, or the common opinions of mankind.

To assist in rendering religious, moral and political instruction more effectual upon the minds of our youth, it will be necessary to subject their bodies to physical discipline. To obviate the inconveniences of their studious and sedentary mode of life, they should live upon a temperate diet, consisting chiefly of broths, milk and vegetables. The black broth of Sparta, and the barley broth of Scotland, have been alike celebrated for their beneficial effects upon the minds of young people. They should avoid tasting spirituous liquors. They should also be accustomed occasionally to work with their hands, in the intervals of study, and in the busy seasons of the year in the country. Moderate sleep, silence, occasional solitude and cleanliness, should be inculcated upon them, and the utmost advantage should be taken of a proper direction of those great principles in human conduct, — sensibility, habit, imitations and association.

The influence of these physical causes will be powerful upon the intellects, as well as upon the principles and morals of young people.

To those who have studied human nature, it will not appear paradoxical to recommend, in this essay, a particular attention to vocal music. Its mechanical effects in civilizing the mind, and thereby preparing it for the influence of religion and government, have been so often felt and recorded, that it will be unnecessary to mention facts in favour of its usefulness, in order to excite a proper attention to it.

I cannot help bearing a testimony, in this place, against the custom, which prevails in some parts of America, (but which is daily falling into disuse in Europe) of crowding boys together under one roof for the purpose of education. The practice is the gloomy remains of monkish ignorance, and is as unfavorable to the improvement of the mind in useful learning, as monasteries are to the spirit of religion. I grant this mode of secluding boys from the intercourse of private families, has a tendency to make them scholars, but our business is to make them men, citizens and Christians. The vices of young people are generally learned from each other. The vices of adults seldom infect them. By separating them from each other, therefore, in their hours of relaxation from study, we secure their morals from a principal source of corruption, while we improve their manners, by subjecting them to those restraints which the difference of age and sex, naturally produce in private families.

From the observations that have been made it is plain, that I consider it is possible to convert men into republican machines. This must be done, if we expect them to perform their parts properly, in the great machine of the government of the state. That republic is sophisticated with monarchy or aristocracy that does not revolve upon the wills of the people, and these must be fitted to each other by means of education before they can be made to produce regularity and unison in government.

Having pointed out those general principles, which should be inculcated alike in all the schools of the state, I proceed now to make a few remarks upon the method of conducting, what is commonly called, a liberal or learned education in a republic.

I shall begin this part of my subject, by bearing a testimony against the common practice of attempting to teach boys the learned languages, and the arts and sciences too early in life. The first twelve years of life are barely sufficient to instruct a boy in reading, writing and arithmetic. With these, he may be taught those modern languages which are necessary for him to speak. The state of the memory, in early life, is favorable to the acquisition of languages, especially when they are conveyed to the mind, through the ear. It is, moreover, in early life only, that the organs of speech yield in such a manner as to favour the just pronunciation of foreign languages.

Too much pains cannot be taken to teach our youth to read and write our American language with propriety and elegance. The study of the Greek language constituted a material part of the literature of the Athenians, hence the sublimity, purity and immortality of so many of their writings. The advantages of a perfect knowledge of our language to young men intended for the professions of law, physic, or divinity are too obvious to be mentioned, but in a state which boasts of the first commercial city in America, I wish to see it cultivated by young men, who are intended for the compting house, for many such, I hope, will be educated in our colleges. The time is past when an academical education was thought to be unnecessary to qualify a young man for merchandize. I conceive no profession is capable of receiving more embellishments from it. The French and German languages should likewise be carefully taught in all our colleges. They abound with useful books upon all subjects. So important and necessary are those languages, that a degree should never be conferred upon a young man who cannot speak or translate them.

Connected with the study of languages is the study of eloquence. It is well known how great a part it constituted of the Roman education. It is the first accomplishment in a republic, and often sets the whole machine of government in motion. Let our youth, therefore, be instructed in this art. We do not extol it too highly when we attribute as much to the power of eloquence as to the sword, in bringing about the American Revolution.

With the usual arts and sciences that are taught in our American colleges, I wish to see a regular course of lectures given upon History and Chronology. The science of government, whether it relates to constitutions or laws, can only be advanced by a careful selection of facts, and these are to be found chiefly in history. Above all, let our youth be instructed in the history of the different states of Europe. I wish likewise to see the numerous facts that relate to the origin and present state of commerce, together with the nature and principles of money, reduced to such a system, as to be intelligible and agreeable to a young man. If we consider the commerce of our metropolis only as the avenue of the wealth of the state, the study of it merits a place in a young man's education; but, I consider commerce in a much higher light when I recommend the study of it in republican seminaries. I view it as the best security against the influence of hereditary monopolies of land, and, therefore, the surest protection against aristocracy. I consider its effects as next to those of religion in humanizing mankind, and lastly, I view it as the means of uniting the different nations of the world together by the ties of mutual wants and obligations.

Chemistry by unfolding to us the effects of heat and mixture, enlarges our acquaintance with the wonders of nature and the mysteries of art; hence it has become, in most of the universities of Europe, a necessary branch of a gentleman's education. In a young country, where improvements in agriculture and manufactures are so much to be desired, the cultivation of this science, which explains the principles of both of them, should be considered as an object of the utmost importance.

Again, let your youth be instructed in all the means of promoting national prosperity and independence, whether they relate to improvements in agriculture, manufactures, or inland navigation. Let him be instructed further in the general principles of legislation, whether they relate to revenue, or to the preservation of life, liberty or property. Let him be directed frequently to attend the courts of justice, where he will have the best opportunities of acquiring habits of comparing, and arranging his ideas by observing the discovery of truth, in the examination of witnesses, and where he will hear the laws of the state explained, with all the advantages of that species of eloquence which belongs to the bar. Of so much importance do I conceive it to be, to a young man, to attend occasionally to the decisions of our courts of law, that I wish to see our colleges established, only in county towns.

But further, considering the nature of our connection with the United States, it will be necessary to make our pupil acquainted with all the prerogatives of the national government. He must be instructed in the nature and variety of treaties. He must know the difference in the powers and duties of the several species of ambassadors. He must be taught wherein the obligations of individuals and of states are the same, and wherein they differ. In short, he must acquire a general knowledge of all those laws and forms, which unite the sovereigns of the earth, or separate them from each other.

I beg pardon for having delayed so long to say any thing of the separate and peculiar mode of education proper for women in a republic. I am sensible that they must concur in all our plans of education for young men, or no laws will ever render them effectual. To qualify our women for this purpose, they should not only be instructed in the usual branches of female education, but they should be taught the principles of liberty and government; and the obligations of patriotism should be inculcated upon them. The opinions and conduct of men are often regulated by the women in the most arduous enterprizes of life; and their approbation is frequently the principal reward of the hero's dangers, and the patriot's toils. Besides, the first impressions upon the minds of children are generally derived from the women. Of how much consequence, therefore, is it in a republic, that they should think justly upon the great subject of liberty and government!

The complaints that have been made against religion, liberty and learning, have been, against each of them in a separate state. Perhaps like certain liquors, they should only be used in a state of mixture. They mutually assist in correcting the abuses, and in improving the good effects of each other. From the combined and reciprocal influence of religion, liberty and learning upon the morals, manners and knowledge of individuals, of these, upon government, and of government, upon individuals, it is impossible to measure the degrees of happiness and perfection to which mankind may be raised. For my part, I can form no ideas of the golden age, so much celebrated by the poets, more delightful, than the contemplation of that happiness which it is now in the power of the legislature of Pennsylvania to confer upon her citizens, by establishing proper modes and places of education in every part of the state.

EDUCATION AGREEABLE TO A REPUBLICAN
FORM OF GOVERNMENT*

Before I proceed to the subject of this essay, I shall point out, in a few words, the influence and advantages of learning upon mankind.

I. It is friendly to religion, inasmuch as it assists in removing prejudice, superstition and enthusiasm, in promoting just notions of the Deity, and in enlarging our knowledge of his works.

II. It is favourable to liberty. Freedom can exist only in the society of knowledge. Without learning, men are incapable of knowing their rights, and where learning is confined to a few people, liberty can be neither equal nor universal.

III. It promotes just ideas of laws and government. "When the clouds of ignorance are dispelled (says the Marquis of Beccaria) by the radiance of knowledge, power trembles, but the authority of laws remains immovable."

IV. It is friendly to manners. Learning in all countries, promotes civilization, and the pleasures of society and conversation.

V. It promotes agriculture, the great basis of national wealth and happiness. Agriculture is as much a science as hydraulics, or optics, and has been equally indebted to the experiments and researches of learned men. The highly cultivated state, and the immense profits of the farms in England, are derived wholly from the patronage which agriculture has received in that country, from learned men and learned societies.

VI. Manufactures of all kinds owe their perfection chiefly to learning — hence the nations of Europe advance in manufactures, knowledge, and commerce, only in proportion as they cultivate the arts and sciences.

For the purpose of diffusing knowledge through every part of the state, I beg leave to propose the following simple plan.

I. Let there be one university in the state, and let this be established in the capital. Let law, physic, divinity, the law of nature and nations, economy, &c. be taught in it by public lectures in the winter season, after the manner of the European universities, and

* From *The Selected Writings of Benjamin Rush,* edited by Dagobert D. Runes (New York: Philosophical Library, 1947).

let the professors receive such salaries from the state as will enable them to deliver their lectures at a moderate price.

II. Let there be four colleges. One in Philadelphia; one at Carlisle; a third, for the benefit of our German fellow citizens, at Lancaster; and a fourth, some years hence at Pittsburgh. In these colleges, let young men be instructed in mathematics and in the higher branches of science, in the same manner that they are now taught in our American colleges. After they have received a testimonial from one of these colleges, let them, if they can afford it, complete their studies by spending a season or two in attending the lectures in the university. I prefer four colleges in the state to one or two, for there is a certain size of colleges as there is of towns and armies, that is most favourable to morals and good government. Oxford and Cambridge in England are the seats of dissipation, while the more numerous, and less crowded universities and colleges in Scotland, are remarkable for the order, diligence, and decent behaviour of their students.

III. Let there be free schools established in every township, or in districts consisting of one hundred families. In these schools let children be taught to read and write the English and German languages, and the use of figures. Such of them as have parents that can afford to send them from home, and are disposed to extend their educations, may remove their children from the free school to one of the colleges.

By this plan the whole state will be tied together by one system of education. The university will in time furnish masters for the colleges, and the colleges will furnish masters for the free schools, while the free schools, in their turn, will supply the colleges and the university with scholars, students and pupils. The same systems of grammar, oratory and philosophy, will be taught in every part of the state, and the literary features of Pennsylvania will thus designate one great, and equally enlightened family.

But, how shall we bear the expense of these literary institutions? — I answer — These institutions will *lessen* our taxes. They will enlighten us in the great business of finance — they will teach us to increase the ability of the state to support government, by increasing the profits of agriculture, and by promoting manufactures.

They will teach us all the modern improvements and advantages of inland navigation. They will defend us from hasty and expensive experiments in government, by unfolding to us the experience and folly of past ages, and thus, instead of adding to our taxes and debts, they will furnish us with the true secret of lessening and discharging both of them.

But, shall the states of orphans, bachelors and persons who have no children, be taxed to pay for the support of schools from which they can derive no benefit? I answer in the affirmative, to the first part of the objection, and I deny the truth of the latter part of it. Every member of the community is interested in the propagation of virtue and knowledge in the state. But I will go further, and add, it will be true economy in individuals to support public schools. The bachelor will in time save his tax for this purpose, by being able to sleep with fewer bolts and locks to his doors — the estates of orphans will in time be benefited, by being protected from the ravages of unprincipled and idle boys, and the children of wealthy parents will be less tempted, by bad company, to extravagance. Fewer pillories and whipping posts, and smaller gaols, with their usual expenses and taxes, will be necessary when our youth are properly educated, than at present; I believe it could be proved, that the expenses of confining, trying and executing criminals, amount every year, in most of the counties, to more money than would be sufficient to maintain all the schools that would be necessary in each county. The confessions of these criminals generally show us, that their vices and punishments are the fatal consequences of the want of a proper education in early life.

I submit these detached hints to the consideration of the legislature and of the citizens of Pennsylvania. The plan for the free schools is taken chiefly from the plans which have long been used with success in Scotland, and in the eastern states of America, where the influence of learning in promoting religion, morals, manners and good government, has never been exceeded in any country.

The manner in which these schools should be supported and governed — the modes of determining the characters and qualifications of schoolmasters, and the arrangement of families in each district, so that children of the same religious sect and nation, may be educated as much as possible together, will form a proper part of a law for the establishment of schools, and therefore does not come within the limits of this plan.

BERTRAND RUSSELL

BERTRAND RUSSELL (1872-   ). Generally regarded as the most controversial figure of modern philosophy because of his eloquent championship of individual liberty, Bertrand Russell is also credited with having taken an outstanding part in the foundation of modern mathematical logic. Though primarily a mathematician and philosopher, Lord Russell has for many years lectured and written on educational topics, and more than once has been at the center of educational controversies. His volume *On Education* (1926) advocated methods which were then considered strikingly advanced but which have subsequently found increasing favor among educational theorists.

Born at Trelleck, Wales, on May 18, 1872, he descended from an aristocratic family. He won an open scholarship to Trinity College, where he took high honors in philosophy and in mathematics. Active in the Fabian Society, he stood for election to Parliament but was defeated. He became a fellow of the Royal Society in 1908 and was appointed lecturer at his old college in 1910. He was persecuted and imprisoned because of his pacifist views, which he refused to modify until Nazism gained ascendancy in Germany. During this period he wrote many books, visited Russia, went to Peiping to lecture on philosophy, operated (with his second wife) a school for young children, and came to the United States (1938), where he taught at many of the leading universities. His advanced sociological views aroused strong resentment which brought about cancellation of his appointment to lecture at the College of the City of New York (1940) and for the Barnes Foundation (1943). He returned to England, where he received the Order of Merit in 1949, and the Nobel prize for literature in 1950. Among some fifty books which he has written, the following are important in the field of education: *Principles of Mathematics* (1903), *On Education* (1926), *Education and the Social Order* (1932), *Human Knowledge: Its Scope and Limits* (1948), *Impact of Science on Society* (1951), *New Hopes for a Changing World* (1951), and *Human Society in Ethics and Politics* (1954), *My Philosophical Development* (1959), *Has Man a Future?* (1961), and *Fact and Fiction* (1961). His uncompromising spirit has always made him a controversial figure. Late in 1963, for example, he signed a letter protesting the mistreatment of Jews in Russia; the next year he wrote a letter condemning American actions in Viet-Nam.

The essay that follows comprises one chapter in Lord Russell's *The Will to Doubt*. It reveals something of the breadth of his knowledge and the profundity of his thought. His easy humor and devastating irony are here used with utmost efficiency to discredit the narrowly utilitarian view of education.

*"USELESS" KNOWLEDGE**

Francis Bacon, a man who rose to eminence by betraying his friends, asserted, no doubt as one of the ripe lessons of experience, that "knowledge is power." But this is not true of *all* knowledge. Sir Thomas Browne wished to know what song the sirens sang, but if he had ascertained this it would not have enabled him to rise from being a magistrate to being High Sheriff of his county. The sort of knowledge that Bacon had in mind was that which we call scientific. In emphasizing the importance of science, he was belatedly carrying on the tradition of the Arabs and the early Middle Ages, according to which knowledge consisted mainly of astrology, alchemy, and pharmacology, all of which were branches of science. A learned man was one who, having mastered these studies, had acquired magical powers. In the early eleventh century, Pope Silvester II, for no reason except that he read books, was universally believed to be a magician in league with the devil. Prospero, who in Shakespeare's time was a mere phantasy, represented what had been for centuries the generally received conception of a learned man, so far at least as his powers of sorcery were concerned. Bacon believed — rightly, as we now know — that science could provide a more powerful magician's wand than any that had been dreamed of by the necromancers of former ages.

The Renaissance, which was at its height in England at the time of Bacon, involved a revolt against the utilitarian conception of knowledge. The Greeks had acquired a familiarity with Homer, as we do with music-hall songs, because they enjoyed him, and without feeling that they were engaged in the pursuit of learning. But the men of the sixteenth century could not begin to under-

*From *The Will to Doubt* (New York: Philosophical Library, 1958).

628

stand him without first absorbing a very considerable amount of linguistic erudition. They admired the Greeks, and did not wish to be shut out from their pleasures; they therefore copied them, both in reading the classics and in other less avowable ways. Learning, in the Renaissance, was part of the *joie de vivre,* just as much as drinking or love-making. And this was true not only of literature, but also of sterner studies. Everyone knows the story of Hobbes's first contact with Euclid: opening the book, by chance, at the theorem of Pythagoras, he exclaimed, "By God, this is impossible," and proceeded to read the proofs backwards until reaching the axioms, he became convinced. No one can doubt that this was for him a voluptuous moment, unsullied by the thought of the utility of geometry in measuring fields.

It is true that the Renaissance found a practical use for the ancient languages in connection with theology. One of the earliest results of the new feeling for classical Latin was the discrediting of the forged decretals and the donation of Constantine. The inaccuracies which were discovered in the Vulgate and the Septuagint made Greek and Hebrew a necessary part of the controversial equipment of Protestant divines. The republican maxims of Greece and Rome were invoked to justify the resistance of Puritans to the Stuarts and of Jesuits to monarchs who had thrown off allegiance to the Pope. But all this was an effect, which had been in full swing in Italy for nearly a century before Luther. The main motive of the Renaissance was mental delight, the restoration of a certain richness and freedom in art and speculation which had been lost while ignorance and superstition kept the mind's eye in blinkers.

The Greeks, it was found, had devoted a part of their attention to matters not purely literary or artistic, such as philosophy, geometry, and astronomy. These studies, therefore, were respectable, but other sciences were more open to question. Medicine, it was true, was dignified by the names of Hippocrates and Galen; but in the intervening period it had become almost confined to Arabs and Jews, and inextricably intertwined with magic. Hence the dubious reputation of such men as Paracelsus. Chemistry was in even worse odour, and hardly became respectable until the eighteenth century.

In this way it was brought about that knowledge of Greek and Latin, with a smattering of geometry and perhaps astronomy, came to be considered the intellectual equipment of a gentleman. The Greeks disdained the practical applications of geometry, and it was only in their decadence that they found a use for astronomy in the guise of astrology. The sixteenth and seventeenth centuries, in the main, studied mathematics with Hellenic disinterestedness, and tended to ignore the sciences which had been degraded by their connection with sorcery. A gradual change towards a wider and more practical conception of knowledge, which was going on throughout the eighteenth century, was suddenly accelerated at the end of that period by the French Revolution and the growth of machinery, of which the former gave a blow to gentlemanly culture while the latter offered new and astonishing scope for the exercise of ungentlemanly skill. Throughout the last hundred and fifty years, men have questioned more and more vigorously the value of "useless" knowledge, and have come increasingly to believe that the only knowledge worth having is that which is applicable to some part of the economic life of the community.

In countries such as France and England, which have a traditional educational system, the utilitarian view of knowledge has only partially prevailed. There are still, for example, professors of Chinese in the universities who read the Chinese classics but are unacquainted with the works of Sun Yat-sen, which created modern China. There are still men who know ancient history in so far as it was related by authors whose style was pure, that is to say up to Alexander in Greece and Nero in Rome, but refuse to know the much more important later history because of the literary inferiority of the historians who related it. Even in France and England, however, the old tradition is dying, and in more up-to-date countries, such as Russia and the United States, it is utterly extinct. In America, for example, educational commissions point out that fifteen hundred words are all that most people employ in business correspondence, and therefore suggest that all others should be avoided in the school curriculum. Basic English,

630

a British invention, goes still further, and reduces the necessary vocabulary to eight hundred words. The conception of speech as something capable of aesthetic value is dying out, and it is coming to be thought that the sole purpose of words is to convey practical information. In Russia the pursuit of practical aims is even more whole-hearted than in America: all that is taught in educational institutions is intended to serve some obvious purpose in education or government. The only escape is afforded by theology: the sacred scriptures must be studied by some in the original German, and a few professors must learn philosophy in order to defend dialectical materialism against the criticisms of bourgeois metaphysicians. But as orthodoxy becomes more firmly established, even this tiny loophole will be closed.

Knowledge, everywhere, is coming to be regarded not as a good in itself, or as a means of creating a broad and humane outlook on life in general, but as merely an ingredient in technical skill. This is part of the greater integration of society which has been brought about by scientific technique and military necessity. There is more economic and political interdependence than there was in former times, and therefore there is more social pressure to compel a man to live in a way that his neighbours think useful. Educational establishments except those for the very rich, or (in England) such as have become invulnerable through antiquity, are not allowed to spend their money as they like, but must satisfy the State that they are serving a useful purpose by imparting skill and instilling loyalty. This is part and parcel of the same movement which has led to compulsory military service, boy scouts, the organization of political parties, and the dissemination of political passion by the Press. We are all more aware of our fellow-citizens than we used to be, more anxious, if we are virtuous, to do them good, and in any case to make them do us good. We do not like to think of anyone lazily enjoying life, however refined may be the quality of his enjoyment. We feel that everybody ought to be doing something to help on the great cause (whatever it may be), the more so as so many bad men are working against it and ought to be stopped. We have not leisure of mind, therefore, to acquire

631

any knowledge except such as will help us in the fight for whatever it may happen to be that we think important.

There is much to be said for the narrowly utilitarian view of education. There is not time to learn everything before beginning to make a living, and undoubtedly "useful" knowledge is *very* useful. It has made the modern world. Without it, we should not have machines or motorcars or railways or aeroplanes; it should be added that we should not have modern advertising or modern propaganda. Modern knowledge has brought about an immense improvement in average health and at the same time has discovered how to exterminate large cities by poison gas. Whatever is distinctive of our world, as compared with former times, has its source in "useful" knowledge. No community as yet has enough of it, and undoubtedly education must continue to promote it.

It must also be admitted that a great deal of the traditional cultural education was foolish. Boys spent many years acquiring Latin and Greek grammar, without being, at the end, either capable or desirous (except in a small percentage of cases) of reading a Greek or Latin author. Modern languages and history are preferable, from every point of view, to Latin and Greek. They are not only more useful, but they give much more culture in much less time. For an Italian of the fifteenth century, since practically everything worth reading, if not in his own language, was in Greek or Latin, these languages were the indispensable keys to culture. But since that time great literatures have grown up in various modern languages, and the development of civilization has been so rapid that knowledge of antiquity has become much less useful in understanding our problems than knowledge of modern nations and their comparatively recent history. The traditional schoolmaster's point of view, which was admirable at the time of the revival of learning, became gradually unduly narrow, since it ignored what the world has done since the fifteenth century. And not only history and modern languages, but science also, when properly taught, contributes to culture. It is therefore possible to maintain that education should have other aims than direct utility, without defending the traditional curriculum. Utility and culture, when both are conceived broadly, are found to be less incompatible than they appear to the fanatical advocates of either.

Apart, however, from the cases in which culture and direct utility can be combined, there is indirect utility, of various different kinds, in the possession of knowledge which does not contribute to technical efficiency. I think some of the worst features of the modern world could be improved by a greater encouragement of such knowledge and a less ruthless pursuit of mere professional competence.

When conscious activity is wholly concentrated on some one definite purpose, the ultimate result, for most people, is lack of balance accompanied by some form of nervous disorder. The men who directed German policy during the war of 1914-18 made mistakes, for example, as regards the submarine campaign which brought America on to the side of the Allies, which any person coming fresh to the subject could have seen to be unwise, but which they could not judge sanely owing to mental concentration and lack of holidays. The same sort of thing may be seen wherever bodies of men attempt tasks which put a prolonged strain upon spontaneous impulses. Japanese imperialists, Russian Communists, and German Nazis all had or have a kind of tense fanaticism which comes of living too exclusively in the mental world of certain tasks to be accomplished. When the tasks are as important and as feasible as the fanatics suppose, the result may be magnificent; but in most cases narrowness of outlook has caused oblivion of some powerful counteracting force, or has made all such forces seem the work of the devil, to be met by punishment and terror. Men as well as children have need of play, that is to say, of periods of activity having no purpose beyond present enjoyment. But if play is to serve its purpose, it must be possible to find pleasure and interest in matters not connected with work.

The amusements of modern urban populations tend more and more to be passive and collective, and to consist of inactive observation of the skilled activities of others. Undoubtedly such amusements are much better than none, but they are not as good as would be those of a population which had, through education, a wider range of intelligent interests not connected with work.

633

Better economic organization, allowing mankind to benefit by the productivity of machines, should lead to a very great increase of leisure, and much leisure is apt to be tedious except to those who have considerable intelligent activities and interests. If a leisured population is to be happy, it must be an educated population, and must be educated with a view to mental enjoyment as well as to the direct usefulness of technical knowledge.

The cultural element in the acquisition of knowledge, when it is successfully assimilated, forms the character of a man's thoughts and desires, making them concern themselves, in part at least, with large impersonal objects, not only with matters of immediate importance to himself. It has been too readily assumed that, when a man has acquired certain capacities by means of knowledge, he will use them in ways that are socially beneficial. The narrowly utilitarian conception of education ignores the necessity of training a man's purposes as well as his skill. There is in untrained human nature a very considerable element of cruelty, which shows itself in many ways, great and small. Boys at school tend to be unkind to a new boy, or to one whose clothes are not quite conventional. Many women (and not a few men) inflict as much pain as they can by means of malicious gossip. The Spaniards enjoy bullfights; the British enjoy hunting and shooting. The same cruel impulses take more serious forms in the hunters of Jews in Germany and kulaks in Russia. All imperialism affords scope for them, and in war they become sanctified as the highest form of public duty.

Now while it must be admitted that highly educated people are sometimes cruel, I think there can be no doubt that they are less often so than people whose minds have lain fallow. The bully in a school is seldom a boy whose proficiency in learning is up to the average. When a lynching takes place, the ringleaders are almost invariably very ignorant men. This is not because mental cultivation produces positive humanitarian feelings, though it may do so; it is rather because it gives other interests than the ill-treatment of neighbours, and other sources of self-respect than the assertion of domination. The two things most universally desired are power and admiration. Ignorant men can, as a rule, only achieve either by brutal means, involving the acquisition of physical mastery. Culture gives a man less harmful forms of power and more deserving ways of making himself admired. Galileo did more than any monarch has done to change the world, and his power immeasurably exceeded that of his persecutors. He had therefore no need to aim at becoming a persecutor in his turn.

Perhaps the most important advantage of "useless" knowledge is that it promotes a contemplative habit of mind. There is in the world much too much readiness, not only for action without adequate previous reflection, but also for some sort of action on occasions on which wisdom would consel inaction. People show their bias on this matter in various curious ways. Mephistopheles tells the young student that theory is grey but the tree of life is green, and everyone quotes this as if it were Goethe's opinion, instead of what he supposes the devil would be likely to say to an undergraduate. Hamlet is held up as an awful warning against thought without action, but no one holds up Othello as a warning against action without thought. Professors such as Bergson, from a kind of snobbery towards the practical man, decry philosophy, and say that life at its best should resemble a cavalry charge. For my part, I think action is best when it emerges from a profound apprehension of the universe and human destiny, not from some wildly passionate impulse of romantic but disproportioned self-assertion. A habit of finding pleasure in thought rather than in action is a safeguard against unwisdom and excessive love of power, a means of preserving serenity in misfortune and peace of mind among worries. A life confined to what is personal is likely, sooner or later, to become unbearably painful; it is only by windows into a larger and less fretful cosmos that the more tragic parts of life become endurable.

A contemplative habit of mind has advantages ranging from the most trivial to the most profound. To begin with minor vexations, such as fleas, missing trains, or cantankerous business associates. Such troubles seem hardly worthy to be met by reflections on the excellence of heroism or the transitoriness of all human ills, and yet the irritation to which they give rise destroys many people's good temper and enjoyment of life. On such occasions, there is much consolation to be found in out-of-the-way bits of knowledge which have some real or fancied connection with the troubles of the moment; or even if they have none, they serve to obliterate the present from one's thoughts. When assailed by people who are white with fury, it is pleasant to remember the chapter in Descartes's *Treatise on the Passions* entitled "Why those who grow pale with rage are more to be feared than those who grow red." When one feels impatient over the difficulty of securing international co-operation, one's impatience is diminished if one happens to think of the sainted King Louis IX, before embarking on his crusade, allying himself with the Old Man of the Mountain, who appears in the Arabian Nights as the dark source of half the wickedness in the world. When the rapacity of capitalists grows oppressive, one may be suddenly consoled by the recollection that Brutus, that exemplar of republican virtue, lent money to a city at 40 per cent, and hired a private army to besiege it when it failed to pay the interest.

Curious learning not only makes unpleasant things less unpleasant, but also makes pleasant things more pleasant. I have enjoyed peaches and apricots more since I have known that they were first cultivated in China in the early days of the Han dynasty; that Chinese hostages held by the great King Kaniska introduced them into India, whence they spread to Persia, reaching the Roman Empire in the first century of our era; that the word "apricot" is derived from the same Latin source as the word "precocious," because the apricot ripens early; and that the A at the beginning was added by mistake, owing to a false etymology. All this makes the fruit taste much sweeter.

About a hundred years ago, a number of well-meaning philanthropists started societies "for the diffusion of useful knowledge," with the results that people have ceased to appreciate the delicious savour of "useless" knowledge. Opening Burton's *Anatomy of Melancholy* at haphazard on a day when I was threatened by that mood, I learn that there is a "melancholy matter," but that, while some think it may be engendered of all four humours, "Galen holds that it may be engendered of three alone, excluding phlegm or pituita, whose true assertion Valerius and Menardus stiffly maintain, and so doth Fuscius, Montaltus, Montanus. How (say they) can white become black?" In spite of this unanswerable argument, Hercules de Saxonia and Cardan, Guianerius and Laurentius, are (so Burton tells us) of the opposite opinion. Soothed by these historical reflections, my melancholy, whether due to three humours or to four, was dissipated. As a cure for too much zeal, I can imagine few measures more effective than a course of such ancient controversies.

But while the trivial pleasures of culture have their place as a relief from the trivial worries of practical life, the more important merits of contemplation are in relation to the greater evils of life, death and pain and cruelty, and the blind march of nations into unnecessary disaster. For those to whom dogmatic religion can no longer bring comfort, there is need of some substitute, if life is not to become dusty and harsh and filled with trivial self-assertion. The world at present is full of angry self-centered groups, each incapable of viewing human life as a whole, each willing to destroy civilization rather than yield an inch. To this narrowness no amount of technical instruction will provide an antidote. The antidote, in so far as it is matter of individual psychology, is to be found in history, biology, astronomy, and all those studies which, without destroying self-respect, enable the individual to see himself in his proper perspective. What is needed is not this or that specific piece of information, but such knowledge as inspires a conception of the ends of human life as a whole: art and history, acquaintance with the lives of heroic individuals, and some understanding of the strangely accidental and ephemeral position of man in the cosmos — all this touched with an emotion of pride in what is distinctively human, the power to see and to know, to feel magnanimously and to think with understanding. It is from large perceptions combined with impersonal emotion that wisdom most readily springs.

Life, at all times full of pain, is more painful in our time than in the two centuries that preceded it. The attempt to escape from pain drives men to triviality, to self-deception, to the invention of vast collective myths. But these momentary alleviations do but increase the sources of suffering in the long run. Both private and public misfortune can only be mastered by a process in which will and intelligence interact: the part of will is to refuse to shirk the evil or accept an unreal solution, while the part of intelligence is to understand it, to find a cure if it is curable, and, if not, to make it bearable by seeing it in its relations, accepting it as unavoidable, and remembering what lies outside it in other regions, other ages, and the abysses of interstellar space.

SENECA

SENECA (c. 4 B. C. - 65 A. D.). Until the time of his disgrace and suicide Lucius Annaeus Seneca was generally considered "the man in letters and in government." Respected in his own time by pagans and Christians alike, he was admired even more by Renaissance thinkers, and his Stoicism penetrated into the minds of Montaigne, Rabelais, and Bacon.

Seneca was born at Cordoba, Spain, about 4 B. C. He studied at Rome under the Stoic Attalus but took up the legal profession at his father's request and attained eminence at the bar. Nero became his pupil at the age of eleven. After Nero came to the throne Seneca fell under suspicion and withdrew entirely from public life. In 65 A. D. Nero suspected him of complicity and ordered him to end his life. Refused even a tablet to make his will, "he turned to his friends and said that, since he was prevented from rewarding their services, he would leave them the one thing, and yet the best thing, that he had to leave — the pattern of his life."

Seneca enjoyed unrivaled popularity in his own time. The most important of his works are his philosophical writings in which he preaches a modified Stoicism. The selections that follow are from his treatise *On Anger* (c. 50 A. D.) and *Essays*. Here, as in his other writings, he enjoins reverence toward God and charity toward men. He considers philosophy the highest of the liberal sciences and, more than any of the other ancient writers, stresses moral values in education.

ON THE EDUCATION OF CHILDREN*

It is, I assure you, of the greatest service to boys that they should be soundly brought up, yet to regulate their education is difficult, because it is our duty to be careful neither to cherish a habit of anger in them, nor to blunt the edge of their spirit. This needs careful watching, for both qualities, those which are to be encouraged, and those which are to be checked, are fed

*From *On Anger*, translated by Aubrey Stuart. Published in Bohn's Classical Library.

by the same things; and even a careful watcher may be deceived by their likeness. A boy's spirit is increased by freedom and depressed by slavery; it rises when praised, and is led to conceive great expectations of itself; yet this same treatment produces arrogance and quickness of temper. We must, therefore, guide him between these two extremes, using the curb at one time and the spur at another. He must undergo no servile or degrading treatment; he never must beg abjectly for anything, nor must he gain anything by begging. Let him rather receive it for his own sake, for his past good behavior, or for his promises of future good conduct.

In contests with his comrades we ought not to allow him to become sulky or fly into a passion; let us see that he be on friendly terms with those whom he contends with, so that in the struggle itself he may learn to wish not to hurt his antagonist but to conquer him. Whenever he has gained the day or done something praiseworthy, we should allow him to enjoy the victory, but not to rush into transports of delight; for joy leads to exultation, and exultation leads to swaggering and excessive self-esteem.

We ought to allow him some relaxation, yet not yield him up to sloth and laziness, and we ought to keep him far beyond the reach of luxury, for nothing makes children more prone to anger than a soft and fond bringing-up, so that the more children are indulged, and the more liberty is given them, the more they are corrupted. He to whom nothing is ever denied, will not be able to endure a rebuff, whose anxious mother always wipes away his tears, whose pedagogue is made to pay for his shortcomings.

Do you not observe how a man's anger becomes more violent as he rises in station? This shows itself especially in those who are rich and noble, or in great place, when the favoring gale has roused all the most empty and trivial passions of their minds. Prosperity fosters anger, when a man's proud ears are surrounded by a mob of flatterers, saying, "That man answer you! you do not act according to your dignity, you lower yourself." And so forth, with all the language which can hardly be resisted even by healthy and originally well-principled minds. Flattery, then, must be kept well out of the way of children.

Let a child hear the truth, and sometimes fear it; let him always reverence it. Let him rise in the presence of his elders. Let him obtain nothing by flying into a passion; let him be given when he is quiet what was refused him when he cried for it. Let him behold, but not makes use of his father's wealth; let him be reproved for what he does wrong.

It will be advantageous to furnish boys with even-tempered teachers and pedagogues; what is soft and unformed clings to what is near, and takes its shape. The habits of young men reproduce those of their nurses and pedagogues. Once a boy, who was brought up in Plato's house, went home to his parents, and, on seeing his father shouting with passion, said, "I never saw any one at Plato's house act like that." I doubt not that he learned to imitate his father sooner than he learned to imitate Plato.

Above all, let his food be scanty, his dress not costly, and of the same fashion as that of his comrades. If you begin by putting him on a level with many others, he will not be angry when some one is compared with him.

ON THE HAPPY LIFE*

A happy life consists in a mind which is free, upright, undaunted and steadfast beyond the influence of fear or desire. A man must be accompanied by a continual cheerfulness, a high happiness, which comes indeed from on high because he delights in what he has. If we attain to this, then there will dawn upon us those invaluable blessings, the repose of a mind that is at rest in a safe haven, its lofty imaginings, its great and steady delight at casting out errors and learning to know the truth, its courtesy and its cheerfulness, in all of which we shall take delight.

Virtue is a lofty quality, sublime, royal, unconquerable, untiring. You will meet virtue in the temple, the market-place, the senate-house, manning the walls, covered with dust, sunburnt,

*From Essays. Reprinted in Treasury of Philosophy, edited by Dagobert D. Runes (New York: Philosophical Library, 1955).

641

horny-handed; you will find pleasure sulking out of sight, seeking for shady nooks.

The highest good is immortal. It knows no ending, and does not admit of either satiety or regret; for a right-thinking mind never alters or becomes hateful to itself, nor do the best things ever undergo any change. But pleasure dies at the very moment when it charms us most. It has no great scope, and therefore it soon cloys and wearies us, and fades away as soon as its first impulse is over. Indeed, we cannot depend upon anything whose nature is to change.

A man should be unbiased and ought not to be conquered by external things. He ought to feel confidence in his own spirit, and so order his life as to be ready alike for good or bad fortune. But let not his confidence be without knowledge, nor his knowledge without steadfastness. Let him abide by what he has determined, and let there be no erasure in his doctrine.

* * *

Let reason be encouraged by the senses to seek for the truth, and draw its first principles from thence. Indeed, it has no other base of operations or place from which to start in pursuit of truth: it must fall back upon itself. Even the all-embracing universe and God who is its guide extends Himself forth into outward things, and yet altogether returns from all sides back to Himself. Let our mind do the same thing.

By this means we shall obtain a strength and an ability which are united; we shall derive from it that reason which never halts between two opinions, nor is dull in forming its perceptions, beliefs or convictions. Such a mind, when it has ranged itself in order, made its various parts agree together, and, if I may so express myself, harmonized them, has attained to the highest good. For it has nothing evil or hazardous remaining, nothing to shake it or make it stumble. It will do everything under the guidance of its own will, and nothing unexpected will befall it, but whatever may be done by it will turn out well, and that, too, readily and easily, without the doer having recourse to any underhanded devices.

642

You may, then, boldly declare that the highest good is single-
ness of mind, for where agreement and unity are, there must the
virtues be. It is the vices that are at war with one another.

B. F. SKINNER

B. F. SKINNER (1904-   ). "Teaching machines," "step-increment learning," "reinforcement," "programed instruction," "behaviorism" — all these
terms immediately evoke the name of Burrhus Frederic Skinner, the leading American exponent of behaviorism. Building on the foundation laid
by such men as John B. Watson and Ivan Pavlov, Skinner has been
particularly interested in operant conditioning, in which instrumental behavior is strengthened by reinforcement. He interprets behavior in terms
of the physiological responses of an organism to environmental stimuli
and shows how it is possible to devise a series of minute steps through
which the organism will acquire a complex pattern of behavior (for example, he has shown that pigeons can be taught to play ping-pong by
rewarding each correct movement with a grain of corn). For the past
decade his name has been associated with promising developments in the
application of behaviorist principles to programed learning.

Born at Susquehanna, Pennsylvania, on March 20, 1904, Skinner graduated from Hamilton College in 1926 and earned his doctorate at Harvard
in 1931. He returned to Harvard in 1948, after teaching at the universities
of Minnesota and Indiana, and since then has concentrated on the study
of behavior in lower organisms and man, verbal behavior in man, and
automated instruction. Through his teaching he has influenced a whole
generation of experimental psychologists. He has lectured widely and has
written many articles and books, among them *The Behavior of Organisms* (1938), *Walden Two* (1948), *Science and Human Behavior* (1953),
and *Verbal Behavior* (1957).

In the following article Professor Skinner, in summing up his reflections
on developments in the field of automated instruction, observes that "No
field is in greater need of our most powerful intellectual resources."

REFLECTIONS ON A DECADE
OF TEACHING MACHINES*

To the general public, and to many educators as well, the nature and scope of teaching machines are by no means clear. There is an extraordinary need for more and better teaching, and any enterprise which may help to meet it will not be left to develop normally. The demand for information about teaching machines has been excessive. Articles and books have been published and lectures given; symposia have been arranged, and conferences and workshops have been held and courses taught. Those who have had anything useful to say have said it far too often, and those who have had nothing to say have been no more reticent.

Education is big business. Teaching machines were soon heralded as a growth industry, and fantastic predictions of the sales of programed texts were circulated. Devices have been sold as teaching machines which were not well built or designed with any understanding of their function or the practical exigencies of their use. No author was ever more warmly received by a publisher than the author of a programed text. Many programs, to be used either with machines or in textbook form, have been marketed without adequate evaluation.

Teachers and Devices

The "mechanizing of education" has been taken literally in the sense of doing by machine what was formerly done by people. Some of the so-called computer-based teaching machines are designed simply to duplicate the behavior of teachers. To automate education with mechanical teachers is like automating bank-

*From Teachers College Record, LXV (1963-1964), pp. 168-77. Reprinted by permission of Dr. Skinner and the editor of *Teachers College Record*.

ing with mechanical tellers and bookkeepers. What is needed in both cases is an analysis of the functions to be served, followed by the design of appropriate equipment. Nothing we now know about the learning process calls for very elaborate instrumentation.

Educational specialists have added to the confusion by trying to assimilate the principles upon which teaching machines are based to older theories of learning and teaching.

In the broadest sense, teaching machines are simply devices which make it possible to apply our technical knowledge of human behavior to the practical field of education. Teaching is the expediting of learning. Students learn without teaching, but the teacher arranges conditions under which they learn more rapidly and effectively. In recent years, the experimental analysis of behavior has revealed many new facts about relevant conditions. The growing effectiveness of an experimental analysis is still not widely recognized, even within the behavioral sciences themselves, but the implications of some of its achievements for education can no longer be ignored.

An important condition is the relation between behavior and its consequences; learning occurs when behavior is "reinforced." The power of reinforcement is not easily appreciated by those who have not had firsthand experience in its use or have not at least seen some sort of experimental demonstration. Extensive changes in behavior can be brought about by arranging so-called contingencies of reinforcement. Various kinds of contingencies are concealed in the teacher's discussions with his students, in the books he gives them to read, in the charts and other materials he shows them, in the questions he asks them, and in the comments he makes on their answers. An experimental analysis clarifies these contingencies and suggests many improvements.

Shaping by Program

An important contribution has been the so-called "programing" of knowledge and skills — the construction of carefully arranged sequences of contingencies leading to the terminal performances which are the object of education. The teacher begins with whatever behavior the student brings to the instructional situation; by selective reinforcement, he changes that behavior so that a given terminal performance is more and more closely approximated. Even with lower organisms, quite complex behaviors can be "shaped" in this way with surprising speed; the human organism is presumably far more sensitive. So important is the principle of programing that it is often regarded as the main contribution of the teaching-machine movement, but the experimental analysis of behavior has much more to contribute to a technology of education.

The direct contact which often exists between teacher and student favors the construction of programed sequences, and the teacher who understands the process can profit from the opportunity to improvise programs as he goes. Programs can be constructed in advance, however, which will successfully shape the behavior of most students without local modifications, and many of them can conveniently be mediated by mechanical devices. Laboratory studies have shown that contingencies emphasizing subtle properties of behavior can often be arranged *only* through instrumentation. There are potentially as many different kinds of teaching machines as there are kinds of contingencies of reinforcement.

Teaching machines which present material to the student and differentially reinforce his responses in well constructed programs differ in several ways from self-testing devices and self-scoring test forms, as well as from the training devices which have long been used by industry and the armed services. As Pressey pointed out many years ago, a student will learn while taking a multiple-choice test if he is told immediately whether his answers are right or wrong. He learns not to give wrong answers again, and his right answers are strengthened. But testing has traditionally been distinguished from teaching for good reason. Before using a self-testing device, the student must already have studied the subject and, presumably, learned most of what he is to learn about it. Tests usually occupy only a small part of his time. Their main effect is motivational: A poor score induces him to study harder and possibly more effectively. Materials designed to be used in self-testing devices have recently been programed, but the contingencies which prevail during a test are not favorable to the shaping and maintaining of behavior.

Conventional training devices arrange conditions under which students learn, usually by simulating the conditions under which they eventually perform. Their original purpose was to prevent injury or waste during early stages of learning, but attention has recently been given to programing the actual behaviors they are designed to teach. To the extent that they expedite learning, they are teaching machines. Terminal performances have usually been selected for practical reasons, but a more promising possibility is the analysis and programing of basic motor and perceptual skills — a goal which should have an important place in any statement of educational policy.

In arranging contingencies of reinforcement, machines do many of the things teachers do; in that sense, they teach. The resulting instruction is not impersonal, however. A machine presents a program designed by someone who knew what was to be taught and could prepare an appropriate series of contingencies. It is most effective if used by a teacher who knows the student, has followed his progress, and can adapt available machines and materials to his needs. Instrumentation simply makes it possible for programer and teacher to provide conditions which maximally expedite learning. Instrumentation is thus secondary, but it is nevertheless inevitable if what is now known about behavior is to be used in an effective technology.

The New Pedagogy

Any practical application of basic knowledge about teaching and learning is, of course, pedagogy. In the United States at least, the term is now discredited, but by emphasizing an analysis of learning processes, teaching machines and programed instruction have been responsible for some improvement in its status. The significance of the teaching machine movement can be indicated by noting the astonishing lack of interest which other proposals

648

for the improvement of education show in the teaching process.

Find better teachers. In his *Talks to Teachers,* William James insisted that there was nothing wrong with the American school system which could not be corrected by "impregnating it with geniuses." It is an old formula: If you cannot solve a problem, find someone who can. If you do not know how to teach, find someone who knows or can find out for himself. But geniuses are in short supply, and good teachers do not come ready-made. Education would no doubt be improved if, as Conant has repeatedly pointed out, good teachers who know and like the subjects they teach could be attracted and retained. But something more is needed. It is not true that "the two essentials of a good teacher are (a) enthusiasm and (b) thorough knowledge of and interest in his subject." A third essential is knowing how to teach.

Emulate model schools. Rickover's criticism of the present American school system is well-known. His only important positive suggestion is to set up model schools, staffed by model teachers. The implication is that we already have, or at least can have for the asking, schools which need no improvement and whose methods can be widely copied. This is a dangerous assumption if it discourages further inquiry into instruction.

Simplify what is to be learned. Unsuccessful instruction is often blamed on refractory subject matters. Difficulties in teaching the verbal arts are often attributed to the inconsistencies and unnecessary complexities of a language. The pupil is taught manuscript handwriting because it more closely resembles printed forms. He is taught to spell only those words he is likely to use. Phonetic alphabets are devised to help him learn to read. It may be easier to teach such materials, but teaching itself is not thereby improved. Effective teaching would correct these pessimistic estimates of available instructional power.

Reorganize what is to be learned. The proper structuring of a subject matter is perhaps a part of pedagogy, but it can also serve as a mode of escape. Proposals for improving education by reorganizing what is to be learned usually contain an implicit assumption that students will automatically perceive and remember

649

anything which has "good form" — a doctrine probably traceable to Gestalt psychology. Current revisions of high school curricula often seem to lean heavily on the belief that if what the student is to be taught has been "structured," he cannot help understanding and remembering it. Other purposes of such revisions cannot be questioned: Materials should be up to date and well organized. But a high school presentation acceptable to a current physicist is no more easily taught or easily remembered than the out-of-date and erroneous material to be found in texts of a decade or more ago. Similarly, the accent of a native speaker encountered in a language laboratory is no more easily learned than a bad accent. No matter how well structured a subject matter may be, it must still be taught.

Improve presentation. Pedagogy can also be avoided if what is to be learned can be made memorable. Audio-visual devices are often recommended for this purpose. Many of their other purposes are easily defended. It is not always easy to bring the student into contact with the things he is to learn about. Words are easily imported into the classroom, and books, lectures, and discussions are therefore staples of education; but this is often an unfortunate bias. Audio-visual devices can enlarge the student's nonverbal experience. They can also serve to present material clearly and conveniently. Their use in attracting and holding the student's attention and in dramatizing a subject matter in such a way that it is almost automatically remembered must be questioned, however. It is especially tempting to turn to them for these purposes when the teacher does not use punitive methods to "make students study." But the result is not the same. When a student observes or attends to something in order to see it more clearly or remember it more effectively, his behavior must have been shaped and maintained by reinforcement. The temporal order was important. Certain reinforcing events must have occurred *after* the student looked at, read, and perhaps tested himself on the material. But when colored displays, attractive objects, filmed episodes, and other potentially reinforcing materials are used to attract attention, they must occur *before* the student engages in these activities. Nothing can reinforce a student for *paying* attention if it has already been used to *attract* his attention. Material which attracts attention fails to prepare the student to attend to material which is not interesting on its face, and material which is naturally memorable fails to prepare him to study and recall things which are not, in themselves, unforgettable. A well prepared instructional film may appear to be successful in arousing interest in a given subject, and parts of it may be remembered without effort, but it has not taught the student that a subject may *become* interesting when more closely examined or that intensive study of something which is likely to be overlooked may have reinforcing consequences.

Multiply contacts between teacher and students. Audio-visual devices, particularly when adapted to television, are also used to improve education by bringing one teacher into contact with an indefinitely large number of students. This can be done, of course, without analyzing how the teacher teaches, and it emphasizes a mode of communication which has two serious disadvantages: The teacher cannot see the effect he is having on his students, and large numbers of students must proceed at the same pace. Contributions to pedagogy may be made in designing programs for educational television, but the mere multiplication of contacts is not itself an improvement in teaching.

Expand the educational system. Inadequate education may be corrected by building more schools and recruiting more teachers so that the total quantity of education is increased, even though there is no change in efficiency.

Raise standards. Least effective in improving teaching are demands for higher standards. We may agree that students will be better educated when they learn more, but how are they to be induced to do so? Demands for higher standards usually come from critics who have least to offer in improving teaching itself.

The movement symbolized by the teaching machine differs from other proposals in two ways. It emphasizes the direct improvement of teaching on the principle that no enterprise can improve itself to the fullest extent without examining its basic processes. In the second place, it emphasizes the implementation of basic knowledge. If instructional practices violate many basic principles, it is only in part because these principles are not widely known. The teacher cannot put what he knows into practice in the classroom. Teaching machines and programed instruction constitute a direct attack on the problem of implementation. With appropriate administrative changes, they may bridge the gap between an effective pedagogical theory and actual practice.

Educational Goals

An effective technology of teaching calls for a re-examination of educational objectives. What is the teacher's actual assignment? Educational policy is usually stated in traditional terms: The teacher is to "impart knowledge," "improve skills," "develop rational faculties," and so on. That education is best, says Dr. Hutchins, which develops "intellectual power." The task of the teacher is to change certain inner processes or states. He is to improve the mind.

The role of the teacher in fostering mental prowess has a certain prestige. It has always been held superior to the role of the trainer of motor skills. And it has the great advantage of being almost invulnerable to criticism. In reply to the complaint that he has not produced observable results, the teacher of the mind can lay claim to invisible achievements. His students may not be able to read, but he has only been trying to make sure they wanted to learn. They may not be able to solve problems, but he has been teaching them simply to think creatively. They may be ignorant of specific facts, but he has been primarily concerned with their general interest in a field.

Traditional specifications of the goals of education have never told the teacher what to do upon a given occasion. No one knows how to alter a mental process or strengthen a mental power, and no one can be sure that he has done so when he has tried. There have been many good teachers who have supposed themselves to be working on the minds of their students, but their actual practices and the results of those practices can be analyzed in other ways. The well educated student is distinguished by certain characteristics. What are they, and how can they be produced?

652

Perhaps we could answer by redefining traditional goals: Instead of imparting knowledge, we could undertake to bring about those changes in behavior which are said to be the conspicuous manifestations of knowledge, or we could set up the behavior which is the mark of a man possessing well developed rational power. But mentalistic formulations are warped by irrelevant historical accidents. The behavior of the educated student is much more effectively analyzed directly as such.

Contrary to frequent assertions, a behavioristic formulation of human behavior is not a crude positivism which rejects mental processes because they are not accessible to the scientific public. It does not emphasize the rote learning of verbal responses. It does not neglect the complex systems of verbal behavior which are said to show that a student has had an idea, or developed a concept, or entertained a proposition. It does not ignore the behavior involved in the intellectual and ethical problem solving called "thinking." It does not overlook the value judgments said to be invoked when we decide to teach one thing rather than another or when we defend the time and effort given to education. It is merely an effective formulation of those activities of teacher and student which have always been the concern of educational specialists.

Not all behavioristic theories of learning are relevant, however. A distinction is commonly drawn between learning and performance. Learning is said to be a change in some special part of the organism, possibly the nervous system, of which behavior is merely the external and often erratic sign. With modern techniques, however, behavior can be much more successfully studied and manipulated than any such inner system, even when inferences about the latter are drawn from the behavior with the help of sophisticated statistics. An analysis of learning which concentrates on the behavior applies most directly to a technology, for the task of the teacher is to bring about changes in the student's behavior. His methods are equally conspicuous: He makes changes in the environment. A teaching method is simply a way of arranging an environment which expedites learning.

653

Such a formulation is not easily assimilated to the traditional psychology of learning. The teacher may arrange contingencies of reinforcement to set up new *forms* of response, as in teaching handwriting and speech or nonverbal forms of behavior in the arts, crafts, and sports. He may arrange contingencies to bring responses under new kinds of *stimulus control,* as in teaching the student to read or draw from copy, or to behave effectively upon other kinds of occasions. Current instructional programs designed to fulfill such assignments are mainly verbal, but comparable contingencies generate nonverbal behavior, including perceptual and motor skills and various kinds of intellectual and ethical self-management.

A second kind of programing maintains the student's behavior in strength. The form of the response and the stimulus control may not change; the student is simply more likely to respond. Some relevant methods are traditionally discussed under the heading of motivation. For example, we can strengthen behavior by introducing new reinforcers or making old ones more effective, as in giving the student better reasons for getting an education. The experimental analysis of behavior suggests another important possibility: Schedule available reinforcers more effectively. Appropriate terminal schedules of reinforcement will maintain the student's interest, make him industrious and persevering, stimulate his curiosity, and so on; but less demanding schedules, carefully designed to maintain the behavior at every stage, must come first. The programing of schedules of reinforcement is a promising alternative to the aversive control which, in spite of repeated reforms, still prevails in educational practice.

In neglecting programing, teaching methods have merely followed the lead of the experimental psychology of learning, where the almost universal practice has been to submit an organism immediately to terminal contingencies of reinforcement. A maze or a discrimination problem, for example, is learned only if the subject acquires appropriate behavior before the behavior he brings to the experiment has extinguished. The intermediate contingencies are largely accidental. The differences in behavior and in rate of learning which appear under these conditions are often attributed to inherited differences in ability.

In maximizing the student's success, programed instruction differs from so-called trial-and-error learning where the student is said to learn from his mistakes. At best, he learns not to make mistakes again. A successful response may survive, but trial-and-error teaching makes little provision for actually strengthening it. The method seems inevitably committed to aversive control. For the same reason, programed instruction does not closely resemble teaching patterned on everyday communication. It is usually not enough simply to tell the student something or induce him to read a book; he must be told or must read and then be questioned. In this "tell-and-test" pattern, the test is not given to measure what he has learned, but to show him what he has not learned and thus induce him to listen and read more carefully in the future. A similar basically aversive pattern is widespread at the college level, where the instructor assigns material and then examines on it. The student may learn to read carefully, to make notes, to discover for himself how to study, and so on, because in doing so he avoids aversive consequences, but he has not necessarily been taught. Assigning-and-testing is not teaching. The aversive by-products, familiar to everyone in the field of education, can be avoided through the use of programed positive reinforcement.

Many facts and principles derived from the experimental analysis of behavior are relevant to the construction of effective programs leading to terminal contingencies. The facts and principles are often difficult, but they make up an indispensable armamentarium of the effective teacher and educational specialist. We have long since passed the point at which our basic knowledge of human behavior can be applied to education through the use of a few general principles.

The difference between general principles and an effective technology can be seen in certain efforts to assimilate the principles of programed instruction to earlier theories. Programed instruction has, for example, been called "Socratic." It is true that Socrates proceeded by small steps and often led his students through an argument with a series of verbal prompts, but the example often cited to illustrate his method suggests that he was unaware of an important detail — namely, that prompts must eventually be "vanished" in order to put the student on his own. In the famous scene in the *Meno,* Socrates demonstrates his theory that learning is simply recollection by leading an uneducated slave boy through Pythagoras's Golden Theorem. The boy responds with the rather timid compliance to be expected under the circumstances and never without help. Although Socrates himself and some of those among his listeners who were already familiar with the theorem may have understood the proof better at the end of the scene, there is no evidence whatsoever that the boy understood it or could reconstruct it. In this example of Socratic instruction, at least, the student almost certainly learned nothing.

A seventeenth-century anticipation of programmed instruction has also been found in the work of Comenius, who advocated teaching in small steps, no step being too great for the student who was about to take it. Programing is sometimes described simply as breaking material into a large number of small pieces, arranged in a plausible generic order. But size of step is not enough. Something must happen to help the student take each step, and something must happen as he takes it. An effective program is usually composed of small steps, but the whole story is not to be found in Comenius's philosophy of education.

Another venerable principle is that the student should not proceed until he has fully understood what he is to learn at a given stage. Several writers have quoted E. L. Thorndike to this effect, who wrote in 1912,

If, by a miracle of mechanical ingenuity, a book could be so arranged that only to him who had done what was directed on page one would page two become visible, and so on, much that now requires personal instruction could be managed by print.

In commenting on this passage, Finn and Perrin have written, ". . . Here are the insights of a genius. History can very often teach us a lesson in humility — and it does here. The interesting question is: Why couldn't we see it then?" We might also ask, why couldn't Thorndike see it then? He remained active in education for at least 30 years, but he turned from this extraordinarily promising principle to another and — as it proved — less profitable approach to educational psychology.

It is always tempting to argue that earlier ideas would have been effective if people had only paid attention to them. But a good idea must be more than right. It must command attention; it must make its own way because of what it does. Education does not need principles which will improve education as soon as people observe them; it needs a technology so powerful that it cannot be ignored. No matter how insightful the anticipation of modern principles in earlier writers may seem to have been, something was lacking or education would be much further advanced. We are on the threshold of a technology which will be not only right but effective.

Criteria of Research

A science of behavior makes its principal contribution to a technology of education through the analysis of useful contingencies of reinforcement. It also suggests a new kind of educational research. Thorndike never realized the potentialities of his early work on learning because he turned to the measurement of mental abilities and to matched-group comparisons of teaching practices. He pioneered in a kind of research which, with the encouragement offered by promising new statistical techniques, was to dominate educational psychology for decades. It led to a serious neglect of the process of instruction.

657

There are practical reasons why we want to know whether a given method of instruction is successful or whether it is more successful than another. We may want to know what changes it brings about in the student, possibly in addition to those it was designed to effect. The more reliable our answers to such questions, the better. But reliability is not enough. Correlations between test scores and significant differences between group means tell us less about the behavior of the student in the act of learning than results obtained when the investigator can manipulate variables and assess their effects in a manner characteristic of laboratory research. The practices evaluated in studies of groups of students have usually not been suggested by earlier research of a similar nature, but have been drawn from tradition, from the improvisations of skillful teachers, or from suggestions made by theorists working intuitively or with other kinds of facts. No matter how much they may have stimulated the insightful or inventive researcher, the evaluations have seldom led directly to the design of improved practices.

The contrast between statistical evaluation and the experimental analysis of teaching has an illuminating parallel in the field of medicine. Various drugs, regimens, surgical procedures, and so on, must be examined with respect to a very practical question: Does the health of the patient improve? But "health" is only a general description of specific physiological processes, and "improvement" is, so to speak, merely a by-product of the changes in these processes induced by a given treatment. Medicine has reached the point where research on specific processes is a much more fertile source of new kinds of therapy than evaluations in terms of improvement in health. Similarly, in education, no matter how important improvement in the student's performance may be, it remains a by-product of specific changes in behavior resulting from the specific changes in the environment wrought by the teacher. Educational research patterned on an experimental analysis of behavior leads to a much better understanding of these basic processes. Research directed toward the behavior of the individual student has, of course, a long history, but it can still profit greatly from the support supplied by an experimental analysis of behavior.

This distinction explains why those concerned with experimental analyses of learning are not likely to take matched-group evaluations of teaching machines and programed instruction very seriously. It is not possible, of course, to evaluate either machines or programs *in general* because only specific instances can be tested, and available examples by no means represent all the possibilities; but even the evaluation of a given machine or program in the traditional manner may not give an accurate account of its effects. For example, those who are concerned with improvement are likely to test the student's capacity to give right answers. Being right has, of course, practical importance, but it is only one result of instruction. It is a doubtful measure of "knowledge" in any useful sense. We say that a student "knows the answer" if he can select it from an array of choices, but this does not mean that he could have given it without help. The right answer to one question does not imply right answers to all questions said to show the "possession of the same fact." Instructional programs are often criticized as repetitious or redundant when they are actually designed to put the student in possession of a number of different responses "expressing the same proposition." Whether such instruction is successful is not shown by any one right answer.

Correct or Educated?

A preoccupation with correct answers has led to a common misunderstanding of programed materials. Since a sentence with a blank to be filled in by the student resembles a test item, it is often supposed that the response demanded by the blank is what is learned. In that case, a student could not be learning much because he may respond correctly in 19 out of 20 frames and must therefore already have known 95 per cent of the answers. The instruction which occurs as he completes an item comes from having responded to other parts of it. The extent of this instruction cannot be estimated from the fact that he is right 19 out of 20 times, either while pursuing a program *or on a subsequent test*. Nor will this statistic tell us whether other conditions are important. Is it most profitable for the student to execute the response by writing it out, by speaking it aloud, by speaking it silently, or by reading it in some other way? These procedures may or may not have different effects on a selected "right-answer" statistic, but no one statistic will cover all their effects.

Research in teaching must not, of course, lose sight of its main objective — to make education more effective. But improvement as such is a questionable dimension of the behavior of either teacher or student. Dimensions which are much more intimately related to the conditions the teacher arranges to expedite learning must be studied even though they do not contribute to improvement or contribute to it in a way which is not immediately obvious.

The changes in the behavior of the individual student brought about by manipulating the environment are usually immediate and specific. The results of statistical comparisons of group performances usually are not. From his study of the behavior of the individual student, the investigator gains a special kind of confidence. He usually knows what he has done to get one effect and what he must do to get another.

Confidence *in* education is another possible result of an effective technology of teaching. Competition between the various cultures of the world, warlike or friendly, is now an accepted fact, and the role played by education in strengthening and perpetuating a given way of life is clear. No field is in greater need of our most powerful intellectual resources. An effective educational technology based upon an experimental analysis will bring it support commensurate with its importance in the world today.

SOCRATES

SOCRATES (c. 470-399 B. C.). The Delphic Oracle, when asked whether there was any man wiser than Socrates, stated unequivocally (in contrast to its usual manner of couching answers in obscure language) that no one was wiser. Though he disclaimed possession of any knowledge, posterity recognizes him as the noblest teacher of Greece, concerned above all else with finding pure truth and directing the strivings of his pupils toward virtue rather than utility.

The son of a stone-cutter and a midwife, Socrates liked to draw a parallel between his method of revealing truth to people and his mother's calling. From his own estimate of his age at the time of his trial, he would appear to have been born in Athens in 470 B. C. He studied with Archelaus and was an associate of the Periclean circle. He distinguished himself on the field of battle but took as little part in politics as he could. Charged with "corrupting the youth" and "neglecting the gods," he was tried and put to death in 399 B. C.

Socrates' entire philosophical activity had a strong educational tendency. His method was to appear ignorant and to encourage his students to teach him. In the dialogues which he conducted with his students, truth gradually emerged from a mass of confused opinions. He called his method *"maeuthics"* or parturition because it brought to birth ideas which already existed in the minds of his students. His teaching was oral, and our knowledge of him is based wholly on secondary sources. One of the two accounts of his defense of his teaching is preserved in Xenophon's *Memorabilia,* the other in Plato's *Apology,* from which the following selection is taken.

Considerable sections of the *Apology* probably reproduce Socrates' own words, for Plato, who loved and admired his teacher, was present at the trial. Faithful to his principles, Socrates never questions the right of the city to prosecute him, but he clings stubbornly to his right to formulate and teach his own opinions. Convinced that he is carrying out a divine mission in his search for truth and in his attempts to lead men to the virtuous life, he makes capital use of Socratic irony (pretending ignorance in order to expose the fallacies in the logic of an opponent) and of the Socratic method (asking a series of easily answered questions designed to lead someone to the logical conclusion foreseen by the questioner). Though he irritated his accusers and failed to win acquittal, his influence spread after his death. The ancient system through which the Athenian youth was prepared for citizenship through imitative practice and association with his elders in the household gave way to a particular institution grounded on rational instruction — the university, of which the prototype was the Academy founded by Plato, the illustrious disciple of Socrates.

THE APOLOGY*

How you have felt, O men of Athens, at hearing the speeches of my accusers, I cannot tell; but I know that their persuasive words almost made me forget who I was, such was the effect of them, and yet they have hardly spoken a word of truth. But many as their falsehoods were, there was one of them which quite amazed me: I mean when they told you to be upon your guard, and not to let yourself be deceived by the force of my eloquence. They ought to have been ashamed of saying this, because they were sure to be detected as soon as I opened my lips and displayed my deficiency; they certainly did appear to be most shameless in saying this, unless by the force of eloquence they mean the force of truth; for then I do indeed admit that I am eloquent. But in how different a way from theirs! Well, as I was saying, they have hardly uttered a word, or not more than a word, of truth; but you shall hear from me the whole truth: not, however, delivered after their manner, in a set oration duly ornamented with words and phrases. No, indeed! but I shall use the words and arguments which occur to me at the moment; for I am certain that this is right, and that at my time of life I ought not to be appearing before you, O men of Athens, in the character of a juvenile orator: let no one expect this of me. And I must beg of you to grant me one favor, which is this — if you hear me using the same words in my defence which I have been in the habit of using, and which most of you may have heard in the *agora*, and at the tables of the money-changers, or anywhere else, I would ask you not to be surprised at this, and not to interrupt me. For I am more than seventy years of age, and this is the first time that I have ever appeared in a court of law, and I am quite a stranger to the ways of the place; and therefore

*From *Dialogues of Plato,* translated by Benjamin Jowett (New York: The Colonial Press, 1900).

I would have you regard me as if I were really a stranger, whom you would excuse if he spoke in his native tongue, and after the fashion of his country: that I think is not an unfair request. Never mind the manner, which may or may not be good; but think only of the justice of my case, and give heed to that: let the judge decide justly and the speaker speak truly.

And first, I have to reply to the older charges and to my first accusers, and then I will go on to the later ones. For I have had many accusers, who accused me of old, and their false charges have continued during many years; and I am more afraid of them than of Anytus and his associates, who are dangerous, too, in their own way. But far more dangerous are these, who began when you were children, and took possession of your minds with their falsehoods, telling of one Socrates, a wise man, who speculated about the heaven above, and searched into the earth beneath, and made the worse appear the better cause. These are the accusers whom I dread; for they are the circulators of this rumor, and their hearers are too apt to fancy that speculators of this sort do not believe in the gods. And they are many, and their charges against me are of ancient date, and they made them in days when you were impressible — in childhood, or perhaps in youth — and the cause when heard went by default, for there was none to answer. And hardest of all, their names I do not know and cannot tell; unless in the chance case of a comic poet. But the main body of these slanderers who from envy and malice have wrought upon you — and there are some of them who are convinced themselves, and impart their convictions to others — all these, I saw, are most difficult to deal with; for I cannot have them up here, and examine them, and therefore I must simply fight with shadows in my own defence, and examine when there is no one who answers. I will ask you then to assume with me, as I was saying, that my opponents are of two kinds — one recent, the other ancient; and I hope that you will see the propriety of my answering the latter first, for these accusations you heard long before the others, and much oftener.

Well, then, I will make my defence, and I will endeavor in the short time which is allowed to do away with this evil opinion of me which you have held for such a long time; and I hope that I may succeed, if this be well for you and me, and that my words may find favor with you. But I know that to accomplish this is not easy — I quite see the nature of the task. Let the event be as God wills: in obedience to the law I make my defence.

I will begin at the beginning, and ask what the accusation is which has given rise to this slander of me, and which has encouraged Meletus to proceed against me. What do the slanderers say? They shall be my prosecutors, and I will sum up their words in an affidavit: "Socrates is an evildoer, and a curious person, who searches into things under the earth and in heaven, and he makes the worse appear the better cause; and he teaches the aforesaid doctrines to others." That is the nature of the accusation, and that is what you have seen yourselves in the comedy of Aristophanes, who has introduced a man whom he calls Socrates, going about and saying that he can walk in the air, and talking a deal of nonsense concerning matters of which I do not pretend to know either much or little — not that I mean to say anything disparaging of anyone who is a student of natural philosophy. I should be very sorry if Meletus could lay that to my charge. But the simple truth is, O Athenians, that I have nothing to do with these studies. Very many of those here present are witnesses to the truth of this, and to them I appeal. Speak then, you who have heard me, and tell your neighbors whether any of you have ever known me hold forth in few words or in many upon matters of this sort. . . . You hear their answer. And from what they say of this you will be able to judge of the truth of the rest. . . .

Men of Athens, this reputation of mine has come of a certain sort of wisdom which I possess. If you ask me what kind of wisdom, I reply, such wisdom as is attainable by man, for to that extent I am inclined to believe that I am wise; whereas the persons of whom I was speaking have a superhuman wisdom, which I may fail to describe, because I have it not myself; and he who says that I have, speaks falsely, and is taking away my character. And here, O men of Athens, I must beg you not to interrupt me, even if I seem to say something extravagant. For

664

the word which I speak is not mine. I will refer you to a witness who is worthy of credit, and will tell you about my wisdom — whether I have any, and of what sort — and that witness shall be the god of Delphi. You must have known Chaerephon; he was early a friend of mine, and also a friend of yours, for he shared in the exile of the people, and returned with you. Well Chaerephon, as you know, was very impetuous in all his doings, and he went to Delphi and boldly asked the oracle to tell him whether — as I was saying, I must beg you not to interrupt — he asked the oracle to tell him whether there was anyone wiser than I was, and the Pythian prophetess answered that there was no man wiser. Chaerephon is dead himself, but his brother, who is in court, will confirm the truth of this story.

Why do I mention this? Because I am going to explain to you why I have such an evil name. When I heard the answer, I said to myself, What can the god mean? and what is the interpretation of this riddle? for I know that I have no wisdom, small or great. What can he mean when he says that I am the wisest of men? And yet he is a god and cannot lie; that would be against his nature. After a long consideration, I at last thought of a method of trying the question. I reflected that if I could only find a man wiser than myself, then I might go to the god with a refutation in my hand. I should say to him, "Here is a man who is wiser than I am; but you said that I was the wisest!" Accordingly I went to one who had the reputation of wisdom and observed to him — his name I need not mention; he was a politician whom I selected for examination — and the result was as follows: When I began to talk with him, I could not help thinking that he was not really wise, although he was thought wise by many, and wiser still by myself; and I went and tried to explain to him that he thought himself wise, but was not really wise; and the consequence was that he hated me, and his enmity was shared by several who were present and heard me. So I left him, saying to myself, as I went away: Well, although I do not suppose that either of us knows anything really beautiful and good, I am better off than he is — for he knows nothing, and thinks that he knows. I neither know nor think that I know. In this latter particular, then, I seem to have slightly the advantage of him. Then I went to another, who had still higher philosophical pretensions, and my conclusion was exactly the same. I made another enemy of him, and of many others besides him. . . .

At last I went to the artisans, for I was conscious that I knew nothing at all, as I may say, and I was sure that they knew many fine things; and in this I was not mistaken, for they did know many things of which I was ignorant, and in this they certainly were wiser than I was. But I observed that even the good artisans fell into the same error as the poets; because they were good workmen they thought that they also knew all sorts of high matters, and this defect in them overshadowed their wisdom — therefore I asked myself on behalf of the oracle, whether I would like to be as I was, neither having their knowledge nor their ignorance, or like them in both; and I made answer to myself and the oracle that I was better off as I was.

This investigation has led to my having many enemies of the worst and most dangerous kind, and has given occasion also to many calumnies. And I am called wise, for my hearers always imagine that I myself possess the wisdom which I find wanting in others: but the truth is, O men of Athens, that God only is wise; and in this oracle he means to say that the wisdom of men is little or nothing; he is not speaking of Socrates, he is only using my name as an illustration, as if he said, He, O men, is the wisest, who, like Socrates, knows that his wisdom is in truth worth nothing. And so I go my way, obedient to the god, and make inquisition into the wisdom of anyone, whether citizen or stranger, who appears to be wise; and if he is not wise, then in vindication of the oracle I show him that he is not wise; and this occupation quite absorbs me, and I have no time to give either to any public matter of interest or to any concern of my own, but I am in utter poverty by reason of my devotion to the god.

There is another thing: — young men of the richer classes, who have not much to do, come about me of their own accord; they like to hear the pretenders examined, and they often imitate me, and examine others themselves; there are plenty of persons, as they soon enough discover, who think that they know something, but really know little or nothing; and then those who are examined by them instead of being angry with themselves are angry with me: This confounded Socrates, they say; this villainous misleader of youth! — and then if somebody asks them, Why, what evil does he practise or teach? they do not know, and cannot tell; but in order that they may not appear to be at a loss, they repeat the ready-made charges which are used against all philosophers about teaching things up in the clouds and under the earth, and having no gods, and making the worse appear the better cause; for they do not like to confess that their pretence of knowledge has been detected — which is the truth: and as they are numerous and ambitious and energetic, and are all in battle array and have persuasive tongues, they have filled your ears with their loud and inveterate calumnies. And this is the reason why my three accusers, Meletus and Anytus and Lycon, have set upon me: Meletus, who has a quarrel with me on behalf of the poets; Anytus, on behalf of the craftsmen; Lycon, on behalf of the rhetoricians: and as I said at the beginning, I cannot expect to get rid of this mass of calumny all in a moment. And this, O men of Athens, is the truth and the whole truth; I have concealed nothing, I have dissembled nothing. And yet I know that this plainness of speech makes them hate me, and what is their hatred but a proof that I am speaking the truth? — this is the occasion and reason of their slander of me, as you will find out either in this or in any future inquiry. . . .

Come hither, Meletus, and let me ask a question of you. You think a great deal about the improvement of youth?

Yes, I do.

Tell the judges, then, who is their improver: for you must know, as you have taken the pains to discover their corrupter, and are citing and accusing me before them. Speak, then, and tell the judges who their improver is. Observe, Meletus, that you are silent, and have nothing to say. But is not this rather disgraceful, and a very considerable proof of what I was saying, that you have no interest in the matter? Speak up, friend, and tell us who their improver is.

The laws.

But that, my good sir, is not my meaning. I want to know who the person is, who, in the first place, knows the laws.

The judges, Socrates, who are present in court.

What do you mean to say, Meletus, that they are able to instruct and improve youth?

Certainly they are.

What, all of them, or some only and not others?

All of them.

By the goddess Hera, that is good news! There are plenty of improvers, then. And what do you say of the audience — do they improve them?

Yes, they do.

And the Senators?

Yes, the Senators improve them.

But perhaps the ecclesiasts corrupt them? — or do they too improve them?

They improve them.

Then every Athenian improves and elevates them; all with the exception of myself; and I alone am their corrupter? Is that what you affirm?

That is what I stoutly affirm.

I am very unfortunate if that is true. But suppose I ask you a question: Would you say that this also holds true in the case of horses? Does one man do them harm and all the world good? Is not the exact opposite of this true? One man is able to do them good, or at least not many; the trainer of horses, that is to say, does them good, and others who have to do with them rather injure them? Is not that true, Meletus, of horses, or any other animals? Yes, certainly. Whether you and Anytus say yes or no, that is no matter. Happy indeed would be the condition of youth if they had one corrupter only, and all the rest of the world were their improvers. And you, Meletus, have sufficiently shown that you never had a thought about the young: your carelessness is seen in your not caring about the matters spoken of in this very indictment.

I have shown, Athenians, as I was saying, that Meletus has no care at all, great or small, about the matter. But still I should like to know, Meletus, in what I am affirmed to corrupt the young. I suppose you mean, as I infer from your indictment, that I teach them not to acknowledge the gods which the State acknowledges, but some other new divinities or spiritual agencies in their stead. These are the lessons which corrupt the youth, as you say.

Yes, that I say emphatically.

Then, by the gods, Meletus, of whom we are speaking, tell me and the court, in somewhat plainer terms, what you mean! for I do not as yet understand whether you affirm that I teach others to acknowledge some gods, and therefore do believe in gods and am not an entire atheist — this you do not lay to my charge; but only that they are not the same gods which the city recognizes — the charge is that they are different gods. Or, do you mean to say that I am an atheist simply, and a teacher of atheism?

I mean the latter — that you are a complete atheist.

That is an extraordinary statement, Meletus. Why do you say that? Do you mean that I do not believe in the godhead of the sun or moon, which is the common creed of all men?

I assure you, judges, that he does not believe in them; for he says that the sun is stone, and the moon earth.

Friend Meletus, you think that you are accusing Anaxagoras: and you have but a bad opinion of the judges if you fancy them ignorant to such a degree as not to know that those doctrines are found in the books of Anaxagoras the Clazomenian, who is full of them. And these are the doctrines which the youth are said to learn of Socrates, when there are not unfrequently exhibitions of them at the theatre (price of admission one drachma at the most); and they might cheaply purchase them, and laugh at Socrates if he pretends to father such eccentricities. And so, Meletus, you really think that I do not believe in any god?

I swear by Zeus that you believe absolutely in none at all.

You are a liar, Meletus, not believed even by yourself. For I cannot help thinking, O men of Athens, that Meletus is reckless and impudent, and that he has written this indictment in a spirit of mere wantonness and youthful bravado. Has he not compounded a riddle, thinking to try me? He said to himself: I shall

669

see whether this wise Socrates will discover my ingenious contradiction, or whether I shall be able to deceive him and the rest of them. For he certainly does appear to me to contradict himself in the indictment as much as if he said that Socrates is guilty of not believing in the gods, and yet of believing in them — but this surely is a piece of fun.

I should like you, O men of Athens, to join me in examining what I conceive to be his inconsistency; and do you, Meletus, answer. And I must remind you that you are not to interrupt me if I speak in my accustomed manner.

Did ever man, Meletus, believe in the existence of human things, and not of human beings? . . . I wish, men of Athens, that he would answer, and not be always trying to get up an interruption. Did ever any man believe in horsemanship, and not in horses? or in flute-playing, and not in flute-players? No, my friend; I will answer to you and to the court, as you refuse to answer for yourself. There is no man who ever did. But now please to answer the next question: Can a man believe in spiritual and divine agencies, and not in spirits or demigods?

He cannot.

I am glad that I have extracted that answer, by the assistance of the court; nevertheless you swear in the indictment that I teach and believe in divine or spiritual agencies (new or old, no matter for that); at any rate, I believe in spiritual agencies, as you say and swear in the affidavit; but if I believe in divine beings, I must believe in spirits or demigods; is not that true? Yes, that is true, for I may assume that your silence gives assent to that. Now what are spirits or demigods? are they not either gods or the sons of gods? Is that true?

Yes, that is true.

But this is just the ingenious riddle of which I was speaking: the demigods or spirits are gods, and you say first that I don't believe in gods, and then again that I do believe in gods; that is, if I believe in demigods. For if the demigods are the illegitimate sons of gods, whether by the Nymphs or by any other mothers, as is thought, that, as all men will allow, necessarily implies the existence of their parents. You might as well affirm the existence

670

of mules, and deny that of horses and asses. Such nonsense, Meletus, could only have been intended by you as a trial of me. You have put this into the indictment because you had nothing real of which to accuse me. But no one who has a particle of understanding will ever be convinced by you that the same man can believe in divine and superhuman things, and yet not believe that there are gods and demigods and heroes.

I have said enough in answer to the charge of Meletus: any elaborate defence is unnecessary; but as I was saying before, I certainly have many enemies, and this is what will be my destruction if I am destroyed; of that I am certain; not Meletus, nor yet Anytus, but the envy and detraction of the world, which has been the death of many good men, and will probably be the death of many more; there is no danger of my being the last of them.

Someone will say: And are you not ashamed, Socrates, of a course of life which is likely to bring you to an untimely end? To him I may fairly answer: There you are mistaken: a man who is good for anything ought not to calculate the chance of living or dying; he ought only to consider whether in doing anything he is doing right or wrong — acting the part of a good man or of a bad. . . .

Strange, indeed, would be my conduct, O men of Athens, if I who, when I was ordered by the generals whom you chose to command me at Potidæa and Amphipolis and Delium, remained where they placed me, like any other man, facing death — if, I say, now, when, as I conceive and imagine, God orders me to fulfil the philosopher's mission of searching into myself and other men, I were to desert my post through fear of death, or any other fear; that would indeed be strange, and I might justly be arraigned in court for denying the existence of the gods, if I disobeyed the oracle because I was afraid of death: then I should be fancying that I was wise when I was not wise. For this fear of death is indeed the pretence of wisdom, and not real wisdom, being the appearance of knowing the unknown; since no one knows whether death, which they in their fear apprehend to be the greatest evil, may not be the greatest good.

HERBERT SPENCER

HERBERT SPENCER (1820-1903). Before he died at Brighton, England, on December 8, 1903, "The greatest intellect since Aristotle" was also credited with being the father of modern social science, the author of evolutionism and Social Darwinism, and the father of social science. Educators praised the writings of Herbert Spencer (his book *Education* appeared in 1861, and his *Essays* appeared in three series between 1857 and 1874) and declared that his question, "What Knowledge Is of Most Worth?" had thrown schoolmen into dismay. He provided a basis for building a curriculum to prepare students "for complete living" by identifying five categories of education: (1) self-preservation, (2) securing the necessities of life, (3) rearing and disciplining children, (4) maintaining appropriate social and political relations, and (5) leisure and the qualifications of taste and feelings. Spencer was convinced that *science* (both natural science and social science) contributed most toward preparing students for a complete life.

Born at Derby, England, on April 27, 1820, he received little formal education but managed to acquire an astonishing intellectual self-reliance. He worked for a time as an engineer and as a journalist. At the age of thirty-two he received from his uncle a legacy which enabled him to devote himself fully to his writing. His transformation from a semi-educated engineer into a philosopher capable of synthesizing all human knowledge (the first thinker since Francis Bacon to accomplish this feat) brought him universal acclaim. In his educational theories he was influenced by the writings of Rousseau, but the two great themes that were forever present in his thinking were utilitarianism, the individualistic doctrine which extolled liberty and happiness as the supreme end of man, and evolution. His popularity was due largely to his ability to harmonize the prodigious scientific advances of his century, the universal belief in human freedom and human dignity, and the newly formulated doctrine of inevitable progress to perfection through the operation of a pitiless nature. In trying to construct his unified system, however, he has been accused of looking for what confirmed his theories and ignoring or reinterpreting what conflicted with them. Toward the end of his life he became less optimistic about the future of humanity.

The selection presented here is from the essay, "What Knowledge Is of Most Worth?" In his classic essay Spencer defines the intimate relationship between the organization of the school curriculum and the aims of education. The knowledge of most worth will determine the content of the curriculum. It is generally agreed that Spencer's functional analysis of human needs resulted in the modern era of curriculum reform in England and in the United States.

WHAT KNOWLEDGE IS OF MOST WORTH?*

It behooves us to set before ourselves, and ever to keep clearly in view, complete living as the end to be achieved; so that in bringing up our children we may choose subjects and methods of instruction, with deliberate reference to this end. Not only ought we to cease from the mere unthinking adoption of the current fashion in education, which has no better warrant than any other fashion; but we must also rise above that rude, empirical style of judging displayed by those more intelligent people who do bestow some care in overseeing the cultivation of their children's minds. It must not suffice simply to *think* that such or such information will be useful in after life, or that this kind of knowledge is of more practical value than that; but we must seek out some process of estimating their respective values, so that as far as possible we may positively *know* which are most deserving of attention.

Doubtless the task is difficult — perhaps never to be more than approximately achieved. But, considering the vastness of the interests at stake, its difficulty is no reason for pusillanimously passing it by; but rather for devoting every energy to its mastery. And if we only proceed systematically, we may very soon get at results of no small moment.

Our first step must obviously be to classify, in the order of their importance, the leading kinds of activity which constitute human life. They may be naturally arranged into: — 1. those activities which directly minister to self-preservation; 2. those activities which, by securing the necessaries of life, indirectly minister to

*From *What Knowledge Is of Most Worth?* (London, 1859). Reprinted in *Essays on Education* (London: J. M. Dent and Sons Ltd., 1911).

self-preservation; 3. those activities which have for their end the rearing and discipline of offspring; 4. those activities which are involved in the maintenance of proper social and political relations; 5. those miscellaneous activities which fill up the leisure part of life, devoted to the gratification of the tastes and feelings.

That these stand in something like their true order of subordination, it needs no long consideration to show. The actions and precautions by which, from moment to moment, we secure personal safety, must clearly take precedence of all others. Could there be a man, ignorant as an infant of surrounding objects and movements, or how to guide himself among them, he would pretty certainly lose his life the first time he went into the street; notwithstanding any amount of learning he might have on other matters. And as entire ignorance in all other directions would be less promptly fatal than entire ignorance in this direction, it must be admitted that knowledge immediately conducive to self-preservation is of primary importance.

That next after direct self-preservation comes the indirect self-preservation which consists in acquiring the means of living, none will question. That a man's industrial functions must be considered before his parental ones, is manifest from the fact that, speaking generally, the discharge of the parental functions is made possible only by the previous discharge of the industrial ones. The power of self-maintenance necessarily preceding the power of maintaining offspring, it follows that knowledge needful for self-maintenance has stronger claims than knowledge needful for family welfare — is second in value to none save knowledge needful for immediate self-preservation.

As the family comes before the State in order of time — the bringing up of children is possible before the State exists, or when it has ceased to be, whereas the State is rendered possible only by the bringing up of children; it follows that the duties of the parent demand closer attention than those of the citizen. Or, to use a further argument — since the goodness of a society ultimately depends on the nature of its citizens; and since the nature of its citizens is more modifiable by early training than by anything else; we must conclude that the welfare of the family

674

underlies the welfare of society. And hence knowledge directly conducing to the first, must take precedence of knowledge directly conducing to the last.

Those various forms of pleasurable occupation which fill up the leisure left by graver occupations — the enjoyments of music, poetry, painting, etc. — manifestly imply a pre-existing society. Not only is a considerable development of them impossible without a long-established social union; but their very subject-matter consists in great part of social sentiments and sympathies. Not only does society supply the conditions to their growth; but also the ideas and sentiments they express. And, consequently, that part of human conduct which constitutes good citizenship, is of more moment than that which goes out in accomplishments or exercise of the tastes; and, in education, preparation for the one must rank before preparation for the other.

Such then, we repeat, is something like the rational order of subordination: — That education which prepares for direct self-preservation; that which prepares for indirect self-preservation; that which prepares for parenthood; that which prepares for the miscellaneous refinements of life. . . .

One further preliminary. Acquirement of every kind has two values — value as *knowledge* and value as *discipline*. Besides its use for guiding conduct, the acquisition of each order of facts has also its use as mental exercise; and its effects as a preparative for complete living have to be considered under both these heads.

These, then, are the general ideas with which we must set out in discussing a *curriculum*: — Life as divided into several kinds of activity, intrinsically, quasi-intrinsically, and conventionally; and their regulative influences estimated both as knowledge and discipline.

Happily, that all-important part of education which goes to secure direct self-preservation, is in great part already provided for. Too momentous to be left to our blundering, Nature takes it into her own hands. While yet in its nurse's arms, the infant, by hiding its face and crying at the sight of a stranger, shows the dawning instinct to attain safety by flying from that which is unknown and may be dangerous; and when it can walk, the terror it

675

manifests if an unfamiliar dog comes near, or the screams with which it runs to its mother after any startling sight or sound, shows this instinct further developed. Moreover, knowledge subserving direct self-preservation is that which it is chiefly busied in acquiring from hour to hour. How to balance its body; how to control its movements so as to avoid collisions; what objects are hard, and will hurt if struck; what objects are heavy, and injure if they fall on the limbs; which things will bear the weight of the body, and which not; the pains inflicted by fire, by missiles, by sharp instruments — these, and various other pieces of information needful for the avoidance of death or accident, it is ever learning. . . .

Knowledge which subserves direct self-preservation by preventing loss of health is of primary importance. We do not contend that possession of such knowledge would by any means wholly remedy the evil. It is clear that in our present phase of civilisation, men's necessities often compel them to transgress. And it is further clear that, even in the absence of such compulsion, their inclinations would frequently lead them, spite of their convictions, to sacrifice future good to present gratification. But we *do* contend that the right knowledge impressed in the right way would effect much; and we further contend that as the laws of health must be recognised before they can be fully conformed to, the imparting of such knowledge must precede a more rational living — come when that may. We infer that as vigorous health and its accompanying high spirits are larger elements of happiness than any other things whatever, the teaching how to maintain them is a teaching that yields in moment to no other whatever. And therefore we assert that such a course of physiology as is needful for the comprehension of its general truths, and their bearings on daily conduct, is an all-esential part of a rational education.

Strange that the assertion should need making! Stranger still that it should need defending! Yet are there not a few by whom such a proposition will be received with something approaching to derision. Men who would blush if caught saying Iphigénia, instead of Iphigenía, or would resent as an insult any imputation of ignorance respecting the fabled labours of a fabled demi-god, show not the slightest shame in confessing that they do not know where the Eustachian tubes are, what are the actions of the spinal cord, what is the normal rate of pulsation, or how the lungs are inflated. While anxious that their sons should be well up in the superstitions of two thousand years ago, they care not that they should be taught anything about the structure and functions of their own bodies — nay, even wish them not to be so taught. So overwhelming is the influence of established routine! So terribly in our education does the ornamental over-ride the useful!

We need not insist on the value of that knowledge which aids indirect self-preservation by facilitating the gaining of a livelihood. This is admitted by all; and, indeed, by the mass is perhaps too exclusively regarded as the end of education. But while every one is ready to endorse the abstract proposition that instruction fitting youths for the business of life is of high importance, or even to consider it of supreme importance; yet scarcely any inquire what instruction will so fit them. It is true that reading, writing, and arithmetic are taught with an intelligent appreciation of their uses. But when we have said this we have said nearly all. While the great bulk of what else is acquired has no bearing on the industrial activities, an immensity of information that has a direct bearing on the industrial activities is entirely passed over.

For, leaving out only some very small classes, what are all men employed in? They are employed in the production, preparation, and distribution of commodities. And on what does efficiency in the production, preparation, and distribution of commodities depend? It depends on the use of methods fitted to the respective natures of these commodities; it depends on an adequate acquaintance with their physical, chemical, or vital properties, as the case may be; that is, it depends on Science. This order of knowledge which is in great part ignored in our school-courses, is the order of knowledge underlying the right performance of those processes by which civilised life is made possible. Undeniable as is this truth, there seems to be no living consciousness of it: its very familiarity makes it unregarded. . . .

Thus, to all such as are occupied in the production, exchange, or distribution of commodities, acquaintance with Science in some

677

of its departments, is of fundamental importance. Each man who is immediately or remotely implicated in any form of industry (and few are not) has in some way to deal with the mathematical, physical, and chemical properties of things; perhaps, also, has a direct interest in biology; and certainly has in sociology. Whether he does or does not succeed well in that indirect self-preservation which we call getting a good livelihood, depends in a great degree on his knowledge of one or more of these sciences: not, it may be, a rational knowledge; but still a knowledge, though empirical. For what we call learning a business, really implies learning the science involved in it; though not perhaps under the name of science. And hence a grounding in science is of great importance, both because it prepares for all this and because rational knowledge has an immense superiority over empirical knowledge. . . .

That which our school-courses leave almost entirely out, we thus find to be that which most nearly concerns the business of life. Our industries would cease, were it not for the information which men begin to acquire, as they best may, after their education is said to be finished. And were it not for this information, from age to age accumulated and spread by unofficial means, these industries would never have existed. Had there been no teaching but such as goes on in our public schools, England would now be what it was in feudal times. That increasing acquaintance with the laws of phenomena, which has through successive ages enabled us to subjugate Nature to our needs, and in these days gives the common labourer comforts which a few centuries ago kings could not purchase, is scarcely in any degree owed to the appointed means of instructing our youth. The vital knowledge— that by which we have grown as a nation to what we are, and which now underlies our whole existence, is a knowledge that has got itself taught in nooks and corners; while the ordained agencies for teaching have been mumbling little else but dead formulas.

We come now to the third great division of human activities —a division for which no preparation whatever is made. If by some strange chance not a vestige of us descended to the remote future save a pile of our school-books or some college examina-

678

tion papers, we may imagine how puzzled an antiquary of the period would be on finding in them no sign that the learners were ever likely to be parents. "This must have been the *curriculum* for their celibates," we may fancy him concluding. "I perceive here an elaborate preparation for many things; especially for reading the books of extinct nations and of co-existing nations (from which indeed it seems clear that these people had very little worth reading in their own tongue); but I find no reference whatever to the bringing up of children. They could not have been so absurd as to omit all training for this gravest of responsibilities. Evidently then, this was the school-course of one of their monastic orders."

Seriously, is it not an astonishing fact, that though on the treatment of offspring depend their lives or deaths, and their moral welfare or ruin; yet not one word of instruction on the treatment of offspring is ever given to those who will by and by be parents? Is it not monstrous that the fate of a new generation should be left to the chances of unreasoning custom, impulse, fancy — joined with the suggestions of ignorant nurses and the prejudiced counsel of grandmothers? If a merchant commenced business without any knowledge of arithmetic and book-keeping, we should exclaim at his folly, and look for disastrous consequences. Or if, before studying anatomy, a man set up as a surgical operator, we should wonder at his audacity and pity his patients. But that parents should begin the difficult task of rearing children, without ever having given a thought to the principles — physical, moral, or intellectual — which ought to guide them, excites neither surprise at the actors nor pity for their victims. . . .

Equally great are the ignorance and the consequent injury, when we turn from physical training to moral training. Consider the young mother and her nursery-legislation. But a few years ago she was at school, where her memory was crammed with words, and names, and dates, and her reflective faculties scarcely in the slightest degree exercised — where not one idea was given her respecting the methods of dealing with the opening mind of childhood; and where her discipline did not in the least fit her for thinking out methods of her own. The intervening years have

679

been given to the grave responsibilities of maternity; and scarcely any of that solid intellectual culture obtained which would be some preparation for such responsibilities. . . .

And then the culture of the intellect — is not this, too, mis-managed in a similar manner? Grant that the phenomena of intelligence conform to laws; grant that the evolution of intelligence in a child also conforms to laws; and it follows inevitably that education cannot be rightly guided without a knowledge of these laws. To suppose that you can properly regulate this process of forming and accumulating ideas, without understanding the nature of the process, is absurd. How widely, then, must teaching as it is differ from teaching as it should be; when hardly any parents, and but few tutors, know anything about psychology. As might be expected, the established system is grievously at fault, alike in matter and in manner. While the right class of facts is withheld, the wrong class is forcibly administered in the wrong way and in the wrong order. Under that common limited idea of education which confines it to knowledge gained from books, parents thrust primers into the hands of their little ones years too soon, to their great injury. Not recognising the truth that the function of books is supplementary — that they form an indirect means to knowledge when direct means fail — a means of seeing through other men what you cannot see for yourself; teachers are eager to give second-hand facts in place of first-hand facts. Not perceiving the enormous value of that spontaneous education which goes on in early years — not perceiving that a child's restless observation, instead of being ignored or checked, should be diligently ministered to, and made as accurate and complete as possible; they insist on occupying, its eyes and thoughts with things that are, for the time being, incomprehensible and repugnant. . . .

Thus we find the facts to be such as might have been inferred *a priori*. The training of children — physical, moral, and intellectual — is dreadfully defective. And in great measure it is so because parents are devoid of that knowledge by which this training can alone be rightly guided. What is to be expected when one of the most intricate of problems is undertaken by those who have given scarcely a thought to the principles on which its solution depends? For shoe-making or house-building, for the management of a ship or a locomotive engine, a long apprenticeship is needful. Is it, then, that the unfolding of a human being in body and mind is so comparatively simple a process that any one may superintend and regulate it wth no preparation whatever? If not — if the process is, with one exception, more complex than any in Nature, and the task of ministering to it one of surpassing difficulty; is it not madness to make no provision for such a task? Better sacrifice accomplishments than omit this all-essential instruction. When a father, acting on false dogmas adopted without examination, has alienated his sons, driven them into rebellion by his harsh treatment, ruined them, and made himself miserable; he might reflect that the study of Ethology would have been worth pursuing, even at the cost of knowing nothing about Aeschylus. When a mother is mourning over a first-born that has sunk under the sequelæ of scarlet-fever — when perhaps a candid medical man has confirmed her suspicion that her child would have recovered had not its system been enfeebled by over-study — when she is prostrate under the pangs of combined grief and remorse; it is but a small consolation that she can read Dante in the original.

Thus we see that for regulating the third great division of human activities, a knowledge of the laws of life is the one thing needful. Some acquaintance with the first principles of physiology and the elementary truths of psychology, is indispensable for the right bringing up of children. We doubt not that many will read this assertion with a smile. That parents in general should be expected to acquire a knowledge of subjects so abstruse will seem to them an absurdity. And if we proposed that an exhaustive knowledge of these subjects should be obtained by all fathers and mothers, the absurdity would indeed be glaring enough. But we do not. General principles only, accompanied by such illustrations as may be needed to make them understood, would suffice. And these might be readily taught — if not rationally, then dogmatically. Be this as it may, however, here are the indisputable facts: — that the development of children in mind and body follows certain laws; that unless these laws are in some degree conformed to by parents, death is inevitable; that unless they are in a great degree conformed to, there must result serious physical and mental defects; and that only when they are completely conformed to, can a perfect maturity be reached. Judge, then, whether all who may one day be parents, should not strive with some anxiety to learn what these laws are.

From the parental functions let us pass now to the functions of the citizen. We have here to inquire what knowledge fits a man for the discharge of these functions. It cannot be alleged that the need for knowledge fitting him for these functions is wholly overlooked; for our school-courses contain certain studies, which, nominally at least, bear upon political and social duties. Of these the only one that occupies a prominent place is History. . . .

But now mark, that even supposing an adequate stock of this truly valuable historical knowledge has been acquired, it is of comparatively little use without the key. And the key is to be found only in Science. In the absence of the generalisations of biology and psychology, rational interpretation of social phenomena is impossible. Only in proportion as men draw certain rude, empirical inferences respecting human nature, are they enabled to understand even the simplest facts of social life: as, for instance, the relation between supply and demand. And if the most elementary truths of sociology cannot be reached until some knowledge is obtained of how men generally think, feel, and act under given circumstances; then it is manifest that there can be nothing like a wide comprehension of sociology, unless through a competent acquaintance with man in all his faculties, bodily, and mental. Consider the matter in the abstract, and this conclusion is self-evident. Thus: — Society is made up of individuals; all that is done in society is done by the combined actions of individuals; and therefore, in individual actions only can be found the solutions of social phenomena. But the actions of individuals depend on the laws of their natures; and their actions cannot be understood until these laws are understood. These laws, however, when reduced to their simplest expressions, prove to be corollaries from the laws of body and mind in general. Hence it follows, that biology and psychology are indispensable as interpreters of so-

682

ciology. Or, to state the conclusions still more simply: — all social phenomena are phenomena of life — are the most complex manifestations of life — must conform to the laws of life — and can be understood only when the laws of life are understood. Thus, then, for the regulation of this fourth division of human activities, we are, as before, dependent on Science. Of the knowledge commonly imparted in educational courses, very little is of service for guiding a man in his conduct as a citizen. Only a small part of the history he reads is of practical value; and of this small part he is not prepared to make proper use. He lacks not only the materials for, but the very conception of, descriptive sociology; and he also lacks those generalisations of the organic sciences, without which even descriptive sociology can give him but small aid.

And now we come to that remaining division of human life which includes the relaxations and amusements filling leisure hours. After considering what training best fits for self-preservation, for the obtainment of sustenance, for the discharge of parental duties, and for the regulation of social and political conduct; we have now to consider what training best fits for the miscellaneous ends not included in these — for the enjoyment of Nature, of Literature, and of the Fine Arts, in all their forms. Postponing them as we do to things that bear more vitally upon human welfare; and bringing everything, as we have, to the test of actual value; it will perhaps be inferred that we are inclined to slight these less essential things. No greater mistake could be made, however. We yield to none in the value we attach to æsthetic culture and its pleasures. Without painting, sculpture, music, poetry, and the emotions produced by natural beauty of every kind, life would lose half its charm. So far from regarding the training and gratification of the tastes as unimportant, we believe that in time to come they will occupy a much larger share of human life than now. When the forces of Nature have been fully conquered to man's use — when the means of production have been brought to perfection — when labour has been economised to the highest degree — when education has been so systematised that a preparation for the more essential activities may be made with comparative rapidity — and when, consequently, there is a great increase of spare time; then will the beautiful, both in Art and Nature, rightly fill a large space in the minds of all.

But it is one thing to approve of æsthetic culture as largely conducive to human happiness; and another thing to admit that is a fundamental requisite to human happiness. However important it may be, it must yield precedence to those kinds of culture which bear directly upon daily duties. As before hinted, literature and the fine arts are made possible by those activities which make individual and social life possible; and manifestly, that which is made possible, must be postponed to that which makes it possible. A florist cultivates a plant for the sake of its flower; and regards the roots and leaves as of value, chiefly because they are instrumental in producing the flower. But while, as an ultimate product, the flower is the thing to which everything else is subordinate, the florist has learnt that the root and leaves are intrinsically of greater importance; because on them the evolution of the flower depends. He bestows every care in rearing a healthy plant; and knows it would be folly if, in his anxiety to obtain the flower, he were to neglect the plant. Similarly in the case before us. Architecture, sculpture, painting, music, and poetry, may truly be called the efflorescence of civilised life. But even supposing they are of such transcendent worth as to subordinate the civilised life out of which they grow (which can hardly be asserted), it will still be admitted that the production of a healthy civilised life must be the first consideration; and that culture subserving this must occupy the highest place.

And here we see most distinctly the vice of our educational system. It neglects the plant for the sake of the flower. In anxiety for elegance, it forgets substance. While it gives no knowledge conducive to self-preservation — while of knowledge that facilitates gaining a livelihood it gives but the rudiments, and leaves the greater part to be picked up anyhow in after life — while for the discharge of parental functions it makes not the slightest provision — and while for the duties of citizenship it prepares by imparting a mass of facts, most of which are irrelevant, and the rest without a key; it is diligent in teaching whatever adds to refinement, polish, éclat. Fully as we may admit that extensive acquaintance with modern languages is a valuable accomplishment, which, through reading, conversation, and travel, aids in giving a certain finish; it by no means follows that this result is rightly purchased at the cost of the vitally important knowledge sacrificed to it. Supposing it true that classical education conduces to elegance and correctness of style; it cannot be said that elegance and correctness of style are comparable in importance to a familiarity with the principles that should guide the rearing of children. Grant that the taste may be improved by reading the poetry written in extinct languages; yet it is not to be inferred that such improvement of taste is equivalent in value to an acquaintance with the laws of health. Accomplishments, the fine arts, *belles-lettres,* and all those things which, as we say, constitute the efflorescence of civilisation, should be wholly subordinate to that instruction and discipline in which civilisation rests. *As they occupy the leisure part of life, so should they occupy the leisure part of education. . . .*

Every artist, in the course of his education and after-life, accumulates a stock of maxims by which his practice is regulated. Trace such maxims to their roots, and they inevitably lead you down to psychological principles. And only when the artist understands these psychological principles and their various corollaries can he work in harmony with them.

We do not for a moment believe that science will make an artist. While we contend that the leading laws both of objective and subjective phenomena must be understood by him, we by no means contend that knowledge of such laws will serve in place of natural perception. Not the poet only, but the artist of every type, is born, not made. What we assert is, that innate faculty cannot dispense with the aid of organised knowledge. Intuition will do much, but it will not do all. Only when Genius is married to Science can the highest results be produced.

As we have above asserted, Science is necessary not only for the most successful production, but also for the full appreciation, of the fine arts. In what consists the greater ability of a man than of a child to perceive the beauties of a picture; unless it is in his more extended knowledge of those truths in nature or life which the picture renders? How happens the cultivated gentleman to enjoy a fine poem so much more than a boor does; if it is not because his wider acquaintance with objects and actions enables him to see in the poem much that the boor cannot see? And if, as is here so obvious, there must be some familiarity with the things represented, before the representation can be appreciated, then, the representation can be completely appreciated only when the things represented are completely understood. The fact is, that every additional truth which a word of art expresses, gives an additional pleasure to the percipient mind — a pleasure that is missed by those ignorant of this truth. The more realities an artist indicates in any given amount of work, the more faculties does he appeal to; the more numerous ideas does he suggest; the more gratification does he afford. But to receive this gratification the spectator, listener, or reader, must know the realities which the artist has indicated; and to know these realities is to have that much science.

And now let us not overlook the further great fact, that not only does science underlie sculpture, painting, music, poetry, but that science is itself poetic. The current opinion that science and poetry are opposed, is a delusion. It is doubtless true that as states of consciousness, cognition and emotion tend to exclude each other. And it is doubtless also true that an extreme activity of the reflective powers tends to deaden the feelings; while an extreme activity of the feeling tends to deaden the reflective powers: in which sense, indeed, all orders of activity are antagonistic to each other. But it is not true that the facts of science are unpoetical; or that the cultivation of science is necessarily unfriendly to the exercise of imagination and the love of the beautiful. On the contrary, science opens up realms of poetry where to the unscientific all is a blank. Those engaged in scientific researches constantly show us that they realise not less vividly, but more vividly, than others, the poetry of their subjects. Whoso will dip into Hugh Miller's works of geology, or read Mr. Lewes's *Seaside Studies*, will perceive that science excites poetry rather than extinguishes it. And he who contemplates the life of Goethe, must see that the poet and the man of science can co-

686

exist in equal activity. Is it not, indeed, an absurd and almost a sacrilegious belief, that the more a man studies Nature the less he reveres it? Think you that a drop of water, which to the vulgar eye is but a drop of water, loses anything in the eye of the physicist who knows that its elements are held together by a force which, if suddenly liberated, would produce a flash of lightning? Think you that what is carelessly looked upon by the uninitiated as a mere snow-flake, does not suggest higher associations to one who had seen through a microscope the wondrously-varied and elegant forms of snow-crystals? Think you that the rounded rock marked with parallel scratches, calls up as much poetry in an ignorant mind as in the mind of a geologist, who knows that over this rock a glacier slid a million years ago? The truth is, that those who have never entered upon scientific pursuits are blind to most of the poetry by which they are surrounded. Whoever has not in youth collected plants and insects, knows not half the halo of interest which lanes and hedge-rows can assume. Whoever has not sought for fossils, has little idea of the poetical associations that surround the places where imbedded treasures were found. Whoever at the sea-side has not had a microscope and aquarium, has yet to learn what the highest pleasures of the sea-side are. Sad, indeed, is it to see how men occupy themselves with trivialities, and are indifferent to the grandest phenomena — care not to understand the architecture of the Heavens, but are deeply interested in some contemptible controversy about the intrigues of Mary Queen of Scots! — are learnedly critical over a Greek ode, and pass by without a glance that grand epic written by the finger of God upon the strata of the Earth!

We find, then, that even for this remaining division of human activities, scientific culture is the proper preparation. We find that æsthetics in general are necessarily based upon scientific principles; and can be pursued with complete success only through an acquaintance with these principles. We find that for the criticism and due appreciation of works of art, a knowledge of the constitution of things, or in other words, a knowledge of science, is requisite. And we not only find that science is the handmaid to all forms of art and poetry, but that, rightly regarded, science is itself poetic.

Thus far our question has been, the worth of knowledge of this or that kind for purposes of guidance. We have now to judge the relative value of different kinds of knowledge for purposes of discipline. This division of our subject we are obliged to treat with comparative brevity; and happily, no very lengthened treatment of it is needed. Having found what is best for the one end, we have by implication found what is best for the other. We may be quite sure that the acquirement of those classes of facts which are most useful for regulating conduct, involves a mental exercise best fitted for strengthening the faculties. It would be utterly contrary to the beautiful economy of Nature, if one kind of culture were needed as a mental gymnastic. Everywhere throughout creation we find faculties developed through the performance of those functions which it is their office to perform; not through the performance of artificial exercises devised to fit them for those functions. The Red Indian acquires the swiftness and agility which make him a successful hunter, by the actual pursuit of animals; and through the miscellaneous activities of his life, he gains a better balance of physical powers than gymnastics ever give. That skill in tracking enemies and prey which he had reached after long practice, implies a subtlety of perception far exceeding anything produced by artificial training. And similarly in all cases. From the Bushman whose eye, habitually employed in identifying distant objects that are to be pursued or fled from, has acquired a telescopic range, to the accountant whose daily practice enables him to add up several columns of figures simultaneously; we find that the highest power of a faculty results from the discharge of those duties which the conditions of life require it to discharge. And we may be certain, *a priori,* that the same law holds throughout education. The education of most value for guidance, must at the same time be the education of most value for discipline. Let us consider the evidence.

One advantage claimed for that devotion to language-learning which forms so prominent a feature in the ordinary *curriculum,* is, that the memory is thereby strengthened. This is assumed to be an advantage peculiar to the study of words. But the truth is, that the sciences afford far wider fields for the exercise of memory. It is no slight task to remember everything about our solar system; much more to remember all that is known concerning the structure of our galaxy. The number of compound substances, to which chemistry daily adds, is so great that few, save professors, can enumerate them; and to recollect the atomic constitutions and affinities of all these compounds, is scarcely possible without making chemistry the occupation of life. In the enormous mass of phenomena presented by the Earth's crust, and in the still more enormous mass of phenomena presented by the fossils it contains, there is matter which it takes the geological student years of application to master. Each leading division of physics — sound, heat, light, electricity — includes facts numerous enough to alarm any one proposing to learn them all. And when we pass to the organic sciences, the effort of memory required becomes still greater. In human anatomy alone, the quantity of detail is so great, that the young surgeon has commonly to get it up half-a-dozen times before he can permanently retain it. The number of species of plants which botanists distinguish, amounts to some 320,000; while the varied forms of animal life with which the zoologist deals are estimated at some 2,000,000. So vast is the accumulation of facts which men of science have before them, that only by dividing and subdividing their labours can they deal with it. To a detailed knowledge of his own division, each adds but a general knowledge of the allied ones; joined perhaps to a rudimentary acquaintance with some others. Surely, then, science, cultivated even to a very moderate extent, affords adequate exercise for memory. To say the very least, it involves quite as good a discipline for this faculty as language does.

But now mark that while, for the training of mere memory, science is as good as, if not better than, language; it has an immense superiority in the kind of memory it trains. In the acquirement of a language, the connections of ideas to be established in the mind correspond to facts that are in great measure accidental; whereas, in the acquirement of science, the connections of ideas to be established in the mind correspond to facts that are mostly necessary. It is true that the relations of words to their meanings are in one sense natural; that the genesis of these relations may be traced back a certain distance, though rarely to the beginning; and that the laws of this genesis form a branch of mental science — the science of philology. But since it will not be contended that in the acquisition of languages, as ordinarily carried on, these natural relations between words and their meanings are habitually traced, and their laws explained; it must be admitted that they are commonly learned as fortuitous relations. On the other hand, the relations which science presents are causal relations; and, when properly taught, are understood as such. While language familiarises with nonrational relations, science familiarises with rational relations. While the one exercises memory only, the other exercises both memory and understanding.

Observe next, that a great superiority of science over language as a means of discipline, is, that it cultivates the judgment. As, in a lecture on mental education delivered at the Royal Institution, Professor Faraday well remarks, the most common intellectual fault is deficiency of judgment. "Society, speaking generally," he says, "is not only ignorant as respects education of the judgment, but it is also ignorant of its ignorance." And the cause to which he ascribes this state, is want of scientific culture. The truth of his conclusion is obvious. Correct judgment with regard to surrounding objects, events, and consequences, becomes possible only through knowledge of the way in which surrounding phenomena depend on each other. No extent of acquaintance with the meanings of words, will guarantee correct inferences respecting causes and effects. The habit of drawing conclusions from data, and then of verifying those conclusions by observation and experiment, can alone give the power of judging correctly. And that it necessitates this habit is one of the immense advantages of science.

Not only, however, for intellectual discipline is science the best; but also for *moral* discipline. The learning of languages tends, if anything, further to increase the already undue respect for authority. Such and such are the meanings of these words, says the teacher of the dictionary. So and so is the rule in this case, says the grammar. By the pupil these dicta are received as unquestionable. His constant attitude of mind is that of submission to dogmatic teaching. And a necessary result is a tendency to accept without inquiry whatever is established. Quite opposite is the mental tone generated by the cultivation of science. Science makes constant appeal to individual reason. Its truths are not accepted on authority alone; but all are at liberty to test them — nay, in many cases, the pupil is required to think out his own conclusions. Every step in a scientific investigation is submitted to his judgment. He is not asked to admit it without seeing it to be true. And the trust in his own powers thus produced is further increased by the uniformity with which Nature justifies his inferences when they are correctly drawn. From all which there flows that independence which is a most valuable element in character. Nor is this the only moral benefit bequeathed by scientific culture. When carried on, as it should always be, as much as possible under the form of original research, it exercises perseverance and sincerity. As says Professor Tyndall of inductive inquiry, "It requires patient industry, and an humble and conscientious acceptance of what Nature reveals. The first condition of success is an honest receptivity and a willingness to abandon all preconceived notions, however cherished, if they be found to contradict the truth. Believe me, a self-renunciation which has something noble in it, and of which the world never hears, is often enacted in the private experience of the true votary of science."

Lastly we have to assert — and the assertion will, we doubt not, cause extreme surprise — that the discipline of science is superior to that of our ordinary education, because of the *religious* culture that it gives. Of course we do not here use the words scientific and religious in their ordinary limited acceptations; but in their widest and highest acceptations. Doubtless, to the superstitions that pass under the name of religion, science is antagonistic; but not to the essential religion which these superstitions merely hide. Doubtless, too, in much of the science that is current, there is a pervading spirit of irreligion; but not in that true science which had passed beyond the superficial into the profound.

"True science and true religion," says Professor Huxley at the close of a recent course of lectures, "are twin-sisters, and the separation of either from the other is sure to prove the death of both. Science prospers exactly in proportion as it is religious; and religion flourishes in exact proportion to the the scientific depth and firmness of its basis. The great deeds of philosophers have been less the fruit of their intellect than of the direction of that intellect by an eminently religious tone of mind. Truth has yielded herself rather to their patience, their love, their single-heartedness, and their self-denial, than to their logical acumen."

So far from science being irreligious, as many think, it is the neglect of science that is irreligious — it is the refusal to study the surrounding creation that is irreligious. Take a humble simile. Suppose a writer were daily saluted with praises couched in super-lative language. Suppose the wisdom, the grandeur, the beauty of his works, were the constant topics of the eulogies addressed to him. Suppose those who unceasingly uttered these eulogies on his works were content with looking at the outsides of them; and had never opened them, much less tried to understand them. What value should we put upon their praise? What should we think of their sincerity? Yet, comparing small things to great, such is the conduct of mankind in general, in reference to the Universe and its Cause. Nay, it is worse. Not only do they pass by without study, these things which they daily proclaim to be so wonderful; but very frequently they condemn as mere triflers those who give time to the observation of Nature — they actually scorn those who show any active interest in these marvels. We repeat, then, that not science, but the neglect of science, is irreligi-ous. Devotion to science, is a tacit worship — a recognition of worth in the things studied; and by implication in their Cause. It is not a mere lip-homage, but a homage expressed in actions — not a mere professed respect, but a respect proved by the sacrifice of time, thought, and labour.

Nor is it thus only that true science is essentially religious. It is religious, too, inasmuch as it generates a profound respect for, and an implicit faith in, those uniformities of action which all things disclose. By accumulated experiences the man of science acquires a thorough belief in the unchanging relations of phenomena — in the invariable connection of cause and consequence — in the necessity of good or evil results. Instead of the rewards and punishments of traditional belief, which people vaguely hope they may gain, or escape, spite of their disobedience; he finds that there are rewards and punishments in the ordained constitution of things; and that the evil results of disobedience are inevitable. He sees that the laws to which we must submit are both inexorable and beneficent. He sees that in conforming to them, the process of things is ever towards a greater perfection and a higher happiness. Hence he is led constantly to insist on them, and is indignant when they are disregarded. And thus does he, by asserting the eternal principles of things and the necessity of obeying them, prove himself intrinsically religious.

Add lastly the further religious aspect of science, that it alone can give us true conceptions of ourselves and our relation to the mysteries of existence. At the same time that it shows us all which can be known, it shows us the limits beyond which we can know nothing. Not by dogmatic assertion, does it teach the impossibility of comprehending the Ultimate Cause of things; but it leads us clearly to recognise this impossibility by bringing us in every direction to boundaries we cannot cross. It realises to us in a way which nothing else can, the littleness of human intelligence in the face of that which transcends human intelligence. While towards the traditions and authorities of men its attitude may be proud, before the impenetrable veil which hides the Absolute its attitude is humble — a true pride and a true humility. Only the sincere man of science (and by this title we do not mean the mere calculator of distances, or analyser of compounds, or labeller of species; but him who through lower truths seeks higher, and eventually the highest) — only the genuine man of science, we say, can truly know how utterly beyond, not only human knowledge but human conception, is the Universal Power of which Nature, and Life, and Thought are manifestations.

We conclude, then, that for discipline, as well as for guidance, science is of chiefest value. In all its effects, learning the meanings of things, is better than learning the meanings of words. Whether for intellectual, moral, or religious training, the study of surrounding phenomena is immensely superior to the study of grammars and lexicons.

Thus to the question we set out with — What knowledge is of most worth? — the uniform reply is — Science. This is the verdict on all the counts. For direct self-preservation, or the maintenance of life and health, the all-important knowledge is — Science. For that indirect self-preservation which we call gaining a livelihood, the knowledge of greatest value is — Science. For the due discharge of parental functions, the proper guidance is to be found only in — Science. For that interpretation of national life, past and present, without which the citizen cannot rightly regulate his conduct, the indispensable key is — Science. Alike for the most perfect production and highest enjoyment of art in all its forms, the needful preparation is still — Science. And for purposes of discipline — intellectual, moral, religious — the most efficient study is, once more — Science. The question which at first seemed so perplexed, has become, in the course of our inquiry, comparatively simple. We have not to estimate the degrees of importance of different orders of human activity, and different studies as severally fitting us for them; since we find that the study of Science, in its most comprehensive meaning, is the best preparation for all these orders of activity. We have not to decide between the claims of knowledge of great though conventional value, and knowledge of less though intrinsic value; seeing that the knowledge which proves to be of most value in all other respects, is intrinsically most valuable: its worth is not dependent upon opinion, but is as fixed as is the relation of man to the surrounding world. Necessary and eternal as are its truths, all Science concerns all mankind for all time. Equally at present and in the remotest future, must it be of incalculable importance for the regulation of their conduct, that men should understand the science of life, physical, mental, and social; and that they should understand all other science as a key to the science of life.

And yet this study, immensely transcending all others in importance, is that which, in an age of boasted education, receives the least attention. While what we call civilisation could never have arisen had it not been for science, science forms scarcely an appreciable element in our so-called civilised training. Though to the progress of science we owe it, that millions find support where once there was food only for thousands; yet of these millions but a few thousands pay any respect to that which has made their existence possible. Though increasing knowledge of the properties and relations of things has not only enabled wandering tribes to grow into populous nations, but has given to the countless members of these populous nations, comforts and pleasures which their few naked ancestors never even conceived, or could have believed, yet is this kind of knowledge only now receiving a grudging recognition in our highest educational institutions. To the slowly growing acquaintance with the uniform co-existences and sequences of phenomena — to the establishment of invariable laws, we owe our emancipation from the grossest superstitions. But for science we should be still worshipping fetishes; or with hecatombs of victims, propitiating diabolical deities. And yet this science, which, in place of the most degrading conceptions of things, has given us some insight into the grandeurs of creation, is written against in our theologies and frowned upon from our pulpits.

Paraphrasing an Eastern fable, we may say that in the family of knowledges, Science is the household drudge, who, in obscurity, hides unrecognised perfections. To her has been committed all the works; by her skill, intelligence, and devotion, have all conveniences and gratifications been obtained; and while ceaselessly ministering to the rest, she has been kept in the background, that her haughty sisters might flaunt their fripperies in the eyes of the world. The parallel holds yet further. For we are fast coming to the *dénouement,* when the positions will be changed; and while these haughty sisters sink into merited neglect, Science, proclaimed as highest alike in worth and beauty, will reign supreme.

EDWARD L. THORNDIKE

EDWARD L. THORNDIKE (1874-1949). The American psychologist, educator, and lexicographer who pioneered in developing methods of testing and measuring intelligence, reading ability, and other factors involved in the learning process was unusually creative and productive as a scholar. Alone or with his collaborators, Edward L. Thorndike published more than five hundred books and articles. His laws of learning, elaborated in his three-volume work *Educational Psychology* (1913-1914), occupy a central place in contemporary theories of learning.

Born at Williamsburg, Massachusetts, on August 9, 1874, he was associated with Teachers College, Columbia University, throughout most of his professional career. He played an important part in developing programs of adult education, in establishing animal psychology as a natural science, and in compiling word-frequency lists. He was largely responsible for the development of the field of psychology in the United States and for applying its principles to teaching and learning. In addition to *Educational Psychology,* his influential writings include *Mental and Social Measurements* (1904); *Animal Intelligence* (1911); *Fundamentals of Learning* (1933); and *Human Nature and the Social Order* (1940).

Notwithstanding his disclaimer, in the address that follows Thorndike manages to do more than report the contribution that recent psychology has to offer to the "work of making schools more efficient." Though he does not attempt to outline an educational creed, he shows that "educational science needs as its basal equipment an exact and adequate inventory of the original nature of man" and that "a flawless architecture of human affairs will not be attained" until that need has been met.

THE FOUNDATIONS OF EDUCATIONAL ACHIEVEMENT*

A minister of the gospel who was asked to enumerate the foundations of the religious life answered, "Everything in God's world and its proper use. Doubtless the proper use of everything in the

*From *Journal of the Proceedings and Addresses of the National Education Association* (1914), pp. 199-206. Reprinted by permission of the editor of the *Journal.*

world of knowledge and skill and conduct is not too wide a description of the fundamentals of educational achievement. You do not, however, expect anybody to outline an entire educational creed and practice in thirty minutes. What you wish, I judge, is that, as a representative of educational psychology, I should report any contribution that recent psychology has to offer to your work of making schools more efficient — of increasing educational achievement.

There is such a contribution, and, as I hope to convince you, an important one in the general view of human nature which recent studies of human thought and action support.

About fifteen years ago the point of view of students of human nature showed the first clear signs of what has been a rather abrupt change toward thinking of a man's mind as the sum total of connections between the situations which life offers and the responses which the man makes. Up till then the mind had been thought of primarily as a set of magical faculties or powers — attention, memory, inference, reasoning, choice, and the like — or as a collection of certain contents — sensations, images, thoughts, volitions, and the like. Today the progressives in psychology think of a man's mind as the organized system of connections or bonds or associations whereby he responds or reacts by this or that thought or feeling or act to each of the millions of situations or circumstances or events that befall him. Their customary name for the mind is the connection-system; their ideal of psychology is a science which can predict what any given situation or stimulus will connect with or evoke in the way of thought, feeling, word, or deed in any given man; their offering to education is an offering of knowledge of the laws whereby connections in thought and behavior are made and broken, are preserved and weakened, and are of help and hindrance one to another.

From this point of view educational achievement consists, not in strengthening mystical general powers of the mind, but in establishing connections, binding appropriate responses to life's situations, "training the pupil to behavior" ("behavior" being the name we use for "every possible sort of reaction on the circumstances into which he may find himself brought"), building up a hierarchy of habits, strengthening and weakening bonds whereby one thing leads to another in a man's life.

The first suggestion resulting is the obvious and simple but profitable one that nothing is achieved by schools unless some connection is influenced, that we cannot assume change in any pupil unless bonds have been made or broken so as to cause him to respond as he did not before. The connection may be one leading only to an attitude, say of interest or enjoyment. It may be only partly made, guaranteeing the possibility of a certain response, not its surety. It may be hidden, showing itself only indirectly, or only after years, or in some subtle modification of intellect or character. It may lead from some elusive element or feature of a situation, such as the "place-value" of a number or the subjunctiveness of a subjunctive, to some general element or feature of many responses, such as open-mindedness, or cheerfulness, or readiness to do what one accepts as right. But if anything is achieved, some actual connection or bond has been made, strengthened, weakened, or broken. A child's mind is never a witch's pot to be set in action by educational incantations. Its defects are not curable by faith. To discipline it means to improve its specific habits. To develop it means to add bonds productive of desirable responses and to weaken their opposites. Learning is connecting. It never becomes so spiritual, so general, or so involved as to evade expression in terms of concrete couplings between real happenings to a man and real responses by him. Of any assumed educational achievement that does evade such expression, we should be suspicious. Probably its only existence is in our hopes or fears.

What bonds are being formed, what is being put with what in the pupil's experience, then becomes a fundamental question concerning school achievement. It is of course the old, old question of what knowledge, what habits, what interests, what skills, and what ideals are being taught, but put so as to encourage real rather than verbal, and detailed rather than vague, answers. We need to ask it. For this new point of view protects us against careless omissions and mistakes. For example, I venture to prophesy that more will be achieved in arithmetic by special exercises

in teaching the addition-combinations with the higher decades —
that is, in forming the connections 26 and 5 are 31, 26 and 6 are
32, 26 and 7 are 33 — than by leaving them to be deduced from
the previously formed connections 6 and 5 are 11, 6 and 6 are
12, 6 and 7 are 13, and so on. Whether or not these particular
bonds do need special drill or may be left to come by transfer,
the general rule, not to assume that a bond exists unless you find
it or make it, is sound. Again, I venture to prophesy that written
single-column addition with sums of 10 or more and without carrying should and will disappear as a preparation for addition with
carrying. A child who adds 6 and 4 and 3 and writes down the 13 is
forming a habit that he will have to break when in two-place addition he has to write down only the 3 and use the 1 in adding.
The answers in the preliminary drill may be better announced
orally. However this particular case be, the general rule, other
things being equal, not to form any connection that will have to
be broken, is sound. Again, I venture to prophesy that soon the
millions of connections formed in the present teaching of arithmetic
and algebra only to test the existence of some other connections
will be replaced by connections that do this disciplinary and drill
work as well and also serve some intrinsically worthy end. For
the psychology of connection-forming carries the educational cor-
ollary, "Other things being equal, favor those situations which
life itself will offer and those responses which life itself demands.
Form connections for use."

Let me read you one or two problems, all from arithmetics published within the last ten years, and ask you to consider whether,
if the writers had thought of just what bonds or connections these
problems formed, they would have printed them.

1. The step of an ostrich measures 5 feet. How many yards
does it travel in taking 120 steps?

2. At 5/8 of a cent apiece how many dozen eggs can I buy
for $60?

3. Eight (8) times the number of stripes in our flag is the
number of years from 1800 until Roosevelt was elected
President. In what year was he elected President?

4. In a school there are 12 classes and an average of 50 pupils in a class. If everyone in the school should make 500 straight marks on each side of his slate, how many would be made in all?

These needed connections now neglected, avoidable connections now formed only to be broken, and wasteful connections formed only for the sake of some principle or power which really useful connections could illustrate or exercise as well, I have illustrated in the case of arithmetic only. But any other school subject would have served as well or better. If each of you will master the psychology of learning, and then scrutinize each page of your approved textbooks and each exercise prescribed by our course of study, asking, line by line, "What connections are formed by this?" the importance of the fact and the point of view for criticism and for construction will soon be proved.

I turn now to a second fundamental principle for school achievement, the order of formation of the connections. The bonds to be formed having been chosen, the next step is to arrange for their most economical order of formation — to arrange to have each help the others as much as possible, or, as we psychologists say, to get the maximum of facilitation and minimum of inhibition.

You have heard so many discussions and read so many treatises concerning the sequence of topics, the correlation of studies, and the like, that you perhaps shrink from re-examining a minute inventory of all school work and reconsidering its best possible arrangement as a system or hierarchy of connections to be formed, each with the interests of all the others in view. It must, indeed, be admitted that the work is long and also tedious, unless one has a scientific interest in minute matters of education efficiency and in principles whereby to adjudicate them. It is, however, important for economy in educational achievement means that we form the most desirable connections in the most useful order. And it is needed; for, in spite of the very great advance of the past hundred years, texbooks and courses of study still follow mere traditional customs or the order which happens to appeal to some individual expositor.

700

I may illustrate this need in the simple case of the bonds between printed words and their meanings that should be formed before, or at the time that, certain work in arithmetic is to be done. It is obvious that to follow printed directions and to solve printed problems a pupil needs to be able to read the directions and problems — that is, to have formed the bonds leading from the sight of certain words and phrases to their meanings. What I propose to show is that even the best of our modern arithmetical textbooks presuppose, at stage after stage, "word-meaning" connections which, at that stage, have not been and should not have been formed; and that, on the other hand, they and the textbooks in reading fail to form in early grades certain connections which would enormously facilitate the arithmetical learning for these grades.

I shall first read you a list of words all of which occur within the first fifty pages of one or more of four elementary beginning arithmetics intended for pupils in Grade II (or Grade III at the latest). I submit that the majority of the children in question will not have formed the connections in question and should not be expected to have done so, and that to make achievement in arithmetic hang on knowledge of these words as a pre-requisite is a monstrous offense against rational organization of learning. The words beginning with "c" are:

cabbage	California	camped	camphor	candles
cardboard	carriage	charity	Clara	Charlotte
Carrie's	circus	circumference	closet	cloudy
clothespin	cocoa	collected	combinations	committee
covered	county	cradles	crane	cranberries
crew	crumbs	currants		

These four books show in the first fifty pages at least four hundred words which not half of the children at the middle of Grade II can read or should be expected to read. For example, in one or more of the four may be found a galaxy of seventy proper names which these children must master before they can understand their problems.

I submit that so long as such offenses come in our best textbooks a scrutiny of the order of formation of bonds, in school work is no empty psychological amusement, but a vital concern for educational policy.

On the other hand, consider the bonds between these words and their meanings:

How much, how many, count, with, together, add, sum, difference, take away, is left, are left, once, twice, two times, three times, four times, half of, some, all, in all, any, not any, equal, part, whole, greater, less, longer, shorter, cost, buy, bought, sell, sold, measure.

The existence and sure action of connections between these words and their meanings must precede or accompany early work in arithmetic, if it is to be efficient, yet few books or courses of study in arithmetic provide for their formation save hit-or-miss; and surely the primers and first and second readers do not. The four books in arithmetic which I examined actually avoid forming these bonds. The word "difference," for example, occurs only once in twenty pages, the pupils' time being spent in getting acquainted with such words as

dairyman	depot
department	Dorothy
discharged	dishwater

Two of the four do not use the word "sum" in these fifty pages, yet find room for Samuel, Susan, Susie, swimming, syllable, syrup, soldiers, sparrows, strips, stripes, and so on.

Bear in mind that the textbook writers who thus leave unformed important facilitating connections, and burden the beginners of arithmetic with the task of learning to read the names of rare food products, strange vehicles, and the Adele, Byron, Dorothy, Esther series, are from our best — that without such a deliberate warning to consider the place of every connection in the hierarchy as I have given not one of us would have done better. Bear in mind also that textbooks in elementary geography show a similar state of affairs.

A psychologist examining the connections made by the school subjects with a view to their arrangement in an optimum order finds many of these chances for sure improvement and also many problematic cases where, it appears, experimentation has a fair probability of showing ways to increase school achievement. Any few of these problems for investigation will serve as illustrations. Consider, for example, teaching certain facts about pints and quarts, feet and yards, cents, dimes, and dollars, very early as an introduction to and confirmation of knowledge of our system of decimal notation and of the processes of "carrying" in addition and "borrowing" in subtraction. The later decimal-system habits would undoubtedly then be more intelligent and less productive of interference. Whether this gain would be outbalanced by other losses can best be discovered by experiment. Or consider, for example, teaching the metric system as an introduction to, instead of as a consequence of, decimal fractions. This change may seem preposterous, but I venture to remind you that doing just this in the case of United States money is one of the most successful features of the arrangement of modern textbooks.

Or consider teaching much of United States history first in the reverse chronological order — from aeroplanes to automobiles, to the electric trolley, to the steam railroad, to the stagecoach; from the building of the schoolhouse to the settlement of the town, to pioneer days, to the Pilgrims; from the discovery of America by Isidore Strauss to the discovery by Columbus — reviewing and expanding and co-ordinating later in a direct chronological account. As romance or panorama, history begins with centuries back, but as a science, it may perhaps best begin at home, and with facts near and verifiable, as we have found it profitable for geography to do.

Or consider the order of acquaintance with the words in a foreign language. The commonest bonds found among words are those binding words to their opposites (good-bad, father-son, boy-girl, hot-cold, up-down, and the like), yet I have searched a score of Latin, French, and German language books without finding any systematic use of this fact. Again the word-meaning connections of most help in facilitating reading are with the relational words, conjunctions, auxiliary verbs, prepositions, pronouns, and directive adverbs. Yet these words are very rarely given early or extensive or ingenious treatment. Indeed, I do not find much

703

recognition of any principles of economical arrangement of vocabularies save the utterly obvious one that words not fitting the grammatical and translational exercises are kept out, and the common word or words used in the "first five books of Caesar" or the like are worked in. Yet the maximum of achievement demands that there should be a reason for every word taught and for teaching it at just that time and no other.

Such problems as these in mental mechanics — problems in choosing, ordering and, manipulating the mind's connections — are now the growing-point of experimental education. By skilful analysis of human learning into the millions of elementary connections between situation and response which constitute it and by experimental study of the ways in which these connections are best formed, preserved, organized, and used, the psychologist hopes to get both comprehension and control of the foundations of educational achievement.

The foundations of educational achievement are these connections or bonds or habits of response, but these habits themselves lead us back farther to the unlearned, original capacities and tendencies of man. Human beings, as you well know, are not indifferent clay to be molded at will by the teacher's art. They are themselves active forces to help or hinder. They inherit as a human birthright instincts and interests of which education from the start and thruout must take account. Educational achievement is small or great in proportion as it neglects these natural untaught tendencies in man or utilizes them to further his ideal aims. And educational science needs as its basal equipment an exact and adequate inventory of the original nature of man as a species and of the idiosyncrasies of individual men.

No choice of the habits of thought or action to be formed by schools is sound which gives technique irrespective of needs felt by the pupil, or adds knowledge without any motive for its use, or tries to cultivate artificial virtues in disregard of the crude forms of courage, kindliness, zeal, and helpfulness which nature already affords.

No arrangement of the mind's connections is economical which fails to use the inborn organizing power of curiosity, the problem-attitude, and the desire to test and verify or refute by eyes and hands.

No manipulation of bonds in learning is efficient which disregards the pupil's own sense of sociability, kindness, and achievement during the learning process. The original proclivities of the human animal are as real as its laws of learning and condition these thruout. Every habit is formed in the service of some instinctive interest.

The inborn interests of man in movement, novelty, color, life, the behavior of other human beings, sociability, cheerfulness, notice, approval, mastery, and self-activity are not ultimate aims of education, nor is their presence a guaranty that school work is well directed and efficient. But we double achievement if we get them on our side and we enrich life enormously at little cost if we turn these fundamental passions into line with higher nature and the common good.

I hold no brief in favor of avoiding in schools anything necessary for human welfare, either because it is hard or because it is disliked. I find many of the tendencies born in man to be archaic, useless, immoral, adaptations to such a life as man lived in the woods a hundred thousand years ago, when affection had not spread beyond the family, or justice beyond the tribe, or science beyond the needs of tomorrow, and when truth was only the undisputed and goodness only the unrebuked. That the natural is the good is a superstition which psychology cannot tolerate. Still less, however, can psychology tolerate the superstition that there can be any foundation for educational achievement other than the best that human nature itself affords. Truth is only what the best in human intellect accepts; goodness is only what the best in human nature craves. We mean by the rational, ideal, and impersonal aims of education only the nobler inborn human interests purified of their crude accompaniments and broadened to harmonize with the common good. We must not find too much fault with human nature; for ultimately it is all we have! Its best elements are the best the world has or ever will have.

What psychology offers education today is thus a matter-of-fact view of human nature as a set of original unlearned connections or tendencies to respond, which we redirect and to which we add by arranging the situations of life so that new and better connections are formed. The efficiency with which we do this work will depend on our knowledge of man's inborn equipment, our wisdom in choosing and arranging the connections to be formed, and our justice and ingenuity in maneuvering these forces of instinct and habit for human betterment. A flawless architecture of human affairs will not be attained until every possible response of every variety of human being to every situation of life is thus understood and controlled by human reason in the interest of human welfare. However, each minute addition of scientific knowledge of man's nature means one more stone (or at least one molecule of cement!) of wise placing in the foundation for education's building.

JUAN LUIS VIVES

JUAN LUIS VIVES (1492-1540). The ideal of the highest culture of the past as a basis for the training of youth was not peculiar to Juan Luis Vives. Erasmus and other humanists held similar views, but they were concerned mainly with training proper to a class of scholars. The Spanish humanist went much further than his contemporaries: he advocated that the basis of education be broadened by using the vernacular as the medium of instruction, wrote treatises on the education of women, stressed the training of teachers, and introduced new concepts in philosophical method and in psychology.

Born in Valencia in the year of the discovery of America, Vives studied at Paris and taught the humanities at Louvain. In England he acted as tutor to Mary, daughter of Henry VIII and Catherine of Aragon, and lectured on philosophy at Oxford, where he received the degree of doctor of laws. In 1527 he opposed the royal divorce and was imprisoned for six weeks, after which he returned to the Netherlands and devoted his time to writing. He died on May 6, 1540.

Like Erasmus, Vives attacked the old scholastic education and sought to combine Christianity with humanism. Seeing the fallacy of arguing from the general assumptions of the scholastics, he helped to establish the deductive method by showing that a general idea or principle must be based on facts drawn from sense experience. Realizing that sense experience was to be gained in many places, he anticipated Rousseau (whose Emile was to learn by entering workshop, farm, and forge) by stating that "the student should not be ashamed to enter shops and factories and to ask the craftsmen questions in order that he may understand the details of their work." He held that knowledge was of value only when put to use, and in his writings he stressed the application to present and future life of moral precepts drawn from both pagan and Christian sources. With respect to psychology and methodology, he considered the M. A. training as insufficient for the teacher of youth and suggested that academic preparation be supplemented by a specialized course for teachers. He discussed the nature of memory, association of ideas, mnemonics, and the importance of the mind of the individual learner, together with the principle that instruction must be suited to that particular mind.

The works which brought Vives acclaim in his own century were those on education. These writings include *An Introduction to Wisdom* (1540), *On Education* (1531), and the book from which the following selection is taken — *The Instruction of a Christian Woman* (1524).

THE INSTRUCTION OF A CHRISTIAN WOMAN*

There are some women who have no talent for learning, just as there are men; other women have such talent that they seem to have been born for learning, or at least it is not difficult for them. The former should not be urged to learn; the latter should not be hindered from learning, but should rather be coaxed and attracted to it and encouraged toward the virtue to which they are inclined.

I see some that regard women skilled in letters with suspicion, since it seems to them that to give women instruction is to throw oil on the fire, adding sagacity to the natural cunning which some of them have. As for me, I would not condone, nor would I wish to behold, woman astute and sagacious in the reading of those evil books which open the path to misdeeds and lead virtue, purity, and goodness astray; let her read, rather, good books composed by holy men who have been diligent in teaching others to live well, as they themselves have lived. This seems to me not only useful, but even necessary.

Speaking of jesters, minstrels, and buffoons, Aristotle asks why they are good for nothing except wasting their lives in vanities and vices. The reason for this is, the philosopher himself replies, that they are always present at parties, feasts, and banquets and never hear precepts of philosophy which might set them on the path of a good and chaste life. They have never in their lives done anything better, nor have they seen anything better done, nor do they know how to do anything better. Their minds do not reach beyond that which they have learned, which has all been bestial and extraneous, among the shouts and confusion of those who dance, frolic, and laugh, who eat and drink, steeped only in vice. Never appearing where virtue might be found, they have

*Published in 1524. Translated by Gene Franks. Used by permission of the translator.

abandoned all concern for who they are and for what purpose they were born.

Whereby it is constrained (as they say) that they practice the profession which they have learned, inasmuch as its practice is second nature. For example, there is no land, no matter how great its worth, which does not become sterile and fruitless if it lacks the hand of the skillful farmer, nor is there any tree which will not become barren and twisted if there is no one to care for it. Any horse will acquire bad habits if unattended by the rein and the hand of the horseman; likewise, there is no good woman who lacks breeding and instruction. You will find no bad woman except the ignorant one and she who neither knows nor considers the great worth of chastity, who does not think of the evil she does in losing it, nor of the incomparable worth of the article which she barters for a false appearance of lascivious, brief, and fading pleasure. She does not see how many evils she brings upon herself by casting aside her virginal goodness. She does not examine how vain, how mad, and how bestial a thing is the pleasure of the flesh, a pleasure for which she should not move one finger, much less lose the greatest and most esteemed good to be found in woman.

The girl who through instruction has learned to lend attention to these and similar matters, having fortified her spirit with virtuous counsel, will not fear the attacks of her enemy the tempter, nor will she be inclined to surrender her goodness to the devil. And should she fall in sin, so much good counsel, admonition, reprehension, and correction having been unable to defend her, one can see quite well how soon she would have been lost without them. If we turn our glance to the paths of past ages in search of examples of this, we shall find scarcely a single learned woman who has fallen or who has been of bad character. By chance you will bring up Sappho, the great poetess who had an affair with Phaon, and Leontium, who was the "friend" of Metrodorus, and who wrote against Theophrastus, the philosopher and orator, and Sempronia, trained and skilled in Greek and Latin letters, who, Sallust tells us, lived somewhat unchastely.

As if I could not call to mind instead of these three a thou-

709

sand other ladies who increased their natural gifts with embellishment attained through learning. But before doing this, I wish to say something about these three whom I have named. I have sources of great authority which say that Sappho of Lesbos, that highly learned woman who composed in lyrical meters, was not that Sappho who loved Phaon, but another Sappho, since the former was as good in character as she was great in learning. Likewise, Leontium did not bring her learning to Metrodorus' home, but rather acquired it after she was in his power. Furthermore, her learning was not such as was appropriate to make her virtuous, for it was from the writings of Epicurus, who placed all good in corporal delight and pleasure alone. The scholarship of Sempronia is not that which I would condone for the virtuous woman, which is studying moral subjects and learning how to conduct herself. Sempronia, however, dedicated herself to the subject of eloquent speech, a matter to which I do not wish our virgin to give so much attention. We could say the same of Sappho. But now, if to the field we call our squadrons, forth will sally many illustrious ladies.

Forth will come Cornelia, mother of the Gracchi, who, being a pure model of chastity, taught letters to her sons Gaius and Tiberius. Forth will come Laelius' daughters, and Brutus' wife Porcia, who attained a great part of the wisdom and learning of her father Cato. Likewise, Cleobuline, daughter of Cleobulus, one of the Seven Sages of Athens, was so devoted to learning and wisdom that, scorning all carnality, she remained forever a virgin. Her example was followed by the daughter of Pythagoras, who, after her father's death, revived his teachings and, opening a school, was given charge of the young ladies of the entire land. In the same class was Theano of Metapontium, who had the gift of prophecy and who radiated a singular chastity.

The ten Sibyls, St. Jerome tells us, were virgins, and we read that Cassandra and Chryseis, priestesses of Apollo and Juno, were virgins as well. Chastity was common to almost all the women who served the idols. Pythia, who gave the replies at Delphi to those who went to consult the oracle of Apollo, was nothing less than a virgin. Of this group as well was Phemonoë, who is said to have invented the heroic meter. Sulpicia, wife of Calenus, wrote a very saintly book on matrimony, a matter which she put in practice before in writing. Martial has these words to say of her: "All wives who wish to please one man alone should read Sulpicia. All husbands who wish to please one woman alone should read Sulpicia. She teaches chaste and gentle affections, deceits, gentilities and delicacies; one who carefully considers her verses will say that a more saintly lady does not exist." From this it is clear that in that age no man was more fortunate nor was any man better married than Calenus with Sulpicia.

Hortensia, daughter of the orator Hortensius, equaled her father in rhetoric to such a degree that she composed an argument to the triumviri favoring statutes of the republic defending women. Her oration was read by subsequent generations, who not only marveled at her womanly eloquence but even imitated it along with the orations and writings of Demosthenes and Tullius. Edesia of Alexandria, a relative of the philosopher Syrianus, was esteemed and considered a miracle of her age in learning and in the purity of her life. Corinna, a most chaste lady, defeated the poet Pindar five times in verse contests. Paulina, the wife of Seneca, filled with the doctrine of her husband, imitated his life as well. Seneca himself laments in one of his epistles that his mother Helvia* did not complete the learning of the precepts of the sages which she had undertaken at her husband's petition.

Argentaria Polla, wife of the poet Lucan, not only revised her husband's *Pharsalia* after his death, but it is said that she even aided him in composing it while he was alive. She was a woman illustrious in lineage, wealth, beauty, genius, and chastity. The muse Caliope, speaking of her in Statius' *Thebaid*, says to Lucan: "Not only shall I grant you the gift for singing in meters worthy of remembrance, but as well I shall endow you with a wife suitable to your indisputable genius, such as gentle Venus or the goddess Juno would give you, adorned with beauty, purity, gentleness, wealth, lineage, grace, and goodness." Diodorus the dialec-

*Vives uses the name Albina, an error unless the reference is to the mother of Paulina. [Tr.]

titian had five daughters, celebrated for their learning and chastity, whose story was recorded by Philo, teacher of Carneades. Zenobia, queen of the Palmyrenians, learned Greek and Latin and wrote on the history of Alexandria and the Orient. We shall deal with her continence and virtue, along with that of other ladies, in the following book. These women mentioned all were Gentiles.

Now, what shall we say of the Christians? Shall I speak by chance of Thecla, disciple of St. Paul, who was worthy of so great a teacher, or of Catherine of Alexandria, daughter of Konstos, who defeated great and practiced philosophers in debates? St. Catherine of Siena, a most learned virgin, left us works of her illustrious genius in which the purity of her saintly spirit glitters like a pearl of the Orient. In the age of St. Jerome all women were very wise. And would to God that many of the elderly men of this age of ours, and even those who pass themselves off as intellectuals, could equal those ladies in learning. St. Jerome wrote to Paula, Laeta, Eustochium, Fabiola, Marcella, Furia, Demetria, Salvina, and Hierontia; St. Augustine wrote to some, St. Ambrose to others. All were worthy of admiration for their genius, their learning, and their lives.

Proba* who loved only her husband Marullus, drew from the verses of Virgil and composed a work to the praise and glory of our Redeemer Jesus Christ. Eudoxia, wife of Theodosius II, was not, writers tell us, less celebrated for her learning and goodness than she was extolled for her sovereign position, and she is said to have written centones drawn from Homer. The German Hildegard, a virgin, wrote epistles and books of great erudition which are read today. Our age has seen the daughters of Queen Isabel, who has been mentioned earlier, attain great learning. In all parts of this land I am told, with great praise and admiration, of Queen Juana, wife of King Philip and mother of our

---

*Vives uses the name Valeria Proba, perhaps through confusion with Anicia Faltonia Proba (long assumed to be the author of centones now attributed to her niece Proba, who was the wife not of Marullus but of Claudius Calcinus Adalphius), or with Marcus Valerius Probus, widely known for his commentary on Virgil. [Tr.]

712

emperor King Charles, who has replied promptly in Latin to those who have addressed her, as it is customary to do with new rulers, in the cities and villages which she has visited. The same is said by the English of their Spanish queen Catherine, the sister of Queen Juana and of the other two who died as queens of Portugal. Of these four sisters we can certainly say that no other women in the memory of men have been adorned with more spotless fame or with chastity more pure, nor have any been better loved by their populace, more loving to their husbands or more obedient to them; none have more carefully preserved themselves and their loved ones from blemish, and to none other have turpitude and immodesty seemed so vile. In a word, no other ladies have so fully arrived at that pinnacle which belongs to the completely perfect woman. Should these ladies, being queens, permit following them the mention of ladies of private means, I would add to this select group the daughters of Thomas More.

More's daughters, Margaret, Elizabeth, and Cecily, and their relative Margaret Giggs, together with the noble and extremely chaste Angela Mercader Zapata from my Valencia, had parents who were not content that their daughters should be merely virtuous, but who wished that they be instructed as well, wisely judging that in this fashion their daughters would be more truly and firmly virtuous. In this they were not in error, nor are other parents who believe the same, for the mind is of such a nature that with liberty it goes astray, with levity it grows proud, with sagacity it penetrates, with activity it understands, and with ignorance it wastes itself. All corporal ailments which can come to mortals medicine can cure, reason can remedy, time can heal, or death can cut short; only the mind which is obfuscated by error, depraved by malice, and corrupted by vice cannot be cured by medicine, set straight by reason, or aided by any other remedy. Thus it is necessary with time to elevate the mind to lofty matters before it can sink to abject and lowly ones. All this being carefully considered, we will find nothing as necessary for raising the understanding to matters of virtue as the study of letters, which is in itself such a noble thing that it captivates the mind and magnifies within it the knowledge of that which is superhuman, while it does not allow the mind to descend to that which is vile and mundane and to that which delights in the carnal. For study has within it its own divine and spiritual manna.

It is for this reason, I believe, that Pallas, goddess of wisdom and household skills, and the muses were fancied by antiquity to be virgins. And not only will the mind which is given to wisdom abhor vice, just as whiteness detests soot and cleanliness shrinks from filth, but it will withdraw as well from all vain desire for pleasure, which takes possession of the imprudent spirits of young girls in the form of dances, songs, and other things of this type, all of which are vain, foolish, and fruitless. As the celebrated philosopher Plutarch says, "The woman inclined to learning will never delight in dancing." Of this and other vanities with which young ladies willingly occupy themselves we shall speak more in detail later, and in the following chapter we shall take note of the books from which the young lady is to study. Here let us only say that her studies should be in subjects which formulate breeding and manners, teach behavior, teach action in accordance with virtue, guide the reasoning faculty, and, finally, show the young lady how to live, causing harm neither to others nor to herself.

For eloquent speech I have little concern, for just as the greatest virtue of water is to be tasteless and odorless, the greatest virtue of the young lady's speech is to be pure and without artifice. The young lady needs less to be a clever speaker than to be good, honest, and wise, for it is not improper for a lady to keep silent; it is extremely improper, though, for her to be ignorant of virtue, and abominable for her to do evil. Though I do not condemn or censure eloquent speech, which Quintilian and after him St. Jerome praised in Cornelia, mother of the Gracchi, and in Hortensia, daughter of Hortensius, I highly esteem silence and consider it more useful for virtuous living, especially when there is no great necessity to speak. Speaking can never be greatly necessary for the young lady, except when silence might do harm to her goodness or speaking aid it. We must keep

714

in mind that the empty vessel is the most resonant and that those who have little in their heads are most talkative. But this subject will be taken up in greater detail in other parts of this work, as it is a matter especially necessary in the honest and virtuous life of a lady.

Now, as for the young lady's teacher, I prefer that she have a woman rather than a man. It is best that the teacher be her mother, her aunt, or her sister rather than an outsider. If she must be an outsider, however, she should be known by the family and, if possible, she should have the following qualifications: she should be advanced in years, clean in behavior, esteemed in reputation, tranquil in temperament, and skilled in learning. With all of these qualifications, I would regard her highly, but if a lady with all of the qualities cannot be obtained, the teacher must at least possess good reputation and skill in learning. If a lady with these last two qualities cannot be found, select with great care an old man who has proven himself worthy in behavior, reputation, and scholarship. If possible, he should be a married man rather than a bachelor; his wife should be sufficiently attractive and he should get on well with her, for if this is the case he will not be driven to covet other women, being satisfied with his own. These things were such as could not be left unsaid, for in the raising of a girl nothing must be guarded more carefully than decency and purity.

She should be taught to read using good, virtuous books, for all water is not for drinking. In learning to write, she should not be given vain, idle materials, but rather something taken from the Holy Scripture or some chaste sentence borrowed from the precepts of philosophy, for as she copies this material many times it will become firmly imprinted in her memory. Both mother and teacher must take care to keep her continually beneath the wings of discipline if they do not wish the girl's mind to become addled and, instead of the desired benefit, to reap only grief. All things of this world cease to move forward when they fall idle: the traveler who does not travel makes no progress; the ship at sea which does not sail never arrives at port; the mind, however, when it does not advance in virtue not only ceases to make progress toward good but even loses ground and slips toward evil. The young are more prone to fall into this vice than adults, and women are more prone to it than men. For this reason the wise poet Horace told us in his *Art of Poetry* that the clay must be worked while it is moist and that the vase is not shaped by resting the wheel. As the popular saying puts it, "Strike while the iron is hot."

I would fix no length of time for woman to study, nor would I fix such for man, except to say that I would wish man to have a broader range of knowledge both for his own benefit and for the benefit which the nation receives when he teaches others. But woman should be concerned only with that part of learning which will teach her to live with virtue and which will put order in her habits, breeding, and behavior. I would have her learn for the sake of knowing, and not in order to display before others what she knows, for it is good that she keep silent and allow her virtue to speak for her. Land with subterranean water, when viewed from a distance before sunrise, gives off a sort of vapor or mist; a woman, likewise, who is truly wise or virtuous, although she makes no outward show of it, continually does things which allow the careful observer to note that beneath her silence are virtue and goodness.

As I have said that woman should make no show of her knowledge, I shall go further to say that she should not teach or have a school for the teaching of children of others. St. Jerome as well censures this. As for teaching her own children or sisters in her own home, however, I not only grant it but would even implore her to do it, granted, of course, that she is well instructed in what she is to teach, for otherwise it is not to be permitted. The Apostle Paul, the chosen vessel, giving his regulations to the Corinthians writes as follows: "Let your women keep silence in the churches; for it is not permitted unto them to speak: but they are commanded to be under obedience, as also saith the law. And if they will learn anything, let them ask their husbands at home. . . ." The Apostle in another place writes to his disciple Timothy as follows: "Let the woman learn in silence with all subjection. But I suffer not a woman to teach, nor to usurp authority over the man, but to be in silence. For Adam was first formed, then Eve. And Adam was not deceived, but the woman being deceived was in the transgression." Therefore, because woman is by nature a tainted creature and her judgment is not in all matters sound, because she can be very easily deceived, as our mother Eve demonstrated, allowing the devil to make a fool of her over a mere trifle, and because of other reasons which I shall not mention, it is not well for woman to teach. She should not teach so that she will not in her capacity as teacher pass on to those who listen to her some false notion which might have entered her head and thus lead others into the same mistake, especially since disciples follow their teacher willingly into error.

ALFRED NORTH WHITEHEAD

ALFRED NORTH WHITEHEAD (1861-1947). The publication of three works outlining the philosophy of organism (*Science and the Modern World*, 1925; *Process and Reality: An Essay in Cosmology*, 1929; *Adventures in Ideas*, 1933) made Alfred North Whitehead the outstanding metaphysician of his time. His philosophy of education, which stressed individuality, exact knowledge, imagination, and creative interaction, was particularly influential in England.

Born in Ramsgate, England, on February 15, 1861, he studied mathematics at Cambridge and became a fellow at Trinity College, where he began teaching mathematics in 1885. He was elected to the Royal Society in 1903. A decade of collaboration with his most brilliant pupil, Bertrand Russell, produced *Principia Mathematica,* a monumental three-volume study of the structure of logical thought (1910-1913). Upon leaving Cambridge in 1910, he became interested in mass education, particularly in science and mathematics, and was active in a number of educational institutions in London. He was also professor of mathematics and later dean of the faculty of science at the Imperial College of Science and Technology. During the same period he published his theory of the philosophical foundations of physics. He was sixty-three when he gave up his position in London to become professor of philosophy at Harvard, where he elaborated his famous theory. Organism assumes that an occasion of experience has its origin in the physical activities of the whole organism and is a process ("concrescence") of past experiences and of external factors, which are incorporated ("prehended") into its own particular unity. His cosmology is based on the principle that all final realities are occasions of experience. One implication of his philosophical system is a return to the idea of the ancient Greeks, who held that the moral and the esthetic belong together. Whitehead published the *Aims of Education* in 1929. Later works include *Modes of Thought* (1938) and *Science and Philosophy* (1946). He died on December 30, 1947, at Cambridge, Massachusetts.

The essay that follows, "Science in General Education," is typical of much of his writing with respect both to its style and its content. A sparkling, mildly ironic humor does not detract from the wisdom of his words. Though his ideas are at times expressed in abstruse language, illuminating references to familiar experiences clarify his meaning. Here as in his other writings he warns against overemphasis on science and teaching of vague general principles. "Interest depends upon background," he observes, "that is to say, upon the relations of the new element of thought or perception to the pre-existing mental furniture. . . . Again facts are exciting to the imagination in so far as they illuminate some scheme of thought." He maintains that training in science should issue "in a stimulus toward creativeness," and that "science and poetry have the same root in human nature."

SCIENCE IN GENERAL EDUCATION*

We are becoming aware that in adjusting a curriculum, it is not sufficient to agree that some specific subject should be taught. We have to ask many questions and to make many experiments before we can determine its best relation to the whole body of educational influences which are to mould the pupil.

In the first place it is necessary to keep before our minds that nine-tenths of the pupil's time is, and must be, occupied in the apprehension of a succession of details — it may be facts of history, it may be the translation of a definite paragraph of Thucydides, it may be the observable effects in some definite physical experiment. You cannot learn Science, *passim;* what you do learn in some definite hour of work is perhaps the effect on the temperature of a given weight of boiling water obtained by dropping into it a given weight of lead at another definite temperature, or some analogous detailed set of facts. It is true that all teaching has its rhetorical moments when attention is directed to aesthetic values or to momentous issues. But practical schoolmasters will tell you that the main structure of successful education is formed out of the accurate accomplishment of a succession of detailed tasks. It is necessary to enforce this point at the very beginning of discussion, and to keep it in mind throughout, because the enthusiasm of reformers so naturally dwells on what we may term "the rhetoric of education."

Our second step in thought must be to envisage the principles which should govern the arrangement of the detailed lessons in

*From *Science and Philosophy* (New York: Philosophical Library, 1948).

the subject. An educational cynic will tell you that it does not make much difference what you teach the pupils: they are bound to forget it all when they leave school; the one important thing is, to get the children into the habit of concentrating their thoughts, of applying their minds to definite tasks, and of doing what they are told. In fact, according to this school of thought, discipline, mental and physical, is the final benefit of education, and the content of the ideas is practically valueless. An exception is made for pupils of unusual ability or of unusual twist of interest. I conceive this summary solution of the educational problem to be based on an entirely false psychology, and to be in disagreement with experience. It depends for its plausibility on the erroneous analogy of the intellectual organism with some kind of mechanical instrument such as a knife, which you first sharpen on a hard stone, and then set to cut a number of different things quite disconnected with the stone and the process of sharpening. The other sources of the theory are the disillusionment of tired teachers, and the trenchant judgments of those who will not give the time to think out a complex question. But as this opinion is not likely to be largely represented among members of the Congress, further contemplation of it is unnecessary. In considering the general principles which are to govern our selection of details, we must remember that we are concerned with general education. Accordingly we must be careful to avoid conceiving science either in quantity or quality as it would be presented to the specialists in that subject. We must not assume ample time or unusual scientific ability. Also in recent years the congestion of subjects in the curriculum, combined with the opposing claims of specialism, has led practically all English Schools and the Board of Education to adopt certain principles regulating the relations between general education and special subjects. Our discussion must take these for granted, if we wish to be practical. Education up to the age of sixteen, or sixteen-and-a-half, is to be dominated by the claims of general education, and extended attention to any special subject is to be limited by the claims of the whole balanced curriculum. In the case of a pupil of any reasonable ability there will be time for some specialism; but the

720

ruling principle is, that where the claims of the two clash, the specialism is to be sacrificed to the general education. But after the age of sixteen, the position is reversed. The pupil is expected to devote the larger proportion of his time to some adequate special subject, such as classics, science, mathematics, or history, and the remaining portion to suitably contrasted subsidiary subjects, such as modern languages, for a scientist or a mathematician. In other words, before sixteen the special subject is subsidiary to the general education, and after sixteen the general education is subsidiary to the special subject. Accordingly our discussion divides into two sections, namely, science in general education before the age of sixteen, and after the age of sixteen. The second division may also be taken to cover the University stage. This principle of a preliminary general education has set to educationalists a new problem which has not as yet been adequately worked on in any subject. Indeed it is only just dawning on responsible people in its full urgency. But on its solution depends the success of that modern system of education to which we are now committed.

The problem is this: In all schools, with negligible exceptions, the general education has to be arranged with practical uniformity for the school as a whole. In the first place it is not very certain who among the pupils are the future scientists, who the future classical scholars, or who are the future historians. For the greater number, the desirable differentiation will only gradually disclose itself. Secondly, we may not assume that the majority of boys or girls in secondary schools will remain at school after the age of seventeen, and thus continue any portion of the general education after the first period. Accordingly for both these reasons, the preliminary general training in each subject should form a self-contained course, finding its justification in what it has done for the pupil at its termination. If it is not justified then, it never will be, since at this point, in the vast majority of instances, the formal study of the subject ends.

If we examine the cause of the educational dissatisfaction at the end of the last and at the beginning of this century, we shall find that it centres round the fact that the subjects in the curriculum were taught as incomplete fragments. The children were taught their elementary mathematics exactly as though they were to proceed in later years to take their degrees as high wranglers. Of course most of them collapsed at the first stage; and nobody — least of all the children — knew why they had been taught just that selection of meaningless elaborate preliminaries. Anyhow, as they soon forgot it all, it did not seem much to matter. The same criticism applied to the classics, and to other subjects. Accordingly, every subject in the preliminary training must be so conceived and shaped as yielding, during that period, general aptitudes, general ideas, and knowledge of special facts, which, taken in conjunction, form a body of acquirement essential to educated people. Furthermore it must be shown that the valuable part of that body of acquirement could not be more easily and quickly gained in some other way, by some other combination of subjects.

In considering the framing of a scientific curriculum subject to these conditions, we must beware of the fallacy of the soft option. It is this pitfall which has ruined so many promising schemes of reform. It seems such an easy solution, that, in order to gain time, we should shape a course comprising merely the interesting descriptive facts of the subject and the more important and exciting generalizations. In this way our course is self-contained and can easily be compressed into a reasonable time. It will certainly be a failure, and the reason of the failure illustrates the difficulty or the art of education. In order to explain this, let us recur to the educational cynic whom I introduced at the beginning of this paper; for he really is a formidable critic. He will point out that in a few years your pupil will have forgotten the precise nature of any facts which you teach him, and will almost certainly have muddled your generalizations into incorrect forms. The cynic will ask, What is the use of a vague remembrance of the wrong date for the last glacial epoch, and of a totally erroneous idea of the meaning of "the survival of the fittest"? Furthermore, we may well doubt whether your science, as thus taught, will be really interesting. Interest depends upon background, that is to say, upon the relations of the new element of thought or perception to the pre-existing mental furniture. If your children have not got the right background, even "the survival of the fittest" will fail to enthuse them. The interest of a sweeping generalization is the interest of a broad high road to men who know what travel is; and the pleasure of the road has its roots in the labour of the journey. Again facts are exciting to the imagination in so far as they illuminate some scheme of thought, perhaps only dimly discerned or realized, some day-dreams begotten by old racial experience, or some clear-cut theory exactly comprehended. The complex of both factors of interest satisfies the cravings inherent in that mysterious reaching out of experience from sensation to knowledge, and from blind instinct to thoughtful purpose.

The conclusion is that you can only elicit sustained interest from a process of instruction which sets before the pupils definite tasks which keep their minds at stretch in determining facts, in illustrating these facts by ideas, and in illustrating ideas by their application to complex facts. I am simply enforcing the truism that no reform in education can abolish the necessity for hard work and exact knowledge.

Every subject in the general education must pull its weight in contribution to the building up of the disciplined power of definitely controlled thought. Experience amply proves that no one special training is adequate for this purpose; the classical scholar cannot necessarily focus on mathematical ideas, and the mathematician may be a slovenly thinker outside his science, and neither classic nor mathematician may have acquired the habits of procedure requisite for observation and analysis of natural phenomena. In this connection the function of the study of a subject is not so much to produce knowledge as to form habits. It is its business to transmute thought into an instinct which does not smother thought but directs it, to generate the feeling for the important sort of scientific ideas and for the important ways of scientific analysis, to implant the habit of seeking for causes and of classifying by similarities. Equally important is the habit of definitely controlled observation. It is the besetting fallacy of over-intellectual people to assume that education consists in training people in the abstract power of thought. What is important in the welding of thought to observation is to make observation exact. You cannot make an exact determination of the passing phenomena of experience unless you have predetermined what it is you are going to observe, so as to fix attention on just those elements of the perceptual field. It is this habit of predetermined perception and the instinctive recognition of its importance which is one of the greatest gifts of science to general education. It is here that practical work in the laboratory, or field work in noting geological or botanical characteristics, is so important. Such work must be made interesting to obtain the proper engrossment of attention, and it must be linked with general ideas and with adequate theory to train in the habit of pre-determining observation by thought. Every training impresses on its recipient a certain character; and the various elements in the general education must be so handled as to enrich the final character of the pupil by their contribution. We have been discussing the peculiar value of science in this respect. It should elicit the habit of first-hand observation, and should train the pupil to relate general ideas to immediate perceptions, and thereby obtain exactness of observation and fruitfulness of thought. I repeat that primarily this acquirement is not an access of knowledge but a modification of character by the impress of habit. Literary people have a way of relegating science to the category of useful knowledge, and of conceiving the impress on character as gained from literature alone. Accordingly I have emphasized this point.

We have, however, not yet exhausted the analysis of the impress on character due to science. The imagination is disciplined and strengthened. The process of thinking ahead of the phenomena is essentially a work of the imagination. Of course it involves only one specific type of imaginative functioning which is thus strengthened, just as poetic literature strengthens another specific type. Undoubtedly there will be some interplay between the types, but we must not conceive the imagination as a definite faculty which is strengthened as a whole by any particular imaginative act of a specific type. Accordingly science should give something to the imagination which cannot be otherwise obtained. If we are finally to sum up in one phrase the peculiar impress on character to be obtained from a scientific training, I would say that it is a certain type of instinctive direction in thought and observation of nature, and a facility of imagination in respect to the objects thus contemplated, issuing in a stimulus towards creativeness. We now turn to the other aspect of science. It is the systematization of supremely useful knowledge. In the modern world men and women must possess a necessary minimum of this knowledge, in an explicit form, and beyond this, their minds must be so trained that they can increase this knowledge as occasion demands. Accordingly the general education during the "pre-sixteen" period must include some descriptive summaries of physiological, botanical, physical, chemical, astronomical, and geological facts, even although it is not possible to choose all those sciences as subjects for serious study in the school curriculum. Especially is this important in the case of physiology owing to the accidental circumstance that we all have bodies.

We see therefore that the scientific curriculum must have a soft element and a hard element. The hard element will consist in the attainment of exact knowledge based on first-hand observation. The laboratory work will be so framed as to illustrate such concepts and theoretical generalizations as the pupil is to know. I would insist that science in this stage of education loses nearly all its value, if its concepts and generalizations are not illustrated and tested by practical work. This union of acquirement of concepts, of comprehension of general laws, of reasoning from them, and of testing by experiment will go slowly at first, because the child's powers of mind have to be built up. The pupil has not got the requisite generalizing faculty ready made, and it is the very purpose of the education to give it to him. Furthermore little bits of diverse sciences are useless for the purpose; with such excessive dispersion the systematic character of science is lost, nor does the knowledge go deep enough to be interesting. We must beware of presenting science as a set of pretentious names for obvious facts or as a set of verbal phrases. Accordingly the hard element in the scientific training should be confined to one or at most two sciences, for example, physics and chemistry. These sciences have also the advantage of being key sciences

725

without which it is hardly possible to understand the others. By the age of sixteen every pupil should have done some hard work at these two sciences, and — generally speaking — it is scarcely possible that there will have been any time for analogous work in any other natural science, after the necessary mathematical time has been allotted. Probably in a four years' course the best quantitative division would be two years of physics and two years of chemistry, and mathematics all the time. But assuredly it is not desirable to do all the physics in the first period of two years, and all the chemistry in the second period. The first simple ideas clustering round the most elementary experiments will undoubtedly be physical and mechanical. But as some serious progress is made the two sciences illustrate each other, and also relieve each other by the width of interests thus developed. For example, the influence of physical conditions, such as temperature, on the rate, and even the possibility, of chemical transformation is an elementary lesson on the unity of nature more valuable than abstract formulation of statement on the subject.

Two factors should go to form the soft element in scientific education. The first and most important is browsing, with the very slightest external direction, and mainly dependent on the wayward impulses of a student's inward springs of interest. No scheme for education, and least of all for scientific education, can be complete without some facility and encouragement for browsing. The dangers of our modern efficient schemes remind one of Matthew Arnold's line "For rigorous teachers seized my youth." Poor youth! Unless we are careful, we shall organize genius out of existence; and some measure of genius is the rightful inheritance of every man. Such browsing will normally take the form either of chemical experiments, or of field work in geology, or in zoology, or in botany, or of astronomical observation with a small telescope. Anyhow, if he can be got to do so, encourage the child to do something for himself according to his own fancy. Such work will reflect back interest on to the hard part of his training. Here the collector's instinct is the ally of science, as well as of art. Also it is surprising how many people — Shelley, for example — whose main interests are literary derive the keenest

726

pleasure from divagations into some scientific pursuit. In his youth, the born poet often wavers between science and literature; and his choice is determined by the chance attraction of one or other of the alternative modes of expressing his imaginative joy in nature. It is essential to keep in mind, that science and poetry have the same root in human nature. Forgetfulness of this fact will ruin, and is ruining, our educational system. Efficient gentlemen are sitting on boards determining how best to adapt the curriculum to a uniform examination. Let them beware lest, proving themselves descendants of Wordsworth's bad man, they

> "Take the radiance from the clouds
> In which the sun his setting shrouds."

The other factor should consist of descriptive lectures, designed for the purpose of giving necessary scientific information on subjects such as physiology, and also for the purpose of exciting general interest in the various sciences. No great amount of time need be taken up in this way. I am thinking of about three to six lectures a term. It should be possible to convey some arresting information about most sciences in this way, and in addition to concentrate on the necessary information on particular points which it is desired to emphasize. The difficulty about such lectures is that comparatively few people are able to give them successfully. It requires a peculiar knack. For this reason I suggest that there should be an exchange of lectures between schools, and also that successful extension lecturers should be asked to take up this kind of work. It is evident that with a little organization and co-operation the thing could be done, though some care would be required in the arrangement of details. Finally we come to the position of science in general education after the age of sixteen. The pupil is now rapidly maturing and the problem assumes entirely a new aspect. We must remember that he is now engaged mainly in studying a special subject such as classics, or history, which he will continue during his subsequent University course. Among other things, his power of abstract thought is growing, and he is taking a keen delight in generalizations. I am thinking of boys in the sixth form and of undergraduates. I suggest that in general practical work should be dropped, so far as any official enforcement is concerned. What the pupil now wants is a series of lectures on some general aspects of sciences, for example, on the conservation of energy, on the theory of evolution and controversies connected with it, such as the inheritance of acquired characters, on the electromagnetic theory of matter and the constitutions of the molecule, and other analogous topics. Furthermore, the applications of science should not be neglected — machinery and its connection with the economic revolution at the beginning of the nineteenth century, the importance of nitrates and their artificial production, coal-tar, aeronautics, and other topics. As in the case of lectures at the earlier stage, not much time should be occupied by them, and also there is the same difficulty in finding the lecturers. I believe that these lectures are easier to give than the more elementary ones. But I think that it will still be found necessary to create some organization so that local talent can be supplemented by external aid.

Also at this stage books can be brought in to help; for example, Marett's *Anthropology* and Myres' *Dawn of History,* both in "The Home University Library," will form a bridge conducting the historians from the general theory of zoological evolution to the classical history which forms the commencement of their own special studies. I merely give this instance to show the sort of thing, and the scale of treatment, that I am thinking about. But this general treatment of science in the later stage of education will lose most of its value, if there is no sound basis laid in the education before the age of sixteen.

I will conclude with a general caution which summarizes the guiding principle of the preceding remarks: There is very little time, and so in the formal teaching above all things we must avoid both an aimless aggregation of details either in class or in laboratory and the enunciation of verbal statements which bring no concrete ideas to the minds of the pupils.